The Routledge Reader in

CARIBBEAN LITERATURE

The Routledge Reader in Caribbean Literature is an outstanding compilation which stages some of the central debates about cultural and aesthetic value that have animated both writers and critics of Caribbean literature throughout the twentieth century. It brings previously unknown or inaccessible texts to greater attention and draws more familiar texts into a new range of contexts. The *Reader* offers new critical configurations, new connections, new ways of reading and new notions of Caribbean literary praxis.

Both the renowned and the less well known are given a voice in this remarkable anthology which encompasses poetry, short stories, essays, articles and interviews. Amongst the many represented are the writers: C.L.R. James; George Lamming; Jean Rhys; Benjamin Zephaniah; Claude McKay; Jamaica Kincaid; Sylvia Wynter; Derek Walcott; David Dabydeen; and Grace Nichols.

The editors probe some of the sore points of the Caribbean literary tradition, areas which previous publications have disavowed for varying reasons, particularly Creole writing, writing in Creole writing which works with (rather than against) colonial and eurocentric forms and early, especially early women's, Caribbean literature.

The Routledge Reader in Caribbean Literature provides an accessible historical and cultural framework to the texts through a series of introductions making the anthology an ideal teaching tool as well as a fascinating collection for anyone interested in the wealth of Caribbean literary traditions.

Dr Alison Donnell lectures in post-colonial literatures at Nottingham Trent University, England. **Dr Sarah Lawson Welsh** lectures in English and post-colonial literatures at the University College of Ripon & York St John, England.

In Memory of My Father
Derrick Donnell (1933–1993)
And
For My Son
Max Donnell Ford (b.1995)

A.D.

To My Parents
And
In Memory of My Grandmothers
Frances Samler and Ivy Lawson

S.L.W.

The Routledge Reader in

CARIBBEAN LITERATURE

Edited by
ALISON DONNELL *and*
SARAH LAWSON WELSH

LONDON AND NEW YORK

First published 1996
by Routledge
2 Park Square, Milton Park, Abingdon, Oxon, OX14 4RN
270 Madison Ave, New York NY 10016

Transferred to Digital Printing 2005

Routledge is an International Thompson Publishing company

Typeset in Janson 11/13 by
Florencetype Ltd, Stoodleigh, Devon

British Library Cataloguing in Publication Data
A catalogue record for this book is available from the British Library

Library of Congress Cataloging in Publication Data
The Routledge reader in Caribbean literature / [compiled by] Alison
Donnell and Sarah Lawson Welsh.
p. cm.
Includes biographical references and index.
1. Caribbean literature (English) 2. Caribbean Area – Literary
collections. I. Donnell, Alison. II. Lawson Welsh, Sarah.
PR9205.5.R68 1996
820.8'09729–dc20 95–48494
ISBN 0–415–12048–9 (hbk)
ISBN 0–415–12049–7 (pbk).

Contents

[v]

CONTENTS

1950–65

CONTENTS

Acknowledgements

We should like to offer our thanks to Professor John Thieme, Professor Roger Bromley, Dr David Dabydeen and Sue Hodges for their comments and practical support at different stages during the writing of the *Reader*. Thanks also go to Sue Hodges and Jenny Rogers for their help in typing the manuscript, and to those writers and critics who were generous in giving their work.

Alison Donnell would like to thank her students of Caribbean Literature at Cheltenham, Leeds and Nottingham who have suffered my enthusiam and have helped to keep my ideas moving. I am grateful for the support I have received from my colleagues in the field, especially Manzu Islam, Elleke Boehmer and Patrick Williams, and from friends, especially Caroline Hencher and Tracey Donnell. Lynnette Turner deserves special thanks for listening to various ideas, as well as for making me talk about other things. Thanks also go to Michael Gilkes for making Caribbean Literature an irresistible challenge ten years ago, and to Henry Swanzy and Cedric Lindo (deceased) who gave generously of their time to share memories. All possible thanks go to my mother for her unconditional support and love, and for her skill and patience as a grandmother. Finally, immense gratitude goes to Jeremy for his unfailing ability to make things work out, and to my baby son, Max, whose arrival in the middle of this project made life both more chaotic and more worthwhile.

Sarah Lawson Welsh sends her special thanks to her New Literatures' students who taught me a great deal and to all my colleagues at the University College of Ripon and York St John, particularly Mary Eagleton and Judy Giles for their unremitting moral support! I am grateful to the College for its generosity in funding secretarial support and to Anne Price for arranging a period of study leave. Finally I should like to thank all my friends and family, especially David Welsh, Janet Baverstock, Daniel Lawson and Roy Wooley for their good humour, patience and support throughout what has been a long and exhausting project. I should also like to express my gratitude to Jimmy Darius and his daughter Sandra for first awakening my interest in the Caribbean many years ago.

Sources

All entries marked * indicate an extract is selected from the whole.

1900–29

*Tropica (Mary Adella Wolcott), *Island of Sunshine* (New York: Knickerbocker Press, 1904): 'The Undertone', p. 26, and 'Nana', pp. 39–41

Claude McKay
   'My Native Land My Home' pp. 84–5, 'A Midnight Woman To The Bobby', pp. 74–6 in *Songs of Jamaica* (Kingston: A.W. Gardner & Co., 1912)
   'The Apple-Woman's Complaint', pp. 57–8 in *Constab Ballads* (London: Watts & Co., 1912)
   'In Bondage', p. 39 and 'Outcast', p. 41 in Max Eastman (ed.) *Selected Poems of Claude McKay* (Harcourt Brace Jovanovitch: San Diego, 1953)

Voices from Summerland, J.E.C. McFarlane (ed.) (London: Fowler Wright Ltd., 1929)
   H.S. Bunbury, 'The Spell of the Tropics', p. 39
   Astley Clerk, 'Islets Mid Silver Seas', p. 58
   J.E.C. McFarlane, 'The Fleet of the Empire', pp. 138–9; 'My Country', pp. 135–7, reprinted in *Selected Shorter Poems* (Kingston, Jamaica: Pioneer Press, 1954) pp. 32–4
   Claude McKay, 'Flame-Heart', p. 152; 'I Shall Return', p. 157
   Eva Nicholas, 'A Country Idyl', pp. 217–8
   Tom Redcam, 'My Beautiful Home', p. 265; '"O, Little Green Island Far Over the Sea"', pp. 279–80
   Tropica (Mary Adella Wolcott), 'Busha's Song', pp. 293–4

*J.E.C. McFarlane, *A Treasury of Jamaican Poetry*, London: University of London Press, 1949) [revised edition of *Voices* (1929)]
   Clara Maude Garrett, 'One', p. 32
   P.M. Sherlock, 'Pocomania', pp. 103–4
   H.D. Carberry, 'Epitaph', p. 105

Songs of Empire, edited by Constance Hollar (Kingston: Gleaner, 1932)
   Albinia Hutton, 'The Empire's Flag', pp. 8–9; 'A Plea', pp. 31–2
   Tom Redcam, 'Jamaica's Coronation Ode', pp. 13–4

*H.G. De Lisser, *Jane's Career*, (Kingston: Gleaner, 1914; London: Heinemann, 1971)

*A.R.F. Webber, *Those That be in Bondage – A Tale of Indian Indentures and Sunlit Western Waters* (Guyana, Georgetown: The Daily Chronicle Printing Press, 1917; reprinted by Calaloux Publications, 1988) pp. 1–8

*C.L.R. James, 'Triumph', *Trinidad* (Christmas 1929), reprinted in Reinhard Sander (ed.), *From Trinidad* (London: Hodder and Stoughton Educational, 1978)
*Leo Oakley, 'Ideas of Patriotism and National Dignity in Some Jamaican Writings', *Jamaica Journal*, 4 (1970), pp. 16–21
*Harvey Clarke, 'Miss Jamaica', *Planters' Punch*, 2 (1929), p. 5
*McFarlane, J.E.C., 'Claude McKay' in *A Literature in the Making* (Kingston: Pioneer Press, 1956), pp. 85–91
*Edward Baugh, *West Indian Poetry 1900–1970: A Study in Cultural Decolonisation* (Kingston, Jamaica: Savacou Publications, 1971)
*Amy J. Garvey, 'Women as Leaders' (1925) in Margaret Busby (ed.) *Daughters of Africa*, (London: Jonathan Cape Ltd., 1993), pp. 209–11; originally editorial in *Negro World* (US)

1930–49

Una Marson *Tropic Reveries* (Kingston: Gleaner, 1930), 'If', p. 84; 'In Vain', p. 27; 'Renunciation', p. 20; 'Jamaica', pp. 60–1; 'In Jamaica', p. 82 [40] in *Heights and Depths* (Kingston: Gleaner, 1931); 'Quashie Comes to London', pp. 17–21; 'Kinky Hair Blues', 'Cinema Eyes', pp. 87–8 IN *The Moth and the Star* (Kingston: Author, 1937); 'Nigger', *The Keys* (July 1933), pp. 8–9
George Campbell, 'Holy', 'Oh! You Build a House' in *First Poems*; reprinted in Pamela Mordecai (ed.) *From Our Yard: Jamaican Poetry Since Independence*, (Kingston: Institute of Jamaica Publications Ltd: 1987)
Louise Bennett 'Jamaican Oman' (pp. 21–3); 'Bed Time Story' (p. 6); 'Proverbs' (pp. 53–4); 'Tan a Yuh Yard' (pp. 110–11) in *Selected Poems*, Mervyn Morris (ed.) (Kingston: Sangster's Book Stores Ltd., 1982)
   'Beeny Bud (Mussirolinkina)' in *Anancy Stories and Dialect Verse* (Kingston: Pioneer Press, 1957)
Mighty Chalkdust, 'Brain Drain', (1968) reprinted in Paula Burnett (ed.) *The Penguin Book of Caribbean Verse* (Penguin, 1986), p. 46
Mighty Sparrow, 'Dan is the Man' (1963) reprinted in Brown, Morris & Rohlehr, *Voiceprint*, (Longman, 1989) pp. 129–30
*Roger Mais, 'Listen The Wind' in *The Green Antilles*, Barbara Howes (ed.) (London: Panter Books Ltd, 1971) pp. 103–108
Vera Bell, 'Ancestor on the Auction Block', *Focus* (1948) p. 187; reprinted in D.G. Wilson (ed.) *New Ships: An Anthology of West Indian Poems* (Oxford: Oxford University Press, 1975), pp. 42–3
A.J. Seymour, 'Sun is a Shapely Fire' (1944) in Elma Seymour (ed.) *Sun is a Shapely Fire* (Georgetown, Guyana, 1973); originally in *Sun's in my Blood* (Georgetown, Guyana Standard, 1944)
*C.L.R. James, 'Discovering Literature in Trinidad: two experiences, *Journal of Commonwealth Literature* (1969), pp. 73–80 [co-authored with Michael Anthony]
*Albert Gomes, *Through a Maze of Colour*, (Trinidad: Key Books, 1974)
*Editorials *The Beacon* 'Local Fiction' and 'Local Poetry' (Jan.–Feb. 1932) in Sander (ed.) *op cit.*
*Alison Donnell, 'Contradictory (W)omens?: Gender Consciousness in the Poetry of Una Marson', *Kunapipi* (1996)

*J.E.C. McFarlane, 'The Challenge of Our Time' (1935) in *The Challenge of Our Time*, J.E.C. McFarlane (Kingston: New Dawn Press, 1945)

*Una Marson, 'We Want Books – But Do We Encourage Our Writers?', *Daily Gleaner* (23 Oct. 1949), p. 7

*Victor Stafford Reid, 'The Cultural Revolution in Jamaica after 1938' (address delivered at the Institute of Jamaica [1978])

Roger Mais, 'Where the Roots Lie', *Public Opinion*, (9 March 1940), p. 12

*Mervyn Morris, 'On Reading Louise Bennett, Seriously', *Jamaica Journal*, 1/1 (1967), pp. 69–74

*Gordon Rohlehr, 'Images of Men and Women in 1930s Calypsoes', in *Gender in Caribbean Development*, edited by P. Mohammed and C. Shepard (U.W.I. Women and Development Project, 1988), pp. 232–306

1950–65

*Martin Carter, *Poems of Resistance* (1954) in *Poems of Succession* (New Beacon Books, 1977) 'The University of Hunger', pp. 34–5; 'I Come from the Nigger Yard', pp. 38–9; 'I Am No Soldier', pp. 49–50

*Karl Sealey 'My Fathers before Me', (*Bim* 7,27, June 1958, pp. 135–8) in *West Indian Stories*, Andrew Salkey (ed.) (London: Faber and Faber 1960)

Elma Napier, 'Carnival in Martinique', *Bim*, 4,15 (Dec. 1951), pp. 155–7

Samuel Selvon, 'Waiting for Aunty to Cough' (1957) in *Ways of Sunlight* (Longman Drumbeat, 1979), pp. 139–145

Jean Rhys, 'The Day They Burnt the Books' in *Tales of the Wide Caribbean* , K. Ramchand (ed.) (London: Heinemann 1985); originally in *London Magazine*, 7 July 1960, pp. 42–6

Henry Swanzy, 'The Literary Situation in the Caribbean', *Books Abroad*, vol. 30, (1956), pp. 266–74

*George Lamming, 'The Occasion for Speaking' in *The Pleasures of Exile* (London: Michael Joseph, 1960), pp. 23–50

*Evelyn O'Callaghan, 'The Outsider's Voice: White Creole Women Novelists in the Caribbean Literary Tradition', *Journal of West Indian Literature*, 1/1 (1986), pp. 74–88

*Reinhard Sander and Ian Munro, 'The Making of a Writer – a Conversation with George Lamming', *Caribbean Quarterly*, 17/3 & 4 (1971), pp. 9–20

Sarah Lawson Welsh, 'New Wine in New Bottles: The reception of West Indian Writing in Britain in the 1950s and Early 1960s' (1991)

1966–79

Dennis Scott, 'Squatter's Rites', 'Grampa' from *Uncle Time* (Pittsburgh: University of Pittsburgh Press, 1973); reprinted in Pamela Mordecai (ed.) *From Our Yard* (Kingston:Institute of Jamaica Publications, 1987) p. 205; p. 206

Anthony McNeill, 'Residue' in Pamela Mordecai (ed.) *From Our Yard* (Kingston: Institute of Jamaica Publications, 1987) from *Reel from the Life-Movie* (Jamaica: Savacou, 1975), p. 139

Christine Craig, 'Elsa's Version', in Pamela Mordecai (ed.) *From Our Yard* (Kingston: Institute of Jamaica Publications, 1987), p. 57

Mahadai Das, 'They Came in Ships', in *India in the Caribbean* (London: Hansib Publications Ltd 1987), pp. 288–9

Rajkumari Singh, 'Per Ajie' in *Days of the Sahib Are Over* (Georgetown, Guyana: Whirl of Papers and Author 1971), pp. 15–16

*Sylvia Wynter, 'We Must Learn to Sit Down Together and Discuss a Little Culture', Parts I and II, *Jamaican Journal*, 2/4 (1968) pp. 24–32 & 3/1 (1969) pp. 27–42

*Derek Walcott, 'The Muse of History', in *Is Massa Day Dead* edited by Orde Coombs (New York: Doubleday/Anchor Press, 1974)

*Kamau Brathwaite, 'Jazz and the West Indian Novel I, II & III', *Bim*, 12/44 (1967), pp. 275–81, 12/45 (1967), pp. 39–51 & 12/46 (1968/9), pp. 115–25

*Gerald Moore, 'Review: Use Men Language', *Bim*, 15/57 (1974), pp. 69–76

*Gordon Rohlehr, 'West Indian Poetry: Some Problems of Assessment' I and II, *Bim*, 14/54 (1972–3?), pp. 80–7 & *Bim*, 14/55 (1972–3?), pp. 134–44; 'Afterthoughts', *Bim*, 14/56 (1973), pp. 227–32

*Kamau Brathwaite, 'Timehri', *Savacou* 2 (1970), pp. 35–44

*James Berry, 'Introduction' to *Bluefoot Traveller* (London: Limehouse Publications, 1976), pp. 9–10

Rajkumari Singh, 'I am a Coolie', *Heritage* 2 (Georgetown, Guyana: Sept. 1973) pp. 25–7

1980–89

Lorna Goodison 'On Houses', p. 44; 'My Late Friend', p. 32; 'Guyana Lovesong', p. 31 in *Tamarind Season*, (Kingston: Institute of Jamaica Publications, 1980) 'For My Mother (May I Inherit Half Her Strength)', 'I Am Becoming My Mother', in *I Am Becoming My Mother* (London: New Beacon Books, 1986)

James Berry 'Lucy's Letter', 'From Lucy: Holiday Reflections' in *Lucy's Letters and Loving* (London: New Beacon Books, 1982) pp. 39–40; pp. 42–3 'Caribbean Proverb Poems 1 and 2' in *Chain of Days* (Oxford: Oxford University Press, 1984) p. 3

Grace Nichols, 'One Continent/To Another' pp. 6–8; 'Your Blessing', pp. 52–5 *i is a long memoried woman* (London: Karnak House, 1983)

Jane King, 'Intercity Dub, For Jean' (for Jean Binta Breeze) in *Confluence: Nine St Lucian Poems* (Castries, St Lucia: The Source, 1988), pp. 23–5

Jamaica Kincaid, 'Columbus in Chains', in *Annie John* (London: Picador, 1985), pp. 72–84

Linton Kwesi Johnson, 'Street 66' in *Dread Beat 'An Blood* (London: Bogle L'Ouverture, 1975) p. 19–20, 'Reggae fi Dada' in *Tings and Times* (Newcastle upon Tyne: Bloodaxe, 1991), pp. 34–6

Harry Narain, 'A Letter to the Prime Minister' in *Grass-Roots People* (Cuba: Casa de las Americas, 1981), pp. 7–12

Mikey Smith, 'Black and White' in *It A Come*, Mervyn Morris (ed.) (London: Race Today Publications, 1986), p. 57

*David Dabydeen, 'On Not Being Milton: Nigger Talk in England Today', *Tibisiri* (Coventry: Dangaroo Press, 1989) pp. 121–135

*Ramabai Espinet, 'The Invisible Women in West Indian Literature', *World Literature Written in English*, 29/2 (1989), pp. 16–26

The 1990s

*David Dabydeen, *The Counting House* (London: Jonathan Cape Ltd, 1996)

Jean Binta Breeze, 'Testament' from *Spring Cleaning* (London: Virago, 1992) pp. 7–11

Benjamin Zephaniah, 'A Modern Slave Song' in *City Psalms* (Newcastle upon Tyne: Bloodaxe Books Ltd, 1992) p. 52

Mutabaruka, 'dis poem', *Jamaican Journal*, 24, 2 (March 1992), p. 52

*Carolyn Cooper, 'Writing Oral History', *After Europe* (Coventry: Dangaroo Press, 1989) pp. 49–57

*Sylvia Wynter, 'Beyond Miranda's Meanings: Un/silencing the "Demonic Ground" of Caliban's "Women"' in *Out of the Kumbla: Caribbean Women and Literature* Carole Boyce Davies and Elaine Savory Fido (eds) (Trenton, N.J.: Africa World Press, 1990)

*Alison Donnell, 'Dreaming of Daffodils: Cultural Resistance in the Narratives of Theory, *Kunapipi* xiv, 2 (1992) pp. 45–52

*Merle Hodge, 'Challenges of the Struggle of Sovereignty' in *Caribbean Women Writers*, (Massachusetts: Calaloux Publications, 1990), pp. 202–208

Jean Binta Breeze, 'Can a Dub Poet be a Women?' *Women: a Cultural Review*, 1/1 (1990), pp. 47–9

*Derek Walcott, 'The Antilles: Fragments of Epic Memory' (The Nobel Lecture), (London: The Nobel Foundation and Faber and Faber, 1992)

*John Vidal, 'By Word of Mouth – John Vidal gets in tune with dub poet, Benjamin Zephaniah', *The Guardian* 15/9/88

General introduction

A R/reader in the 1990s

Each editor of a Reader has different notions of what a Reader can be; in formulating the present Reader we have been guided by a strong awareness of the politics concerning the reception of Readers in the 1990s, and in particular by certain negative expectations. Readers are frequently viewed as 'short-circuit' mechanisms to navigate a literature, as textual packages which promise a spurious comprehensiveness but, in actuality, can dissuade readers from further exploratory reading. There is good sense in these objections and we share some of the frustrations at the limitations inherent in the Reader format. Working within the field of Caribbean literary studies, we have been especially concerned that the Reader could be perceived as a 'quick fix' sampling of the exotica of a marginal literature. However, working in this field has also convinced us of the value and potential of such a text. It is probably not surprising that publishers are reluctant to reissue entire works by writers who are little known and have been long out of print. A Reader in Caribbean literature can offer a valuable space for such material and therefore function not just cynically to 'feed' a market but importantly to lead a market.

The primary aim of this publication is to generate more readers of Caribbean literature and readers of more Caribbean literature. This Reader brings little-known texts to greater attention, but it also brings more familiar texts into a range of contexts which re-inflect their possible meanings. In this way, a Reader can be not merely recuperative but also re-evaluative – offering not only new texts but new critical configurations. It is our aim that this Reader will 'write in' those who have been 'written off' or 'written over', not as an act of prescriptive recuperation or counter-canonization, but as a way of generating new connections, new ways of reading and new notions of Caribbean literary praxis.

[1]

We hope not only to construct a Reader in Caribbean literature but also a reader of Caribbean literature – conceiving of the project as a joint production of text and living reader. The R/reader is multiple: just as the reader is always constructed by the overlapping functions of gender, class, education and cultural identity, so too the Reader resists any single intellectual perspective and aims to be open to a range of positions. The R/reader is a site of discensus and of process. During the course of co-production we found that we disagreed not only with each other but with ourselves in relation to selections and ways of reading; and we wanted, as far as possible, to emphasize this potential in our readership and to allow the reader to plot their own pathways through the Reader. In a profound sense the Reader is never 'finished' but passes to the reader for a series of partial and provisional acts of meaning, stable only for a moment within a matrix of mobile interconnections. Indeed, our own affectionate title for the work in process was the 'rebellious Reader', as the manuscript constantly shape-shifted and presented new challenges for selection. Although it has finally conformed to the neat contours of the printed page, we would like to think that the rebellious spirit which it demonstrated in process remains. However, we are equally aware that the notion of the dissenting R/reader is in itself in danger of becoming a new orthodoxy, with the constant privileging of writing which conforms to .non-conformity and a critical impasse which cannot move beyond celebration of the 'other' in radical form.

Evidently all anthologies are instruments of canon-formation, shaped partly by the biases of their editors and located in a specific time and place. Our aim is to work against the consolidation of the few (writers) which has led to the neglect of the many, and to open up rather than to close down interpretative possibilities, which may well be regarded in time as a characteristic of the 1990s Reader. However, we should be delighted if this text prompts readers to search even deeper into the forgotten files and crumbling newspapers of a Caribbean archive and to make the necessity for such a Reader as this an historical phenomenon.

For the present, we have deliberately probed some of the sore points of the Caribbean literary tradition, those areas which previous critics have sought to disavow. These include Creole writing and writing which works with rather than against colonial and eurocentric forms. We have also sought to stage some of the central debates about cultural and aesthetic value which have animated writers and critics of Caribbean literature through the twentieth century. Our criteria for inclusion of pieces were driven by a desire to represent as wide a range of Anglophone Caribbean literary discourse as possible. This was in part enabled by our decision not to include Caribbean theatre texts which have recently received significant critical attention (Omostoso 1982, Corbsie 1984, Hill 1992, Banham, Hill and Woodyard 1994, Stone 1994). This genre proved unproductive to represent due to its performance element and its form, which is difficult to extract from successfully. We have sought to privilege inaccessible texts as well as pieces which have made important contributions to key critical debates, with the aim of supplementing available texts. It is for this reason that we have settled for significant omissions; the poetry of Derek Walcott and the fiction of V.S. Naipaul may be crucial to an understanding of Caribbean literature and certainly of the literary and academic establishments' reception of this literature, but they are also widely available. Another aim was to give a reasonably representative sampling of literary range from different periods, ethnic groups, genres, genders and regions. However, our guiding principle was not so much comprehensiveness as to give space to those pieces most likely to produce a useful 'abrasiveness', as pieces within the whole rubbed up against each other and generated new readings and cross-connections.

We hope to have selected pieces which will have value in different ways for different readers: the value of challenging dominant readings (**Wynter 1968** and **1969, 1990, Kincaid 1985**); the value of being a prime example of a received colonial mindset and aesthetic (**McFarlane, Bunbury, Clerk 1929, McFarlane 1945**); the value of presenting a clear overview (**Rohlehr 1972–3, 1973**); the value of the writer-critic's perspective (**Lamming 1960, Walcott 1974, Binta Breeze 1990**) which problematizes the demarcation between primary and critical writing. We were also keen to include texts which are valuable in ways that are not normally credited in academic publications: the enjoyable or humorous read (**Clarke 1929, *The Beacon Editorials* 1932, Selvon 1957, Gomes 1974,** Kincaid 1985); and lively, polemical writings (**Rajkumari Singh 1973, Dabydeen 1989**) in order to question the notion of post-colonial 'worthiness'. It is also worth mentioning what could not be included: the costly (a factor in the omission of Walcott and Naipaul), the difficult to access (*Singers Quarterly* and certain of Walter MacA. Lawrence's poems) and those about which we were unable to find sufficient information (this was particularly pertinent to literature from some of the smaller islands). We have attempted to overcome the bias towards Jamaican and Trinidadian material in our selection as far as possible, but it must be noted that the dominance of these islands reflects not only our own particular specialisms, but also what has been most widely circulated and commented upon, with the exception of work by St Lucian Derek Walcott and Barbadians George Lamming and Kamau Brathwaite.

Notions of a Caribbean literature

The genesis of a Caribbean aesthetic has been traced by many scholars of the tradition to a desire to decolonize and indigenize imaginatively and to claim a voice for a history, a geography and a people which had been dominated by British Victorians – both literally and literarily. Certainly this desire to reclaim and restore alter/native cultural traditions has been a prime motivating factor for many Caribbean writers throughout the twentieth century, and any attempt to assess a Caribbean aesthetic must clearly take into account the influence which British colonial educational policy and colonial policy more generally would have exercised over notions of the literary and of emerging post-colonial identities.

Colonial institutions had played a primary role in determining the nature and value of literature in the West Indies. The literature selected for dissemination served the interests of colonial policy and as such was 'ideologically motivated in the very essence of seeming to be devoid of ideology' (Donnell 1992: 50). Many of the texts which were promoted by school syllabuses as unproblematically apolitical are interesting subjects for trans-contextual analysis. The much-referred-to 'Daffodils' by Wordsworth is an excellent example, as its political orientation is implicit. Written by a white man about flowers native to England, within anglocentric culture, it is seemingly both objective and purely aesthetic. However, the poem cannot be identified as ideologically neutral within a Caribbean context where daffodils are unfamiliar and perhaps defamilarizing. Indeed, the cultural politics of the canon and the way in which the now familiar notion of English literature was constructed in line with the colonial project to educate 'the natives' has generated interesting debates within Caribbean writing itself (**Lamming 1960, James 1969**).

Many early twentieth-century texts continue to operate within colonial expectations of literature at the level of both form and content. However, from the start of this century gestures towards distinct local literature emerged. Many of these, like **Thomas MacDermot**'s 'All Jamaica Library', were ventures of those white Creoles with the money and social profile to publish. The Jamaican poet **Claude McKay** is the exceptional black writer of this period, although it is a mark of the ambivalent attitude towards black folk culture at this time that McKay was encouraged to write poetry in creole by a white folklorist, Walter Jekyll.

Although it is **our** aim to bring texts from this period into the frame of Caribbean literature, most writers at this time would have seen themselves as contributing to local traditions rather than regional ones. It seems important to be aware that the idea of a West Indian or Caribbean aesthetic really only emerged during the 1930s and 1940s and although it appears as an issue for debate in early editorials of *The Beacon* in Trinidad and *Kyk-over-al* in British Guyana, many writers and critics at this time remained focused on the task of consolidating local traditions. It is also relevant to consider that at this time the use of the term 'West Indian' was more likely to occur within colonial contexts, as perhaps the strongest common factor amongst West Indian territories was their shared experience of colonialism. Consequently when the term 'West Indian' appears during the pre-1950 period, it does not usually represent any radical anti-imperialist sentiment or vision of a pan-Caribbean culture. However, around 1950 a profusion of articles began to appear in which the term 'West Indian' was used in order to explore the possibilities for a unified regional identity (Blackman 1949: 7, Hearne 1950: 6, Seymour 1950, 1953/4). It would appear that the activities of the most federalist Caribbean journals, such as *Kyk-over-al*, enabled some writers and critics to gain a sense of an emergent West Indian literature, as opposed to separate island literatures – what **Brathwaite** has termed as a shift from 'West Indian island to Caribbean matrix' (1977a: 54). It could be argued that this sentiment was strengthened as West Indian Federation loomed larger in the late 1950s and, although short-lived, became an actuality in the early 1960s. However, the surge of nationalisms in many Anglophone Caribbean territories in this period, especially those such as Jamaica and Trinidad which were to gain their independence in 1962, tended to cut across this move towards a West Indian literature and to re-establish a sense of individual literatures.

The project to establish an 'independent' cultural identity and literary identity was probably more fraught in the Caribbean than other post-colonial societies. With the indigenous Caribs, Arawaks and Amerindians all but annihilated (although interestingly Amerindians are now re-gaining political and cultural prominence in Guyana), there was no pre-colonial culture to turn to, and with such an ethnic admixture still living in the region, the problem of a common cultural base was acute. Although one might argue that this absence of a stable, homogeneous culture has made the role of imaginative forms more vital during periods of nationalist struggle, it has also made the relationship between 'Caribbeanness' and literature less easy to define. The search for a Caribbean aesthetic has been renegotiated and refined in the decades since Independence. In a plural culture there can be no single notion of 'Caribbeanness', rather there is a growing acceptance of a syncretic (centreless) model of cultural definition which is inclusive and accepts diversity and hybridity as the foundation for both Caribbean aesthetics and cultural identities.

Although in the 1980s and 1990s the notion of a West Indian/ Caribbean literature has gained a popular currency within the academy and in international contexts, the idea of a cognate and unified field is still importantly contested by critics in the field who wish to retain the emphasis on diversity and discensus (Breiner 1986). In the last decade also, certain Caribbean writers have gained an increasingly high media and academic profile. The culmination to this came in 1992 with the Nobel Prize for literature being awarded to **Derek Walcott**, the St Lucian poet and playwright. The international and popular recognition of Caribbean literature is arguably overdue, but this form of incorporation may also produce an unduly neat and packaged version of the literature. If Caribbean literature is to preserve its varied and mongrel nature then these are trends which writers and critics must observe carefully.

We have elected to use the term 'Caribbean' in preference to 'West Indian' (a term used to differentiate former and current British colonies) as it is more suggestive of a literature freed from the (re-)centring tendencies of a colonial and Commonwealth framework,

[6]

and in every case we use Caribbean as synonymous with Anglophone Caribbean as a practical necessity.

Locating a tradition

The Caribbean canon has been traditionally dominated by a number of seminal works from the 1950s and 1960s, the period when Caribbean literature 'boomed' in the metropolitan motherland, London. The writings of V.S. Naipaul, **George Lamming**, **Sam Selvon**, Wilson Harris, **Derek Walcott** and **Kamau Brathwaite** have been the staple diet of Caribbean literature studies and undergraduate courses for the past two decades. The formation of this canon needs to be read in its own historical moment. In the political context of the 1960s and 1970s (with the majority of English colonies achieving Independence and an emphasis on black consciousness and emergent Black Power movements) it is unsurprising that the critical axes were shifting away from the aesthetic productions of the educational and social elite which had previously achieved the recognition for literary endeavour in the region. Works by black and anti-colonial writers which celebrated and validated the regional and the populist traditions of 'the folk' were particularly crucial to the new agendas of indigeneity and creolization. This phase of ideological repositioning in relation to literary history can be most obviously located, and its strategic essentialism identified, in Kamau Brathwaite's often cited rejection of **Jean Rhys** as a *bone fide* Caribbean writer (see Brathwaite 1974, 1995). This exclusion is particularly ironic given that Rhys herself is now usually the one Creole and woman writer to be admitted into the canon alongside the male writers listed earlier.

However, while the cultural separatism of this project has not endured, the canon proposed by this general movement towards a new literary agenda remains remarkably unscathed. A version of Caribbean literature predicated on the works of the above writers is limited both in its narrow historical range and in its male and African-Caribbean bias. Furthermore, the same critical studies of the 1960s and 1970s which ventured these writers as the literature's central figures also demarcated the paradigms for a critical approach to Caribbean literature, outlining the dominant tropes, thematic preoccupations, and stylistic devices (Coulthard 1962, Ramchand 1970, Coombes 1974, Baugh 1978, Brown 1978, King 1979). The critical

[7]

preoccupations with naming the landscape; validating the local; the architecture of a literature; accommodation; alienation; personhood and community; the autobiographical mode; childhood and matrilineal links; exile; nostalgia; rewriting histories; and a realist tradition, persist as classic areas of enquiry. Indeed, the degree to which these survey texts remain significant resources even today cannot be stressed enough. The above litany of approved sites for critical intervention is now both formulaic and out-moded, and yet has retained its status as the assumed Caribbean rubric. These 1970s text-books have strongly shaped notions of a Caribbean literary archive by suggesting a teleological framework, championing a select group of writers in virtual consensus and often refusing to address the vexed question of literary value in relation to early twentieth-century writings. It is precisely this recycling of a limited number of texts and issues which the canon now represents which we believe is positively damaging both to Caribbean texts and to critical practices.

It is our aim in the Reader to trace the dominant Caribbean literary traditions which have emerged through the course of the twentieth century, but it is equally our hope to open up these traditions for further enquiry and to read them alongside other potential traditions. By challenging the stasis of the Caribbean canon, we wish to dissuade readers from taking a convenient but rather unadventurous short-cut through the literature and to encourage them to enjoy the variety of pace and of terrain which a meandering journey entails.

In its deliberate inclusiveness, this Reader contrasts with previous anthologies which have tended to separate texts along lines of regional, generational, ethnic and gender differences, as well as the more obvious categorizations according to genre, and primary or secondary material. Some recent examples include *From Our Yard*, edited by Pamela Mordecai (1987) (Jamaican post-Independence poetry), *Her True-True Name* edited by Pamela Mordecai and Betty Wilson (1989) (women's short fiction from throughout the region), *Hinterland: Caribbean Poetry from the West Indies and Britain*, edited by E.A. Markham (1989) (contemporary Anglophone poetry), *Voiceprint: An Anthology of Oral and Related Poetry from the Caribbean*, edited by Stewart Brown *et al.* (1989), *Out of the Kumbla: Caribbean Women and Literature*, edited by Carole Boyce Davies and Elaine Savory Fido (1990) (secondary sourcebook on women's writing and feminist criticism), *India in the Caribbean*, edited by David Dabydeen and Brinsley Samaroo (interdisciplinary essays on the Indo-Caribbean experience), and *Green Cane and Juicy Flotsam: Short Stories by Caribbean Women*, edited by Carmen C. Esteves and Lizabeth Paravisini-Gebert (1991) (pan-Caribbean women's short fiction).

Such anthologies have clear agendas and are often helpful in reconfiguring notions of Caribbean literature, but they also constrain readers to comply with the editor's vision. In contrast, we seek to stress the connections and interactions between these groups and writings, whilst at the same time retaining a strong sense of the hy'iridity and plurality which characterizes the Caribbean experience. This Reader offers a range of texts which can usefully displace both the belief in a limited configuration of writers and the exclusive concentration on certain critical paradigms which have emerged alongside these writings.

Locating theory

As a discipline which has almost wholly gained status in Western and European forms, the application of critical theory to Caribbean literature could be perceived as a means through which to reassert the dominance of European cultures – a neo-colonial intellectual device. The unquestioning adoption of a privileged and possibly even alienating discourse in order to discuss the work of writers who have constantly, and often fiercely, had to struggle against such intellectual orthodoxies in order to achieve recognition would seem a little misplaced. Nevertheless, we would argue that certain theoretical positions do have important functions in relation to literary works in the Caribbean (see pp. 440–50). Although 'theory-speak' can disguise its own value-laden assumptions within a cumbersome costume of elaborate language games, it can also work to unmask areas of intellectual activity in which covert and somehow naturalized cultural biases masquerade as clarity and universal truth. Post-colonial theory with its foregrounding of cultural difference as a key determinant within evaluation has been enabling to both the analysis and the promotion of Caribbean literature. The interrogation of the ideological biases which inform the production and reception of post-colonial texts has also been helpful. However, the complexity of the reference of a term such as 'post-colonial' needs to be attended to, if post-colonial theory is not to become an homogenizing narrative which tends to collapse regions as diverse as Australia and Africa into a space of (implied equal) otherness, oppression and silencing. Also, whilst post-colonial theory has successfully highlighted the resistance and subversion of colonialist discourse within post-colonial texts, it has been less ready to embrace a position which refuses centrality to the tyranny of colonialism by envisaging ways of being and of writing outside of its boundaries of definition.

It is our aim here to represent some of the most salient developments in Caribbean literary theory and to take a broad definition of theory which accepts Barbara Christian's proposition that 'people of colour have always theorized – but in forms quite different from the Western form of abstract logic. And I am inclined to say that our theorizing is often in narrative forms, in the stories we create, in riddles and proverbs, in the play with language, since dynamic rather than fixed ideas seem more to our liking' (Christian 1989: 226). We trust that by representing a range of voices the value of a plurality of positions in which no utterance can hold absolute authority may become apparent, in addition to the value of each. In the 1990s climate of the fetishization of theory, it is also our aim to alert readers to the problems of constantly proliferating critical discourse without an accompanying attentiveness to literary texts.

Language politics: defining the ground

The language situation in the Caribbean is as fascinating as it is complex and needs to be foregrounded in any appreciation of the literature itself. Key terms important to an understanding of the language debates include: creole, nation language and 'the creole continuum'. We therefore seek to clarify our use of these terms. The term 'Creole' is often confused with the linguistic term 'creole'. Both derive from the Spanish *criollo* which denotes 'born in, native to, committed to the area of living' (Brathwaite 1971: xv). Creole is often used to describe those of predominantly European descent who regard the Caribbean as home, or those who are 'functionally white' (Saakana 1987). However, the variety of different names accorded to those of European descent resident within the Caribbean – white West Indians, Creoles, Euro-Creoles, expatriates, 'red legs' – suggests a continuum of cultural involvement and allegiance to colonial powers along which such individuals might position themselves or be positioned by different historical narratives, as well as the difficulties of definition.

The term 'creole' denotes the linguistic forms which are closest to dialect or nation language (a term coined by Kamau Brathwaite) and which are often erroneously considered to be broken or approximate language systems. In fact, creoles are language systems in their own right, with syntax and lexicons of considerable sophistication, and are found globally. 'Nation language' is a more culturally specific and less neutral term which affirms a positive status for Caribbean non-'standard' linguistic forms. Dialect and patois (or patwa[h]) are more pejorative (see Brathwaite 1984: 13) and less linguistically accurate terms for what we call creole or nation language. However, as with other traditionally denigrated terms, these have been re-appropriated and re-inflected as positive terms of cultural resistance by certain writers. The Jamaican theatre group, Sistren, whose groundbreaking *Lionheart Gal: Life Stories of Jamaican Women* was published in 1986, both reclaimed (and re-spelt) 'patwah' as their language.

Indeed, the importance of the status accorded to creole or nation language in the attribution of literary value should not be underestimated. Some early commentators on the literature of the region were progressive in suggesting the primary orality of creole and its capacity to express a range of emotions. For example, the white amanuensis of **Claude McKay**'s early poetry, Walter Jekyll, had this to say in his preface to McKay's *Songs of Jamaica* (1912):

> What Italian is to Latin, that in regard to English is the negro variant thereof. It shortens, softens, rejects the harder sounds alike of consonants and vowels; I might almost say, refines. In its soft tones we have an expression of the languorous sweetness of the South: it is a feminine version of masculine English; pre-eminently a language of love, as all will feel who setting prejudice aside, will allow the charmingly naive love-songs of this volume to make their due impression upon them. But this can only happen when the verses are read aloud and those unacquainted with the Jamaican language may thus welcome a few hints as to pronunciation.
>
> (Jekyll 1912: 5)

Jekyll does fall back on some stock-responses to creole (e.g. that it is 'charmingly naive') and his need to offer 'hints as to pronunciation' foregrounds questions of audience and the packaging of creole poetry as a quaintly exoticized poetic medium. However, in comparison with the later comments of J.E.C. McFarlane, also discussing McKay's poetry, they are positively radical. In *A Literature in the Making*, McFarlane declared: 'Dialect . . . is a "broken tongue" with which it is impossible to build an edifice of verse possessing the perfect symmetry of finished art' (**McFarlane 1956**: 85). Indeed, even as late as the 1960s, the poet **Louise Bennett** was seen to be 'doing dialect' rather than literature and her work was anthologized only in appendices to poetry collections (Lindo 1962). In the same decade, writers and commentators appear frequently at odds with each other as to the status of creole and its literary value. Mervyn Morris lamented in 1967 that: 'The language which . . . maids and yard boys [use] is not yet accepted simply as one of our Jamaican ways of speech' (**Morris 1967**: 69). Yet Rex Nettleford referred to creole as an 'unruly substance' and 'an idiom whose limitations as a bastard tongue are all too evident' (Nettleford 1966: 9–10), in his otherwise sensitive and supportive introduction to Bennett's *Jamaica Labrish* (1966).

The status of creole received a massive boost with the publication of certain ground-breaking linguistic studies of Caribbean creoles from the 1960s onwards (Cassidy 1961, Bailey 1966, Cassidy and Le Page 1967, Hymes (ed.) 1971, Bickerton 1973, Sutcliffe 1982, Pollard 1982, 1983, 1984, 1986, Daphinis 1985, Devonish 1986, Sutcliffe and Wong 1986, Rickford 1987). The emphasis on indigenous, grassroots and 'folk' resources in the critical praxis of the 1970s furthered the literary use of creoles. This has not necessarily been accompanied by a shift in popular attitudes to creoles, both within and outside the Caribbean (Lawson Welsh 1991); nor has any comfortable usage of nation language penetrated academic discourse, which is why **Carolyn Cooper**'s creole journalism and critical evaluation in creole of *Lionheart Gal* (**1989**) are so very significant.

The strongest statements in favour of creole so far have been those of Brathwaite (1984) and **Hodge (1990)**. Brathwaite traces the historical origins of the low status accorded to creole to the prohibitive language policies of the slave plantations where the slaves' African languages were severely undermined in favour of the European 'standard'. This led, Brathwaite argues, to the formation of a 'submerged language' (Brathwaite 1984: 7) with the potential for cultural resistance, and it is this which makes creole or nation language simultaneously powerless (without official status) and empowering (with great subversive potential). Hodge holds a similar view of creole as an empowering medium and in **'Challenges of the Struggle for Sovereignty'**, she makes a direct and impassioned plea for its recognition: 'We speak creole, we need creole, we cannot function without creole, for our deepest thought processes are bound up in the structure of creole, but we hold creole in contempt' (Hodge 1990: 204).

One useful concept for literary analysis originating in linguistic theory is that of the creole continuum, or, more accurately, the 'post-creole speech continuum'. As Hodge notes, almost all Caribbean people use some form of a creole language some of the time. The term *post-creole continuum* refers to the range of possible speech variants in a single speech community which might be plotted along a continuum between the most creolized forms at one end and language forms which are closer to (and virtually indistinguishable from) a standard language at the other end (David Decamp 1971: 349–70). In practice, most individuals command competence of a small range of varieties along the linguistic continuum, 'the breadth of the span depending on the breadth of [their] social contacts' (Decamp 1971: 350). The process of switching between different speech varieties according to social context is called *code-switching*. Significantly, both the concept of a linguistic continuum and of the individual's ability to 'code-switch' have been appropriated by certain Caribbean writers and theorists and adapted to refer more generally to the cultural variety and aesthetic choices open to the Caribbean writer (see **O'Callaghan 1986**: 75–6 and Rohlehr 1986).

Creolizing the canon

(i) Literature before the boom

Very little attention has been paid to the period of Caribbean literature before the 'boom' years of the 1950s. As late as 1966, A.J. Seymour declared that 'the 1920s were a period when the British Caribbean was still literarily asleep' (Seymour 1966: 180), and in 1970, despite paying it considerable attention, the pre-1930 period was branded by Kenneth Ramchand as 'life without fiction'. In fact, literary works by black West Indians date back to the eighteenth century with Francis Williams's 'Ode to Governor Haldane' (1759), and important contributions to a white cultural archive can be traced back to 1764 with James Grainger's 'The Sugar Cane: A poem in four parts'. In the nineteenth century significant works include narratives and journals by European travellers and white plantation-owners such as the gothic novels and journal of Mathew 'Monk' Lewis, the 1801–6 diaries of Lady Maria Nugent (the American wife of a governor of Jamaica) (Nugent, 1966) and J.W. Orderson's novel *Creoleana* (1842). Texts that redressed the outsider bias of colonial narratives during this period, whether consciously or unconsciously, include the poetry of Guyanese Egbert Martin ('Leo'), Mary Seacole's *The Wonderful Adventures of Mrs Seacole* (1857) and the early creole works of S.E. Wills and Michael McTurk ('Quow'). The remarkable counter-discourse of black Trinidadian J.J. Thomas's *Froudacity* (1889), which was a direct response to Oxford Emeritus Professor of History Anthony Froude's *The English in the West Indies or The Bow of Ulysses* (1888), deserves special mention.

As **Henry Swanzy** has pointed out: 'it is significant that the work [of the first writers in the West Indies] was mainly conversational, never literary in the pure sense' (Swanzy 1956: 267). Perhaps the unorthodox and diverse profile of early literary endeavour in the region is one of the reasons why an acknowledgement of a Caribbean literary history was slow to arrive. Nevertheless, journals and 'histories' such as those mentioned above should not be perceived merely as examples of a subgenre or anomalies in the line of Caribbean literary production. Indeed, in Jamaica, for example, the long existence of *Singers Quarterly* (a scrap-book of poetry and other writings produced and circulated by a circle of fourteen from 1932 into the 1960s) and more recently the emergence of Sistren's working-class autobiographies (1986) suggest that the cultural status of 'literature' is still conceived of more flexibly. Our decision to represent interviews, polemics, autobiographical writings and fictionalized letters in this Reader is in part motivated by a desire to retain this more fluid definition of literary enterprise.

Regarded as somewhat embarrassing and naïve, literature from the period 1900–29 is frequently disinherited. Lacking both the' sophistication and maturity of later works, it is constructed only as a precursor to later praxis. Moreover, a number of critics have dismissed the work of early poets such as **Thomas MacDermot** ('Tom Redcam'), W. Adolphe Roberts, **J.E.C. McFarlane** and Walter

MacA. Lawrence as 'almost exclusively historical in interest' (**Edward Baugh** 1971: 5). Other critics have admitted a select few of these writers – **Claude McKay, H.G. De Lisser** and Thomas MacDermot – into the canon as key pioneering voices (Ramchand 1970, Gilkes 1981) and others still have attempted to document more fully the range of voices but have found it difficult to offer any positive evaluation or sustained analysis of the texts themselves (Boxhill in King 1979). Evidently, a major obstacle to a full coverage of this period is the inaccessibility of many of the texts. Although the absence of early writing may often be one of recognition as much as of text, the material difficulties of locating texts cannot be underestimated. It would seem that during the first half of this century little care was taken to ensure that a substantial literary archive survived and it was certainly not anticipated that critics might wish to take up material at a later date. A significant number of the early texts we include might not have survived if the writers themselves, or their friends and relatives, had not felt that their work was worthy of national attention and so donated copies to the West India Reference Library or to literary figures of their time. Of the material problems associated with establishing and compiling an archive, the dating of material is extremely difficult, as collections may only appear at the end of a life, or have been reprinted several times (e.g. McFarlane 1956, Elma Seymour ed. 1973).

The matrix of various modes of oppression (lack of education, self-censorship, lack of access to publishing houses, or money to print manuscripts) has prevented the works of many early Caribbean writers from being included in this study, but their presence, even as ellipses in a tradition (undiscovered texts in a bibliography, e.g. S.N. Cobham's *Rupert Gray: A Tale of Black and White Trinidad*, 1907) still testifies to the spaces of resistance that were mobilized in a cultural regime which operated silencing as power (their silence now being powerful). Their absence also conveys the vulnerability of any sustained or communal literary movements during the first half of the twentieth century. Against this backdrop of neglect, dismissal or compromised recognition, we felt it important to represent texts from the pre-1930 period. One valuable outcome of this inclusion is to force a reconsideration of what exactly constitutes Anglophone twentieth-century Caribbean literature and to challenge an unduly constraining developmental trajectory.

Although it is often suggested that the 1930s were the watershed years in terms of a genesis of 'authentic' Caribbean literary voices, a detailed examination of writings from the 1930s and 1940s reveals that these too are not well catalogued or regarded. In **'Discovering Literature in Trinidad', C.L.R. James** comments that he did not 'know much about West Indian Literature in the 1930s – there wasn't much to know' (James 1969: 73). Even more recent survey texts of the region's literary activity such as Brown (1978), King (1979), Gilkes (1981) demonstrate an alarming propensity to represent pre-1950 writing as an undifferentiated and unchallenging corpus, with the same few individual writers singled out for attention. This is probably due to the often ambivalent relation which writings of this period still bear in relation to colonial culture, despite powerful moves towards social realism and a new political commitment to anti-colonial writings. Moreover, the explicit 'political' status of some literature written in this period can in itself be a licence for neglect (e.g. De Boissiere's novel *Crown Jewel* started in 1935 and eventually published in Australia in 1952, which chronicles the volatile period of strikes and unrest in Trinidad and Tobago between 1935 and 1937). The current lack of critical interest in pre-1950s literature can be usefully attributed to the establishment of critical agendas in the 1960s and 1970s. Writings from the first half of the twentieth century were at best marginal to these works that were motivated by the quest to establish post-Independence regional and national literatures.

The critical sidelining of early writers has continued into recent decades, and many remain problematic subjects for post-colonial theorists in both their Creole identities and their workings with colonial forms. Others, despite offering themes and forms concurrent with the new critical agendas, still remained beyond critical sight. However, it was in the 1970s and 1980s that much of this writing was recuperated by academics such as Reinhard Sander (1978) and Rhonda Cobham-Sander (1981), and other committed individuals such as Anson Gonzalez, Trinidadian broadcaster and editor of *New Voices* magazine and John La Rose, London-based publisher and founder of New Beacon Books. Nevertheless, it is perhaps not until the 1990s that re-evaluations, as opposed to recuperations, of pre-1950 texts began to take place on a significant scale (Cudjoe 1988, 1990, **Donnell 1995**, Cooper 1993).

[16]

It is two of the main aims of this Reader to present writers from the early period of literary activity who do not conform to the assumed colonial profile, and to offer ways of rethinking both Creole and so-called 'imitative' writing. It is our contention that much of this early writing, with its complex and often contradictory positioning in relation to colonial and national ideology and to literature as aesthetic expression and as cultural expression, presents equally interesting and significant texts for a R/reader of Caribbean literature.

(ii) Accommodating women

One of the key motivations in compiling this Reader was to give space to the historical range, the thematic and formal diversity, and the colluding and colliding ideological positions which characterize twentieth-century Caribbean women's writing. While the positive move towards woman-centred scholarship in the field of Caribbean literature during the last two decades has ensured both recognition and serious critical attention for contemporary Caribbean women writers, there remains a notable dearth of research and academic attention on women's writing in the region which predates the 1970s. Even *Out of the Kumbla*, the recent study of Caribbean women and literature, suggests that: 'Out of this voicelessness and absence, contemporary Caribbean women writers are beginning some bold steps to creative expression' (Boyce Davies and Savory Fido 1990: 2). However, the fact that women writers have not been heard in an international context does not mean that they have been voiceless. Although we trust that it is with a heavy note of irony that Selwyn Cudjoe claims the first International Conference of Caribbean Women Writers at Wellesley, US, in 1988 to be 'the founding event of Caribbean women's writing' (Cudjoe 1990: 5), his sweeping assertion does clarify how little awareness and attention has been focused on the wealth of women's writing from within region from the beginning of the twentieth century and before.

As late as 1987, **Evelyn O'Callaghan** acknowledged that 'attempts to "discover" early Caribbean women writers are still in progress, so it is difficult to identify a female literary tradition' (O'Callaghan 1987: 9). Perhaps one of the most important and previously unacknowledged problems with accrediting worth to Caribbean women writers is that their work was only really admitted to the 'tradition' once criticism of male writing had established an agenda of themes, tropes and aesthetic trends characteristic of the region's output. A strong analogy with Indo-Caribbean writing can be drawn here. The reluctance to admit that Caribbean literature does also have a tradition and even a canon – with all the attendant notions of stasis, monologism and privilege – has prevented critics from revising or dismantling preconceptions about the region's literary activity which might have militated against women writers achieving equal recognition. By the late 1970s and 1980s when a serious, sustained and 'mainstream' interest was being taken in Caribbean women's writing as a tradition in its own right (with all the problematics such a term implies), it would seem that the critical and evaluative agendas for reading these texts had already been inscribed according to the then comparatively well-established body of post-1950s Caribbean male writing and the Anglo-American and French schools of feminist literary criticism which had developed in parallel to the women's movement in the early 1970s.

Early identified tropes which derived from an analysis of male writing still dominated, and dominate, discussions of a Caribbean aesthetic. This tendency is evidenced by recent readings of Caribbean women's writing which continue to foreground these literary concerns and thereby to emphasize areas of similarity within women's writing rather than areas of difference (Boyce Davies and Savory Fido 1990: 66). The formation of a proto-canon of Caribbean writing was prompted by critical response to the 1950s boom period and, although conceptions of possible traditions and characteristics of Caribbean writing have changed since this period, the consensus over crucial markers of national identity (e.g. use of nation language, naming of the Caribbean landscape, exile and return motifs) has remained unquestioned within much critical work. Similarly, issues of economic independence, autonomy from heterosexual structures and fragmentation of masculinist narratives which were highlighted by Western feminist thought during its early phase of prominence have retained a high priority with reference to other historical and cultural contexts. While many of these content-based and structural considerations were, and indeed remain, pertinent to readings of Caribbean women's writing, this does not preclude the possibility of a more suitable agenda which accounts for the particular nexus of

[18]

gender and cultural positioning. The foregrounding of similarity is a convenient critical practice through which to manage a complex matrix of sexual–textual difference, but it can also slip into a means by which simply to overlook the specific nature and effects of those differences.

Indeed, while both of these alternative agendas of Caribbean and Western feminist writing might have been liberating in their rejection of the criteria of a eurocentric, patriarchal canon, they too have become restrictive. Both bodies of scholarship were seeking to give voice to the silenced, and no consideration was given to the fact that their own vociferousness might be drowning out more subtle and marginalized tones still striving to be heard. Among these less defined cadences were Creole writings, Indo-Caribbean and Chinese-Caribbean writings and importantly, women's writing which was not easily accommodated by, was even resistant to, the agendas which had been established.

During the process of constructing the Reader, we playfully termed the latter 'unaccommodating women' and those which were more easily absorbed (although not necessarily complicit, e.g. **Kincaid**'s *Annie John* (1985)): 'accommodating women'. Accommodation is a key trope of criticism established in response to an androcentric canon and a reference to the containing process of canonization itself. It is important to stress that not all 'unaccommodating' women writers have deliberately sought a separatist space by establishing a single-sex context and writing against masculinist versions of both literature and criticism, although there have been important gestures in this direction (e.g. Mordecai and Wilson (1989), Boyce-Davies and Savory-Fido (1990)). Others have sought to evade accommodation, not only to the canon but also to comfortable, transparent or appropriative readings, in unaccommodating texts which are critical as well as creative. Certain texts are so unaccommodating that they challenge all established critical paradigms with a 'demonic' searching for a space outside interpretation and representation (**Wynter 1990**, Brodber 1980, 1988).

We hope that the collection of women writers represented in this Reader, although only a fraction of the voices we would like to have included, may at least be suggestive of the range of works and of names which have not yet been fully acknowledged and which await serious critical attention.

(iii) Coolie connections

Most readers of Caribbean literature are aware of the Indian populations who crossed the *kala pani* to indentureship after the abolition of slavery in the British West Indies and they know that the vast majority of these settled in Guyana and Trinidad, where over half of the current population are Caribbean people of East Indian descent. However, few know the unfolding history of these peoples to the present day or are familiar with many Indo-Caribbean literary works. As **David Dabydeen** has pointed out:

> Scholarly research has been focused overwhelmingly on the African dimension, and in the resulting Afro-centric view of the Caribbean, the Indo-Caribbean is relegated to a footnote. (The same can be said of Amerindian studies; the annihilation of the Amerindians has been both physical and intellectual). Such academic marginalisation of Indo-Caribbeans, which leads to a flawed conception of the region, has been paralleled, and perhaps reinforced, by the deliberate efforts to withhold economic and political power from them.
>
> (Dabydeen and Samaroo eds 1987: 10)

Dominant histories often do not adequately account for Indo-Caribbean experience. For example, the canefield riots are far less known and noted than the oil-workers strike of 1937 and the General Strike of 1938 in Trinidad, and yet the riots are probably equally important to notions of mass unrest and discontent which have come to mark the 1930s period. Another little-known fact is that Indo-Trinidadians were offered passports to go back to the newly independent India in the post-Independence years. This invisibility has also characterized literary histories, as Ramabai Espinet points out in her article which re-examines the status of particular representations of the Indo-Caribbean woman (**Espinet 1989**).

Naipaul and **Selvon**, two of the best-known writers from the region, are Indo-Caribbean writers but their ethnic identities are often unspoken by critics, and their own success has seemingly not helped to correct the marginalization of other Indo-Caribbean writers. This tendency can be traced back to as early as 1931 with the publication of Norman Cameron's *Guianese Poetry 1831–1931*. This volume sought to represent Afro-Guyanese writers against a literary profile which was otherwise white but offered no Indo-Caribbean verses at all, despite the relatively high profile of Joseph Ruhoman. It is interesting that in Guyana in 1934 a separate collection appeared entitled *An Anthology of Local Indian Verse*; however, there was little about the poetry itself which registered this cultural specificity. Nevertheless, the cultural profile of the Indo-Caribbean population in this period is demonstrated by the achievements of the British Guiana Dramatic Society between 1929 and 1947 in which women (including Rajkumari Singh) actively participated. In Trinidad, also, similar activity is signalled by the establishment in 1924 of the East Indian Literary Club and East Indian League of Trinidad.

There has been an on-going Indo-Caribbean contribution to literary journals of the region, such as *Kyk-over-al*, *Kaie*, *Heritage*, *Amar Jyoti* and *Corlit* from Guyana and *The New Voices* from Trinidad, but relatively little had been collected and republished until recently. Jeremy Poynting's academic research, cataloguing of an archive and commitment to publishing texts by Indo-Caribbean writers (Peepal Tree Press, founded in 1985) have been crucial in this respect (Poynting, 1985, 1987, 1990). He has also been instrumental in foregrounding Indo-Caribbean women's writing and in locating the sparsity of this archive within a socio-political context. As he comments:

> The domestic, educational, occupational and social disadvantages suffered by Indo-Caribbean women are reason enough not to be surprised at the small quantity of imaginative writing they have produced. To date some forty individuals have contributed poems and stories to local journals; one collection of short stories and a dozen slim volumes of poetry have been published; as yet no novel has appeared.
>
> (Poynting 1985)

This is not to say that there have not been Indo-Caribbean women writers of note, of which we wish to emphasize the works of **Rajkumari Singh** (1965, 1971, 1977), Shana Yardan (1976) and **Mahadai Das** (1977, 1982, 1988) amid an archive which would clearly reward further exploration.

Despite the acknowledgement due to writers of earlier generations such as Seepersad Naipaul, Shiva and V.S. Naipaul and Ismith Khan (1961, 1964, 1987, 1994), the current focus on the contemporary within post-colonial scholarship has made us most aware of recent writing. Writers and works of note include *India in the Caribbean*

[21]

(1987) edited by David Dabydeen and Brinsley Samaroo, *Johaji Bhai: An Anthology of Indo-Caribbean Literature* (1988) edited by Frank Birbalsingh, and the works of Trindadian Sonny Ladoo (1972, 1974), Trinidadian Clyde Hosein (1980), Guyanese Harry Narain (1981), Trinidadian Canadian Neil Bisoondath (1985), Guyanese writer and poet Rooplall Monar (1985), Guyanese British David Dabydeen (1984, 1988, 1991, 1993, 1994), Guyanese Canadian Cyril Dabydeen (1980, 1985, 1988, 1989, 1994), Churaumanie Bissundyal (1994) and Guyanese Harischandra Khemraj (1994).

Although we have chosen to designate these writers by their ethnic identities, this is only in the face of the homogenizing and effacing propensity of a dominant Caribbean literature and a critical approach which articulates only an Indo-Caribbean as opposed to a territory specific identity. We do not in any way wish to advocate prescriptive agendas in which ethnicity is elevated as the governing preoccupation in acts of writing and reading, especially in a Caribbean context where cultural identities are inherently unstable and syncretic. Neither do we wish to omit mention of the literary practice of 'other ethnicities' in the Caribbean (such as Chinese, Irish, Portuguese, and Syrians) and writers such as Marion Patrick Jones (1973, 1976), Willi Chen (1988), Janice Shinebourne (1986, 1988) and Meiling Jin (1995) merit consideration.

(iv) 'The new orality': towards a performance aesthetic

One of the most exciting developments to emerge from the 'explosion of grassroots artistic/intellectual activity' in the late 1960s and 1970s (Brathwaite 1977a: 58) was dub poetry. Dub poets such as Oku Onuora, **Michael Smith** and **Mutabaruka** in Jamaica, **Linton Kwesi Johnson** and others in Britain, were strongly influenced by Rastafarianism and the politics of an ascendant black power movement on both sides of the Atlantic. Although dub poetry had specific roots in Jamaican popular culture, it also found fertile soil in the newly militant atmosphere and confrontational politics of 1970s Britain; the 'touch-paper' of two decades of discrimination against blacks in Britain being lit with the sparks of high black (especially youth) unemployment and the perception of heightened police intolerance and brutality in urban multi-racial areas (this period is satirized in Selvon 1975).

Britain became an interesting, although not exclusive, diasporic centre for this activity. The pioneering voice in Britain was that of Linton Kwesi Johnson, who soon gained tremendous popularity for his forceful vocalization of a highly politicized standpoint in relation to issues affecting the Afro-Caribbean population in London, as well as for his links with reggae music and his striking performative style. However, the oppositional or subversive stance of much of his early work has not always worked in favour of the reception of dub poetry. Chiefly, it has acted to 'muddy the waters' of any critical appreciation by instigating the notion that dub poetry dealt only in the kind of protest rhetoric which James Berry warned against in his preface to a collection of black poets in Britain, *Bluefoot Traveller* (**Berry 1976**: 10). There remains a common belief that dub is at best a limited form, at worst – with familiar echoes of the early reception of **Louise Bennett**'s work – not really 'literature' at all. Although dub poetry should not necessarily be privileged over and above the wider range of black British writing (in itself a contested term, see Fred D'Aguiar 1989, Lawson Welsh 1996) of the 1980s, we wanted to represent some of the more interesting critical and primary texts concerning this poetic form, which is still subject to critical marginalization (Brown *et al.* eds, *Voiceprint – An Anthology of Oral and Related Poetry from the Caribbean* (1989), is an important exception and an excellent introduction to the field).

Mervyn Morris's recognition that such poetry exists as part of a continuum of usages and influences which range from the literate/scribal to the oral, from the musical to gestural and other elements of what could be called a theatrical repertoire, is a crucial one. We hold the view that sharp demarcations of the oral from the literate, even if they could be made, are counter-productive because they exclude much 'performance poetry' as something unconnected and separate from written literature. In practice, most 'practitioners like Breeze and Smith who are both literate and orate employ the conceptual conventions of both discourses' (Cooper 1993: 81). Just as creole can no longer be exclusively defined as the language of orality because of its increased use in education and a growing literary use of creole in written form, so performance poetry, although it privileges the oral, is dependent to varying degrees on the conventions of writing and scribal culture. Indeed, much poetry constructed in a creole idiom, but not normally termed 'performance poetry', displays just this inter-relation of oral and literate characteristics. To this end, Carolyn Cooper has coined the useful term 'oraliterary', which could be applied to much of the literary praxis with which we are concerned in this Reader.

The performative form can be problematic for readers and critics more accustomed to written literature, in that it encompasses much greater textual variation, and like theatre (many of the dub poets, such as Smith and Breeze having received a theatrical training) demands attention to gesture, intonation and the role of audience in the holistic context of the performance. In many respects the live performance is superior to both written and recorded texts, and constitutes a kind of 'privileged reading' (Cooper 1989) which retains the gestural and other kinetic features of the performed poem in its total context. It is also an aim of this Reader to encourage a wider reading and teaching of dub poetry, even if only in textual form, for, as Moore reminds us, this 'is a poetry which restores the need for immediate audience, even though it can be relished in solitary reading also' (Moore 1974).

Although the accessibility of both primary and secondary materials on dub have greatly improved in the last decade or so (e.g. Sutcliffe and Wong 1986), there is still commonly a reluctance to critically engage with this form in any sustained way, or – with the exception of a small number of poems – to admit it to academic syllabuses, due to its perceived 'borderline' literary status and the confusion as to what kinds of critical standards can be applied. **Jean Binta Breeze** has commented (of a black British context) that she 'had rather we had only two or three artists in our community that represented what is finest and truest about ourselves than a host of poseurs who have been allowed to take on the title of artist just because they are black. In a society that loves to represent black mediocrity, it is the black community that must maintain standards' (Stuart 1988: 44–5). Certainly, much dub poetry has been compromised by the demands of popularity and more stringent standards are needed if dub is to survive as an art form of quality. Cooper terms as 'meta-dub' that dub poetry which has 'come of age', conscious of its own weaknesses, as in **Mutabaruka**'s 'Revolutionary Poets' and his self-satirical '**dis poem**' or Breeze's 'Dubbed Out', which satirizes the problems of over-reliance on the dub beat. More importantly, meta-dub poetry provides a sophisticated 'script' which stands in textual form as well as enabling a powerful 'performative transference [which] gets across the closure of the printed page' (Cooper 1993: 68).

Clearly, since **Rohlehr** (1970, 1972–3, 1973, 1975), Moore (1974), **Brathwaite** (1970–1, 1979), De Boissiere (cited in Moore 1969: 6) and others first signalled the literary potential of oral, or residually oral, and musically influenced Caribbean forms such as dub and calypso, and the explosion of activity in the late 1970s, dub has continued to develop and diversify. In any critical response to dub or performance poetry in creole, it is crucial to grasp this hetero-geneity, especially in means of composition (see Johnson and Smith interviews in Markham, 1989), in performance style, and in the pres-ence of a wide range of oraliterary characteristics along a continuum between the residually oral or performative to the radically so.

New connections

Our emphasis on process, on continuums and on creolization in this introduction may be read as an academic fashion statement, but it is also a statement of the lived realities of those from the Caribbean. The literature from this region, like its history, has by necessity devel-oped from acts of negotiation and crossing between different cultures. It could be argued that in the 1990s Caribbean literature does not have a centre; the majority of the writers are based in diasporic cities in Britain, Canada and the United States, with many continuing part-time residence in the Caribbean. Yet this dispersal from a centre, both in terms of geography and in terms of an aesthetic consensus, need not be read as a sign of the collapse of Caribbean literature as a cultural entity, but rather as a continuation of its initial extraordi-nary flexibility in both intellectual and spatial terms.

As readers in the 1990s, we are now familiar with literatures of movement, with mobile cultural identities, and with flexible notions of aesthetic and cultural value. As readers of Caribbean literature we need to be aware that these seemingly postmodern tropes do not arrive as abstract theory but rather emerge from the lived reality of mobility, plurality and relativity over the centuries. The cultural speci-ficity of Caribbean literature is not at risk in this almost postmodern configuration as these features are distinctly Caribbean ones. Indeed, with several of the region's writers (V.S. Naipaul, Jean Rhys and Derek Walcott) now esteemed and established figures within the tradition of literature in English, it seems important to rethink the cultural status of Caribbean works within an international market.

Although it may be argued that at present all cultural forms are in peril of being re-appropriated by the new cultural hegemonies beamed globally via satellite or by the new intellectual meta-narratives of Western theory, it may also be argued that Caribbean literature, with its remarkable history of creative struggle, adaptation and fusion, is the least likely to fall victim to these. To our minds, Caribbean literature throughout the twentieth century has been a literature of colossal aspirations and achievements, as Eduoard Glissant suggested at the threshold to the 1990s: 'We will perhaps be the ones to teach others a new poetic and, leaving behind the poetics of not-knowing, will initiate others into a new chapter in the history of mankind' (Glissant, 1989: 169). Indeed, it is in the works which appropriate and creolize these new cultural authorities that we are beginning to see striking and strident Caribbean works which venture new intellectual and creative positions (**Cooper 1989, Wynter 1990**).

As editors, we remain enthralled by the moving feast that is Caribbean literature and we hope that some of our excitement and enjoyment will be passed on to the R/reader. Ours is not a definitive navigation of this literature, only a map which hopes to raise some new sign-posts alongside the old, and to suggest some of the abandoned oases which merit attention. It is a map which we encourage readers to stray across and hopefully beyond to bookshops, libraries and archives.

1900–29

Introduction

Early twentieth-century texts have not been widely circulated or paid critical attention and the assumption that they are simply absent appears to have gained credibility both within non-specialist and specialist readerships. The fact that the majority of writing from this period is by Creoles (whose work tends to celebrate Caribbean culture and geography within the context of colonialism) has undoubtably affected both the quality and quantity of critical responses to literature before 1930 (**McFarlane 1957, Baugh 1971**). Yet, despite this mythology of absence, it is during these first decades of the twentieth century that local poetry leagues, other writing groups and several publishing ventures emerged which facilitated and inspired future literary production in the region. In Jamaica, **Thomas MacDermot's** (Tom Redcam's) series 'The All Jamaica Library' (1904–9) is one such example which was sponsored by *The Jamaica Times*, the leading literary newspaper which MacDermot edited from 1900 to 1920. This project became a valuable outlet for cheap editions of local writers, designed to be accessible to a Jamaican reading public and guided by a manifesto: 'to present to a Jamaican public at a price so small as to make each publication generally purchasable, a literary embodiment of Jamaican subjects. Poetry, Fiction, History and Essays, will be included, all dealing with Jamaica, and Jamaicans and written by Jamaicans' (MacDermot, 'Foreword' to 1904). The fact that MacDermot's 'library' could not be sustained beyond four volumes, two of which were his own works (1904, 1909), is less important than the call for an acknowledgement of Jamaican culture which it issued. This culturally focused and committed project instigated by a member of the Creole elite has been commented on by **Mervyn Morris** as 'pushing cultural nationalism further than many of us would think sensible even today' (Morris 1972: 47). Indeed, MacDermot's call for a nationalist culture finds a response almost half a century later in the equally committed but somewhat differently positioned Jamaican writer and critic, **Roger Mais**, and his comment that his own *Face and Other Stories* was an 'all Jamaica story written by a Jamaican' (Mais, 1946). As editor of *The Jamaica Times*, MacDermot took other practical steps to nurture local literary activity, publishing early works by **Claude McKay, H.G. De Lisser** and W. Adolphe Roberts, amongst others. MacDermot's efforts at the turn of the century certainly testify to an opening up of the cultural divisions embedded in colonialism and a gradual fracturing of its ethnic and social hierarchies. It was during these opening decades that the ascendancy and empowerment of the black middle classes began to take shape in the form of (pan)African and Indian associations, and civil rights campaigns, which in the 1930s were to become mass suffrage and trade union labour movements, started to find a platform.

At this time, there was also a flourishing of literary clubs and leagues which functioned as important forums for local literary activity. In Jamaica, the James Hill Literary Society, founded in 1912, is an early example of a proto-nationalistic event where the work of writers could be shared across colonial divides, as MacDermot reported: 'the descendants of slaves and their masters equally taking their places in the field of literature'. However, it was the Poetry League of Jamaica, formally initiated in 1923, which most clearly served to raise the profile of poetic activity in the island, with its public meetings, lectures, prizes and Year Books (published by New Dawn Press from 1939). Although in its early years the League provided a valuable space in which poetry could be shared and discussed, it became (along with its President, J.E.C. McFarlane) increasingly out of step with the changing cultural profile of poetry in Jamaica.

Indeed, by the early 1930s it would appear that the usefulness of these groups had been exhausted. Their rather precious and defensive notions of aesthetic activity as spiritually rather than socially committed were increasingly under attack. Albert Gomes's editorial in *The Beacon* in Trinidad expresses his anathema for the literary club in general.

Our opinion of the literary club movement remains unchanged. As far as we can see their very existence constitutes a flagrant prostitution of the word 'Literature.' ... If a group of energetic adolescents wish to amuse themselves over a few tea-cups why must Wordsworth's grave be disturbed? No one wants to deny these simple souls the right to acquire culture or side-step ennui ... The very atmosphere of the 'literary' club reeks of an unctuousness, a stupid formality and a hypocrisy, from which any man or woman of true artistic sensibilities would flee in disgust.

(Gomes 1933)

These early gatherings and collective notions of aesthetic taste became moulds waiting to be broken.

It is certainly the case that the writings which were generated by such early stirrings of cultural nationalism are not always easy to locate or to access at the end of the twentieth century. It is only the relatively recent interest of critics attempting to rethink charges of cultural inauthenticity and aesthetic dependency which has prompted a revision of this scattered and disintegrating archive (Gonzalez 1972, **Sander 1978**, Cobham-Sander 1981, Cudjoe 1988, and **Donnell 1995**). Although these critics present re-readings which often gesture towards new critical frameworks, so-called 'early texts' can remain difficult for readers familar only with later texts which write from more distinctly non- and anti-colonial models of experience and aesthetic practices. It is therefore our aim in introducing this material to suggest ways of, as well as contexts for, reading.

From plantation to barrackyard: voicing the working-class experience

Against a backdrop of high (colonial) literary idolatry, it is important to note an awareness of alternative cultural authorities within literary works which is strengthened throughout the first half of the century. In particular, there is an interest in folklore and folk tradition which demonstrates both an insight into and recognition of non-colonial cultural resources, and which most importantly allows for cultural activity to be directed from the life of the 'folk' upwards. Again, Jamaica was the focus for many of the early studies, with central texts including Walter Jekyll's *Jamaican Song and Story* (1907) and Martha Beckwith's *Jamaica Anansi Stories* (1924) and *Jamaica Proverbs* (1925). However, the relationship between folklore and folk-directed literature is not only to be traced in Jekyll's positive promotion of folk material and language in the work of his protégé, McKay, as **Louise Bennett** has been conducting scholarly research in this area for a long time and **C.L.R. James** engaged in a more direct method of research when he rented rooms in a yard environment in order to observe his future literary subjects. Certainly, folklore's capacity to legitimate the experiences and voices of the majority population paralleled several writers' attempts to relate those lives previously excluded from literary attentions. This gesture of giving cultural value to folk traditions was to be powerfully and politically reiterated in the 1970s 'grassroots' movements (Brathwaite 1977a).

It is hard now to imagine how groundbreaking, even outrageous, it was merely to represent the working-class folk as literary subjects and to allow their language to be printed in literary forms. It is in 'barrackyard fiction', which gained popularity in the 1930s and 1940s, that this project of representing lower-class life in socially 'real' fiction found its fullest expression. Nevertheless, we have included three earlier texts (**De Lisser 1914, Webber 1917** and **James 1929**) which can also be usefully read in the context of this genre.

H.G. De Lisser was a high-profile figure in Jamaican literary circles. He became editor of the *Gleaner* newspaper in 1904 at the age of 26, and remained so until his death in 1944. In addition he was a prolific writer, publishing ten novels, with the last appearing posthumously in 1958. *Jane's Career*, along with *Susan Proudleigh* (1915), are strange eruptions of interest in working-class female subjects in an *œuvre* which is mainly characterized by middle-class portraits and values, and by an increasingly conservative, even reactionary, belief system. Nevertheless, both women protagonists in these first two novels are strong and sensible, sympathetically sketched by De Lisser in narratives which explore the hardships and oppressive structures governing working-class Jamaican life.

In his introduction to the 1971 reprint of *Jane's Career* (1914), Kenneth Ramchand describes this text as: 'the first West Indian novel in which the peasant is given full status as a human person capable of spontaneity and a delicacy of response to people and situations, and one involved in a range of thoughts and feelings hitherto denied in literature to the slave or ex-slave' (Ramchand 1971: xiv). Indeed, the significance of a black female protagonist cannot be underestimated. Neither should De Lisser's depiction of an oppressive social order which merely substituted domestic servitude for its less palatable predecessor be overlooked. *Jane's Career* chronicles the life of a young woman who leaves her rural home for Kingston in search of excitement and personal achievement. This urban migration, along with migrations to Costa Rica and Panama, is a key feature of this period hit by an agricultural depression, as well as of its literary representations. In reality such migration is entry into a system of brutality and prejudice which operates in both the middle-class home and the workplace, and which is perpetrated by both men and women. Although Jane resists first the tyranny of her mistress and then the sexual advances of her predatory boss, she can ultimately achieve social mobility and recognition only through marriage. While it may well be De Lisser's aim to convince his readership of Jane's emotional depth and moral wholeness, as well as of the exploitative nature of their own social system, it is clearly not his brief to critique a patri- archal colonial society in which independent womanhood must be sacrificed to the cause of social integration and success.

A.R.F. Webber emigrated to Guyana from Tobago, where he was born, at the age of 19 and contributed vigorously to both literary and political activity in Guyana for the rest of his life (see Cudjoe, 1988). In several respects, Webber occupied a similiar position in Guyana to that of De Lisser in Jamaica. Both edited newspapers which gave them ready avenues through which to publish their own works. Both took an interest in recording the history of their local- ities, although Webber more seriously so (De Lisser 1913, Webber 1931), and they worked together for the West Indian Press Association founded in 1929. Possibly the most significant difference between the two was Webber's demonstrable commitment to the causes of the working-class populations in Guyana and his opposi- tion to colonial rule.

Those That Be in Bondage – A Tale of Indian Indentures and Sunlit Western Waters is the first known of Webber's works and was published in 1917, significantly the year in which indentureship was banned by the Colonial Office, although it was not until 1921 that the system finally ceased. The recovery of this text is particu- larly important as it deals with a range of issues not commonly found in literary works of this period: indentureship, the uneasy social positions of the overseers and the Creoles, and the tense sexual relationships endemic to plantation life. Webber's narrative can be usefully linked to other literary works which examine the Indo-Caribbean experience, particularly those which focus on first-generation experiences, such as **Singh (1971)** and **Dabydeen (1995)**. The intertextual relationship to *The Counting House* is further strengthened by the foregrounding in both of gender relations in a context of 'the uneven sex ratio of men to women [and] an inevitable increase of intercaste marriages, the opposite of which was a fundamental principle of maintaining the caste system in India' (Saakana 1987: 95). However, although this text offers a sustained exploration of the various modes of 'bondage' in a situation of colonial rule, it is less confident stylistically, slipping from an almost documentary, realist mode into romance, and even into sentimental portraiture.

The representations of De Lisser's and Webber's novels (and of many barrackyard works) may have been more authentic to the lived experience of the majority population, in their emphasis upon hardship, poverty and struggle. However, their status as truth-telling documents was always in tension with the status of their authors as members of the educated, middle-class, Creole minority. Indeed, the cultural gap between those being represented and those representing was particularly acute for those Creole members of the 1930s *Beacon* group (Mendes and Gomes), who sought to articulate a black oppositional perspective. C.L.R. James, himself a member of this group, points to the social consequences of racial difference in the face of political consensus: 'We went one way; these white boys all went the other way. We were black and the only way we could do anything along the lines we were interested in was by going abroad' **(James 1969: 75)**. It is important not to discredit the interesting works which these writers produced, along with others such as **Jean Rhys**, whose *Left Bank and Other Stories* (which explored questions concerning belonging and identity most notably interrogated in her 1966 novel *Wide Sargasso Sea)* was published in 1927. However, James's observation and experience are significant in documenting the operations of a 'racial politics' within a colonial society, a politics of exclusion by denial and neglect which becomes evident when we consider the dearth of published black writers before 1950 and the large-scale migration of these writers in the 1950s. Indeed, problems of striving to give voice to an oppositional consciousness across

educational, class and ethnic divides has remained a serious dilemma
for socially engaged writers throughout the century (see **Hodge 1990**)
although it could be argued that the issue came to a critical 'head'
in the 1970s.

C.L.R. James (1901–89) was the most influential and insightful
intellectual of the twentieth-century Caribbean; James's sharp and
sophisticated mind turned its attentions to politics (especially to the
reconstruction of Marxism), revisionary history (*Black Jacobins* of 1938
is a central and celebrated text) and cricket, as well as to creative
writing and literary criticism. His first publishing venture, with
Alfred Mendes, the magazine *Trinidad*, appeared in 1929 and was
received with great commotion by a middle-class educated audience
to whose tastes it deliberately chose not to cater. **'Triumph'** which
was originally published in *Trinidad* was one of many pieces to
stir up controversy with its depiction of supposedly unsuitable, crude
material. Reflecting back on his work in 1980, James spoke of
'Triumph' as: 'one of the best things I have ever written', believing
that it successfully represented his 'concern with ordinary people,
quite ordinary people who were not members of any union, were
not politically advanced, but they were there' (Cumber Dance, 1992:
111). This story remains distinct in its period because it is not simply
interested in documenting oppressive structures but also, crucially,
in telling the qualities of unacknowledged lives, and therefore
in giving value to those people previously deemed unworthy of
middle-class notice and literary notation. The self-conscious 'preface'
paragraph to this story most clearly demonstrates its status as a literary
work which speaks of rather than speaking for the folk, and the
middle-class eye of the narrator is a less instrusive presence than in
the two Creole novels (**1914, 1917**). 'Triumph' is also not an isolated
statement of James's interest in the life of those less privileged and
less educated than himself; it was also in 1929 that James wrote *Minty
Alley*, an extended portrait of yard life (which was the first Caribbean
novel to be published in England in 1936).

These end-of-decade works gesture towards a new socially motivated agenda for literary works, and even an awareness of the problems
which this would bring in terms of the necessary downward mobility
of the artistic gaze. However, it is a striking register of cultural in-
consistencies and of future 'cultural contests' that the first anthology
of Jamaican poetry, *Voices from Summerland*, which is dominated

by Creole poetry in the pastoral and romantic vein, was also published, directly for the Jamaican schoolroom, in 1929 (a revised version appeared as *A Treasury of Jamaican Poetry* twenty years later).

Colony and nation: a poetics of belonging

Probably the clearest statement of cultural politics within the poetic archive of this time can be found in Constance Hollar's title for her 1932 anthology, *Songs of Empire* (included here as the poems were mainly written during the 1920s). Sir William Morrison's 'Foreword' to this anthology declares its colonial allegiances in an unqualified manner.

> The songs themselves although pitched in various keys and from different outlooks all express unbounded loyalty and devotion of the people of Jamaica to Their Majesties the King and Queen and to the Members of the Royal family and the intense love which all the inhabitants of this ancient and loyal Colony bear to the Motherland.

Certainly the presence of colonial ideology cannot be ignored within the majority of the poetic works included, although it is often less stable and less centred than Morrison suggests. In a similar gesture of colonial filiation David M. Mitchell's introduction to *Voices from Summerland*, proudly pronounces:

> Once more our restless sea-borne race has explored the wine-dark ocean and founded new homes for its children over not one but many seas. And of its ever loyal cherishing of our English poetic tradition this volume is proof.

The confident assertion concerning the achievements of 'our race' which Mitchell makes here suggests an almost supremacist attitude and a clear relation between the cultural form of this poetry and the cultural politics of Empire. Furthermore, his argument based on 'our race' shows no recognition of the ethnic diversity of the writers whose work is published within this volume (poems by both Claude McKay and J.E.C. McFarlane, the volume's editor, appear), and certainly no engagement with the fact that work by 'colonial subjects' may form part of a Caribbean poetic tradition. The eurocentrism of this comment is corroborated by the title of this volume; it is only when defined within a European conceptual framework that Jamaica is a

[34]

'summerland' (**Webber's** *Those That Be in Bondage – A Tale of Indian Indentures and Sunlit Western Waters* is another example). However, this particular representation of Jamaica within the cultural reference system of Europe is not an isolated, or incidental, coding of the Caribbean. Located on the cusp between colonial imagination and island nation, poetry ostensibly 'about' the Caribbean in both volumes is commonly composed of European myths of beauty and bounty relocated within the tropics (see **Clerk** and **Bunbury**). Even **Carberry's 'Epitaph'** which is formally distinct in its adoption of a modernist aesthetic could be read ultimately as a transposition of a eurocentric vision which provides 'The Waste Land' for the West Indies.

While the commitment to Empire and to European sensibility does find strong expression in many of the poems written during this period, it is not uncommon for works to offer more complex representations of nationalist sentiment. J.E.C. McFarlane draws attention to the cultural ambivalence which informs notions of the homeland in several Creole works in his critical estimation of Tom Redcam's poetry.

> The ruling passion of his verse [is] loyalty to Britain and love for Jamaica. In the pattern of his soul and of his poetry these two affections so blend into a harmony of sound and colour as to be incapable of a separate existence.
>
> (McFarlane 1957: 8)

Indeed, Redcam's **'O, Little Green Island Far Over The Sea'**, written when the poet was ill in London, expresses exactly this designation of England as the site for 'loyalty' (political belonging) and Jamaica for 'love' (emotional belonging). This expression of nationalism which looks in two directions is relevant to McFarlane's **'My Country'** which also figures England as the mother/lover. Indeed, Leo Oakley suggests that this ambivalent configuration of cultural placing is symptomatic of those works produced whilst 'the Cobwebs of colonialism had held the creative arts chokingly enmeshed' (**Oakley 1970: 16**).

In Albinia Catherine Hutton's most famous poem, **'The Empire's Flag'**, the Union Jack is transformed into an oracle of patriotic interest. The image of the flag bursting through geographical boundaries with the 'progress' of Empire may be a clear indication of this poem's cultural affiliations. However, the celebrated 'banner of the free' and the conflation of ideologies suggested by formulations such as 'colonial nationalism' and 'colonial freedom' foregrounds the complicated and involved pattern of nationalist thought amongst the cultural elite at this time.

The gendering of colonial affiliation is also present in this poem in which the flag itself becomes the colonial mother. This same figuring appears in Hutton's **'A Plea'**; in this absolute antithesis of a call for Independence, the trope of the mother as caring custodian works in nationalist terms to signal (or appeal to) the nature of the motherland as guardian, a construction which demands loyalty and attachment as well as offering security and recognition. The gendering of nationalistic sentiment is figured rather differently in Tom Redcam's **'Jamaica's Coronation Ode'**, which focuses on both the masculinity and the muscularity of Jamaica's path of progress. This emphasis upon an aggressive movement, although here more explicitly of colonial might rather than of nationalist campaign, is also suggested by the refrain of J.E.C. McFarlane's **'The Fleet of The Empire (Reflections on the Visit of the Special Service Squadron)'**.

Perhaps the most surprising representation of Jamaica can be found in Tropica's **'The Undertone'**, which foregrounds a violent history of slavery and thus declares its interest not in the obvious beauty of nature, but in the less visible and less reassuring histories which this focus might conceal. Saakana has noted that: 'It was safer to extol the virtues of the landscape than of the people who toiled on it' (Saakana 1987: 36). With this in mind, it is interesting that Tropica not only offers a more challenging version of a Caribbean cultural geography but also of the people who inhabited it. In her volume *The Island of Sunshine* (1904), the earliest work represented here (E.A. Dodd's *Maroon Medicine* (1905) was the first collection of Jamaican short fiction), the ethnographic dimension of the work is suggested by photographs of black people at work and of Jamaican scenes printed alongside the poems. Tropica's **'Nana'**, set alongside a picture of a black nanny holding a white child, is an elegy which draws attention to the cultural traditions (African retentions) which will fade away with the nana's passing. But the description of these 'weird' stories and remedies suggests that they have a 'curiosity value' more than a cultural value. Moreover, it is important to be aware that this elegy is also to the plantation house-based society and economy which secured the loyalty and devotion of this black woman to 'Massa' and the white children in her care.

In **'Busha's Song'** (1929), the figure of the plantation overseer is romanticized. Within the poetic frame the busha becomes a pastor, but the fact that plantation life is not an innocent, simple, carefree existence is never addressed. Another equally comforting representation, or perhaps projection, of the working population can be found in Eva Nicholas's **'A Country Idyl'**. Not only does this idyll present working life as a pastoral indulgence, it also suggests a romanticized simplicity of the 'folk', who emerge only as bodies and voices.

Indeed, from an analysis of these poetic cross-cultural representations, it would appear that a voyeuristic and objectifying approach to both the Caribbean island and the people is the norm. The absence of clear attempts to differentiate the Jamaican nation from the imperial mother-land and to authenticate a language and experience of its people which had been denied, is notable. However, it may be less puzzling that poetry written by members of an often remote Creole elite does not present any clear expressions of nationalism, than that it forwards nationalistic sentiments at all.

It is to the work of Claude McKay that a reader of Caribbean literature may usefully turn in order to locate the beginnings of the now familiar tradition. Contrary to Baugh's suggestion that McKay was: 'weakly derivative [and] ... did not inspire any immediate successors in this [nation language] medium' (**Baugh 1971: 7**), we would argue that McKay's first two volumes *Songs of Jamaica* (1912) and *Constab Ballads* (1912) should be recognized as important forerunners of creole monologues such as those of Bennett, **Berry**, Bloom, **Dabydeen** and D'Aguiar. Furthermore, Inez Sibley's *Quashie's Reflections in Jamaican creole* (which appeared in *The Daily Gleaner* in the 1930s), Una Marson's **'Quashie Comes to London'** (1937: 17–21), and **Louise Bennett**'s first volume *Jamaica Dialect Verses* (1942) could be read as significant poetic works which continue McKay's creole poetics. In general, it seems important to stress the value of these first two critically neglected (creole) collections by McKay. McFarlane reads McKay's relinquishing of creole as a poetic idiom as a sign of his greater poetic sophistication and assurance (**McFarlane 1956: 85**). In contrast, we would argue that these early creole collections offer altogether fresher, more vigorous and interesting examples of Jamaican poetry in the early twentieth century.

For Leo Oakley, McKay was 'the first to show his countrymen ... that there was music in the dialect they spoke' (1970: 19). However, for some readers the uneasy oscillation between creole and standard idioms and a tendency to rely on an archaic vocabulary and sentimental themes of Victorian and Georgian English poetry may be seen to weaken many of his ballads. Nevertheless, the question of how any 'authentic Jamaica' may have been conceived and mapped out, given the constant recourse to British culture (even for representations of nature) and the saturation of British cultural forms, clearly needs to inform any evaluation of the status of these representations and idioms.

Lloyd Brown in *West Indian Poetry* (Brown 1984: 48) warns of the 'potentially stultifying rhyme scheme of McKay's dialect verse'. However in McKay's finest creole poems, such as the dramatic monologues **'A Midnight Woman to the Bobby'** and **'The Apple-Woman's Complaint'** he combines the immediacy and resilience of spoken language with a strong sense of the ballad form, as a residually oral form geared to the ebb and flow of speech itself. The dialogue form which is little used in these collections does not emerge again until James Berry's experimentation with the form in *Lucy's Letters and Loving* (Berry 1982) which offers another extended poetic adaptation of this most basic of contrapuntal structures found in traditional balladry and folk song.

Although the reputation of McKay remains high within Caribbean literary histories, his migration to the United States in 1912 led to the incorporation of his future writings within the 'Harlem Renaissance' movement there. His move abroad also inaugurated the tradition of literary exile to diasporic centres which has become characteristic of Caribbean writers at the end of the century.

Women subjects

Herbert De Lisser's magazine, *Planter's Punch*, is a fascinating subject for an analysis of both gender and cultural politics. Established in 1920, De Lisser used this annual as a vehicle for publishing all of his novels subsequent to *Jane's Career* in an affordable and popular format for a Jamaican public (2,000 copies were sold). However, his secondary intention appears to have been a reinforcement of colonial and patriarchal values amongst those with social power. The conspicuous and relentless promotion of European graces and beauty and the concentration on the white female body offers an interesting location of colonial beliefs. Despite the inclusion of a significant amount of women's verse, the magazine's interest is never wholly poetic, given its excessive interest in measuring women as bodily objects. In **'Miss Jamaica'** by Sub-Inspector Harvey Clarke, this propensity is clearly visible. The black Jamaican woman is a conspicuous absence in this consideration of Jamaica's female population and is symptomatic of her negation as a legitimate subject of enquiry. The only black women to receive mention are the 'fat, perspiring, black cook' and the 'kindly old black "Nana"' (1929: 5), neither of whom have a positive status; they are both stereotyped and marginal to the article's interests and the society it describes. Clarke's arrogant idiom and amazing confidence in an evaluative model, which is not only blatantly sexist but implicitly racist, positions this piece in a tradition of colonial discourse which effaces and silences black women, and objectifies white women. His approach to the subject of the island's 'beauty queen' is in sharp contrast to **Una Marson's** 1931 article in *The Cosmopolitan*, the magazine which she founded, in which she expresses her contempt for the insistent idealization of white beauty, epitomized by the recent announcement of yet another 'blond and blue-eyed' Miss Jamaica. It is Marson's suggestion that the title should have been awarded to a 'girl who is more truly representative of the majority of Jamaicans'. It is also interesting to contextualize Clarke's piece alongside early twentieth-century attempts at female eurocentric socialization, in particular the 1917 Social Purity Association of Jamaica, designed to reduce venereal disease and immoral behaviour, and the 1918 Women's Social Service Club which aimed to 'uplift womanhood' (Reddock 1990: 65). It is clear that any attention and interest directed specifically at Jamaican women at this time served merely to reinforce their position within a male-dominated society and to establish codes of normalized moral behaviour and attitudes in line with eurocentric conceptions of femininity.

Amy Garvey's **'Women As Leaders'** contrasts both starkly and instructively with these attempts and with Clarke's 'Miss Jamaica', most emphatically in her declaration that 'the doll-baby type of woman is a thing of the past'. This is the very construction of Jamaican femininity which Clarke both relishes and endorses. The clear feminist inflections of Garvey's piece need to be foregrounded, as does the way in which it offers a positive model of women's issues being given space within a black consciousness and anti-colonialist movement. This exploration of gender politics within a racist culture and the assertion of a black womanist identity and voice can be usefully traced through **Marson** (**1937**) and **Bennett** (**1982**), to **Nichols** (**1983**), and **Wynter** (**1990**).

However, the context in which this piece originally appeared and the relationship which Amy Garvey (his wife) bore to Marcus Garvey and certain political projects are also crucial to consider. The UNIA (Universal Negro Improvement Association) was founded by Marcus Garvey in Jamaica in 1914 and based after 1916 in the United States (with twenty island affiliations in the Caribbean), and gave rise to Garvey's 1922 'Back-to-Africa' repatriation movement. As an editorial in *Negro World*, the newspaper published by the UNIA, this piece needs to be read as an early example of polemical writing which assumes an oppositional stance to both colonial politics and morality. *Negro World* featured articles by some of the leaders of trade unions and strikes in the Caribbean and had a substantial influence on a number of working-class leaders coming to power in the Anglophone Caribbean in the 1930s. It is perhaps unsurprising that in its choice of writers, its direct and confrontational mode of address, as well as in its insistent articulation of an empowered black consciousness, this paper was to clash with the colonial institutional powers. *Negro World* was impounded on entry to the Caribbean according to war censorship and there is evidence to suggest that 'the colonial office considered [Marcus] Garvey as spreading dangerous race consciousness and hatred' (Saakana 1987:67) in a situation of growing discontent. Furthermore, in 1920 a number of Caribbean states passed a bill specifically aimed at *Negro World* and *The Crusader*, another Afro-Caribbean newspaper published in the states.

This early example of censorship needs to be situated as but the first example of further tangible restraints being imposed on Caribbean writers and writing during the twentieth century. It is in this context of censorship that Gomes's account of the police visit to his home (under suspicion of writing material with incitement to racial violence) and the censorship of calypsos in the 1930s should be read (see **Gomes 1974**). Also important is the brief imprisonment for sedition of **Roger Mais** in Jamaica in 1944 for his essay 'Now We Know' which, it was alleged, could incite disaffection in wartime. Indeed, the imprisonment of **Martin Carter** in Guyana in 1953 under British direct rule, and of **C.L.R. James** on Ellis Island, United States, in 1956 and later his house arrest under the Trinidadian government of his one-time political ally Dr Eric Williams, along with that of Abdul Malik in Trinidad in 1970 with its atmosphere of grim censorship (which Rohlehr speaks of in 'A Carrion Time', 1975), provide further examples of the perceived threat of cultural representation to the security of political representation in the region. Perhaps the most alarming and tragic example of the actual dangers presented by political activity for Caribbean writers is **Mikey Smith**'s death by stoning at the hands of his political opponents in 1983 in Jamaica.

All of these examples attest to the long and volatile relationship between literature and politics in the Caribbean, a relationship which was to become particularly highly charged in the 1930s and 1940s as a more fierce and conscious forging of the alliance between cultural forms and cultural politics emerged.

Tropica (Mary Adella Wolcott)

The Undertone

But Hearing oftentimes
The still, sad music of humanity.
Wordsworth

Beneath the brightness of the Southern day
I seem to hear a dull, half-stifled moan;
Beneath the mirthful sound of children's play
A low, complaining note – the undertone.

The far, faint cry of wounded slaves in chains;
The struggle of some falling soul alone;
The blood that darkens with its crimson stains
A girlish hand – these are the undertone.

The sins and sorrows of those far-off times
Whose echoes are to us so faintly blown;
The cruel deeds beneath the flowering limes
(As fair as now) – these are the undertone.

Beneath the brightness of the Southern day
I seem to hear a dull, half-stifled moan;
'Old nurses' tales!' 'All nonsense!' do you say?
Ah, mind your words! Hark – hear the undertone!

(1904)

Nana

With the old homes are going
  The Nanas of past days,
With their gay stiff-starched kerchiefs
  And dear old-fashioned ways;
They disappeared with other
  Quaint things too good to last;
And seldom now we see them –
  Those pictures of the past!

The strange 'Anancy' stories,
  And legends weird and old
Which after patient coaxing

Were in the twilight told
To breathless, wide-eyed children –
    We hardly hear to – day;
A few faint echoes linger –
    The rest have passed away.

But in the days of plenty,
    When 'Old Jamaica' flowed,
And heavy, lumbering coaches
    Rolled o'er the dusty road, –
When railway, street car, tourist,
    Were to the isle unknown, –
Then each true household boasted
    A 'Nanna' of its own.

The children came to Nana
    With every trifling tear.
And feared no foe in armour
    When her strong arm was near;
For childish ills no doctor
    Was torn from sleep at night;
A cup of Nana's 'bush-tea,' –
    And all would soon be right.

At christenings and weddings
    She played a shining part,
And every household function
    Owned Nana as its heart;
At balls she peeped through doorways
    To see 'Young Missis' dance,
And beamed if for a moment
    She caught the girl's bright glance.

Whilst all else changed around her
    She kept the same old place,
Till like some faithful guide-post
    Became the kindly face;
For to 'Ole Massa's fam'ly'
    Her life was rooted fast:
In fancy we can see her –
    The Nana of the past!

                                    (1904)

Busha's song[1]

The soldier loves the battle,
The sailor loves the sea;
To each his heart's desire –
The busha's life for me!
A soul that's one with Nature,
A mind that's free from care,
And riding, ever riding,
On the hills in the open air.

   Chorus
   O it's riding, always riding,
   Out in the sun and dew;
   O it's riding, always riding,
   Over the mountains blue;
   O it's riding, always riding,
   While the sun-kissed cheek grows brown,
   And the careless heart beats lighter –
   Riding up and down.

Give me the lunch snatched gaily
Down by the wayside hut;
The roasted yam, the water
Fresh from the great green nut;
Give me the sparkling river,
The plunge in the deep 'blue-hole';
These are the simple pleasures
That are life to the busha's soul!

Give me the slopes of logwood
Veiled in the morning haze;
Arches of breezy bamboos
Screening the noonday blaze;
Give me the fragrant evenings
When shining blinkeys peep;
The scent of the starry jasmine –
And at night, the dreamless sleep.

(1929)

NOTE

1 A Busha is the overseer of a property, usually of a cane or banana plantation.

Tom Redcam (Thomas MacDermot)

My Beautiful Home

(*For music*)

I sing of the Island I love,
Jamaica, the land of my birth,
Of summer-lit heavens above,
An Island the fairest on earth.

I sing of Jamaica, my home,
Begirt with the azure of seas,
And kissed by the white-gleaming foam,
And fanned by the balm of the breeze.

I sing of the cloud reaching height,
Of the roar of the wind-waving wood,
Of the torrent descending in might,
Of the sweep of the swift-gleaming flood.

There slumbers the Mango in gloom,
There flings the Marengo its snows,
And, dark where Convolvuli bloom,
Slow-motioned, the deep river flows.

There, towers the Ceiba sublime,
The breezes sing glad through its bloom,
When bursts the perfume of the Lime
In the twilight's ear-silencing gloom.

Oh! Land that art dearest to me,
Though unworthy of thee is my song,
Wherever I wander, for thee
My love is abiding and strong.

(1929)

O, Little Green Island Far Over the Sea

O, little Green Island, in far away seas!
Now the swift Tropic shadows stride over thy leas;
The evenings' Elf-bugles call over the land,
And ocean's low lapping falls soft on the strand.
Then down the far West, towards the portals of Night,
Gleam the glory of orange and rich chrysolite.
Day endeth its splendour; the Night is at hand;
My heart groweth tender, dear, far away land.

For England is England, the strong and the true,
Whose word is her bond in her march through the blue.
For England is England, who mothers my soul,
Truth, bare in its glory, with her deep self-control.
With red in her flag, the white and the blue.
For England is England, brave, patient and true.

But my little Green Island, far over the sea,
At eve-tide, Jamaica, my heart turns to thee.
Then the querulous Hopping Dick seeks for repose;
On the white, winding roadway the lone peasant goes;
Pass flocks of swift White Wings, aslant the air way,
Where the West is aflame with the embers of Day.
Orion's gemmed blade shall soon flash from the sky;
And the great Southern Cross shall be lifted on high.

Here I lie in great London, in her hugeness I rest;
An atom least heeded, I lie on her breast.
O London is London, she mouldeth the fate
Of the Mighty to ruin, to triumph, the Great;
For London is London, she sitteth on high;
On her multiple ways do her millions pass by;
And order, sure order, is the pulse of her will;
Not till day draweth nigh doth her labour grow still.

But my little Green Island, far over the sea,
At eve-tide, Jamaica, my heart is with thee.

(1929)

Jamaica's Coronation Ode

Here where Nelson led we follow
In the light of Duty's star,
Where Jamaica's blue hills dreaming,
See her torrents streaming far.
From the mango-shadowed village
Where unresting bamboos sigh,
Where the dew-empearled banana
Gleams beneath the morning sky.

We are marching to conquer the Future,
We are sons of Jamaica the free,
We are true to our King and our Country,
We are heirs of the ages to be.

Where the great stars o'er the blackness
Of our mountain ridges flame,
Where our sun-kissed seas are foaming.
Once the Royal Sailor came,
Now his people file before him,
And the Isles their homage bring,
Loud amid the gathering nations,
Let Jamaica's anthem ring.

We are marching to conquer the Future,
We are sons of Jamaica the free,
We are true to our King and our Country,
We are heirs of the ages to be.

King! The land that Nelson guarded,
Where victorious Rodney came,
Her bright streams and wooded mountains
Pour to thee their loud acclaim
Unto thee be salutation!
Round thy throne forever be
Equal Justice, Mercy's power,
Strength to smite and grace to free,

We are true to the flag that has floated
Above us in tempest and strife,
In the steps where our fathers have trodden

[47]

We march on the Highway of Life.

We are marching to conquer the Future,
We are sons of Jamaica the free,
We are true to our King and our Country,
We are heirs of the ages to be.

(1932)

J.E. Clare McFarlane

The Fleet of the Empire

(Reflections on the visit of the Special Service Squadron)
July, 1924

From Britain's fog-bound coast they come –
From shrouded skies and steel-gray seas;
With pennants streaming on the breeze,
They wander o'er their ocean home;
Out from grim portals of the North,
Into the South's effulgent day,
They come, the symbols of her worth,
The heralds of Britannia's way. –
  For dauntless, undismayed as they,
  Forward, whatever tempests sweep,
  Our Empire plunges thro' the deep
  Into the dawn of greater day.

No flaunting boast of Pride are they,
No gestures of relentless Power;
But watch-dogs of the Evil Hour –
A terror unto those who prey!
Love-tokens from a Mother's soul,
They breathe rememb'rance, and a prayer
That wafts unto the nearing goal;
That urges to a high desire. –
  For dauntless, undismayed as they,
  Forward, whatever tempests sweep,
  Our Empire plunges thro' the deep
  Into the dawn of greater day.

Like them, the great Dominions wait –
Great units of a greater whole –
The promise which the years unroll:
The consummation of their fate.
And love their triple armour be;
And Truth and Freedom man their guns;
And at their helm sit Equity
And Honour, bright as rising suns.

[49]

For dauntless, undismayed as they,
Forward, whatever tempests sweep,
Our Empire plunges thro' the deep
Into the dawn of greater day.

Whether beneath the North's grey dome,
Or in the Southland's shining zone,
On separate keels they stand as one,
To dare whatever foes may come;
To breast whatever men conspire,
And bear aloft in steel and flame
The challenge of a great Empire
To whomso'er defies her name!
  For dauntless, undismayed as they,
  Forward, whatever tempests sweep,
  Our Empire plunges thro' the deep
  Into the dawn of greater day.

(1929)

My Country

If e'er I tread the highways of the world,
'Twill be for thee, my country! For thy name
I am most zealous; unto thee I owe
All the imaginings of beauty sown
Deep in my soul; and unto thee I bring
What thou has given. While on thy breast I lay
In helpless childhood, I have felt thy breath,
Moist with the mountain-dew, and seen thy face
Aflush with Eden's earliest dawn; have heard
Thy whispers 'midst vast silences, when noon
Held breathless Earth and Sea.

                              And thou has nursed me
From season unto season, year to year,
Till dawning consciousness in me revealed
The graces of thy form. Well I remember
The vague and subtle sense of joy which stole
Into my pulses as I gazed upon
Thy fields of flowering grasses, 'neath the wind
Rising and falling, like a reedy pond

Half-blown to life; and well do I recall
Thy first sweet favour, my first love: a flower,
Star-like and tender, whose perfumèd breath
Wafted my soul into the enchanted land
Of dreams and fairies.

                    – Or thou would'st lead me
Through labyrinthine ways where murmuring flowed
The shadow-full waters of some lonely stream,
Dappl'd with glimmerings where the sun
Pierc'd with his prying eye the sanctuary
Hallow'd by solitude.

                    Alone with thee,
And in such mood as each sequestered spot
Would lend, and with the gather'd Presences
Of Years whose summers lay beneath my feet,
I heard thy wondrous story, saw thy tears,
Thy laughter 'midst thy tears I heard and saw;
And with entrancèd vision did behold
Phantom Romances that at noon-tide dream
Upon thy hills, and in thy valleys sleep.

There is a world-old pain within thine eyes
E'en while they sparkle mirth; a shadowy trouble
That sits on thy fair brow; a spectral languor
That cleaves to thine immortal youth, and casts
A damp upon thy warmest impulse. Oft
In the still watches of the night I've heard
Thy stifled moan and, like the homeless wind,
Warring against opposing shutters, oft
Thy sighs have come to me.

                    And I have sought,
Uneasy with thy hidden pain, the woods
On summer nights, to listen to the leaves
Whispering in solemn conclave, or to scan
Their black and golden tracery, images
And symbols of thine own mysterious fate,
Dark with forebodings, golden with lure
And promise of thy matchless loveliness;

And, baffled, I have lifted searching eyes
Unto thy mist-veiled mountains, where the peace
And majesty of heaven linger yet.
– They loom against the sky-line; seem to yearn
Pulsating towards high heaven; are silent still.
Tense with an anguished waiting.

                And now I sink,
Vanquished, beneath the burden of thy grief;
And now a deathless impulse bears me on
To dare for thee, to spend myself for thee,
To take the rugged path, nor heed the pain,
To grapple with the thorns of sacrifice,
The sneers of cowards, the malice of the proud –
If I might win thee to a nobler self,
And see thee stand triumphant on the heights,
Steadfast like thine own mountain-range and flush'd
With the bright splendour of a new-born day.

O bless me now, my Mother, bless me now!
And be the music of thy thousand streams
In me a song of triumph! The fleet winds
That haunt thy shadowy passes be the wings
That shall upbear my fancy; let it glow
Like thine own ardent noonday, and resound
With the o'erpowering harmony that swells
From thine encircling seas!

                And that strange peace
Be mine, that broods above thy mist-filled vales
At twilight, and upon thy purple hills;
Not silence, but a hushed expectancy,
A brimming joy that greets night unafraid,
When Life stands tiptoe on the brink of time
And waits with fluttering pulses for the last
Sweet benediction, and the touch of hands;
And Hope aspires toward the Evening Star.

                           (1929)

Albinia Hutton

The Empire's Flag

Flag of our loyal worship, flag of our nation's pride,
Salt from the old sea battles, with heroes' life-blood dyed,
Casting they shelt'ring shadow o'er all the Empire wide.
Whence comes the wond'rous glamour woven in every fold?
What have the mighty nations given to thee of old?
Tell us the ancient secrets, tell us the tales untold.

'Fragrance of old-world gardens, fragments of early rhyme,
Peace of her old Cathedrals heard in their distant chime,
Grace to her banner bringing adown the paths of time.
She who grew great by sorrow, strong when she suffered loss,
She who in quest of Honour counted her gold but dross,
I am the Flag of England, I am St George's Cross.'

'Spirits of loch and forest, mountain, and flood, and field,
Ballads of ancient battles, men who would never yield,
Tender-eyed mountain maidens on whose brows peace is sealed.
Kin to the Scottish Lion, borne high o'er heath and moss,
High in my silver splendour, wings to the winds I toss,
I am the Flag of Scotland, I am St Andrew's Cross.'

'Sprite of a land of beauty known as "The Isle o' Green,"
Breath of her lakes and rivers, fairest were ever seen,
Dreams of her radiant daughters, dearer than all I ween.
Spirit am I of Erin, measure her gain or loss
By the red sign of glory that aye aloft I toss,
I am the Flag of Ireland, I am St Patrick's Cross.'

'All the great deeds of nations as one together bound,
Souls of their ancient heroes in friendship hover round.
A wond'rous triple glory whose like has ne'er been found.
No hand has ever ta'en me, no army borne me back,
My children gather round me, no homage do I lack,
Flag of the three great Kingdoms, I am the Union Jack.'

'Grown too large for my birthplace, they bore me thence afar,
Over the distant ocean, 'neath many a stranger star,
Seeking the lands that lay far over the silver bar.

[53]

Bought once for all with life-blood, courage that could not flag,
Planted me there in triumph, called me "The dear Old Rag."
I am their gallant symbol, I am the Empire's Flag.'

'I fly where'er the birds fly, where'er the sun doth shine,
I've sons of every colour, in every land and clime;
I witch them all with beauty, and make them forever mine.
Set on the crests of mountains, Queen of the boundless sea,
Proudly they walk beneath me, they who are truly free.
I am the Flag of Freedom, where'er my children be.'

'Over Jamaica's mountains, where seldom foot has trod,
There where fond Nature drinketh her fill of the Wine of God,
And pays it back in beauty and richness of her sod.
O'er her once famous seaport, watch Nelson's spirit keeps,
Over her quiet city where Benbow sleeps,
Wave I in glowing splendour, crown I her topmost steeps.'

So through the countless ages, honour and grandeur cling
Round thee, O Flag of Beauty! List while thy praise we sing!
When with one voice they children their loyal homage bring.
Draw around us, O Mother! thy mantle's ample fold;
Let it ne'er leave us naked, out in the dark and cold;
God keep us 'neath thy banner as we have been of old.

(1932)

A Plea

Britain our Mother, lend to us thine ear,
Listen to our petitioning to-day;
We, the descendants of thy children dear,
Though born in far-off lands and living there
For generations, love thee even as they.

We pray thee do not call us colonies,
Nor even say 'The Empire.' Nor speak
About Colonials, knowing well how these,
Taught by their fathers, love thee on their knees.
O, Mother, let us love thee cheek to cheek!

Give us thy name in filial pride to wear,
And, from that loved, but distant land, thy throne,

Extend thy sceptre to thy kindred here;
We know thou wilt not sell thy children dear:
That we are irrevocably thine own.

Children are called by their parents' name
Else would there be confusion, and we pray
That we may be so also. Wrap thy fame
Around our littleness, a garb of flame
To guard thine own, a banner bright and gay.

We have our Christian names, and what they are
Thou knowest, nay, who knowest half so well
As thou dost, thou the Mother? Canada,
South Africa, Australia, India,
New Zealand. Far too numerous to tell,

With them a host of smaller gems as fair,
Sweet pearls ingathered from the Summer Seas
And strung together for a necklet rare
To deck thy queenly bosom, shining there
In loveliness. Jamaica is of these.

One of the smallest pearls upon that string
Is she, we know, but she is wholly thine,
Amongst thy first-born, and her children sing
Thy praises, while her beauty grace doth bring
Not all unworthy of that necklet fine.

And we, thy children, as a boon, do claim
The right to proudly boast our heritage,
Oh, give us Greater Britain for surname,
That all the world may know we share thy fame.
The glory that endures from age to age!

And call us not Colonials, we who dwell
Where still the echoes whisper 'midst the trees
The names of famous sons who served thee well;
Nay, let our name, their victories to tell,
Be honoured as 'The Britons Overseas.'

(1932)

[55]

H.S. Bunbury

The Spell of the Tropics

When the fever of daytime has fallen
And the pulse of existence subsides,
When the stars are drowned in the moonlight,
And the earth is adrift in its tides,

Then the spell of the tropics is deepest,
Most subtle and sweet their power;
And there blossoms the love of a life-time
From the passions, perhaps, of an hour.

So the tropics remain as the mistress;
They reign in a region apart;
And he holds them, that northern lover,
In the innermost shrines of his heart.

From beyond the mist-ridden horizons
Of his pallid tempestuous skies,
For that Eden of palms and of moonlight,
And the ocean of love where it lies,
Comes the ache of an infinite longing
That is set to a cadence of sighs.

(1929)

Astley Clerk

Islets Mid Silver Seas

Islets of brown-tinged clouds
Resting mid silver seas,
Each friezed with the same soft passioned sigh,
Breath of the Western breeze.

And between each light-girt isle
Falls a shower of golden beams,
(Like pathways leading from Heaven to Earth)
Into the realms of dreams.

Oh! 'tis the magic touch
Of the Lord of the golden lands
That colours these fairy islets all
And the shining silver strands;

He has hidden his own fair face,
As he drives in his chariot bright,
So that I, and his children all, might paint
The picture in dreams to – night.

(1929)

P.M. Sherlock

Pocomania

Long Mountain, rise,
Lift you' shoulder, blot the moon.
Black the stars, hide the skies,
Long Mountain, rise, lift you' shoulder high.
Black of skin and white of gown
Black of night and candle light
White against the black of trees
And altar white against the gloom,
Black of mountain high up there
Long Mountain rise,
Lift you' shoulder, blot the moon,
Black the stars, black the sky.

Africa among the trees
Asia with her mysteries
Weaving white in flowing gown
Black Long Mountain looking down
Sees the shepherd and his flock
Dance and sing and wisdom mock,
Dance and sing and falls away
All the civilized to-day
Dance and sing and fears let loose;
Here the ancient gods that choose

Man for victim, man for hate
Man for sacrifice to fate
Hate and fear and madness black
Dance before the altar white
Comes the circle closer still
Shepherd weave your pattern old
Africa among the trees
Asia with her mysteries.

Black of night and white of gown
White of altar black of trees
'Swing de circle wide again
Fall and cry me sister now

Let de spirit come again
Fling away de flesh an' bone
Let de spirit have a home.'
Grunting low and in the dark
White of gown and circling dance
Gone to-day and all control
Here the dead are in control
Power of the past returns
Africa among the trees
Asia with her mysteries.

Black the stars, hide the sky
Lift you' shoulder, blot the moon
Long Mountain rise.

(1949)

Eva Nicholas

A Country Idyl

Fragrant loads of green pimento
On the barbecue,
Crushed green leaves among the berries
Giving perfume too;
Voices mellowed by the distance,
Sounding sweet and low;
Gay pimento pickers moving
Briskly to and fro.

Graceful bamboos imitating
Soft sounds of the sea;
'Hush! Hush! Hush!' They seem to whisper,
Bending over me.
Crimson poincianas, blushing
Yet a brighter red,
As the honey bees, in passing,
Kiss the rose instead.

Cloudlets forming moving pictures
In the azure skies;
Hill tops crowned with golden sunshine –
Yellow butterflies,
Just like buttercups, are flitting
Near me as I pass,
Where the withered leaves are hiding
In the velvet grass.

Am'rous breezes telling orchids
Of their loveliness,
Wooing, too, the guava blossoms
In their simple dress.
Softly pleading with the roses
And the maidenhair;
How the dainty fronds are quiv'ring
At the words they hear!

Stately penguins in the hollows
Stretching prickly arms
To embrace the clinging creepers –
Oh! What glowing charms
Are the luscious fruits displaying
On the branching trees,
As the shining leaflet's flutter
In the scented breeze.

Would that I could find expression
Mother Nature fair!
Gladsome songs of all thy beauties
And perfections rare
I would sing to all thy children –
Voice the music sweet
Of the wanton breezes, strewing
Dead leaves at my feet.

But, Alas! my voice is feeble;
Locked within my breast
I must keep this joyous music,
Ever unexpressed.
Just relieved by plaintive pipings,
Or some simple song,
Lost amid the dulcet measures
Of the poet throng.

(1929)

Clara Maude Garrett

One

O I am one with the banana tree
And one am I with every swaying palm;
In thunder of the hurricane or calm
I am as one with my Caribbean Sea.

The thousand peaks that lift their seeking heads
Storming the sunset clouds are of me too:
Orchids that bend beneath the mountain dew
Are fraught with me: I am their gold and reds.

There is a wedding of my soul with all
From whence I came, whereof my flesh is made:
The tissue of my thought is Island laid
In my warm earth. The solitaire's strange call
Is but my spirit's cry: there is no glade
But holds my inmost ME in deathless thrall.

(1949)

H.D. Carberry

Epitaph

I think they will remember this as the age of lamentations,
The age of broken minds and broken souls,
The age of hurt creatures sobbing out their sorrow to the
    rhythm of the blues –
The music of lost Africa's desolation become the music of
    the town.

The age of failure of splendid things,
The age of the deformity of splendid things,
The age of old young men and bitter children,
The age of treachery and of a great new faith.
The age of madness and machines,
Of broken bodies and fear twisted hearts,

The age of frenzied fumbling and possessive lusts –
And yet, deep down, an age unsatisfied by dirt and guns,
An age which though choked by the selfishness of the few
    who owned their bodies and their souls,
Still struggled blindly to the end,
And in their time reached out magnificently
Even for the very stars themselves.

(1949)

Claude McKay

My Native Land My Home

Dere is no land dat can compare
Wid you where'er I roam;
In all de wul' none like you fair,
My native land, my home.

Jamaica is de nigger's place,
No mind whe' some declare;
Although dem call we 'no-land race',
I know we home is here.

You give me life an' nourishment,
No udder land I know;
My lub I neber can repent,
For all to you I owe.

E'en ef you mek me beggar die,
I'll trust you all the same,
An' none de less on you rely,
Nor saddle you wid blame.

Though you cas'¹ me from your breas'
An' trample me to deaf;
My heart will trus' you none de less,
My land I won't feget.

An' I hope none o' your sons would
Refuse deir strengt' to lend,
An' drain de last drop o' deir blood
Their country to defend.

You draw de t'ousan' from deir shore,
An' all 'long keep dem please;²
de invalid come here fe cure,
You heal all deir disease.

Your fertile soil grow all o' tings³
To full de naygur's wants,
'Tis seamed wid neber-failing springs⁴
To give dew to de plants.⁵

[64]

You hab all t'ings fe mek life bles',
But buccra 'poil de whole
Wid gove'mint⁶ an all de res',
Fe worry naygur soul.

Still all dem little chupidness⁷
Caan' tek away me lub;
De time when I'll tu'nn' gains' you is
When you can't give me grub.

(1912)

NOTES

1 Cast
2 And keep them amused and happy all along (all the time of their stay
3 All of (the) things
4 Brooks
5 The dew falls heavily in the valley-bottoms
6 Government
7 Those little stupidnesses

A Midnight Woman to the Bobby

No palm me up,¹ you dutty brute
You 'jma mout' mash² like ripe bread-fruit;
You fas'n now, but wait lee ya,³
I'll see you grunt under de law.

You t'ink you wise,⁴ but we wi see;
You not de fus' one fas wid me
I'll lib fe see dem tu'n you out,
As sure as you got dat mash' mout'.

I born right do'n beneath' de clack⁵
 (You ugly brute, you tu'n you' back?)
Don't t'ink dat I'm a come-aroun;⁶
I born right 'way in 'panish Town.

Care how you try, you caan' do mo'
Dan many dat was hyah befo';⁷
Yet whe' dey all o' dem te-day?⁸
De buccra dem no kick dem' way?⁹

Ko'¹⁰ pon you' jam samplatta¹¹ nose:
'Cos you wear Mis'r Koshaw clo'es¹²

[65]

You t'ink say you's de only man,[13]
Yet fus'[14] time ko how you be'n 'tan'[15]

You big an' ugly ole tu'n-foot[16]
Be'n neber know fe wear a boot;
An' chigger nyam you' tumpa toe,[17]
Till nit full i' like herrin' roe.

You come from mountain naked' kin[18]
An' Lard a mussy! You be'n thin,
For all de bread-fruit dem be'n done,
Bein' 'poil' up by de tearin' sun:[19]

De coco'[20] couldn' bear at all,
For, Lard! de groun' was pure white-marl;
An' t'rough de rain part[21] o' de year
De mango tree dem couldn' bear.

An' when de pinch o' time you feel
A' pur you a you' chigger heel,[22]
You lef' you' district, big an coarse,
An come join[23] buccra Police Force.

An' now you don't wait fe you' glass,[24]
But trouble me wid you jam fas';[25]
But wait, me frien; you' day wi' come,
I'll see you go same lak a some.[26]

Say wha'? 'res' me?[27] – you go to hell!
You t'ink Judge don't know unno well?[28]
You t'ink him gwin' go sentance[29] me
Widout a soul fe witness i'?

(1912)

NOTES

1 Don't put your hands on me
2 Your d—d mouth is all awry
3 You are fast (meddling, officious) now but wait a little, d'you hear?
4 You think you're wise
5 The clock on the public buildings at Spanish Town
6 Day-labourers, men and women, in Kingston streets and wharves, famous for the heavy weights they carry, are called 'come-arounds'
7 No matter how you try, you can't do more than your predecessors (all that were here before)

8 Yet where are they all today?
9 Did not the buccra (white man) kick them away (dismiss them)?
10 Look
11 A piece of leather cut somewhat larger than the size of the foot, and tied sandal-wise to it; said of anything that is flat and broad
12 Mr Kershaw's clothes i.e. police uniform. Col. Kershaw, Inspector General of Police in 1911 and for many years before
13 A mighty fine fellow
14 When I knew you first
15 Look what sort of figure you cut
16 Turned-in foot
17 And chigoes (burrowing fleas) had eaten your maimed toe and nits (young chigoes) had filled it
18 Naked skin, i.e. with your shirt and trousers full of holes
19 Having been spoilt by the hot sun. Pronounce 'bein' as a monosyllable
20 An edible root
21 During some months
22 When you felt hard times spurring you in your chigger-eaten heel
23 Came and joined
24 You don't wait for the right and proper moment
25 With all your infernal forwardness and officiousness
26 Same like some, just as others before you did
27 What's that? – arrest me?
28 D'you think the magistrate doesn't know your tricks? 'unno' or 'Onnoo' is an African word, meaning 'you' collectively
29 Pronounce the a 'ah', but without accent.

The Apple-Woman's Complaint

While me deh walk 'long in de street,
Policeman's yawnin' on his beat;
An' dis de wud him chiefta'n say –
Me mus'n' car' me apple-tray.

Ef me no wuk, me boun' fe tief;
S'pose dat will please de police chief
De prison dem mus' be wan' full[1]
Mek dem's 'pon we like ravin' bull.

Black nigger wukin' lada cow
An' wipin' sweat-drops from his brow.
Dough him is dyin' sake o' need.
P'lice an' dem headman boun' fe feed.

[67]

P'lice an' dem headman gamble too,
Dey shuffle card an bet fe true;
Yet ef me Charlie gamble, – well,
Dem try fe' queeze him laka hell.

De headman fe de town police
Mind neber know a little peace
'Cep' when him an' him heartless ban
Hab sufferin' nigger in dem han'.²

Ah son-son! dough you're bastard, yah,
An' deres no one you can call pa,
Jes' try to ha' you' mudder's min'
An Police Force you'll neber jine.

But how judge believe policemen,
Dem dutty mout' wid lyin' stain'?
While we go batterin' along
Dem doin' we all sort o' wrong.

We hab fe barter-out we soul
To lib t'rough dis ungodly wul';
O massa Jesus! don't you see
How police is oppressin' we?

Dem wan' fe see we in de street
Dah foler dem all' pon dem beat;
An' after, 'dout a drop o' shame,
Say we be'n dah solicit dem.

Ah massa Jesus! in your love
Jes' look do'n from you' t'rone above,
An' show me how a poo' weak gal
Can lib good life in dis ya wul.

(1912)

NOTES

1 The prisons must want occupants, and that is why they are down upon us
like angry bulls
2 The mind of the chief of the town police is never happy, except, etc.

In Bondage

I would be wandering in distant fields
Where man, and bird, and beast, lives leisurely,
And the old earth is kind, and ever yields
Her goodly gifts to all her children free;
Where life is fairer, lighter, less demanding,
And boys and girls have time and space for play
Before they come to years of understanding –
Somewhere I would be singing, far away.
For life is greater than the thousand wars
Men wage for it in their insatiate lust,
And will remain like the eternal stars,
When all that shines to-day is drift and dust.

But I am bound with you in your mean graves,
O black men, simple slaves of ruthless slaves.

(1953)

Outcast

For the dim regions whence my fathers came
My spirit, bondaged by the body, longs.
Words felt, but never heard, my lips would frame;
My soul would sing forgotten jungle songs.
I would go back to darkness and to peace,
But the great western world holds me in fee,
And I may never hope for full release
While to its alien gods I bend my knee.
Something in me is lost, forever lost,
Some vital thing has one out of my heart,
And I must walk the way of life a ghost
Among the sons of earth, a thing apart.

For I was born, far from my native clime,
Under the white man's menace, out of time.

(1953)

[69]

Flame-Heart

So much have I forgotten in ten years,
  So much in ten brief years! I have forgot
What time the purple apples come to juice,
  And what month brings the shy forget-me-not.
I have forgot the special, startling season
  Of the pimento's flowering and fruiting;
What time of year the ground doves brown the fields
  And fill the noonday with their curious fluting.
I have forgotten much, but still remember
The poinsettia's red, blood-red in warm December.

I still recall the honey-fever grass,
  But cannot recollect the high days when
We rooted them out of the ping-wing path
  To stop the mad bees in the rabbit pen.
I often try to think in what sweet month
  The languid painted ladies used to dapple
The yellow by-road mazing from the main,
  Sweet with the golden threads of the rose-apple.
I have forgotten – strange – but quite remember
The poinsettia's red, blood-red in warm December.

What weeks, what months, what time of the mild year
  We cheated school to have our fling at tops?
What days our wine-thrilled bodies pulsed with joy
  Feasting upon blackberries in the copse?
Oh some I know! I have embalmed the days,
  Even the sacred moments when we played,
All innocent of passion, uncorrupt,
  At noon and evening in the flame-heart's shade.
We were so happy, happy, I remember,
Beneath the poinsettia's red in warm December.

(1954)

[70]

I Shall Return

I shall return again; I shall return
To laugh and love and watch with wonder-eyes
At golden noon the forest fires burn,
Wafting their blue-black smoke to sapphire skies.
I shall return to loiter by the streams
That bathe the brown blades of the bending grasses,
And realize once more my thousand dreams
Of waters rushing down the mountain passes.
I shall return to hear the fiddle and fife
Of village dances, dear delicious tunes
That stir the hidden depths of native life,
Stray melodies of dim remembered runes.
I shall return, I shall return again,
To ease my mind of long, long years of pain.

(1954)

H.G. De Lisser

Jane's Career

The thought of earning a shilling a day – six shillings a week, if she worked on Saturdays – filled the heart of Jane with inexpressible joy. Here were riches and comparative independence within her grasp; here was escape from domestic servitude; here was a future made bright with hope. She thanked God very devoutly that night. It was only two weeks before that she had met Sathyra, and a casual acquaintanceship, begun in a Chinaman's shop, had rapidly ripened into friendship in the course of a day or two. Jane told Sathyra of her troubles, and Sathyra, with the memories of her own early youth still fresh in her mind, listened sympathetically. She was living alone just then. Her last 'friend' had left her rather suddenly, having had a dispute with her on the subject of expenditure; her one child had died some two years before, and her craving for companionship, as well as financial considerations, made it necessary that she should have some one to share her room and her living expenses with her, go to picnics with her, converse with her, and help to make her happy.

'Why don't y'u leave you' employer?' she had one day suggested to Jane.

'But where to go to?' was Jane's very natural question.

'You can stop wid me till you get a job. I am workin' downtown. There is no vacancy where I am now, but I will tell you if I hear of anything.'

And Sathyra did hear of something within the next couple of weeks. Not far from the office where she worked was an establishment belonging to one of the liquor merchants of the town. Here, on the average, some twenty girls and women were employed in the corking and labelling of bottles, and changes in the personnel of the staff were not infrequent. Sathyra heard that two assistants were wanted, and went immediately to bespeak one of the vacant positions for Jane. This was on a Friday. Meeting Jane on the following day, by arrangement, she told her of the job she had secured for her. It was she who had planned Jane's method of escape, for the latter shrank from boldly defying Mrs Mason and walking out of the yard in the full light of day, a mode of taking leave which Sathyra at first advised and would have much preferred.

Thus aided and abetted by her friend, Jane had made her great essay towards freedom and financial betterment. It never occurred to Mrs Mason, when she was sending Amanda about her business, that Jane's programme was already mapped out and that the hour of her emancipation was at hand. Cecil had not divined that what he termed the 'rudeness' of Jane was but the first expression of her feeling of independence. Jane would have gone in any case on that Sunday night, would have gone whether Amanda had been sent away or not, whether or not Mrs Mason had held the terror of a Monday morning reprimand over her head. She had not the slightest intention of being turned off 'like a dog'. And fortune had so arranged it that she should leave a poor situation for a good one.

The change pleased her. She was engaged on the Monday morning at the liquor establishment, and turned in to work at once. Seated on a box in front of a sort of counter laden with bottles, equipped with a batch of labels and a jug of mucilage, she plunged into her task. She was but one of a line of other workers, all of whom were very young women. Her job was simple, quickness being the only qualification for the work after she had been shown how to paste the labels on. Sometimes the women sang, a Catholic hymn preferably, though most of them were Protestants; at other times they talked, but conversation was not always easy when they wanted to get through a lot of work. They were paid by results, a shilling a day being the average amount earned; but a very quick girl could earn more, one or two making as much as eight shillings in six days.

The other girls became friendly with Jane after the first hour or so. Learning her name, they addressed her as Miss Burrell; indeed, it was a matter of etiquette with them to speak to one another as Miss So-and-so; only close personal friends calling each other by their Christian names. This was a change from (and an improvement on) the customs and manners of domestic service, and Jane highly appreciated it. She had gone up more than one step on the social ladder.

From seven till twelve she worked, then they ceased for an hour for lunch. Lunch cost her three pence; it was provided by a woman who came in with a tray filled with little plates, each plate containing a bit of stewed meat or some boiled salt fish, a piece of yam or a sweet potato, and some rice. It was not a large meal, but it would serve to sustain her until dinner-time; she ate it with the knife and fork supplied by the caterer, and, lunch over, she lounged on her box, placing her back against the wall of the building, stretched out her legs, and composed herself to rest, like the most of the others, for the balance of the hour.

Jane's companions were not all of the same complexion; some were of a light-brown hue, some were chocolate-coloured, a few were black. Every one chatted gaily as though not one of them had a care in the world. They screamed with merriment over some feeble joke, such as when one of them declared that she would never marry a cigar maker because she did not smoke, or when another affirmed that she should not marry at all because she could not undertake to support a husband. Jane laughed with the rest, and thought it fine to be addressed as 'Miss'. True, the work was tiresome, and her back ached; but what an emancipation it was from Mrs Mason's petty tyranny!

'Where y'u was before y'u come here, Miss Burrell?' asked one of her neighbours when the general conversation lagged a little.

'I was workin' wid a lady, but I leave her. She follow me up too much,' was Jane's reply.

'Tcho! dat is a life wouldn't suit me at all,' commented her questioner. 'I wouldn't be a servant to anybody – I would prefer to sell fruit in de street. Them want to treat you too bad, ma'am, an de work is hard. This work hard too,' she added reflectively; 'but you can earn more money, and you is o-you' own mistress after five o'clock.'

'Them employ y'u all the time?' asked Jane.

'No; sometimes there is noten to do, and then them knock you off. However, what's de use of fretten, me love? God is in heaven, an' we mus' trust to Him. Besides, some of us lucky enough to have a back force.'

The expression was new to Jane.

'What is a "back force"?' she asked.

The innocent query drew forth a scream of laughter from those who heard it. These called out to the others –

'Miss Burrell want to know what a "back force" is!' and then they exploded anew. Such simplicity was as astonishing as it was diverting. Then one girl condescended to explain. 'It is a "friend",' she said.

So once again Jane learnt that the inevitable solution, or partial solution, of the problem of living for most women was to be found in assistance from a 'friend'. There was, it seemed, no other way, for few of these young women earned enough to live easily upon, and their wants were always increasing. She reverted to the question of domestic service. 'I doan't like to work in a house,' she stated with conviction.

'But some lady is very kind,' said one of the girls to her. 'Them treat y'u well. I never work with them myself, but I know some who is very kind.'

'True, my love,' agreed another; 'but I wouldn't like de work: it doan't suit me. I prefer to be me own mistress . . .'

This was the general sentiment, and had Jane been a judge of character she would have perceived that these young women were either of a more independent disposition or of a somewhat better class than those who remained domestic servants nearly all their lives. They were rebels; they had no humility in them; in their own way they had aspirations; they wanted to be free. Most of them (city born) had never been domestics. One or two others had early emancipated themselves from that form of service. On the whole they knew very little about it, but that little was sufficient for them. As for Jane, her experience has been a hard one, and so she could cordially agree with the views of her new acquaintances.

At one o'clock they straggled back to work, and from that hour until five they pasted labels and hummed hymns, only stopping now and then to have their bottles inspected and checked. Sometimes there was a sharp dispute between them and the man who examined their work. Their inveterate inclination was to think that he was cheating or that he wished to be unreasonable. Jane shared the sentiments of her colleagues, and once during the day she even ventured upon a feeble protest against the man's complaint. She was quite wrong but this effort at self-assertion pleased her. She had already begun to feel herself 'her own woman'.

She was thoroughly tired when she reached home that afternoon, and for some time she sat idly by the threshold of her little room, watching Sathyra prepare dinner for both of them. Sathyra placed a small box very near to the door, and under the single window which the room possessed. On the box she set a little iron stove filled with burning charcoal, and on this an iron pot. She sat beside the impromptu fireplace, a second box forming her seat, and in a very short space of time she had peeled the bit of yam, scraped the four sweet potatoes, and stripped the skin from the stout green plantain that was to form the staple of their evening meal. It was a salt-fish dinner: half a pound of salt fish and three farthings' worth of pork would be adequate flavouring for the breadkind. Sathyra would not ask Jane to assist her just then, knowing that the girl had been tired out by work that was strange to her; as for herself, she was accustomed to cooking her meals after going home, and to doing her own washing after that, and Jane would be able to help in a very short time. She talked as she worked; talked business.

'Dis room is eight shillings a month, and you will pay half. About five shillin's a week should give us breakfast in de morning, an' dinner – sometimes it may be six shillin's, if we get anyt'ing extra. You will have to pay for you'own lunch downtown, which is one an' sixpence a week, so you will only have a few pence leave over for snowball¹ or a car ticket. But we can't do no better. I doan't think you will ever earn much more than six shillin's a week at the start: however, somebody may fall in love wid y'u an' then you will be all right . . .'

'I doan't think anybody gwine to fall in love wid me,' Jane observed, crooking one of her legs and crossing her hands over the knee. She did not believe what she said, but wanted to hear from her friend the latter's opinion of her charms and prospects.

'You is all right,' returned Sathyra, glancing at her for a moment and nodding her head. 'You are young an' y'u have good looks. You are all right.'

Jane was flattered. She wished to return the compliment.

'You all right too,' she replied. 'But you doan't have nobody now?'

'Not now; but it must be soon. I never too long widout an admirer. But I doan't accustom to teckin' any-and-everybody, an' as I have a good job I can afford to pick and choose.'

The breadkind being nearly ready, Sathyra tied the salt fish in a clean bag and plunged it into the pot. All along the front of the low range of rooms cooking was going on, and in the gathering darkness the line of lights from half a score of stoves gave a touch of picturesqueness to the simple, homely scene. Some of the people of the yard were washing their clothes; some were standing by their room doors waiting patiently till dinner should be ready; others were tidying up their little rooms. The smallest number of persons in a room was two, while as many as six could be found in one of these

[76]

places. These six represented a family. Where only two occupied a room, they were either a man and his wife or two women who had clubbed together for companionship and urgent reasons of economy. Although living in the same yard, some of these people were strangers to one another. They knew each other by sight and name, but there was no particularly friendly intercourse between them beyond a courteous salutation and an occasional brief conversation. The yard was like a section of a street, and one chose one's friends without regard to proximity.

Sathyra soon lifted the pot off the fire, threw the bit of pork into a frying-pan, and placed this upon the blazing coals. The sharp fizzing sound and pleasant odour of the melting pork whetted the appetite of the girls, and Jane, considerably rested, busied herself to help in the final preparations for their meal.

She went into the room and brought out three plates, into one of which the salt fish was put, the melted fat being poured over it. Into the other two plates the breadkind, equally divided, was served. Jane carried the three laden plates inside, while Sathyra scooped the live coals out of the stove and extinguished them, putting them aside for use on the following morning. This done, she followed her friend into the room, beat up the fish with a fork so as to mix it well with the grease, divided it between herself and Jane, and sat down on a chair (the plate in her lap) to dine. They ate with forks, slowly and with evident enjoyment. It was, if coarse, a palatable and sufficient meal, and more than ever did Jane feel satisfied with her newly-won freedom and independence.

(1914)

NOTE

1 'Snowball' is a mixture of crushed ice and syrup sold in the streets of Kingston.

A.R.F. Webber

Those That Be in Bondage – A Tale of Indian Indentures and Sunlit Western Waters

'Jim, what are you going to do?'

Me? Just one other before dinner: but see that he does put more Gin than Angostura.'

'My goodness, man, I am not talking about your comfortable self, but of my troubles.'

Thus opened the first skirmish, and so spake the fair chatelaine of the House of Walton: Walton the Big man. John James Walton: forty, hale and hearty – Sugar oracle and Planting Attorney of the firm of Rickets & Co., whose vast sugar plantations spread from the Mahaica River on the sea coast of British Guiana to far up the Corentyne River on the Dutch border of the same.

British Guiana! So few do know thee – except colloquially as 'Demerara', the home of grocery crystals. Few stay-at-home people realise that you are a vast inheritance – and the only one – of some 100,000 square miles, snugly stowed away on the shoulder of the great South American continent, and the natural highway to the upper reaches of the fertile but turbulent Amazon. But these are things beyond this time of writing, and the scribe must his tale unfold.

To – day but a fringe on the sea coast of this magnificent domain is beneficially occupied, and that almost entirely by the dominating interest of sugar-growing. Sugar-growing to give to the world the famous Demerara crystals: something to be proud of and to enjoy; and something to be imitated by rotten German beets, which destroy the bees that venture to feed on its sugar. This is the great work – the original not the imitation – that John James Walton spends his life time on; while he divides up his recreation between his swizzles and the petting of his pretty and affectionate spouse. This is the great work that has created for its well being a system of labour immigration, alike the wonder of economists and the anathema of Cobden school purists, from far-off India, across two oceans to the shores of the sunlit Caribbean.

Walton watched his under-managers and heard their tales of woe: he watched his canes and argued about seedlings; but he saw not the great tragedy that grew at his feet; a tragedy born of that system of immigration which was at once his pride and his worry. A tragedy deep as night, warm as the sun in his cane-fields, and subtle as the centuries whose guile and song have changed but little the hearts of women and the fancies of men.

At the check-up from his wife, recorded above, 'Honest John', as he was known to his intimates, sat up. He turned the leaves of his memory back: he weaned himself from the half-pleasant contemplation of a swizzle, ill-made enough to give cause for an honest grumble, well made enough to enjoy; and turned to the wholly unpleasant subject which his wife would hark back to. His mental comment being, 'Women are so worrisome.' He had hoped to 'jolly along' the subject with her until it reached the limbo of forgetfulness, or, at least, the easy toleration he had seen so many others win. Aloud he replied:

'Well, Marion, what would you have me do? I have selected the best-managed estate under me: Old Rapfuller is the best planter alive. Things are run so on 'Never Out' that the boy will learn more about the great work of agriculture and sugar making there, in six months, than perhaps he would in six years on some of the very much larger estates, where each subject is so very much farther away from the other. The boy, I tell you, is all right! What about the swizzles we spoke about?'

'Swizzles *we* spoke about?' echoed Mrs Walton. 'I did not hear myself in that conversation. Anyway, I'll ring, and then perhaps you will listen to me.'

Walton rolled in his Berbice chair: that science of comfort; so called because it was first 'practised' in the colony province of that name; being 'invented' by an old soldier of India in the evening of his days, which he had spent in Berbice as a planter. 'Honest John' took down one leg, from the chair's comfort-giving arm, and put up the other on the far side. He was clearly cornered and had to be rustling up the old arguments – getting the old brain away, as he would put it, from facts to fancies – so he needs must roost himself in comfort.

'Look here, Jim,' she persisted, 'You know I am uneasy about the boy. I have not a word against old Rapfuller – except, perhaps that if he had less of lean and lanky sisters, and more of plump and pleasing nieces, the road might be easier.'

'Jim', as she called him in imitation of the fat grey mule which he sometimes rode and which owned to the name of 'Big

Jim', grumbled that he did not know what the lean and lankiness of 'old Raps' sisters had to do with it and, moreover, if they had not been lean and lanky, Mrs Walton might have been someone else's wife. Marion, however, was not taking any such red herring trail, but headed straight back.

'Jim,' she espostulated [sic], 'you are not giving the matter sufficient consideration. Edwin, I have no doubt, is learning a great deal about planting; but what I am worried about is that he seems to be learning a great deal about other things too.'

'Learning! and he from a Public School!' was all that poor Walton could ejaculate; and then he turned to contemplate the rosy sparkle and swallow the tempting swizzle, which by then was by his elbow.

Even that caustic comment could not deter my lady: she knew her mind, and that mind she was determined to speak.

'I have heard,' she resumed, 'on the best authority, that he is far too much wrapped up with that smooth-skinned, bare-toed East Indian young lady. And I do hate these entanglements when a boy is young.'

Walton squirmed piteously, and remembered two bright eyed Eurasian boys, well placed in the local Civil Service, by an invisible hand: carrying another name than his own, but recalling some of the roystering [sic] days of his youth, under a dead and gone worthy whose only demand of conduct was that his staff should ride in 'for orders' – sober, or seemingly so – under his verandah window in sun or rain at 5.30 every morning. Then, as now, the overseers, or 'staff', were fed from the manager's table, because they 'cannot be trusted with their board allowance.' Outside of that their domestic concerns in those days were their own. Cut off from marriage under this rotten system, they found their wives among their neighbours', or, perhaps, shared another with some complaisant immigrant. For, despite Des Veoux – the civil servant originator of a great Commission on the treatment of immigrants – some immigrants will remain complaisant, and even invite such relationships, for the gain it brings them.

'Well, you know, my dear,' the now fairly uncomfortable Jim replied, 'the boy is young. Like the measles or teething, with sympathetic management, he will get over it. I'll tell 'Old Raps' to have a quiet look at the situation and keep me posted. And, moreover, I do think after all this dry-earth talk I am entitled to another swizzle before sitting down.'

Saying which Jim suited his action to his word and took the reins in his own hands. The proximity of dinner revived his drooping spirits, and soon his cheery voice was heard echoing down the spacious verandah demanding 'another rosy,' and bespeaking a special 'pony one for the missy, yeh!'

During dinner the subject cropped up and up again; and 'Honest John' carefully repeated his plans. If things were really going to bad, 'Old Raps' would know. 'Old Raps' was a wonderful man, and one to be depended upon in every respect. If it became absolutely necessary he would remove the boy to some other Estate; or get the indentures of that particular family transferred to some far away plantation. He would send the boy back to England. As 'Honest John's' heart expanded under the pressure of good food and wine, and the charming influence of his wife, who made a capital hostess, whether company was present or not, he threw himself with zest into the plans for saving his wife's younger brother: for such, in fact, was the much discussed 'boy'. So, by the time dinner was through, he and his wife were well at one on the subject nearest her heart. As they rose and adjourned to the verandah, Mrs Walton heaved one last sigh and gave voice to her hope:

'That the day would soon come when there would be more marriages and giving in marriage among sugar estate overseers; when there would be more of a social and home life among them, in keeping with their own walks in life.'

Poor woman; she could not grasp the rotten economic conditions which made her hope a vain one, and condemned all overseers, irrespective of inclination, to a life of enforced celibacy: without the freedom from temptation of the cloister, or the safeguard of vows.

'Honest John's' counterpart of his wife's sigh and voiced hope, was the lighting of a cigar and the registering of a solemn, but inward, wish that she would drop the subject. For, he was resolved that Planting Attorneys had quite enough worry, chasing after seedlings, and agitators, and Immigration Circulars, without being hamstrung by their own wives over overseers and *their* domestic affairs. 'It's all these agitators' he finally, and still inwardly, commented with charming inconsistence: as though agitators had anything to do with the subject ...

Meanwhile, Edwin Hamilton, the subject of all the worry, slowly wove the mesh of his fate around himself and a generation ahead,

[81]

amid the gibes and good natured sallies of his brother 'celibates'. Young and impressionable, on the threshold of his twenties, a little bookish by heart, he had dabbled in Socialism; he had flirted with Darwin and with Mendel, and had been captivated by Eugenics. Whilst, originally, he had set out in the study of Darwin and Mendel for their influence on the calling which he had been encouraged to make his own, they ended by influencing his whole outlook on the question of sex.

Had Edwin's temperament and learning been carefully measured by some accurate instrument, he would have been the last person to be sent on a sugar estate, where the whole atmosphere reeks of sex and its trying complications. Reared far from Colonial influences he was too prone to think a man 'a man for a' that'; and a girl just a girl, without reference to the hue of her skin, or her immediate position in the world's economics. Bred in the atmosphere of an English public school, he had absorbed to a hyper-sensitive degree its spirit of fair play, until it obsessed him and dwarfed his every other instinct. With such a spirit, 'expediency' has no place, and 'the balance of convenience' may as well have been expressed in unknown characters.

The problems of sex on a sugar estate are the problems of that immigration system on which the very existence of the sugar industry, and consequently the whole industrial life of the colony, may be said to be at stake. It is a paradox, but one easily understood by the initiated, that in a world where the female element so largely preponderates, the proportion of females among the 100,000 immigrant population in British Guiana is frightfully meagre. This develops a fierceness of sentiment, on questions of sex, which is horrible to behold. While there are immigrants, like some men of every community, who are complaisant with respect to their wives and daughters for their own gain, those are but the exceptions, and the remainder fiercely resent any poaching of such a nature. Wife slayers are hanged by the score; here a woman may be seen noseless or, another, with both her hands lopp[e]d off, because some fiercely jealous lord and master had been wronged. Fierce, perhaps, as much because of the wrong that has been done him, as because of the difficulty with which he is faced in filling her place, with that freedom of choice, that would obtain under less strained conditions of proportion.

Add to all of this that other disturbing factor, thought of by Mrs Walton as the absence of social life among overseers – the lords of the pay, comfort and very existence of the immigrants. These overseers, barracked under a most unholy system, under conditions worse than soldiering, what wonder they deteriorate in mind, morals and manners. Denied the soldier's right to married privileges and quarters, they must borrow or steal a wife. If the borrowed or stolen wife is the property of an immigrant, discovery means serious disaster; this, as is inevitable with human nature, supplying the element of danger and romance that make an irresistible appeal to adventurous spirits. Then again, an overseer may not quit the confines of his plantation, or entertain any friends on it to lunch or dinner, until he has obtained the sanction of his manager, to whom every detail and even, possibly, every reason has to be stated. Thus, denied mastership of his table, board or leisure, it is little wonder if the overseer finds scope for the practice of the most clamant instinct of the human race on underlings and immigrants.

Such in brief are the conditions which make sex, and the complications arising from the attempt to force celibacy on overseers, such a burning immigration question.

Such was the atmosphere in which Edwin Hamilton found himself at twenty-two – lord of his hours of meditation, but not of his physical liberty; lord of the liberty of scores of immigrants, but not of his own. The very readiness with which 'Old Raps' gave him leave to 'quit boundaries' was in itself an embarrassment; for less favoured and less deserving ones were not slow to chaff him about his favoured relationship, and the privileges it brought.

(1917)

C.L.R. James

Triumph

Where people in England and America say slums, Trinidadians say barrack-yards. Probably the word is a relic of the days when England relied as much on garrisons of soldiers as on her fleet to protect her valuable sugar-producing colonies. Every street in Port-of-Spain proper can show you numerous examples of the type: a narrow gateway leading into a fairly big yard, on either side of which run long low buildings, consisting of anything from four to eighteen rooms, each about twelve feet square. In these live, and have always lived the porters, prostitutes, carter-men, washer-women, and domestic servants of the city.

In one corner of the yard is the hopelessly inadequate water-closet, unmistakable to the nose if not to the eye; sometimes there is a structure with the title of bath-room: a courtesy title, for he or she who would wash in it with decent privacy must cover the person as if bathing on the Lido; the kitchen happily presents no difficulty: never is there one and each barrack-yarder cooks before her door. In the centre of the yard is a heap of stones. On these the half-laundered clothes are bleached before being finally spread out to dry on the wire lines which in every yard cross and recross each other in all directions. Not only to Minerva have these stones been dedicated. Time was when they would have had an honoured shrine in a local temple to Mars, for they were the major source of ammunition for the homicidal strife which in times past so often flared up in barrack-yards. As late as 1915, the local bard, practising his band for the annual carnival (which still flourishes in Trinidad alone of the British West Indian islands) – as late as 1915 he could sing:

> When the rumour went round the town
> That the Germans was comin' to blow us down,
> When the rumour went round the town
> That the Germans was comin' to blow us down,
> Some like cowards remain at home
> Others come forth with bottle and stone
> Old lady couldn't bring stone but she come with the
> pot-chambre.

The stones from 'the bleach' were to help even in the repelling of the German invader. A poetic idea, and as is not uncommon with poetry, an anachronism. No longer do the barrack-yarders live the picturesque life of twenty-five years ago. Then, practising for the carnival, rival singers, Will, Jean, and Freddie, porter, wharf-man, or loafer, in ordinary life, but for that season ennobled by some such striking sobriquet as The Duke of Normandy or The Lord Invincible, and carrying with dignity homage such as young aspirants to literature would pay to Mr Kipling or Mr Shaw, thirty years ago. They sang in competition from seven in the evening until far into the early morning, stimulated by the applause of their listeners and the excellence and copiousness of the rum; night after night the stick-men practised their dangerous and skilful game; the 'pierrots', after elaborate preface of complimentary speech, belaboured each other with riding whips; while around the performers the spectators pressed thick and good-humoured, until mimic warfare was transformed into real, and stones from 'the bleach' flew thick. But today that life is dead. All carnival practice must cease at ten o'clock. The policeman is to the stick-fighter and 'pierrot' as the sanitary inspector to mosquito larvae. At nights the streets are bright with electric light, the arm of the law is longer, its grip stronger. Gone are the old lawlessness and picturesqueness. Barrack-yard life has lost its savour. Luckily, prohibition in Trinidad is still but a word. And life, dull and drab as it is in comparison, can still offer its great moments.

On a Sunday morning in one of the rooms of a barrack in Abercromby Street sat Mamitz. Accustomed as is squalid adversity to reign unchallenged in these quarters, yet in this room it was more than usually triumphant, sitting, as it were, high on a throne of royal state, so depressed was the woman and depressing her surroundings.

The only representatives of the brighter side of life were three full-page pictures torn from illustrated periodicals, photographs of Lindbergh, Bernard Shaw, and Sargent's 'Portrait of a Woman', and these owed their presence solely to the fact that no pawnshop would have accepted them. They looked with unseeing eyes upon a room devoid of furniture save for a few bags spread upon the floor to form a bed. Mamitz sat on the door-step talking to, or rather being talked to, by her friend Celestine who stood astride the concrete canal which ran in front of the door.

'Somebody do you something,' said Celestine with conviction. 'Nobody goin' to change my mind from that. An' if you do what I tell you, you will t'row off this black spirit that on you. A nice woman like you, and you carn' get a man to keep you! You carn' get nothing to do!'

Mamitz said nothing. Had Celestine said the exact opposite, Mamitz's reply would have been the same.

She was a black woman, too black to be pure negro, probably with some Madrasi East Indian blood in her, a suspicion which was made a certainty by the long thick plaits of her plentiful hair. She was shortish and fat, voluptuously developed, tremendously developed, and as a creole loves development in a woman more than any other extraneous allure, Mamitz (like the rest of her sex in all stations of life) saw to it when she moved that you missed none of her charms. But for the last nine weeks she had been 'in derricks', to use Celestine's phrase. First of all the tram conductor who used to keep her (seven dollars every Saturday night, out of which Mamitz usually got three) had accused her of infidelity and beaten her. Neither the accusation nor the beating had worried Mamitz. To her and her type those were minor incidents of exist-ence; from their knowledge of life and men, the kept woman's inevitable fate. But after a temporary reconciliation he had beaten her once more, very badly indeed, and then left her. Even this was not an irremediable catastrophe. But thenceforward, Mamitz, from being the most prosperous woman in the yard, had sunk gradually to being the most destitute. Despite her very obvious attractions, no man took notice of her. She went out asking for washing or for work as a cook. No success. Luckily, in the days of her prosperity, she had been generous to Celestine, who now kept her from actual starvation. One stroke of luck she had had. The agent for the barracks had suddenly taken a fancy to her, and Mamitz had not found it difficult to persuade him to give her a chance with the rent. But that respite was over; he was pressing for the money, and Mamitz had neither money to pay nor hope of refuge when she was turned out. Celestine would have taken her in, but Celestine's keeper was a policeman who visited her three or four nights a week, and to one in that position a fifteen-foot room does not offer much scope for housing the homeless. Yet Celestine was grieved that she could do nothing to help Mamitz in her troubles,

which she attributed to the evil and supernatural machinations of
Irene, their common enemy.

'Take it from me, that woman do you something. I's she put
Nathan against you. When was the quarrel again?'

'It was two or three days after Nathan gave me the first beating.'

Nathan then had started on his evil courses before the quarrel
with Irene took place, but Celestine brushed away that objection.

'She must 'a' had it in her mind for you from before. You didn't
see how she fly out at you? ... As long as you livin' here an' I
cookin' I wouldn' see you want a cup o' tea an' a spoonful o' rice
... But I carn' help with the rent ... An' you ain' have nobody
here!'

Mamitz shook her head. She was from Demerara.

'If you could only cross the sea – that will cut any spirit that on
you ... Look the animal!'

Irene had come out of her room on the opposite side of the yard.
She could not fail to see Celestine and Mamitz and she called loudly
to a neighbour lower down the yard:

'Hey Jo-Jo! What is the time? Ten o' clock a'ready? Le' me start
to cook me chicken, that me man buy for me – even if 'e have a so'-
foot ... I don't know how long it will last, before 'e get drunk and
kick me out o' here. Then I will have to go dawgin' round other
po' people to see if I could pick up what they t'row 'way.'

She fixed a box in front of her door, put her coal-pot on it, and
started to attend to her chicken.

Sunday morning in barrack-yards is pot-parade. Of the sixteen
tenants in the yard twelve had their pots out, and they lifted the
meat with long iron forks to turn it, or threw water into the pot so
that it steamed to the heavens and every woman could tell what her
neighbour was cooking – beef, or pork, or chicken. It didn't matter
what you cooked in the week, it didn't matter if you didn't cook at
all. But to cook salt-fish, or ribs, or hog-head, or pig-tail on a Sunday
morning was a disgrace. You put your pot inside your house and
cooked it there.

Mamitz, fat, easy-going, and cowed by many days of semi-starva-
tion, took little notice of Irene. But Celestine, a thin little whip of
a brown-skinned woman, bubbled over with repressed rage.

'By Christ, if it wasn't for one thing I'd rip every piece o' clothes
she have of off'er.'

'Don' bother wid 'er. What is the use o' gettin' you'self in trouble with Jimmy?'

Jimmy was the policeman. He was a steady, reliable man but he believed in discipline, and when he spoke, he spoke. He had made Celestine understand that she was not to fight: he wasn't going to find himself mixed up in court as the keeper of any brawling woman. Celestine's wrath, deprived of its natural outlet, burned none the less implacably.

'I tell you something, Mamitz. I goin' to talk to the agent in the mornin'. I goin' to tell him to give you to the end o' the month. I's only five days . . . I goin' to give you a bath. Try an' see if you could get some gully-root and so on this afternoon . . . Tonight I g'on' give you . . . An' I will give you some prayers to read. God stronger than the devil. We g'on' break this t'ing that on you. Cheer up. I g'on' send you a plate with you' chicken an' rice as soon as it finish. Meanwhile, burn you' little candle, say you' little prayers, console you' little mind. I g'on' give you that bath tonight. You ain' kill priest. You ain't cuss you' mudder. So you ain' have cause to 'fraid nothin'.'

Celestine would never trust herself to indulge in abuse with Irene; the chances that it would end in a fight were too great. So she contented herself with casting a look of the most murderous hate and scorn and defiance at her enemy, and then went to her own pot which was calling for attention.

And yet three months before, Mamitz, Celestine, and Irene had been good friends. They shared their rum and their joys and troubles together; and on Sunday afternoons they used to sit before Mamitz's room singing hymns: 'Abide with me', 'Jesu, lover of my soul', 'Onward! Christian soldiers'. Celestine and Irene sang soprano and Irene sang well. Mamitz was a naturally fine contralto and had a fine ear, while Nathan who was a Barbadian and consequently knew vocal music used to sing bass whenever he happened to be in. The singing would put him in a good mood and he would send off to buy more rum and everything would be peaceful and happy. But Irene was a jealous woman, not only jealous of her man, but jealous of Mamitz's steady three dollars a week and Celestine's policeman with his twenty-eight dollars at the end of the month. She lived with a cab-man whose income, though good enough was irregular. And he was a married man, with a wife and children to support. Irene had to do washing to help her out, while Mamitz and Celestine did nothing, merely cooked and washed clothes for their men. So gradually a state of dissatisfaction arose. Then one damp evening, Mamitz passing near the bamboo pole which supported a clothes line overburdened with Irene's clothes, brought it down with her broad expansive person. The line burst, and night-gowns, sheets, pillowcases, white suits, and tablecloths fluttered to the mud. It had been a rainy week with little sun, and already it would have been difficult to get the clothes ready in time for Saturday morning; after this it was impossible. And hot and fiery was the altercation. Celestine who tried to make peace was drawn into the quarrel by Irene's comprehensive and incendiary invective.

'You comin' to put you' mouth in this. You think because you livin' with a policeman you is a magistrate. Mind you' business, woman, mind you' business. The two o' all you don't do nothing for you' livin'. You only sittin' down an' eatin' out the men all you livin' wid. An' I wo'k so hard an' put out me clo'es on the line. And this one like some blame cab-horse knock it down, and when I tell 'er about it you comin' to meddle! Le' me tell you . . .'

So the wordy warfare raged, Celestine's policeman coming in for rough treatment at the tongue of Irene. Celestine, even though she was keeping herself in check, was a match for any barrack-yard woman Port-of-Spain could produce, but yet it was Mamitz who clinched the victory.

'Don't min' Celestine livin' with a policeman. You will be glad to get 'im for you'self. An' it better than livin' wid any stinkin' so'-foot man.'

For Irene's cab-man had a sore on his foot, which he had had for thirty years and would carry with him to the grave even if he lived for thirty years more. Syphilis, congenital and acquired, and his copious boozing would see to it that there was no recovery. Irene had stupidly hoped that nobody in the yard knew. But in Trinidad when His Excellency the Governor and his wife have a quarrel, the street boys speak of it the day after, and Richard's bad foot had long been a secret topic of conversation in the yard. But it was Mamitz who had made it public property, and Irene hated Mamitz with a virulent hatred, and had promised to 'do' for her. Three days before, Nathan, the tram-conductor had given Mamitz the first beating; but even at the time of the quarrel there was no hint of his swift defection and Mamitz's rapid descent to her present plight. So that

[89]

Celestine, an errant but staunch religionist, was convinced that Mamitz's troubles were due to Irene's trafficking with the devil, if not personally, at least through one of his numerous agents who ply their profitable trade in every part of Port-of-Spain. Secure of her own immunity from any thing that Irene might 'put on her', she daily regretted that she couldn't rip the woman to pieces. 'Oh Jesus! If it wasn't for Jimmy I'd tear the wretch lim' from lim'.' But the energy that she could not put into the destruction of Irene she spent in upholding Mamitz. The fiery Celestine had a real affection for the placid Mamitz, whose quiet ways were so soothing. But, more than this, she was determined not to see Mamitz go down. In the bitter antagonism she nursed against Irene, it would have been a galling defeat if Mamitz went to the wall. Further, her reputation as a woman who knew things and could put crooked people straight was at stake. Once she had seen to Jimmy's food and clothes and creature comforts she set herself to devise ways and means of supporting the weak, easily crushed Mamitz.

Celestine's policeman being on duty that night, she herself was off duty and free to attend to her own affairs. At mid-night with the necessary rites and ceremonies, Ave Marias and Pater Nosters, she bathed Mamitz in a large bath-pan full of water prepared with gully-root, fever-grass, lime leaves, gueerir tout, herbe a femmes, and other roots, leaves, and grasses noted for their efficacy, (when properly applied) against malign plots and influences.

(1929)

Leo Oakley

Ideas of Patriotism and National Dignity

Jamaica, having only recently shaken off the shackles of colonialism, falls within the category of 'developing nations', and its literature is still developing, still in the making. For a long time the Cobwebs of colonialism had held the creative arts chokingly enmeshed, and much of the Literary stuff produced during our colonial experience showed a love for Jamaica inseparably bound up with a love for England, the so-called 'Mother Country' and her Empire. Indeed, to be a good patriot in those days one had to be an Anglophil[e] and an empire man! No wonder then that the colonial climate generated writings with a colonial patriotic bias ...

On the early 20th century Jamaican literary scene appeared names like Tom Redcam (Thomas Henry MacDermot), H.S. Bunbury, Albinia Catherine Hutton, Clara Maude Garrett, Arthur Nicolas, H.G. De Lisser, Adolphe Roberts, Claude McKay, Lena Kent and Una Marson. Indeed, it could be said that modern Jamaican writings by Jamaicans about Jamaica began on a professional scale with Tom Redcam (1870–1933) who founded a Jamaican literary movement and who did much to encourage young Jamaican writers. But what of Redcam's idea of patriotism? Referring to eighteenth century Spanish Town he had written in rolling phrases:

> *Death is life's bivouac round the fires of faith.*
> *Grey town and time-worn church, we come to thee.*
> *Shrine of our history, about the tombs*
> *The patriot's spirit lingers reverently.*

And it is safe to assume that his *'patriot's spirit'* was an imperial, not Jamaican, one.

In posthumously making him Poet Laureate of Jamaica in 1933, the Jamaica Branch of the Poetry League had referred to his *'merit as poet, **patriot** and interpreter of the hearts of the people'* and his *'abiding interest in the child life of his country'*. There is no doubt that Redcam loved Jamaica and had a passion for Jamaican history. But all this was evidently circumscribed by loyalty to the British Empire ...

Constance Hollar too loved Jamaica, but, like so many at that time, she seemed bound up by the historical situation within which

[91]

she found herself. '*Poinciana is rushing to my heart with all its magic beauty*', she wrote, '*Storming the highways and byways of it*', and she appeared quite sincere about her '*Songs of the Empire*' publication in 1932. There was also nothing denoting 'pure' Jamaican patriotism in the writings of Albinia Catherine Hutton. In '*The Empire's Flag*', the Union Jack, she could see a '*gallant symbol*', or what she regarded as '*the Flag of Freedom*'. Commenting on the '*Empire's Flag*', J.E. Clare McFarlane wrote: *I do not hesitate to predict that to a generation to come it will be counted among the classics of its kind. The admirable restraint with which the poem is written lends to it that touch of power in tranquility which a contemplation of the Union Jack brings.* McFarlane's predictions have been, to say the least, far off track and such comments revealed the man's thinking at that time. No doubt such writings and comments would have found favour with our ex-colonial masters whose system taught our community to look outside of itself for leadership and excellence. After all, those were the days of sheer Crown Colony Government . . .

As it were, Colonial Jamaica was never encouraged to have any sense of national dignity – at least not until the 'Mother Country' saw which way the wind was blowing. We were to have instead a sort of Empire dignity, and the literature was really a by-product of an educational system geared to ensure loyalty to England, and designed to make us look outside for standards and values . . .

Claude McKay was somewhat different, however, from those writers already mentioned. It is a pity that Jamaica never saw more of the ex-constable who became an internationally recognized writer after leaving Jamaica as a young man for the United States of America in 1912. McKay made his literary name in America but he never did forget his homeland and continued to sing of it, if nostalgically and sentimentally, in poems like '*Flame-Heart*' which tells of honey-fever grass and the poinsettia among other things seen on the Jamaican Countryside which he dearly loved. It is said that McKay could be described as '*the Robbie Burns of Jamaica*', having been the first to reveal to his countrymen in '*Songs of Jamaica*' and '*Constab Ballads*' that there was music in the dialect they spoke. His was indeed an assertion of a Jamaican way of life . . . McKay's Autobiography, '*A Long Way from Home*' and his sentimental poem '*I Shall Return*' show up his love, his longing, indeed his patriotism, for Jamaica, and this was not adulterated with imperial sentiments.

But it was left to the late 1930s to throw up a different brand of writers in Jamaica, who did not hesitate to assert their Jamaicanism, their nationalism. They could not identify themselves with England and English ways. They were for things Jamaican, and they gave voice to the nationalist movement of the time. That upsurge of literary activity took the form, as Adolphe Roberts pointed out, of '*unrhymed modern verse and plotless fiction. The idea, I suppose, was to react as brusquely as possible from the prevailing standard*'. The idea was also to assert Jamaican patriotism and national dignity and to cease being blindly imitative. As G.R. Coulthard in '*Caribbean Literature – An Anthology*' rightly said: *There was definitely a connection in the British Caribbean between the awakening of a national consciousness and a desire for independence and the burgeoning of a new national literature, which set itself higher standards than those hitherto accepted. Writing in the first number of Magazine Focus in 1943, Mrs Edna Manley said, 'Great and irrevocable change[s] have swept this land in the last few years and out of these changes a new art is springing*'. She too was right. And from that 'new art' group sprang George Campbell, M.G. Smith, Roger Mais, Vic Reid, H.D. Carberry, and others like P.M. Sherlock who preceded and nurtured the new nationalist awakening.

There was a conscious attempt by these writers to break away from Victorianism and to associate with the Jamaican independence movement ...

Yes, we must help Jamaica as it grows from foundations laid by patriotic sweat and blood and nourished by the inspiration of writings which continue to reflect patriotism and national dignity. And this is all for the good, providing that we never become blinded by chauvinism or insularism.

(1970)

Harvey Clarke

Miss Jamaica

Before I begin I desire to convince one and all that I am entirely serious and in earnest, and that I am *not* laughing. It is too serious a subject to laugh at. Being utterly incapable of writing down anything about women – or girls rather, – like all writers on this elusive, intangible subject I must endeavour to appear, myself, intangible and elusive. If then you cannot grasp the clear meaning of any part of this – or all of it – put it down to my intangibility. Wonderful world Wonderful subject! Any man who in writing about women deliberately sets to catalogue their virtues and their vices with a stupidness only equalled by rural correspondents to local papers, is merely asking to be told a few home truths about his miserable person and characters. Therefore, gentle reader, I will hie me to my subject with required vagueness and, or, respect for the truth, *naturally*.

The Jamaican girl is fascinating. There, you immediately exclaim, there you go doing just what you said you despised – summarising. Not so. Fascination is a quality sufficiently elusive and slippery to set down without any hedging. The particular fascination peculiar to Jamaica and the Jamaica creole – by which I mean anyone born in the island – is one made up of such components as languor, sudden sparkle, as sudden stillness, a caress given unexpectedly, sulkiness – for even this has its own low – quick temper as quickly quiet, and silence. I have to admit it, but unless she has grown to know you very well or is one of the exceptions, the Jamaican girl has not an easy flow of conversation. Yet even in that you get a very singular type of fascination which appeals to the inborn vanity of man, who loves to unburden himself of his woes, fears, hopes, desires and conquests to some sympathetic girl – and the Jamaican girl is an excellent listener. Silence, even if it conceals but little (and here I do not by any means infer that the silence of the Jamaican girl means a void within), silence carries with it a challenge to probe – to endeavour to find out what lies beneath that silence. Silence, I grant, can be a fearsome thing carried to embarrassment and uneasiness, but silence judiciously used as it is by girls out here can stir men and, as every man's urge is, challenge him. Perhaps, being very young, I err terribly and irrevocably, but I state boldly as I said I was not going to – that coupled with silence a man loves an occasional flickering of gossip, and here I am quite decided to start afresh, with a new paragraph.

GOSSIP! It always behoves a man writer to use, if with discretion, exclamation marks. I use one here. I use it without apology and I use it merely as a means of sensation. After all, sensation is life, and where, oh! where in the name of the seven Parables of Woman, would life be without gossip? Life in Jamaica is necessarily narrow and insular, in however large a community, however broad-minded a nation or sect, where is the one to be found whose women do not (just very, very occasionally) indulge in an exchange of views regarding their own or someone else's neighbours?

In this a woman – I very nearly said 'through practice' – is cleverer than a man, more subtle, more tangible. The Jamaican girl really has few excitements and fewer pleasures. Her English or American cousins have a larger scope of amusements, entertainments and general 'pass-her-times' compared with the Jamaican girl. So scandal as spoken out here is naturally of vital importance to girls budding out into life – to life in which A knows to a sixpence how much B earns a year, and when that affair ended between Mrs B and old X, and how long Miss B has been wearing 'that rather terrible little cloche hat she got cheap at Johnson and Johnson's sale last June'. Let him who is without sin chuck the first jolly old pebble. Personally I dislike stones. The Jamaican girl is too good a hand to fling stones about. She lobs a *bread crumb* perfectly deliciously, and I take off – haven't got one, but if I had – I'd take off my hat to her.

We all were, more or less I suppose, in a natural state in the Beginning. The Jamaican girl is natural even to primitiveness at times. Secretly men like that although they are attracted at times by artificiality carried to a pitch bordering on the absurd. But this palls. So does nature unadulterated. The Creole, however, can pour tea with the best, dine with the highest in the land, conversing in correct if rather stilted English, attend a garden party where 'form' is everything, then go home and indulge in a wordy battle in the native vernacular with a fat, perspiring, black cook. She – the creole, not the cook – carries a slight air of boredom which is really languor brought about by our steamy hot climatic conditions. In that state she is given to moody fits lasting according to company or circumstances . . .

Finally, and in conclusion, I will add that Jamaica is a land where oranges grow. On the orange tree is found orange blossom. Orange blossom is used in weddings and ... well, the average Jamaican girl is much too good for the average Jamaican man. But she seems to bear her burden with fortitude and remarkable courage, marrying him and making an excellent wife and mother despite her numerous and ardent critics. All Jamaican men should agree with this view ...

(1929)

J.E. Clare McFarlane

Claude McKay

Claude McKay has been often referred to as the Bobby Burns of Jamaica; and the comparison is more than superficial. Like Burns he expresses the soul of his people in a medium created by his people. It is small wonder that his dialect poetry went immediately to their hearts and that, although he is still unread by the majority, his name has become something of a legend among them. The masses do not read him because his work has never been issued in an edition sufficiently large and cheap to encourage its easy circulation among them; but many of his phrases have passed from lip to lip and have become household words. For McKay has caught up within his verse the spontaneous humour and infectious laughter of his people; he reflects their ability to make a jest of their own dilemmas and illustrates their capacity for tender emotion.

But as characteristic and valuable as are these dialect poems they do not embrace, any more than did those of Burns, the full range of McKay's poetic powers. Dialect, as I have pointed out elsewhere, is a 'broken tongue' with which it is impossible to build an edifice of verse possessing the perfect symmetry of finished art. It can be forceful and impressive in conveying ideas within the power of the people, whose natural vehicle it is, to express; but it can never transcend them in the way that their own spiritual qualities transcend their physical and intellectual limitations. So it must fail in any attempt to explain the people fully to themselves; it may serve as an admirable record of feeling, but not as an interpreter of that record.

McKay, long ago, became conscious of this limitation and sought the more spacious ways of orthodox language for the full expression of his powers. Halting and uncertain in *Spring in New Hampshire*, his verse achieved the stride of self-confidence in *Harlem Shadows*. To his native gifts he was able to add the fruits of experience acquired in the course of a life which shunned no avenue that led to knowledge. With this later work, however, few of his countrymen are acquainted, save for such pieces as have been made familiar by repeated quotation in magazines and newspapers ...

Whatever his shortcomings, it must be admitted that McKay's genius has made an indelible impression on the literary history of this country. One may disagree with the philosophy expressed in most of his writings, but one cannot deny his outstanding gifts. His faults are very largely the faults of his age. His excellencies are his own.

(1956)

E. Baugh

West Indian Poetry 1900–1970: A Study in Cultural Decolonisation

Author's Note: This title is intended as an allusion to Henry Swanzy's pioneering article 'Writing in the British Caribbean: a study in cultural devolution', *Overdrup witt de West Indische gids*, 32.4: 217–40 ('s-Gravenhage, M. Nijhoff [1952]).

The publication of books of poetry by Edward Brathwaite and Derek Walcott makes a fair claim to having provided the most talked-about events on the West Indian literary scene during the last two years (1968–70). Almost every West Indian newspaper of note and every little magazine has contributed to the minor spate of articles and comprehensive reviews on the work of these two poets. The tendency to compare the work of the two, to see them as opponents in a struggle for the 'West Indian poetry championship', has added to the excitement. West Indian poetry seems to have come into its own.

During the efflorescence of the West Indian novel in the 1950s people asked, 'Where are the poets?' But the poets were not quite as non-existent as may have been thought. The truth is that it was harder, and still is, for the poet than for the novelist to get his work published and recognised. Very few of the people who now know something about Walcott and Brathwaite know that they had been assiduously and consistently practising their craft, publishing wherever they could find an outlet (i.e. almost exclusively in *Bim* and on the *Caribbean Voices* programme), for many years before they came to international prominence ... And there were other poets publishing in the 1940s and 1950s who, if they had had enough encouragement and guidance, might also have persevered to become considerable forces in West Indian poetry today. One thinks of people like E.M. Roach and Harold Telemaque of Trinidad, Owen Campbell and Daniel Williams of St. Vincent, M.G. Smith and Basil McFarlane of Jamaica ...

A.J. Seymour of Guyana, one of the great patrons of West Indian poetry and himself a poet, wrote recently:

When I was younger, I sometimes got the feeling from the educated and well placed individuals around me that it was positively indecent

that a young Guyanese should want to write poetry. That sort of
activity was for a person born in another country. You should read
about it happening in England or America but in a colony it meant
that you were young and conceited and so should be taken down a
peg or two . . .

I remember one or two persons in 1937 asking me why should I
want to publish a book of poems at all. It hadn't been done, at least
not for years and years.

The reference to the colonial aspect of the problem is important.
The development of poetry in the West Indies reflects the colonial
experience of the region.

Even those West Indians of Seymour's time who may have been
hoping for a West Indian poetry had, by today's standards, very
modest expectations. In *Bim*, No. 7 (c. Dec. 1945), Bryan King, a
Kittitian who had gone to study in England . . . published an article
entitled 'What Poetry Means to Me' . . .

King then explained what he had hoped to find in verse which
was West Indian: 'West Indian subject matter' and 'West Indian
imagery' . . . He admits . . . what he should have been looking for
. . . was not West Indian *subjects* and *imagery* but West Indian *poets*,
who, as he says in an unfortunate image, 'with one foot soaring in
the air . . . will have the other foot firmly planted on a West Indian
soil' (p. 46). It would be interesting to know what King thinks of
'Mulatta', a poem dedicated to him by Brathwaite, which recently
appeared in *Bim* (No. 50, Jan.–June 1970). A poem like this goes far
beyond King's early expectations.

There were 16 poems, by 12 poets, in the same number of *Bim*
in which King's article appeared. Most of this poetry is bad and very
little of it now seems 'firmly rooted in a West Indian soil'. Much of
it is still set squarely in the convention of the bulk of the poetry
which had been written in the West Indies during the preceding half
century or so.

What did the pioneers produce – men like Tom Redcam (Thomas
Henry MacDermot, 1870–1933), W. Adolphe Roberts (1866–1962)
and J.E. Clare McFarlane (1894–1962) of Jamaica and Walter MacA.
Lawrence (1896–1936) of Guyana? Such interest as their work can
hold now is almost exclusively historical. In each case not more than
one or two poems are still in any way memorable for their own sake.
The poets of the post-1940 mainstream do not consider themselves

to be descendants of these forerunners, who produced a strictly colonial poetry. It is as if one of their chief aims was to show that natives of the colonies could write verse like that which poets of the 'mother country' had written.

Since the chief influences on the young colonials growing up at the end of the last century and the beginning of the present century were, first the Victorian poets and, filtered through the Victorians, the Romantics, and behind the Romantics, dimly, Neo-classical decorum, didacticism and 'poetic diction', one could easily guess what the colonials would produce. But perhaps the trouble was not so much the fact of imitation as the relative feebleness of the imaginations which were imitating . . .

One of the dominant notes in this early poetry, and very strong in Tom Redcam, is that of a pedestrian, lofty-sounding moralising. Besides, 'local' poems are local only by virtue of the names of places and plants. The bird in H. Gillies Clerk's 'Ode to the Jamaica Mocking Bird' is a most 'loyal subject':

> Hail Seraph of Jamaica! Hail, sweet bird!
> Sweet when throughout the day,
> The joyful roundelay,
> Pouring through all the latticed-leaved trees is heard;
> Or when pimento branches glist'ning play
> Fragrant accompaniments to thy wondrous song;
> Perched on thy dry twig rostrum –
> Throne of thy wide-spread kingdom,
> Whence thou dost rule the world with thy melodious song.

Patriotic verses abound in this period. The Great War brought out the worst in our poets; the influence of the 'Rule, Britannia' school was strong. Here are a few lines from Redcam's 'Jamaica's Coronation Ode':

> Here where Nelson led we follow
> In the light of Duty's star,
> Where Jamaica's blue hills dreaming,
> See her torrents streaming far.
> From the mango-shadowed village
> Where unresting bamboos sigh,
> Where the dew-empearled banana
> Gleams beneath the morning sky . . .

This poem appeared in a volume entitled *Songs of Empire*, 'collected and arranged by Constance Hollar with foreword by Sir William Morrison, Kt.' (Kingston: The Gleaner Co., 1932, p. 13).

Roberts, while being no less derivative than his contemporaries, was more gifted than they, with a reasonably good ear for the melodious and richly sensuous line. He is a by-product of the English 'decadent' school of the 1890s and could have held his own in that company:

> The braided iron of the balconies
> Is like locked hands fastidiously set
> To bar the world. But the proud mysteries
> Showed me a glamour I could not forget:
> Your face, camellia-white upon the stair,
> Framed in the midnight garden of your hair.

An overall mood broadly similar to that generated by Roberts is to be found in the work of another Jamaican of an even more self-assured gift – Vivian Virtue (b. 1911), whose collection, *Wings of the Morning*, was published by New Dawn Press, Kingston, in 1938. He is very much the aesthete and has about him the air of a man single-mindedly cultivating his own dream of a world, coolly regardless of what the world-at-large might consider to be most important. His quality is Parnassian and the following translation by him of a sonnet from the French of Jose-Maria de Heredia is typical of his work:

> *The Conquistadores*
> Like noble falcons from their native height
> Winging, wearying of their wretchedness,
> From Palos de Mogeur they forward press,
> Adventurers in search of honour and fight.
> They go to seize the fabulous metal bright
> Cipango hoards in far-off mines, through stress
> Of winds that bend their masts, down loneliness
> of seas unknown fronting the New World's might.
> Each set of sun, dreaming an epic rise,
> The mirrored burning of the tropic skies
> With its mirage of glory charms their rest;
> Where the white caravels with leaning spars
> Towards the trackless limits of the West
> Dip under the swift uprising of strange stars.

Virtue brought to a high point of craftsmanship the tradition, broadly speaking, within which we may conveniently place the pioneers. And speaking of pioneers, we must not forget the dialect poetry of the Jamaican Claude McKay (1890–1948). But this too was weakly derivative, Burns without the tang of wit and humour, without the acuity and depth of perception. McKay abandoned dialect poetry very early and did not inspire any immediate successors in this medium.

A.J. Seymour of Guyana (b. 1914) is a transitional figure between the poetry of the pioneers and the more progressive poetry of the post-1940 period. He belongs in large measure to the old ornamental tradition of routinely noble sentiments and 'local' poetry which is really a grafting of local names on to borrowed stock. At the same time he vigorously encouraged the idea of a new cultural awakening which would produce a truly West Indian literature. He actively promoted this idea in his critical writings and in his editing of *Kyk-over-al*, a little magazine which in its time was one of the very few local outlets for West Indian writers. In his own poetry we find him purposefully digging about in Guyanese history and legend, asserting continuities, going back to the Amerindians in the search for a Guyanese spirit. But with him history is really not much more than romance . . .

Frank Collymore of Barbados (b. 1893) occupies a place somewhat similar to Seymour's. Although in strict chronological terms he is contemporary with most of those whom I have called pioneers, he did not flourish as a poet until the 1940s. His influences are correspondingly more twentieth century than those of his coevals. His poetic ambitions are not as high as Seymour's but on the whole his quality is more consistent. Within his very limited range and depth he achieves an appreciable variation of tone and rhythm. His is a quiet and careful poetry, conservative and hardly disturbing; but it does usually leave an impression, even when it is only playing on the surfaces of things, of an honest reaction to the poet's particular environment and experiences. To this extent it marks something of an advance in West Indian poetry.

If Seymour and Collymore have hardly influenced younger poets through their own poetry, they have certainly been of inestimable value for the outlet and encouragement which they have provided through their little magazines, *Bim* and *Kyk-over-al* (1945–61). Together with the BBC programme *Caribbean Voices* (1945–58), these magazines help to account for the upsurge in West Indian poetry which becomes increasingly evident during the 1940s. [. . .]

(1971)

Amy J. Garvey

Women as Leaders

The exigencies of this present age require that women take their places beside their men. White women are rallying all their forces and uniting regardless of national boundaries to save their race from destruction and preserve its ideals for posterity ... White men have begun to realize that as women are the backbone of the home, so can they, by their economic experience and their aptitude for details, participate effectively in guiding the destiny of nation and race.

No line of endeavor remains closed for long to the modern woman. She agitates for equal opportunities and gets them; she makes good on the job and gains the respect of men who heretofore opposed her. She prefers to be a bread-winner than a half-starved wife at home. She is not afraid of hard work, and by being independent she gets more out of the present-day husband than her grandmother did in the good old days.

The women of the East, both yellow and black, are slowly but surely imitating the women of the Western world, and as the white women are bolstering up a decaying white civilization, even so women of the darker races are sallying forth to help their men establish a civilization according to their own standards, and to strive for world leadership.

Women of all climes and races have as great a part to play in the development of their particular group as the men. Some readers may not agree with us on the issue, but do they not mould the minds of their children, the future men and women? Even before birth a mother can so direct her thoughts and conduct as to bring into the world either a genius or an idiot. Imagine the early years of contact between mother and child, when she directs his form of speech, and is responsible for his conduct and deportment. Many a man has risen from the depths of poverty and obscurity and made his mark in life because of the advices and councils of a good mother whose influence guided his footsteps throughout his life.

Women therefore are extending this holy influence outside the realms of the home, softening the ills of the world by their gracious and kindly contact.

Some men may argue that the home will be broken up and women will become coarse and lose their gentle appeal. We do not think so, because everything can be done with moderation ... The doll-baby type of woman is a thing of the past, and the wide-awake woman is forging ahead prepared for all emergencies, and ready to answer any call, even if it be to face the cannons on the battlefield.

New York has a woman Secretary of State. Two States have women Governors, and we would not be surprised if within the next ten years a woman graces the White House in Washington D.C. Women are also filling diplomatic positions, and from time immemorial women have been used as spies to get information for their country.

White women have greater opportunities to display their ability because of the standing of both races, and due to the fact that black men are less appreciative of their women than white men. The former will more readily sing the praises of white women than their own; yet who is more deserving of admiration than the black woman, she who has borne the rigors of slavery, the deprivations consequent on a pauperized race, and the indignities heaped upon a weak and defenseless people? Yet she has suffered all with fortitude, and stands ever ready to help in the onward march to freedom and power.

Be not discouraged, black women of the world, but push forward, regardless of the lack of appreciation shown you. A race must be saved, a country must be redeemed, and unless you strengthen the leadership of vacillating Negro men, we will remain marking time until the Yellow race gains leadership of the world, and we be forced to subserviency under them, or extermination.

We are tired of hearing Negro men say, 'There is a better day coming,' while they do nothing to usher in the day. We are becoming so impatient that we are getting in the front ranks, and serve notice on the world that we will brush aside the halting, cowardly Negro men, and with prayer on our lips and arms prepared for any fray, we will press on and on until victory is ours.

Africa must be for Africans, and Negroes everywhere must be independent, God being our guide. Mr Black man, watch your step! Ethiopia's queens will reign again, and her Amazons protect her shores and people. Strengthen your shaking knees, and move forward, or we will displace you and lead on to victory and to glory.

(1925)

1930–49

Introduction

Creative disturbances

The 1930s and 1940s represent a time of great change both politically and culturally within the Caribbean region. The poor social
conditions, low wages and high infant mortality which the strikes and
demonstrations of this period sought to draw attention to were clearly
legacies of the long history of colonial rule and neglect. However,
the crumbling economic climate of the late 1920s and 1930s was the
main catalyst in provoking both social crisis and change. The Wall
Street Crash of 1929 and the Depression impacted on the Caribbean
as well as the motherland; crop prices and workers' wages fell dramatically, and the economic escape route of emigration to the Canal
Zone was now exhausted. In this context, both trade-union and
nationalist movements, and a black and mixed-race middle class,
gained popular support, and the authority of the colonial administration began to appear less secure. Calls for political platform,
representation and self-government for the majority populations
became louder and increasingly difficult to manage. In Trinidad and
Tobago, there were demonstrations and strikes by sugar-workers in
1934, and an oil-workers strike in 1937 (led by Grenadian-born Uriah
Butler) escalated to a general strike. Disturbances rapidly became
more widespread throughout the region with a wave of riots and
strikes moving across Barbados, British Guiana and Jamaica, as well
as Trinidad. In 1938 the conflict between colonial law and workers'
power came to a head with the dock-workers strike in Jamaica.

In response to this 'up-rising', the colonial authorities appointed
a West India Royal Commission to investigate the problems and
report on policy 'solutions' for the British West Indies. A key policy

was the partial advancement of self-rule, a political opportunity which the newly formed trade union-based political parties capitalized on. In 1944 universal adult suffrage was granted in Jamaica, in 1945 electoral franchise was substantially extended in British Guiana, in 1946 Trinidad held its first elections with adult suffrage, and in 1950 and 1952 universal suffrage was achieved in Barbados and in the Leeward and Windward islands respectively.

Speaking of Barbados, **Lamming** described these events as: 'dramatic moments on a small island, which had always seemed on the surface very stable and calm'. Indeed, the apparent order of the British colonies had been permanently shaken by these demonstrations of mass discontent and of political agency. Even though full independence was not secured for the Anglophone Caribbean until the 1960s and even later (Antigua 1981), it is the period of the 1930s and 1940s which seems to represent a moment of changed (national) consciousness in which the mentality and security of colonial domination was permanently fractured. As Victor Stafford Reid has stated of Jamaica post-1938, the collective sense of unrest and the solidarity of the working-class majority was a public declaration of a 'new brand of loyalty' which expressed itself not only outside, but importantly in opposition to, colonial rule (**Reid 1978**: 4).

Events outside the region also played a role in the changing culture, in particular the Italian invasion of Abyssinia (Ethiopia) in 1936. Ethiopianism as a political ideology dating from the 1890s was important in the decade following the crowning of Haile Selassie as Emperor in 1930, and the fact that Britain chose not to support Ethiopia contributed to the loss of moral faith in the motherland. The most important manifestation of this new questioning of Europe was the birth of the Ras Tafari movement in Jamaica in 1930. Jamaicans familiar with the Old Testament prophecies of the coming of the messiah and Marcus Garvey's more recent politicized prophecies of the same, were swift to interpret the crowning of Selassie (who claimed ancient lineage to the biblical kings) as the fulfilment of these prophecies – Jah Ras Tafari. Rastafarianism soon spread to other parts of the Caribbean and has become a culturally complex global phenomenon (**Rohlehr 1972-3**: 86-7, **1973**: 137-40, Pollard 1982, 1984, 1986, Sutcliffe and Wong 1986: 37-51). The 1941 Anglo-American agreement which permitted the establishment of United States military bases in the region also influenced the cultural as

well as economic climate in an interesting way: the 'American occupation' demolished the myth of white superiority; Trinidadians saw
white Americans perform hard manual labour, and laughed at the
antics of drunken 'bad behaviour' sailors. The automatic deference
to a white face became a thing of the past (Brereton 1981: 192) (see
Selvon 1952, 'Wartime Activities' in Selvon 1957). The American
government also paid higher wages and offered better working conditions, thus forcing social expectations upwards.

It would be naïve to perceive the 1930s and 1940s as a period
of unqualified raised consciousness and cultural revision in the
Anglophone Caribbean. There could be no 'quick fix' for the long
history of colonization during which 'economic exploitation went
hand in hand with cultural subjugation by way of deracination,
psychological conditioning ... and systematic cultural denigration'
(Nettleford 1978: 2). Nevertheless, with the interdependence of
colonial political, moral and cultural authorities in mind, it is perhaps
important to realize how those who were campaigning for political
freedom in the Caribbean saw cultural decolonization as an important
ally. This was certainly true of the Manley government of Jamaica
which gave high priority to cultural activities in the process of national
self-determination. However, there is no unproblematic correlation
between political and cultural liberation, and the diversity of cultural
awareness and affiliation can be glimpsed by a brief comparison of
events. In 1929, the charismatic and influential Marcus Garvey came
back to Jamaica in order to represent his theories on 'black pride'
and African consciousness (which were consolidated in the 1940s by
the developing profile of the *negritude* movement, associated in the
Caribbean with the Martiniquan poet, Aimé Césaire). Yet, as **Mervyn
Morris** relates 'referring to an art competition in the 1930s, the
sculptress, Edna Manley, tells of entries in which Jamaican market
women had been portrayed with Caucasian features. Blackness was
inconceivable' (Morris 1975: 9).

Critical voices:
towards an aesthetic of social engagement

In this period of flux in terms of political and social definition, it is
not surprising that Caribbean cultural identities were mobile and
hybrid. However, it is also the case that serious differences in cultural

direction between certain individuals and their associated organizations and publications can be traced. In these differences we can map pathways through the key debates pertinent to the literature of this period.

J.E.C. McFarlane, the Jamaican poet and critic, has left a careful record of his offerings to the island's cultural scene through collections of lectures which he delivered at the Institute of Jamaica, and documents detailing his involvement as President with the Poetry League of Jamaica. Although McFarlane's prose attacks on Caribbean civil, economic and Christian institutions reveal him as politically forward thinking, his attitude to poetry was far more conventional. It had always been his position to defend the worth of poetry on the grounds that it was acultural and apolitical, and must therefore transcend the immediate in favour of the eternal and 'universal'. In the context of a society undergoing fundamental political and cultural change, his position did not falter but was more fiercely guarded.

McFarlane's insistence upon the duty of poetry to forge spiritual growth led him to resist the necessity of both aesthetic and social change. In his 1924 address to the Poetry League, McFarlane spoke of poetry as being 'of greatest service to humanity: in restoring the lost outline, in raising it from the maze of sensuous things into the clear atmosphere of the spirit' (McFarlane 1945: 107). Despite the evident unrest in the social and political atmosphere which had marked the intervening decade, he maintained this emphasis on poetry as transcending 'crisis' in his 1935 address **'The Challenge of Our Time'**. Speaking for the League, McFarlane declared:

> As representatives of a great tradition we offer you Poetry, upon which we feel certain the true foundation of this Empire rests and by which it will be preserved throughout the storm that hangs above the horizon of civilization.
>
> (McFarlane 1935: 29)

As an imperial preservative, McFarlane's recipe for poetry declares its cultural orientation towards the motherland and in favour of a Leavisite vision of moral education. It also promotes a version of poetry in which Anglocentric canonical criteria and texts remain unchallenged. Yet, while McFarlane stood firm in his own convictions, his suggestion that poetry might serve the 'hungry and ragged populace' through moral rather than social amelioration became increasingly untenable in the worsening conditions of the late 1930s. His attack on 'narrow nationalism' was similarly soon out of step with the rise of nationalist activity in the 1940s.

However, McFarlane was not alone in his vociferous defence of poetry against the changing reality of the Caribbean, and the modern world at large. In Trinidad, E.A. Carr was also attempting to defend the apolitical status of Art.

> Many good artists today are deliberately denying ... the essential part tradition plays in art. The flouting of this fact has something even of the fanaticism of a crusade ... It seems the political unrest of the age has seeped into and infected the serenity of the sphere of Art.
>
> (Carr 1933)

Carr opposes modern poetic praxis by defining poetry proper in terms of the received rather than the experienced or the experimental, thereby endorsing the derivative and orthodox. He was particularly critical of the writers of 'New Poetry' whom he perceived as 'young people who parade their bitterness and disillusion as virtue' (Carr 1933). It may be surprising that Carr's opinion was published in *The Beacon*, as this was the magazine most clearly associated with disillusioned, even bitter, writers (although not poets). However, as Albert Gomes points out (**1974**), the magazine began as a 'rather staid affair' and became progressively radical.

Indeed, despite the continuance of aesthetic conformity and colonial allegiance, the 1930s did mark the period when significant change could no longer be deferred. As V.S. Reid records 'culturally, our concern was with Keats; our fascination was with the View from Westminster Bridge ... But a sense of renewal was surging against those bonds of remembered bondage' (**Reid 1978**: 3). Leo Oakley further comments that the 1930s produced 'a different brand of writers ... who did not hesitate to assert their Jamaicanness, their nationalism. They could not identify with England and English ways. They were for things Jamaican, and they gave voice to the nationalist movement of the time' (**Oakley 1970**: 19). It was certainly this shift in cultural identification which motivated *The Beacon* group in Trinidad and the *Public Opinion* group in Jamaica, and provoked their open dissent from received aesthetic and moral ideals.

During the 1930s several politically engaged magazines emerged, including *Picong, Progress, The Forum* and *Callaloo*. The most prominent of these, *The Beacon*, developed from the two-issue *Trinidad* started by Alfred Mendes and **C.L.R. James**. It was founded by Albert Gomes and involved Mendes, James, De Wilton, A.M. Clarke, Jean De Boissiere and Neville Giuseppi. This magazine, which ran for two years, was committed to publishing local material and to establishing cultural awareness, literary ethics and critical standards. In 1937 *Public Opinion*, a political weekly which foregrounded issues of cultural politics and ran a literature page, began in Jamaica. It is worth noting that it was staffed by many of the island's culturally active women; Edna Manley (the artist wife of Norman Manley) was editor, Una Marson and Amy Bailey (a campaigner for women's rights) were board members and the artist and poet Gloria Escoffery was the editor of the literature page. As *Public Opinion* faded, the skeleton group went on to produce *Focus* from 1943 which had a short but interesting publishing history, continuing to campaign for Jamaican cultural nationalism.

The writers associated with both *The Beacon* and *Public Opinion* sought to re-align literary sensibilities and were willing to court the discontent of a whole range of authorities (the colonial administration and the Catholic Church included) in their pursuit of a Caribbean cultural consciousness. In both their own creative writings and their articles, these writers foregrounded a validation of the local in order to break the bonds between culture and colonialism.

In opposition to the orthodox and static versions of cultural production advocated by McFarlane and Carr (which amounted to an aesthetic of social and cultural denial), these groups advocated an aesthetic of social engagement. As well as a strident commitment to the legitimation of a Caribbean lived reality, these writers promoted an acknowledgement of the present in terms of twentieth-century literary forms. This dual agenda can be observed at work in **Mais's 'Listen the Wind'**. A current of the modern blows through this story which depicts the harsh realities of yard life, and is particularly evident in its ending which attempts (in a fashion reminiscent of D.H. Lawrence) to capture the workings of the unconscious.

Gomes describes *The Beacon* group as 'angry young men of the thirties' (**1974**: 18) and it is clear even from the two editorials included here (**1932**) that these writers were deliberately abrasive and abusive in their style. They functioned as cultural agitators, disturbing the comfortable reliance on outdated and redundant models: 'Why so many of the poems we receive are imitations of Ella Wheeler Wilcox is a question we have been asking ourselves for quite some time. We realize, of course, that intellectual dropsy is a popular form of ailment in Trinidad' (*The Beacon* 1932). As the most acerbic voice of *Public Opinion*, the writer Roger Mais also attempted to shock Jamaican writers into a new perspective.

> As to your dogged refusal to accept the more modern form; that in itself constitutes an insult to my mentality. I refuse to be hurled back into the dark ages, or to be dragged there supinely on the back of a sure-footed, nimble quadruped.
>
> (**Mais** 1940: 12)

These statements are demands for serious cultural development in the region's creative consciousness. After his most vitriolic attack, **Mais** confesses: 'I am deliberately saying all these unpleasant things about us in the hope that somebody will rise up in self-righteous indignation, and try to justify us' (Mais 1940: 12). In their provocative assaults on the gentile and colonial notion of literary activity dominant in their localities, both Mais and *The Beacon* group were enacting the 'protest . . . against or about ourselves' which **Brathwaite** calls for in the early 1970s (Brathwaite 1970–1: 70).

The issue central to most acts of protest was cultural validity. The basic criteria for cultural reorientation was to leave behind any stylistic or content-based striving towards pseudo-Britishness. Albert Gomes's article in *The Beacon*, 'A West Indian Literature', sets out a manifesto for the establishment of an indigenous literature.

> It is important, moreover, that we break away as far as possible from the English tradition; and the fact that some of us are still slaves to Scott and Dickens is merely because we lack the necessary artistic individuality and sensibility in order to see how incongruous that tradition is with the West Indian scene and spirit . . . the sooner we throw off the veneer of culture that our colonisation has brought us the better for our artistic aims . . . One has only to glance through the various periodicals published in this and the other islands to see what slaves we still are to English culture and tradition. There are some who lay great store by this conscious aping of another man's culture but to us it merely seems a sign of the immaturity of our own spirit.
>
> (Gomes 1933)

As a corrective to this colonial dependency, the nationalist writers advocated socially realist writings and a literary naming of the landscape. It was hoped that seemingly simple gestures such as writing sonnets to the hibiscus rather than the rose would collectively achieve a nationalization of consciousness. During the 1930s and 1940s there were a variety of signs which pointed to the success of this venture. The publication of regionally focused works such as Norman Cameron's *Guianese Poetry 1831–1931* (1931) and Albert Gomes's *From Trinidad: A Selection from the Fiction and Verse of the Island of Trinidad* (1937) helped to consolidate a sense of the local. Journals such as *Bim* in Barbados from 1942 and *Kyk-over-al* founded in 1945 in Guyana, as well as the BBC *Caribbean Voices* radio programme of the same year (originally conceived by **Una Marson** in 1939 as 'Calling The West Indies' for those West Indians on active service to send messages back home), helped to provide forums for material from across the region, allowing both for cultural specificity and exchange. Debates concerning the cultural validity of writing continued to flourish, with a cluster of articles towards the end of the decade. In 1948 Peter Blackman published his article 'Is There A West Indian Literature?' in *Life and Letters* (reprinted in Jamaica's *Sunday Gleaner* in 1949). In 1950 **A.J. Seymour** attempted to synthesize and comment on emergent trends in his special edition of *Kyk-over-al*, 'The Literary Adventure in the West Indies', and in 1952 *Public Opinion* conducted an extended debate (which ran from August to December) questioning 'Has Literature in Jamaica Died?'. Certainly the direction of literary development was a serious issue during this period.

Although many of the works written during this period demonstrated commitment to the project of cultural decolonization, **Vic Reid**'s *New Day* (1949) was a landmark narrative. Tracing Jamaican society from the Morant Bay Rebellion of 1865 to the new constitution of 1944 through the character of Johnny Campbell, *New Day* is important both in its particular approach to the historical novel and for its use of nation language as the language of narration. This novel tells the history of Jamaica from the perspective of the Jamaican participants and raises consciousness in relation to their struggle and resistance often suppressed in narratives of colonialism and oppression. For Reid, this novel was designed to 'tell the Jamaicans who they are, to remind [them] . . . where they came from, to show them that the then self government we were aiming for, the then change in the constitution that we were getting, was not entirely a gift' (Daryl Cumber Dance 1992: 207). This emphasis upon resistance, rooted-ness, and agency is also echoed in Reid's lecture (1978) which privileges insurgent texts, anticipating the later critical bias in favour of 'resistant readings'.

Traditional values

It was clearly the project of many writers at this time of rising nationalism both to expose and to oppose the powerful influence exercised by colonial education and its laudation of all that was British – including racism, sexism and imperialism. For **Roger Mais**, a key obstacle to the creation of a local literature was that 'minds stopped growing in the schoolroom', and the pernicious influence of certain 'set texts' is foregrounded by *The Beacon* editorials. The calypso **'Dan is the Man'** by The Mighty Sparrow also participates in this debate by turning the value of colonial education on its head: 'But in my days in school they teach me like a fool / The things they teach me I should be a block-headed mule'. In **The Occasion For Speaking (1960)**, George Lamming makes explicit his perception of the colonial education system as a means of ideological control which suffocated any expression of a Caribbean consciousness. All of these objections point to the eurocentric saturation of literary consciousness.

However, in **'Discovering Literature in Trinidad'**, C.L.R. James offers a different version of colonial education. In stating that 'the origins of my work and my thoughts are to be found in Western European literature, Western European history and Western European thought' (**James 1969**: 73). James declares his ease and fluency in a medium that he not only explored but also surpassed. This pride in claiming a rich intellectual heritage as his own is an echo of his earlier claim that he was 'a British intellectual before [he] was ten' (1963: 28). Yet James's position here is not only a significant departure from that of Mais and Lamming. The centrality of a formal education advanced by James is almost antithetical to the stance forwarded by Brathwaite in **'Timehri' (1970)**. James wishes to emphasize his deliberate apprenticeship to Western literature: 'I didn't learn literature from the mango tree, or bathing on the shore and getting the sun of colonial countries; I set out to master the literature' (James 1969: 73). In 'Timehri' Brathwaite, on the other hand, emphasizes the importance of an informal education which admitted folk elements: 'My education and background, though nominally "middle class", is ... not of this nature at all. I had spent most of my boyhood on the beach and in the sea with the "beach boys", or in the country, at my grandfather's with country boys and girls' (Brathwaite 1970: 37). Nevertheless it would be too simplistic to draw a divide of cultural orientation between James and Lamming or Mais, just as it is too easy to oppose Walcott (who also claims an enabling affiliation to Western tradition) and Brathwaite in the same way.

As a central figure in Trinidad's anti-colonial movements, C.L.R. James 'discovered' that the intellectual heritage of Western Europe was not ideologically fixed even though ideologically informed. He was able to draw upon his 'mastery' of classical literature in his quest to make Trinidadians see themselves, their society and their own literature as distinctive and of value, and as in his hijacking of cricket as a West Indian sport, James cleverly appropriates the colonial for the national.

The relationship of English literature to the works of those writers from (ex)colonial societies is now mainly characterized by a counter-discursive (writing back) approach (Sparrow 1963, Rhys 1966, Lamming 1971, 1972, Selvon 1975, 1983, Walcott 1978, Phillips 1991). Nevertheless the work of Walcott, most notably his epic poem *Omeros* (1990) which writes alongside Homer's *Odyssey*, has ensured that readers of Caribbean literature remain aware of the creative and positive possibilities for intertextual relations with classical and canonical works.

Poetry and the people

Una Marson's 1937 article 'Wanted: Writers and Publishers' speaks clearly to its cultural moment in calling for writers and publishers who can validate the experiences and voices of the Jamaican people – a step which she herself took in her poetry published in this year. It is often suggested that there was a significant disparity between poetry and prose during this period in terms of cultural engagement. With regard to Trinidad, Peter Ayres has drawn attention to the contrast between 'iconoclastic, aggressively anti-bourgeois element in the prose work', and poetry reliant on 'sin, despair, world weariness, and religious ennui' (Ayres 1978: 18). The stark difference in orientation between **'Triumph'** and **'Listen the Wind'** compared to *Voices from Summerland* and *Songs of Empire* may ostensibly confirm this thesis. However, the poetry of **Una Marson, Louise Bennett, Vera Bell** and **George Campbell** can be more easily approached through the dominant prose agenda of a cultural nationalism, with the active inscription of the realities of everyday experience.

Campbell's poetry, which **Reid** identifies as engaged in the cultural struggles of this period, meditates upon what it means to be 'West Indian' and is thus involved in the broad cultural project towards self-definition. As a more inclusive litany than the familiar Christian one, **'Holy'** is an acknowledgement and benediction of the ethnic plurality on which a Caribbean nation could be built. This idea of nation-building is translated from the sacramental to the mainly secular in **'Oh! You Build A House'** which explores the reconstruction and rebirth of both the island homeland and the individual's identity. Alongside the important task of literally re-building the society, Campbell suggests the construction of an emotional and intellectual space in which belonging and peace can be achieved. This emphasis upon accommodation and belonging was to become central to many fictional and critical texts of the 1950s (see 1950–9 section introduction, pp. 206–21).

Vera Bell's **'Ancestor on the Auction Block'**, which originally appeared in the 1948 *Focus* anthology, examines the responsibility of the present to the past, and also engages with the task of reconstruction: 'Yours was the task to clear the ground / Mine be the task to build'. The poem arrives at this positive awareness of how to move into the future through the acceptance of a unifying and redemptive spirituality which transforms the shame and humiliation of slave history. In its acknowledgement of a painful history and its hope for a future free from guilt and anguish, Bell's poem locates the nationalist optimism of this period and also anticipates Walcott's revisioning of history (**1974**). Indeed, the 18-year-old Walcott's first volume of poems, *25 Poems*, was also published in 1948. Bell herself emigrated to Britain in 1955.

Poetic foremothers

While it may not be surprising that two major black Caribbean (Jamaican) women poets of the twentieth century, Una Marson and Louise Bennett, began publishing during a period of social and cultural change in which 'dissenting' voices were finally being listened to, it is interesting that this was not a context particularly favourable to women. It has been suggested that in Jamaica the period from 1938 to 1944 represented a phase of carefully gendered policies which effectively served to 'blunt the militancy of women ... [and] make [them] second-hand beneficiaries of the reforms implemented after '38' (French 1988: 38). Indeed, the findings of the Royal Commission chaired by Lord Moyne suggested that the 'woman question' was at the very heart of Jamaica's problems, and thus the very focus for its 'solution', which was a society based on monogamous male-headed marriages. Moreover, the wider state apparatus after 1938 still functioned as a powerful agency of patriarchal power. Married women were not allowed to pursue careers as civil servants, the school curriculum was revised with female education as matrimonial training in 1939, and the 1941 Committee on Concubinage and Illegitimacy chaired by the Lord Bishop recommended that working-class women be directed into domestic duties.

Despite the fact that such policies were clearly intended and enforced in order to protect the interests of the minority, the assumption that working-class women would simply obey the edicts was not always correct, as evidenced by the failure of the 'mass marriage' campaign in the late 1940s. As historical evidence nearly always emerges from and tends to support middle-class lives and perspectives, it is difficult to know or even to speculate about the actual changes to Jamaican working-class women's lives which this sustained twentieth-century campaign of feminine socialization effected. Nevertheless, it is important that both Una Marson and Louise Bennett, writing at this time, took issue with this 'mission' to shape womanhood in their own poetic works. Both poets explicitly engage with notions of a Caribbean female identity, but they also negate prescriptive versions of femininity by addressing a wide range of social and cultural issues.

In comparison with the work of her fellow Caribbean poets publishing in the late 1920s and 1930s (**McFarlane 1929, Hollar**

1932), with the exception of **Claude McKay,** Una Marson's poetry offers a far more challenging and critical engagement with the issues of cultural and gender politics. It is our aim here to enact a partial recuperation of Marson by representing a range of her material. As **Donnell (1995)** points out, readings of Marson's work have been both scanty and hesitant to date and it is her project, like **Morris's (1969),** to demonstrate the value and complexity of poetry which has previously been critically devalued. In opposition to those critics who point to derivativeness as an almost inevitable sign of poetic weakness and failing (**Baugh** on McKay **1970:** 5, **Rohlehr** on Roach **1973:** 141–2), Donnell re-reads imitation as a possible aesthetic of subversion and resistance, thus opening up a critical avenue into Marson's early poetry and, by implication, the work of many other poets from this period.

Given the propensity to re-inscribe the Caribbean within eurocentric mythic frameworks in the works of Creole writers (**Webber 1917, McFarlane 1929**), it is interesting to consider how the most persistent myth, that of the prelapsarian paradise, surfaces in Una Marson's poetry. The allusion to an Edenic vision appears in *Tropic Reveries* in **'Jamaica'.** The Jamaican landscape is first presented as a positive inversion of its English counterpart: 'No fields and streams are covered o'er with snow, / But one grand summer all the year through'. This celebration of the absence of snow can certainly be read as a positive representation, given **Brathwaite**'s observation that 'in terms of what we write, we are more conscious of the falling snow ... than the force of the hurricane' (Brathwaite 1984: 8). However, the fashioning of the Jamaican climate as 'one long summer' returns the island to an Anglocentric gaze. The fact that the representations of both the British and the Jamaican landscape resort to a 'picture postcard' vocabulary seems to suggest the way in which these landscapes are always already culturally mediated, as in Claude McKay's poetry.

However, **'In Jamaica'**, in *Heights and Depths*, offers a self-conscious representation of Jamaica as prelapsarian world. The ambivalence of the first stanza: 'It's a lazy life that we live here, / Tho' we carry a fair share of work' develops into a clearly defined picture of a society ethnically and economically divided. The references to the divides between tourists and slum-dwellers, and between black and white Jamaicans reveals a paradise island to be an ideal imposed on the real island divided by colonization, and its help-mate tourism.

Marson spent the years from 1932 to 1937 in England. This period gave her a chance to experience the reality behind the promises of the 'mother-land'. In England, working as a secretary for the League of Coloured Peoples and later for the exiled Ethiopian Emperor HIM Haile Selassie, Marson was involved in and committed to the promotion of anti-racist philosophy. The one poem known to have been written and published during Marson's first stay in England powerfully communicates her awareness of racism. 'Nigger' appeared in *The Keys*, the quarterly magazine published by the League of Coloured Peoples, in July 1933. Despite the fact that the League was moderate in its approach to racial politics, emphasizing harmony and unity, 'Nigger' voices an anger and fury unique within Marson's work. The word 'nigger' forces itself brutally and painfully upon the reader, linguistically rehearsing the hurt and damage of racial abuse. However, the repetition of 'you' is equally important in the poem as it serves as a substitute term of denigration. Marson traces the word 'nigger' to a discourse of power and of hatred established through the fatal history of her people, making the links between actual violence and the violence of language and of inscription explicit. Marson's appropriation of 'nigger' here can be usefully read alongside **Singh**'s reappropriation of 'coolie' (**1973**), as both seek to reclaim agency for the victim of racist language.

The Moth and the Star, published in Jamaica in 1937, conveys the strong sense of nationalism generated at this time, and explores both the contemporary problems and the future potential of a society striving to define itself. Marson's poetry reflects a new sense of urgency and a more direct engagement with the issues of cultural politics. In **'Quashie Comes To London'**, which anticipates **Louise Bennett**'s poem 'Colonization in Reverse' (1966: 179), Marson shifts the dominant gaze from a colonial view of the Caribbean to Quashie's Jamaican perspective on England. Rehearsing the voyeurism of colonial exploits, he writes with both benevolence and bravado of his life in the 'motherland'. Although eager to report good news and present himself as the urbane traveller, Quashie's humorous tone fails at the end of the poem. Recalling the 'pigeon feed' which leaves him hungry, he signs off with a sense of his cultural hunger, reasserting Jamaica as 'home' and London as the temporary venue for entertainment in this missive of a colonial encounter in reverse.

The use of the epistolary form to dramatize dialogue, or more generally monologue, has been one of the most successful adaptations of the oral to the scribal in Caribbean poetry. This 'letter home' form has been variously reworked by Bennett (1982: 70-1, 'Labrish') and later practitioners such as Valerie Bloom (1983: 50-1, 'Letter from home'), **James Berry** (1982: 37-56, *Lucy's Letters*), Fred D'Aguiar (1985: 20-1, 'Letter from Mama Dot'), **Linton Kwesi Johnson** (1980: 11-13, 'Sonny's Lettah'), and **David Dabydeen** (1988: 17, 'The Toilet Attendant Writes Home'). Ironically, the 'letter home' has provided an equally fine opportunity for the development of poetry dependant on the power and potentialities of the creole-speaking voice as much so-called performance poetry.

In both **'Kinky Hair Blues'** and **'Cinema Eyes'** Marson explores the interaction of gender and cultural politics in order to trace how the structures of colonialism and patriarchy are intimately enmeshed in the constitution of the black woman as social subject. 'Kinky Hair Blues' confronts the way in which a black woman's sense of 'self' is constantly disfigured by the white male ethos of sexuality. It is significant then that the black female subject of this poem, written during a period of fierce discrimination, does not feel inherently unhappy with her own appearance: 'I like me black face / And me kinky hair', but is forced to perceive herself as a physical aberration by the pressure of male indifference. Within a colonial society, our protagonist is made aware that 'right' equals 'white', and that the only promise of 'correction' lies in the beauty shop where the trappings of a white physical ideal can be purchased. This 'ironed hair' and 'dat bleaching skin' which represents an attempt to europeanize the African face is a bizarre ritual of self-humiliation and deformation which remains an issue high on the agenda of Caribbean women's writing even today (Hodge 1970, Brodber 1980, **Goodison 1980,** Senior 1995).

'Cinema Eyes' also confronts the pressure which black women face to conform to the false icon of white beauty, although now the source of perversion moves from the shop to the cinema, from the crude commodification of needs and desires to the glamorous indoctrination of them. Although the poem centres on an exploration of the cinema's promotion of white beauty, it does not aim simply to expose but also to counter this ethic by promoting black beauty. The panegyric representations of the African Caribbean physical presence here are evidently disproportionate to the 'no' which prefaces this eulogy. The poem is therefore able to offer a positive sense of self and particularly of the body which is fundamentally denied by both the beauty shop and the cinema.

Although the poetry of **Louise Bennett** has received significant critical attention in recent years, the aesthetic status of her poetry has been under dispute for virtually her entire career. Bennett, probably more than any other Caribbean writer, has successfully bridged 'the gulf' between artist and audience. She trained at the Royal Academy of Dramatic Arts in London and returned to Jamaica in 1955. As Cobham-Sander points out: 'By the time she left for England at the end of 1949 Bennett had established herself as a leading performer and scriptwriter in the Little Theatre movement's annual Jamaican pantomime and "Miss Lou" had become a household name for Jamaicans at all social levels' (Cobham-Sander 1981: 101). The very fact that a 'poet' could attract such popular support points to Bennett's unconventional status in this role and her unique relationship to the Jamaican people whom she seeks to give a voice through her work:

> Then I started to write and I realized more and more that this is what I should do because this is what I understand and this is what the people were saying. More was being said in that language than in any other thing and nobody was listening to them.
>
> (Haniff 1988: 58)

Bennett's insistence on the value of everyday speech and experience also relates to her sustained interest in folk traditions, represented here in the anancy story **'Beeny Bud'**. Yet despite, indeed probably because of, her popular appeal and her rare ability to speak about the working-class population without 'speaking for' them or 'speaking down' to them, Bennett has encountered real problems in terms of an academic reception. Looking back on her early working years, Bennett pointed out that she had never been invited to a Poetry League of Jamaica meeting and recalled that: 'most people thought that . . . they couldn't discourse with me at all because I was going to talk to them in Jamaican dialect which they couldn't understand' (Scott 1968: 98). Indeed, it is the language of Bennett's poems, along with their performative style, which have been the most significant obstacles to positive readings within the academy with its slow, seemingly reluctant, recognition of creole as a serious literary medium. Interestingly, in their performed version, Bennett's poems were featured between 1947 and 1958 on the *Caribbean Voices* programme broadcast in London.

Like Marson's poetry, Bennett's work does not fit comfortably within the ready-made literary critical paradigms and its reception has suffered for this. Mervyn Morris's **'On Reading Louise Bennett, Seriously'** was first published in 1964 in Jamaica's *Sunday Gleaner* as a prize-winning essay by a young literary scholar. This is a key critical piece which seeks to establish Bennett as a serious literary figure and to validate the literary use of creole. For Morris, who was to edit Bennett's *Selected Poems* in 1982, the repeated failure of anthologies to include Bennett's work represented the omission of an exciting and culturally creative voice in a poetic portfolio dominated by bland and 'faked' works. Indeed, the fact that Morris points to McFarlane's *A Literature in the Making* as 'an absurd little volume' and also highlights the limitations of much of the work included in *A Treasury of Jamaican Poetry* is suggestive of the successful revision of critical criteria initiated during the 1930s and 1940s. Morris here denigrates the 'borrowed sensibilities' of Redcam, McFarlane and (oddly Bennett's creole antecedent) McKay and champions the cultural values advocated by *The Beacon* and *Public Opinion* groups. Yet it is important to note that while Morris is able to foreground questions of literary value, he remains hesitant in this piece, and cannot make an unqualified assertion of nation language as an equal language for literary expression.

'Jamaica Oman', one in a series of poems by Bennett which stages the multiple assets of the Jamaican (w)oman, celebrates archetypal female strength and versatility. This poem importantly overturns the common assumption that feminism is a movement instigated in Europe and exported to the Caribbean: 'An long before Oman lib bruck out / Over foreign lan / Jamaica female wasa work / Her liberated plan!' As **Sylvia Wynter** points out in her interrogation of Western feminism (**1990**), the difference between Caribbean defined and 'foreign' feminism is that liberation has necessarily been defined within anti-colonial struggles in the Caribbean. Moreover, as **Carolyn Cooper** indicates in her analysis of the creative capacity of this 'Jamaica Oman', Bennett relates the imperatives of the everyday in 'the tenuous compromise that Jamaican women often make in order to live with their men' (Cooper 1993: 50). In this way, the poem relates to 'the context of survivalism in which both men and women were placed', which Rohlehr deems to be a key structure governing the depiction of gender relations in calypsos of this period (**Rohlehr 1988**: 303).

'**Proverbs**' takes this primary oral form as its thematic and structural principle. Bennett's use of proverbs, aphorisms and other familiar Jamaican expressions in her poetry situates her work in a popular base which is the shared resource of her characters and audiences. Situating the text close to a recognizable world of human experience is a characteristic shared by almost all oral literatures, and one which is central to the validation of the communal over the individual. In the work of other Caribbean performance poets, proverbs are extended almost allegorically in order to reveal their terrifying appositeness to a new and more disturbing urban reality of violence, grinding poverty and human degradation (Mikey Smith, 'I an I' (Smith 1986: 28)).

'**Bed-time Story**' also offers an inventive use of the residually oral form of nursery rhyme, here to suggest dual levels of signification – the comforting child's bedtime story and the discomforting resonances as interpreted by the adult listener. The poem blurs the worlds of innocence and experience, with the characters and actions taking on a decidedly harsher complexion than in the usual world of nursery rhyme. 'Bed-time Story' is an important precursor to **Mikey Smith**'s later experimentation with nursery rhyme in 'Mi Cyaan Believe It' (1986: 13–15), and **Mutabaruka**'s 'Nursery Rhyme Lament' (Mordecai 1987: 178–9); in both of these poems the thematic and aural expectations of the nursery rhyme are exploded by a similar incursion of socio-economic and political dimensions.

It is perhaps less easy to identify the orality of Bennett's story '**Beeny Bud**', a regional variant on an archetypal folk-tale (familiar to many readers as 'Rapunzel'). However, the authorial interjections in parentheses such as: 'wat a pity me kean sing a song fe unnon', suggest the presence of a voice and remind the reader of the story-telling context, only ever partially rendered in textual form. This story not only looks back to a folk tradition brought with the slaves to the Caribbean but also looks forward to the creole narratives and testimonies found in Sistren's *Lionheart Gal* and discussed in **Cooper** (**1989**).

In framing the work of these poetic foremothers, we encourage our readers to explore the work of Marson which remains critically neglected, but we also suggest that we *still* 'ought to read [Bennett] ... more seriously for she is worth it'!

Politicizing the popular

The popularity of Miss Lou is usefully contextualized within the rising profile of other popular cultural forms, particularly the calypso. Indeed, the shift in a cultural focus from the canonical writers of Empire to those representatives of a popular indigenous tradition is given literary representation in the treatment of calypsonians at the beginning of James's **'Triumph'** (James 1929: 87). As Errol Hill carefully documents in his historical grounding of the calypso, this foı.m originated in West African griots and developed alongside other traditional Caribbean songs to incorporate elements of 'digging songs chanted by people at work; belair and calinda songs when they play; shango and shouter baptist revival songs when they worship; and insurrectionary songs such as were sung by slaves in revolt' (Hill 1971: 23; see also Warner 1982). The calypso has remained a cultural form which speaks of and to an often illiterate working-class audience, as Hill points out: 'The one great leveller was the calypsonian. He sang with courage and wit, debunking the great and defending the small' (Hill 1971: 24). It is perhaps in calypsos that we can finally locate a working-class uneducated voice representing its own perception of cultural and social issues, as opposed to the conscious downward gaze of the intellectual and writer.

However, as **Rohlehr (1988)** points out the calypsos do not offer unproblematic or transparent representations of working-class life. His exploration of sexual and racial politics of this popular form is instructive in its exploration of the calypsonian as a public figure who through performance conjured a male ego in the face of dire and disempowering social circumstances. Carole Boyce Davies also discusses the particularly hostility to women of the calypso during this period and perceives its verbal aggression as both sexual and social in origin: 'a distinct economic factor and a concomitant need to "put women in their place" are the most important factors determining the treatment of women' (Boyce Davies 1990: 185). Rohlehr's comment that many calypsos were 'not about women at all, but about masked inter-racial conflict' is particularly interesting, given the arrival on the contemporary calypso scene of Drupatee, an Indo Caribbean woman calypsonian who claims a voice for those most consistently stereotyped during the 1930s and 1940s, and whose presence and popularity signals a shift in terms of a popular cultural base.

We have included only later examples here because calypsos of this period are, by their very nature, transient and difficult to locate. Both **'Brain Drain'** (1968) and **'Dan is the Man'** (1963) engage in the debates concerning cultural validity. Both seek to ruffle dominant expectations: 'Dan is the Man' questions the worth of a standard(izing) education to a Caribbean citizen and 'Brain Drain' questions the root of cultural dilution. **The Mighty Chalkdust** suggests that the real threat to 'Caribbeanness' is not the migration of the educated to the motherland, which was to become so prominent in the 1950s, but rather the erosion of distinct cultural practices and the commodification of certain cultural products for the outsider's eye: 'While the calypsonians must sing for rum, / And when steelbandsmen teach outsiders / To tune a pan for kisses and favours – / All that is what I call Brain Drain'. This is a topic other Caribbean writers have also explored (Lovelace 1979, Rohlehr 1989: 8–9, **Hodge 1990**: 203, Cooper 1993: 190–1).

The Mighty Sparrow's 'Dan is the Man' needs to be read as a 'sustained comic attack' (Thieme 1994) on Capt. J.O. Cutteridge's *West Indian Readers* (1926 to 1929), a six-volume textbook widely used in the Caribbean for three decades. Like Brodber 1988, it stages the 'infantilizing of the colonial subject' through the education system and points to the irony of the calypsonian's adept articulation of his escape from the fate of becoming 'a block headed mule'. As John Thieme has argued (1994), in its 'parodic approach' and the use of mimicry and irony this calypso is located firmly within a carnival discourse which is both playful and powerfully subversive. Thieme goes as far as to suggest that calypso itself constructs an 'alternative discursive universe' in which hierarchies are overturned and 'comic inventiveness, the ex-centric and the individualistic' are all validated. 'Dan is the Man' is also in part a 'plea for orality' (Thieme 1994). Not only is it crucial to account for the performance element in any assessment of the calypso form, but calypsos also intervene significantly in cultural debates regarding the privileged status of written texts and the nature of literature itself. Indeed, **Rohlehr** (1970, **1988**,

1989) and **Brathwaite** (1984), among others, have progressively argued that the calypso should be regarded not merely as an available model for Caribbean literature, but a literary form itself.

The texts from this period were clearly both shaped by and instrumental in the major cultural transitions which re-made national subjects from colonial subjects and Caribbean home-lands from imperial motherlands. Yet, although the critics and writers of the 1930s and 1940s believed that they had fought the battles of cultural decolonization with their defiant and committed texts, the ambivalent cultural allegiances and orthodox aesthetic models of many works produced in the ensuing decades testify to the powerful legacy of the dominant colonial culture. Indeed, to read much of the criticism of the 1970s which celebrates the passing of 'alien restraints' (**Moore 1974**: 71) and calls for a literature rooted in the culture of the majority is to realize how little impact these texts achieved, and perhaps how narrow an audience they reached. Two events at the end of this decade offer possible explanations. In 1949 the University College of the West Indies gained its Royal Charter, offering a place of belonging for the Caribbean intellectual, although it was to be another twenty years before a course in Caribbean literature was admitted on to the syllabus. A year earlier, on 22 June 1948, 492 Jamaicans disembarked from the *Empire Windrush* and thus began the pattern of migration to the motherland which was to powerfully influence the direction of Caribbean literature in the coming decade.

Una Marson

Renunciation

For me the sunbeams dance and dart
And song birds sing with merry heart,
For me the winds are whispering low
And laughing flowers in hedges grow.

For me the brook runs merrily
With soothing song to seek the sea,
For me Diana sheds her light
And steadfast stars shine thro' the night.

For me the waves of ocean sigh
Or dance with sunbeams darting by,
For me the shades of twilight fall
And beauty doth the earth enthrall:

But not for me what most I crave, –
To call thee mine, – to be thy slave.

(1930)

In Vain

In vain I build me stately mansions fair,
And set thee as my king upon the throne
And place a lowly stool beside thee there,
Thus, as thy slave to come into my own.

In vain I deck the halls with roses sweet
And strew the paths with petals rich and rare,
And list with throbbing heart sounds of thy feet,
The welcome voice that tells me thou art near.

In vain I watch the dawn break in the sky
And hope that thou wilt come with coming day:
Alas, Diana calmly sails on high,
But thou, king of my heart, art far away.

In vain one boon from life's great store I crave,
No more the king comes to his waiting slave.

(1930)

If

If you can keep him true when all about you
The girls are making eyes and being kind,
If you can make him spend the evenings with you
When fifty Jims and Jacks are on his mind;
If you can wait and not be tired by waiting,
Or when he comes at one, be calm and sleep,
And do not oversleep, but early waking
Smile o'er the tea cups, and ne'er think to weep.

If you can love and not make love your master,
If you can serve yet do not be his slave.
If you can hear bright tales and quit them faster,
And, for your peace of mind, think him no knave;
If you can bear to hear the truth you tell him
Twisted around to make you seem a fool,
Or see the Capstan on your bureau burning
And move the noxious weed, and still keep cool.

If you can make one heap of all he gives you
And try to budget so that it's enough,
And add, subtract and multiply the issue,
So that the Grocer will not cut up rough;
If you can force your dress, and hat, and stocking
To serve their turn long after they are worn,
And pass the 'sales,' and do not think it shocking
To wear a garment that has once been torn:

If you can walk when he takes out the Ford
And teaches girls to drive before you learn,
And list to tales of tyres without a rye word,
And let him feel you're glad for his return:
If you can fill the unforgiving minute
With sixty seconds work and prayer and smile,
Yours is the world and everything that's in it,
And what is more, you'll be a wife worth while.

(With apologies to Kipling)
(1930)

Jamaica

Thou fairest Island of the Western Sea,
What tribute has the Muse to pay to thee?
Oh, that some tender lay she could inspire
That we might sing they praises and ne'er tire.
Oh lovely Island where the sun shines bright
And scarce one week withholds her cheery light;
No chilly winter wind doth o'er thee blow,
No fields and streams are covered o'er with snow,
But one grand summer all the long year through
Dost thou enjoy beneath a sky of blue.

Among thy woods the birds with carols gay
From morn till night are merrily at play;
The hum of bees upon the flowering trees
Makes sweetest music with the summer breeze.
The fields are covered o'er with Daisies bright
Which nod their pretty heads in sheer delight;
By babbling brooks the shady palms arise,
While wandering near, earth seems a Paradise.

The brilliance of the myriad stars by night
Unto the weary traveller giveth light;
Among thy woods the flitting fireflies
Form one grand starland with their fiery eyes.
And when Diana rising o'er yon hill
Sheds her pale light, while all the earth is still,
Ah, then, what bliss to wander hand in hand
Like lovers 'neath the bowers in Fairyland.

All hail to thee! Fair Island of the West,
Where thy dear people are forever blest
With beauteous gifts from nature's blessed hand,
Lavished in rich profusion o'er the land.
Welcome be all who journey many a mile
To share the joys of this our lovely Isle:
Fond nature still invites, – 'Come be my guest
And I will give thee gladness, peace and rest!'

(1930)

In Jamaica

O! the sun shines warm in Jamaica,
From one year's end to the next,
The flowers bloom on in Jamaica,
And songbirds are never perplexed;
It's a lazy life that we live here,
Tho' we carry a fair share of work;
And tho' the warmth makes us weary,
It's seldom we really do shirk.

O! the darkies smile on in Jamaica,
And whistle or sing all the day;
There's always a song ringing somewhere,
To them it is always bright May.
It's little we need for our comfort,
When we live in a wee cosy cot
In the heart of the hills where kind Nature
Gives all, and the towns are forgot.

O! it's a glorious life in Jamaica
For the man who has merely enough,
But it's a dreary life for the beggars,
And the large slums are all pretty rough.
It's a gay life too for the children
Not poor, and whose skin is light,
But the darker set are striving
And facing a very stiff fight.

O, it's a wonderful life in Jamaica
For the tourists who visit this shore,
There's golf, there's dancing, and swimming,
And charms that they ne'er saw before.
They call it a garden of Eden,
They love the fair hills of St. Ann,
And they say on the white sands of Mo. Bay
They get such a wonderful tan!

O, there's beauty in most every country,
And scenes that bring thrills of delight,
But there's no place like sunny Jamaica,

And no people whose hearts are so light.
Should I leave these fair shores for another,
Be that land yet the fairest of all,
I should pine for the hills of Jamaica
And hasten to answer her call.

(1931)

Quashie Comes To London

I gwine tell you 'bout de English
And I aint gwine tell no lie,
'Cause I come quite here to Englan'
Fe see wid me own eye.

I tell you fuss 'bout London town,
Hi man, it big fe true,
If you get lass as you often will
Is de Corpie put you troo.

An' talking 'bout de Bobbie dem,
Dem is nice as nice can be,
An' some o' dem is tall me boy
Mos' like a coconut tree.

But dem neber fas' wid you me frien'
Dem eben pass a fight,
An' fe see dem guide de traffic,
Man, it is a pretty sight.

I tink I love dem bes' of all
Dem people in dis town,
For dem seem to hab some life in dem
An' you nebber see dem frown.

I know you wan' fe hear jus' now
What I tink of dese white girls,
Well I tell you straight, dem smile 'pon me,
But I prefer black pearls!

You see dem always coated up,
It's no good fe go to a show
Fe see a crowd of lovely dames
All sitting in a row,

'Cause dem always hab a cloak
Or someting fe kip dem warm,
So you can't admire dem in truth
And dat is jes' de harm.

An' dat takes me fe talk 'bout shows:
Now dem is someting gran'
An' if you neber see one here
You jes' can't understand.

Dem hab de shows fe fit all taste
De highbrow and de low,
An' 'cording to de mood I hab
I choose de one fe go.

If I is feeling full o' pep
I choose variety,
Dem call dem all de nonstop show
An' 'tis dere you want to be.

Some of de numbers ain't so fine,
But dat you mus' expec'
But boy, I tell you, some again
Is surely full o' pep.

You hear some fun an' see some sights
Dem frown upon out dere,
But dough dem say dese people col'
De hot stuff gets de cheer.

An' sometimes jes when I feel gran'
Dere sitting all alone,
Dem play some tune dat takes me home
In sweet and soulful tone.

An' de tears dem well up in me eyes
An' I try fe brush dem 'way,
But me heart gets full and dough I try
Dem simply come fe stay.

For de orchestra is really gran'
I mean de bes' one dem,

For hot stuff gie me Harry Roy,
For sweet, Geraldo's men.

Sometimes de jazz gets in me bones
Me feet dem can't keep still,
I wants fe get right up and dance
But I use me good strong will.

I see some ob me own folks dem
In dese here music hall,
An' if you hear Paul Robeson sing
You feel you wan' fe bawl.

De folks dem love him here fe true,
An' all de coloured stars,
Dem love de darkies' tunes me frien'
An' try fe play guitars.

Dem love we songs, and I wan' tell you
Dat dough dem tink dem great,
Wid no glad darkies in de worl'
'Twould be a sad sad fate.

Now de oder times I go to plays
When I feel fe someting more
An' I hear English as she is spoke
An' it please me heart fe sure.

I don't go much to de Movie show
For I see so much back home,
Dem all is nice but jes' de same
Dem is but de ocean's foam.

But de organs dere delight me heart,
Dem stir me to me soul,
Dem tek me to dose pastures green
An' I hear Jordan roll.

An' dat minds me fe tell you now
'Bout de Parks dem in dis town,
Boy, if you wants something dat's fine
Jes' come along right down.

[134]

In Spring you feel you heart astir
When you hear de birdies sing,
An' de flowers bloom and de leaves come out
An' de kids dance in a ring.

As quick as de sun can show his light
An' de air is a little warm,
Out to de Parks dem everywhere
You wan' see people swarm.

Dem sit like flies in Mango time
Under de lovely trees,
But all de same dem wear a coat
As if dem gwine fe freeze.

Man, some of de Parks is really fine,
Dem hab little lakes dem mek,
An' if you know fe row a boat
A nice one you can get.

If you walk de Parks on a real hot day
You'd a swear dat all de folk
Ain't got a blooming ting fe do
But sit in de sun fe joke.

For London town hab people man,
Dem jes' like gingy fly,
Dem say its 'bout eight million
But a figure dat dem lie.

I mos' feget fe tell you now
About de place fe eat,
Massy massa, dere's a ting,
Now here's one big treat.

One day me walk upon de Stran'
Me see one place mark LYONS,
Me say Now Quashie, here's some fun
You better hol' you irons.

Me grab me umbrella real tight,
Yes man, me carry dat,

I step right in fe see de brutes
I fraid fe lif me hat.

But guess me what I fin' in dere
Not eben a lion's tail,
But a jazz ban' playing like it mad
An' folks eating grub wholesale.

I fin' a table to meself
An' I smile and look quite calm,
A little gal in black and white
Come speak to me wid charm.

She says 'What can I get you sir?'
I says 'Some ripe breadfruit,
Some fresh ackee and saltfish too
An' dumplins hot will suit.'

She look pon me like say she lass,
A say 'Why what's de row?'
She say 'Sorry, but we have none sir'
An' I feel fe laugh somehow.

She gie me Menu fe go read,
You know I's good at dat,
But I say 'no tanks, jes' bring me den
Some red herring an' sprat.

'An' anyting you habe fe food
Because I wan' a feed,'
You should see de dainty ting she bring,
It look like pigeon feed!

It's den I miss me home sweet home
Me good ole rice an' peas
An' I say I is a fool fe come
To dis lan' of starve an' sneeze.

But dis missive is too mighty long,
I will write more news nex time,
Me love fe all de gay spree boys
An' dat buxom gal o' mine.

It not gwine be anoder year
Before you see me face,
Dere's plenty dat is really nice
But I sick fe see white face.

(1937)

Kinky Hair Blues

Gwine find a beauty shop
Cause I ain't a belle.
Gwine find a beauty shop
Cause I ain't a lovely belle.
The boys pass me by,
The say I's not swell.

See oder young gals
So slick and smart.
See dose oder young gals
So slick and smart.
I jes gwine die on de shelf
If I don't mek a start.

I hate dat ironed hair
And dat bleaching skin.
Hate dat ironed hair
And dat bleaching skin.
But I'll be all alone
If I don't fall in.

Lord 'tis you did gie me
All dis kinky hair.
'Tis you did gie me
All dis kinky hair,
And I don't envy gals
What got dose locks so fair.

I like me black face
And me kinky hair.
I like me black face
And me kinky hair.
But nobody loves dem,
I jes don't tink it's fair.

[137]

Now I's gwine press me hair
And bleach me skin.
I's gwine press me hair
And bleach me skin.
What won't a gal do
Some kind of man to win.

(1937)

Cinema Eyes

Don't want you to go to the Cinema –
Yes, I know you are eighteen,
I know your friends go,
I know you want to go.

I used to go to the Cinema
To see beautiful white faces.
How I worshipped them!
How beautiful they seemed –
I grew up with a cinema mind.

My ideal man would be a Cinema type –
No kinky haired man for me,
No black face, no black children for me.
I would take care
Not to get sun burnt,
To care my half indian hair
To look like my cinema stars.

I saw no beauty in black faces,
The tender light and beauty
Of their eyes I did not see;
The smoothness of their skin,
The mellow music of their voice,
The stateliness of their walk,
The tenderness of their hearts
No, they were black
And therefore had no virtue.

A handsome youth came
To woo me at twenty;
I did not think him handsome then –

He was black and not my fancy.
I turned my back on him –
My instinct told me he was good and true,
My reason told me he was black
I turned my back on him.

Another came to woo me –
How fair he was! How like
My ideal built up in my heart –
I gave to him my heart,
My life, my soul, my all;
And how in hell he tortured me,
My dream lover – my husband –
Then you were born,
But I remained disconsolate.

He too saw no beauty in black faces,
You came dark like your grandmother;
He was peeved. I thought
You just a little like
My first handsome suitor
Who so long had gone away; –
He would have been more kind –
More tender – So I thought aloud
One day and he o'erheard me.

Soon this black god came from far
And called to greet me.
My husband, in fury and in drink,
Watched us as we talked –
And as he rose to go
Followed him calmly out,
And shot him, ere he reached the gate.
Another bullet sound,
And he too was gone;
And we were left alone.

I know that love
Laughs at barriers,
Of race and creed and colour.
But I know that black folk

Fed on movie lore
Lose pride of race.
I would not have you so.

Come, I will let you go
When black beauties
Are chosen for the screen;
That you may know
Your own sweet beauty
And not the white loveliness
Of others for envy.

(1937)

Nigger

They called me 'Nigger',
Those little white urchins,
They laughed and shouted
As I passed along the street,
They flung it at me:
'Nigger! Nigger! Nigger!'

What made me keep my fingers
From choking the words in their throats?
What made my face grow hot,
The blood boil in my veins
And tears spring to my eyes?
What made me go to my room
And sob my heart away
Because white urchins
Called me 'Nigger'?

What makes the dark West Indian
Fight at being called a Nigger?
What is there in that word
That should strike like a dagger
To the heart of Coloured men
And make them wince?

You of the white skinned Race,
You who profess such innocence,
I'll tell you why 'tis sin to tell

Your offspring Coloured folk are queer.
Black men are bogies and inferior far
To any creature with a skin made white.

You who feel that you are 'sprung
Of earth's first blood', your eyes
Are blinded now with arrogance.
With ruthlessness you seared
My people's flesh, and now you still
Would crush their very soul,
Add fierce insult to vilest injury.

We will not be called 'Niggers'
Since this was the favourite curse
Of those who drove the Negroes
To their death in days of slavery.
'A good for nothing Nigger',
'Only one more Nigger gone'
They would repeat as though
He were a chicken or a rat.
That word then meant contempt,
All that was low and base,
And too refined for lower animals.

In later years when singing Negroes
Caused white men to laugh,
And show some interest in their art
They talked of 'Nigger Minstrels'
And patronised the Negro,
And laughing at his songs
They could in nowise see
The thorns that pierced his heart.
'Nigger' was raised then to a Burlesque Show
And thus from Curse to Clown progressed
A coloured man was cause for merriment.
And though to-day he soars in every field
Some shrunken souls still say
'Look at that Nigger there'
As though they saw a green bloodhound
Or a pink puppy.

God keep my soul from hating such mean souls,
God keep my soul from hating
Those who preach the Christ
And say with churlish smile
'This place is not for "Niggers"'
God save their souls from this great sin
Of hurting human hearts that live
And think and feel in unison
With all humanity.

(1933)

George Campbell

Holy

Holy be the white head of a Negro.
Sacred be the black flax of a black child.
Holy be
The golden down
That will stream in the waves of the winds
And will thin like dispersing cloud.
Holy be
Heads of Chinese hair
Sea calm sea impersonal
Deep flowering of the mellow and traditional.
Heads of peoples fair
Bright shimmering from the riches of their species;
Heads of Indians
With feeling of distance and space and dusk:
Heads of wheaten gold,
Heads of peoples dark
So strong so original:
All of the earth and the sun!

(1987)

Oh! You Build a House

Oh! you build a house as a woman
Builds a child in her time, building
With the inner vision of her eyes
The knowingness of her being
The whole of her living, turned inward, creating.

Here you build a cottage in the hills
And raise up trees every leaf of them
As parents build up their children, wilfully.

Who would construct the sky?
Do you know how many visions
Of space to fill the view of your vision?
Where are the unseeing hands that would
Lift up one transfiguration of space

[143]

That a child would dream?

Yet you build like the builder of space
The weaver of silences, the construction of hills
With hands of existence, your purpose, the light of your way.
I would not tell you that, were it not natural,
Else I would turn away, mad like a man
From a mirror who sees the sky in his face
And the resolutions of horror and peace in his face.

Here you build your peace in your hills
Reconstructing your silences, like a child
Being endlessly born in its mother.
Here you construct your space, every forgetfulness.
Every pocket of silence, every atom of thought.
Here is the reconstruction of peace, never outside one,
But where a man can turn his energies
To his innermost being, to his own infiniteness.

Where are the succession of stars that are
The glory to one's mind.
Where is the space and time that can be
The peace that man should know?

Yes! It's good that you build your cottage
And the external comforts of home.
'Tis the same process and reality backward . . .

The reconstruction that is rebirth in motherhood,
The working of a plot of land,
The building of a house in the dirt,
The growing of grass, warm roses and trees
Reconstruction of the hills, mass upon mass
Resurrection of the sky, space beyond space:
The infinity of peace.

(1987)

Louise Bennett

Jamaica Oman

Jamaica oman, cunny, sah!
Is how dem jinnal so?
Look how long dem liberated
An de man dem never know!

Look how long Jamaica oman
– Modder, sister, wife, sweetheart –
Outa road an eena yard deh pon
A dominate her part!

From Maroon Nanny teck her body
Bounce bullet back pon man,
To when nowadays gal-pickney tun
Spellin-Bee champion.

From de grass root to de hill-top,
In profession, skill an trade,
Jamaica oman teck her time
Dah mount an meck de grade.

Some backa man a push, some side-a
Man a hole him han,
Some a lick sense eena man head,
Some a guide him pon him plan!

Neck an neck an foot an foot wid man
She buckle hole her own;
While man a call her 'so-so rib'
Oman a tun backbone!

An long before Oman Lib bruck out
Over foreign lan
Jamaica female wasa work
Her liberated plan!

Jamaica oman know she strong,
She know she tallawah,
But she no want here pickney-dem
Fi start call her 'Puppa'.

[145]

So de cunny Jamma oman
Gwan like pants-suit is a style,
An Jamaica man no know she wear
De trousiz all de while!

So Jamaica oman coaxin
Fambly budget from explode
A so Jamaica man a sing
'Oman a heaby load!'

But de cunny Jamma oman
Ban her belly, bite here tongue,
Ketch water, put pot pon fire
An jus dig her toe a grung.

For 'Oman luck deh a dungle',
Some rooted more dan some,
But as long as fowl a scratch dungle heap
Oman luck mus come!

Lickle by lickle man start praise her,
Day by day de praise a grow;
So him praise her, so it sweet her,
For she wonder if him know.

(1982)

Bed-time Story

Ah long fi see yuh tell ah short!
Whe yuh deh all dis time?
Dah pickinni yah woan go sleep,
She waan me tell her rhyme.

Mary had a little lamb
– Miss Mattie li bwoy Joe
Go kick May slap pon har doorway –
His feet was white as snow.

An everywhere dat Mary went
– Him modder never know,
An when she ear she ongle seh –
De lamb was sure to go.

She ongle seh de bwoy too bad
An tell May nuffi bawl
– Jack and Jill went up de hill –
An dat was all an all.

May mighta go to hospital
– To catch a pail of water;
Jack fell down an bruck him crown –
Jus like Miss Mattie daughter.

Yuh never know de baby bawn?
Him pa gi him name Marta.
Teng God him drop eento a doze
– An Jill come tumblin after.

(1982)

Proverbs

'When ashes cowl dawg sleep in deh';
For sence Ma dead, yuh see,
All kine a ole black nayga start
Teck liberty wid me.

Me no wrap wid dem, for me
Pick an choose me company:
Ma always tell me seh: 'Yuh sleep
Wid dawg yuh ketch him flea.'

Me know plenty a dem no like me,
An doah de time so hard
Me kip fur from dem, for 'Cockroach
No biniz a fowl yard.'

Ah teck time gwan me ways an doan
Fas eena dem affair;
Me tell dem mawnin, for 'Howdy
An tenky bruck no square.'

Sometime me go a parson yard
Sidung lickle an chat –
'Ef yuh no go a man fir-side, yuh no know
Ow much fire-stick a bwile him pot.'

Sake-a dat, as lickle news get bout
Dem call me po gal name;
Me bear it, for doah 'All fish nyam man,
Dah shark one get de blame.'

But when me go look fi parson
Me ongle talk bout me soul,
For Ma use fi tell me: 'Sweet mout fly
Follow coffin go a hole.'

Das why ah miss me mumma, yaw:
Ef she wasa live tedeh
All dem liberty couldn teck wid me,
Dem couldn a seh me seh.

She was me shiel an buckler,
She was me rod an staff.
But 'Back no know weh ole shut do fi i
So tell ole shut tear off.'

(1982)

Tan a Yuh Yard

Teng Gad, massa, yuh neber go!
Tan weh yuh deh, Mas Jone!
Quiet yuhself, no meck no fuss –
Lef Merica alone!

Gwan do yuh lickle bolo job,
Glad fi yuh lickle pay;
Me wi tun me han an we can live
Pon de four-bit a day.

Win yuh mine offa foreign lan –
Koo how some a de man-dem
Run back home like foreigner
Dis set bad dog pon dem!

Ef backra even poas ticket
Come gi yuh, bwoy, refuse i!
Better yuh tan home fight yuh life
Dan go a sea go lose i.

[148]

De same sinting weh sweet man mout
Wi meck him lose him head –
Me read eena newspaper seh
Two farm-man meet dem dead!

Ef a lie, a no me tell i,
Ef a label, me no know!
So me buy i, so me sell it,
So me reap, a so me sow.

But whedder true or lie, me bwoy,
Coward man kip soun bone;
Tan a yuh yard an satisfy –
Lef Merica alone.

(1982)

Beeny Bud (Mussirolinkina)

Once upon a time dere was a oman an she had a nice gal pickney. From de pickney bawn she was soh pretty an her hair was soh long dat her mada did know sey wen she grow big plenty man hooda want her fe married to. Soh, as mada all ovah, fe proteck de gal, she meek up her mine fe gi de pickney a long juice of a name dat ongle she an de gal wi know, an any man want her fe married to hooda haffe guess de name fus. Well, she call de gal 'Mussirolinkina'. Wen she grow big, nuff–nuff man come fe cou'ten her, but dem nevah know de name, soh dem fail.

Bredda Anancy hear bout dis boonoonoonoos gal, an swear sey dat him mus get her fe him wife. Soh one day, Anancy hide himself outa de river side weh de oman wasa wash her daughta clothes. Him se' de oman wash out one wite frock an 'pread i' out pon some stone fe dry, an Anancy walla up himself eena dutty an crawl ovah de frock. Wen de oman come back wid piece more clothes fe 'pread out an she se de dirt pon de fus frock, she say, 'Ah wanda who dutty up me pickney clothes doah!' Anancy nevah hear wat him did want fe hear. Soh, as de oman tun her back again him walla up himself wussara an nasy up de gal clothes. Dis time wen de gal muma come back (fe 'pread out more clothes) she did so bex fe se all de nasyness pon de frock dem, dat she bust out an sey, 'But is who dah nasy up me pickney Mussirolinkina clothes doah?' Baps, Anancy ket de name.

Hear him, 'Mussirolinkina, Mussirolinkina,' an all de way to him yard him sey de name ovah an ovah. (Dat time him stick up him big toe eena de air, fe hinda him buck i' an fegat de name.)

Wen him ketch home, Anancy gi himself name Mr Bogle an him borrow some clothes and a buggy an a figgle. Him dress off himself, goh eena de buggy, chap him ten, an start play de figgle an sing:

> Ring ding ding Mussirolinkina
> Mussirolinkina, Mr Bogle a come
> Ringga dingga ding a
> Ringga dingga ding a ling.

(Wat a pity me kean sing de song fe unoon.) Wen de gal hear Anancy song, hear her, 'Mada, Mada my lover is comin.' An she run go a winda go look out pon Anancy eena de buggy. Dem invite him eena de house an gi him plenty tings fe eat an him married de gal. Well dem start fe drive goh to fe Anancy house. All of a sudden Anancy hat fly offa him head. Hear him wife, 'Husban your hat is off'; hear Anancy, 'Meck it stay, it gwine to de owna.' De po gal frighten, but she noh sey nutten till Anancy jacket fly off she sey, 'Husban you jacket is off.' Him sey, 'Meck it stay, it gwine to de owna.'

Dem galang galang soh till everything fly offa 'Nancy. Unoo jus guess how de po gal feel bad! At las dem ketch a one ole empty house, but wen Anancy kea de gal een deh, she bawl out fe her Muma an she meck so much nize dat Anancy get fraid an jump up eena de house top. Lickle afta, her Muma come an teck her wey back to dem yard. An from dat day Anancy live up eena house top, an man dah run wey leff dem wife, and Muma dah goh back fe dem daughta wen husban maltreat dem. Is Anancy start it. Jack Mandoora, me noh choose none.

(1957)

Roger Mais

Extract from 'Listen, the Wind'

The banging of the shutter jerked her out of unconsciousness, just as she was dropping off again.

All night long she lay awake and listened to the gossip of the wind. Strange how tonight the wind was full of foreboding . . . like the tongues of those gossiping old women – only worse, much worse, for the words that told of the evil to come were her own words, shaped in her own consciousness.

She turned over on her side and tried not to listen to the things that the wind whispered about the trees outside, that the wind against the banging shutter was telegraphing to her waking brain.

Tomorrow was washday. She would take the large round bath pan full of washing down to the river, where all the women of the village would be. Above the noise of the paddles with which they beat the clothes, with the soap in them, against smooth, round boulders to get the deep dirt out of them would be heard the tongues of the women, the cruel tongues that tore secrets from the innermost recesses of homes and spread them out before the world as washing was spread upon the river bank; the idle tongues, never for a moment quiet, that slavered over another's wounds with gloating and laughter.

But her secret would be locked within her breast, and she would smile deep down inside herself. That smile would be etched upon the corners of her mouth, but that would only be a reflection of the other, just as the white shifts of the women shone up at the men passing over the bridge above, from the placid surface of the pool.

The hearty cries of the younger women and girls who had waded higher upstream to bathe naked under the shadows of some trees, reached her in occasional gusts. Once there was a wild scattering of shrill laughter, and little shrieks of terror what were without sincerity, as some young men, for the mischief of it, sauntered down to the pool where they knew the girls were bathing.

There was a bold exchange of challenges, retorts, spiced with elemental, good-natured teasing, that would have sounded coarse to the ears of their more sophisticated sisters. But these black girls were of an innocence and naiveté that defied the conventions of what was regarded as the licence that might be allowed between men and women. The nakedness of their bodies, under the frankly covetous stares of the men, left them not one scrap ashamed. Their hiding behind boulders and frantic splashing of water to form a curtain around them was not because they were ashamed to be caught thus, without their clothes on, but in reproof of those impudent young men who would reveal the secrets of their bodies' loveliness.

She had left Joel at home busy working out the details of his latest scheme to get his hands on to a lump of cash so he could go into business like his uncle, who was making a fortune out of buying produce from small settlers and selling it to the big merchants in the city and, more recently, had even been exporting it himself.

He had armed himself with hammer and nails with the intention of mending the broken shutter. He was all contrition in the morning when she told him of her sleepless night.

He found the ladder in the fowl house; the fowl had been using it as a roost. It too needed mending. As she was going out with the pan of washing on her head, he had just looked up from the ladder, his mouth full of nails, and waggled the hammer at her.

A gaunt old woman with the stringy, pimpled neck and sharp face of a crow was saying in her cracked voice, that had an edge to it that reminded one of a saw, 'He'll break your heart, my fine hussy. You take my word for it. He'll spoil your sweet face for you, and that smile too.'

A stout woman laughed. Her strong arms were bare to the elbows, and she was wielding a paddle with savage grunts that seemed to indicate the satisfaction she got out of pounding at something . . . anything.

'That Joel of yours needs a strong woman to make a man out of him – to make him do something besides fritter away his time with women and dice. None of your milk-and-water kind for him, honey. After the first flavor wears off, he'll be sorry he ever tied himself to you, because you're the sort of weak creature that will never do no good to him. When he was foolin' round my Estelle – now there was a gal would have been a match for him – I told him straight he'd have to get a real job first, or else work the land his father left him. That sent him on his way. Then he took up with you.'

She plied her paddle with powerful strokes, as though driving home her words.

It was getting dusk when she left the river with her burden of clean linen heaped up in a white bundle that flowed over the rim of the pan. She walked with the grace of a goddess, balancing her load upon her head with a perfect sense of rhythm, going up even the steepest incline.

She had to hurry home in order to prepare supper in time.

They were vultures, all of them, great flapping black vultures circling above the still-living flesh upon which they hoped to feast.

The sound of an axe met her as she was coming through the gate. Somehow that sound cheered her. It was Joel splitting firewood to cook their supper. The steady rhythm of the axe contrasted comfortingly with the quick feminine staccato thwacks of the women's paddles that still echoed about her ears. It was a homely agreeable sound. The slow smooth rhythm of it flowed about her, filling her breast. She smiled deep down inside her, taking out her secret as she did in quiet moments of revealment like these, to look at it with wonder, and a sort of gentle longing.

She sought to reconcile all things with the quotient of that . . . the fixed and constant idea of him that she held in her mind's ideal imaging . . . that rapturous idea of *her* Joel that she kept locked away in the secret place of her heart . . . the revelation of him that looked up at her and made demands upon all her woman's store of compassion and faith and understanding . . . How could she make these things known to those soulless harpies who would rob her of her happiness for the barren satisfaction of knowing that she too had succumbed to the dross and canker of uninspired living . . .

She cooked rice cakes and dumplings and set them before him with a hash made from what was left of Sunday's joint.

He ate ravenously without saying much. He was thoughtful and subdued this evening as though he had something on his mind. She recognized the mood. It meant that he was being driven by his thoughts into channels of exploration down which her simple mind could not follow him. When he tried to explain his plans to her, her inability to keep pace with his nimble thinking irritated him. She had learned, when he had moods like these, not to ply him with questions.

She thought, with that secret smile of hers, that those other women would have construed it differently. Their suspicious minds would instantly have accused him of infidelity. They would say, 'He got some mischief on his mind. Ten chances to one it's another woman he's thinking about.' But she knew differently.

[153]

He said, suddenly pushing his plate away from him, 'Why the hell you don't say something, instead of just standing there, staring at me like an idiot all the time? God, I didn't know I was marrying a dummy, a woman without any mind of her own!'

He pushed the chair away from under him so savagely that it was overturned, and strode past her through the door. She felt as though he had struck her.

Numbed, unthinking, she started mechanically to clear the dishes from the table.

Hours later, as she lay awake in bed, the portentous stillness of night suffocatingly thrown about her, shutting her off from those emotions that moved deeply within her like currents of tide and wind moving across the face of the deep, she heard him coming up the path, singing lightheartedly as though he had not a care in the world.

She heard him stop just outside the door of their bedroom and remove his boots. He came into the room in his bare feet, so as not to awaken her. She felt his breath on her cheek as he bent over to kiss her long and tenderly.

She longed with all her heart to take his head upon her breast then, to tell him that all was right and as it should be between them . . . that she would not have had anything of all that changed.

She was surprised that he should have been able to fall asleep so soon, so soundly, leaving her, a little shaken, a little bewildered, with a feeling of unfulfillment, on the brink of this new and wonderful revelation of himself. Almost she could have been the tiniest bit resentful of this . . .

And then she too slipped quietly into the unconsciousness of sleep. How long she slept she did not know. It may have been an hour or a matter of moments. She was awakened by the banging of the broken shutter that Joel had set about mending that morning. It went through her with a nerve-racking insistency, until her body became numb and feelingless under the bludgeoning of that dreadful sound.

And the wind spoke to her . . . telling her wild and terrible things . . . telegraphing them to the sounding board of her unconscious self that translated those ominous whisperings and noises into words, heavy with portent . . .

And all that night she lay awake and listened to the wind.

(1967)

[154]

Vera Bell

Ancestor on the Auction Block

Ancestor on the auction block
Across the years your eyes seek mine
Compelling me to look
I see your shackled feet
Your primitive black face
I see your humiliation
And turn away
Ashamed.

Across the years your eyes seek mine
Compelling me to look
Is this mean creature that I see
Myself?
Ashamed to look
Because of myself ashamed
Shackled by my own ignorance
I stand
A slave.

Humiliated
I cry to the eternal abyss
For understanding
Ancestor on the auction block
Across the years your eyes meet mine
Electric
I am transformed
My freedom is within myself.

I look you in the eyes and see
The spirit of God eternal
Of this only need I be ashamed
Of blindness to the God within me
The same God who dwelt within you
The same eternal God
Who shall dwell
In generations yet unborn.

Ancestor on the auction block
Across the years
I look
I see you sweating, toiling, suffering
Within your loins I see the seed
Of multitudes
From your labour
Grow roads, aqueducts, cultivation
A new country is born
Yours was the task to clear the ground
Mine be the task to build.

(1948)

A.J. Seymour

Sun is a Shapely Fire

Sun is a shapely fire turning in air
Fed by white springs and earth's a powerless sun.

I have the sun today deep in my bones
Sun's in my blood, light heaps beneath my skin.
Sun is a badge of power pouring in
A darkening star that rains its glory down.

The trees and I are cousins. Those tall trees
That tier their branches in the hollow sky
And, high up, hold small swaying hands of leaves
Up to divinity, their name for sun
And sometimes mine. We're cousins.

Sheet light, white power comes falling through the air,
– All the light here is equal-vertical –
Plays magic with green leaves and, touching, wakes
The small sweet springs of breathing scent and bloom
That break out on the boughs
And sun has made
Civilisation flower from a river's mud
With his gossamer rays of steel

II

These regions wear sharp shadows from deep suns.
The sun gives back her earth its ancient right
The gift of violence.

Life here is ringed with the half of the sun's wheel
And limbs and passions grow in leaps of power
Suddenly flowing up to touch the arc.

Upon this energy kin to the sun
To learn the trick of discipline and slow skill.
Squaring in towns upon an empty map
Hitching rivers to great water wheels.
Taming the fire to domesticity.

[157]

III

Sun is a shapely fire floating in air
Watched by God's eye. The distance makes it cool
With the slow circling retinue of worlds
Hanging upon it.

Indifferently near
Move other stars with their attendant groups
Keeping and breaking pace in the afternoon
Till the enormous ballet music fades
And dies away.

Sun is a shapely fire
Turning in air
Sun's in my blood.

(1944)

'The Mighty Chalkdust'

Brain Drain

Just because some teachers go away
To improve their status and their pay,
Many people calling this thing Brain Drain,
But I say they should be shame.
They ain't see Horace James and Errol John
Teaching drums to foreign sons,
They would never see our best footballer
In the States as professionals.
  Police and soldiers went to Expo
  And only one true Calypsonian go,
  And when foreign artistes come
  They does get lump sum,
  While calypsonians must sing for rum,
  And when steelbandsmen teach outsiders
  To tune a pan for kisses and favours –
  All that is what I call Brain Drain.

So many good technicians away,
So many doctors and engineers don't stay,
But on teachers and nurses they put a stain,
And when *they* leave, people bawl 'Brain Drain!'
Look, C.L.R. James, that great writer,
He should be at U.W.I teaching literature.
Cricketers like Legall and Ramdeen
Still teaching the English to bat and spin.
  Foreign artistes coming here and getting jobs,
  And Andrew Beddal can't make some bobs!
  Why not put in every school a Steelbandsman
  To train children to beat pan?
  Our children don't know what's B-flat an pan,
  While the U.S. Army and all have Steelband!
  That is what I call Brain Drain.

Men like Peter Farquhar and Sukie
Should be given jobs in the Ministry.
We wasting brain in this our nation –
Forget party affiliation! –

[159]

And we does use we Drain to make we mas:
Tourist come click-click in photograph –
All we mas pictures in America
And Saldenah getting cah-cah-dah!
   Our culture fruits are draining away,
   And we ain't doing nothing to make them stay!
   Tobago goat race, crab race, bongo, limbo,
   And stickfighting draining out slow.
   O yes, we are living on yankee sad songs like bugs,
   While we parang and folk song going to dogs.
   This is what I call Brain Drain!

                                  (1968)

The Mighty Sparrow (Slinger Francisco)

Dan is the Man

I

According to the education you get when you small
You'll grow up with true ambition and respect from one an all
But in days in school they teach me like a fool
The things they teach me I should be a block-headed mule.

Pussy has finished his work long ago
And now he resting and thing
Solomon Agundy was born on a Monday
The Ass in the Lion skin
Winkin Blinkin and Nod
Sail off in a wooden shoe
How the Agouti lose he tail and Alligator trying to get
    monkey liver soup.

II

The poems and the lessons they write and send from England
Impress me they were trying to cultivate comedians
Comic books made more sense
You know it was fictitious without pretence
But like Cutteridge wanted to keep us in ignorance.

Humpty Dumpty sat on a wall
Humpty Dumpty did fall
Goosey Goosey Gander
Where shall I wander
Ding dong dell . . . Pussy in the well
RIKKI . . . TIKKI TAVI.
Rikki Tikki Tavi

III

Well Cutteridge he was plenty times more advanced than
    them scientists
I aint believe that no one man could write so much foolishness

Aeroplane and rockets didn't come too soon
Scientist used to make the grade in balloon
This time Cutteridge done make a cow jump over the moon.

Tom Tom the piper son
Stole the pig and away he ran
Once there was a woman who lived in a shoe
She had so many children she didn't know what to do
Dickery Dickery Dock
The mouse run up the Clock
The lion and the mouse
A woman pushing a cow up a ladder to eat grass on top a
     house.

IV

How I happen to get some education my friends I don't
     know
All they teach me is about Brer Rabbit and Rumplestilskin
     ... O
They wanted to keep me down indeed
They tried their best but didn't succeed
You see I was dunce and up to now I can't read.

Peter Peter was a pumpkin eater
And the Lilliput people tie Gulliver
When I was sick and lay abed
I had two pillows at my head
I see the Goose that lay the golden egg
The Spider and the Fly
Morocoy with wings flying in the sky
They beat me like a dog to learn that in school
If me head was bright I woulda be a damn fool.

(1989)

C.L.R. James

Discovering Literature in Trinidad

I don't know much about West Indian literature in the 1930s – there wasn't much to know. But at any rate I want to give some idea of how I grew up in the thirties and became the kind of writer that I am. I want to make it clear that the origins of my work and my thoughts are to be found in Western European literature, Western European history and Western European thought. To avoid misunderstanding, I must say that I think the people of the underdeveloped countries accept me and feel that I have had a lot to say that is valid about the underdeveloped countries. That is important. But what I want to make clear is that I learnt this quality in the literature, history and philosophy of Western Europe. I didn't *have* to be a member of an underdeveloped country, though I know a lot of people who are, and yet don't know anything about those countries. I didn't *have* to be an exploited African. It is in the history and philosophy and literature of Western Europe that I have gained my understanding not only of Western Europe's civilisation, but of the importance of the underdeveloped countries. And that is still my outlook.

The atmosphere in which I came to maturity, and which has developed me along the lines that I have gone, is the atmosphere of the literature of Western Europe. In my youth we lived according to the tenets of Matthew Arnold; we spread sweetness and light, and we studied the best that there was in literature in order to transmit it to the people – as we thought, the poor, backward West Indian people ... I didn't learn literature from the mango-tree, or bathing on the shore and getting the sun of the colonial countries; I set out to master the literature, philosophy and ideas of Western civilisation. That is where I have come from, and I would not pretend to be anything else ...

In the 1930s there were a number of us in the West Indies who were to become writers – in Trinidad, myself and George Padmore (we were boys together, and used to bathe in the Arima River, underneath the ice factory); in Martinique there was Aimé Césaire. We hadn't the faintest idea that the time would come when we would be in the forefront of the revolution for African independence.

Among my contemporaries was Grantley Adams, who is now a very distinguished citizen. When I was talking to him a few years ago, he told me that before he left Harrison College he had read Homer, Hesiod, Euripides, Sophocles and Aristophanes, and he was a great master of Aeschylus; he could read Greek almost as well as he could read English. That is the way he was educated, and later he went to an English university and studied law. That was the way that generation was brought up ... We were educated not only in the literature and material life of Western civilisation, but we also became marxists and were educated by marxism ...

There were some of us who were not black men. There was Carpenter the violinist. There was Alfred Mendes. There was a tall, handsome boy, a very able boy, called Frank Evans, a white boy. There was Daly who had an extremely sharp wit, and was light-skinned. There was De Boissiere. There was Albert Gomes. We went one way; these white boys all went the other way. We were black and the only way we could do anything along the lines we were interested in was by going abroad; that's how I grew up ...

Albert Gomes told me the other day: 'You know the difference between all of you and me? You all went away; I stayed.' I didn't tell him what I could have told him: 'You stayed not only because your parents had money but because your skin was white; there was a chance for you, but for us there wasn't – except to be a civil servant and hand papers, take them from the men downstairs and hand them to the man upstairs.' We *had* to go, whereas Mendes could go to the United States and learn to practise his writing, because he was white and had money. But we had to make our money. I came to Europe because Learie Constantine told me: 'You come. I'll see that you go on all right. I'll see that nothing happens to you.' It reminds me of what Khrushchev said at the Twentieth Party Congress, when he claimed that Stalin used to do this and used to do that, and they asked him, 'But if that is so, what did *you* do?' And he answered, 'Boys, it was tough.' That was the general atmosphere, and all of us black writers in the Caribbean went that way, suffered from that ...

By the thirties some of us were feeling our way to something, but we had to leave. After the Second World War those who began to feel that they had some possibility had also, *of necessity*, to leave. What I want to make clear is that all of us were writers of a certain type.

All of us had this literary tradition; all of us had the European training; all of us wrote in the definite tradition of English literature. For us in the thirties there was no literature otherwise ...

At the present time I have discovered in two writers of the Caribbean – Earl Lovelace and Michael Anthony – a new type of West Indian writer. They are not writing with all the echoes and traditions of English literature in their minds. As I see them (and I know the West Indies and particularly Trinidad very well), they are native writers in the sense that their prose and the things that they are dealing with, spring from below, and are not seen through a European-educated literary sieve, as some of the finest writing in the West Indies up to today has been.

(1969)

Albert Gomes

Through a Maze of Colour

I had been away in the United States during 1928–1930. While there, someone had sent me a copy of a collection of poems, short-stories and essays by Trinidadians and others that Alfred H. Mendes, another Trinidadian of Portuguese ancestry, had compiled and published. It was elegantly put together, its form suggesting the influence of the 'London Mercury', J.C. Squire's English monthly of the time. I was very excited by Mendes' publication. Did this really mean that a cultural breakthrough was imminent in Trinidad? At 17 or 18 one desires passionately that events should bear witness to one's dreams and hopes.

Back in Trinidad, I discovered that Mendes had gathered around him a small circle of young men who shared his interest in literature and music. They met regularly and informally at Mendes' home where they listened to recorded music, argued way into the night, and read excerpts from each other's writings. This was the tiny oasis of artistic appreciation I found in the vast philistine desert of Trinidad on my return in 1930; and from it arose the movement of the Thirties that played such an important part in the literary development of the island, later extending its seminal influences to the entire West Indies. It was around my magazine 'The Beacon' that this movement grew, the movement, giving 'The Beacon' the initial push forward.

The members of the group to which Mendes introduced me were held together by a common bond of detestation of the hypocrisy, obscurantism and general claustrophobia of Trinidad society and a gallant resolve to lay seige to all these evils. They spurned the values of the society and withdrew from it into the corner of their choice. Here they could better assert their own values, in a dispensation all their own. But they soon lapsed into a self-flattering aestheticism. Perhaps because they were themselves so much the products of the system they condemned they were constrained to this protest of derisive withdrawal. Withdrawn, they developed a sense of their own uniqueness and another form of snobbery. They were, I think, among the earliest romantics of the social reform movement in the West Indies; for such acts of protest as they later engineered consisted in the main of adolescent cocking-the-snook at the mildewed Victorianism then prevalent. Significantly, only two of them, C.L.R. James and R.A.C. De Boissiere, rose from this comfortable armchair aestheticism to affirmation of political views. The others, in time, either gravitated towards the status quo and ceased to protest, or continued to find solace from its humiliations in dilettante devotion to the arts, or, embittered, derived a masochistic comfort from endless sterile protestation.

Once I had decided that the Island needed a magazine and that I should be its editor and publisher I did my best to persuade my mother that the idea was a good one, and hoped that she in turn would persuade my father to finance it. It lost money consistently during its two years of publication, even though it eventually achieved a popularity, most unusual, and certainly most unexpected, for a publication of the kind in the Trinidad of that time. Its provision of a much-needed safety valve for the pent-up feelings of many must have been timely, the basis of its popularity. But the businessmen, after all, are the ones who decide whether to give or not to give advertisements; their support being indispensable to successful publication. During the magazine's brief but turbulent life, these businessmen were under constant pressure from various groups in the community, who feared the rising popularity of a magazine that so unequivocally and irreverently opposed their cherished convictions ...

'The Beacon', while it lasted, never compromised its views. In the end, faced with a choice between compromise and discontinuance, I chose the latter. I remember one month when the Catholic Guild conducted such a well-organised campaign among our advertisers that at the penultimate hour nearly every advertisement was withdrawn; it became necessary to make good by other means nearly the entire cost of printing. Yet that issue appeared, and the one following, and the one following that.

The small group gathered around Mendes, once publication of the magazine had begun, rallied round it, becoming its contributors and ardent propagandists. Soon the circle spread. From far and wide men and women who had long felt as members of the Mendes circle did, but, believing themselves solitary and isolated, had become afflicted by a kind of costive despair and succumbed to inertia, discovered, at long last, that they were not alone. They made their presence known by contributing either an article, a poem or a short story to

'The Beacon' and so earned their right to be accepted as one of us. And we too, of course, discovered to our surprise and pleasure, that there were many others like us in the community, as eager to sweep away the ancient incrustation of psychic mildew and cobweb that lay thick and heavy on everything and everyone around us. It was in this way that 'The Beacon' became much more than just a literary magazine and mouthpiece of a clique. Indeed, it became the focus of a movement of enlightenment spearheaded by Trinidad's angry young men of the Thirties. It was the torpor, the smugness and the hypocrisy of the Trinidad of the period that provoked the response which produced both the magazine and the defiant bohemianism of the movement that was built around it.

So deep had the community sunk in its obscurantism that the mere existence of such a group, thinking and behaving as we did, aroused the collective imagination to all sorts of fantastic and hysterical speculations about its secret activities ... In fact, I continued to live fairly conventionally, even though involved in the editorship and publication of a journal that was regarded by many as the vanguard of Red Revolution and *avant-garde* morality. However, like most of the other members of our circle I enjoyed the fact that our efforts were having such a convulsive effect on the community. After all, that was precisely what we were after, and it was encouraging to know that we were succeeding.

But this kind of public response to our activities was hardly surprising, since the group included some members who in addition to expressing unpopular views in print, flaunted unpopular attitudes. Jean De Boissiere – 'Tony' to us all – was one such ... Tony found some relief in the extraordinary magazine 'Callaloo' which he edited and published; for while it appeased his relentless bitchery, it at the same time excoriated aspects of Trinidad life which cried out for just that kind of harsh therapy ...

The hullabaloo over the Divorce Bill of 1932 marked a turning point in the careers of both 'The Beacon' and its little group; it was our first and only venture into active politics. It very nearly precipitated premature death for the magazine, since the pressures from the Church increased so alarmingly at this stage that we could not obtain advertisements. Yet, miraculously, we continued. In its chequered two years of existence 'The Beacon' was involved in a libel action, frequent visits from the police, denunciation from the pulpit, pressure from both church and state, increasing opposition from the commercial community, and chronic lack of funds. For myself, in ad'ition to my own struggles to exist, I had monthly to face the fierce struggle to persuade my father to give the magazine yet another chance. When I think that this ordeal was repeated every month and was successful on every occasion, for two years, I wonder how we (my mother and I) managed the miracle, especially since editorial wrath fell with equal fury on everyone ...

The first number of the magazine was a rather staid affair; it gave no indication of the character that would emerge later. If anything, it read more like *The Hibbert Journal* than the debunker of bourgeois morality, obscurantist religion and primitive capitalism it soon became. Starchiness and pretentiousness combined to give it an air of intellectual pomposity. This made the second number, which provided a fair sample of what was to come, a startling contrast. My contribution to this number ('editorial notes', which became a permanent feature, had not yet started) was an article written in staccato phrases – an obvious imitation of Sherwood Anderson. It was entitled 'Black Man' and painted a depressing picture of racial persecution of the Negro in the Southern United States. The tone of protest was shrill, the mood informing it, in its indiscipline, inclining somewhat to the hysterical. But it was by any standards, except of course those of the Trinidad of that period, a gauche and innocuous (and not well written) article on the subject. On the basis of its true importance it should have been ignored. The attention it received from the Trinidad Establishment of the day was gratuitously flattering. They must have felt that it could be an upsetting reminder to the Trinidad Negro of the invidious position he occupied in the society and might even give him ideas about what he should do about it ...

I well remember the afternoon the police car pulled up outside our house and the four plain-clothes men, one of whom was well known to my family, walked up the steps and asked to see me ...

Three of the policemen who came to interrogate me were Negroes, the senior officer being an Englishman. This was the first of many similar experiences I have had and, as I have always been since, I was struck then by the monumental inanity of the questions asked.

'How did I come to write the article?'
'How did I get the information I used?'
'How did I know that the information was reliable?'
'Had I ever witnessed racial violence in the United States?'
'How did I know that the reports I had read were true?'
'Did I know that this sort of writing was dangerous in Trinidad?'
'Was I in communication with any organisations in the United States?'
'Who were my contacts?'
'Was the magazine getting any financial backing from the United States?'
'I did of course know that matters were different in Trinidad?
'I was aware – wasn't I – that Negroes were treated quite differently here?'. . .

Our group preserved its essentially informal character throughout. For this I must claim some credit. I find that people react much more naturally and give much more of their true selves, their talents and idiosyncracies, when they are not contained in any formal social crucible, especially one of the kind that gives importance to rules of parliamentary procedure, which, effective and indispensable as they may be in guaranteeing the discipline of legislative bodies, invariably lead to a stratification of normal reflexes into self-conscious attitudes of pomposity and pretence when applied to less formal patterns of social coalescence. Hence, my insistence throughout the life of our group that we should eschew chairmen and standing orders and all other aspects of the paraphernalia by which men impose controls upon themselves when they become committees. We met at each other's homes and never around a table, except, of course, one on which there were bottles and glasses.

The policy of the magazine was really the absence of one, for although the editorial notes reflected more or less my own views, in all other sections contributors of most riotously conflicting views co-existed. If we wrote something attacking some aspect of church policy and a defender appeared who was prepared to state his views in writing, these views were published. The same privilege was granted to any other person, from whatever section or vested interest in the community, who wished to do likewise. Thus controversies, always the best boost to circulation, were frequent. When they did not occur spontaneously we deliberately engineered them . . .

I found early that if the magazine was to serve the purpose we intended the editorial discipline had to be relaxed, not only as regards points of view but even in relation to standards of writing and general literacy. A rigorous standard of selection would inevitably result in such exclusion of potential new contributors as to make the magazine eventually the mouthpiece of a self-perpetuating elite; something I wished to avoid. From the second and third issues manuscripts began to pour into my home from all parts of the Island, some written by persons so illiterate that it was pathetic to observe the failure of their valiant attempts to express their views. Not all expressed ignorant views because they were not learned or even literate. And it was this realisation that influenced my policy. On many occasions when I received a manuscript that I felt could become a good article or short-story after some revision, I wrote to the author asking him to come to see me, and when he came, if I saw that he was the sort of person whose pride was not above a little advice and guidance, I tactfully offered my help . . .

Life was exciting and unpredictable while 'The Beacon' lasted . . .

(1974)

The Beacon Editorials

Local Fiction

We regret to write that few good stories have been received for th[e Short Story] Competition. The majority of local fiction-writers obviously believe that gross exaggerations contribute to the artistic value of their stories. Several of the stories we have received read like advertisements for the enhancement of our tourist trade: others, like anecdotes from the Good Book, and still more, like extracts from *True Story*. This, however, might easily be attributed to that deep religious consciousness of which Trinidadians are so proud. We fail utterly to understand, however, why anyone should want to see Trinidad as a miniature *Paradiso*, where grave-diggers speak like English MPs and vice versa. The answer is obviously that the average Trinidad writer regards his fellow-countrymen as his inferiors, an uninteresting people who are not worth his while. He genuinely feels (and by this, of course, asserts his own feeling of inferiority) that with his people as characters his stories would be worth nothing. It is for this reason that he peoples them with creatures from other planets, American gangsters and English MPs; and revives familiar plots and characters from *True Story* and other *nth* rate periodicals. It would be difficult to convince him that the exotic quality of his plot is immaterial and that it is difficult to write well of persons and things beyond one's ken. For those clerics and stern moralists who are always preaching and parading the moral cleanliness of 'our fair isle' there are abundant surprises in the stories received for the competition. Sex is still 'the dirty secret', but the aspiring local writer treats it with religious fervour ... We have never seen such bad love scenes before ... We advise the local writer ... however, to spend less time on florid descriptions of our hills, valleys and the moonlight on the Queen's Park Savannah. Those things are only incidental to a good story. It is, moreover, better to spend two days trying to analyse the sensations of your last toothache than to continue to nibble away indefinitely at the distorted psyche of some New York gangster. Why is the local writer so eager to attach mystery to cut and dried Trinidad?

Local Poetry

Why so many of the poems we receive are imitations of Ella Wheeler Wilcox is a question we have been asking ourselves for quite some time. We realize, of course, that intellectual dropsy is a popular form of ailment in Trinidad. Wilcox dealt with the obvious and commonplace all her life, and the mood of the average Trinidadian is still surface. Whatever pleases his aggravated sentiments is *very good* to him.

His universe is a marshmallow and anyone who assists him in nibbling at its cardinal points is feted like a prince. Reality he refuses and every Sunday he may be seen seeking an escape from life in the bosom of an evangelist. Wilcox was an evangelist. She painted a picture of life which is both inartistic and unreal. She became disgustingly popular. Her fame spread like wildfire and she died in extreme wealth. Both the intellectual and economic progress of the world has followed a similar line of development. There has been an amazing increase in the number of persons who attain a high intellectual level, but a majority-class remains, however on an intellectual level slightly above that of an intelligent ape . . .

[Wilcox] wrote *trash* and there is a larger market for trash than for any other literature. Here in Trinidad there are two large libraries with the majority of the classics on their shelves but to every individual who patronises Keats or Shelley there are a few thousand who will pay exorbitant prices for books by Wilcox and her kind.

(1932)

J.E. Clare McFarlane

The Challenge of Our Time

The death of Tom Redcam which took place at the commencement of our last working year may be considered to have marked the close of a definite epoch in literary effort of this country. It is not my purpose here to consider the significance of the work which has been accomplished or initiated during that period. For this, other occasions and opportunities will serve. But I desire to point out that we have received a very definite heritage and hold in trust a tradition which we cannot regard with levity. It is fashionable to talk about Art for Art's sake; and perhaps more fashionable to talk about Art for Money's sake. But every artist, whatever be his medium, who is not a mere craftsman, a mere pedlar of tinsel and paste, knows that the vision with which he is endowed and the message he has received lay upon him a solemn obligation to declare, as far as his voice will carry, what he has heard and seen.

We live in the twilight of an age. We are privileged to witness the passing of a civilization and the birth of a new culture – both painful processes. Those of us who are now approaching, or have attained, our prime are conscious, as our fathers never were, of a deep anguish at the heart of life. We are filled with an inexpressible regret for the apparent waste of the last twenty years ...

There is not much that we can do now for the old order which is passing away; it has fulfilled its destiny; it moves to its appointed doom. But the new order demands much of us; it offers us a challenge. We are men in our prime; and we cannot avoid without dishonour the obligation to see that the dawn which is visiting mankind is ushered in under the best auspices of which we are capable. How shall we meet this new opportunity? ...

Now Europe is breaking up under the weight of her own thought. Communism aims at being a world force; so does Fascism; Germany would extend her borders; Britain is already the centre of a world Empire. It is clear that narrow national boundaries must give way before this all-conquering desire to extend. Narrow Nationalism in this day is illogical and contrary to the tendency of things. In the midst of human selfishness and greed, the idea of human unity stands like a gleaming cross – a challenge to the contending nations, each of whom desires to swallow the rest and at the same time remain separate and distinct. This new idea of human unity is implied in the Commonwealth of Nations known as the British Empire, in the United States of America which is a meeting ground of all nations and races – and in little Jamaica which for its size is probably the most cosmopolitan country on Earth.

It is clear that Nature has chosen us to be one of the important centres in this new experiment in human relations. The time has therefore arrived when we should cease to regard ourselves as an insignificant little Island in the Caribbean and realise that we are called to great responsibilities. The new order of human affairs will be affected very profoundly by the results we show; and the results we show will depend upon the thoughts we think to-day.

Therefore as representatives of a great tradition we offer you Poetry, upon which we feel certain the true foundation of this Empire rests and by which it will be preserved throughout the storm that now hangs above the horizon of civilization. We of the Poetry League as you will observe from our programme for this Session propose to initiate a study of European Philosophy and History as a necessary step toward an understanding of the Past, but we go forward into the future assured that only on the highest principles of human conduct as enunciated in the immortal poetry of all ages can we proceed to any lasting human good. Poetry; not the facile jingle of recurrent rhymes or the collection of apt phrases, but living symbols of the soul's travail and exultation; the quintessence of human experience, lifted momentarily into the rhythm of universal life; courage and magnanimity and hope and faith and justice and sympathy and love: all the essential qualities which distinguish the Religion of Jesus Christ; words of life and power; a light about our feet in days of darkness! . . .

We have paid, and are willing to pay. He is a fool who identifies heaven with ease, or fails to realise that laughter is the counterpart of tears, or is blind to the fact that the spiritual elevation of a people must be built upon the solid foundation of its material well-being and for which those of us who care must pay with our hearts' blood. It may be possible for a poet to starve and yet produce immortal poetry; but it is not possible to teach the beauties of poetry and the meaning of higher living to a hungry and ragged populace; and it is with this, which may be called the mission of poetry, that we are primarily concerned at this moment. The greatest bane of our present existence is to be found in the over-emphasis which has been laid upon material things by the very fact of the lack of them. We desire that the people have enough of these necessary things so that they may not assume in their minds an importance out of all proportion to the value. And if we give you Poetry we give it not as an opiate that you may forget your wretchedness; but as an elixir by whose aid you may gather strength sufficient to win from out the nightmare pit of your present existence . . .

The Poetry League is proposing to you that you begin the change of your environment and the improvement of the quality of your public men by changing and improving the pattern and quality of your individual thought: by the cultivation of a mind in which generous impulses will have free play. We offer you the inexhaustible riches of poetry with which to do this. This is the contribution which we have been commissioned to make to the future welfare of this country. It is fundamental work; it is a quality which will be built into the fabric of the generations to come; an ingredient which will slowly but surely transfigure life like a new dawn above the hills of Time. The opportunity is ours; the challenge is to us.

(1935)

Victor Stafford Reid

The Cultural Revolution in Jamaica after 1938

Significantly, and happily for symbolic historians, 1938 in Jamaica occurred exactly one hundred years after Emancipation. A full century of a freedom that was phony. A freedom that with some enthusiasm, arranged to slay us in infancy, drove us out of school at fifteen, enabled a few by a carefully limited skill to enter the company of mechanics – whether of field, factory or the humbler schoolrooms; and at the same time, yet managed to rouse among us, many fine voices singing *Rule Britannia*.

It was a funny freedom. The purchasing of bodies by documents was behind us. The whip and branding iron had joined the archaeological artifacts which up to then had consisted only of Arawak skulls. Yet we now know that the documents of purchase had merely changed form and become the paybills of the sugar estates; binding a land-less majority through the threat of loosening them into starvation. The whip had changed form, and become the *law* of racism.

But what of the branding iron? Fortunately, the iron had not changed. It had merely entered our souls.

Few people can have had less reason to believe in the presence of iron. For the most part, we were impoverished, illiterate, ignorant of our history, easily sold on the idea of our inferiority, considering that it had been drummed into us by the presence of a master race in every area of authority and learning; by the pictures, the books, the music, particularly among those of us who exposed ourselves to it for the quite laudable reason of a desire to 'succeed' . . .

And as it was politically and socially, and very much as it was economically, so it was culturally. We had nothing but the words, the music, the images, the plays of the conqueror; and these were merely discards from the work benches of the familiar alien.

But gradually, slowly, painfully, our fingers found new holds in place of the long worn ones. We had not, it turned out, lost the knack of aching and yearning; as we had not lost the knack of hunting down the tormentors.

The adaptation had its moments of fun. We danced the European quadrilles under the tropical sun, sang the European madrigals beneath the mango trees, sat at European afternoon teas belted and

[177]

brass-buttoned in our woollen suits in the flaring heat. (I sometimes believe that high among the traumatic adventures of the newly arrived ancestral Africans, coming from a culture in which the hat was frequently unknown, save the religious reasons, the custom of head-gear must have been particularly evil. By such simple savagery were his days made unbearable.)

But the adaptation was made; and we kept *in* ourselves, and *for* ourselves, a trace of the rhythm that synthesizes our Caribbean cultural forms . . .

And so we walked into the twentieth century, contented in a way, I assume, as fish born in a tank are contented. The memory of the open sea, the swirl and leap and flash of it, lies buried. Or so it seems.

The few on whom we had pinned some hope had galloped over the hill. Claude McKay to America. W. Adolphe Roberts, also. But we were making politicians by the handsful.

The brave young Marxists and black nationalists were stirring us with new ideas, new visions, new brands of bravery, and even some sensibly wrought bravura that scared the authorities into believing they had been given the keys to the Kremlin. But culturally, our concern was with Keats; our fascination was with the View from Westminster Bridge. Even those two best among our political and social awakeners, N.W. Manley and his cousin Alexander Bustamante, were not immune to matters of King and Empire. Jamaica was a cultural wasteland that exiled sanity.

But a sense of renewal was surging against those bonds of remembered bondage.

One of the earliest breaks from the cultural traditions, that is, our strongest turning-away from the English countryside in the budding month of May, appeared in N.W. Manley's household, in the poetry of his virtual protege, George Campbell. It was George who gave us the first agonising look, the angry look at women in 'pregnant frocks . . . hammering rocks', a view that like no other exposed the squalid-ness inside 'beautiful Jamaica'.

In 1938 came the first clearcut victory ever won by the working-class; i.e., all the poor people of Jamaica. A new brand of loyalty emerged in which *need* stepped aside for *principle*. It was a general strike . . .

It was clearly a good year in which to see powerful forces, for after all, the two most powerful men in the country were working hand in glove. For it was Manley who had employed his clout and legal skill in obtaining Busta's release. Together, they had beaten the Establishment. For the first time in the centuries since the Maroons, since the Establishment became really established, they had been beaten. Ahead lay probabilities, lay hope.

And it was poetry that provided the opening hope, even if rhetoric was its outrider.

And you know, the long limb of poetry, longer even than the law, the limb that has been known to reach down years, and touch a truth in men, has reached down the years to a young poet, unborn at thirty-eight and at school in the cold north, and caused Anthony McNeill to write:

> Tonight, circled by snow / in a foreign country / I
> praise one of the children / who stood alone /
> hearing old drums / under the bam bam bangarang /
> who passed into manhood / through the eye of the sun /
> and smelted lonely calypsoes and soul / against the
> long morning of English rule.

It was poetry that provided the hope even if rhetoric was its outrider ...

Except for religion, or the exercises that pass for it, poetry had been for long the staple of a tiny coterie, stepping its careful way through the familiar-alien. It provided us back in 1933, with what I desperately hope is unique in the Caribbean, a poet laureate. The form acknowledges its beginnings in the man often called the father of Jamaican poetry, T.H. MacDermot, or as he is better known, Tom Redcam. He was the man they made a poet laureate. But posthumously, since he died just before they could get to him. However, nineteen years later, another Jamaican poet, J.E. Clare McFarlane, was robed and garlanded on the stage of the Ward, before a large and mystified audience, as our second poet laureate. It seemed late in the day of the revolution to be holding coronations; but the tenacity of poets, especially when strengthened by an Empire Poetry League, is legendary.

But not to get ahead of myself, the new wave of poets was not many, nor prolific, but telling in their dues, in their contribution, in their early recognition before the Americans could reach it, that black was beautiful. Or as George Campbell sang it:

[179]

> Say, is my skin beautiful? And (is) my mind
> like bright sunlight?

And again, with the true sensitivity and understanding of his land as a melting pot of the races, Campbell could say:

> Dark peoples singing in my veins / Fair peoples singing in
> soft strains / Oh, when I pray, I bow with blue eyes
> Dark hands, red hair
> My prayer is life . . .

But Campbell, and Philip Sherlock and Roger Mais, and Louise Bennett, whose nationalism in dialect made her defy the Back-to-Africa cry by declaiming: 'Back to Africa, Miss Matty / Yuh no know weh yuh da seh / Yuh haffe come from somewhey fus / Before you go back deh'; all these were the orthodox poets.

Spread out into the woodlands, in the mountain villages and seaside fishing towns were scores of other poets, the young activists Sam Hinds, McBean, who wrote the political songs that would rouse a generation of voters to *Come rally to the PNP*. For you must know that, by that time, the break had occurred; and it was clear that the old starry-eyed hope of a Manley/Bustamante tandem of political and union leaders leading the country to the promised land, was over.

If it seems peculiar that nothing has been said to suggest that there was a similar cultural quality in the wake, or with, the Busta party, it is because such was never identified. The Bustamante charisma tended to the workingman, rather than the middleclass – or those with the leanings, and it is true to say that the cultural revolution was having its spurs fitted among the aspirants to a middleclass, and the younger, and consequently, better educated Jamaicans, of this emergent society . . .

Now then the new movements in the arts had created a restlessness, a sense of inadequacy, a need to move outward, while we searched inward. And so, many of our writers went abroad, to do their works of dissent in the culture with which their precursors had consented. England was mecca. They never thought, then, that she would prove a peculiarly unloving mother. However, they wrote. It could have been the usefully unhappy relationship that made them work . . .

Literature has spoken full-throatedly, rightly or wrongly. In sport, we of the West Indies have been world champions in cricket,

individual Olympic gold medallists, and even evolved a new competition: champion coconut husker. Every creative cultural happening
since that month of May has been a portion of the revolution. The
process, of course, continues.

(1978)

Roger Mais

Where the Roots Lie

The fault is with us. We are soft. We have sat back and allowed ourselves to get soft. We have allowed the heat to get us. It goes over us in great waves. Our poetry is drugged with the lassitude of this heat, the langours fostering this scabrous blight of softness – this scrofula of superficiality!

'We are Jamaicans, are we not?' This is the way we talk to ourselves subconsciously. We are Jamaicans writing for Jamaicans. Let us for the sake of illustration turn this proper noun into a commonplace adjective. Let us say instead 'We are Jamaicans writing for a Jamaican Public.' This is what you get, – we, from the heights of Parnassus are writing down to you fellows below there! Because the adjective 'Jamaican', prefixing certain nouns, – notably 'taste' 'public,' 'thought,' 'culture,' and the rest, – becomes not so much an adjective as an implied slur.

It is a slur that implies mediocrity – oh, quite unconsciously, of course. I can hear some people arguing that this thing has its roots within our constitution, in the fact that we are a subject people. Be that as it may just thinking so is too much like sugar-coating the pill. The real root of the trouble lies in ourselves. We have fed ourselves upon the pap of inferiority, till now we have not got any real bones in our bodies, only gristle, and not too much of that either.

Nothing is intrinsically wrong with our reading public, and *I* don't take our would-be serious writers seriously – not more of them than may be counted on the fingers of one hand. I resent being 'written down to', I resent this implication of mediocrity, therefore I refuse to read your poems, because they teem with little simpering *clichés* – in the thoughts that inspire (?) the words, if not in the phraseology itself.

As to your dogged refusal to accept the more modern form; that in itself constitutes an insult to my mentality. I refuse to be hurled back into the dark ages, or to be dragged there supinely on the back of a sure-footed, nimble quadruped. If I am to enjoy your company, or even to be bored by it, I must do the journey by car, or by aeroplane.

Think; your minds grew until they caught up with Chaucer, Milton, Shakespeare – the eras in which these men wrote, – and then they stopped growing. In a word they stopped growing with the school syllabus. And when you stop growing you become stagnant!

If you would only wake up for long enough to give the matter some thought you would realise that these men in their day were the last syllable in modernity! Chaucer broke new ground and a lot of traditions, so did Milton, so did Shakespeare. In his last three plays or so Shakespeare started writing verse so 'free', so modern, that it might make Eliot himself take thought.

So you see you are not really true disciples of these ancient masters. You are disciples in the *letter* only, not the spirit. Chaucer would have laughed in his beard to watch you mimicking him, if he lived today. He would exclaim: 'What are these stuffed dummies trying to do, imitating that dead stuff! Why don't they try to break new ground for themselves, like I am doing! I took a book or two to say then what I say now in a short poem of six lines or so. That was because I was learning. The world hadn't got beyond that point, in those da‾s. I was way ahead of the others. In those days we thought three miles per hour was some going. But today, why people are zooming through the air at 300 mph. If all the world of letters and of art kept creeping backward into the dark ages, in a little time we should be moving around on our bellies. What we want to do is to go forward until we learn to grow wings, and having grown them, we won't stop there!'

Because we as writers have sold ourselves the idea that the Jamaican public is an ass, a simpering sort of ass – quite unconsciously! – we feel that we must talk their language, or rather, write it – oh, quite unconsciously! – and so we put a period to our own efforts.

I am deliberately saying all these unpleasant things about us in the hope that somebody will rise up in self-righteous indignation, and try to justify us.

I am spoiling for a scrap. I want [to] climb right up somebody's chest, and take them apart. In order to do that I would gladly mix a hell-broth of revolt in Jamaican letters, let alone a couple of metaphors.

One of the troubles with people who write poetry, is that they have picked that medium. It is not a medium that lends itself to practising nothing more than the modicum of mediocrity. Poetry is to letters what the violin is to music, if you feel that you must express something, and realise at the same time that you are only just 'so–so', it would be better for you to learn to play the drum, or the harmonica.

I am not trying to disparage these instruments, God forbid! – but while I can sit and listen placidly to a drum or a harmonica being played just 'so-so', not so with a violin. I invariably feel that person ought not to be trying to play a violin, he should start practising with a drum, to see if he has got any music in him. *Voilà* as the French say, with a simultaneous shrug of hands and shoulders. It is just one of those things that I cannot help!

So with poetry!

Why go to all that pains to say in rhymed lines, what you would be ashamed to say in indifferent prose? Do you think you can hide superficiality behind assonance or alliteration, or successfully camouflage the trite between a sequence of rhymes?

(1940)

Una Marson

We Want Books – But Do We Encourage Our Writers?

In the nineteen twenties and early nineteen thirties there were many active Debating Societies in Jamaica.

A favourite subject for debate used to be 'Resolved that the Pen is mightier than the sword'.

There are many hackneyed platitudes about writers and writing.

'Reading maketh a full man and
Writing maketh a ready man'.
'Give me the songs of a country and I care not who makes its laws'.
'A good book is the precious livelihood of a master spirit'.

In our island home the writers who have reached professional status can be counted on the fingers of one hand. Nevertheless many others have made contributions that will outlive them. But far too few.

Most people are ready to explain that lack of adequate remuneration and means of publication have combined to discourage and thwart the would-be writer.

There is undoubtedly truth in this statement, but it is not the whole truth . . .

During the war a taxi driver named Hodges was induced to broadcast his experiences as a London taxi driver during the Bombing of London. He became a popular broadcaster. Doubtless you heard him in Jamaica. To-day he has several books to his credit.

The other day a story was told of a street sweeper in London who carried text books in his pocket and studied while he had a pint of beer and a sausage. He sat up nights studying. Now he is doing a course with a University extra Mural Department.

When men who come from the poorest sections of a community produce work of a high literary standard by dint of hard work and application they are not discouraged and kept outside the pale of public acclamation and appreciation because they were not born with a silver spoon in the mouth . . .

Now, I am told and I know that in Jamaica the young writer is regarded as a little queer.

If he is a Civil Servant his superiors think he would be a better civil servant if he was not interested in literature and had no literary ambitions. In fact everything is done by his superiors to discourage him to attain – even his promotion in the Service is soft pedalled.

In the home he hides his poems or essays for fear of being laughed at.

The truth is that it has not yet come home to the hearts and minds of the people of this island that our status in the way of nationhood is more to be enhanced by our literary output than by rum and bananas. In fact, that 'man shall not live by bread alone'.

We have to realise that it is as vital to encourage the spark of creative genius as it is to encourage the spark of genius that shows in youth aptitude for a materialistic money making career.

Writers of a country are respected and revered even tho' they are never rich . . .

I do not know how many people who entertain encouraged Vic Reid on his new success as a novelist. This apart from functions organised by his colleagues for him.

I do not think the public knows what our leading writers look like – nor is it interested.

Our writers have no Guggenheim, Rockefeller or Rosenwald Scholarship to keep them while they spend a couple of years on research for the production of a book.

Indeed, they have not even the consciousness that their fellow Jamaicans are supporting them spiritually.

Perhaps that is an exaggeration.

There has been some little awakening recently – 'one swallow does not make a Summer – but it tells that Summer is coming' – the Summer of warm, generous and true encouragement to our young writers – the Summer of a real, and not just a mythical cultural Renaissance.

Politics, Federation – money, yes – but even with all these things – 'where there is no vision the people perish'.

(1949)

Alison Donnell

Contradictory (W)omens?: Gender Consciousness in the Poetry of Una Marson

Scholarship during the last decade has successfully highlighted the wealth of creative talent and literary innovation from contemporary Caribbean women writers, yet there remains a dearth of research and criticism on early women's writing in the region ...

One of these early writers, Una Marson, is now well recognized as an important literary role model for Caribbean women and there is no shortage of tributes to her ... [Yet] there has been no detailed or substantive reading of her work. Even those critics who have pioneered a literary recognition of Una Marson's work have adhered to criteria which make an uncompromised acknowledgement problematic. The elements of mimicry and pastiche within her poetry, along with her use of orthodox poetic forms and archaic language continue to elicit embarrassed critical silences or excuses ...

My project here is to ... engage in a close reading of two of Marson's early poems, 'In Vain' (a love sonnet) and 'If' (a Kipling parody), in order to place what have previously been seen as oppositional poetic and ideological positions side by side and thus put forward a different, consciously speculative, reading of Marson's troubling texts ...

For the majority of critics, the writing of Una Marson, and moreover the whole of the early period of Caribbean literature, does not advance beyond blatant aesthetic mimicry or crude political posturing ...

Certainly the commonest criticism of Jamaican poetry during the first half of the twentieth century was its reliance upon British models and its lack of experimentation and 'authenticity'. Aesthetic critics challenged the worth of the poetry on the basis that it relied too heavily upon poetic models to offer any exciting or innovative insights into the possibilities of language, imagery or form. Cultural critics disputed the poetry's worth on the basis that it was too dependent upon the experiences and ideas of the colonial centre to merit the label 'Jamaican'. Both charges reveal that imitation was seen as the principal stumbling block to real literary achievement ...

[187]

Yet, some critics have moved beyond excusing the practice [of mimicry] by offering historical and cultural reasoning for it, in order to re-evaluate the process itself and assess the potential it holds for subverting from within and mobilizing the very conventions which it appears to submit to. The line between a mere imitation of a European literary model and a re-writing of it is difficult to draw and in many cases is as reliant upon a politics of reading as of writing. The use of stylized English language and the conscious adoption of British literary models should be viewed suspiciously by the critic searching for an imitative lineage in order to substantiate claims of unbroken colonial domination in the work of both white and black writers ... .

I have chosen to look at 'In Vain' because it disrupts the assumption that a poem written in a form as conventional as a sonnet will be proportionately reliant on that structure's eurocentrically gendered system of signification. This poem also raises the issue of mimicry, as it has many echoes of Elizabethan and courtly love poetry but is crucially different to that genre ...

The language and imagery of imperialism, which surfaces in a number of Marson's 'love poems' with such disturbing and shocking effect, could be traced to the Elizabethan sonneteers. Both offer the same classical framework, in which the lover is apotheosized with the characteristic blurring of religious and amatory imagery. The frustration of fulfilment (all is 'in vain') could also be seen as mere convention, the portrayal of necessary cruelty and indifference on the part of the lover. Marson does present an inverted imitation of the paradigm of courtly love; the man is unattainable, placed on a throne rather than a pedestal, and the woman is actively, and inevitably unsuccessfully, wooing.

Yet, by inverting the gender roles, Marson brings new meaning to the genre. The adoration of woman and her fictive ability to wield power through indifference and abstinence within male courtly love poetry is revealed as playful and even derisory, since the real power structures of society frustrate any such notion of female power, an issue especially pertinent in the Caribbean. The politics of courtly love poetry exist then in the space between art and life whereas in Marson's poem it is relation between the art and life of a black woman which makes the 'slave image' such a disturbing, difficult and fascinating one. However, while this poem obviously provokes consideration of the power politics of eroticism and relationships within heterosexual, patriarchal, colonial societies, I would suggest that it takes us beyond a commentary on what has elsewhere been termed 'the pornography of Empire'.

As I have already stated, criticism to date has attempted to either suppress or dismiss sonnets such as this one, which is part of a thirteen-poem sonnet sequence. These approaches are strongly suggestive of the fact that such poetry is considered to be a saccharine sub-genre of gendered verse and embarrassingly colonial. Within the Jamaican context 'A Lover's Discourse' is not only 'unwarranted' (to quote Barthes); the sentimental and sacrificial proves a particularly treacherous territory for the post-colonial feminist critic for whom such poems occasion a fighting back both of charges of emotional excess and of literary dependency.

However, the poem 'In Vain' seems to offer us a point from which to resist these readings. The proposition of the first stanza that submission and servitude represent an opportunity 'to come into my own' undermines any static notion of conditioned feminine self-sacrifice or cultural masochism. At the point of submission the slave should be owned; it is a moment which traditionally signifies the denial of subjectivity, not the acquisition of it. By calling the issue of ownership into question, Marson's poem reveals how taking control of submission can be an act of transgression. Indeed, we might wish to extend this principle to a consideration of Marson's poetics here and suggest that by consciously crafting a poem in which subordination is undermined, any relationship of 'In Vain' to the European sonnet tradition is similarly subverted. Thus by rehearsing a position of servitude – to poetic convention as well as to the lover/master figure – this poem is able to articulate a space in which the subject can position itself even within the structure of slavery, which might be seen as a place of no resistance. By operating within convention, the poem explores but does not endorse the surrender of self, which might be seen as the traditional destiny of the female and colonial subject. It is this ambivalent representation of woman as slave within the poem which disturbs any easy reading of Marson's gender politics; the ultimate undecidability as to the parodic or sincere nature of this genre of her poetry demands that we engage with the complexity of sexual and cultural identity.

If we pursue the possibility of subversion as textual allegory further, the title of this volume, *Tropic Reveries*, might be construed rather differently from the obvious romantic and climatic interpretation. Indeed, we might wish to consider this volume as a dreaming up of alternative tropes for the Caribbean woman writer, as a series of poems which engage in irreverent reveries concerning dominant tropes. Certainly, the figure desiring mastery is not the only trope of woman to undergo revision in this volume. Indeed, it is in *Tropic Reveries*, the volume most densely populated by these seemingly self-sacrificial love poems, that we also find the most acerbic attacks on 'matrimony' – the expected epitome of heterosexual romance. In this volume Marson re-models two of the 'sacred' speeches of English literature, Kipling's 'If' and Hamlet's soliloquy 'To be or not to be ...', playfully shifting the poetic axis from a discussion of 'man's condition' to an exploration of woman's.

Although much of the text [of 'If'] ... is taken directly from Kipling, the effect of the poem as a whole is far from mimetic. Reconstruction on the levels of diction and form serves to facilitate deconstruction on the level of ideas. It is clear that the Jamaican woman poet is not bidding to be a pale imitation of a brilliant predecessor, but is rather choosing models and forms best suited to elucidate her own ideas and express a state of consciousness and a social role which has been left uninterrogated by patriarchy and colonialism.

The parody of Kipling's grand recipe for manhood has an interesting subtext with reference to him as colonial writer, but I want to concentrate here on gender politics. While Kipling's poem inscribes the ethos of imperial masculinity *par excellence*, Marson's parody appropriates this framework with daring and decorum in order to communicate the consciously anti-heroic role of a 'wife worth while' ... The trials which mark a boy's rite of passage into manhood are travestied by the domestic obstacle course which faces a prospective bride. In the poem, the initiation into matrimony is revealed to be an exercise requiring practical skills, dissimulation and self-delusion. Indeed, although Kipling writes of maturity and Marson of matrimony, the ultimate subject of both poems is significantly the same in terms of a discussion of masculine fulfilment, and yet crucially different. Marson's poem effectively re-defines and re-aligns the status of this achievement, again raising a question mark over established notions of value. The references within the third stanza of the poem point to the very real problems of budgeting, but also suggest that to be contented and worthwhile a wife must learn to play with the concept of value. The manipulation of figures which the wife must learn standing figuratively for the creative accounting with her own happiness which she must perform in order for her marriage to balance emotionally.

In this poem, Marson acknowledges and 'plays off' the primary text with critical awareness, thus making the ideological inflections of the poem far more explicit. To undervalue parody as either a sign of the writer's inability to escape received models (a potential post-colonial reading) or of a penchant for apolitical play (a potential postmodern reading) would be to miss the radical relationship which these poems establish between different models of experience and different participants within an established discourse. As Helen Tiffin has pointed out:

> Pastiche and parody ... offer a key to the destabilisation and decon-struction of a repressive European archive. Far from endlessly deferring or denying meaning, these same tropes function as potential de-colonising strategies which invest (or re-invest) devalued 'peripheries' with meaning.[1]

It is woman and domestic politics as periphery which Marson addresses in her parodies. As Linda Hutcheon points out, parody 'establishes difference at the heart of similarity. No integration into a new context can avoid altering meaning, and perhaps even value'.[2] Indeed, it is crucial that the transcontextual act becomes transvalua-tive as the issue of sexual difference is written into Marson's versions.

Rhonda Cobham-Sander has described Marson's parodies as 'of slight literary merit ... probably written while Marson was still at school for the entertainment of school friends'.[3] Although this sugges-tion of commonplace schoolgirl activity is purely speculative it might be interesting to pursue this line of enquiry a little further. Rather than indicating the lesser value of these poems (Cobham-Sander's comment implies that they are somehow inconsequential and aesthet-ically immature), this idea that the poems were produced as a direct response to and in the context of the colonial education system serves to highlight their inherently subversive quality. The pedagogic imper-ative for repetition which was instilled by this system is here radically revised through parodies of high literary discourses. By choosing to travesty such well-established texts, Marson is able to demonstrate her knowledge of tradition, whilst asserting a counter-discourse via the substitution of woman's experience.

The apology to Kipling at the end of the parody does not signal the filial relationship with indifference. Marson deliberately foregrounds the 'original creator' and text and thus ironically references the consciously disobedient nature of this poem through a gesture of mock humility. Although such explicit intertextuality may suggest that the meanings in operation here can only come into 'play' because of their textual (and colonial) antecedents, the counter-textuality of this poem illustrates that Marson's relationship to tradition is not passive or derivative in nature.

While Cobham-Sander seeks to give agency to the education system, with Marson simply in the role of reactor, my reading seeks to highlight how this poem actually reclaims agency from an institution founded on a belief in the hierarchy of discourses in order to communicate a consciously non- (if not anti-) elitist perspective. Far from being any incidental act of verbal play, this parody presents ideological rivalry, offering Marson an opportunity to radically dislocate tradition from authority and to question the gender politics of such an authoritative text.

Indeed, far from reading this parody as an insignificant experiment with poetry or as a 'miscellaneous' work unrelated to the volume as a whole, I wish to propose that Marson's parody be read as a paradigmatic text for an analysis of the tensions between imitation and creation within much of her work where intertextuality operates more subtly. Parody with its possibility for split signification works both within and against the colonial imperative to mimic, making a double demand on meaning which I would suggest is also operating in some of Marson's 'love poems' on a less explicit level.

With these links in mind, it is interesting to consider the elements of self-parody to be found within *Tropic Reveries*. In 'To Wed Or Not To Wed', Marson ironizes women who 'pine and sigh under a single life', an agenda which a less generous critic may accuse her love poems earlier in the volume of fulfilling, and in 'If' she seems to satirize 'In Vain' with the counsel to 'serve yet do not be his slave'. Perhaps then, having arrived at the parodies, which are the penultimate poems of the volume, we can laugh at these earlier poems as unenlightened, if, that is, the parodies give us anything legitimate to laugh at? Perhaps we should laugh at the wonderful sense of contradiction which is embraced by Marson within one volume? Would this be an embarrassed laughter at the fact that Marson failed to spot her own discrepancies, or at the fact that no single version is more 'true' even though they may appear to be mutually exclusive?

If we laugh at these parodies, I think that it should be because they dare to confront paradox, embrace their constructed 'other' (the slave sonnets), and thereby tell the 'whole truth' which is necessarily partial. By communicating both versions of female destiny, Marson is able to disclose the multiplicity of identities, breaking free of the fiction of a 'unified self', to reveal the complex and contradictory constitution of a black woman's subjectivity within a colonial and patriarchal society.

(1995)

NOTES

1 Introduction to *Past the Last Post: Theorizing Post-Colonialism and Post Modernism*, edited by Ian Adam and Helen Tiffin (London: Harvester Wheatsheaf, 1991), p. x.
2 Linda Hutcheon, *A Theory of Parody: The Teachings of Twentieth Century Art Forms* (London: Routledge, 1985), p. 8.
3 Rhonda Cobham-Sander, 'The Creative Writer and West Indian Society: Jamaica 1900–1950' (unpublished PhD dissertation, University of St Andrews, 1981), p. 218.

Mervyn Morris

On Reading Louise Bennett, Seriously

I believe Louise Bennett to be a poet. By many people whose taste
and judgement on other matters I respect she is regarded more or
less as a local joke; a good, high-spirited joke, but, in the end, only
a joke. I believe it is time we took Louise Bennett more seriously;
and the purpose of this essay is to suggest literary reasons for doing
so . . .

I am told (I think on good authority) that Miss Bennett had been
writing and speaking her poems for many years before she won
general acceptance even as an entertainer. The Jamaican middle-class
was slow to acknowledge an interest in dialect which represented for
most of them the speech-forms of a lower class from whom they
wished to be distinguished. Our political and social history since
about 1940 confirms the assertion that the Jamaican middle-class
have moved only very gradually towards an awareness of Jamaican
identity; we have moved gradually from an unthinking acceptance of
a British heritage to a more critical awareness of our origins and
a greater willingness to acknowledge African elements of our past as
part of our national personality . . .

Gradually, Louise Bennett won middle-class acceptance; though
one may well wonder for what reasons. Is it not possible that many
middle-class audiences laugh at dialect verse or drama for uncomfortable psychological reasons? My own observation suggests this. If
one reads Louise Bennett to middle-class school children they are
apt to laugh not only at wit and humour but at the language itself.
The language which their maids and yardboys use is not yet accepted
simply as one of our Jamaican ways of speech.

I write particularly of the middle-class because it is that class which
must necessarily form at present the mass of a Jamaican reading-
public, and which has so far been the bulk of our theatre audiences.
It is for that class mainly, that Louise Bennett has so far written and
performed.

The middle-class, then, came to accept Louise Bennett as an
entertainer; they bought her poems – her early volumes are now
unpurchasable – and they laughed delightedly (or in embarrassment)
at her performances.

[194]

It was not perhaps fair to expect that many of those who enjoyed Louise Bennett should have thought much about literary value. But one might surely have expected this of those who read other poetry. They were not many; and most of these few were busy over-rating the borrowed sensibilities and fake poems of Tom Redcam, Claude McKay and . . . J.E. Clare McFarlane. The Poetry League was formed; they crowned McFarlane Poet-Laureate. McFarlane himself wrote an absurd little volume called *A Literature in the Making* in which he praised fulsomely a number of poets who, whatever their merits, scarcely deserved the adulation heaped upon them . . .

Anyone who has read *A Treasury of Jamaican Poetry* (edited by Clare McFarlane) may well wonder whether the Redcam poems chosen do justice to such talent.

There are some interesting (though one would be foolish to say 'great') poems in that anthology; notably, competent work by Philip Sherlock ('Pocomania', 'A Beauty Too'), Roger Mais ('All Men Come to the Hills'), H.D. Carberry ('Nature') and Adolphe Roberts ('The Cat'). But this anthology of Jamaican poetry, some of it startlingly inept, finds no place for Louise Bennett.

To *Caribbean Quarterly* Vol. 7 No. 3, Dr R.J. Owens contributed a convincing judicial article on 'West Indian Poetry' . . . Apart from its faint praise for Walcott, the most remarkable thing about the article is that it does not mention Louise Bennett, even although it offers some interesting comments on the vernacular and poetry. The article was based primarily on the two anthologies of West Indian Poetry, *Kyk-over-al* No. 22 (1957), and *Caribbean Quarterly* Vol. 5 No. 3 (1958); neither of these anthologies included any Louise Bennett . . .

It is in the foreword to *Laugh With Louise* (1961) that one finds a member of . . . Jamaican cultural establishment saying plainly that he thinks Miss Bennett valuable. Mr Robert Verity writes:

Louise Bennett, by the authenticity of her dialect verse, has given sensitive and penetrating artistic expression to our National Character. Her sympathetic, humorous and humanitarian observation of Jamaicans and our way of life, has been given literary expression in a medium which is 'popular' in the original and authentic meaning of that much abused word.

Her work has constituted an invaluable contribution to the discovery and development of an indigenous culture and her verses are valid social documents reflecting the way we think and feel and live.

That seems to me something approaching justice ...

In the *Independence Anthology of Jamaican Literature* (edited by A.L. Hendriks and Cedric Linto) Miss Bennett does appear. But she is not regarded as a poet. The poetry section does not include Miss Bennett. Her place is at the back of the book tucked away under 'Humour', keeping company with the hard-working jocosity of Mr. A.E.T. Henry.

Louise Bennett, then, has been accepted as an entertainer but, with the glowing (but, as to her being a poet, slightly equivocal) exception of Mr Verity, not as a poet.

I do not believe that Louise Bennett is a considerable poet. But a poet, and, in her best work, a better poet than most other Jamaican writers, she certainly is. She does not offer her readers any great insight into the nature of life or human experience but she recreates human experience vividly, delightfully and intelligently. She is rarely pretentious – the most common fault in West Indian poetry; she is not derived from other poets – she has her own interesting voice; and she is invariably sane ...

The form most often chosen by Miss Bennett is dramatic monologue. This is hardly surprising in a poet who often performs her work. She writes for the voice and the ear, and when her poems are expertly performed something more, movement, added ...

[In] The Candy-Seller [she] is addressing a number of different people in a number of different tones of voice ... As in a Browning monologue, the entire dramatic situation is made clear without the direct intervention of the author. The whole poem convinces; it has a vitality that seems perfectly to match the imagined context ...

Sometimes the situation is presented through the poet as story-teller rather than directly through characters. A good example of this is 'Dry Foot Bwoy' in which the affected speech of a boy just home from England is dramatically contrasted with the story-teller's Jamaican dialect ...

In some of her poems Louise Bennett is not just a story-teller but is herself the central character. 'Television' is an example of this ...

Louise Bennett ... is always attacking pretension by laughter, and sometimes by hard logic. An example of logic would be 'Back to Africa' in which an argument is ruthlessly followed through ...

It takes a shape very eighteenth-century in its careful balance, the balance helping to point the strictly logical operation of a keen intelligence . . .

It is not my main purpose in this essay to demonstrate Miss Bennett's weaknesses, but it may be well to mention some of her problems or faults and to attempt to define her limitations.

I think her most central difficulty is choice of subject. Many of her poems are a sort of comic-verse-journalism; she is quick to tackle the topical . . . One willingly says good-bye to numerous poems about new Governors, new pantomimes, Paul Robeson's visit, a Test match victory, and so on, where interest has not survived the topicality of the subject. As in the same periods as her very topical poems she wrote others of more lasting interest, we can hardly complain: we can only regret that so much of the journalism has been published in book form. It would be a service to her readers if Miss Bennett would present a Collected Poems, dropping all the ephemera and choosing the best of the others . . .

To trace Louise Bennett's development is interesting. She develops, I think, from the high-spirited monologist to a more purposeful thinker writing in dialect: it is not for nothing that the mature irony of 'Independence' or the logic of 'Back to Africa' are recent, and the best dramatic monologues are early . . .

A weakness, particularly in the early poems, is for direct and unsubtle moralising. In the later poems any sentimentality or tendency to moralise is usually redeemed by irony or wit . . .

Louise Bennett, then, is a poet of serious merit, although like all poets, she has her limitations. Like most poets she is, I have tried to show, developing. And she is so much more rewarding a poet than many to whom we in Jamaica give the name, that it seems reasonable to expect more of those who claim an interest in poetry to give her more attention. She is sane; throughout, her poems imply that sound common sense and generous love and understanding of people are worthwhile assets. Jamaican dialect is, of course, limiting (in more senses than one); but within its limitations Louise Bennett works well. Hers is a precious talent. We ought to read her more seriously; for she is worth it.

(1967)

Gordon Rohlehr

Images of Men and Women in the 1930s Calypsoes

FROM GAYELLE TO ROAD TO BARRACK ROOM

Kalinda songs of the nineteenth and early twentieth centuries glorified the prowess of stickfighters and were primarily concerned with the courage and skill of men in a situation of physical encounter. Female stickfighters did exist, some indeed achieving legendary status, but the world of the batonnier was predominantly male, and its songs were a celebration of heroic conflict which was essentially male. Elder (1969: 91, 110) mentions the prevalence of female banter songs, or carisoes, which were sung in the intervals between stickfights. There are also several references in nineteenth century newspapers to the 'obscene' dancing and 'profane' singing of women, who then, as now, were the focal point of much moralizing commentary.

Elder suggests that the curtailment of stickfighting activities after the 1884 Peace Preservation Ordinance deprived the kalinda chantwels of a context for their battle songs, and led them to appropriate the feminine cariso mode of banter, gossip and abuse. There may be some truth in this, though many of the qualities of the cariso also existed in the kalinda and in the earlier African song forms from which both derived. After the 1880s, the song – kalinda, cariso or belair – became increasingly and almost exclusively a form for the fiercely competing egos of male chantwels, and by the turn of the century virtually all the singers were male. It is possible that the continuous pressure of 'respectable' public opinion against 'jamette' women in Carnival, along with the gradual emergence of orderly well-dressed and well-behaved 'social unions', could have led to the withdrawal of the old time 'matador' woman into the background. Bands ... consciously sought to abolish the image of scandal and scurrility which had surrounded earlier jamettes ...

The famous Sans Humanité of the Oratorical period (1860–1920) was characterized by the fierce and fanciful verbal conflict of singers such as Lord Executor, The Duke of Marlborough, Norman le Blanc and Senior Inventor, in a context where the calypso singer acquired great status among his peers as acknowledged 'man-of-words' ... What marks the differences between the 1900–1920 and the

1920–1940 periods is the fact that to the delight in a purely verbal self-inflation were added two elements: a growing concern for social and political issues and the calypsonian's self-celebration as a 'sweet man', a macho man in 'control' of several women, or a man who lived in the barrack-yard and could therefore impart intimate knowledge of its 'comesse', scandal and 'bacchanal.'

The latter concern involved a certain domestication of the heroic persona, in that the perceived arena of encounter within the fictional world of the calypso, which had once been the stickfighter's gayelle or the road, and had between 1900 and 1920 been the bamboo and cocoyea tent, now also became the barrack-room, and would later with a few singers also become the bedroom. One lacked privacy, space or silence in the barrack-yard. Life was a perpetual public drama, in which the thin and incomplete partition separating rooms, made one privy to the secrets, the sex life, the eating habits and the peculiarities of one's neighbour and gave him or her a similar familiarity with yours. This environment was the breeding ground of the 'ballad' calypso.

The barrack room of the 1920s had altered little from its 1880s predecessor and despite the Slum Clearance Ordinance of 1935, barrack-yards continued to exist and to provide calypsonians with themes, well into the 1950s ... The protagonist of the typical 'barrack-yard calypso' is a 'macho', a peeping Tom, a gossip or simply a reporter of incidents which he always claims to have personally witnessed ... The stereotype of the inquisitive and contentious neighbour becomes soundly established by calypsoes [sic] ... and is later reinforced by a series of plays set in the barrack-yard.

The shift in the locus of encounter from gayelle and road to barrack-room, was accompanied by a transformation in the form of calypso, from the litanic kalinda which formally incorporated the tension and shared reciprocity between individual and group, through Sans Humanite whose fixed formulaic melody made it possible for singers to concentrate on the improvisation of picong to the ballad form, where at last the calypso became the vehicle for narratives about the everyday lives of ordinary Trinidadians.

Calypsonians were now confronted with the challenge to create fictions from observed domestic situations, current events read of in the newspapers, and rumours. Scandals from the lives of the ruling elite or burgeoning middle class provided a particular choice source of calypso fiction; one that was fed by gossip-mongers from among the very middle class who enjoyed the indecent exposure of their own group to public scrutiny.

In the process of fictionalizing domestic lower-class situations, calypsonians brought into focus the confrontation of males and females, in a context where both were battling for economic survival. Never before has this confrontation received such close, varied and extensive scrutiny as in the post-1920s period. While the lyrics of most of the songs between 1920 and the early thirties have been lost, there was substantial recording of calypsoes [sic] between 1934 and the late forties ... [which] afford us our first really sustained look into the life-style, attitudes, confusions, contradictions, weaknesses, fantasies, grim realities, tough resilience, courage, emerging humour, dreams and strength of the ordinary folk, as perceived through the fictions of fifteen full-time singers.

They tell these stories not only as observers, but as participants in a life which had many facets and dimensions. This does not, of course, mean that these calypsoes [sic] are autobiographical. Like the emerging novels and short stories of the period, they were a fictionalizing of observed or imagined social reality, and one must always be conscious of the element of making, of craftsmanship, and all that this involves. There are often distances between the eye or I that perceives and the fiction which it creates out of what it has seen or imagined. The impersonal, dramatic 'I' provides the narrative voice of many calypsoes [sic] of this period. While there are points of coincidence between the calypsonian and his persona, the artist and his mask, such coincidence should never be simply assumed.

THE CONTEXT OF HUNGER

We are never far away from the context of hunger, unemployment, economic depression, worker militancy, desperation, struggle and sheer survivalism out of which the fictions of the thirties were shaped. This context provides the frame for the domestic encounter of male and female ...

THE INDIAN WOMAN AND THE INDIAN FEAST

In 1930 the Duke of Normandy sang about his affair with an Indian woman in a calypso of which Beginner could remember only two lines: 'After she gave me parata / She had me cooraja.' From that time the Indian woman was generally presented against the background of the Indian feast, and many calypsoes [sic] in which such women appear are really not about the women at all, but about masked inter-racial conflict, in which the feast becomes a point of, or arena of ethnic confrontation. In Atilla's *Dookanii* (1939), the one calypso where the singer attempts a portrait, she is presented as an exotic: ideal lovable but unattainable:

> *She was the prettiest thing I'd ever met*
> *Her resplendent beauty I can't forget*
> *With her wonderful, dark bewitching eyes*
> *I used to gaze in them hypnotized . . .*
> *She was exotic, kind and loving too*
> *All her charms I could never describe to you . . .*

In Executor's *My Indian Girl Love* (1939) the Indian woman is also named Dookanii . . . He meets her while he is singing at a tent in Caroni during the *Hosein* festival:

> *It was on a night of the Hosein*
> *That gala Indian fete I mean to say . . .*
> *An Indian man was holding a piece of wire*
> *One passing right through the fire*
> *One had a ram goat he was killing*
> *With rum their bodies they flinging*
> *Songs laughter and yelling*
> *All the time her love was proving.*

The calypso is true to form. The many calypsoes [sic] of the period which deal with festivals or religious rites (e.g. Shango, Baptists) usually focus on their exotic externals, their 'eccentric' features, from which they might try to extract humour . . .

Dookanii is little more than a feature of the exotic scene and it is against this background that she declares her love . . . Dookanii's speech, which is stereotypical East Indian pidgin, establishes her identity as an unsophisticated rural maiden and would probably have evoked laughter from Executor's audience. The rapid arrangement of marriage in which, in contravention of all codes, Dookanii proposed, secures a signed contract of agreement and then tells her father, would also have struck Executor's audience as absurd ...

Humour in inter-racial situations usually masks even from the joker himself the underlying seriousness of the issue which is being joked about. The stereotype of the Indians was that of a people who wanted to preserve ethnic purity, and were totally against its violation, particularly via the marriage or sexual cohabitation of Indian woman and Creole man. Long before, the 1930s the stereotype had emerged of the jealous Indian man – father, brother, or husband – defending with sharp cutlass the honour of daughter, sister or wife, or saving face after having been cuckolded by chopping up his woman and her lover. Executor deliberately excludes this type of possibility in his calypso; but it undoubtedly underlies future calypsoes [sic] on the same theme, such as Dictator's *Moonia* (early 1950s), Fighter's *Indian Wedding* (1957) and Sparrow's *Maharajin's Sister* (1983).

Fighter's *Indian Wedding* ... merits comparison with Executor's *My Indian Girl Love*. Its protagonist, an Afro-Creole, attends all Indian receptions where, disguised as a Hindu, he sings Hindu melodies. So skilled is he at both singing and disguise that he is mistaken one Phagwa night for a true Hindu, entrances the gathering, and is offered an Indian girl in marriage. This is where the disguise slips. He is discovered to be Black ('Hoota! Hoota! Black man, Hoota!') and given a severe beating ('Awee gwine marsaray you beef'). He can't escape, but doesn't seem to mind, since his only interest in the festivals has been the food.

Where Executor excludes the idea of hostile encounter from his calypso, Fighter, coming out of the Guyana of 1957, where 'Aphan Jaat' ('Our own [race] for own [race]') was a current political slogan among supporters of the Jagan faction of the split People's Progressive Party (PPP), assumes that it is a 'given' in his world. Yet, a similar hostility existed between indentured Indian workers and the Creole community of Executor's day. The oral testimony of one such worker indicates that East Indian workers considered their Sundays as liberated space. They would then gather to sing, dance and read the Ramayana, and would beat anyone who tried to interrupt these occasions. Much of their aggression was directed against Blacks who would try to join in the fete ...

Such segregation applied even though Indians and Creoles (kirwal) might work side by side, digging canals, say, on the plantation ...

Executor, then ignores the reality of conflict inherent in the situation, while Fighter engages more deeply and less indirectly with the awkwardness and pain of Afro-Indian social relations. His humour includes the mask of a triumphant insouciance by which one celebrates a hostile and deprecatory stereotype which one knows the Other holds of one. Fighter's protagonist, threatened with death, flippantly declares:

> *Ah say 'Well if allyuh kill me,*
> *I would like to bury by dat tray o' dhalpourie'* . . .

Fighter 'accepts' and celebrates the stereotype of the Afro-Creole as glutton. This is certainly not because he is unaware of its underlying aggressive intent. He enters the situation with a full understanding of the possibility of hostile encounter. He has to mask in order to attend the feast; he will be beaten if discovered and killed if he interferes with any of the women. So he knowingly assumes the role of trickster in order to penetrate into the secret or private lifestyle of the Other and to consume their dhalpourie, and maybe marry the princess too, which is the price they must pay for having a different and exclusive lifestyle.

His behaviour follows the shape of archetypal myth. Anansi is depicted as gate-crasher, disguiser and trickster. He is also frequently threatened with violence, when it is discovered that an uninvited and undesirable guest has found his way into the feast . . . The laughter of Fighter's protagonist at himself as glutton, hero, and successful then unmasked trickster contains an unconscious criticism of the hostility of the Other, as well as an unconscious desire to be accepted by the Other.

This is counterbalanced by a conscious rejection of the Other's otherness. We see this in both Executor's calypso and Fighter's. In the one Indian pidgin is parodied, in the other a hotchpotch of presumably 'Hindi' words is rattled off in a fashion calculated to evoke laughter:

> *Mahabir, mahaba, puja koray* . . .
> *Cobanay talkarie* . . .

But ridicule, and even apparently gentler forms of humour are, particularly in the case of competitive ethnoses, forms of sublimated aggression, the counterpart to corresponding aggression and contempt, in the Other. As we have seen, such contempt could co-exist with the gesture of welcome and goodwill: the East Indian feast. Africans knew this from experience and included this knowledge, either openly or in disguised form, in their calypsoes [sic]. This is why calypsoes about real or imagined affairs between African men and Indian women tell us very little about the women, and much more about the open or secret confrontation of the two ethnoses. The women don't really exist as persons, but rather as omens of the neurosis which surrounds the idea of inter-racial contact; a neurosis which involved on the one hand fear of violation and on the other fear of violent reprisal . . .

SUMMARY

This study . . . views male/female conflict . . . as the logical product of the context of survivalism in which both men and women were placed.

Its subjects are landless urban dwellers whose only resource is their labour, in a period when the labour market is contracting and wages are low and undergoing erosion. Calypsoes [sic] from the thirties reflect the asperities of a culture of survivalism in which a shrewd self-centredness in the quest for food is, perhaps, the most basic ingredient in human relationships. People are loved not for themselves but for what they can provide. The provider, whether male or female, tends to regard the dependant as a parasite, and to seek to exercise absolute proprietory rights over the dependent. Given the harshness of economic circumstance, either the provider or the dependent may renege on the understood marital contract, a situation which inevitably increases tension and conflict in the relationship . . .

A marginalized people on the edge of the economy still share certain ideals of bourgeois society, particularly those which state that the male should be provider and the female housewife. Calypsoes [sic] tend to reveal the inapplicability of these ideals to marginalized people, as well as the shattering of the male ego in situations where the man cannot fulfil his ideal role . . . Several male strategies of ego-retrieval were examined, including the creation of a fantasy world in which the good life is achieved; the projection of a mask of machismo; the recourse to 'robustness' or violence in relationships with women; the use of wit and humour to restore the ego by means of the reduction of the threatening Other.

The study recognizes the presence of the 'rebel woman' who refuses to be taken advantage of, seeks recourse to law and sometimes physically beats her men, or expels them from the home.

The study recognizes the limitations of the data. Virtually all the singers of that era were men, though Lady Trinidad did record her *Advice to Every Young Woman* (1937) warning young women not to be taken in by the guile of faithless young men. There were, clearly, many women's stories needing to be fictionalized from the women's point of view in the same way that the male calypsonians were presenting observed reality from male perspectives. One has, therefore, to imagine the presence of an unheard voice answering the men ... Tiger in *Lazy Man* and *Miss Marie's Advice*, Growler in *Boysie Darling*, Caresser in *Don't Knock Me Joe* and Lion in *Sweet Emily*, all try to let us hear something of this voice. But in these calypsoes [sic], women's alternative presence is reflected more in what they do – quarrel, evict, refuse, reduce, rebel – than in what they say ...

[H]ow men dealt with women was an extension of how they dealt with each other: with a comic reductivity whose vehicle was sharp, harsh vituperation or refined insult; in a spirit of confrontation in which there were rigidly demarcated sex role barriers that were not to be crossed; with a sense of ego perpetually under threat of attack. If other men – from stickfighters and horner men to resurrected old Casanovas and crafty policemen – were the Other to a Self which was always under attack, women were the most extreme example of the Other. They needed to be contained, controlled:

(i) by stereotyped roles which men sought to define and in which they tried to fix women
(ii) by mockery or abuse of those women who either failed or refused to be confined in those stereotypes or roles ...

[S]ome of the main roots of an emerging tradition of the comic in Trinidad, are to be found in gender and ethnic conflict.

(1988)

1950–65

Introduction

Literature of the boom

The burgeoning literary production of this period, often referred to as the 'boom period' in Caribbean literature, was, paradoxically, largely a function of the exile of a significant number of Caribbean writers to the metropoli of Europe, with London fast becoming the 'literary capital' of the West Indies. The phenomenon of exile was and is not exclusive to the Caribbean or to this period, as Lamming points out (**1960**: 24) and **Sealey**'s short story (**1958**) usefully illustrates. However, it is productive to grasp the wider historical context of migration in this period. British subjects from the Caribbean and elsewhere in the former Empire were actively recruited to Britain to provide labour in certain (particularly service) industries after the Second World War and were attracted by the promise of better training and employment prospects in the 'motherland' more generally. This migratory pull and the establishment of a growing diasporic population in Europe intensified debate concerning Caribbean cultural production. Important questions were raised regarding the viability (or desirability) of a Caribbean literature produced in Europe and consumed by largely European audiences, and the long-term implications of the exodus of so many of the Caribbean's most promising writers.

Finding West Indian identity in Britain

The writers themselves gave a range of related reasons for exile. Lamming (**1960**) and **Marson** (**1949**), who came to England in 1950 and 1932 respectively, both speak of the crippling devaluation of the

writer within the Caribbean and of the need to give greater 'encouragement [to] our writers' (Marson 1949). Others, such as **Brathwaite**,
reflected, with striking echoes of earlier commentators (**Gomes 1974**:
16, **Swanzy 1956**: 267):

> The West Indies could be written about and explored. But only from
> the vantage point outside the West Indies. It was no point going
> back. No writer could live in that stifling atmosphere of middle class
> materialism and philistinism.
>
> (Brathwaite 1970: 37)

Ironically, Brathwaite was to do precisely this, disillusioned by his
experiences as a Cambridge undergraduate and by metropolitan attitudes to his work:

> I felt that I had arrived; I was possessing the landscape. But I turned
> to find that my 'fellow Englishmen' were not particularly prepossessed
> with me . . . the Cambridge magazines didn't take my poems. Or rather,
> they only took those which had West Indian – to me, 'exotic' – flavour.
> I felt neglected and misunderstood.
>
> (Brathwaite 1970: 37)

Even those who did not return to live in the Caribbean, such as V.S.
Naipaul, express this ambivalence: acknowledging the positive bene-
fits afforded to the Caribbean writer in London and an 'indebtedness'
to the wider English literary tradition but simultaneously feeling that
one exists in a 'kind of limbo', a 'refugee . . . always peripheral' to
the same (Naipaul 1974: 122).

In a particularly sardonic passage of his seminal analysis of the
writer-in-exile, *The Pleasures of Exile*, from which we include an
extract in this section, Lamming writes:

> The [names of the] West Indian novelists living in a state of chosen
> exile . . . make temporary noise in the right West Indian circles. Their
> books have become handy broomsticks which the new nationalist will
> wave at a foreigner who asks the rude question: 'What can your people
> do except doze?' . . . They are afraid of returning . . . because they feel
> that sooner or later they will be ignored in and by a society about
> which they have been at once articulate and authentic . . . In spite of
> all that happened in the last ten years, I doubt that any one of the
> West Indian writers could truly say that he would be happy to go
> back.
>
> (Lamming 1960: 46–7)

However, the location of so many Caribbean writers in London at this time ultimately enabled a clearer sense of a developing Caribbean literature and West Indian consciousness to be developed. As Lamming reflected in 1960:

> No Barbadian, no Trinidadian, no St Lucian, no islander from the West Indies sees himself as a West Indian until he encounters another islander in a foreign country ... In this sense most West Indians of my generation were born in England.
>
> (Lamming 1960: 214)

As Susheila Nasta has commented: despite the difficulties of 'com[ing] to terms with the idea of London as an illusion ... a dream built on the foundations of the colonial myth ... ironically, it was London that created the possibility, in many cases, of a bridge between the past ... and the present, which posited a strong need to establish West Indian "cultural pedigree"' (Nasta 1995: 80). However, there were still notes of caution and uncertainty in some contemporary comments: back in the Caribbean, Marson hoped for 'a real, and not just a mythical cultural Renaissance' in Caribbean literature (Marson 1949: 7). Henry Swanzy, producer of the influential BBC *Caribbean Voices* programme, acknowledged the difficulties of 'defin[ing] a trend, among so many scattered units, at such an early stage' (Swanzy 1956: 270) and expressed some doubt about the 'lesser names beneath the peaks' (273) in his West Indian contribution to a survey of world literature. Similarly, Barbadian writer and long term editor of *Bim* Frank Collymore reflected:

> What the future holds for West Indian writing remains to be seen. The potential is there, encouragement has been much more notice-able in recent years, the awareness of nationalism has done much to overcome the note of protest of 'colonialism' which was so noticeable in the writing of twenty years ago ... these ... are hopeful signs but against them must be matched the realization that ... Until ... a large leisured class interested in the arts emerges, the dedicated writer or artist must seek a living abroad.
>
> (1960: 123–4)

In his *The Pleasures of Exile*, published in the same year, Lamming discusses the lack of a Caribbean audience and the sense of 'in-adequacy' and 'irrelevance of function' consequently felt by many Caribbean writers in their own societies. In his emphasis on 'imported culture', the transfer of ideas or expectations as well as people in a longer colonial history of unequal 'exchange', he anticipates the similarly polemical cultural criticism of **Sylvia Wynter** later in the decade (**1968, 1969**). Although Lamming's criticism is frequently idiosyncratic, this key text accurately reflects the dominant critical concerns of the period.

Language and the 'problem of idiom'

As **Lawson Welsh** (**1991**) argues in this section, British reviews of Caribbean writing published in London during this period frequently frame Caribbean writing as 'problematic' to approach. Chief amongst these was what one reviewer termed 'the problem of idiom' – the tension between a desire to make literary use of Caribbean creoles and the need to cater for a non-Caribbean metropolitan audience. This issue found particular resonance in reviews of **Selvon**'s novels, which are characterized by a radical experimentation with creole as the language of narration, not merely of dialogue. Many of the English reviewers of Selvon in the 1950s and 1960s were simply unable to perceive his ability to create a unique literary language, neither purely creole/Caribbean nor purely 'standard'/English: a 'modified dialect' achieved by assimilating features of both language varieties into his style. The fact that compromise was seen as culturally unacceptable is witnessed by the way in which Selvon has since justified his use of an adapted rather than a naturalistic dialect in his novels, by expressing a conviction that: 'I could [not] have said what I wanted to say without modifying the dialect ... the pure dialect would have been obscure and difficult to understand ... Greek to a lot of people' (Selvon 1982: 60).

However, many reviewers persisted in the belief that Selvon retained his Caribbean idiom only for reasons of literary exoticism. One reviewer warned:

> Unless he narrows the range artificially or returns to the West Indies he has no alternative. The problem of idiom can only increase as the circle of his identity expands.
>
> (Anon 1958: 57)

Ironically, Selvon's later novel *Moses Ascending* (1975) was to demonstrate exactly the opposite: a widening of linguistic and literary range by the use of an experimental idiom which synthesized a wide range of spoken-language varieties and written styles, successfully subverting, in the process, the hegemonies of more standardized and 'traditional' forms.

Subject matter: strangeness and exotica

Many British reviews of Caribbean writing in this period foreground the perceived strangeness and exotica of the literature and return to a number of stereotypes which limited the possibilities for critical appreciation of other aspects of this writing (see Anon 1952, 1955, 1957, 1958a, 1958b, 1960a, 1960b, and Lawson Welsh 1991). The West Indian's perspective on London was deemed so alien by one reviewer that in reference to Andrew Salkey's (1960a) novel of diasporic experience, *Escape to An Autumn Pavement*, he could comment:

> Mr Salkey, concentrating on the impact of London on an educated Jamaican succeeds in making parts of that city as foreign to the English as Babylon and Buenos Aires – but then today they are.
>
> (Anon 1960: 15)

Ironically, this was the whole point to this and other novels such as Selvon (1956) and Lamming (1954) which dealt with the realities of cross-cultural encounter in the 'mother country'. Descriptions of the loneliness, alienation and disorientation of the newly arrived immigrant finding his bearings in a city at once familiar (part of the mythology of empire) and strange were the strengths of these narratives.

However, reviews in themselves were not the most important factor in ensuring the continued promotion of new and emergent literary voices from the Caribbean. Henry Swanzy was amongst those to suggest the ironies of this critical attention without a commensurate commitment to publishing short works, in the English press:

> I hope that . . . as it is not so impossible in these days, a really good anthology of West Indian writing of the modern age is made . . . In the meantime, I should like to suggest that newspapers show the same alacrity in printing poems and short stories as they show in reprinting the criticism of writers in England.
>
> (1949: 28)

'The power of the provincial'

Other contemporary commentators mounted a persuasive counter-criticism of the apparent necessity for Caribbean writers to exile themselves in this way. **Derek Walcott** proved the exception to the norm in this period, establishing himself with three poetry collections (1948, 1962, 1965) and in 1959 founding the Trinidad Theatre Workshop, a significant outlet for his and other Caribbean dramatists' work (Walcott 1950, 1952, 1954, 1956, 1957, 1958, 1959, 1967), which then was successfully performed in London, Canada and the United States. Based in Trinidad for most of this period, Walcott termed the contrary pull to remain in the Caribbean 'the power of the provincial'. Another example of the powerfully provincial writer is that of Guyanese **A.J. Seymour**, editor of the journal *Kyk-over-al* between 1945 and 1961, who in 1951 launched the Miniature Poet Series (an offprint of Jamaica's Pioneer Press which ran to 1955), with the aim to publish in the Caribbean new and established Caribbean poets. Indeed, with its 1950 special edition 'The Literary Adventure of the West Indies' (2.10. 1950), 1952 *Anthology of West Indian Poetry* and 1954 *Anthology of Guianese Poetry*, *Kyk* under Seymour's guidance was a crucial literary platform.

We include a selection of poems from another very important figure who 'remained' in the Caribbean: Martin Carter's **Poems of Resistance from British Guiana (1954)**. Carter was a member of the People's Progressive Party-led Government which was dissolved by the British authorities in October 1953 on the grounds of a feared 'communist subversion of the government and a dangerous crisis both in public order and economic affairs' (cited in Latin America Bureau 1984: 33). An interim administration replaced the elected government and a number of former members and activists, including Carter, were imprisoned. It was in this context that many of the *Poems of Resistance* were written.

Carter's work may also be read within a larger protest tradition in Caribbean literature. Asein, for example, has argued that a trajectory can be traced from early sites of textual resistance to colonialism, and criticism of racial and social injustice, through some of **Claude McKay**'s work (largely that produced in exile, in America), to the poetry of **George Campbell** in 1940s Jamaica. Carter's poetry shares something of Campbell's social commitment and deep humanism and he similarly 'identifi[es] himself with the disinherited poor in an a-racial universalism' of approach (Asein 1972: 44). However, his 'performance' of his poems on the streets of Georgetown to large and attentive audiences and the hostile reception of his most politicized, protest-orientated work in some quarters (see Asein 1972; 45), link him with later Caribbean artists such as the radical and most politicized dub poets of the 1970s. *Poems of Resistance* have been described as 'basically situational; intensely personal in the exclusiveness of the private experiences and responses, but representative and contemporary in their stunning reflection of a bleak slice of Guyanese history' (Asein 1972: 44).

One of the fiercest critics of the writer-in-exile was Margaret Blundell. She reiterated *The Beacon*'s earlier call for the establishment of a local literature, in a polemical piece which strikingly anticipates **Wynter's** similar call in the late 1960s (**1968, 1969**):

> Can a people achieve a real literature if it only produces for export? A society produces writers and artists of ability and imagination. The society can provide its authors with the raw material for their arts, but can the finished work continue to be valid when it is continually played to an alien audience ... After ten years in exile, writing about the Caribbean of ten years ago, the writer is in danger of creating the equivalent of the stage Irishman, a sort of never-never calypso man of Caribbean fiction designed to amuse the fog-bound silent Englishmen.
>
> (Blundell 1966: 164)

Like **Lamming (1971)**, Blundell draws attention to the potential 'problems of audience' created by this situation especially in relation to language:

> Not enough of our poets speak to us through our own vernacular. Inevitably when they are moulded, consciously and unconsciously by far wider reading than most literate West Indians, there is a gap in communication ... Sometimes the acclaim of an absentee and largely urban audience makes the situation worse as the intellectual qualities of poetry are over-emphasized at the expense of the more imaginative and intuitive qualities. *There is scarcely any local West Indian audience to speak to in this literary idiom.*
>
> (Blundell 1966: 167)

Indeed, considering the allure of the metropolis which so affected the dynamics of Caribbean literary production during this period, it is important to note the level of commitment which some writers and cultural activists demonstrated to non-colonial traditions and institutions. Probably the most ardent example of these 'culturally corrective' movements is Rastafarianism, which in its adaption and promotion of African cultural forms offered a very different notion of a Caribbean cultural trajectory to the canonical in its peak years of 1963 and 1964 (see Brathwaite 1979a). Novels which most directly represent the Rastafarian experience include Wynter (1962), Mais 1953, 1954) and Patterson (1964).

The Caribbean Little Magazines

In the Caribbean, the inadequacies of external criticism and, for some critics, the palpable danger of Caribbean writing being 'annexed' to the English canon, did not go unnoticed. The commitment to 'estab-lish[ing] an authoritative regional criticism [as] an almost fundamental corollary to the establishment of a regional literature' (Allis 1986: 1) had been a salient feature of the Caribbean Little Magazine or cultural journal since the heady days of *The Beacon*. Journal activity was particularly intense in the 1940s and 1950s with a flush of new journals emerging in the British West Indies, buoyed up by growing nationalist sentiment and independence movements in various terri-tories. Although it is true that a number of these journals did not outlive the 1962 breakdown of hopes for an enduring West Indian Federation, (e.g. Jamaican *Focus*, edited by Edna Manley, spanned only four issues between 1943 and 1960 and Guyanese *Kyk-over-al*, edited by A.J. Seymour, launched in 1945, folded in 1961) it is impor-tant not to limit any evaluation of the Caribbean literary magazines' contribution to a nationalist framework. Indeed, a number of jour-nals, including *Bim*, which Lamming described as 'a kind of oasis in that lonely desert of mass indifference, and educated middle-class treachery' (1960: 41), were to outlive this period and continue to play a key role in subsequent decades.

The task of promoting Guyanese writers and a wider Caribbean literature to which *Kyk-over-al* had been so committed, was taken over by a new government magazine *Kaie*, the official organ of the Guyanese National History and Arts Council in 1965. In Trinidad between 1964 and 1966 Clifford Sealy edited *Voices*, a literary maga-zine important in launching a series of younger writers. In Jamaica, interdisciplinary journals such as *Caribbean Quarterly* were launched by the Extra-Mural Department of the University of the West Indies in 1949, and the enormously important *Jamaica Journal* by the Institute of Jamaica (also a publishing outlet and library resource) in 1961. Barbadian-based *Bim*, which Lamming (1971) discusses, published some important short fiction during the 1950s and early 1960s of which we include two pieces in this volume (**Napier 1951, Sealey 1958**). In its fifty-year history (with some breaks in the 1970s) *Bim* has featured the work of key writers such as Michael Anthony, Walcott, John Hearne, Lamming, Brathwaite, and Timothy Callender. Although its literary inclusions have tended to be less adventurous. and radical than younger little journals such as the Jamaican-based *Savacou* it has, like *Savacou* (Journal of the Caribbean Arts Movement) from 1974, published what have frequently become seminal critical essays on Caribbean literary and cultural issues. Notable among these are essays by **Brathwaite** (1959, 1960, 1961, 1967a, 1967b, 1968, 1977a, 1977b, 1978a, 1979a) and **Gordon Rohlehr** (1972a, 1972b, 1973, 1975). One of *Bim*'s distinctive features is that it has expanded the geographical range of its writers and writing to include most of the Anglophone Caribbean whilst still retaining its characters as a 'regional magazine', without the negative connotations of parochialism which this might imply.

BBC Caribbean Voices

One sympathetic and liberal ear in London was **Henry Swanzy's** at the BBC and because of this, many aspiring Caribbean poets and writers submitted scripts to him for broadcast back to the Caribbean. The BBC *Caribbean Voices* programme (originally conceived by **Una Marson** in 1939 as 'calling the West Indies' for the purpose of relaying messages back home from those West Indians on active service) was to become a supportive forum for many Caribbean writers between 1945 and 1951. The programme formed a network between writers in (and from) different islands based in London and in the Caribbean. As Swanzy the editor, reflected at the time:

> The main value of a programme like *Caribbean Voices* is to provide an outlet for writers who would otherwise be mute, a means of inter-communication with like minds, and, if anything so sordid can be mentioned, money, for it must not be forgotten that the BBC is

subsidising West Indian writing to the tune of £1,500 a year in programme fees alone. It is for this reason that we encourage 'local' writing, descriptive and otherwise, as well as for the more obvious reason that people write and speak best about the things they have made most their own ... the time allowed is of course not enough to build up a cumulative effect; but if at any time there appears a talent (usually a prose talent) which needs 3,200 words to make its effect, and not 1,600 only, they may rest assured that they will be given the outlet.

(1948: 28)

Indeed, the openmindedness and generosity of Swanzy has been widely acknowledged (Lamming 1971). The contribution of *Caribbean Voices* cannot be overestimated, featuring creative writing and critical comment by Naipaul, **Selvon**, Lamming, Salkey, Mittelholzer, Trinidadian dramatist Errol Hill, Jamaican poet John Figueroa and many other less well-known figures such as Canadian-born Jamaican poet H.D. Carberry and Emily Lockhart, short story writers Willy Richardson and Gordon Woodford. Symposiums with other commentators also facilitated some useful, if uneven and often undeveloped, debates such as the perceived lack of a Caribbean literary tradition and audience, the role and responsibility of the writer and the need for a more thorough critical response to Caribbean writing. Many contributors have since acknowledged the invaluable role of the programme in providing a publishing outlet and critical forum for writers to meet and discuss each other's work, much as the Caribbean Artists Movement, set up in London in 1966 by John La Rose, Andrew Salkey and **Kamau Brathwaite** would continue to do in the late 1960s and 1970s (see Walmsley 1992).

However, the programme's format had its limitations and the ironies of a London-based focus for Caribbean writing and cultural exchange were not lost on a number of writers and critics. Lamming, for example, sardonically noted the echoes of the sugar trade in the dynamics of the programme's operation:

Taking the raw material [the literature] and sending it back [to the Caribbean] almost like sugar, which is planted there in the West Indies. Cut, sent abroad to be refined, and gets back in the finished form.

(**Lamming** 1971: 9)

Despite its pivotal role in the literature of this period, *Caribbean Voices* could not help but privilege literary production at the metropolitan 'centre' and thus perpetuated notions of literature happening 'else-where'. Although the literary expectations of the programme were often far from neo-colonial, in many ways *Caribbean Voices* constructed an eccentric/ex-centric notion of Caribbean literature and its critical commentary could emerge from conservative rather than progressive positionalities.

It would be the task of Caribbean-based critics such as Brathwaite to explore more fully the 'contradiction between our expatriate artistic selves and the local existential reality' (Brathwaite 1978a: 185), a dichotomy opened up by a decade of artistic exile and approaching political independence for countries such as Guyana, Jamaica and Trinidad in the early 1960s.

Establishing the canon and agendas for popular criticism

Looking back, Lamming called the period between 1948 and 1958 'the decade that has really witnessed the "emergence" of the novel as an imaginative interpretation of West Indian society by West Indians' (**1960**: 41) and certainly a large proportion of the one hundred or so novels published during this period formed what is often regarded as the canon of Caribbean Literature. Even today it is difficult to conceive of a course in Caribbean literature which would not include Lamming's *In the Castle of My Skin* (1957), Naipaul's *A House for Mr Biswas* (1961) and Harris's *Palace of the Peacock* (1960). Significantly, almost all these writers, Samuel Selvon, V.S. Naipaul, Lamming, Andrew Salkey, Wilson Harris, Edgar Mittelholzer, Kamau Brathwaite, John Hearne, Jan Carew, V.S. Reid, Walcott, were male, educated, middle class and – with very few exceptions – based in England at this time.

In this section, we include two short stories by male authors. Although Selvon's **'Waiting for Aunty to Cough'** was written and based in Britain and Sealey's **'My Fathers before Me'** in the Caribbean, both stories deal with the phenomena of exile and cross-cultural encounter. Selvon migrated to Britain in 1950 and remained there until the mid-1980s when he moved to Canada. His story is notable for its use of the 'lime' and extended anecdote as narrative strategy, which gives a dominantly oral feel to his writing, and for its linguistic playfulness which anticipates that of his later novel *Moses Ascending* (1975). As in Selvon's other 'London novels' (e.g. 1956,

1975), 'Waiting for Aunty to Cough' includes a litany of street and place names which reflect the colonial idea of England, which **Lamming** discusses (**1960**), and yet, also like his other works, this 'idea' is one which the substance of the narrative seeks to unpack.

Karl Sealy's 'My Fathers Before Me' was published in the Barbadian Little Magazine, *Bim*, in 1958 and mounts a fascinating interrogation of questions of empire, allegiance and national identity, as Dick tries to explain to his mother, sister and lover the reasons for his own imminent migration to England, as located within a larger socio-historical and filial context. This poignant and beautifully controlled story manages to examine the individual consequences of migration, and to indict some dominant colonialist narratives for omitting and obscuring the importance of such individual histories or testimonies. These narratives also stand accused of overlooking the contribution of the colonies in historical events such as the Boer War of 1899–1902 and two world wars.

It is impossible to over-estimate how influential this canon of writers has been in framing notions of a developing Caribbean literature and in establishing agendas for popular criticism, which have prevailed despite the fact that Caribbean writers and the writing itself have continued to develop and diversify. Kenneth Ramchand's influential critical text, *The West Indian Novel and its Background* (1970) and the more philosophical approach of Wilson Harris's *Tradition, the Writer and Society* (1967), both set the critical axis firmly towards male writers by articulating and affirming a particular idea of the writer and many of the themes and tropes for criticism, as found in this canon of writing. These included notions of tradition and Caribbean literary 'precursors'; the relationship between literature and society; questions of audience and the responsibility of the artist; alienation and the isolated individual; a privileging of the autobiographical and/or novel of childhood as formative to an emergent Caribbean literature; accommodation in its full figurative and allegorical dimensions (the West Indian as 'unhoused'; the centrality of the building process as explored in texts such as Naipaul (1961) and **Campbell, 'Oh! You Build a House' (1945)**, and an emergent sense of the 'architecture' of a literature). Other key themes established in this and other critical works of this period (eg. Baugh ed. 1978) include stylistic and linguistic experimentation with creole (see Reid 1949, Selvon, Naipaul 1959) and a shift away from the monologic narrator; the dual pulls of Africa and Europe and the educated (middle-class) appropriation of the peasant or 'folk' as literary subject (**Lamming 1960**).

Much criticism of this period is also characterized by a homogenizing subscription to the (since much contested) Arnoldian/ Leavisite tenets of 'moral worth', 'universality' and a rather imprecise notion of 'the best that has been said and written' as a critical touchstone (see Roach, cited in **Rohlehr 1972–3**). As Rohlehr has argued (1975) such criticism, however closely argued and well intentioned, tended to erase rather than foreground the importance of context and other material specificities which are important to Caribbean writing, and particularly to women's writing. Nevertheless, critiques of reading methodologies remain easier to locate than suggested reformulations and the question of a set of criteria appropriate to the aesthetic and cultural practices of the Caribbean remains vexed.

Women writers and the canon

The continued dominance of critical agendas based on the male writer-in-exile inevitably marginalized Caribbean-based and women writers. Yet there was much literary activity by a range of Caribbean women prior to and during this period, including Phyllis Shand Allfrey, Kathleen Archibald, Eliot Bliss, **Vera Bell**, Estha Chapman, Barbara Ferland, Arabel Moulton-Barrett, Clara Maude Garrett, Lena Kent, Hilda McDonald, **Elma Napier**, **Eva Nicholas**, M.M. and Stephanie Ormsby, Ada Quayle, **Jean Rhys**, Inez Sibley, **Sylvia Wynter** and Olga Yaatoff, to which list we could add the English publications of Allfrey (1953), Wynter (1962) and Rhys (1966). Furthermore, the Jamaican poet and activist Una Marson had a relatively high profile in the *Caribbean Voices* radio programme and as a director of the Jamaican *Gleaner's* publishing house, Pioneer Press, which forwarded the project of cultural nationalism at this time. Nevertheless, most Caribbean women writers were excluded from the canon and continued to suffer critical neglect, even 'invisibility', until relatively recently (see Morris 1971, **O'Callaghan 1986**, Boyce Davies 1988, Cudjoe ed. 1990, **Donnell 1995**, for important recuperative critiques). An example of this is to be found in the 1952 *Kyk-over-al Anthology of West Indian Poetry*, edited by **A.J. Seymour**, which included only two women poets: **Una Marson** and Hilda McDonald.

The work of Creole women writers such as Allfrey and Bliss and – to a lesser extent – Rhys, also suffered critical neglect during this period as O'Callaghan (1986) discusses, because their writing dealt with the 'ultimate outsider', situated uncomfortably on the cusp of coloniality, divided between different worlds (black / white / indigenous / expatriate / public / private) and belonging fully to none. Despite their similar exile to European metropoli during this and previous decades, and some shared concerns with their male counterparts (as Campbell argues in Cudjoe 1990: 123), it is a testimony to the exclusionary practices of canonical formation that the diasporic dynamics of Rhys's and Allfrey's works are rarely interrogated alongside those of their male contemporaries (Nasta 1995 is one recent exception).

We include Rhys's short story **'The Day They Burnt the Books'** as one of only two new pieces of published fiction produced by Rhys between 1945 and the publication of *Wide Sargasso Sea* in 1966 (the other was 'Let Them Call It Jazz' reprinted in Ramchand 1985). 'The Day They Burnt the Books' was 'probably developed out of her Creole memories of the fifties' and 'a more recent addition' (Angier 1990: 479) to an earlier collection of short stories which Rhys called *The Sound of the River*. In the 1950s her friend and fellow writer Francis Wyndham brought this volume to the attention of John Lehmann, editor of *The London Magazine*, and he published two stories: 'The Day They Burnt the Books' and 'Till September, Petronella' which were republished under the title *Tigers are Better Looking* (1968). 'The Day They Burnt the Books' like *Wide Sargasso Sea*, is set in the Caribbean. Like **Lamming (1960)** and **Sealey (1958)**, Rhys partly explores colonial constructions of the 'motherland'; however, as in the work of other Creole writers (which **O'Callaghan** analyses in this section) the child narrator's cultural confusion and doubts about 'home', meaning 'England', are part of a deeply ambivalent relationship to the metropole and are enmeshed in a complex matrix of ethnic and class prejudice. The story is also interesting for its sustained engagement with the issue of literary value. In sorting through those books to be sold and those to be burnt after her husband's death, Mrs Sawyer re-inscribes a preference for ideologically influential and colonially endorsed European texts: the educational (*Encyclopedia Britannica*) and the canonical English poets (Milton, Byron). Moreover, her marked distaste for women writers ('by a flicker in [her] eyes I knew that worse than men who wrote books were women who wrote books') and her selection of books according to their appearance rather than content, is part of a fiercely satirical portrait of the middle-class 'materialism and philistinism' of which *The Beacon*, **Gomes**, **Lamming**, **Brathwaite** and **Swanzy** all speak. Yet Rhys allows the children to enact their own unknowing acts of textual decolonization: they rescue a copy of Kipling's ideologically important text *Kim* – only to find the first nineteen pages are missing and the appropriately titled *Fort Comme La Mort* which disappoints 'because it is in French and seemed dull'. In this respect, **Rhys**'s story can be usefully read alongside her 1966 novel, in which European texts are similarly abandoned; and later texts such as **Kincaid** (**1985, 1991**) which also address European intertexts with irony and a confidently different value system.

We also include an interesting short story set in the Francophone territory of Martinique by **Elma Napier**. Napier belongs to the same generation as Eliot Bliss and Jean Rhys, and like them was published in the 1930s. Napier has been described as representing 'the meeting of expatriate writer and native-born writer' (O'Callaghan 1984b: 356). She came to Dominica in 1932, having already published a book of travel stories *Nothing So Blue* (1928) and (like fellow Dominican writer Allfrey) combined a political and literary career. 'Two novels with Dominican backgrounds, *Duet in Discord* (1935) and *A Flying Fish Whispered* (1938), two autobiographical works, *Youth is a Blunder* (1944) and *Winter is in July* (1948), were all published in London; a number of short stories about Dominica were published in the *Manchester Guardian*, *Blackwood's Magazine*, *The West Indian Review* and *Bim*' (O'Callaghan 1984b: 357). Napier 'was elected to the Dominica legislature in 1940, the first woman in Dominica and the West Indies to hold such a post' (Herdeck 1979: 162), and in her committed political career led a popular protest to gain better roads for Dominica. She died in 1973.

'**Carnival in Martinique**' is one of several of Napier's stories published in Caribbean Little Magazines in the 1950s. Its exploration of the gendered and class determinants of Jeannette's domestically circumscribed life and the juxtaposition of her 'immobility' against the 'journeyings' of the male guests at the Pension allows it to be usefully read alongside Goodison's **'On Houses'** later in this volume. In its treatment of the Empress Josephine (Martiniquan-born wife of Napoleon Bonaparte) as Jeannette's confused role model and in its clever meshing of myth and realities, the story also stages the complexities of identification with colonial icons. In a sense, Josephine has been twice colonized: she is the indigenous inhabitant become European Empress, and she is sexually as well as geographically colonized by her Emperor, Bonaparte. Throughout the story, motifs of clothing (shoes, masks, carnival costumes) are foregrounded as Napier explores issues of gender identity, appearances and disguise. Jeannette's gauche romanticism and honourable sense of tradition (as manifest in her donning of her mother's unambiguously feminine carnival costume) are contrasted with the slippery insincerity of Jules and the gender subversion of the two girls 'dressed in men's pyjamas' and masked from head to hand, thus also effectively rendering them racially indeterminate. The fact that this story, which interestingly engages with so many of the collective concerns of Caribbean literature at this time, remains virtually unknown is further evidence of a metropolitan, male bias.

Martin Carter

University of Hunger

is the university of hunger the wide waste.
is the pilgrimage of man the long march.
The print of hunger wanders in the land.
The green tree bends above the long forgotten.
The plains of life rise up and fall in spasms.
The huts of men are fused in misery.

They come treading in the hoofmarks of the mule
passing the ancient bridge
the grave of pride
the sudden flight
the terror and the time.

They come from the distant village of the flood
passing from middle air to middle earth
in the common hours of nakedness.
Twin bars of hunger mark their metal brows
twin seasons mock them
parching drought and flood.

is the dark ones
the half sunken in the land.
is they who had no voice in the emptiness
in the unbelievable
in the shadowless.

They come treading on the mud floor of the year
mingling with dark heavy waters
and the sea sound of the eyeless flitting bat.
O long is the march of men and long is the life
and wide is the span.
O cold is the cruel wind blowing.
O cold is the hoe in the ground.

They come like sea birds
flapping in the wake of a boat
is the torture of sunset in purple bandages
is the powder of fire spread like dust in the twilight

is the water melodies of white foam on wrinkled sand.

The long streets of night move up and down
baring the thighs of a woman
and the cavern of generation.
The beating drum returns and dies away.
The bearded men fall down and go to sleep.
The cocks of dawn stand up and crow like bugles.

is they who rose early in the morning
watching the moon die in the dawn.
is they who heard the shell blow and the iron clang.
is they who had no voice in the emptiness
in the unbelievable
in the shadowless.
O long is the march of men and long is the life
and wide is the span.

(1954)

I Come from the Nigger Yard

I come from the nigger yard of yesterday
leaping from the oppressors hate
and the scorn of myself;
from the agony of the dark hut in the shadow
and the hurt of things;
from the long days of cruelty and the long nights of pain
down to the wide streets of to-morrow, of the next day
leaping I come, who cannot see will hear.

In the nigger yard I was naked like the new born
naked like a stone or a star.
It was a cradle of blind days rocking in time
torn like the skin from the back of a slave.
It was an aching floor on which I crept
on my hands and my knees
searching the dust for the trace of a root
or the mark of a leaf or the shape of a flower.

It was me always walking with bare feet,
meeting strange faces like those in dreams or fever

when the whole world turns upside down
and no one knows which is the sky or the land
which heart is his among the torn or wounded
which face is his among the strange and terrible
walking about, groaning between the wind.

And there was always sad music somewhere in the land
like a bugle and a drum between the houses
voices of women singing far away
pauses of silence, then a flood of sound.
But these were things like ghosts or spirits of wind.
It was only a big world spinning outside
and men, born in agony, torn in torture, twisted and broken
    like a leaf,
and the uncomfortable morning, the beds of hunger stained
    and sordid
like the world, big and cruel, spinning outside.

Sitting sometimes in the twilight near the forest
where all the light is gone and every bird
I notice a tiny star neighbouring a leaf
a little drop of light a piece of glass
straining over heaven tiny bright
like a spark seed in the destiny of gloom.
O it was the heart like this tiny star near to the sorrows
straining against the whole world and the long twilight
spark of man's dream conquering the night
moving in darkness stubborn and fierce
till leaves of sunset change from green to blue
and shadows grow like giants everywhere.

So was I born again stubborn and fierce
screaming in a slum.
It was a city and coffin space for home
a river running, prisons, hospitals
men drunk and dying, judges full of scorn
priests and parsons fooling gods with words
and me, like a dog tangled in rags
spotted with sores powdered with dust
screaming with hunger, angry with life and men.

It was a child born from a mother full of her blood
weaving her features bleeding her life in clots.
It was pain lasting from hours to months and to years
weaving a pattern telling a tale leaving a mark
on the face and the brow.
Until there came the iron days cast in a foundry
Where men make hammers things that cannot break
and anvils heavy hard and cold like ice.

And so again I became one of the ten thousands
one of the uncountable miseries owning the land.
When the moon rose up only the whores could dance
the brazen jazz of music throbbed and groaned
filling the night air full of rhythmic questions.
It was the husk and the seed challenging fire
birth and the grave challenging life.

Until to-day in the middle of the tumult
when the land changes and the world's all convulsed
when different voices join to say the same
and different hearts beat out in unison
where on the aching floor of where I live
the shifting earth is twisting into shape
I take again my nigger life, my scorn
and fling it in the face of those who hate me.
It is me the nigger boy turning to manhood
linking my fingers, welding my flesh to freedom.

I come from the nigger yard of yesterday
leaping from the oppressor's hate
and the scorn of myself.
I come to the world with scars upon my soul
wounds on my body, fury in my hands.
I turn to the histories of men and the lives of the peoples.
I examine the shower of sparks the wealth of the dreams.
I am pleased with the glories and sad with the sorrows
rich with the riches, poor with the loss.
From the nigger yard of yesterday I come with my burden.
To the world of to-morrow I turn with my strength.

(1954)

I Am No Soldier

Wherever you fall comrade I shall arise.
Wherever and whenever the sun vanishes into an arctic night
there will I come.
I am no soldier with a cold gun on my shoulder
no hunter of men, no human dog of death.
I am my poem, I come to you in particular gladness.
In this hopeful dawn of earth I rise with you dear friend.

O comrade unknown to me falling somewhere in blood.
In the insurgent geography of my life
the latitudes of anguish
pass through the poles of my frozen agonies, my regions of
    grief.
O my heart is a magnet
electrified by passion, emitting sparks of love,
swinging in me around the burning compass of to-morrow
and pointing at my grandfather's continent, unhappy Africa
unhappy lake of sunlight
moon of terror . . .

But now the huge noise of night surrounds me for a
    moment.
I clutch the iron bars of my nocturnal cell
peeping at daylight.
There is a dark island in a dark river.
O forest of torture!
O current of pain and channel of endurance!
The nausea of a deep sorrow hardens in my bowels
and the sky's black paint cracks falling into fragments
Cold rain is mist! is air, is all my breath!

There is a night mare bandaged on my brow.
A long hempen pendulum marks the hour of courage
swinging over the bloody dust of a comrade
one minute and one hour and one year –
O life's mapmaker chart me now an ocean
Vast ship go sailing, keel and metal rudder.

It began when the sun was younger, when the moon was
    dull.
But wherever you fall comrade I shall arise.
If it is in Malaya where new barbarians eat your flesh, like
beasts
I shall arise.
If it is in Kenya, where your skin is dark with the stain of
famine
I shall arise.
If it is in Korea of my tears where land is desolate
I shall wipe my eyes and see you
Comrade unknown to me . . .

I will come to the brave when they dream of the red and
yellow flowers blooming in the tall mountains of their
nobility . . .
I will come to each and to every comrade led by my heart
Led by my magnet of freedom which draws me far and wide
over the sun's acres of children and of mornings. . ..

O wherever you fall comrade I shall arise.
In the whirling cosmos of my soul there are galaxies of
    happiness
Stalin's people and the brothers of Mao Tse-tung
And Accabreh's breed, my mother's powerful loin
And my father's song and my people's deathless drum.
O come astronomer of freedom.
Come comrade stargazer.
Look at the sky I told you I had seen.
The glittering seeds that germinate in darkness.
And the planet in my hand's revolving wheel.
And the planet in my breast and in my head
and in my dream and in my furious blood.
Let me rise up wherever he may fall.
I am no soldier hunting in a jungle
I am this poem like a sacrifice.

(1954)

Elma Napier

Carnival in Martinique

In the yard there were two fowls tied together by eighteen inches of string. Very early in the morning, before the stars had quite faded out of the sky, Jeannette carried them across the street and tethered them under a sand-box tree on the savannah. Twice a day she took food and water to them, and in the evening she brought them back to the yard. Jeannette loved the fowls better than she loved anybody else at the Pension.

Her next duty was to make Madame's coffee and take it up to her room Madame was not a pretty sight in bed. Asleep the Chinese blood in her triumphed over the negress. Clean of paint her skin was yellow, and her nostrils gaped hideously. Always she woke with a snarl, and her clacking tongue began to scold automatically. Her wit and her smile were reserved for the dining-room. Then Jeannette had to prepare the boarders' breakfasts, but today was Sunday, the last Sunday before Lent, and she knew that nobody would wake until late. She would have time to finish cleaning the shoes before anybody opened their door and bellowed: 'Jeannette! Cafe! A toute vitesse!' There was a great many shoes. First of all Madame's, incredibly tiny and high-heeled. No wonder, thought Jeannette, that she never goes out into the street. Then there were the large white shoes of the purser of the St Raphael, shoes that vanished for three weeks at a time when the St Raphael went south to St Lucia and Trinidad and Cayenne. The Pension was quieter and sadder when the St Raphael was not in port. And there were the neat black shoes of the purser of the Antilles, shoes that went north to St Bartelmey, where the cattle are slung on board in chains, and to Porto Rico and San Domingo. She thought as she cleaned them how far they travelled, these the shoes, while she stayed always on the staircase, gazing out of the open window across the red-tiled roofs at the palm trees raising their royal heads into the sky. There was no escape, save in dreams, for Jeannette, the half-caste servant girl. In dreams she wandered through the mazes of her ancestry; in dreams she found herself in the African jungle or at the gay Court of France.

Never had the boarders been so slow over their lunch. They wasted time drinking their 'petits ponches', they wasted time fooling with

Madame. The spirit of the carnival was abroad, and they had found paper caps in a drawer of the ice-chest. It was late before the washing-up was done and the beds made and she was free. Then she took off her white cotte[sic]n frock and put on the old red silk gown that had been her mother's, a traditional costume of their race, with lace and muslin petticoat and a turbanned handkerchief to wear about her head. She looked prettier in her working frocks; the old-fashioned dress added years to her age, but she was enchanted with herself and curtsied to her reflection in the glass. Other girls dressed up as men for the carnival, ran about the streets in shirts and silk pants, or in pyjamas, but Jeannette would be dignified as became her mother's frock, and Jules would be pleased with her and see that she was different. Jules worked in the Ford garage next door. Sometimes, when she was feeding the fowls on the savannah, she would see him standing outside the shop and think how handsome he looked in blue overalls and cloth cap, with a cigarette behind his ear.

She slipped out of the Pension and made her way into the main-street. Never was street so crowded. Men, women, and children, some disguised, some merely sight-seeing, walked up and down and back-wards and forwards, screaming, gaping, laughing in the sunshine. Here were the stalls of the vendors of sweetmeats, of biscuits and wafers, of doughnuts and fruit. Old women made fritters on the curb, dipping a paste of breadfruit into a white, creamy mixture and frying it over coals. There was a tightrope dancer, and a man dressed as a skeleton carrying a scythe, who played out a grim pantomime every few minutes. There were men who had bound cows' horns upon their foreheads and wore women's corsets outside their clothes. For a long time Jeannette stood watching a wheel of fortune, and at last ventured a franc herself, winning a china cup. It was sweetly pretty and she loved it, but there was nowhere to put it, and when she saw Jules she forgot that she was carrying it and so it broke. He was not wearing dungarees now but a beautifully cut white suit and a solar topee, under which his black face shone like the purser's boots. And under each arm there hung a girl, a girl wearing one of those pink wire masks with hideously vacant expression that were on sale in every shop; their necks and heads were wrapped in towels and their arms cased in gloves, so that none could see their skins or guess their colour. They were dressed in men's pyjamas, vulgar flaming garments that hung upon them in folds. Jeannette pressed towards them, and

Jules smiled, but there was no invitation in his smile, and when Jeannette would have spoken the two masks dragged him away, shrieking with laughter and gibing, in the shrill falsetto they used to disguise their real voices, at her old-fashioned clothes. Jeannette walked on as though in a nightmare. She held her head high and her little red figure was dignity incarnate, but she saw and heard nothing more of the noisy crowd about her.

On the stairs of the Pension she met the happy purser, and he said: 'Que tu es gentille comme ça,' and he took her by the shoulders and turned her round to look at her dress, but she twitched herself free and ran away. The boarders were Madame's preserve. Woe to Jeannette if she trespassed! She tore off her silk frock and her turbaned handkerchief, and flinging herself down by the window she rested her head on the sill and wept. And when she had done crying and lifted up her head to look across the savannah the sun was sinking and touching with a pink wand the burned-up grass, the grey walls of the fort, and the white statue of Josephine standing in its circle of palm trees. Had she been dignified, Jeannette wondered, that Martiniquan girl who had become an empress and who now immortalised in stone with a coronet upon her head, stood forever gazing across the bay at the little town where she was born? How had she done it? Had she tried to be sweet and gentle and have nice manners, or had she rushed screaming to grab her man in a pink mask and pyjamas. The light faded and the stars came out, and in the little kiosks where they sell aperitifs barmaids flicked chairs with dusters and put syphons and syrup upon the rickety iron tables. Suddenly from under the sand-box came the subdued crow of rooster, the half-hearted cry of a bird who feels that his world has gone wrong. Jeannette flung on her white working frock and ran down into the street. What did Jules matter, or Josephine, or the spirit of carnival? She had forgotten to bring the fowls back into the yard.

(1951)

Samuel Selvon

Waiting for Aunty to Cough

It had a late lime what few of the boys acquainted with. That don't mean to say was anything exclusive, but as far as I know Brackley was the only fellar who get in with a thing that living far from London, and had was to see the piece home every night, going out of the city and coming back late, missing bus and train and having to hustle or else stay stranded in one of them places behind God back.

I mean, some people might say a place like where Brackley used to go ain't far, and argue even that it still included in London, but to the city boys, as soon as you start to hit Clapham Common or Chiswick or Mile End or Highgate, that mean you living in the country, and they out to give you tone like: 'Mind you miss the last bus home, old man,' and, 'When next you coming to town?' or, 'You could get some fresh eggs for me where you living?'

Well Brackley in fact settle down nicely in Central, a two and ten room in Ladbroke Grove, with easy communications for liming out in the evenings after work, and the old Portobello road near by to buy rations like saltfish and red beans and pig foot and pig tail. And almost every evening he would meet the boys and they would lime by the Arch, or the Gate, and have a cup of coffee (it have place like stupidness now all over London selling coffee, you notice?) and coast a talk and keep a weather eye open for whatever might appear on the horizon.

But a time come, when the boys begin to miss Brackley.

'Anybody see Brackley?'

'I ain't see Brackley a long time, man. He must be move.'

'He uses to be in this coffee shop regular, but these days I can't see him at all.'

All this time, Brackley on one of them green trains you does catch in Charing Cross or Waterloo, taking a ride and seeing the girl home.

Though Brackley living in London for eight years, is as if he start to discover a new world. Brackley never hear name like what he reading as they pass them stations – Gypsy Hill, Penge West, Forest Hill.

'You sure we on the right train?' Brackley frighten like hell the first time, feeling as if they going to Scotland or something. 'How far from London you say this place is?'

'It is in London, I keep telling you,' the girl say patiently.

'All of this is London?' Brackley look out and see a station name Honor Oak Park. Houses fading away and down there real grim as if is a place far out in the country.

'Yes,' Beatrice say.

'And every day, you have to come all this way to work in London?'

'Yes.'

'Oh, you must be one of those commuter people I read about in the papers.'

Brackley look at his wristwatch. 'I don't like this lime,' he say.

'Oh, you'll get accustomed to it,' Beatrice say. 'It is like nothing to me now.'

'I wonder what the boys doing in the coffee shop in town,' Brackley mutter.

'That is all you ever worry about – wasting your time,' Beatrice start to sulk.

'It ain't have no high spots this side of the world?' Brackley ask. 'If it have, we could go out down here instead of staying in London and coming home late every night.'

'You know I like to go out in the city,' Beatrice pout. 'The only place we could go to down here is near to Croydon.'

'Croydon!' Brackley repeat. 'Where the aeroplanes come from all over the world? You mean to say we so far from London?'

'There are frequent trains,' Beatrice say anxiously.

'Frequent trains!' Brackley repeat. 'Frequent planes, you mean! I don't like the lime at all.'

But all the same, Brackley like the thing and he was seeing she home every night.

Well he start to extend his geographical knowledge from the time he going out with Beatrice, and when he was explaining his absence from the city to the boys, he making it sound as if is a grand lime.

'Man,' he boasting, 'you-all don't know London! You think London is the Gate and the Arch and Trafalgar Square, but them places is nothing. You ever hear about Honor Oak Rise?'

'Which part that is, behind God back?'

'That is a place in London, man! I mean, look at it this way. You live in London so long, and up to now you don't know where that is. You see what I mean?'

'Man Brackley, you only full of guile. This time so that woman have you stupid and travelling all over the country, when you could be liming here. You staying tonight? It have two sharp things does come for coffee here – I think they from Sweden, and you know over there ain't have no inhibition.'

'I can't stay tonight.'

'Today is Saturday, no night bus.'

But Brackley in hot with Beatrice at this stage and that ain't worrying him. What happen that night was he find himself walking to Kent afterwards, thinking that he was on the way to London, and he would have found himself picking hops or something if a fellar didn't put him right.

One night Brackley was taking a cuppa and a roll in a little place it have near Charing Cross, what does stay open all night for stragglers like him. The set-up is this: three-four frowsy women, and some tests who look as if they only come out at night. I mean, if you really want to meet some characters, is to lime out there by the Embankment after midnight, and you sure to meet some individuals.

That night, two fellars playing dominoes. A group stand up round a fire that they light with wood to keep warm. Suddenly a big commotion start, because the police take Olive and a test say it serve her right.

A woman start to 'buse the fellar who say it serve Olive right.

'What do you know about it?' the woman snarl. 'Keep your —ing mouth shut.'

She start to scratch her thigh. Same time another woman come hustling up with the stale news that the police take Olive.

'Yes,' the first woman say, 'and this bastard here say that it served her right.' She turn to the fellar again, 'Keep your —ing mouth shut,' she say, though the fellar ain't saying anything.

Suddenly she turn on Brackley and start to 'buse him, saying that he was responsible. Poor Brackley ain't have a clue what the woman talking about, but three-four frowsy-looking sports gather around him and want to beat him up.

Brackley ease away and start to go up by Whitehall, and the starlings kicking up hell on the sides of the tall buildings, and is almost three o'clock in the morning and he thinking what a hell of a thing life is, how he never hear about any Olive and look how them women wanted to beat him up.

Well to get back to the heart of the ballad, one rainy night Brackley and Beatrice went theatre, and theatre over late, and they catch the last train out of town. While they on the train – and Brackley like a regular commuter these days, reading the *Standard* while Beatrice catching up on some knitting – Beatrice suddenly open her handbag and say: 'Gosh, I think I've lost my key!'

'You could always get another one,' Brackley say, reading How The Other Half Laughs.

'You don't understand,' Beatrice moan. 'Aunty is always complaining about my coming in late, and by the time we get home it will be long after midnight, and the door will be shut.'

'Ring the bell,' Brackley say, laughing at a joke in the paper.

'I daren't wake Aunty at that hour,' Beatrice say, putting aside the knitting to worry better.

'Don't worry, I will open a window for you,' Brackley say.

But when they get to where Beatrice living she was still worrying what to do. She tell Brackley to wait by the gate. She went inside and pick up a tiny pebble and throw at the window, which was on the first floor. It make a sound ping! but nothing happen. After a little while she throw another one ping! but still nothing happen.

Brackley stand up there watching her.

She turn to Brackley helplessly. 'I can't wake Aunty,' she say.

Brackley open the gate and come inside and pick up a big brick from the garden to pelt at the people glass window. Beatrice barely had time to hold his hand.

'Are you mad?' she say in a fierce whisper.

'Well,' Brackley say, 'you don't want to get inside?'

'You are making too much noise already,' Beatrice whisper. 'I will have to stay on the steps until Aunty gets up.'

'What time is that?' Brackley ask.

'About six o'clock,' Beatrice say. 'She is an early riser.'

'You mean to say,' Brackley say, 'you spending the night here in the damp? Why you don't make a big noise and wake she up?'

'No no,' Beatrice say quickly, 'we musn't make any noise. The neighbours are very troublesome. Let us wait here until Aunty gets up. She is restless at night. When I hear her coughing I will throw another stone.'

So Brackley and Beatrice sit down on the wet steps, waiting for Aunty to cough.

One o'clock come and gone, two o'clock come and gone. Three o'clock rain start to pelt slantways and fall on the steps wetting Brackley. This time so, as Brackley look around, the world grim. Rain and fog around him, and Beatrice sleeping on his shoulder.

He shake her.

Beatrice open her eyes and say, 'What is it, did you hear Aunty cough?'

'No. It look as if her cold get better, I don't think she going to cough tonight at all.'

'She always coughs in the night. As soon as she does I will throw some stones again.'

'Why you don't make a big noise and finish with it? Back home in Trinidad, you think this could happen? Why –'

'Hush, you are speaking too loudly. I told you it would cause trouble with the neighbours.'

'Why you don't wake up the people on the ground floor?'

'Nobody is there – they work nights.'

'I ain't even a cigarette,' Brackley grumble, wondering what the boys doing, if they get in with the two girls from Sweden and gone to sleep in a nice warm room.

Beatrice went back to sleep, using poor Brackley as pillow.

Four o'clock come, five o'clock come, and still Brackley waiting for Aunty to cough and she wouldn't cough. This time so he have a sizeable stone in his hand and he make up his mind that the moment Aunty cough he going to fling the stone at the window even if he wake up everybody in the street. Sleep killing Brackley but the doorway small and he bend up there like a piece of wire, catching cramp and unable to shift position. In fact, between five and half past Brackley think he hear Aunty cough and he make to get up and couldn't move, all the joints frozen in the damp and cold.

He shake Beatrice roughly. 'Aunty cough,' he say.

'I didn't hear,' Beatrice say.

'I hear,' Brackley say, and he stretch out slowly and get up.

Brackley augment the stone he had with three others and he fling his hand back and he pelt the stones on the people glass window before Beatrice know what he doing.

Well glass cracks and break and splinters fly all about and the noise sound as if the glasshouse in Kew Gardens falling down. Same time Aunty start one set of coughing.

'You see?' Brackley say, 'I tell you Aunty was coughing!'

'You fool!' Beatrice say. 'Look what you have done! You had better go quickly before you cause further trouble.'

And before Brackley know what happening Beatrice hustle him out to the pavement and shut the gate.

Well a kind of fore-day light was falling at that hour of the morning and when Aunty fling open the window to see what happening, she see Brackley stand up out there. Only, she not so sure, because Brackley blend in nicely with the kind of half-light half-dark. But all the same, Aunty begin to scream murder and thief.

Brackley take off as if he on the Ascot racecourse.

Some nights later he tell the boys the episode, making it sound like a good joke though at the time he was frighten like hell. But that was a mistake he make, because since that time whenever the boys see him they hailing out:

'Brackley! You still waiting for Aunty to cough?'

(1957)

Jean Rhys

The Day They Burnt the Books

My friend Eddie was a small, thin boy. You could see the blue veins in his wrists and temples. People said that he had consumption and wasn't long for this world. I loved, but sometimes despised him.

His father, Mr Sawyer, was a strange man. Nobody could make out what he was doing in our part of the world at all. He was not a planter or a doctor or a lawyer or a banker. He didn't keep a store. He wasn't a schoolmaster or a government official. He wasn't – that was the point – a gentleman. We had several resident romantics who had fallen in love with the moon on the Caribees – they were all gentlemen and quite unlike Mr Sawyer who hadn't an 'h' in his composition. Besides, he detested the moon and everything else about the Caribbean and he didn't mind telling you so.

He was agent for a small steamship line which in those days linked up Venezuela and Trinidad with the smaller islands, but he couldn't make much out of that. He must have a private income, people decided, but they never decided why he had chosen to settle in a place he didn't like and to marry a coloured woman. Though a decent, respectable, nicely educated coloured woman, mind you.

Mrs Sawyer must have been very pretty once but, what with one thing and another, that was in days gone by.

When Mr Sawyer was drunk – this often happened – he used to be very rude to her. She never answered him.

'Look at the nigger showing off,' he would say; and she would smile as if she knew she ought to see the joke but couldn't. 'You damned, long-eyed gloomy half-caste, you don't smell right,' he would say; and she never answered, not even to whisper, 'You don't smell right to me, either.'

The story went that once they had ventured to give a dinner party and that when the servant, Mildred, was bringing in coffee, he had pulled Mrs Sawyer's hair. 'Not a wig, you see,' he bawled. Even then, if you can believe it, Mrs Sawyer had laughed and tried to pretend that it was all part of the joke, this mysterious, obscure, sacred English joke.

But Mildred told the other servants in the town that her eyes had gone wicked, like soucriant's eyes, and that afterwards she had picked up some of the hair he pulled out and put it in an envelope, and that Mr Sawyer ought to look out (hair is obeah as well as hands).

Of course, Mrs Sawyer had her compensations. They lived in a very pleasant house in Hill Street. The garden was large and they had a fine mango tree, which bore prolifically. The fruit was small, round, very sweet and juicy – a lovely, red-and-yellow colour when it was ripe. Perhaps it was one of the compensations, I used to think.

Mr Sawyer built a room on to the back of this house. It was unpainted inside and the wood smelt very sweet. Bookshelves lined the walls. Every time the Royal Mail steamer came in it brought a package for him, and gradually the empty shelves filled.

Once I went there with Eddie to borrow *The Arabian Nights*. That was on a Saturday afternoon, one of those hot, still afternoons when you felt that everything had gone to sleep, even the water in the gutters. But Mrs Sawyer was not asleep. She put her head in at the door and looked at us, and I knew that she hated the room and hated the books.

It was Eddie with the pale blue eyes and straw-coloured hair – the living image of his father, though often as silent as his mother – who first infected me with doubts about 'home', meaning England. He would be so quiet when others who had never seen it – none of us had ever seen it – were talking about its delights, gesticulating freely as we talked – London, the beautiful, rosy-cheeked ladies, the theatres, the shops, the fog, the blazing coal fires in winter, the exotic food (whitebait eaten to the sound of violins), strawberries and cream – the word 'strawberries' always spoken with a guttural and throaty sound which we imagined to be the proper English pronunciation.

'I don't like strawberries,' Eddie said on one occasion.

'You *don't like* strawberries?'

'No, and I don't like daffodils either. Dad's always going on about them. He says they lick the flowers here into a cocked hat and I bet that's a lie.'

We were all too shocked to say, 'You don't know a thing about it.' We were so shocked that nobody spoke to him for the rest of the day. But I for one admired him. I also was tired of learning and reciting poems in praise of daffodils, and my relations with the few 'real' English boys and girls I had met were awkward. I had discovered that if I called myself English they would snub me haughtily: 'You're not English; you're a horrid colonial.' 'Well, I don't much want to be English,' I would say. 'It's much more fun to be French or Spanish or something like that – and, as a matter of fact, I am a bit.' Then I was too killingly funny, quite ridiculous. Not only a horrid colonial, but also ridiculous. Heads I win, tails you lose – that was the English. I had thought about all this, and thought hard, but I had never dared to tell anybody what I thought and I realized that Eddie had been very bold.

But he was bold, and stronger than you think. For one thing, he never felt the heat; some coldness in his fair skin resisted it. He didn't burn red or brown, he didn't freckle much.

Hot days seem to make him feel especially energetic. 'Now we'll run twice round the lawn and then you can pretend you're dying of thirst in the desert and that I'm an Arab chieftain bringing you water.'

'You must drink slowly,' he would say, 'for if you're very thirsty and you drink quickly you die.'

So I learnt the voluptuousness of drinking slowly when you are very thirsty – small mouthful by small mouthful, until the glass of pink, iced Coca-Cola was empty.

Just after my twelfth birthday, Mr Sawyer died suddenly, and as Eddie's special friend I went to the funeral, wearing a new white dress. My straight hair was damped with sugar and water the night before and plaited into tight little plaits, so that it should be fluffy for the occasion.

When it was all over everybody said how nice Mrs Sawyer had looked, walking like a queen behind the coffin and crying her eyeballs out at the right moment, and wasn't Eddie a funny boy? He hadn't cried at all.

After this Eddie and I took possession of the room with the books. No one else ever entered it, except Mildred to sweep and dust in the mornings, and gradually the ghost of Mr Sawyer pulling Mrs Sawyer's hair faded though this took a little time. The blinds were always half-way down and going in out of the sun was like stepping into a pool of brown-green water. It was empty except for the book-shelves, a desk with a green baize top and a wicker rocking-chair.

'My room,' Eddie called it. 'My books,' he would say, 'my books.'

I don't know how long this lasted. I don't know whether it was weeks after Mr Sawyer's death or months after, that I see myself and Eddie in the room. But there we are and there, unexpectedly, are Mrs Sawyer and Mildred. Mrs Sawyer's mouth tight, her eyes pleased.

She is pulling all the books out of the shelves and piling them into two heaps. The big, fat glossy ones – the good-looking ones, Mildred explains in a whisper – lie in one heap. The *Encyclopedia Britannica*, *British Flowers, Birds and Beasts*, various histories, books with maps, Froude's *English in the West Indies* and so on – they are going to be sold. The unimportant books, with paper covers or damaged covers or torn pages, lie in another heap. They are going to be burnt – yes, burnt.

Mildred's expression was extraordinary as she said that – half hugely delighted, half-shocked, even frightened. And as for Mrs Sawyer – well, I knew bad temper (I had often seen it). I knew rage, but this was hate. I recognized the difference at once and stared at them curiously. I edged closer to her so that I could see the titles of the books she was handling.

It was the poetry shelf. *Poems*, Lord Byron, *Poetical Works*, Milton, and so on. Vlung, vlung, vlung – all thrown into the heap that were to be sold. But a book by Christina Rossetti, though also bound in leather, went into the heap that was to be burnt, and by a flicker in Mrs Sawyer's eyes I knew that worse than men who wrote books were women who wrote books – infinitely worse. Men could be mercifully shot; women must be tortured.

Mrs Sawyer did not seem to notice that we were there, but she was breathing free and easy and her hands had got the rhythm of tearing and pitching. She looked beautiful, too – beautiful as the sky outside which was a very dark blue, or the mango tree, long sprays of brown and gold.

When Eddie said 'No,' she did not even glance at him.

'No', he said again in a high voice. 'Not that one. I was reading that one.'

She laughed and he rushed at her, his eyes starting out of his head, shrieking, 'Now I've got to hate you too. Now I hate you too.'

He snatched the book out of her hand and gave her a violent push. She fell into the rocking-chair.

Well, I wasn't going to be left out of all this, so I grabbed a book from the condemned pile and dived under Mildred's outstretched arm.

Then we were both in the garden. We ran along the path, bordered with crotons. We pelted down the path, though they did not follow us and we could hear Mildred laughing – kyah, kyah, kyah, kyah. As

I ran I put the book I had taken into the loose front of my brown holland dress. It felt warm and alive.

When we got into the street we walked sedately, for we feared the black children's ridicule. I felt very happy, because I had saved this book and it was my book and I would read it from the beginning to the triumphant words 'The End'. But I was uneasy when I thought of Mrs Sawyer.

'What will she do?' I said.

'Nothing,' Eddie said. 'Not to me.'

He was white as a ghost in his sailor suit, a blue-white even in the setting sun, and his father's sneer was clamped on his face.

'But she'll tell your mother all sorts of lies about you,' he said. 'She's an awful liar. She can't make up a story to save her life, but she makes up lies about people all right.'

'My mother won't take any notice of her,' I said. Though I was not at all sure.

'Why not? Because she's . . . because she isn't white?'

Well, I knew the answer to that one. Whenever the subject was brought up – people's relations and whether they had a drop of coloured blood or whether they hadn't – my father would grow impatient and interrupt. 'Who's white?' he would say. 'Damned few.'

So I said, 'Who's white? Damned few.'

'You can go to the devil,' Eddie said. 'She's prettier than your mother. When she's asleep her mouth smiles and she has curling eyelashes and quantities and quantities and *quantities* of hair.'

'Yes,' I said truthfully. 'She's prettier than my mother.'

It was a red sunset that evening, a huge, sad, frightening sunset.

'Look, let's go back,' I said. 'If you're sure she won't be vexed with you, let's go back. It'll be dark soon.'

At the gate he asked me not to go. 'Don't go yet, don't go yet.'

We sat under the mango tree and I was holding his hand when he began to cry. Drops fell on my hand like the water from the dripstone in the filter in our yard. Then I began to cry too and when I felt my own tears on my hand I thought, 'Now perhaps we're married.'

'Yes, certainly, now we're married,' I thought. But I didn't say anything. I didn't say a thing until I was sure he had stopped. Then I asked, 'What's your book?'

'It's *Kim*,' he said. 'But it got torn. It starts at page twenty now. What's the one you took?'

'I don't know; its too dark to see,' I said.

When I got home I rushed into my bedroom and locked the door because I knew that this book was the most important thing that had ever happened to me and I did not want anybody to be there when I looked at it.

But I was very disappointed, because it was in French and seemed dull. *Fort Comme La Mort*, it was called . . .

(1960)

Karl Sealey

My Fathers before Me

Dick, the yard man, took the big Rhode Island cock from the run and, tucking it under his arm, went back to the kitchen steps where he had been sitting.

He held the cock fast between his legs and, squeezing its mouth open with his left hand, took a pinch of ashes from the small heap beside him, between right thumb and forefinger. This he rubbed on to the bird's tongue, and began to peel the hard, horny growth from the tongue's end.

His grandmother, who had spent most of her usefulness with the family, came shambling from the house behind him, eating cassava farina soaked in water and sugar. She stood looking down at him for some time, her eyes, the colour of dry bracken, tender, before she took a spoonful of farina from the glass and, bending with the stiffness of years, put it from behind into his mouth. Through the farina in his mouth Dick said, like a man continuing his thought in speech:

'And your age, Granny? You've spent a lifetime here. How many summers have you seen?'

'More than you'll ever see if you go to England,' she said, letting herself down on the step above him. 'Eighty-four years come October, God spare life. Whole fourteen above-and-beyond what the good Lord says.'

'Hmm,' Dick said, and taking the cock to the run, returned with a hen as white as a swan.

The old woman said: 'Just think of it, Dick, just think of it. Come this time tomorrow you'll be miles away, with oceans of water separating you from everybody who loves you, and going to a land where you ent got a bird in the cotton tree, where nobody'll care a straw whether you sink or swim, and where black ent altogether liked.' She scraped the last of the farina from the glass, and once more put the spoon to his mouth.

'You ent mind leaving us, Dick?' she said. 'You ent mind leaving your poor old Granny and Ma? And Vere? What about Vere? You ent got no feelings in that belly of ye'n, Dick?'

Sucking farina from his teeth with his tongue, Dick said: 'I'll send for Vere as soon as I can. Maybe Ma, too.'

[243]

The old woman continued as though she had not heard: 'No more Dick about the house to put your hands 'pon. Maybe some lazy wringneck governor in your place whose only interest'll be his week's pay.'

'Time enough too, and welcome,' Dick said.

From an upstairs window, whose curtains she had been pulling against the evening sun, Bessie saw her mother sitting on the concrete step above Dick. Going down to the servants' room she took a cushion from the sofa and went out to where they were sitting. She said:

'Up, Ma. Think you're young, sitting on this cold step?'

The old woman raised herself a few inches, and Bessie pushed the cushion under her.

'I's just been telling Dick, Bessie, how no good ent ever come to our family leaving our land and going into nobody else country,'

'True enough,' said Bessie. 'Look at my Dick and Panama.'

Then the old woman asked: 'Ever teach you who the Boers was at school, Dick?'

'I ent ever learn for sure who the Boers were,' said Dick, 'save that they couldn't stand up to bayonets.'

'That's right,' Bessie said. 'At the bayonet charge the Boers surrender.'

'British bayonets,' Dick remarked.

'Don't you let nobody fool you with that, Dick,' said the old woman. 'There wasn't all no British bayonets. Your gran'dad's bayonet was there, too.'

'Oh, well, we're all British. At least that's the way I look at it.'

'But British or no British,' said the old woman, 'your gran'dad came back to me and his four children with a foot less, and as I often told him after, it served him in a way right. For what in the name of heaven had the Boers ever done him, whoever in God's name they was, that he should leave off peaceful shoeing horses, and go in their own country to fight them for it? What right had he, Dick, answer that question, nuh?'

Dick, having peeled the pip off the hen's tongue, handed the bird up to Bessie, who laid it in her lap and began to stroke its feathers.

'Didn't it serve him in a way right, don't you think, Dick?' the old woman insisted. 'Going to kill those Boers who'd never done him a single thing? Speak from your conscience, Dick.'

Dick said, turning the bit of callus from the hen's tongue round his fingertips: 'Well, he went to fight for his kind. To defend the Empire.'

'The Empire?'

'The Empire,' Dick said.

'What Empire?'

'The British Empire!'

'Listen, Dick,' said the old woman. 'I can't ever get this straight though I must have tried dozen of times to get the old man to put it right in my brain before he died: Ent Britain England?'

'Sure. Britain is England,' said Dick.

'And ent British come from Britain?'

Dick said, perhaps not too sure of himself: 'Well . . . yes. British from Britain.'

And how come that your gran'dad lost a leg at a place called Mother River in Africa, as he was so fond of relating, and you says that he went to fight for the king of England in Africa? What right had the king of England in Africa?'

'Well, I don't think that the king of England was there in person,' said Dick. 'But he had, well . . . interests there.'

'Interests?' said the old woman.

Well, it's like this,' said Dick. 'Years ago, just as we from the West Indies are going to England now, English men and women, British if you like, went and made their homes in other lands, Canada –'

'That's where Vere's sister gone to a hotel to do waitressing,' interrupted Bessie.

'. . . Australia, Africa, and so on,' continued Dick. 'And these places where the British made their homes became British and made up the British Empire. So the king of England had a right to interfere of any other nation tried to pinch the places where these English had made their homes, as the Boers wanted to do.'

'Oh, I see,' said the old woman, shaking her head up and down. 'It's a bit clearer now than I's ever understood it before. But how come you's all flocking to England like a parcel of sheep? Vere says she gets sixty-seven cents on every dollar that her sister sends her. Why don't some of you try and work for Canadian dollars to send back home? Ent you just told me we's all British?'

Dick said: 'Well, it's like this: A man had, say, twelve children. As the years passed by, the oldest grew up and left the old man and went and made their own homes. Mind you, you couldn't interfere with the old man and the younger kids they'd left at home for them to know, but at the same time the old man couldn't tell them who to let come in their houses and who not to. Well, it's like that with Canada and Australia and South Africa. They have grown up and are running their own homes, and they say they don't want us West Indians to come into them and that's the end of it.'

'But we can still run about in the backyard of the old home,' said the old woman. 'Is that what you mean?'

'Exactly. If you put it that way.'

'I see it all now. I see. Your gran'dad was never given to explaining. Still, I don't feel that your gran'dad had any right going to fight those Boers,' she persisted. 'Just as I don't feel you've got any right leaving bright, sunny Barbados and going to that bleak England, though I's often thought that with your reading and quickness maybe you could do better than you're doing.'

'I've thought so too, for a long time.'

The evening sun has struck through the leaves into his eyes, and letting himself down upon the lowest step he sprawled back, making a rest for his head with his interlocked fingers. The women looked down on his face, and when he spoke his eyes had a faraway look into the sky.

Bessie said: 'Your dad thought the same thing, and it didn't do him no good.'

Vere, the young cook, appeared round the corner in the yard, carrying a basket of groceries in her hand.

She rested her basket on the ground and sat beside Dick with a sigh, leaning her body heavily upon him.

'Your dad thought Barbados was too slow for him too,' said Bessie. 'He swaggered about singing the foolish songs of the money they'd made digging the Canal with the other fools just like, as Ma says, our dad used to sing about the "pound and a crown for every Boer they down". Only he hadn't the luck that your gran'dad had. He didn't ever come back.'

The old woman said: 'Died like a rotten sheep in Panama mud. No, no good ent ever come to our family leaving our land and forking ourselves in nobody else's. Not one bit of good.'

'Three for luck,' Dick laughed.

Bessie got stiffly to her feet, walked over to the fowl run, and put the white fowl in. Then she came back and stood looking down at Vere.

'You's a foolish girl, Vere,' said Bessie, after a time. 'Why don't you tell this Dick not to go to England?'

''Cause it wouldn't be any use,' said Vere.

'No use, nuh?' said the old woman. 'Hm.'

Vere said, sitting up and half-turning so that her word might be taken in by both women:

'You two had husband mind you, and nothing you could say or do could stop them from going away once their minds was made up. I ent see how I's been more foolish than either of you 'cause I ent been able to stop Dick here from going.'

Dick executed a long stretch before he said: 'My grandfather was sick of cleaning up the mess that Miss Barbara's dogs made in the morning, sick of watering the gardens under the big evergreen, sick of cleaning pips off these stupid fowls, sick of waiting for the few paltry shilling at the end of the week, just as heartily sick of the whole deuced show as I am myself now.

'And so when the chance of going to Panama came along nothing nobody could say could stop him from going, just as nothing nobody can say will stop me from going to England. My grandfather and dad didn't go because they wanted rid of their wives and children. They didn't go because they wanted an easy life. They didn't go for a spree. They went because their souls cried out for better opportunities and better breaks, and just like them, I'm going for the same thing.'

Bessie was still standing there her hand akimbo, looking down at Dick. When Dick finished speaking her eyes switched their measure to Vere, and with a fleeting lightening of her harsh face which none of the others saw she decided to play her last card.

'Still, Vere,' said Bessie, 'you're a foolish girl.'

Vere pouted: 'Say it again. A hundred times. Till you're tired.'

'What're you straightening your hair so for?' Bessie asked.

''Cause other girls do,' said Vere.

'And rouging your face, and plastering that red thing on to your mouth?'

''Cause other girls do.' Vere hugged her knees, rocking herself back and forth on the step.

'You was always a rude brazen little girl. All the same, I hope you's

[247]

got something else to make Dick stick by you. He going to England where he'll see hundreds of girls with real straight hair and really red cheeks and mouths natural like roses. Ten to one, one of them will get him.'

Vere sprang to her feet, her eyes dilated.

'And I'd spent the last cent getting to England, and wherever they was I'd find them out and tear the last straight hair from her head. I'd tear the flesh from her red cheeks to the bone!

'I'd beat her rosy mouth to a bloody pulp! Oh Christ, I'd . . .'

She caught at her breath in a long racking sob, snatched the basket from the ground and ran into the house.

The other three were all standing now, and in the understanding of Vere's love, had drawn involuntarily closer to one another.

The old woman said, knocking a beetle from Dick's shirt with her spoon: 'And will you still go to England, Dick?'

Their ears just barely caught the one word from his lips.

The women turned and, mounting the steps in the setting dusk, made their way together into the house.

The old woman said: 'It's the same with him as it was with them, Bessie. Nothing will ever stop him.'

'No. Nothing,' said Bessie.

(1958)

Henry Swanzy

The Literary Situation in the Contemporary Caribbean

Twenty years ago, I have been told, there did not exist a single separate book shop in Kingston, the capital of Jamaica, a city of over a quarter of a million souls. And doubtless the same attitude to books was shown in the other main centers of population: Port of Spain, Bridgetown, and Georgetown; although it is possible that Bridgetown, the capital of Barbados, may have been a step in advance of the others, remembering its two centuries of higher education. As for the other aspects of the literary profession, the printing presses, apart from the newspapers, the magazines with some critical standards and an assured relationship, they were simply not to be found.[1]

Today, of course, Kingston has a book shop, and what is more, a flourishing Library and Institute, with a junior section, run upon enlightened lines by enthusiasts, one indeed an American (with scientific training). The sense of what books can mean is being spread abroad by a great number of agencies, official or otherwise, the Extra-Mural Department of the new University College of the West Indies (whose Director, Philip Sherlock, is himself a poet), the British Council, the Rockefeller and Carnegie Foundations. They stretch out, directly or indirectly, by means of mobile vans, to the real backbone of the West Indies, the little villages lost in the mountains or strung out along remote and precipitous bays. In the last five years Kingston has even seen a special press, the Pioneer Press, started by the main newspaper, the *Gleaner*, to provide reading material for the new generation of self-awareness that is dawning. It, too, has a poet as director, Una Marson, who has had work published in England and America . . .

This material detail, the social background, is stressed because the literary world is pragmatic like any other, and the canon of literary achievement, the very commerce of ideas, depends so largely on the development of outlets. But perhaps it would be as well to note one further social fact before we come to the purely literary aspect of West Indian writing within the British sphere; that is the provincial, not to say the parochial, aspect of the literary setting. The two magazines, for example, try to be as catholic as possible, admitting writers from any island. This they succeed in doing for the South Caribbean, and particularly for Trinidad, the richest and the most cosmopolitan island of all, with the greatest tensions of race and class, the itch in the oyster that produces the pearl. They have little success in Jamaica, where I have been told that precisely three copies were ordered by the aforesaid book shop in Kingston of the work of the latest and in many ways the most interesting talent in the West Indies, the Barbadian George Lamming, author of the autobiographical novel, *In the Castle of My Skin*.[2] Literary activity in Jamaica is divided equally between a larger and a smaller horizon; the local branch of the International PEN Club, and the Poetry League, which confines most of its enthusiasm to the island, sometimes extending to the writers in neighboring Cuba and the French Antilles. It is a very human attitude, and one not unknown in other regions struggling to find a soul free of the burden of great traditions elsewhere. And indeed, despite this inevitable handicap (which is also a spur), and despite the further handicaps common to all tropical, colonial areas in an industrial age – the climate, philistinism, and materialism . . . it will probably be seen by the percipient reader that it is not easy to define a trend, among so many scattered units, at such an early stage, and in an area where the works of man are apt to follow nature, so lavish yet so brief in its creation. In a symposium of fourteen writers, fortuitously assembled in London in the summer of 1950, it was agreed that there was no such thing as 'West Indian writing'. In fact, any attempt to postulate such a development as desirable is regarded with suspicion, as an outside attempt to impose metropolitan patterns, even to relegate the region to the Atlantic fringe. Most West Indian writers have not really recognized the truth of Chesterton's aphorism that only the local is real – even when they most exhibit its truth in their attitudes . . .

Neither Selvon nor Lamming really set themselves up as critics of life, the rather easy criticism of the protest writer. To that degree, they may lose something, writing for their equals, a foreign audience, which will know, in general, what they are getting at, although missing the local strength. In this, they are like the poet Derek Walcott who is probably the most gifted verbally of any writer in the whole brief course of writing in the region . . . Walcott, more than any other West Indian poet, is least West Indian, or at least, most aware of the Western dilemma, since almost all his inspiration is literary . . .

Perhaps I should not end this rather discursive account without mentioning a small phenomenon of the contemporary Caribbean in which I have some interest, and without which I should have no reason for writing so much *ex cathedra*. All the works we have been considering are published; for what, after all, is literature? Yet some of the writers I have mentioned, and a great many others that I have not, find their outlet through aural rather than visual means. Or rather, many of them combine the cash of the BBC with the credit of *Bim* and to some degree *Kyk-over-al* and the little poets published in Guiana by A.J. Seymour. Most of them, of course, however successful in limited fields, do not rival in importance those who have attained the dignity of print; but one or two of them well deserve it. In Tobago, there is a poet, E.M. Roach, who has the genuine lyrical gift, which he puts at the service of the peasant, with no sense of condescension. So far as I know, he has appeared only in the review published by the University Extra-Mural Department, *Caribbean Quarterly*. In Guiana, there is another poet, Wilson Harris, a land surveyor, who has an astonishing quality of imagination, almost of mysticism, in which he brings back the Grecian heroes and the mysterious heads of Easter Island, for a new vision of the world, in which the beggar is king. (He is very far from being a Communist like another poet of the same type, Martin Carter.) As the mind ranges, it begins, indeed, to wonder whether the lesser names beneath the peaks may not have the real heart of the matter in them, so far as the development of a true canon of self-understanding is concerned. There is the gentle story writer R.L.C. Aarons, with his sense of pity, and the strange imagination of Inez Sibley, which can inject power into old legends of the terrorbull and the taunt song. There is a student Evan Jones, with a wonderful ballad of the banana-man, fresh and vigorous and true, and the East Indian V.S. Naipaul, with his gentle humour, and the brilliant monologue of Cyril Charles, and the sharp sense of form and satire of George Phillips, the occasional lyricism of Harold Telemaque, the delightful fancy of Eula Redhead, the group of poets Keane, Williams, and Campbell, the Catholic truth of Barnabas Ramon Fortune, and dozens more, who shine for a season, as most people do, I suppose, who are not pretentious, and write of what they know; from them, the listener has visited every kind of home in town and village, sat with the fishermen hefting sea-eggs, gone with the pork-knockers into Guiana jungles, followed the sagga boys and the whe-whe players, heard the riddles, the digging-songs, the proverbs, the ghost stories, duppies, La Diablesse, Soukivans, zombies, maljo, obeah, voodoo, shango. He has agonized over the waifs, the unemployed, the mental patients, scoundrels, fallen women, the rich and comfortable in their wall of privilege. Increasingly, he has come up against the double wave of prejudice, the old white prejudice which in many ways is growing. He feels, in short, that the new, creative phase in West Indian writing is only just beginning . . .

(1956)

NOTES

1 This article is part of our survey of the world's various national literatures during the past quarter-century. – *The Editors.*
2 From two lines by St Lucian poet Derek Walcott:

> You in the castle of your skin
> I the swineherd.

George Lamming

The Occasion for Speaking

I want to consider the circumstances as well as the significance of certain writers' migration from the British Caribbean to the London metropolis . . .

Why have they migrated? And what, if any, are the peculiar pleasures of exile? Is their journey part of a hunger for recognition? Do they see such recognition as a confirmation of the fact that they are writers? What is the source of their insecurity in the world of letters? And what, on the evidence of their work, is the range of their ambition as writers whose nourishment is now elsewhere, whose absence is likely to drag into a state of permanent separation from their roots? . . .

The exile is a universal figure. The proximity of our lives to the major issues of our time has demanded of us all some kind of involvement . . . We are made to feel a sense of exile by our inadequacy and our irrelevance of function in a society whose past we can't alter, and whose future is always beyond us. Idleness can easily guide us into accepting this as a condition. Sooner or later, in silence or with rhetoric, we sign a contract whose epitaph reads: To be an exile is to be alive.

When the exile is a man of colonial orientation, and his chosen residence is the country which colonised his own history, then there are certain complications. For each exile has not only got to prove his worth to the other, he has to win the approval of Headquarters, meaning in the case of the West Indian writer, England. If the West Indian writer had taken up residence in America – as Claude McKay did – his development would probably be of a different, indeed, of an opposed order to that of a man who matured in England. One reason is that although the new circumstances are quite different, and even more favourable than those he left in the West Indies, his reservations, his psychology, his whole sense of cultural expectation have not greatly changed. He arrives and travels with the memory, the habitual weight of a colonial relation . . .

I have lately tried to argue, in another connection, that the West Indian student, for example, should not be sent to study in England. Not because England is a bad place for studying, but because

[253]

the student's whole development as a person is thwarted by the memory, the accumulated stuff of a childhood and adolescence which has been maintained and fertilised by England's historic ties with the West Indies ... In England he does not feel the need to try to understand an Englishman, since all relationships begin with an assumption of previous knowledge, a knowledge acquired in the absence of the people known. This relationship with the English is only another aspect of the West Indian's relation to the *idea* of England ...

This *myth* begins in the West Indian from the earliest stages of his education ... It begins with the fact of England's supremacy in taste and judgement: a fact which can only have meaning and weight by a calculated cutting down to size of all non-England. The first to be cut down is the colonial himself ...

This is one of the seeds which much later bear such strange fruit as the West Indian writers' departure from the very landscape which is the raw material of all their books. These men had to leave if they were going to function as writers since books, in that particular colonial conception of literature were not – meaning, too, are not supposed to be – written by natives. Those among the natives who read also believed that; for all the books they had read, their whole introduction to something called culture, all of it, in the form of words, came from outside: Dickens, Jane Austen, Kipling and that sacred gang.

The West Indian's education was imported in much the same way that flour and butter are imported from Canada. Since the cultural negotiation was strictly between England and the natives, and England had acquired, somehow, the divine right to organise the native's reading, it is to be expected that England's export of literature would be English. Deliberately and exclusively English. And the further back in time England went for these treasures, the safer was the English commodity. So the examinations, which would determine that Trinidadian's future in the Civil Service, imposed Shakespeare and Wordsworth, and Jane Austen and George Eliot and the whole tabernacle of dead names, now come alive at the world's greatest summit of literary expression.

How in the name of Heavens could a colonial native taught by an English native within a strict curriculum diligently guarded by yet another English native who functioned as a reliable watch-dog, the favourite clerk of a foreign administration: how could he ever get out from under this ancient mausoleum of historic achievement?

Some people keep asking why the West Indian writers should leave the vitality and freshness (frankly I don't believe in the vitality talk, as I shall explain) for the middle age resignation of England. It seems a mystery to them. The greater mystery is that there should be West Indian writers at all. For a writer cannot function; and, indeed, he has no function as writer if those who read and teach reading in his society have started their education by questioning his very right to write . . .

The historical fact is that the 'emergence' of a dozen or so novelists in the British Caribbean with some fifty books to their credit or disgrace, and all published between 1948 and 1958, is in the nature of a phenomenon . . .

There are, for me, just three important events in British Caribbean history. I am using the term, history, in an active sense. Not a succession of episodes which can easily be given some casual connection. What I mean by historical event is the creation of a situation which offers antagonistic oppositions and a challenge of survival that had to be met by all involved . . .

The first event is the discovery. That began, like most other discoveries, with a journey; a journey inside, or a journey out and across. This was the meaning of Columbus. The original purpose of the journey may sometimes have nothing to do with the results that attend upon it. That journey took place nearly five centuries ago; and the result has been one of the world's most fascinating communities. The next event is the abolition of slavery and the arrival of the East – India and China – in the Caribbean Sea. The world met here, and it was at every level, except administration, a peasant world. In one way or another, through one upheaval after another, these people, forced to use a common language which they did not possess on arrival, have had to make something of their surroundings. What most of the world regard today as the possibility of racial harmony has always been the background of the West Indian prospect . . . The West Indian, though provincial, is perhaps the most cosmopolitan man in the world . . .

The third important event in our history is the discovery of the novel by West Indians as a way of investigating and projecting the inner experiences of the West Indian community. The second event

[255]

is about a hundred and fifty years behind us. The third is hardly two decades ago. What the West Indian writer has done has nothing to do with that English critic's assessments. The West Indian writer is the first to add a new dimension to writing about the West Indian community . . .

As it should be, the novelist was the first to relate the West Indian experience from the inside. He was the first to chart the West Indian memory as far back as he could go. It is to the West Indian novelist – who had no existence twenty years ago – that the anthropologist and all other treatises about West Indians have to turn.

I do not want to make any chauvinistic claim for the West Indian writer. But it is necessary to draw attention to the novelty – not the exotic novelty which inferior colonials and uninformed critics will suggest – but the historic novelty of our situation. We have seen in our lifetime an activity called writing, in the form of the novel, come to fruition without any previous native tradition to draw upon. Mittelholzer and Reid and Selvon and Roger Mais are to the new colonial reader in the West Indies precisely what Fielding and Smollett and the early English novelists would be to the readers of their own generation. These West Indian writers are the earliest pioneers in this method of investigation. They are the first builders of what will become a tradition in West Indian imaginative writing: a tradition which will be taken for granted or for the purpose of critical analysis by West Indians of a later generation.

The novel, as the English critic applies this term, is about two hundred years old, and even then it had a long example of narrative poetry to draw on. The West Indian novel, by which I mean the novel written by the West Indian about the West Indian reality is hardly twenty years old. And here is the fascination of the situation. The education of all these writers is more or less middle-class Western culture, and particularly English culture. But the substance of their books, the general motives and directions, are peasant. One of the most popular complaints made by West Indians against their novelists is the absence of novels about the West Indian Middle Class.

Why is it that Reid, Mittelholzer in his early work, Selvon, Neville Dawes, Roger Mais, Andrew Salkey, Jan Carew – why is it that their work is shot through and through with the urgency of peasant life? And how has it come about that their colonial education should not have made them pursue the general ambitions of non-provincial writers. How is it that they have not to play at being the Eliots and Henry Jameses of the West Indies? Instead, they move nearer to Mark Twain . . .

Unlike the previous governments and departments of educators, unlike the business man importing commodities, the West Indian novelist did not look out across the sea to another source. He looked in and down at what had traditionally been ignored. For the first time the West Indian peasant became other than a cheap source of labour. He became, through the novelist's eye, a living existence, living in silence and joy and fear, involved in riot and carnival. It is the West Indian novel that has restored the West Indian peasant to his true and original status of personality.

Edgar Mittelholzer was born in British Guiana in 1909. He came to Trinidad in 1941; but he was a name to me before I left Barbados to live in Trinidad . . .

Mittelholzer is important because he represents a different generation from Selvon and myself. He had suffered the active discouragement of his own community, and he had had their verdict sanctioned by the consistent rejection of his novels by publishers abroad. And in spite of this he made the decision, before anyone else, *to get out*. That is the phrase which we must remember in considering this question of why the writers are living in England. They simply wanted *to get out* of the place where they were born. They couldn't argue: 'you will see'; and point to similar examples of dejection in earlier West Indian writers who were now regarded as great figures. There were no such West Indians to summon to your aid. We had *to get out*; and in the hope that a change of climate might bring a change of luck. One thing alone kept us going; and that was the literary review, *Bim*, which was published in Barbados by Frank Collymore. This was a kind of oasis in that lonely desert of mass indifference, and educated middle-class treachery.

This experience is true of Trinidad. The story is the same in Barbados. British Guiana would be no different. In Jamaica, with a more virile nationalist spirit, the difference is hardly noticeable. They murdered Roger Mais, and they know it. And when I was there in 1956, Vic Reid, their greatest performer in the novel, was talking to me about going to Britain. Whether for a year or for good, Reid needed to get out. And it's an indication of his thinking and feeling when he said to me that evening in the course of talk about the situation of the West Indian writers: 'You know somethin, George? Roger is the first of us ...' I knew that Mais was dead, but it had never occurred to me to think of him as the first to die, meaning the first of the lot whose work appeared in England from 1948 to 1958. For that is the period we are talking about. This is the decade that has really witnessed the 'emergence' of the novel as an imaginative interpretation of West Indian society by West Indians. And every one of them: Mittelholzer, Reid, Mais, Selvon, Hearne, Carew, Naipaul, Andrew Salkey, Neville Dawes, everyone has felt the need *to get out*. And with the exception of Reid who is now in Canada, every one of them is now resident in England ...

If we accept that the act of writing a book is linked with an expectation, however modest, of having it read; then the situation of a West Indian writer, living and working in his own community, assumes intolerable difficulties. The West Indian of average opportunity and intelligence has not yet been converted to reading as a civilised activity, an activity which justifies itself in the exercise of his mind. Reading seriously, at any age, is still largely associated with reading for examinations. In recent times the political fever has warmed us to the newspapers with their generous and diabolical welcome to join in the correspondence column. But book reading has never been a serious business with us ...

The absence of that public, the refusal of a whole class to respond to an activity which is not honoured by money: it is this dense and grinning atmosphere that helped to murder Roger Mais. Mittelholzer survived it by fleeing the land; and Mr Vic Reid still breathes it, preparing, for all we know, to make a similar flight.

For whom, then, do we write?

The students at University College were always raising that question in their discussion ... Many of the West Indian writers would have passed through the same cultural climate. But the West Indian writer does not write for them; nor does he write for himself. He writes always for the foreign reader. That foreign does not mean English or American exclusively. The word *foreign* means other than West Indian whatever that other may be. He believes that a reader is *there*, somewhere. He can't tell where, precisely, that reader is. His only certain knowledge is that this reader is not the West Indian middle class, taken as a whole ...

An important question, for the English critic, is not what the West Indian novel has brought to English writing. It would be more correct to ask what the West Indian novelists have contributed to English reading. For the language in which these books are written is English which – I must repeat – is a West Indian language; and in spite of the unfamiliarity of its rhythms, it remains accessible to the readers of English anywhere in the world. The West Indian contribution to English reading has been made possible by their relation to their themes which are peasant. This is the great difference between the West Indian novelist and the contemporary English novelist ...

Writers like Selvon and Vic Reid – key novelists for understanding the literacy and social situation in the West Indies – are essentially peasant. I don't care what jobs they did before; what kind or grade of education they got in their different islands; they never really left the land that once claimed their ancestors like trees. That's a great difference between the West Indian novelist and his contemporary in England. For peasants simply don't respond and see like middle-class people. The peasant tongue has its own rhythms which are Selvon's and Reid's rhythms; and no artifice of technique, no sophisticated gimmicks leading to the mutilation of form, can achieve the specific taste and sound of Selvon's prose ...

The West Indian who comes near to being an exception to the peasant feel is John Hearne. His key obsession is with an agricultural middle class in Jamaica. I don't want to suggest that this group of people are not a proper subject for fiction; but I've often wondered whether Hearne's theme, with the loaded concern he shows for a mythological, colonial squirearchy, is not responsible for the fact that his work is, at present, less energetic than the West Indian novels at their best ...

So we come back to the original question of the West Indian novelists living in a state of chosen exile. Their names make temporary noise in the right West Indian circles. Their books have become handy broom-sticks which the new nationalist will wave at a foreigner who asks the rude question: 'What can your people do except doze?'

Why don't these writers return? There are more reasons than I can state now; but one is fear. They are afraid of returning, in any permanent sense, because they feel that sooner or later they will be ignored in and by a society about which they have been at once articulate and authentic. You may say that a similar thing happens to the young English writer in England. There is the important difference that you cannot enjoy anonymity in a small island ...

In spite of all that has happened in the last ten years, I doubt that any one of the West Indian writers could truly say that he would be happy to go back. Some have tried; some would like to try. But no one would feel secure in his decision to return. It could be worse than arriving in England for the first time ...

In the Caribbean we have a glorious opportunity of making some valid and permanent contribution to man's life in this century. But we must stand up; and we must move. The novelists have helped; yet when the new Caribbean emerges it may not be for them. It will be, like the future, an item on the list of possessions which the next generation of writers and builders will claim. I am still young by ordinary standards (thirty-two, to be exact) but already I feel that I have had it (as a writer) where the British Caribbean is concerned. I have lost my place, or my place has deserted me.

This may be the dilemma of the West Indian writer abroad: that he hungers for nourishment from a soil which he (as an ordinary citizen) could not at present endure. The pleasure and paradox of my own exile is that I belong wherever I am. My role, it seems, has rather to do with time and change than with the geography of circumstances; and yet there is always an acre of ground in the New World which keeps growing echoes in my head. I can only hope that these echoes do not die before my work comes to an end.

(1960)

Sarah Lawson Welsh

New Wine in New Bottles:
the Critical Reception of West Indian Writing in Britain
in the 1950s and Early 1960s

The 1950s and early 1960s signalled a period of immense literary activity for those Caribbean writers who had emigrated to Britain in search of jobs and better publishing prospects, but it was also a time of intense re-adjustment. The hasty, ill-informed, occasionally even malicious pronouncements which emanated from some parts of the British critical 'establishment' in relation to this new literary and physical 'arrival' reflected a social, political and cultural climate in which the immigrant was frequently regarded as an interloper, an alien presence or threat. In such a context, the opportunities for reciprocal literary and critical exchange were rarely maximized. Besides, some writers favoured a separatist position. For example, George Lamming offered this cautionary remark in 1960:

> What the West Indian writer has done [is] nothing to do with ...
> English critic[al] assessments ... The discovery of the novel by West
> Indians as a way of investigating and projecting the inner experiences
> of the West Indian community [is an] important event in *our* history.
> (**Lamming, 1960**: 37 and 41, my emphasis)

Others such as V.S. Naipaul have spoken in retrospect of the impossibility of full acceptance by the host society in Britain, rather than this being a conscious choice by the West Indian not to 'integrate'; similarly he recognizes that although the Caribbean writer might choose to ignore the critical pronouncements of the British literary establishment, he could hardly ignore the crucial role played by the 'whole physical apparatus of publishing, of magazines, the BBC' in his and many Caribbean writers' early careers (Naipaul, 1974: 122–3).

It is my contention that the critical response to these 'transferred' voices of West Indians in Britain constitutes a fascinating social archive of popular and critical attitudes to an emergent Caribbean literary canon at its primary site of production during this period: London. It is important to examine this archive of metropolitan critical attitudes to the subjects, form and especially the language of

West Indian literature, as it has tended to be overshadowed by critical attention to the Caribbean contribution to this cross-cultural
encounter of texts and minds in the metropole: the activities of the
BBC's *Caribbean Voices* programme under Henry Swanzy, the Caribbean Artists Movement (see Walmsley, 1994) and the views of writers
such as Naipaul, **Lamming (1960)** and **Marson (1949)**.

Whilst a 'benign point of view' (Allis, 1982: 2) characterized many
of the earliest critical responses in both the popular press and more
specialized literary journals, from the start the English critical establishment was beset by an 'approach [which] tended towards the
patronizing and simplistic' (Allis, 1982: 2). One of the most striking
features of reviews of this time is the over-emphasis on 'certain characteristics associated with the West Indies or considered to be West
Indian' (Allis, 1982: 2). Not only were these often misplaced or generalized assumptions but they acted to divert attention away from the
real issue at stake – the nature and quality of a rapidly growing
Caribbean literature.

Allis argues that this critical propensity towards stereotypes,
involved a view of the West Indies and the West Indian which foregrounded:

> the lushness of the scenery, the passion and
> exoticism of the tropics, and the simple but happy
> native folk with their quaint humorous speech while
> avoiding the harsher realities of poverty,
> deprivation and above all colour, race.
>
> (Allis, 1982: 2)

One such review, which appeared in *The London Sunday Observer*
(Hutchinson, 1956: 11) 'typified Selvon's tragi-comic West Indians
in London as happy-go-lucky wanderers who come here for the richly
dissolute life that London has to offer' (Allis, 1982: 2–3).

As Brathwaite found (**Brathwaite, 1970:** 37), many British reviewers
and editors seemed unable to transcend such expectations of exotica
and go beyond such stereotypical formulations in their reception of
Caribbean literature. The 'happy-go-lucky' West Indian was just
one of a number of related stereotypes including the 'child-like'
(un)sophisticate, the 'uncultured primitive', the threatening or 'savage'
presence and the irredeemably strange 'other', some of which were
derived from a much longer tradition of colonial representation. In

one particularly derogatory American review of Selvon's *A Brighter Sun* in 1949, the reviewer complained that the: 'acute [social] problems introduced in the novel are rather quickly abandoned; they are oddly non-corrosive, viewed as they are by "child-like" primitive eyes' (cited in Allis, 1982: 5–6). Wider analogies between a literature in its 'infancy' and a lack of intellect or sophistication are also to be found. In the case of some critics, this extended to an incredulity that any such writing could emerge from the Caribbean at all (Pritchett, 1953).

Caribbean writers and their work are frequently represented as 'little more than exotic adjuncts to the larger literary tradition of their adopted countries' (Phillips, 1989: 46) in reviews of this period and their writing is subjected to highly inappropriate (English) canonical criteria or to demeaning or insulting comparisons to other (often lesser or quite obscure) English or American works (Anon, 1952: 121). Cultural and linguistic difference is often foregrounded in an attempt to emphasize not only the 'otherness' of these writers and their work, but the potentially 'alienating' effects of their writing as far as metropolitan audiences are concerned; repeatedly, Caribbean writing is re-presented as problematic or 'obscure', as critics struggle with a critical vocabulary inadequate to the task of apprehending this new literary phenomena.

In no respect is this more apparent than in the critical discussion of the literary use of creole or characteristically West Indian linguistic forms. The following review of Selvon's work is not at all unrepresentative in speaking of creole or adapted dialect as an 'oddity': '[Selvon] writes with an engaging oddity – using a kind of Basic English with poetic undertones reminiscent of Uncle Remus – which is presumably the language of his characters' (Allis, 1982: 3). Other reviewers of Selvon make equally crude, if slightly less disparaging analyses. A reviewer of *A Brighter Sun* in *The Times Literary Supplement* writes, 'Mr Selvon writes vividly and poetically and his handling of the picturesque native idiom, which might so easily have become tedious, is excellent' (Anon, 1952: 121). A later reviewer of Selvon's *Ways of Sunlight* in the same newspaper acknowledges the author's 'great skill in handling the West Indian idiom ... [his command of] a poetic tenderness that radiate[s] both place and people' (Anon, 1958: 57). However, the reviewer's starkly polarized view of the language situation facing the Caribbean writer in London fails to recognize the linguistic phenomenon of code-switching along a continuum of language varieties and the radical creative potential of a syncretic approach to literary praxis, grounded in an aesthetic of cultural and linguistic cross-fertilization:

> Selvon's vernacular skill has survived his migration to London though in the process of transplantation he has virtually had to learn another language – perhaps not so much learn it as be obliged to practice it . . . The two idioms (West Indian and 'Standard English') are not always happy together . . . the problem is a real one: Mr Selvon is attempting to become a dual character without losing the bright individuality of his origins.
>
> (Anon, 1958: 57)

Although the reviewer does touch upon an important pressure felt by some Caribbean writers in London, that is, the need to ensure reasonable accessibility to a wider metropolitan audience (Selvon, 1982: 60), he fails to grasp the linguistic basis of Selvon's narrative style as a 'modified' rather than 'naturalistic dialect' and its integral part in his fiction, rather than being merely an exotic stylistic embellishment. Unable or unwilling to envisage a positive inflection to the cross-cultural mappings of diasporic experience in Selvon's writing and the possibility of multiple 'belongings', the reviewer advocates a monoglot, univocal route for Selvon if he is to survive as a writer in Britain: 'Unless he narrows his range artificially or returns to the West Indies he has no alternative. The problem of idiom can only increase as the circle of his identity expands' (Anon, 1958: 57).

The potential problems of decontextualized criticism and the influential role played by some British critics in establishing an agenda for Caribbean literary criticism during this period did not go without comment. Naipaul, for example, reflected:

> The social comedies I write can be fully appreciated only by someone who knows the region I write about. Without that knowledge it is easy for my books to be dismissed as farces and my characters as eccentrics . . . the critic of the *Observer* thinks I get my dialect from Ronald Firbank [1] . . . the critic of the *Yorkshire Post* says she is just fed up with Trinidad and Trinidad dialect . . . It isn't easy for the exotic writer to get his work accepted as being more than something exotic.
>
> (Hamner, 1979: 7)

In 1968 and 1969 Sylvia Wynter was to make the most direct call yet for an end to the 'pretended objectivity and detachment' (Wynter, 1968: 26) of what she termed 'acquiescent criticism' in both Britain and the Caribbean. The enduring strength of Wynter's argument lies in its refusal of simple binary oppositions and any slippage into the all-too-easy validation of 'insider' (i.e. Caribbean) critical readings over 'external', metropolitan ones. Instead, she argues that critics and writers in both locations – the exiled Caribbean writer in London as much as the English critic in the Caribbean – should recognize themselves as involved in the 'same historical process', fixed critical positionalities outside of which are both fraudulent and untenable. More recently Amon Saba Saakana has noted the intervention of English critics such as Colin MacInnes, Louis James and Gerald Moore in literary criticism for Caribbean journals during this period and reiterates something of Wynter's sense of the 'multiple ramifications [of exile] when viewed spectrally' (Saakana, 1987: 109).

The 1950s witnessed an increasing politicization of race as a key issue in Britain. The 1948 Nationality Act had facilitated large-scale immigration from the West Indies and other Commonwealth countries in order to supply urgently needed labour to specific (mainly service) industries in Britain ... However, when:

> the British economy began to take a turn for the worse in the mid 1950s and the shortage of labour in Britain's major industries began to recede ... the social consequences of this mass, unregulated arrival from the Caribbean and, increasingly after 1956, India and Pakistan, began to make a significant impact on British politicians.
>
> (Cashmore and Troyna, 1983: 48)

The heightened racial atmosphere of the mid to late 1950s was directly related to parliamentary pressure for stricter immigration control and the racial disturbances which broke out in the summer of 1958 in Nottingham and then in Notting Hill, London, further fuelled public and parliamentary debate on immigration and the black presence in Britain. Unsurprisingly, this new atmosphere was reflected and registered in the tenor of critical reviews of the work of Caribbean and black writers more generally. Allis cites several examples of this, including a short review of Naipaul's *The Mystic Masseur* in 1957 which warns, 'The characters in it are as excitable as children, while in Trinidad today maybe in the Tottenham Court Rd. tomorrow'

(Anon, 1957: 15).

A review of Selvon's *Turn Again Tiger* and Jan Carew's *The Wild Coast* in *The Times* a year later takes refuge in racial stereotypes by claiming that:

> The books of West Indians are almost as prominent in the bookshops as their physical presence is in the Bayswater Road, and they have a virility about them that cannot be ignored. The people who throng them belong to the world of the same dark-skinned Fielding but in both these novels there are signs that introspection is breaking in and what is more is recognised as the enemy.
>
> (Anon, 1958: 13)

Perhaps the most extreme manifestation of this racial undercurrent is to be found in a much later critical review. Auberon Waugh's 1972 review of Wilson Harris's *Black Marsden* in *The Spectator* displays a racism as overt as its condescendingly superior tone:

> I suppose it was to avoid being typecast as another negro writer that an intelligent and gifted novelist like Mr Harris chose to adopt this high-flown and idiotic style of writing. The expression 'negro writer' does indeed carry disparaging undertones ... I notice that *The Times* avoids this difficulty by describing Mr Harris as a West Indian writer. Perhaps Guyana, from whence he hails, is really part of the West Indies. I confess I am a trifle vague about these things myself.
>
> (Waugh, 1972: 1009)

However, a number of reviewers offer more intelligent and informed critical assessments of Caribbean literature during this period. John Lehmann opened the first edition of *The London Magazine* in 1957 with a foreword that is prescient in its recognition that this efflorescence of Caribbean and other Commonwealth writing would play a key role in changing the face and nature of fiction in the English language. Although Lehmann perhaps underestimated the long-term radical potential of this literature, which would become increasingly politicized and overtly confrontational in the 1970s with the emergence of a new generation of black writers in Britain, he did have the foresight to recommend that critical provisions should be made, based on the 'prophecy that the next few decades will show an immensely varied tradition in literature that uses the English language, because of the rise of literatures of distinct flavours, even with idioms and word forms of their own in the other English-speaking countries overseas' (Lehmann, 1957: 9). The foreword concluded that 'Very soon the literature of this country will be merely the oldest branch of a tree that has other strong branches not only in America but in the Commonwealth as well' (Lehmann, 1957: 9).

With the benefit of hindsight, the West Indian literary contribution in Britain might have been more aptly coined the start of a painful and deeply ingrowing toenail on the foot of the Mother Country – rather than the placid branch-plant metaphor that Lehmann chose to use. The latter was to find its most striking expression in the highly politicized dub poetry of Linton Kwesi Johnson in Britain in the 1970s and in the work of those 'Black British' writers who followed in his footsteps in the late 1970s and 1980s.

Another article, one that appeared in *The Times Literary Supplement* at this time (Anon, 1955: xv–xvii) also showed signs of this willingness to consider more widely the work of the 'other writers in English', including work of those Caribbean writers now based in London. The article explored with some accuracy the pioneering role of the BBC radio programme broadcast from London to the Caribbean, 'Caribbean Voices', and the creative activities of its participant authors. This was a welcome change from the propensity of many reviewers to 'review the writer rather than the book' (Allis, 1982: 5).

One persistent problem which beset the reviewing of Caribbean literature, as Lamming has documented (Lamming, 1960: 28–9), was the tendency of certain critics to use the reviewing space available to them as an arena for personal disputes and rivalries. This neither encouraged a positive response to the works supposedly under consideration, nor did it promote a serious image for Caribbean writers and West Indian literature. Admittedly this was not a problem exclusive to the reviewing of Caribbean texts. However, the relative infancy of this literature and the newness of the writers' sojourn in Britain meant that it was very much more vulnerable to critical neglect or a distorted image through biased or ill-informed critical comment. Lamming's frustration at the 'type of mind [which] cannot register the West Indian writer as a subject for intelligent consideration' (Lamming, 1960: 29) brought into focus a factor which still works against the widespread recognition of all but the most lauded and cosmopolitan Caribbean writers and their work.

(1991)

[267]

NOTE

1 Ronald Firbank's *Prancing Nigger* is a novel set in Cuba, the dialogue of which is written in a highly artificial dialect idiom. It was first published in Britain in 1925 and reissued in 1977 to much critical attention.

Reinhard Sander and Ian Munro

The Making of a Writer –
a Conversation with George Lamming

Qu: The periodical *Bim* remains an important medium of publishing for new writers. Would you comment on its significance to your own generation of writers?

The original meaning of *Bim* was never really fixed. I doubt myself that Frank Collymore realized that it would grow into the kind of journal it is today: the one journal which West Indian writers, at home and those abroad, support, the journal out of which so many established writers have grown ...

It started as the magazine of a little club, where people met to have debates ... the Young Men's Progressive Club, [but] at that it would have been anything but progressive. *Bim* started as a magazine for the members of the YMPC, as distinct from being a magazine even for Barbados.

The importance of Collymore in this respect is that he took *Bim* out of this club – first, into the island itself ... I became a sort of missionary in Trinidad for *Bim* ... Trinidad writers were recruited to send contributions.

Then the wider connection took place 4,000 miles away. Sometime in the 1940s, the BBC Overseas Service started a program called 'Caribbean Voices' and *Bim* served as a kind of pool from which they drew. Since the program went out to the entire Caribbean, *Bim* was brought to the attention of Jamaica and other places. So the BBC played a role of taking the raw material and sending it back, almost like sugar, which is planted there in the West Indies, cut, sent abroad to be refined, and gets back in the finished form.

Qu: West Indian literature has traditionally been a literature of exile, which poses a problem of audience for the writer. Could you define for us the kind of reading public you have in mind for your own work?

I hope it does not seem to contain an element of arrogance to say that a book like *In the Castle of My Skin* seems to me to be a book that is relevant to intelligent and sensitive reading in any part of the English-speaking world, for the reason that the kind of theme, the internal and external drama I am concerned with, is a very universal drama.

I know that there is an accusation by critics that I am a bit difficult. This means that I have to be read more slowly than would be the case with some writers, which I think is a good thing. Within the context of the Caribbean, what has hurt somewhat is that I am in fact cut off because of the lack of training in reading at a mass level of society. My greatest pleasure would be to know that the cane-cutters and the labouring class read and understood *In the Castle*; that would be infinitely more pleasing to me than the verdict of whoever is known as the most sensitive and perceptive critic.

Qu: But you feel, then, that the situation in the West Indies necessarily limits your audience there?

It causes a problem, because the common people are often too busy looking for bread. You know, when a man is really rummaging for bread, you can't be too hard on him when he says, 'I haven't the time for books.' The people whose lives are the substance of the book do not have an opportunity to see that life returned to them in literary form.

I suppose the one corrective to that really is the film; the visual medium is such a powerful thing. Sometimes I wonder if we are not on the eve of the disappearance of the book as a form of entertainment and of instruction . . .

Qu: How would you evaluate the current climate of writing in the West Indies for the individual writer – in comparison, say, to the situation when you first began to write?

Writing, you know, had never really been regarded as a particularly respectable activity in the area until recently. The writers who are respected are to a large extent respected because of their reputations *outside* the Caribbean. In fact, the same books . . . with the same *quality* of writing, had they come out of the West Indies (though I don't see how they would have, since there are no large publishing houses there), it would not have had the same kind of meaning. One of the important contributions that this particular generation of writers, Naipaul, Selvon and so on, has made is that they have made writing an honorable occupation. It is no longer a crazy thing for a young chap to say, 'I think I would like to be a writer.' When I was fifteen or sixteen, that would not only have been crazy, but he would have been frowned on, because what he probably meant was that he had no intention of getting a job, or something like that.

Qu: But has the situation of the young West Indian writer seeking to publish changed much? That is, is he still not dependent primarily on the verdict of the English publishing houses?

The situation has not substantially changed. This is rather disheartening. The London firms are setting up branches in the Caribbean, but publishing houses as indigenous growths, on the scale of doing novels and so on, are not yet there. I have no illusions at all about what one may call the 'commerce of culture'. Publishers are businessmen and books are commodities, and readers are consumers and when those chaps sit around the table after the manuscript has been sent about, they talk in the same way as I imagine people do who are selling detergents. I believe that one of the reasons they have not moved into the Caribbean in a bigger way is for the simple reason that the market is small. Even though their calculation may be, 'yes, an extraordinary body of literature has come out of that place', what do you do with a population of about five million, compared with, for instance, fifty or fifty-five million in Nigeria?

They are small territories, they are poor territories, and let us face it that when, right across the Caribbean you still have something like thirty per cent of the labour force – thirty per cent – unemployed, preoccupation with a publishing house seems a very small matter.

Qu: Your remarks so far seem to show that in order for West Indian writers to establish a reputation, they must still go abroad, as you did.

As a matter of fact, when I was back (I left in 1950, a good twenty years ago) as writer-in-residence at the University of the West Indies in 1957–8, I had graduate students who clearly with a little luck would be good writers, there could be no question about that, and this was the discussion all the time. They were coming for advice about leaving. Now, I would be in a position where it is very difficult for one's advice to be authentic. My advice automatically was, 'You must not', 'You should not', to which they would invariably reply, 'then why aren't you here permanently?'

But there have been just one or two, Derek Walcott for example, who never left. But the writers ten or fifteen years my junior are out of the area or are making preparations for departure – and I regard that, making preparations for departure, to be in some way a partial definition of their relation, the nature of their commitments to the area. It is characterized as a lack of confidence.

Qu: Recently, black literature has been more widely accepted as a valid part of the curriculum of schools in the US and in Europe. Has this development begun to have an effect on West Indian literature?

I'd like to say frankly that it has astonished me to notice in the various prospectuses for what are called 'Black Studies' across the US, the conspicuous omission of Caribbean literature, when it should be an immediate cultural concern for the US, because the Caribbean is part of the Americas . . .

I think that [this] is tied up again with the questions of size. What surprised critics was that in these areas which could almost be regarded as pebbles on the water, and were not associated in their minds with centers of cultivation, the language which they in English would have regarded as theirs exclusively could have been used with such flexibility and precision.

Qu: This problem though – the problem of critical acceptance – has faced all writers writing in English who are outside the traditional bounds of English and American literature, to some extent.

Yes. I think what they did not realize, and should have realized a long time ago, is that the English language does not belong to the Englishman. It belongs to a lot of people who do a lot of things with it; it is really a tree that has grown innumerable branches, and you cannot any longer be alarmed by the size and quality of the branch.

This is something which, as I said, they should have been aware of, because a similar thing happened in the American colonial period.

Matthew Arnold was a little puzzled about why the Americans should want something called an American Literature – I mean, since we had already loaned them the English Language, and after the political break we hadn't taken it back. I remember reading with great amusement in Marcus Cuncliffe's little book, *The Literature of the US* about the extremely derogatory remarks that used to be made.

But one would have thought that by the end of the nineteenth century any serious critic of the English language would have stopped thinking that the language belonged to England, it stopped belonging to England a very long time ago.

(1971)

Evelyn O'Callaghan

'The Outsider's Voice': White Creole Women Novelists in the Caribbean Literary Tradition

By the early 1980s, one could reasonably claim that although West Indian fiction was influenced by previous and contemporary schools of literary theory, there was nonetheless something called a West Indian literary tradition. Its main feature was one shared with the creole languages of the region: Syncretism. So a Caribbean literary tradition was one which created indigenous forms out of the adaptation of imported elements, rather like the genesis and development of West Indian creoles out of language contact situations.

No longer were West Indian writers attempting to imitate European models, nor indeed were they striving to gain admittance to a mainstream literary tradition whose arbiters would always view their function as 'filial and tributary' (Walcott, 'What the Twilight says: An Overture', 1972, p. 21). Neither did they consider their African heritage to be their only inspiration, although this heritage was now acknowledged, even celebrated, and the importance of African retentions in diaspora literature was recognized. Instead, with Walcott West Indian writers saw the lack of existing orthodoxies as a challenge to the creation of a creole tradition:

> Colonials, we began with this malarial enervation: that nothing could ever be built among these rotting shacks, barefooted backyards and moulting shingles ...
> If there was nothing, there was everything to be made.
>
> (Walcott, 1972, p. 4)

The 'creole tradition' was characterised by a concern with West Indian history (official and otherwise), not merely for the sake of analysis and the apportioning of blame, but as the subject of creative reinterpretation ...

In addition, this literary tradition was open-ended, 'elastic' in its approach to language, stylistically exploiting the resources of *all* registers of the creole continuum, and transcending rigid genre boundaries. Just as there is a lack of strict separation between 'the arts' in many West Indian territories – so that dance/drama/music/poetry may blend one into the other – similarly literature crosses oral/scribal,

[274]

sacred/secular boundaries and allows some degree of inter-genre cross fertilization . . .

Above all, this tradition focused on the syncretic qualities of the fiction, preserving survivals, adapting from other sources and creating out of these processes something new; no door was closed to the West Indian writer in the quest for a literary voice. Edward Brathwaite had consistently argued that historically, creolization involved creativity as well as imitative acculturation, and opposed the view of Caribbean culture as a static plural one in favour of the principle of productive friction. In literature too, a 'meaningful federation of cultures' was to be the norm. So, for example, Harris's outline of the Caribbean novel as 'a drama of living consciousness' cited Proust, Dante, Joyce, Patrick White, Tutuola and Malcolm Lowry as partial precursors of such a literary development (*Tradition the Writer and Society*, New Beacon, London (1967) pp. 34–5).

Obviously, this general overview of a literary tradition had to be refined. For example, Edward Brathwaite had raised the issue of whether or not white creole (native born) writers could properly be considered a part of this tradition, and decided that:

> White creoles in the English and French West Indies have separated themselves by too wide a gulf and have contributed too little cultur- ally, as a *group*, to give credence to the notion that they can, given the present structure, meaningfully identify or be identified, with the spiritual world on this side of the Sargasso Sea . . .

His argument seemed to be that the historical *facts* of white colo- nialism put insurmountable ideological barriers between white West Indian writers and the mainstream of West Indian culture, thus preventing novels like Rhys's *Wide Sargasso Sea* from constituting a truthful 'recognition of the realities of the situation' (1974, p. 38): that is, their perception and representation of experience was not true for most West Indians – the underprivileged, non-white majority.

For Brathwaite, the basis of culture in the Caribbean 'lies in the folk' (the Afro-Caribbean majority), and the bulk of his *Contra- dictory Omens* (1974) deals with the ways in which integration of other cultural groups and orientations into this Afro-Caribbean folk 'norm and model' may be achieved . . . Other writers and critics with a similar outlook have further defined and discussed this folk culture in terms of the 'peasant sensibility' which informs Caribbean literature. Clearly, the contribution of the white creole writer added little to the literary representation of this sensibility . . .

I want to claim that while it *is* true that the white creole writer (and protagonist) – especially the female of the species – represents the 'outsider's voice', yet this voice is an integral part of a Caribbean literary tradition. The perspective on West Indian reality articulated by these 'outsiders', 'the other side', cannot be provided by the expatriate European or the native Afro-Caribbean writer. And though this perspective . . . may be outmoded or even archaic, it is after all this reality, experience of and contact with this world-view, which gave impetus to the writing of much of early West Indian 'mainstream' literature . . .

The 'outsider's voice' . . . constitutes an important thread in the fabric of any Caribbean literary tradition, and one can focus on this particular perspective as expressed in three novels: Jean Rhys's *Wide Sargasso Sea* (1966), Eliot Bliss's *Luminous Isle* (1934) and Phyllis Shand Allfrey's *The Orchid House* (1953)[1] . . .

I want to demonstrate that these novels clearly belong within a literary tradition that concerns itself with 'interacting' racial/cultural orientations.

Jean Rhys (born Dominica, 1890) sets *Wide Sargasso Sea* (*WSS*) in Jamaica after the Emancipation Act of 1834; like Rhys's own maternal forebears, the white creole Antoinette's family had owned slaves. The break-down of plantation society and her family's growing poverty isolate Antoinette and her mother, until marriage to an Englishman saves them from economic ruin. But the freed blacks, who had mocked the whites' financial degradation, react with violence to their new wealth and burn the family estate. As a result, the family is split up and Antoinette, after years in the refuge of convent school, is married off to an Englishman, a virtual stranger . . . The novel ends with her incarceration in her husband's English mansion, [like] the Thornfield Hall of Brontë's *Jane Eyre*.

This novel deals with the attempt and failure of dialogue and interculturation: between white creoles and expatriate whites; between white, black and 'coloured' West Indians; between males and females, between colony and metropolis – one can take as the structuring principle Antoinette's assertion that 'there is always the other side. Always.' The mirror image of Antoinette/Tia (p. 38), and the conversation between Antoinette and her husband about the unreality of each other's environment (p. 67) are but two examples of failed attempts to communicate across racial, cultural, social and national barriers ...

Luminous Isle (*LI*) by Eliot Bliss (born Jamaica, 1903) chronicles Emmeline Hibbert's childhood in the white colonial Jamaican society of the early twentieth century. After an English education, Em returns, a young woman, to rejoin her parents and to play 'her part as their daughter in the social rounds of garrison life in a Crown Colony' during the 1920s. But despite her love for the island and her 'affinity' with the black population, Em finds she cannot become integrated into this life of 'perfect Englishness under the hot tropical sun'. As an artist, seeking to lead a free life of the mind without the petty restrictions of class or 'sex-consciousness', she eventually discovers that 'to be sexless, creedless, classless, free' she must leave her beloved Jamaica for a future in the less limiting society of England.

The book anatomizes the life of a privileged child born into the elite white ruling class of a black country. From the first pages of the text, with the distinction between the 'large white houses' and the 'nigger huts' of the two groups, the inter-relationship of races, classes and nationalities (expatriate and creole white values) and the conflicting viewpoints which arise, form the ever-present backdrop to the heroine's development, which in itself leads to the ultimate choice between island colony and metropolis.

Phyllis Shand Allfrey (born Dominica, 1915) sets *The Orchid House* (*OH*) on an island based on post-colonial Dominica, now ruled by coloured merchants, civil servants and the Catholic church. The novel harks back to childhood in the 1920s, but the concern with transitional politics suggests that the bulk of the action takes place in the 1940s–1950s period. Allfrey's theme is a society in change, mirrored in the microcosm of one white creole family. The old dispensation of the benevolent colonial patriarchy – like Rhys, Shand Allfrey's West Indian roots go back centuries – have given way to that of 'the master', emotionally crippled by his war experiences; in turn he passes control to the three daughters, Stella, Joan and Natalie, on whom the narrative focuses ...

OH continues the span of political history covered in the other fictions – from Emancipation through Crown Colony to early representative government. Again, the interculturation of, and changing relations between, white creole elite, coloured middle class and black peasantry are dealt with.

As in the other two novels, implicit questions are raised regarding the place and contribution of the white creole minority in the organization of West Indian society; again, the ambivalent nature of ties between colony and metropole is examined from the perspective of the white creole ...

Despite major differences in subject and treatment, these three writers, through their white creole female characters, collectively evoke an ultimately alienated 'outsider persona' who looks on but is rarely able to take part in the unfolding drama of West Indian socio-history ...

The female characters all belong to families who occupy an insecure position in the socio-economic hierarchy and thus don't quite fit into the rigid class definitions of their society. In *WSS*, Antoinette's background is wealthy planter class of English descent, but in fact her mother is from Martinique, and the family has been reduced to virtual poverty after the post-Emancipation financial crash ...

In Bliss's novel, Em is aware that for all their pretensions, her family's genteel poverty sets them apart ...

Again, the family of *OH* live in reduced circumstances, forced to sell their town house and live quietly in the country supported by their daughter's foreign money ... One should also note that the young women of L'Aromatique, like Allfrey and Rhys, are English-speaking Anglicans in a society which is predominantly French or French Creole speaking and Catholic – this, perhaps, adds to their distinctness and resultant isolation.

Secondly, all three novels describe societies in transition – the old order is disappearing and power is leaving the hands of the white creole elite ... It may be worth pointing out that *LI* was written in the 1930s, a time of growing political unrest throughout the West Indies, and *OH* was composed in the 1950s when most territories were on the brink of independence from British Colonial rule; *WSS* was written over a long period, during which the Caribbean islands gained independence and went through many social and political changes ...

Thirdly and most importantly, these creole women inhabit a kind of vacuum regarding their racial/cultural identity. Supposedly superior to their black compatriots, they are not considered equals by the expatriate whites, English people.

Antoinette's English step-father 'had made me shy about my coloured relatives' (WSS, p. 42); similarly, the girls of OH must deny their 'coloured cousins' to prevent scandal. But neither imitation of, nor pretence of English standards makes the white creole fully acceptable to the expatriate. Antoinette's husband thinks of her as strange, 'alien', perhaps mixed with some debased, 'tainted' blood. Stella, in OH, feels alienated from the metropolitan whites, the 'tamed city-living people' she meets en route to America, and is considered suspiciously strange by her own husband and mother-in-law ...

Wally Look Lai's comment on WSS can be applied, in some degree, to all three novels, in that they all touch on 'the theme of the existential chasm that exists between the white West Indian and his ancestors, and the tragic fate which awaits any attempt to bridge this chasm'.[2]

Look Lai also points out the white creole's 'fundamental closeness to the Negroes in feeling and response, despite the barrier which history has erected between them. This is a fact to which both races in the society are blind, but which is very noticeable to the observer' (p. 24).

In all three novels, white creole children assimilate the customs, folklore, language, music and spiritual beliefs of their black nurses and playmates, and all seek in some way to identify with the black population. Stella, in particular, is emotionally and physically close to Lally in OH, and Joan actually chooses to join with the blacks in their struggle for political representation and labour reform ...

Bliss's heroine, Em, though born of English parents, feels more affinity for black people than white since childhood: 'She liked niggers, they fascinated her. There was something restful about black people, and nothing in the least indecent' (p. 4).

And Antoinette's empathy with Christophine and admiration of the 'superior' Tia, hints at a desire to identify with them that Rhys herself clarifies in Smile Please:

> Once I heard her [mother] say that black babies were prettier than white ones. Was this the reason why I prayed so ardently to be black, and would run to the looking-glass in the morning to see if the miracle had happened?
>
> (Rhys, 1982: 42)

But Antoinette is *rejected* by Tia and viewed with hostility by the blacks because of their recent experience of white exploitation. Look

Lai draws attention to the fact that her choice of union with Tia and the black world at the end of *WSS* is based on an illusory gesture of welcome; just as white creole Anna's communality with the black masqueraders in *Voyage in the Dark* (1934) is achieved only in the realm of dream . . .

A gulf does exist between the races in the West Indies, and Allfrey acknowledges this in showing how different is the viewpoint of even the most well-intentioned of white creoles from the black peasants. For example, both Joan and Stella react against what they perceive as the passivity of the blacks, the refusal or inability of the islanders to struggle against the status quo for their own survival . . . However much they wish to empathize with the black peasantry, those white creole characters implicitly believe in the superiority of their perspectives and ideas . . .

Perhaps the attraction to black people as evidenced by these white creole women is largely an attraction to what they *perceive* as a freer, less restrained way of life. Certainly, sexual morality is far more casual among the blacks (see *OH*, p. 25 for example) and the vitality of black cultural expressions, such as Carnival, is admired, even envied: as Rhys expresses it in *Smile Please*, 'I decided that they [black people] had a better time than we did, they . . . were more alive, more a part of the place than we were' (pp. 50–1).

Certainly, Em's attraction to black people in *LI* is due to what she sees in their natures and values as antithetical to those of artificial white society . . . the point is that Em, alienated from her beloved island by the soul-destroying white society (*of which she is a part* even as she rejects it), projects all that she longs to be, in terms of union with the environment's sensuality, onto black people. In *themselves*, they are no more to her than servants and aesthetic objects; in the abstract, they symbolize an independence from social restrictions and a rootedness in the landscape which she'll never be able to achieve.

Christophine describes Antoinette to her English husband, 'she is not *beke* like you, but she is *beke*, and not like us either' (p. 128); the white creole woman is 'white nigger' to the English, 'white cockroach' to the blacks, and belongs in some indeterminate region between the two. Thus as Helen Tiffin puts it, she is 'a double outsider, condemned to self-consciousness, homelessness, a sense of inescapable difference and even deformity in the two societies by whose judgements she always condemns herself'[3] . . .

I have illustrated some of the ways in which these white West Indian women novelists have built up a *composite* figure of the white woman as ultimate outsider ... This figure is a second-class member of an already precarious social group; she's creole rather than 'real' (English) white, she belongs emotionally and spiritually to no group, despite efforts at partial integration. With neither blackness, nor money and 'Englishness' as a passport to identity, she's a lonely, withdrawn, isolated and marginal figure, subject to cruel paradoxes – such as having privileges with virtually no power, or being oppressed without the support and solidarity of fellow victims.

And as ultimate outsider, her situation presents a new variation on the Caribbean theme of creolization – a negative one. A product of two cultures, she's yet denied and despised by both, and her perceptions can reveal some of the devastating obstacles to true self-definition for the colonized West Indian ...

Interestingly, alienation (produced by historical and societal factors) leading to temporary or permanent exile and thus to artistic creation for these women writers, follows the same pattern as the male West Indian writer's well documented journey in a quest of a literary identity. Thus the factors that drive characters like Stella, Natalie and Em to permanent, wandering exile and Antoinette to madness, seem to have been channelled into creative literary production by their authors ...

It's my contention that these female writers, through their creation of white creole women characters, provide a certain literary perception of historical reality which is unavailable to other West Indians. The consideration of their insights and perceptions, their 'outsider's voices', can aid in the completion of a social history advocated by Erna Brodber as vital to the elucidation of *all* aspects of the West Indian tradition.

(1986)

NOTES

1 The editions quoted from are Penguin (1968), Virago (1984) and Virago (1982) respectively.
2 Wally Look-Lai; 'The Road to Thornfield Hall', *New World Quarterly*, 4; 2 (1968), p. 20.
3 Helen Tiffin; 'Mirror and Mask: Colonial Motifs in the Novels of Jean Rhys', *WLWE* 17 (April 1978), p. 328.

1966–79

Introduction

'Post-Independence blues': towards a Caribbean aesthetic

In his foreword to the first edition of *Savacou Kamau*, the Barbadian poet, critic and cultural historian Brathwaite commented on how:

> The West Indies at the present time, is in a state of post-Independence depression and everywhere we hear the sound of these blues ... there is, perhaps on a scale not experienced before a disillusionment of expectation ...
>
> (Brathwaite 1970–1: 70)

In a later study of the development of a 'Caribbean Aesthetic 1962–1974' he reflected on the sense of mis/indirection which, was a salient feature of the transition toward postcoloniality for many in the Caribbean:

> In 1962, the Federation of the West Indies broke up ... and the second great migration of our talent from the region began. True, we'd been left with universal adult suffrage, and this had taken us into our various independencies and, certainly, especially in Jamaica, there was a certain spirit and expression of nationalism. But our 'actions' had been mainly 'international' gestures: anti-establishment, anti-colonial: not popular, people-based, certainly not native ... The Federation turned out to be a dream of London. Somewhere along the line we'd forgotten Garvey, our grassroot selves, the insurrection of the 1930s.
>
> (Brathwaite 1977a: 56)

The redeeming feature of this period, for Brathwaite at least, was the perception that 'today we are involved with something much nearer ourselves, much more *of* ourselves. The significant protests that we want to make now can only be against or about ourselves' (Brathwaite 1970–1: 70).

Despite, his idealism, Brathwaite did register a palpable trend as a growing number of writers and critics in the post-independence era and years of transition to post-coloniality, turned their attentions inward and, with new vigour and urgency, sought to re-centre cultural and critical activity *in* the Caribbean (rather than the expatriate base of the 1950s). Nowhere was this more apparent than in a series of seminal journal essays which advanced the theorizing of a Caribbean aesthetic and contributed significantly to the debates concerning linguistic and formal experimentation in Caribbean literature – especially in relation to a new generation of writers (Brathwaite 1967, 1968/9, **Rohlehr 1972–3, 1973**, 1975, **Moore 1974**). Such intensified critical activity has led some to dub the 1970s as the 'decade of the critics' (Allis 1990: 31).

Amongst the key critical voices of this period was Cuban-born, Jamaican-based novelist, playwright and critic, Sylvia Wynter. **Wynter (1968, 1969)** called for an end to what she termed 'the appeasing arts'. She pointed to the complicity of Caribbean artists in a nexus of creative and critical praxis predicated on a 'branch plant' mechanism, one which made Caribbean writers and literature little more than commodities for a foreign market, located in and led by a metropolitan literati. Another important contributor, Kenneth Ramchand, commented unsparingly on the inadequacies of metropolitan critics in approaching Caribbean literature (1970: 117) and reflected on 'the enormous critical task waiting to be done' (1969: 83). Others, such as Brathwaite, called for a '(re) assertion of [the] local' which would involve the '(re)establishment . . . [of] links – artistic and intellectual – with the *people*', a need for an 'explosion of grassroots artistic/intellectual activity' (Brathwaite 1977a: 56). His privileging of these features was to have significant ramifications for critical as well as creative writing in the Caribbean. The strong sense of critical dialogue and dissent in this period constituted exactly the kind of 'protest . . . against or about ourselves' (Brathwaite 1970–1: 70) which Brathwaite had hoped for and went some way towards fulfilling his wish that Caribbean writers be provided 'with a way of seeing = thinking/feeling = saying . . . a literary criticism not of description (of parts, of features) [as in the 1950s and early 1960s] but of *explanation*' (Brathwaite 1977a: 184). By 1978, Brathwaite was already confidently stating: 'we are at last experiencing an *aesthetic*, rather than the more limited critical mind in action' (Brathwaite 1978a: 183).

Poetry: beyond Walcott vs. Brathwaite

However, critical dissent could also have negative connotations. In this period, Caribbean poetry was frequently approached via the organizing lens of disputing polarities, of which the so-called 'Brathwaite vs. Walcott' debate is the most (in)famous (see Ismond 1971). Arguably this binarism has been more debilitating than productive. Even the writers themselves contributed to this polarized debate, each at times seeming to fuel the 'feud' (Walcott 1973: 127–8) or appease the other's point of view (Brathwaite 1970–1: 5). As Collier (1985) has pointed out, such emphasis on poetic reputation has tended to occlude the poetry itself and overshadow some interesting connections between their work (especially when the folk base of much of Walcott's drama is taken into account). The high critical profile and tremendous productivity of **Walcott** and Brathwaite also tended to 'drown out' some other interesting poetic voices during this period. They include Jamaicans **Mervyn Morris** (1973, 1976, 1979), **Dennis Scott** (1969, 1973) and **Anthony McNeill** (1972), Trinidadian Victor Questel (1979), as well as the publication of early poems by women writers such as Jamaicans **Christine Craig** and **Lorna Goodison** and Guyanese **Mahadai Das** and **Rajkumari Singh**. The emergence of a new generation of radical, performance/ dub poets who included: Jamaicans Bongo Jerry, **Mutabaruka** (1973, 1976, 1980), Oku Onuora (1977), **Michael Smith**, and in Britain, **Linton Kwesi Johnson** (1974, 1975, 1980) should also be acknowledged. As a corrective gesture, we therefore include poems by Craig, Das, Singh, Scott and McNeill and some of the dub poets but we nevertheless strongly encourage readers to explore the extensive and rewarding poetic archives of Walcott and Brathwaite.

Anthony McNeill's **'Residue'** is a good example of the new expression of cultural confidence in the 'here and now' which Brathwaite noted (1970–1: 9). However, the re-appropriation of the indigenous and the local in the poem is not unproblematic: the pared-down, almost elemental landscape (reminiscent of Walcott's *Castaway*), is also inhabited by 'lolloping tourists' and thoughts 'of Columbus' – both potent reminders of the larger colonial frame. In this respect, 'Residue' may be usefully read alongside the ironic treatment of Columbus in **Kincaid (1985, 1988)**. Jamaican playwright and poet Dennis Scott's **'Squatter's Rites'** is one of a series of poems dealing with the Rastafarian in Caribbean society and can be read alongside Brathwaite (1973: 42–5), **Berry** (1985: 75) and novels such as Wynter's (1962), Mais's (1954, 1955) and Patterson's (1971). The poem charts a shift from country to city as in other Caribbean texts (**De Lisser 1917**, Selvon 1952, Brathwaite 1973) but is more centrally concerned with Old Ras' dispossession from the land, his marginal position soci-etally and the more profound vulnerability and 'unhousedness' of his state (in both senses of the word in this linguistically playful poem). Scott's comments on Rastafarians as 'one of the healthiest phenomena that the New World has thrown up ... in the sense of choosing a life-enhancing value system [and as] a creole development – a group, people, who can trace most of their roots to another continent ... have had to come to terms with an environment which is essentially strange to them ... and to forge some kind of world-view' (Markham ed. 1989: 138–9) are illuminating here – especially to the poem's ending which links father and son as creative artists within a hopeful vision of the future. '**Grampa**' may be productively read alongside other elegies to male figures (**Linton Kwesi Johnson 1984**) and other creole monologues (Bennett, Craig and Berry), as well as the more dominant mythologizing and elegizing of the grandmother figure in Caribbean literature (Senior 1989: 62–75, Brodber 1980, D'Aguiar 1985).

Mahadai Das and the late **Rajkumari Singh** were amongst the first published Indo-Caribbean women writers, an achievement which needs to be contextualized within the persistent marginalization and devolving of Indo-Caribbean culture within the mainstream (see 'Coolie Connections', pp. 20–2). Singh's contribution to the cultural life of Guyana, as poet, dramatist, editor and encourager of the arts – particularly a generation of younger poets, writers, artists and performers – has been highly significant but is often unrecognized outside her native Guyana. We include '**I am a Coolie**' as an important polemical and impassioned essay which argues for the re-inflection and political mobilization of 'Coolie' as a term of affir-mation rather than denigration. In this respect, Singh anticipates Dabydeen's similar project (**1989**), and parallels synonymous reap-propriative projects in the areas of feminist theory and 'queer' theory. Singh's reference in this piece to **Per Ajie** links it to her poem of the same name, which is a more fully realized attempt to pay tribute and give subjectivity to the great-grandmother who emigrated with some 239,000 indentured labourers to Guyana from India between 1838 and 1918. Both pieces by Singh can be profitably read alongside fellow Indo-Guyanese writers **Das (1987)** and **David Dabydeen (1995)**, who are also concerned with this very different 'journey to an expectation' and with the early immigrant life of their people, as well as more recent texts dealing with an Indo-Caribbean peasant experience (Monar 1985, Dabydeen 1989). The gendering of Per Ajie as both an erotic and exotic object in the eyes of a brutal colonial and masculine regime, and as a maternal figure of blessing and redemption is equally important to a reading of this poem and cannot be disentangled in this case from the telling of a founding Indo-Caribbean experience. Craig's **'Elsa's Version'** usefully interrogates the male construction of Jamaican women as idealized signifiers of national identity by foregrounding the wageless work of many women, the slack (obscene) reggae lyrics and other anti-feminist elements of Jamaican society in an impassioned plea to be 'deal[t] wid' as 'I ... a real somebody', an individual and a woman in one's own right.

'Dub and beat and us and dem': journal activity and the 1970 Savacou 'new writing' anthology

Many of the writers' works during this period first appeared in Caribbean 'little magazines', the role of which remained highly significant during this period. Whilst in Barbados *Bim* continued to launch writers such as Timothy Callender, John Wickham and Austin Clarke, other little magazines such as the Trinidad-based *Tapia* (1970–) (now *The Trinidad and Tobago Review*), *Kalaloo*, *New Voices* (1975–), and *Kairi* (with its accompanying activist group of the same name) were also actively encouraging local writing. Arguably, it was the Jamaican-based *Savacou* which was to be most influential in charting the course of a literary aesthetic and in opening up the canon to new forms and voices in Caribbean literature during this period. Two anthology volumes of 1970–1 and 1979, edited and introduced by Brathwaite, 'frame' the decade and as such provide a useful barometer of how far the critical and creative practices of Caribbean literature were undergoing change. They show a shift in concern from anti-colonial, oppositional modes, levelled against inscriptions and ascriptions of non-identities, to more introspective and 'non-colonial' attempts to reclaim a Caribbean subjectivity. They also demonstrate a shift in critical tone, whereas the 1970 introduction constitutes an important statement of hope and of the positive ethics of Caribbean literature, whereas the 1979 introduction acknowledges more fully the extent to which colonial systems were perpetrated and the ideals of freedom/ self-definition problematized by 'two decades of traumatic post-independence change' (Brathwaite 1979). Similarly, the 1969 (July) issue of *The Journal of Commonwealth Literature*, and the 1970 (2.2) issue of *The Literary Half Yearly* have been viewed as 'show[ing] West Indian literature, not as the struggling infant of the pioneering *Tamarack Review* issue of 1960, but as a sophisticated literature with its own themes and motifs, and its own academic critics capable of dealing with them' (Allis 1990: 31).

Savacou developed out of the Caribbean Artist's Movement established by John La Rose, Andrew Salkey and **Kamau Brathwaite** in London in 1965. It maintained both a dual literary-historical focus and British connections via CAM. The publication of the first of an influential series of 'New Writing' editions in 1970 acted as the unsuspecting catalyst to a particularly fierce 'debate about aesthetics, tradition, literary criticism and sensibility in the West Indies' **(Rohlehr 1972–3: 82)** and the role of social and cultural contexts in the assessment of Caribbean poetry (Rohlehr 1972-3, **1973**).

Gerald Moore welcomed the Volume, commenting:

> Gone is the comic intrusion of the creole speaker into the polite circle of the educated ... Gone is the polite tradition, afraid of letting out rude noises, and always looking over its shoulders for approval **outside** the islands. Much of the poetry in *Savacou* 3/4 seems, rather, to exult in its freedom from alien restraints. It is a poetry which restores the need for immediate audience, even though it can be relished by solitary reading also ...
>
> **(Moore 1974: 71)**

Likewise, Gordon Rohlehr welcomed this evidence of 'the confidence with which young writers are trying to shape ordinary speech, and to use some of the musical rhythms which dominate the entire Caribbean environment' (Rohlehr 1972–3: 82). However he noted 'it is precisely this that disturbs some critics of West Indian poetry' **(Rohlehr 1972: 82)**. One of Rohlehr's particular focuses in **'West Indian Poetry: Some Problems of Assessment'** was the Tobagan poet Eric Roach whose criticism of the selection of poems for the *Savacou* 3/4 anthology crystallized a number of issues currently to the fore in the critical reception of Caribbean literature.

Although some of Roach's early poetry had made use of a modi-fied creole in a re-rendering of popular folk tales and myths, his mature work was more studied, formalized and at times mannered, and this is the Roach whom Rohlehr attacks. Rohlehr sees Roach as, in many respects representative of an older generation of West Indian poets, those who privileged standardized 'literary' language and traditional (i.e. European) forms which were culturally divergent, if not opposed to those employed in much of the 'new writing'. The former positionality stressed 'craft' and the 'civilizing' influence of a European tradition and culture: 'One must erect one's own bungalow by the sea out of the full knowledge of the architecture of the English places and cottages' (cited in **Rohlehr 1973**: 141). Furthermore, and importantly distinct from **James (1970)**, with whom Roach may seem to be in some consensus here, it demonstrated a marked distaste or disapproval for the new attention to racial politics and the Afrocentric purchase on Caribbean 'folk' culture which critics such as **Brathwaite** and **Rohlehr** were keen to promote (see Rohlehr 1972: 85) (and novels such as **Roger Mais**'s (1953, 1954, 1955), Namba Roy's *Black Albino* (1961), and **Wynter**'s *The Hills of Hebron* (1966) had already articulated). Roach's prediction was that 'all this soap box street corner ranting and posturing' would be shortlived **(Rohlehr 1973**: 141).

In a related piece Rohlehr (1973–4) articulated this creative tension between a literary and critical praxis which privileged the 'civilizing' influence of a European tradition and culture, and that which clearly did not, in a thinly veiled allusion to fellow critic and academic, Ramchand:

> One can still find the [literary] critic who believes that a thorough grounding in F.R. Leavis, will help us here, and help us to understand why Bongo Jerry [one of the more radical, performative poets included in the *Savacou* 3/4 anthology and analyzed in Rohlehr 1973: 139-40] writes as he does.
>
> (Rohlehr 1973–4: 232)

However, he advised:

> one will have to study the Caribbean people and ... listen to them, before one can learn to make important or relevant critical statements

on the new writers. The critic's business is first to understand the contexts out of which the work that he is examining grows. Our context is simply not Leavis.

(Rohlehr 1973–4: 232)

Matters of audience, the writer and society

This shifting of the critical axis away from the so-called universalist tenets of much criticism of Caribbean writing in the 1950s and early 1960s and towards a stronger appreciation of regional cultural and political contexts was developed further in 'A Carrion Time', where Rohlehr argues, after Brathwaite, for 'alternative ways of seeing both society and the artist ... the possibility of a different relationship between them' (1975: 99). Challenging the dominant literary construction of the Caribbean artist as an alienated individual, part of 'a community of the elite ... elaborately and expensively trained in the graces of the inheritance ... of a great tradition' (Rohlehr 1975: 99), Rohlehr signalled the extent to which conceptions of the writer and his/her audience were shifting. As Brathwaite reflected:

Until recently, the writer was hero ... one of the elite; his distance overseas added to the glamour ... But suddenly ... all that has changed. We now have a mature contributing audience who demand to share in the artistic exploration of our terrain. Not you and me, but us. Not what is happening there, but here.

(Brathwaite 1970–1: 9)

Brathwaite's confidence in the changed relationship between writer and audience – and even in the existence of this audience – was perhaps premature, even if the call to recentre critical as well as literary activity in the Caribbean and to widen the creative and critical terrain to a more heterogenous body of indigenous writers was a positive one. James Berry wrote of the Caribbean writer in Britain: 'He has missed out on the exciting process of rediscovery ... [of] Westindians at home' (**Berry 1976**: 9–10).

However, the optimism of some of these cultural and critical documents is thrown into relief by the testaments of other writer/ critics who found less to celebrate during this period. The 'exciting process of rediscovery' which Berry perceived to be afoot in the Caribbean in the post-independence period and Rohlehr's projected

[289]

inter-connectedness between artist and audience, writer and society were more easily articulated than realized, it would seem. The untimely deaths of Guyanese novelists Edgar Mittelholzer and Roach during this period and **Walcott**'s following comment all testified to a gloomier prognosis, which reflects back to Brathwaite's 'blues': 'It is almost death to the spirit to try to survive as an artist under colonial conditions which haven't really changed with our independent governments' (Walcott 1970: 45).

Since **James**'s and Mendes's 'barrackyard fiction' which had aimed to capture the idiom and milieu of the yard communities of 1930s Trinidad, a 'gulf' of class, education, literacy, exile (or all of these factors) still often separated the middle-class artist from his subject-matter. This 'frightening gap between the writer and the society he describes' (Brathwaite 1968–9: 158) continued to cause concern amongst a number of Caribbean writers and critics (Brathwaite 1968–9, **Lamming 1971**: 10). Despite his own major contribution to the shaping of 'camps' on the contentious critical terrain of this period, Rohlehr's call for 'bridges to be built between the privacy of pain and a rooted sense of community, between the artist who borrows his goggles from the alienated West and the other kind of artist who tries to work with what he finds right in his backyard' (Rohlehr 1975: 108) can still be read as powerfully regenerative given the context in which it was originally voiced, and in the sense of its greater inclusiveness – even more strongly creolized than Brathwaite's call for a return to alter/native forms. More recently, Rohlehr has formulated the idea of code-switching along an aesthetic continuum in Caribbean literature (Rohlehr 1986), a model similarly receptive to the creative possibilities generated by a culturally plural and syncretic framework.

Caribbean criticism: some seminal moments

Brathwaite's cultural analysis anticipates that of Rohlehr in its painstaking yoking of particular details and local events with a broader sense of an emergent aesthetic and both can be located in an iconoclastic or polemical tradition of Caribbean criticism (see *The Beacon* editorials **1932**, Reid **1978**, Lamming **1960**, Singh **1973**, Dabydeen **1989**, Kincaid **1988**). Both subscribed to a belief in the 'revolutionary' possibilities of Caribbean literature at a time which saw an 'inva[sion

of politics into] the private life' (Rohlehr 1975: 94) and increased political instability in many territories (e.g. the heightened racial tensions
of the Burnham years in 1960s Guyana, the Black Power Riots and
popular discontent in Trinidad in 1969–70).

Other seminal critical pieces were important in different ways.
Brathwaite's 'Timehri' (1970) examines a range of issues pertinent to
his own work and to Caribbean literature more generally. Brathwaite
explores creolization, not as yet theorized in terms of a cultural
aesthetic but in terms of distinct 'socio-cultural orientations' created
in the interface between different ethnicities and cultures in the New
World. He outlines the empowering sense of community and the
positive re-scripting of Caribbean culture which might be gained
through the reclamation of aspects of African and Amerindian ancestral cultures in the Caribbean. The value of this ancestral recognition
for the developing Caribbean aesthetic is outlined by Brathwaite
as 'a journeying into the past and hinterland which is at the same
time a movement of possession into present and future ... discovering word for object, image for the word' (Brathwaite 1970: 44).
'Timehri' is also significant in its exploration of the important but
marginalized contribution of Amerindian culture to contemporary
Caribbean art forms. 'Timehri' belongs, in part, to an autobiographical tradition to which Walcott also made key critical (e.g. 1970)
and creative (e.g. 1973) contributions during this period. Interestingly,
Brathwaite constructs a kind of 'revisionist (personal) history' which
minimizes his educated middle-class origins in favour of the lower-
class 'folk' base and Afro-centrist orientation of his experience: a
direction he was increasingly gravitating towards in his poetic and
critical work.

The publication in 1967 of Wilson Harris's *Tradition, the Writer
and Society* marked an important and interesting intervention in
Caribbean criticism and a companion lens to his fictional works, which
date from 1960 with the publication of the influential *Palace of the
Peacock*. Harris's writing, both fictional and critical, is marked by a
unique and complex vision which although widely admired has not
been easily accommodated within Caribbean literary traditions or
critical paradigms and is often categorized as being more akin to the
'magic realism' of South American writing. The work of Gilkes (1975,
1989) and Maes-Jelinek (1976, 1991) has been central in an attempt
to bring Harris's original and challenging writing on myth, history

and cultural wholeness to the attention of a Caribbean readership, but in many other works his elaborate and scholarly conceptualizations of syncretism and universality have been both simplified and bowdlerized in a flattening out of post-colonial and post-modern aesthetics.

Walcott's **'Muse of History'** has been more influential in debates on the writer, ancestry and history, during this period and since (see Naipaul 1962, 'What the Twilight Says', preface to Walcott 1970, Walcott 1974: chapters 19 and 22 and **Rohlehr 1972–3**: 86). Walcott argues for a 'revolutionary philosophy based on a contempt for historic time' and rejects linear narratives in favour of a more fluid, inter-penetrating sense of past and present. For Walcott, once the fictional basis of history is grasped ('history is ... a kind of literature without morality'), the writer may 'successful[ly] confront ... fictions about the past ... [and] determine his own lineaments' (Breiner 1986: 142). In this way Caribbean writers and peoples are liberated from the limiting positionalities of 'recrimination and despair', previously considered axiomatic to any discussion of colonial history. In his emphasis on history as discourse Walcott parallels certain European theories (e.g. most particularly those of Foucault and Hayden White 1973); in his formulation of a cyclical or fluid notion of the past he reflects aspects of Harris's fictional vision, and in his stress on 'maturity [as] the assimilation of all the features of the ancestors' his work anticipates later texts such as Brodber (1980).

Women writers and the beginnings of a gender-based analysis of Caribbean literature

In terms of male authored texts, this period was essentially one of consolidation of established writers, with prolific publications by Walcott, Brathwaite, Naipaul, Harris, **Selvon**, and Salkey. Despite the emergence of a number of new male voices (in addition to those already mentioned) such as St Lucian Garth St Omer, Trinidadians Michael Anthony and Harold Ladoo and Barbadian Timothy Callender, Ramchand commented in 1978: 'No major West Indian talent has emerged since the establishment of Walcott, Harris, Naipaul and Rhys, unless criticism has failed in its responsibility to others besides Garth St Omer and ... Harold Ladoo' (Ramchand 1978: 168). Perhaps if he had attended more closely to the emerging voices of a large number of Caribbean women writers, he might have noticed a major critical failing and thus concluded differently. Those overlooked by Ramchand included Trinidadians **Merle Hodge**, Marion Patrick Jones, Jamaicans Olive Senior, **Lorna Goodison**, **C. Craig**, Pamela Mordecai, Valerie Bloom, Velma Pollard, Beverly Brown, Gloria Escoffery, Jean Goulbourne, Rachel Manley, and Guyanese Shana Yardan, **R. Singh**, **M. Das** and Guyanese British Meiling Jin. The 1970s also saw the beginnings of a more serious, sustained and mainstream interest in Caribbean women's writing as a tradition of its own, as demonstrated by the inclusion of seven women poets in the important *Savacou* 3/4 'New Writing' anthology (1970/1), the publication of an anthology of women's poetry, *Guyana Drums* in 1972, a *Savacou* special edition on Caribbean Woman in 1977 and the groundbreaking publication in 1980 of another anthology of (hitherto largely unpublished) women poets, *Jamaica Woman* (Mordecai and Morris eds 1980).

However, although the emergence of a gender-based analysis in the Caribbean can be traced to this period, early examples still concentrated on the deconstruction of images within male texts and thus still registered the primacy of critical agendas established in relation to the 1950s proto-canon of mainly male writers as the reference points for any discussion of women's writing (Cobham 1981). The critique of male writing, according to these criteria, was followed by a shift towards the discussion of gendered representations in women's writing (Gonzalez 1974, Thorpe 1975, Loncke 1978, 1986, Cobham 1990). However, this too tended to re-confirm the centrality of the 1950s androcentric canon and did little to outweigh the analysis of male writers which still dominated the discussions of a Caribbean aesthetic (see **Brathwaite, Rohlehr, Wynter, Moore**).

One early example of this content-based criticism is Anson Gonzalez's section on women writers in *Trinidad and Tobago Literature on Air* (1974). Interestingly, with the exception of Hodge, Gonzalez chose to focus mainly on earlier and generally critically neglected Trinidadian women writers such as Olga Yaatoff and Kathleen Archibald. He thus makes an early, if slight, contribution to the recuperation of female voices, which became a key part of the critical agendas being established both within the Caribbean and elsewhere in the latter part of this period (Showalter 1977, Olsen 1980). Gonzalez's analysis, although valuable in this respect, is clearly characteristic of this embryonic, early 1970s criticism of Caribbean women's writing: it privileges public over private themes and forms (e.g. love poetry) and tends to read for female economic independence and autonomy from heterosexual structures in rather basic and unproblematized ways, invoking various stereotypes such as the resilient Caribbean woman ('always hard working and fortuitous') (see Brodber 1982 and O'Callaghan 1993: 74 for more on this). Furthermore, Gonzalez's attention to these (still) neglected writers was disappointingly accompanied by an unintentional neglect of, or blindness to, the exciting works of many women writers in the Caribbean contemporary with his analysis, and consequently had little effect in raising the critical profile of women's writing in the region as a whole. Even later, more sophisticated, analyses have been in danger, it would seem, of prematurely establishing agendas which would not be flexible enough to accommodate the range and variety of women's writing emerging at this time.

Despite **Evelyn O'Callaghan**'s claim that the 'admission of women writers into such a [Caribbean] "canon" as exists has not been problematic since this canon is **not** an attempt to shore up the status quo, eschewing any deviant or subversive minority art' (O'Callaghan 1987: 10), the politics of reading Caribbean literature established in the decades immediately preceding and prevalent in the early part of this period, *did* have had a real and lasting impact in engendering a greater invisibility and (under)development of a critical tradition in relation to Caribbean women's writing. The desire to recuperate or uncover a 'tradition' of women's writing in the Caribbean had first to overcome a virtual denial that a 'tradition' might exist in many quarters. For example, Andrew Salkey's substantial short story anthologies from this period (Salkey 1960, 1965, 1967) include no women writers. Although John Figueroa's two poetry anthologies, *Caribbean Voices* I and II (Figueroa ed. 1966, 1970) do include a small number of women poets, curiously even as late as 1982, his *An Anthology of African and Caribbean Writing in English* includes no Caribbean women prose writers. Likewise, the first edition of Bruce King's *West Indian Literature* (1979) contained only one chapter on women's writing: that of **Jean Rhys**, and only brief comments on the works of **Una Marson**, **Louise Bennett** and Barbadian American Paule Marshall (1969); no mention of Hodge's seminal (1970) novel was made. (This study has now been revised with a chapter on women's writing (King

1995)) In the light of the omissions of this and other prominent anthologies and critical studies it is hardly surprising that it is often erroneously assumed there were few or no Anglophone Caribbean women writers before the 1980s.

Moreover, the development of a critical agenda which could evaluate and validate women's writing during this period was much problematized (as well as facilitated) by imported paradigms from Western feminist theory which were held in tension with indigenous formulations of Caribbean women's experience. As the next section evidences, the search for a critical agenda which could account for the particular nexus of gender and cultural identities presented by and in the work of Caribbean women writers was to continue well into the 1980s and beyond.

The beginnings of dub and a black British literature

The 'implosion' of new voices in the form of dub and performance poetry from the mid 1970s onwards in Britain and the Caribbean owed much to previous critical breakthroughs. Although most of Bennett's pioneering work had been published in the 1940s and 1950s, she was still productive in the 1960s and this decade witnessed the first major evaluation of her work as *literature*, with influential criticism by **Morris** (1964, republished **1967**) and Nettleford (1966). Both pieces signalled a dramatic breakthrough in the growing critical receptiveness to oral and performative poetry as literature. Brathwaite was also highly influential in this respect. His 1973 trilogy *The Arrivants* constructed an experimental poetry, which explored the possibilities of making use of black musical rhythms and forms (work-song, spirituals, mento, ska, reggae, steelpan, calypso, jazz, the blues) as St Vincentian, Shake Keane had similarly done (1950, 1952, 1975). He also critically explored the wider possibilities of a poetics of musicality, a Caribbean literary aesthetic based on these black musical influences and forms – primarily jazz (**Brathwaite 1967, 1968, 1969**). '**Jazz and the West Indian Novel**', in which Brathwaite argues jazz is an archetype of 'new world creative protest', uses 'the idea of jazz as an aesthetic model (a way of seeing; a critical tool)' to posit an 'alternative to the European cultural tradition which has been imposed upon us' (1968–9: xxx). Despite the unevenness and even self-contradictory nature of some of Brathwaite's critical writing of this period, such ideas were to be significant in facilitating a new experimentation with form and presentation in Caribbean poetry. By the time Brathwaite's 'electronic lecture' *History of the Voice* was published in 1984, a whole generation of poets had been encouraged and enabled in literary careers, many directly by Brathwaite's anthologizing of their voices in the 1979 *Savacou* anthology, others indirectly by his inspirational critical writing.

The problematics of classifying diasporic literary production intensified during this period. Although a significant number of Caribbean writers had settled in Europe or North America in previous decades, and although there is a documented black presence and textuality in Britain many centuries old (see Edwards and Dabydeen 1991), it is in this period that we first find a number of British-born or British-based writers of Caribbean descent beginning to identify themselves as British, and regarding their work as equally or even predominantly British in concern, a sentiment which many of the West Indian writers arriving in Britain in the 1950s would not or could not have countenanced. This is not to say that the label 'Black British' was universally adopted or accepted; on the contrary it has always been a much contested term (see D'Aguiar 1989, Lawson Welsh 1995), and yet, arguably, it was in this period that contemporary Black British literature was born.

Amongst its pioneers was the young poet and activist, **Linton Kwesi Johnson**, whose groundbreaking collection *Dread Beat and Blood* was published in London in 1975. It was followed by Oku Onuora's *Echo* in Jamaica in 1977 and both poets were included in the *Savacou* anthology of 1979. Although the poetry of both is characterized by the use of nation language, a strong performance aesthetic, the formal and thematic influence of reggae music and stylistic devices such as the use of biblical allusion and a highly politicized content, each differs by being inflected by local particularities. Johnson's poetry is, and has always been, firmly grounded in the realities of life in an urban British context rather than the more abstracted 'Babylon' of some of the other dub poets. The radical nature of his work, especially in linguistic terms, paved the way for the breakthrough of a new generation of Black British poets in the 1980s including V. Bloom, **Jean Binta Breeze, Ben Zephaniah**, Jimi Rand, John Agard, **Grace Nichols**, Jackie Kay, Maud Sulter, Fred D'Aguiar, Amryl Johnson and **David Dabydeen**. The fact that anthologies of

Black British women's writing did not appear for almost another decade (Burford 1984, Ngcobo 1987, Cobham and Collins 1987), is instructive of the particular difficulties which women's writing faces in securing both a popular audience and serious critical reception (see *Feminist Review*, 17, 1984).

Charting this transition from Caribbean to Black British writing were figures such as James Berry and Monserrattian Archie Markham, both of whom had been in Britain since the 1950s. Both poets now turned their attentions to encouraging a new generation of writers by publishing them, many of them for the first time, in a series of groundbreaking anthologies of the late 1970s and 1980s (Berry 1976, 1984, Markham 1989). The Race Today Collective also acted as a significant publishing outlet for new poets such as Johnson, Breeze and **Smith**. Nevertheless Berry's outlook in 1976 was gloomy:

> There is no nourishing atmosphere for the development of black distinctiveness [in Britain] ... Westindians here are a long way away from the dynamic cultural activities of American blacks or their fellow Westindians at home. They are grossly underexplored, underexpressed, underproduced and undercontributing. They have not yet managed to create any steadily developing cultural activity with both a deepening and widening upward trend.
>
> **(Berry 1976: 9)**

Berry's concerns were prescient in relation to the struggle to establish a critical as well as creative tradition in Britain. If his anxieties on the creative front were to be largely allayed by the tremendous energy, diversity and quality of Black British writing produced in the next decade, those on the critical front were not. Whereas the cultural politics of feminist approaches to Caribbean women's writing and theories of post-colonial literature were to be articulated and interrogated with increasing sophistication in the 1980s and 1990s, a specific and cognate critical attention to Black British literature (as opposed to Black British cultural praxis more generally) would continue to be neglected.

Dennis Scott

Squatter's Rites

Peas, corn, potatoes; he had
planted himself
king of a drowsy hill; no one
cared how he came to
such green dignity,
scratching his majesty
among the placid chickens.

But after a time, after
his deposition, the uncivil wind
snarled anarchy through that
small kingdom. Trees, wild birds
troubled the window,
as though to replace the fowl
that wandered and died of summer;
spiders locked the door,
threading the shuddered moths,
and stabbed their twilight needles through
that grey republic. The parliament of dreams
dissolved. The shadows tilted
where leaf-white, senatorial lizards
inhabited his chair.

Though one of his sons made it,
blowing reggae (he
dug city life)
enough to bury the old Ras
with respect
ability and finality,
a hole in his heart;
and at night when the band played
soul, the trumpet
pulse beat
down the hill
to the last post, abandoned,

leaning in its hole
like a sceptre
among the peas, corn, potatoes.

(1973)

Grampa

Look at him. As quiet as a July river-
bed, asleep an' trim' down like a tree.
Jesus! I never know the Lord could
squeeze so dry. When I was four
foot small I used to say
Grampa, how come you t'in so?
an' him tell me, is so I stay
me chile, is so I stay
laughing, an' fine
emptying on me –

laughing? It running from him
like a flood, that old molasses
man. Lord, how I never see?
I never know a man could sweet so, cool
as rain; same way him laugh,

I cry now. Wash him. Lay him out.

I know the earth going burn
all him limb dem
as smooth as bone,
clean as a tree under the river
skin, an' gather us
beside that distant Shore
bright as a river stone.

(1973)

Anthony McNeill

Residue

I

The wind is crisp and carries
a tang of the sea. The flowers
burn richly against the grass.
The grass itself shines and is precious.

II

Ahead, the sky and the ocean
merge in a stain of blue. On the beach
yesterday, lolloping tourists
were posting umbrellas like crosses.

III

This morning I chose to stay home.
To watch the cats and think of
Columbus. And the grass is precious
merely because it belongs to us.

(1975)

Christine Craig

Elsa's Version

Lawd God
I tired fe hear it
I tired fe hear it
so till.
All dem big talk:
'Women are our natural resources
Women are the backbone
of this country'
Me no bone inna
no body back
nor rib outa
no body side.
Is who dem tink
dey a go fool
while dem still a
treat we to no-count wages.
An we shouldn' mind
dat we riding fine
in nuff dutty song
a boom shaka boom
pon every street corner.

You rass man
stop put we down
in dutty song or
high-up editorial.
You can confuse, abuse
an mess wid you own self
till you good an ready
to deal wid I as a real somebody.

Till dat day come
    Lef me alone
    an me modda
    an me sista
    an me gal-pickney.

(1987)

Mahadai Das

They Came in Ships

They came in ships.

From across the seas, they came.
Britain, colonising India, transporting her chains
from Chota Nagpur and the Ganges Plain.

Westwards came the Whitby,
The Hesperus,
the Island-bound Fatel Rozack.

Wooden missions of imperialist design.
Human victims of her Majesty's victory.

They came in fleets.
They came in droves
like cattle
brown like cattle,
eyes limpid, like cattle.

Some came with dreams of milk-and-honey riches,
fleeing famine and death:
dancing girls,
Rajput soldiers, determined, tall,
escaping penalty of pride.
Stolen wives, afraid and despondent
crossing black waters,
Brahmin, Chammar, alike,
hearts brimful of hope.

I saw them dying at streetcorners, alone, hungry
for a crumb of British bread,
and a healing hand's mighty touch.

I recall my grandfather's haunting gaze;
my eye sweeps over history
to my children, unborn
I recall the piracy of innocence,
light snuffed like a candle in their eyes.

I alone today am alive.
I remember logies, barrackrooms, ranges,
nigga-yards. My grandmother worked in the field.
Honourable mention.

Creole gang, child labour.
Second prize.
I recall Lallabhagie, Leonora's strong children,
and Enmore, bitter, determined.

Remember one-third quota, coolie woman.
Was your blood spilled so I might reject my history –
forget tears among the paddy leaves.

At the horizon's edge, I hear
voices crying in the wind. Cuffy shouting:
'Remember 1763!' – John Smith – 'If I am
a man of God, let me join with suffering.'
Akkarra – 'I too had a vision.'

Des Voeux cried,
'I wrote the queen a letter,
for the whimpering of coolies in logies
would not let me rest.'
The cry of coolies echoes round the land.
They came, in droves, at his office door
beseeching him to ease their yoke.

Crosby struck in rage against planters,
in vain. Stripped of rights, he heard
the cry of coolies continue.

Commissioners came,
capital spectacles in British frames
consulting managers about costs of immigration.
The commissioners left, fifty-dollar bounty remained.
Dreams of a cow and endless calves,
and endless reality in chains.

(1987)

Rajkumari Singh

Per Ajie – A Tribute to the First Immigrant Woman

1 Per Ajie
  In my dreams
  I visualise
  Thy dark eyes
  Peering to penetrate
  The misty haze
  Veiling the coast
  Of Guyana.

  Knew'st thou then
  'Twas to land
  Far-flung from home
  Thy bark the seas
  Had skimmed
  Bearing thee
  Thy Kismet to fulfil
  Of Sweat and toil?

2 Per Ajie
  Did bangled-ankles
  Well thy sea-legs bear
  While Sahib's gaze
  Thy exotic
  Gazelle beauty
  Of face and form
  Envelope.

  If later
  Thy chastity
  He violated
  'Tis nought
  'Tis no shame
  To thee
  If man turn brute
  A lotus-soul defiles.

3 Per Ajie
I can see
How in stature
Thou didst grow
Shoulders up
Head held high
The challenge
In thine eye.

Yet none dared
Tell of Sahib
Whipped in fields
Lest
On kith and kin
Of outraged
Woman
Descend vengeance!

4 Per Ajie
Somewhere 'neath
Guyana's skies
In Guyana's soil
Two blades you caused
To grow where first
'Twas
But only one.

Hail dearest one
Thy tears
Shed for
Ganga-desh
Have watered
The blades
Thou didst sow
In my land.

5 Per Ajie
Couldst thou but see
The land's abundance
Of growing things
And thy offsprings

Steeped in thy Philosophy
To bend before
The tempest's blast!

O'er thy head
By burdens hallowed
Malas
Of brightest hue
We place
In reverence
Seeking ever
Thy benediction.

(1971)

Sylvia Wynter

We Must Learn to Sit Down Together and Discuss a Little Culture - Reflections on West Indian Writing and Criticism

My concern is with connections. The first connection to be made is that the critical writing of the English-speaking Caribbean, as a body, is centred at and diffused from the university [of the West Indies].

The second connection to be made is that this critical exploration is conducted, for the most part, under the guidance and within the perspectives of English criticism. This itself reflects the fact, that the University, like the society, is a 'branch plant industry of a metropolitan system'. In all such systems, the creators of original models, i.e. the writers, must cluster at the centre if they are to have the freedom and the opportunity to create. The third connection follows from this last – that whilst the critics are safely 'home and dry' at the university, the writers are scattered, in exile . . .

Our condition is one of uprootedness. Our uprootedness is the original model of the total twentieth century disruption of man. It is not often appreciated that West Indian man, qua African slave, and to a lesser extent, white indentured labourer, was the first labour force that emergent capitalism had totally at its disposal. We anticipated by a century the dispossession that would begin in Europe with the Industrial Revolution. We anticipated, by centuries, that exile, which in our century is now common to all.

The exile of the writer, then, not only from the Caribbean, but from Latin America and from many other neo-colonial territories, is part of a general negation . . . In the West, and the 'free world' over which the West exercises dominance, culture has become a mere appendage to the market mechanism; another industry among others . . .

The concept of 'people', better expressed by the Spanish 'pueblo' is fast vanishing. The writer who returns from exile at the metropolitan centre to 'write for his people'; to seek with them to 'break out of identity imposed by alien circumstances', and to find a new one, must come face to face with the fact that his 'people' has become the 'public'. And the public in the Caribbean, equally like the public in the great metropolitan centres, are being conditioned through television, radio and advertising, to want what the great corporations of production in the culture industry, as in all others, have conditioned them to want. Returning from exile at the metropolitan centre, the writer all too often finds that he returns only to . . . another facet of exile. Yet by not returning, the writer continues to accept his irrelevance.

I returned. I returned because I had no choice. I could not write, my talent did not suffice, except I could return to the lived experience of my own corner of reality. I accepted that writing would have to be done in the interstices of my time. For my writing was not a marketable product in the 'branch plant society' to which I returned. My interpretation of one aspect of European literature could be sold; I had the Good Housekeeping label of a metropolitan university. If the label had been marked English literature rather than Spanish, I would be able to function in my own society as an interpreter of West Indian literature rather than of Spanish literature. But within the 'branch plant' arrangement of my society and its university, I (and others infinitely more gifted than I am) would have no possibility to function as the creator of any such writing.

Given my particular position, I cannot pretend to objectivity nor impartiality in my approach to these critical essays. Nor can I pretend to function purely as a critic in relation to them. I prefer to bear witness to my own reaction on reading what is after all a feed back report on the body of writing now labelled West Indian. And my first reaction on reading these essays was that this critical body of work confronted us with a paradox at once so simple and so complex, that it staggers the imagination, until one remembers that in the upside down reality in which we have our being, paradoxes are 'normal'. For what they show us, these essays, is that the books, as the products of the writers, have a function, at least in academic circles. There they are transformed into texts. West Indian books have a function in West Indian society. West Indian writers have none.

Since the texts are there, to be explained, interpreted, accepted, dismissed, the interpreter replaces the writer; the critic displaces the creator. Yet in displacing the creator, he diminishes his own validity. Criticism is a part of culture and not its instant powder substitute. When the creative instinct is stifled or driven into exile, the critical faculty can survive only as maggots do – feeding on the decaying corpse of that which gives it a brief predatory life. The exclusion of the West Indian writer from West Indian life has even more far-reaching implications than the agony of exile undergone by the writer himself. It implies the acceptance by us ... of an arrangement of society in which the writer in order to find a way of functioning, must go to the metropolitan centre. It implies our complicity with the commissars of the market system. The Communist commissars send their dissident writers to prison. The market commissars by inducing writers to find outlet and function only at the metropolitan centre, sends them into exile. We come to terms with our 'branch plant' existence, our suburban raison d'etre.

To be a colonial, says Lamming, is to be a man in a certain relation. A suburban is a man without a being of his own; a man in a dependent economic and cultural relation with the metropolis. To be in that relation is an example of exile. The air of inauthenticity which pervades the West Indian University, springs from the fact that the university, like its society, only much more so, is in exile from itself ...

In his long and detailed introduction to *The Islands In Between*, Louis James as editor has only this to say about the exile of the West Indian writer:

> *Seen against the various tensions of the area, it is not surprising that many creative Caribbean writers moved away from the West Indies to see their predicament in perspective ... V.S. Naipaul – who entitled an account of his visit to his ancestral homeland 'An Area of Darkness (1964)' – and Samuel Selvon, left permanently for England. Into exile in London too, went many other creative West Indian writers, including George Lamming, Wilson Harris, Andrew Salkey and Edgar Mittelholzer.*

Why does Louis James accept and pass over, as a given fact, a connection without which West Indian writing cannot be properly explained? For James cannot be accused, as W.I. Carr can be, of refusing to see literature in the context of a given time and place. Indeed much of his introduction is given over to a historical sketch of the area which produced West Indian writing, and of the circumstances which helped to define it. Yet this historical sketch is distorted by James' essentially 'branch plant' perspective – a perspective that views the part for the whole; that adjusts new experience to fit an imported model, with a shift here and a shift there; that blinds its horizons in order not to perceive the logical and ultimate connections, that would invalidate the original model that had formed his being and distorted his way of seeing. The 'branch plant' perspective is the perspective of all the 'appeasing arts'; and of their corollary, 'acquiescent criticism'.

What do we mean by this? James does not hesitate to point out the colonial background to West Indian writing. No West Indian, however passionate and anti-colonial could fault him on this. He says all the right things, makes all the right genuflections. If he praises the British presence in the Caribbean,

> *Only an extremist would deny the positive contributions to West Indian social and political life made by England. They are ubiquitous, and deeply ingrained, far more so than in India or Africa. English education opened up a cultural heritage which reached beyond England to Europe, and Asia and Africa. It provided a highly developed tool of language with which a writer like Walcott could explore his own unique predicament, just as the British liberal traditions formed the basis for the struggle for independence from England.*

Louis James is quick to adjust the balance with this:

> *At the same time the English traditions could be destructive. Petrified within the social structure as the standards of respectability they could also, as we have noticed, divide class from class, and constrict the evolution of national ways of life.*

If we examine both the praise and the dispraise, we shall find that James has really evaded the issue. He has, to use a just phrase of T.W. Adorno 'parried by not parrying'. No one, in reading both accounts could fail to see on which side the balance tilts – in favour of England and her 'positive contributions'. Yet an English education provided Walcott with a highly developed tool of language to explore a 'unique predicament' which England's economic interest had created; a predicament which had profited her. If British liberal traditions formed the basis of the West Indian's struggle for independence, it was the British anti-liberal tradition which by making him colonial, caused him to have to struggle in the first place. From this long and anti-liberal tradition England also profited. Her 'destructive English traditions' which divided class from class, were there to serve a purpose. To continue an economic and political arrangement which profited her. The more they profited her, the less they profited the West Indies. The end result is an arrangement by which, with independence attained, the majority of the West Indians were illiterate. The writer wanting market and audience had to go to England . . .

The distortion of Louis James' perspective comes from his avoidance of this connection. He sketches the history of the Caribbean from an Archimedean point outside the historical process. Yet it is a process in which he is as involved as is the West Indian. This pretended objectivity and detachment is the common stance of what I call, for convenience, the 'acquiescent critic'. In attempting to write from outside the process, in pretending detachment, the 'acquiescent critic' accepts the status quo, by accepting his own fixed point outside it. He falls into the trap of which Adorno spoke:

> He, the cultural critic speaks as if he represented either unadulterated nature or a higher historical stage. Yet he is necessarily of the same essence as that to which he fancies himself superior. The insufficiency of the subject . . . which passes judgement . . . becomes intolerable when the subject itself is mediated down to its innermost make-up by the notion to which it opposes itself as independent and sovereign.

James, as an English teacher teaching in a West Indian university, passing judgement on West Indian writing, is mediated to his bones by the colonial experience, by the colonial myth in which he is as involved, though in a different role, as is the West Indian.

It is Lamming the writer and the West Indian, and not James the critic and the Englishman, who sees this vital connection. James' criticism, in the final analysis, is there to reinforce the status quo; Lamming's is there to question it. Lamming, the questioning critic cannot take fixity as his stance; he knows himself and his perspective moulded by a historical process imposed on his being. He writes from a point of view inside the process. He knows that he does. Awareness is all. In the *Pleasures of Exile* he begins his historical sketch of the Caribbean quite differently from James. He speaks to James, not at him. '*We have met before.*' Lamming tells him. '*Four centuries separate our meeting . . .*'

What James and Cameron peddle and what Walcott is at times trapped by is the 'cultural myth' rather than the cultural reality of Europe. The cultural myth under-props the economic and political power of Europe based on its exploitation of non-Europeans; the cultural reality of Europe consistently attacked and opposed this dominance, this concept of Europe as a super-culture, as the end product of Man's glorious march towards 'humanity'. The cultural reality of Europe sees the ambivalence of its own power and glory; and embodies its real creativity best when it is most self-critical . . .

If Walcott has not yet realized the full range of his talent, it has nothing to do with his either accepting Europe or turning his back on Europe. He has no choice. The West Indian experience was 'created' by Europe; and the West Indian experience helped to create Europe as it is today. Besides to *be* West Indian is to be syncretic by nature and circumstance, by choice. It is the *myth* of Europe which rejects; which rejects all other experience, African, Indian, Chinese which contribute to the being of the West Indian. What is important is whether Walcott accepts the myth of Europe for its creative reality. The myth of Europe will alienate him from himself in much the same way as it has alienated European man. The creative reality will give him a complex, if painful, mirror in which to reassemble all the divided fragments of his still indeterminate identity. The dilemma of being either West Indian or European is a false one. To be a West Indian is to accept all the facets of one's being. The over-emphasis on the European facet is a hangover of the myth: and implies a rejection of the others. The swing of the pendulum, now in vogue, will redress the balance towards the myth of Africa. One then hopes that the West Indian and Walcott will work through to the reality of both . . .

As the only institution of comparable size that the Caribbean territories will be able to afford, it is clear that the University must commit itself to the cultural destiny of our territories . . . we may well ask – to which Jamaica, which Caribbean is the University of the West Indies to belong? To the inauthentic, making gestures, and in particular the gesture of 'silence', which is . . . the most typical gesture of those who refuse to explore their reality? Or to that other, 'that invisible heart' which compels exploration and awareness. The critical essays show that the University is still poised between the choice; and leaning more towards the older, the easier, the gesture of silence. Silence, and in silence we include slogans and formulas borrowed from the metropolitan centre and applied without relevance, is more 'academic', conforms to 'established standards'. Silence is more livable with. With silence, the descendants of Prospero and Caliban, ex-colonial master, and ex-colonized, can pretend that the multiple flags waving in place of the Union Jack have bewitched away the past. Yet we can realise our common present only by the exploration of our common past. To replace this exploration by silence as we have mainly done so far, is to give to silence the sound of the school yell that Dawes describes in *The Last Enchantment*: *The unity, the oneness of the same school yell, was superficial, and the much vaunted great harmony among the different races was an inaccurate interpretation of a very precarious compromise.*

Above all, this kind of silence, of the unsaid, has deprived the University, as it does some of these essays, of a genuine sense of purpose. To avoid the past connection between Prospero and Caliban is to ignore what *unites* them in the present; the unity of a *common purpose* ... What then is this common purpose?

Our purpose begins to formulate itself with our awareness of the University as the logical result of a common history stretching over some four centuries; as a place where the descendants of Prospero-slave owner, and Caliban-slave, can, by using the technological knowledge acquired by Prospero from an unjust relation, mount an assault against that historical necessity, that scarcity of food and shelter, which had, in the dark and terrible ages, impelled exploitation of some by others; and still impels it ...

And what, one may well ask, has all this got to do with 'talking about a little culture?' Injustice, based in all its forms, on a concept of elitism, continues, not because the technological means are not available, to provide food, shelter, and freedom from material want for *all*, but because minds, which have for centuries been moulded and preformed to come to terms with the *actuality* of scarcity and therefore of injustice and elitism and division, find it difficult to come to an awareness of the distortion of their own barbaric formation. This formation ... continues to dominate us through the power of the very cultural myths which we had devised as our avenue of escape, our illusionary flight from this necessity. And that is why the twentieth century revolution must essentially be a cultural revolution; a transformation in the way men see and feel. To paraphrase Brecht: '*The Barbarians had their cultures; it is time now that we had ours.*'

It is not, of course, going to be as easy as all that. The Argentinian writer, Ezequiel Estrada, discussing among other things, the cultural failure of the Russian Revolution, also pinpoints the reasons for the failure of the nineteenth century independence movements of Latin America:

Neither here nor elsewhere is there any public awareness of the fact that cultural emancipation is not any easier, although it may be less bloody, than political liberty; and a great part of the failure of our independence movements was due to the fact that our liberators were not liberated from themselves. Mentally freed, they were subconsciously in chains, because they continued to accept the structure of European cultures, changing only their forms and a small part of their content, in the same way as they had done with their political institutions.

This is an exact analysis of our situation, both as society and University today. This situation is reflected in the imitative solutions which we devise to all our problems. This is not to deny that our cultural distortion is a reflection of a power situation in which we are still economically dominated, as was nineteenth-century Latin America, by metropolitan centres. As a University we have attacked the distortion of this *economic* dominance: yet we continue to reflect in our goals, curriculum, 'standards' the cultural corollary of this economic arrangement. The refusal of our society to take us seriously may well spring from the fact that 'culturally' we reflect the very untruths that we denounce. We need a new awareness of our own paradox; and this awareness should be diffused through our praxis, however inadequate, rather than through our sermons.

The cultural image of the University can be said to be embodied in its critical writing, and in its Creative Arts Centre, not in its writers nor in its creative artists. It may be argued that it is the policy of the Centre to invite down writers to become West Indian versions of the English Universities 'writers-in-residence'; for the period of exactly one year. Yet it is clear that the writer-in-residence, brought-down-for-a-year, can be there for no other purpose than for that of being a piece of cultural display; there for his advertising value rather than for the reality of his function. The writer-in-residence-for-a-year is the appeasing gesture used to disguise the fact that as a University, and a society, we acquiesce in the arrangement by which West Indian writers must continue to live in metropolitan centres and thereby be rendered impotent to take part not 'in the talking about culture', but in its creation. And for that, the University, and its society need the writers as much as the writers need them.

If it is argued that there is no place in the present arrangement and curriculum of the University to provide the writer with a function, it can be answered that this may very well be where the change in the arrangement and curriculum ought to begin. It is not by accident that the uprising of the thirties threw up writers and artists at the same time as it threw up politicians; both are at one and the same time, prophets and technicians of change. The failure of a society can depend on the limitations of the vision and the skill of both. The exile of the one or the other creates an imbalance for the society as a whole. The exile of the writer from the University . . . is a serious lack; it is the writer and not the academic who is best able to link the University to that 'invisible heart of the nation'. The link is of the imagination rather than of the intellect; and it is this link which can include Dawes' words of the politician Edgar¹ within the social meaning from which he is so far a stranger. Without writers to give flesh to its interior and without *functioning* artists, the Creative Arts Centre remains but another appeasing gesture; another Ark for the faithful in which the elite and the highbrow can contemplate their intellectual navel, whilst the floods of proletarian disorder sweep over the multitudes outside.

A new 'culture' for us is not a luxury, not and no longer the playmate of an elite soul; it must be instead the agent of man's drive to survive in the twentieth century.

(1968–9)

NOTE

1 In the novel – *The Last Enchantment*.

Gordon Rohlehr

West Indian Poetry: Some Problems of Assessment I

In selecting an anthology of current West Indian writing, I'd have tried as far as possible to determine how far that writing reflected and explored the tensions of the society, and would have used 'genuineness of feeling' as one of my criteria. The question of form or shape is a much more difficult one to settle, since there is no common consensus anywhere in the world today as to what constitutes proper form. I myself admire a wide variety of writing, ranging from the overtly 'dramatic' use of language, which may be concerned only with things like rhythm and tone, to the highly complex and concentrated use of images and symbols, and I welcome the presence of both elements in current West Indian writing. I welcome especially the confidence with which young writers are trying to shape ordinary speech, and to use some of the musical rhythms which dominate the entire Caribbean environment.

Yet it is precisely this that disturbs some critics of West Indian poetry. Eric Roach, for example, reviewed *Savacou* 3/4 in *Trinidad Guardian* (14 July 1971). Restricting his commentary to an examination of *some* of the poetry, Mr Roach described his criteria for determining what was art, and what was good or bad poetry. In so doing, he has joined a sharp debate which is going on about aesthetics, tradition, literary criticism and sensibility in the West Indies. This debate started quite long ago and involves English liberals such as Owens, Carr and Louis James, and just about every Caribbean writer and critic. A great deal of the recent debate can be followed in journals like *Caribbean Quarterly*, *Bim*, *Jamaica Journal*, *Savacou*, and to a lesser extent in *The Journal of Commonwealth Literature*, *New World*, and the Caribbean dailies. Then there are the pronouncements of West Indian writers on writing. The most prolific of these is probably Brathwaite, but Walcott has written considerably on the work of his colleagues, and has recently written a long essay, 'What the Twilight Says: An Overture' (*Dream on Monkey Mountain and Other Plays*, New York, 1970) which deserves the closest attention for its strong auto-biographical content, and its lacerating statements on current developments in Caribbean writing, attitudes, insensibility and politics.

Mr Roach, then, a reviewer of long standing, is part of this debate. Without, perhaps, really intending to, he in his review of *Savacou* 3/4 expressed the attitudes of his generation to what it sees as a number of unsavoury and alarming features in today's youth. In criticising adversely a number of the younger Jamaican writers, Mr Roach also made clear his own assumptions about 'culture' and 'history', and expressed a particular disgust at what he saw as a tendency 'to thresh about wildly ... in the murky waters of race, oppression and dispossession ... to bury one's head in the stinking dunghills of slavery'. He seemed to me to be taking a firm stand against simple rhetorical protest, which, he feels, retards rather than liberates. He stressed the artist's need to learn his craft and to write out of the fullness of his experience, and found most of the poetry in the anthology bad, fanatical, boring and naive. On the other hand, he had every admiration for the work of Derek Walcott, Wayne Brown, A.L. Hendriks and Dennis Scott, of which he found too little.

Syl Lowhar sensed the assumptions about 'culture' and 'history' upon which Mr Roach's review was based, and questioned these in *Trinidad Guardian* (17, 18 July, 1971). Mr Roach's reply on Sunday, 18 July was that his review had nothing to do with racialism or nationalism, but with bad verse as against good, and with standards of judging poetry. He reiterated his arguments against self-consciously asserted racial pride, and said that the quality of the Black man's efforts in the task of survival is sufficient sign of his rich identity.

I do share some of Mr Roach's reservations about the journal. Editing needed to be more selective. There were a number of poems of similar theme, some extremely simple, others much more complex in form and treatment. I would have opted for the more complex abstracts from experience, in preference to simple statement of it. I need to feel that a writer is trying to use language imaginatively – any language in which he chooses to write. I didn't feel that this was happening in all the poems I read. I don't, however, share all Mr Roach's reasons for wanting to exclude some of the writing. The abundance of publication from the late fifties onwards, the bewildering and often inchoate variety of forms, styles and techniques revealed in spite of the frequent mediocrity of the writing, makes me a little less certain about standards than he seems to be. Intimate acquaintance with the pressures which exist throughout the Caribbean, and with the fact that some of the writers Mr Roach rejects feel them even nearer to the bone than I, gives me pause in passing judgement on the sensibility of the youth. Having some knowledge of the sensibility which produces Reggae, and the entirely different one which shapes Kaiso, I cannot but wonder what forms will grow from these roots, and welcome every sincere struggle to make abstracts of the languages and rhythms which constitute the thews and sinews, the inner ground of our sensibility. These languages, ranging from Creole to standard English are often more various than is realized, and all available for exploration.

Mr Roach, however, and there are many like him, feels that West Indian poetry *must* be tempered by a concern for craft which *must* be learned from the great English poets. A closer look at the basis on which he accepts or rejects this or that poet, is revealing. He first gives his general impressions on *Savacou* 3/4:

> Colour, trumpeted on so many pages, gives the impression that one is listening to 'Air on the nigger string', or to the monstrous thumping of a mad shango drummer on his drum 'in sibylline frenzy blind'.

In the two succeeding paragraphs, the words 'fanatical' or 'fanatic' are employed four times, so that one gets the general impression that a great deal of writing in the journal was black, bloody and bad – although Mr Roach deals with none of the prose pieces and only a small fragment of the poetry. He makes no distinction between the style and treatment which different poets brought to bear on the same themes of deprivation, disillusion, and impending rebellion . . .

It is interesting that Mr Roach hears *frenzied* drums in so much of the writing, and that he singles out the poetry of Bongo Jerry for comment. It is unfortunate, though, that he did not choose to illustrate the specific mood of 'frenzy', and that he seems automatically to associate the drum with the monstrous, the animal, and uncontrolled emotion. He asks in some dismay,

> Are we going to tie the drum of Africa to our nails and bay like mad dogs at the Nordic world to which our geography and history tie us?

So Africa, too, seems to hold frightening resonances for Mr Roach as, indeed, it did for people like Froude or Trollope, and Kingsley who was able to see a Negro work-song and satirical dance as signs of the animal-like depravity of the race, while he saw the fine Caucasian features of one native as sufficient sign of that Black's ability to lead his people out of captivity (Kingsley, *At Last, A Christ in the West Indies*, London, 1890, second edn, pp. 16–17 & p. 267).

For Kingsley, it was only necessary for the native to look different from the Caucasian to be damned, and for him to resemble the Caucasian to possess every potential for refinement, and every qualification for humanity. For Mr Roach ... the drum of the Afro–West Indian is associated with an animalistic blood-lust, while 'European culture' is most generously defined, and proffered as a means of Caribbean salvation.

He writes, for example;

> We have been given the European languages and forms of culture – culture in the traditional aesthetic sense, meaning the best that has been thought, said and done.

If by 'we have been given' Mr Roach means 'we can take what we need from; we can assimilate or fruitfully relate to', fine. In this respect there is really no limit to what anyone can choose. The whole world is our 'schoolmaster'. I am not quite certain, however, what is meant by 'the traditional aesthetic sense'. This implies that there has always been a universal conception of good taste, or sensibility, when, in fact, there is in the vast and complex tradition of Europe – not to mention other parts of the world – justification for just about every kind of writing, including the elemental naked statement of emotion which is what Mr Roach says he deprecates in young West Indian writers, and the rhetorical use of local dialects, which Mr Roach seems to view more as limitation than as possibility.

Mr Roach's definition of 'culture' as 'the best that has been thought, said and done' is also fascinating. European writers today are much less confident than he, and are busy trying to come to terms with the ironies of a culture which has produced both Wagner and Hitler, Nietzsche and the gas chambers of six million Jews. These and similar incongruities have turned many writers into nihilistic visionaries, who are uncertain of everything, including the cerebration and rationalism on which their writing depends. West Indians, however, tend to romanticise Europe's staggering achievements, while they gloss over the constant barbarity which has been inalienable from them. It is necessary for the West Indian to acquaint himself not with any one side of European achievement, but with the whole paradoxical movement of human history, precisely because the West Indies were in large measure a product of some of the worst aspects of all history.

Also it seems to me that Mr Roach, like so many others, is begging the question as to what constitutes 'the totality of our history'. Naipaul has already said that we have no history, and recently, Walcott has lamented our lack of 'a tiered concept of a past' (see 'What the Twilight Says'). But we have barely started to write this history, and to examine those admittedly inadequate records of the past. If there seems to be 'no history', it must mean that a great deal remains to be written, not that nothing ever happened or survived. I believe the sense of there being a void to be filled has led to a great deal of freshness, innovation and versatility in West Indian writing, and in Caribbean life-style, while it has also informed their underlying melancholy . . .

Not only must we guard against the assumption that we really understand what happened in the past, but we also need constantly to reinterpret our present in the light of every fresh discovery of the meaning of ourselves. Mr Roach writes as one who is sure that he knows exactly what is good for us. But what *is* the totality of history, environment and feeling of a West Kingston Rastafarian? How is this to be expressed in language, and how will it transform the style of our writing when we learn what it is? No one really knows. Yet, the Rastafarian presence is a felt one in the popular music of Jamaica, which is colonising the Caribbean as surely as calypso used to in the fifties . . .

This is perhaps why the editors of *Savacou* 3/4 included Ras Dizzy and Bongo Jerry. I tried to show how the Rastafarian bec[a]me a symbol of sainthood for Anthony McNeill because the poet realised the sacrificial nature of the Rastafarian's life. He can see how Ras becomes the visible scapegoat of the society, how his pain releases the creativity of some, while it increases the need for absolution which so many others seem to feel . . .

I say all of this as introduction to an examination of Bongo Jerry's poetry, because I believe that that poetry has been deeply influenced by a whole style of rhetoric which surrounds the popular music of Jamaica. I believe, too, that Jerry shares [Jamaican musician Don] Drummond's sense of 'dread', a brooding melancholy which seems always on the verge of explosion, but which is under some sort of formal control . . .

(1972–3)

Gordon Rohlehr

West Indian Poetry: Some Problems of Assessment II

In his 'Sooner or Later' and 'Mabrak', which I find to be more complex poems that either 'The Youth' or 'Black Mother', Jerry relates very closely to traditions of preaching rhetoric and music which most Jamaicans can understand and identify immediately.

The rhetorical style of the Disc Jockeys has developed during the sixties, and has matured in the singing, talking 'scatting' and clowning of people like Hugh Roy. Gibberish, riddles, nonsense rhymes, proverbs and fragments of wisdom all combine in this form of rhetoric, whose aim, as Satchmo's or Ella Fitzgerald's was, is not to make sense in any syntactical way, but to fit words into the shape of a mood, or the fluid rhythm of a line. To understand 'Sooner or Later' and 'Mabrak', one must first have some sympathy for the tradition out of which these grew. Mr Roach takes particular offence at the line,

> so have-gots, have-nots,
> trim-heads, comb-locks, dread-knots
> is sheep from goat.
> find yourself, row your own boat,
> 'be ready for the day'

which he sees simply as 'clap-trap'. Perhaps, but this, when seen in the tradition which I have been suggesting exists, takes on a different complexion. The enumeration of stereotypes 'have-nots, have-gots', etc. indicates impatience on the speaker's part. He has heard the debate over and over and would prefer some action. His aim is to get down to the fundamentals of self-knowledge and independence ... The community for which this poem is meant would accept these aphorisms as meaningful bits of advice, wisdom which they can test by experience. The average reader of *Savacou*, however, comes from a world in which proverbs and aphorisms are meaningless. Yet one reads Louise Bennett's *Jamaica Labrish* and finds it saturated with proverbs, whose function needs carefully to be assessed ...

Bongo Jerry's work ... [carries a] wealth of allusion to the apocalyptic imagery of 'Revelation' and the fascinating, unwritten liturgy of Rastafarianism. One notes, for example, Jerry's usage of the call-

[321]

and-response pattern, which is the root pattern of Jamaican work songs, and Rastafarian or sectarian preaching . . .

Some of the best Ska tunes were clearly based on the classic work-song call-and-response pattern. I think of Don Drummond's *Reburial*, *Fidel*, *Occupation*, *Eastern Standard Time*, *Stampede*, *Street Corner*, *Man on the Street*, all of which are classic examples of his style. The soloists make their statements against the background of a continuously answering chorus. In Rastafarian sermons or even ordinary conversation, the group often answers the speaker with murmurs of 'seen', 'natural', 'true word', 'true story' and so on. In Bongo Jerry we hear and feel it time and again. Leader: 'Sooner or later'. Chorus: 'But mus . . .'. The importance of this pattern of call-and-response, is that it tightens the bond between individual and group, and affirms their mutual acknowledgement of each other's presence. It is, in fact, a basic pattern of *all* negro speech and music . . .

A friend of mine who was at [a recent reading of poetry from *Savacou*] had this to say:

> In *Mabrak* is a different kinda thing happening. Power within the people. Not so much high seriousness as '*dreadness*'. Not prophecy and lyricism and spectral doom but *menace* and *cool* and *menace*.
>
> A different quality sound; and what makes it different is the humour in *Mabrak*. The message doan just register, it resonates . . . This sense of one-ness is upsetting a lot of people.
>
> (14 June, 1971)

In an earlier letter, he had commented that the 'dread' music of Kingston contained 'more elemental honesty of rage and blues and menace' than any of the poetry he had heard emanating from the Mona Campus. This is no new thing. The music generally predicts the course of things in Jamaica . . .

For what really is 'Dreadness'? . . .

Dread is that quality which defines the static fear-bound relationship between the 'have-gots' and the 'have-nots'. It is the historic tension between slaver and slave, between the cruel ineptitude of power on the part of the rulers, and introspective menace and the dream of Apocalypse on the part of the down-trodden. This is why Dread remains a constant quality in Jamaica's creative life . . .

Having identified this quality of Dread as an inalienable part of our past and present, how do we fuse a form capable of containing it, and how do we assess such writing as attempts to do so? People like Mr Roach would have us forget the matter all together though this quality invests the society with a sense of the tragic and a capacity for myth. It may be, also, that similar questions are being asked all over the world, similar quests for form being made, and similar problems arising about standards of judgement. We can gain by identifying these areas of similarity. For example, familiarity with the Wright–Baldwin–Howe–Ellison–Cleaver exchange on 'protest' fiction would redeem a lot of West Indian criticism from its naivete ...

One of the many questions asked by Mr Roach concerns the possible fate of today's generation. His manner in phrasing it suggests that his age was in some way better:

> When today's whirlwind and whirlpool of race and colour in the Caribbean have subsided, where will all this soap box street corner ranting and posturing of the younger poets be?

But perhaps Mr Roach is himself in a better position to answer this question than most people. The question he raised about standards of judgement and his unequivocal rejection of the rhetoric of this generation, sent me back to the earlier anthologies of West Indian poetry, in which a few of Mr Roach's poems appeared. His declaration that:

> To be a Caribbean English language poet is to be aware of the functions and structure of English verse. At the same time one must, like a reptile, shed the skin of learning, disdain, while we revere that cultural dominance and strive for what we would like to call the West Indian thing. One must erect one's own bungalow by the sea out of the full knowledge of the architecture of the English places and cottages.

made me reflect that at no point does Mr Roach stress the need for the West Indian writer examining what he actually has in the West Indies, which, after all, is what he will have to come back to, when, like a soucouyant, he stops flittering about and returns to his skin, which history has already seared with salt, pepper and fire. Secondly, Mr Roach speaks of 'English poetry' rather than of 'poetry in English', forgetting, no doubt, that the English language has long ceased to be the single property of any one people.

I therefore undertook to read his own poetry in the light of his own statement about possibilities and standards, and was surprised to discover in his 'I am the Archipelago' not only the rhetoric of Marlowe and Shakespeare, but a bitterness and imagery reminiscent of some of Martin Carter's *Poems of Resistance*. Roach writes:

> And now
> I drown in the groundswell of poverty
> No love will quell. I am the shanty town
> Banana, sugarcane and cotton man;
> Economies are soldered with my sweat
> Here, everywhere; in hate's dominion;
> In Congo, Kenya, in free, unfree, America.
>
> I herd in my divided skin
> Under a monomaniac sullen sun
> Disnomia deep in artery and marrow.
> I burn the tropic texture from my hair;
> Marry the mongrel woman or the white;
> Let my black spinster sisters tend the church,
> Earn meagre wages, mate illegally,
> Breed secret bastards, murder them in womb ...

In many ways, this reminded me of Martin Carter. There was the general, rhetorical tribal 'I' in which the poet sees himself as the spokesman for the group. He probes, catalogues and summarises the history of the group. Each line becomes a plain self-contained statement of fact, names, catalogues the distress, guilt, and rebellion of the group, like a political pamphlet, or the pioneer historiography of Eric Williams. The lack of enjambment is the result of this desire to catalogue. I can hear in those lines what it felt like to be a conscious young man in the last days of Crown Colony, when one could entertain the slender hope of Federation and self-government ... Because little has changed, the language of rebellion remains the same.

But this is not how the people who taught me English at U.W.I. encourage me to see the verbal rebellion of West Indian writers. Had Marlowe written those lines, they would have been viewed as part of a rhetorical tradition, part of a progression from Beowulf and Kyd, which eventually achieved its fruition in Donne and Shakespeare. But unfortunately, the lines had been penned by Eric Roach. Their dramatic potential was completely ignored, though a poet like Mr Roach, springs from a society with a rich tradition of formalized rhetoric (e.g. robber-talk, sans humanite picong, all kinds of

preaching, *Pierrot Grenade*, etc.) and may well have been attracted to
the Elizabethans, because their use of the language counterpointed
forms which he knew, and which were alive in his own society.

Thus it was that R.J. Owens, one of my tutors in English literature at Mona, could divorce Carter's poetry from the Guyanese
political trauma of 1953, and state simply that Carter confuses rhetoric
with poetry. It would have been more rewarding to discuss Carter's
use of rhetoric, with a view of discovering its sources, how it makes
or mars his verse, and whether it opened any possibilities for
Caribbean verse . . .

It is a discussion which must remain open in island societies which
oscillate between a rich oral tradition, and a growing scribal one.
Owens was even more severe on . . . 'I Am the Archipelago':

> Mr E.M. Roach indulges himself in a breathless rhetorical rodomon-
> tade in *I Am the Archipelago*.
> The highflown tone and disarticulated movement turn the poem
> into a watered down version of minor Elizabethan blank verse . . .
> Mr Roach is clearly an intelligent man and one hopes he will stop atti-
> tudinising and get down to refining the sensibility he shows in his
> *Seven Splendid Cedars*.
>
> (R.J. Owens, 'West Indian Poetry', *Caribbean
> Quarterly*, 7, No. 3, Dec. 1961, pp. 120–7)

While Owens condemns the imitativeness of Caribbean writers, Mr
Roach criticizes them for being too self-conscious and for their
growing refusal to relate to an English tradition of great writing.
Doubtless both extremes need to be avoided. Yet one cannot help
feeling that Dr Owens, in addition to stressing how badly the poets
of Mr Roach's time imitated their English masters, might have
detected the emergence of characteristic ways of looking at Caribbean
landscape and politics which are quite different from what had been
taking place in the thirties and early forties. The reason why the
poets of the forties and fifties so often provided descriptions rather
than explorations of experience was that these pioneers felt the urgent
need simply to name their landscape and give it some being.

It is no surprise that the characteristic mode of the sixties has been
one of introspection, concentration, and sophistication of several of
the techniques which the writers of the forties could only wield
crudely. Seymour's and Carter's interest in history have taken a clearer

and more definite shape in the work of Edward Brathwaite. Keane's interest in the musical rhythms of calypso and jazz has also found apotheosis in Brathwaite, and a growing number of writers. Walcott has learned how to speak with his own voice and to write a tight concentrated dense poetry in which he fuses public and private anxieties . . .

In answer to Mr Roach's question about the possible fate of today's generation of 'soap box bards', I'd venture that in twenty years time, their fate may be no worse than his. The experience of living in the West Indies is sufficiently chastening to temper most rhetoric into reticence. Carter burned out in five years into the sad blue 'Poems of Shape and Motion' (*Kyk-over-al*, Vol. 6, No. 20, 1955), whose doubt was much more movingly shaped into poetry than his earlier oratorical commitment. The weight of compassion, life and time which those poems contain, tells me clearly as anything, how our lives will from generation to generation be denuded slowly into grief, tiredness and silence. In twenty years, if spared by ganja, soul, cacapool rum and the widening barbarity of our politics, most of today's youth will be respectable citizens, without illusions, and terribly afraid of tomorrow's children, whose ears they will try to fill with fables of the swinging seventies.

(1972-3)

Gordon Rohlehr

Afterthoughts

Since this article was first published, I have received a number of comments from friends and associates. Two said that they liked the article itself much more than they did the material which it attempted to 'vindicate'. Now I wasn't really trying to vindicate anything ... What I was doing was simply an attempt to join a growing debate about the nature of the West Indian experience, and to describe the *context* of contemporary West Indian poetry, as I see it. This is probably why I spoke more about what was happening in Reggae and in the folk-urban jazz of Jamaica than about the magazine itself. Mr Roach's article convinced me that a number of people in the West Indies are prepared to talk about literature without understanding much about the context out of which such writing grows. If my article was attempting to do anything, then, it was to sketch in some of the background relevant to an understanding of the material in the *Savacou* [3/4] anthology.

Another comment which I ought to reply to, has been the feedback on the last paragraph of the article, where I said that most of today's strident youth will be little different from last generation's once angry, now tired rebels, after twenty years have elapsed ...

What I wanted to stress was that there would be a continuity of the folly, deceit and grief which one can easily see in the people from Mr Roach's age. If the rest of my article stressed the fact that there was a great deal of creativity in the West Indian people, it also stressed that this creativity existed in spite of Caribbean politics. I view with particular disgust the attempts which politicians are making throughout the West Indies, not to enhance, but to exploit art on all levels. This sort of thing can become tragic when a folk art begins to be used solely as a tourist attraction, or to gain a few more votes for a party in office. Recently here in Trinidad, Derek Walcott has been making a similar point. If in everything I've written I've affirmed a kind of faith in our capacity for survival, I've never underestimated the corrosive nature of absurd politics.

This is why I've seen the experience of Martin Carter as a paradigm of what will be the fate of most of the rebels in the West Indies. Because, if a finer spirit emerges from the carrion of our present, it will be won at the expense of individual defeat, sacrifice, tiredness of spirit and the sickness unto death, attenuation of faith and despair. This seems to me to be the meaning of both Carter's life and Walcott's. It also seems to me to be the experience of many a man who walks the street. I know that young people here feel it to the bone, and that most of them will simply seek one way or another of opting out of whatever struggle presents itself. This is not to say that nothing will be created, but to stress the price at which such creativity will be achieved . . .

Anyone who has lived through 1971 will recognize tiredness and despair as inalienable parts of the landscape here [in Trinidad]. My feeling is that they will increase, until the society creates new means of dealing with them . . . At present, the forces of decay seem to be so much stronger than those of creativity.

Jamaica is a different case. The forces of despair and erosion are even fiercer than those in Trinidad. But Jamaica has a more coherent people and a more continuous line of history. Hence the dismay is counterbalanced by a tremendous vitality . . .

Jamaica, however, because of the greater integrity of its population, has begun to lay the foundations of a vital folk–urban culture. This is why Afro-Jamaican religion, mythology, rhythms, rhetoric and music have begun to saturate the whole consciousness of the place. This accounts for the sound of *Savacou* 3/4, which I can see is simply a beginning . . .

All of these folk–urban manifestations have their roots in the syncretic Afro-Protestantism of Pukkumina, Bedwardism, Garveyism and Rastafarianism. At all times in the history of Black Jamaica, culture has had a religious basis. So also have politics, and the reaction of people to the depredations of politics and politicians has always had a nearly mystical basis. This is why it is difficult today to separate religious music from the music of open rebellion . . .

Now . . . [the] attempt to see the 'criminal' as redeemer, as measure of the society's wound and power to transcend, is by now a commonplace occurrence in West Indian literature. It is there in Mais, in Lamming's *Season of Adventure*, in Harris, too, and appears as major elements of *Savacou* 3/4. The Guyanese Mark Matthews *For Cuffy* is addressed not only to the slave rebel of 1763, but to Clement Cuffy, a convict whose jailbreak in the late fifties resulted in a relentless manhunt in Guyana's backlands. Moreover, both Cuffeys, the rebel and the convict ... are associated with the common man, the eccentric, the grotesque ...

This desire to reclaim the 'criminal' on the part of middle-class writers is partly an attempt to exercise [sic] a guilt at having grown away from roots, or an emptiness at having never known them. It is also a positive attempt to create and deepen conscience in sections of society whose traditional response has been an automatic impulse to repress, beat up, execute and imprison. As such it is to be welcomed. Half in guilt and half in self-vindication, the West Indian writer is declaring his identity with the West Indian people; in their shame, in their degradation, in their in-search, in their mythical eternal journeying, which so many Pukkumina hymns, Baptist hymns in Trinidad, and popular music in Jamaica are today celebrating ...

Self-acceptance is the important thing. It is what Césaire's return really meant, a terrible affirmation in the face of an almost total despair ... Césaire's great act of affirmation will continue to be made, even when it changes little or nothing.

> I accept ... I accept ... entirely, without reservation ...
> My race which no absolution of hyssop
> mingled with lilies can ever purify.
>
> my race gnawed with blemishes
> my race ripe grapes from drunken feet
> my queen of spit and leprosies
> my queen of whips and scrofulae
> (p. 80, Penguin Translation)
>
> At the end of the small hours, lost pols,
> stray smells, stranded hurricanes, dismasted
> boats, old wounds, rotten bones, buoys,
> chained volcanoes, ill-rooted deaths, bitter cries,
> I accept!
> (*Return to My Native Land*, p. 83)

It is this which is beginning to sound in the poetry of the 'Commonwealth' Caribbean. Not surprisingly, some of us cannot recognise or accept the sound. On the political level, all over the West Indies the laws of censorship are being invoked, or, as in Trinidad, grim laws of sedition are being passed to kill this acceptance. On the level of literary criticism, one can still find the critic who believes that a thorough grounding in F.R. Leavis, an understanding of how he rescued English criticism from Bradleyan doldrums in the thirties, will save us here, and help us to understand why Bongo Jerry writes as he does. But one will have to study the Caribbean people and to listen to them, before one can learn to make important or relevant critical statements on the new writers. The critic's business is first to understand the contexts out of which the work that he is examining grows. Our context is simply not Leavis's. The critic, like the writer, will have to learn the meaning of self-acceptance.

(1973)

Gerald Moore

'Review: Use Men Language'

The last two years have seen such remarkable developments in Caribbean writing that it seems a peculiarly apposite time to be celebrating Frank Collymore's eightieth birthday. The distance travelled stylistically and intellectually over the thirty-odd years of *Bim*'s existence received impressive confirmation with the appearance of the *Savacou* special issue in March 1971 and of Andrew Salkey's anthology *Breaklight* in the same year. The very fact of *Bim*'s continued survival throughout this period of gradual cant-clearing and self-discovery will make it of unique interest and importance to all future historians of West Indian cultural growth . . . Wrapped hammock-like in a Union Jack slung between two wicket-posts, lulled by the best of rum and the most genial of climates, Barbados might have slumbered while islands with more chequered, broken and violent histories woke abruptly into self-awareness.

It has happened otherwise. Easy as it would now be to identify the colonial and even sycophantic attitudes which can occasionally be found in the early issues of *Bim*, the key is that it existed and existed in Barbados, to register whatever messages might begin to crackle over the Caribbean air-waves.

The most important of the discoveries made over the intervening thirty years is that the West Indies has languages of its own. Not curiosities for the linguist and ethnologist to study, but living and developing languages which have proved essential to the full revelation of West Indian life in literature. Who can imagine the stories of Norma Hamilton or Timothy Callender, the poems of Bongo Jerry or Audvil King, written otherwise? What would Wilson Harris's *Palace* or *Oudin* be without the deep, salty tang of Guyanese speech, which continually roots his poetic fantasies in social reality?

Such instances make it clear that the representation or creative rehandling of a particular texture of West Indian sound (be it speech or song) is not some sort of verbal decoration, more or less dispensable, but the very material out of which the new literature and drama are being wrought. Gone is the comic intrusion of the Creole-speaker into the polite circle of the educated – strictly comparable with the comic Cockney housemaid or manservant in a pre-war West End play. How can what is indigenous and natural to the vast body of people in a society be presented to them in a comic or eccentric light, except by a kind of cultural confidence trick? This trick, still played by many of those in authority in the islands, takes in fewer people every time.

In West Indian drama we can already see the recognition of this truth in works as early as Walcott's *The Sea at Dauphin* and *Ti-Jean and His Brothers*. In fiction it emerges in the contrast between C.L.R. James's *Minty Alley* (1934) and Roger Mais's *The Hills Were Joyful Together* (1953). Both were middle-class writers reporting on a yardlife out of which they hadn't themselves sprung; but the James novel, interesting and original as it is in its epoch, presents the wrong kind of cultural centre by interposing its hero (with a middle-class background like James's own) between the reader and the yard. Mais suppresses this intervention, because he offers us no figure in the yard with whom we can identify the author himself. We are plunged straight into that life, and hence participate imaginatively in it far more directly than if we were encouraged to cling to the coat-tails of a character who is not really of the yard himself, who experiences and interprets it for us, and thus holds it at a distance from the reader. I don't want to exaggerate the notion of 'literary landmarks'. Mais's achievement had been anticipated in some ways by a book like *New Day*, and his own influence was not evenly or immediately felt, but it did significantly and permanently alter the map of Caribbean fiction ...

Although we might wish the Creole ballads of Louise Bennett and the best of the Calypso lyrics as poetry – indeed I believe we should – they were not perhaps fully apprehended as such by the audiences which first heard them, in the 'forties, 'fifties and even the 'sixties. Poetry was something else, something which appeared in little magazines, on BBC programmes, in rare anthologies and even rarer slim volumes. And it is poetry in these terms (though with the important added dimension of public readings) which has been transformed in the past few years; first by Brathwaite's trilogy, in which a sustained effort was made to identify the language bases (American and Caribbean folk-song, Akan drum rhythms, West Indian popular speech) on which a new poetry might be built; and more recently in the electric vitality of poets like Bongo Jerry:

MABRAK is righting the wrongs and brain-whitening HOW?
Not just by washing out the straightening and wearing dashiki
   t'ing;
MOSTOFTHESTRAIGHTENINGISINTHETONGUE   so HOW?
Save the YOUNG
from the language that MEN teach,
the doctrine the Pope preach
skin bleach.

How ELSE? ... MAN must use MEN language to carry dis message:
SILENCE BABEL TONGUES; recall and
recollect BLACK SPEECH.

Notice how Jerry in this passage chucks the heavy stresses to and fro within the line, demanding vocal agility and a quick eye in his reader. This is a highly rhetorical poem, and it uses rhetoric in much the same way as Brathwaite does in parts of his trilogy, though the devices are broader and less meticulous ... Gone is the polite tradition, afraid of letting out rude noises, and always looking over its shoulder for approval *outside* the islands. Much of the poetry in *Savacou 3-4* seems, rather, to exult in its freedom from alien restraints. It is a poetry which restores the need for immediate audience, even though it can be relished in solitary reading also. It says: 'Try me out. Use all your voice and all your gestures.' Isn't that how West Indians talk, and how their poetry must also, sometimes, speak?

With the exception of Mervyn Morris, who remains generally faithful to the iambic pentameter and to a general stanzaic regularity, most of the poets represented in *Breaklight* and in *Savacou 3-4* have felt the need to make formal changes which accord with their new-found sense of assertion – assertion not merely *against* the relics of colonial order, but *for* the freedom to seek the bases of their music where they will. And in the search for an appropriate rhetoric, it is natural that poets like Bongo Jerry, Ras Dizzy and Audvil King should make use of devices long practised by the preachers, story-tellers and political leaders of the Caribbean; devices which probably go back to the earliest cross-roads meetings that prepared the great slave revolts of the seventeenth and eighteenth centuries ...

Even where the actual words and phrases used offer no dialect features, the diction reflects a much greater awareness of what can be done in English than was to be found in any poet writing in the West Indies fifteen years ago ...

It is interesting to compare this with the development of an older, more established poet like Derek Walcott, whose early work was stamped with the twin influences of the seventeenth century – especially Marvell – and [with] Dylan Thomas. The varied, complex rhythm and difficult rhyme-scheme he employs in a mature poem like 'Laventville' amount to a new poetic voice, free from that slight air of provinciality which clung to a Caribbean poet, however excellent, whose deep love of English poetry was so immediately evident in everything he wrote . . . To see how far Walcott had travelled by the time he wrote this poem, we need only compare it with an earlier piece of descriptive writing from a volume published in the early fifties, 'The Cracked Playground' . . . In this poem . . . the density of exotic reference which is typical of early Walcott . . . immediately situates it in terms of an audience which will appreciate and applaud this learned young colonial. It is the poet, with his 'shameful audacious complexion', who looks like an intruder among this bric-a-brac of classical statues and literary relics. And this derivative relationship is equally reflected in the rather heavy, even movement of the pentameters. In these early poems Walcott . . . captures us by his exuberance, but is often wordy and showy . . .

I don't want to exaggerate the role of distinctively West Indian speech-patterns in the liberation of its poetry which the last few years have brought. Many of its most remarkable and original poets, such as Martin Carter, Dennis Scott and Faustin Charles, have not found it necessary to their purposes to use dialect words or phrases. The question of indigenous rhythms is more subtle and difficult to elicit. Many poets have moved towards a more flexible line-length, with a predominance of short lines and consequently stronger, swifter emphases . . .

The poetic map in the Caribbean then, is full . . . of variety and achievement . . . But beneath all the different choices of language, rhythm, line-length, musical stress and stanzaic form lies a general determination to use English in poetry as uninhibitedly as West Indians have long used it in speech and song. The poet is no longer a kind of putative Rhodes Scholar, learning his craft, his language and his references by way of 'English Literature'. In the words of Knolly La Fortune:

> We've seen through
> the writing on the wall.

There need no longer be any distracting debate about which language they 'ought' to use. From the formal classicism of Mervyn Morris to the drum-beats of Bongo Jerry, these poets have equally something to write about, and their work is driven forward by an equal impulse to deliver it.

(1974)

Kamau Brathwaite

Jazz and the West Indian Novel, I, II and III

The Blues is a special kind of music . . . It is . . . the artistic expression of a particular kind of Negro – the Negro slave and his descendants under the geographical and social conditions of the American South . . .

Jazz, on the other hand, is not 'slave' music at all. It is the emancipated Negro's music: hence its brash brass colouring, the bravado, its parade of syncopation, its emphasis on improvisation, its *swing*. It is the music of the freed man who having left the countryside of his shamed and bitter origins, has moved into the complex, high-life town . . .

Jazz . . . was, and in many ways continues to be, the perfect expression for the rootless, 'cultureless', truly ex-patriate Negro . . .

Jazz has been from the beginning a cry from the heart of the hurt man, the lonely one. We hear this in the saxophone and trumpet. But its significance comes not from this alone, but from its collective blare of protest and its affirmation of the life and rhythm of the group . . .

We should expect that other great creolized and Negro society of the Americas – the Caribbean – also to have its jazz.

But there is no West Indian jazz. The urban, emancipated Negro musical forms in the West Indies, where they appear at all – the calypso in Trinidad, the ska in Jamaica, and the similar, related forms in some of the Spanish and French islands – are concerned with protest only incidentally. They are essentially collective forms, ridiculing individualism, singing the praises of eccentricity, certainly; more often celebrating their own peculiar notions of conformity. The West Indian musical form, where it has any general area of application at all, is basically a music for dancing: a communal, almost tribal form. There is no suggestion of alienation, no note of chaos in calypso . . .

This isn't to say that there was (or is) no protest tradition in the West Indies . . . But West Indian post-emancipation protest, being not concerned like the American with 'civil rights', the place and status of a black minority in a white world, but rather with subtleties of caste and colour, of West Indian against West Indian, has achieved little or no liberating, self-creative expression. There has been, it is true, with the increasing urbanization of Kingston and Port-of-Spain, a growing element of protest (and comfort) in the calypso and the ska. But it is still too early to see this as a positive contribution ... here it has been mainly literary ...

And yet it is here, in the new literary elements in the calypso and ska, and of course in the more sophisticated and elaborate structures of West Indian poetry and novels, [that] we can find a connection, (or rather a correspondence) between jazz (the American Negro expression based on Africa), and a West Indian Negro expression based on Africa ... We will, in other words, be looking for some mode of New World Negro cultural expression, *based* on an African inheritance ... [but] built ... on a superstructure of Euro–American language, attitudes and techniques. Jazz, for instance, is played in an Africanized manner on European instruments ...

My concern ... is ... with the (British) West Indian contribution to the general movement of New World creative protest of which I regard jazz as the archetype. I am asking here whether we can, and if it is worthwhile attempting to, sketch out some kind of aesthetic whereby we may be helped to see West Indian literature in its (it seems to me) proper context of an expression both European and African at the same time ... The West Indian writer is just beginning to enter his own cultural New Orleans. He is expressing in his work of words that joy, that protest, that paradox [of] community and aloneness, that controlled mixture of chaos and order, hope and disillusionment, based on his New World experience, which is at the heart of jazz. It is in the first place mainly a Negro experience; but it is also a folk experience; and it has ... a relevance to the 'modern' predicament as we understand it today ...

Words, then, are the notes of this new New Orleans music. The 'personal urge for words', the West Indian writer's trumpet. But the 'jazz' sound of these novels is not expressed in words alone ...

Word, image and rhythm are only the basic elements of what, within the terms of my definition, would go to make up a jazz aesthetic in the Caribbean novel. What determines the shape and direction of a jazz performance ... is the nature of its improvisation ...

It should be clear by now that what I am attempting in this study is the delineation of a possible alternative to the European cultural tradition which has been imposed upon us and which we have more

[337]

or less accepted and absorbed, for obvious historical reasons, as the only way of going about our business. Or to put it more accurately: I'm trying to outline an alternative to the English Romantic/Victorian cultural tradition which still operates among and on us, despite the 'colonial' breakthrough already achieved by Eliot, Pound and Joyce; and despite the presence among us of a folk tradition which in itself, it seems to me, is the basis of an alternative. Our folk tradition, however, and the urbanized products of this tradition – jazz in the United States, calypso and ska in the islands – has been (with the partial exception of jazz) largely ignored; and where it has been examined, the examination has been usually cursory, uncritical, sometimes patronizing. The assumption has been that these are debased forms; hybrid forms; formless peripheral forms . . .

The resistance to the calypso and related West Indian indigenous forms by West Indians is and continues to be, it seems to me, a very real and pervasive thing. But it is the nature of the objection which is most pertinent to our discussion: the fear of attack on the *moral standards* of the middle class; the objection of *belly centred* bawdy. As Odlum said, quoting from Derek Walcott: 'we must teach our philosophy to reach above the navel'. And yet it is around this very navel that the battle rages. The alternative tradition is belly-centred: in the beat, the drum, the apparent bawdy. This region, as opposed to the middle-class Romantic/Victorian virtues of the 'head', is the centre of Sparrow's art; is the source of Louise Bennett's vitality; is the blood-beat of the ska and jazz . . . And behind this whole revolt, this assertion of an alternative, there lies the deep rhythmical and formal influence of Africa . . .

But . . . this tradition has remained fixed, isolated, a relic, a ruin; a memory that has ceased to move and therefore hardly moves us. Even our novelists, more aware than most others that there is something *there*, have not on the whole made any real concerted attempt to explore or rehabilitate this tradition. After an instinctive, initial (usually autobiographical) attempt to associate with this tradition, they have (most of them), left the islands either physically or spiritually or both, before they have come to grips with these 'alternative' possibilities . . . we still await serious and more than occasional ethno-cultural and *creative* sociological studies on this subject.

It is because of this lack of information, of articulation, that in the search for a possible West Indian aesthetic I have chosen, for the time being, to explore the potentials of jazz as a working model. Jazz is a New World negro form of expression that *has* received study, recognition and a certain measure of acceptance. And it is an urban folk form that has wider and more modern connections and correspondences with the increasingly cosmopolitan world in which we live, than the purely West Indian folk forms ... Most importantly, jazz, in several quarters, is already *seen* to be, or to represent, an alternative to the 'European' tradition ...

It is of course difficult ... to make wholly convincing correspondences from music into literature; and easier to demonstrate relations between jazz improvisation and the folk/oral tradition than it is to do the same with jazz and the more conscious products of the 'written' tradition ... What can be said with some certainty, however, is that ... many folk forms, and those passages on West Indian ... literary works that grapple most closely with folk forms and folk experience, contain elements of improvisation ...

[There] is a folk form improvisation tacked on ... at the end of Neville Dawes' *The Last Enchantment* (1960) ... an almost perfect example of improvisation, in the jazz sense, where tone, rhythm and image come together to create a certain kind of effect ... this same story could be told by different people with infinite degrees of variation ... But this is not jazz improvisation (the novel's concerns are too 'sophisticated' for this) ... no West Indian novelist has, as far as I know, attempted yet to incorporate the Anancy story structure in the form of his work; and this is because, as I have already suggested, most of our novelists, after their initial 'creole' expression, have passed on out of the West Indian orbit, moving to London, New York or Montreal before they can really come to grips with the problem of formally expressing the deep-rooted experiences of the folk aspect of their tradition. Where is the second and third novel written by a West Indian *in* the West Indies about the West Indies? ...

To find 'written' examples of improvisation similar to the Anancy story, we have to turn to those few poets who have remained working in the West Indies ... and who have had ... to come to grips with the oral tradition of the region (e.g. Louise Bennett [in] *Pedestrian Crosses*).

The 'improvisation' here is not only in the variations of tone, made possible by the assumption of dramatic method (as in the calypso), and in the changes of rhythm within the verse structure, but in the 'melody' itself – the variations based on the word 'cross' . . .

Improvisatory effects can also be achieved through repetition of a 'theme' – the jazz 'riff' – a kind of collective response which marks the end of one improvisation and the beginning of the next. This is a form found in many folk literatures . . .

In his train scene in *The Emigrants* (1954) George Lamming uses a similar kind of device, contracted to a single repeated line . . . 'WILL PASSENGERS KEEP THEIR HEADS WITHIN THE TRAIN?' . . .

The 'theme' here is the train journey. The improvisation is in the rhythm, the shifts of tone and rhythm, the repetitions, the apparently spontaneous variations of thought, point of view and comments that make the journey 'happen' . . .

Here at the end of the 'performance' (the journey) the ensemble re-asserts itself ('Remember we keep together'), though still expressing the individual/group dilemma ('But if a man see one single good break goin' . . .') which jazz, on the whole, has so successfully resolved . . .

There are, of course, even more subtle, more 'literary' kinds of improvisation, where the variation takes place not in the word and/or rhythm only, but in the image and metaphor of the theme; so that a kind of transformation of meaning takes place . . . (e.g. Lamming: *The Pleasures of Exile* (1960), p. 121 or Wilson Harris' *The Waiting Room* (1967b) . . .)

Harris' book, taken as a whole, is not a jazz novel. As with Lamming, his concerns remain individual rather than social . . . They move beyond 'mere' regional socio-cultural preoccupations, into the infra-national and cosmopolitan; though their modes of expression and the structures of their work, based as they are on New World experience, remain outside the 'European' tradition . . .

Our concern in this study is with the novel as an expression of West Indian 'creole' experience: a structure taking its form from the pressures of West Indian social reality. My thesis is that faithfulness to this concern discovers a form similar to that evolved by the American negro in jazz; I hope to be able to trace . . . this in . . . Roger Mais' *Brother Man* . . .

Brother Man, significantly, opens with a 'Chorus of People' – musical and social elements . . .

This is the basic rhythm of the book. But playing against it, leaking tension into it (compare the method with say, Vic Reid's *New Day*), there is a staccato counterpoint:

> – Cordy's man get tek-up for' ganga ...
> – Bra Man show de gospel way ...
> – Me-gal still wi' hold wid Bra' Ambo ...
>
> (p. 8)

But after this 'downbeat', this introductory statement of theme, the rhythm changes, as it shifts and changes in jazz, and we hear the entry of the first solo instrument – or rather solo instruments, because two people, a woman and a man (Girlie and Papacita) are involved ...

Gradually, as from within a New Orleans ensemble or a Duke Ellington structure, these two solo instruments begin an interchange; the male voice and action (trumpet) alone first, staccato, challenging the female (clarinet) ...

In the next scene (pp. 12–15) another 'duet' is started, this time between a small boy, Joe, and Jennings, a policeman; both as Mais reveals later, having significant connection with Papacita and Girlie of the first theme. The third theme, also in duet form, introduces two sisters, Cordy and Jesmina (pp. 15–17). And before the introduction of ... Brother Man himself, Mais links Girlie – Papacita and Cordy – Jesmina (p. 16); and brings about the expected resolution of 'conflict' between Girlie and Papacita started in the first theme. This resolution is expressed not only as 'plot', as a literal union of voices; the two individual soloists begin to interchange with each other in a kind of collective improvisation. That is, the solo voices (pronoun notes), instead of being continued to separate paragraphs, now begin to appear together in the same lines ... (pp. 21–2) ...

The introduction of the 'sexual' here ... underlines the social theme of the novel with its emphasis on collectiveness, cohesion and making ... But perhaps most importantly, this scene serves as an introduction and counterpoint to the other and main theme of the book: Brother Man with his sense of spiritual love; and the conflict, within him, as within all men, of this with the physical ...

Mais now moves from clumsy *word* to dramatic *symbol*. And herein lies his integrity as a 'folk' artist. He is able, always, to reinforce what is often quite banal verbalisation with meaningful *image* ... [e.g.] (pp. 25–6).

[341]

This trapped fluttered bird is Minette, is Brother Man, is all the people who live within this novel. It is also the life of Brother Man's spirit, it is the life of 'making the room new' and it is also the life and love within Minette . . . (p. 32) . . . The whole novel, in fact, is structured around this image as a jazz improvisation is based on the few notes of a theme . . .

Brother Man, then, reveals certain rhythmic, thematic and structural features which justify, I think, my comparing it to music. Its specific relationship to New Orleans jazz comes with its peculiar sense of union and unity, its contrasting 'duets', its 'improvisation' and correspondences and above all, its pervading *sense of community* (its *collective* .improvisation). The 'Chorus of People' who introduce each section of the book is only the most obvious instance of this sense of community – and a rather external instance at that. Mais' sense of community goes deeper than a mere device. It informs the very structure of the book . . .

In *Brother Man* the violence is a kind of communal purgation. It involves the entire community of the novel, finally moving beyond the apparent chaos it brings, to that revelation of wholeness that one is aware of at the end of a successful jazz improvisation . . .

Using therefore the idea of jazz as an aesthetic model (a way of seeing; a critical tool), we can perhaps now begin to generalise . . . about the kind of West Indian novel . . . I have called the 'jazz novel'; the most successful, though far from perfect, example of which, so far, has been Roger Mais' *Brother Man*. (The reason why there have not been more of these novels – only Salkey's *A Quality of Violence* could be said to be another; and why Mais' itself is so very flawed . . . is mainly a question of orientation; attitude to 'West Indian' material; the amount of attention given to what we really have; the kinds of models which we have absorbed as paradigms.)

The 'jazz novel' . . . deal[s] with a specific, clearly-defined, folk-type community, [and] will try to express the essence of this community through its form. It will absorb its rhythms from the people of this community; and its concern will be with the community as a whole . . . The conflicts which give this kind of novel meaning will not be Faustian conflicts of self-seeking knowledge or the Existentialist stoicism of alienation . . . We are not here trying to say what anybody should or should not write. We are striving towards a way of *seeing* what they write and relating it to our indigenous experience. There is an argument, of course, that holds that 'our experience' is in fact the world's; by which, I think, is meant West Europe's, certainly Britain['s] and North America's. I do not dispute this; though I would seriously qualify it. But I would also add that those people who delight to see our experience as 'international', as 'cosmopolitan', tend to see it *only* as these things ... It is my contention that *before it is too late*, we must try to find the high ground from which we ourselves will see the world, and towards which the world will look to find us. An 'international' tradition by all means for those that wish it. *But a creole culture as well.* And a creole way of seeing first. It is from this that we must begin ...

(1967–9)

Kamau Brathwaite

Timehri

The most significant feature of West Indian life and imagination since Emancipation has been its sense of rootlessness, of not belonging to the landscape; dissociation, in fact, of art from act of living. This, at least, is the view of the West Indies and the Caribbean that has been accepted and articulated by the small but important 'intellectual' elite of the area; a group – call it the educated middle class – ex-planter and ex-slave – that has been involved in the post-plantation creolizing process that made our colonial polity possible . . .

'Creolization' is a socio-cultural description and explanation of the way the four main culture-carriers of the region: Amerindian, European, African and East Indian: interacted with each other and with their environment to create the new societies of the New World. Two main kinds of creolization may be distinguished: a *mestizo-creolization*: the inter-culturation of Amerindian and European (mainly Iberian) and located primarily in Central and South America, and a *mulatto-creolization*: the inter-culturation of Negro–African and European (mainly Western European) and located primarily in the West Indies and the slave areas of the North American continent. The crucial difference between the two kinds of creolization is that whereas in mestizo-America only one element of the interaction (the European) was immigrant to the area, in mulatto-America both elements in the process were immigrants. In mestizo-America, there was a host environment with an established culture which had to be colonized mainly by force – an attempted eradication of Amerindian spiritual and material structures. In mulatto America, where the indigenous Indians were fewer and more easily destroyed, and blacks were brought from Africa as slaves, colonizing Europe was more easily able to make its imprint both on the environment (the plantation, the North American city), and the cultural orientation of the area . . . In mulatto America . . . the process of creolization began to alter itself with the waning of the colonial regime. It simply fragmented itself into four main socio-cultural orientations: European, African, indigeno-nationalist and folk.

The problem of and for West Indian artists and intellectuals is that having been born and educated within this fragmented culture, they start out in the world without a sense of 'wholeness'. Identification with any one of these orientations can only consolidate the concept of a plural society, a plural vision. Disillusion with the fragmentation leads to a sense of rootlessness. The ideal does not and cannot correspond to perceived and inherited reality. The result: dissociation of the sensibility. The main unconscious concern of many of the most articulate West Indian intellectuals and artists in the early post-colonial period was a description and analysis of this dissociation: C.L.R. James' *Minty Alley*, the work of George Lamming, V.S. Naipaul, Orlando Patterson and M.G. Smith's *The Plural Society in the British West Indies*. The achievement of these writers was to make the society *conscious* of the cultural problem. The second phase of West Indian and Caribbean artistic and intellectual life, on which we are now entering, having become conscious of the problem, is seeking to transcend and heal it.

My own artistic and intellectual concern is, I think, not untypical of this new departure in West Indian and Caribbean cultural life ... I was born in Barbados, from an urban village background, of parents with a 'middle class' orientation. I went to a secondary school originally founded for children of the plantocracy and colonial civil servants and white professionals; but by the time I got there, the social revolution of the '30s was in full swing, and I was able to make friends with boys of stubbornly non-middle class origin. I was fortunate, also, with my teachers. These were (a) ex-patriate Englishmen; (b) local whites; (c) black disillusioned classical scholars. They were (with two or three exceptions) happily inefficient as teachers, and none of them seemed to have a stake or interest in our society. We were literally left alone. We picked up what we could or what we wanted from each other and from the few books prescribed like Holy Scripture. With the help of my parents, I applied to do Modern Studies (History and English) in the Sixth Form ... and succeeded, to everyone's surprise, in winning one of the Island Scholarships that traditionally took the ex-planters' sons 'home' to Oxbridge or London.

The point I am making here is that my education and background, though nominally 'middle class', is, on examination, not of this nature at all. I had spent most of my boyhood on the beach and in the sea with 'beach-boys', or in the country, at my grandfather's with country boys and girls. I was therefore not in a position to make any serious

[345]

intellectual investment in West Indian middle class values. But since I was not then consciously aware of any other West Indian alternative (though in fact I had been *living* that alternative), I found and felt myself 'rootless' on arrival in England and like so many other West Indians of the time, more than ready to accept and absorb the culture of the Mother Country. I was, in other words, a potential Afro-Saxon.

But this didn't work out. When I saw my first snow-fall, I felt that I had come into my own; I had arrived; I was possessing the landscape. But I turned to find that my 'fellow Englishmen' were not particularly prepossessed with me. It was the experience later to be described by Mervyn Morris, Kenneth Ramchand and Elliot Bastien in *Disappointed Guests* (OUP, 1965). I reassured myself that it didn't matter. It made no difference if I was black or white, German, Japanese or Jew. All that mattered was the ego-trip, the self-involving vision. I read Keats, Conrad, Kafka. I was a man of Kulture. But the Cambridge magazines didn't take my poems. Or rather, they only took those which had a West Indian – to me, 'exotic' – flavour. I felt neglected and misunderstood . . .

Then in 1953, George Lamming's *In the Castle of My Skin* appeared and everything was transformed. Here breathing to me from every pore of line and page, was the Barbados I have lived. The words, the rhythms, the cadences, the scenes, the people, their predicament. They all came back. They all were possible. And all the more beautiful for having been published and praised by London, mother of metropolises.

But by now this was the age of the Emigrant. The West Indies could be written about and explored. But only from a point of vantage outside the West Indies. It was no point going back. No writer could live in that stifling atmosphere of middle class materialism and philistinism. It was Lamming again who gave voice to the ambience in *The Emigrants* (1954), and in *The Pleasures of Exile* (1960). His friend Sam Selvon made a ballad about it in *The Lonely Londoners* (1956), and Vidia Naipaul at the start of his brilliant career could write (in *The Middle Passage*):

I had never wanted to stay in Trinidad. When I was in the fourth form I wrote a vow on the endpaper of my Kennedy's *Revised Latin Primer* to leave within five years. I left after six; and for many years afterwards in England, falling asleep in bedsitters with the electric fire on, I had been awakened by the nightmare that I was back in tropical Trinidad . . .

I knew [it] to be unimportant, uncreative, cynical . . . (p. 41). For me, too, child and scion of this time, there was no going back. Accepting my rootlessness, I applied for work in London, Cambridge, Ceylon, New Delhi, Cairo, Kano, Khartoum, Sierra Leone, Carcassone, a monastery in Jerusalem. I was a West Indian, rootless man of the world. I could go, belong, everywhere on the world-wide globe. I ended up in a village in Ghana. It was my beginning . . .

Slowly but surely, during the eight years that I lived there, I was coming to an awareness and understanding of community, of cultural wholeness, of the place of the individual within the tribe, in society. Slowly . . . I came to a sense of identification of myself with these people, my living diviners. I came to connect my history with theirs, the bridge of my mind now linking Atlantic and ancestor, homeland and heartland. When I turned to leave, I was no longer a lonely individual talent; there was something wider, more subtle, more tentative: the self without ego, without I, without arrogance. And I came home to find that I had not really left. That it was still Africa; Africa in the Caribbean. The middle passage had now guessed its end. The connection between my lived, but unheeded non-middle class boyhood, and its Great Tradition on the eastern mainland had been made.

The problem now was how to relate this new awareness to the existing, inherited non-African consciousness of educated West Indian society. How does the artist work and function within a plurally fragmented world? How can a writer speak about 'the people', when, as George Lamming dramatizes in *The Castle of My Skin*, those to whom he refers have no such concept of themselves?

'I like it,' I said. 'That was really very beautiful.'
    'You know the voice?' Trumper asked. He was very serious now. I tried to recall whether I might have heard it. I couldn't. 'Paul Robeson', he said. 'One of the greatest o' my people.' 'What people?' I asked. I was a bit puzzled. 'My People', said Trumper. His tone was insistent. Then he softened into a smile. I didn't know whether he was smiling at my ignorance, or whether he was smiling his satisfaction with the box and the voice and above all Paul Robeson. 'Who are your people?'

I asked. It seemed a kind of huge joke. 'The Negro race,' said Trumper. The smile had left his face, and his manner had turned grave again ... He knew I was puzzled ... At first I thought he meant the village. This allegiance was something bigger. I wanted to understand it ...

(p. 331)

What kind of product will emerge from this gap and dichotomy; from conscious vision and the unwillingly envisioned? It is a problem that Derek Walcott, never leaving the Caribbean and aware of it from his very first lines in 1949, was increasingly to face ...

In 'Hic Jacet' (1969), he seems certain in the knowledge that the source of his art was and is with the people, and now 'Convinced of the power of provincialism', he says: 'Commoner than water I sank to lose my name ...'. But Walcott is a brilliant exceptional, creatively expressing through his work the pressures and dilemmas of his plural society. Here is a humanist in the sense that the scholars and artists of the Italian Renaissance were humanists. He is concerned with converting his heritage into a classical tradition, into a classical statement. But as the folk movement from below his outward looking position begins to make itself felt, there is heard in the title poem of *The Gulf*, a growing note of alienation and despair ... So the question of communal, as opposed to individual wholeness still remains. And returning to London late in 1965, I was more than ever aware of this. For there were the West Indian writers and artists, still rootless, still isolated, even if making a 'name'. It seemed that flung out centrifugally to the perimeter of their possibilities, our boys were failing to find a centre. Salkey's *Escape to an Autumn Pavement* (1960), and *The Adventures of Catullus Kelly* (1968), Naipaul's *The Mimic Men* (1967), and Orlando Patterson's *An Absence of Ruins* (1967), were moving witnesses to this realization ...

In 1966/67, two events of central importance to the growth and direction of the West Indian imagination took place. Stokely Carmichael, the Trinidadian-born American Black Power leader visited London and magnetized a whole set of splintered feelings that had for a long time been seeking a node. Carmichael enunciated a way of seeing the black West Indian that seemed to many to make sense of the entire history of slavery and colonial suppression, of the African diaspora into the New World. And he gave it a name. Links of sympathy, perhaps for the first time, were set up between labouring immigrant, artist/intellectual, and student. Sharing, as he saw it, a

[348]

common history, Carmichael produced images of shared communal values. A black International was possible. West Indians, denied history, denied heroes by their imposed education, responded. From London, (and Black America) the flame spread to the university campuses of the archipelago. It found echoes among the urban restless of the growing island cities. Rastafari art, 'primitive' art, dialect and protest verse suddenly had a new urgency, took on significance. Walter Rodney published *Groundings with My Brothers* (1969); Marina Maxwell started the Yard Theatre; Olive Lewin's Jamaican Folk Singers began to make sense; Mark Matthews in Guyana ... was doing with the dialect of the tribe what critics like Louis James had declared to be impossible. The artist and his society, it seemed, were coming closer together.

The second event, of late 1966, was the founding, in London, of the Caribbean Artists' Movement. The object of CAM was first and foremost to bring West Indian artists 'exiled' in London into private and public contact with each other. It was a simple thing, but it had never happened before. The results were immediate, obvious and fruitful. Painters, sculptors, poets, novelists, literary and art critics, publishers, for the first time saw and could talk to each other ...

Artists such as Orlando Patterson, Andrew Salkey and Marina [Maxwell] were concerned primarily with the ex-African black experience, slavery, the plantation, and their consequences.

But there was also Harris and Aubrey Williams, both black, both from Guyana, who were contributing if not a different vision, then at least a different approach to that vision. Coming from mainland South America, they found themselves involved not with the problem of mulatto-creolization, but with mestizo-creolization. Their starting point, was not the Negro in the Caribbean, but the ancient Amerindian. Williams, speaking at a CAM Symposium in June 1967 had said:

> In art, I have always felt a wild hunger to express the rather unique, human state in the New World ... I find there an amalgam of a lot that has gone before in mankind, in the whole world. It seems to have met there, after Columbus, and we are just on the brink of its development. The forces meeting in the Caribbean ... will eventually, I feel, change this world ... not in the sense of a big civilization in one spot, but as the result of the total of man's experience and groping for the development of his consciousness.

In articulating this faith in the Caribbean, and in emphasising roots rather than 'alien avenues', Williams was connecting with what many West Indian writers are now trying to do. And in emphasizing the importance to himself of primordial man, *local* primordial man, he, like Harris, was extending the boundaries of our sensibility. Most of us, coming from islands, where there was no evident lost civilization – where, in fact, there was an 'absence of ruins', faced a real artistic difficulty in our search for origins. The seed and root of our concern had little material soil to nourish it. Patterson's view was that we should accept this shallow soil, (we begin from an existential absurdity of nothing) and grow our ferns in a kind of moon-dust. Fertility would come later; if not, Naipaul refused to plant at all. He watered the waste with irony. But Williams, coming from Guyana, where he had lived intimately for long periods with the Warraou Indians of the Northwest District, had a more immediate and tactile apprehension of artistic soil . . .

For Williams, this central source is Amerindian. For others of us, the central force of our life of awareness is African. As black people in the Caribbean, that is how we feel it should be. But Williams' choice of the Amerindian motif does not exclude the African. For one thing, Williams claims ancestry from both peoples – he is spiritually a black Carib . . . Africa in the Caribbean at that time was still hidden and/or ignored. But what Williams' work has revealed – and what in my analysis of it I have largely unconsciously stressed – is that the distinction between African and Amerindian in this context is for the most part irrelevant. What is important is the primordial nature of the two cultures and the potent spiritual and artistic connections between them and the present. In the Caribbean, whether it be African or Amerindian, the recognition of an ancestral relationship with the folk or aboriginal culture involves the artist and participant in a journey into the past and hinterland which is at the same time a movement of possession into present and future. Through this movement of possession we become ourselves, truly our own creators, discovering word for object, image for the Word.

(1970)

Rajkumari Singh

I am a Coolie

The first batch of Indentured Labourers from India arrived in British Guiana in May, 1838. To commemorate the 100th Anniversary of the arrival Peter Ruhoman, then a retired Civil Servant, wrote and got published, at a later date, a book entitled 'Centenary History of the East Indians in British Guiana 1838–1938'.

On page six of the volume, this appears:

Note: –

It will be observed in the course of this history, that the term 'coolie' frequently appears in quotations from reports, books and other documents from which the author has drawn his facts. As the word has been grossly misused and in many instances abused some explanation would appear necessary to those unacquainted with its exact connotation.

The term Kuli, commonly spelt coolie or cooly, is of Indian origin and is used in Eastern Countries as a designation for an Indian or Chinese hired labourer and is the equivalent to the use of the word porter or jobber in the Colony or carrier in England.

Webster defines it as follows: –

Coolie, cooly, n., pl. coolies. (Aug.-Ind.)
In the East Indies, a porter or carrier. The term is also extended to emigrant labourers from India, China, and other Eastern countries who are introduced into the East India Islands, British Guiana, Mauritius, and other European Colonies.

Chambers gives its probable origin in the following clear and unmistakable language: –

Coolie, Cooly. n. an Indian or Chinese labourer who has emigrated under contract to a foreign land: a European's name for a hired native labourer in India or China. (Prob. Kuli, a tribe of Guzerat: originally Tamil, of Kuli, hire)

In the Colony the word had hitherto been accepted as a designation for all Indians, regardless of rank, professional status or social position. Happily, there is a tendency now, especially among the educated classes, to correctly evaluate the significance of the term and to refrain from its misuse. The explanation therefore, given both by Webster and Chambers, as to its correct usage, should settle, once and for all, any doubts that might still exist as to its meaning, force and effect.

Let's have a look at the first three lines of the last paragraph, which are in italics for emphasis. Read it again. Good! Now, – at the present time, we have come a far way from the Colonial days. We moved from a Colony to Internal Self-Government to Independence to Republicanism. Yet, can we honestly say that 'the word' is not used in the same context, even in our Co-operative Republic? Even Indo-Guyanese use it to denigrate each other.

Let's take the next set of italicised words. How was 'the word' evaluated by the educated classes? Even word-meanings change with the age or in a special context. And at that time it related to menial occupation and had a menial connotation.

Is it not time that we should think about this word . . . re-think, rather. Peter Ruhoman verifies that it was used in an uncomplimentary connotation. In our time we find it is still used with an uncomplimentary connotation. But where did it all start?

It all started with our forefathers, remember . . . this is the name of our hard-working, economy-building forefathers who were called COOLIE! Think of the word. Mull over this word. What does it mean to YOU? Does it not make you aware of the hardships and trials – mental and physical – that our grandfathers and grandmothers experienced? Does it not remind you that they were brought from their far-off Motherland to save ours from total economic collapse following the Slave Emancipation experience?

The word brings to mind 'rows and rows of toilers' – coolie men and women – with soft mud squelching between their toes, up to their breasts in water, planting rice. And when 'the pregnant paddy sheaves bend low with their grain-burden', do you not recall the bent emaciated bodies of the toilers, and hear their wheezing, coughing, their premature old-age because of water, of bending of intense Tropic sun-heat?

When you see the Sun Belle Dairy vans, huge and small, delivering milk for school children, for them to grow strong and healthy, do you not recall Ahir Baba's early morning song as he roused his cattle at four in the morning to milk them, to supply milk for one and all – and the beauty of it all as he led the cattle out in the early dawn, lowing, trodding their way to the green, green pastures – and of the ghee to keep our sacrificial fires alight?

Did not these Coolies plant sugar-cane, fields and fields of swaying sugar-cane to give the taste of sweetness to us all and to all sorts of people all over the world? And let us not forget how often this sweetness became bitter gall to them for seeking their rights ... remember ... remember ... Lallabagee ... Alice ... remember, and all those others who showed resistance for their rights and died to lay paths of freedom for us ... remember?

Surely you cannot forget Per-Agie our great-Coolie grandmother squatting on her haunches, blowing through the phookni to help the chuha-fire blaze so that your parents and mine could have a hot sadha roti and alloo chokha [sic] before they leave for the fields! Can't you hear her bangles tinkling as she grinds the garam massala to make her curries unforgettable? Does not your gourmet's nostrils still quiver with the smell ... the one and only unforgettable smell of hot oil, garlic, onions, pepper, geera, to chunke the daal that was and still is a must in our daily diet?

Daal, rice and baigan choka, or coconut choka, or alloo choka, or ... so many other delightful, simple peasant food ... clean nourishing ... healthy food.

All this they gave to us and more. In return for our HERITAGE what greater tribute can we pay to them than to keep alive the name by which they were called. COOLIE is a beautiful word that conjures up poignancy, tears, defeats, achievements. The word must not be left to die out, buried and forgotten in the past. It must be given a new lease of life. All that they did and we are doing and our progeny will do, must be stamped with the name COOLIE lest posterity accuse us of not venerating the ancestors.

Remember the Hesperus and the Whitby. They came with blowing sails, riding the waves of our coffee-tinted Atlantic to unload their precious cargo on our Guyana. Brave, courageous, daring, exciting, industrious, thrifty, nation-building, humble folk – our COOLIE ancestors.

Not only in the Guyana context must COOLIE be given new meaning, but in every land of the Caribbean Sea, the Indian Ocean, the seas of the East, in Africa and Europe. Proclaim the word! Identify with the word! Proudly say to the world: 'I AM A COOLIE.'

(1973)

Derek Walcott

The Muse of History

History is the nightmare from which
I am trying to awake.

Joyce

The common experience of the New World, even for its patrician writers whose veneration of the Old is read as the idolatry of the mestizo, is colonialism. They too are victims of tradition, but they remind us of our debt to the great dead, that those who break a tradition first hold it in awe. They perversely encourage disfavour, but because their sense of the past is of a timeless, yet habitable, moment, the New World owes them more than it does those who wrestle with that past, for their veneration subtilises an arrogance which is tougher than violent rejection. They know that by openly fighting tradition we perpetuate it, that revolutionary literature is a filial impulse, and that maturity is the assimilation of the features of every ancestor ...

These writers reject the idea of history as time for its original concept as myth, the partial recall of the race. For them history is fiction, subject to a fitful muse, memory. Their philosophy, based on a contempt for historic time, is revolutionary, for what they repeat to the New World is its simultaneity with the Old. Their vision of man is elemental, a being inhabited by presences, not a creature chained to his past. Yet the method by which we are taught the past, the progress from motive to event, is the same by which we read narrative fiction. In time every event becomes an exertion of memory and is thus subject to invention. The further the facts, the more history petrifies into myth. Thus, as we grow older as a race, we grow aware that history is written, that it is a kind of literature without morality, that in its actuaries the ego of the race is indissoluble and that everything depends on whether we write this fiction through the memory of hero or of victim.

In the New World servitude to the muse of history has produced a literature of recrimination and despair, a literature of revenge written by the descendants of slaves or a literature of remorse written by the descendants of masters. Because this literature serves historical truth, it yellows into polemic or evaporates in pathos. The truly tough aesthetic of the New World neither explains nor forgives history. It refuses to recognise it as a creative or culpable force. This shame and awe of history possess[es] poets of the Third World who think of language as enslavement and who, in a rage for identity, respect only incoherence or nostalgia.

The great poets of the New World, from Whitman to Neruda, reject this sense of history. Their vision of man in the New World is Adamic. In their exuberance he is still capable of enormous wonder. Yet he has paid his accounts to Greece and Rome and walks in a world without monuments and ruins. They exhort him against the fearful magnet of older civilisations . . . Violence is felt with the simultaneity of history. So the death of a gaucho does not merely repeat, but is, the death of Caesar. Fact evaporates into myth. This is not the jaded cynicism which sees nothing new under the sun, it is an elation which sees everything as renewed . . .

New World poets who see the 'classic style' as stasis must see it also as historical degradation, rejecting it as the language of the master. This self-torture arises when the poet also sees history as language, when he limits his memory to the suffering of the victim. Their admirable wish to honour the degraded ancestor limits their language to phonetic pain, the groan of suffering, the curse of revenge. The tone of the past becomes an unbearable burden, for they must abuse the master or hero in his own language, and this implies self-deceit. Their view of Caliban is of the enraged pupil. They cannot separate the rage of Caliban from the beauty of his speech when the speeches of Caliban are equal in their elemental power to those of his tutor. The language of the torturer mastered by the victim. This is viewed as servitude, not as victory.

But who in the New World does not have a horror of the past, whether his ancestor was torturer or victim? Who, in the depth of conscience, is not silently screaming for pardon or for revenge? The pulse of New World history is the racing pulse beat of fear, the tiring cycles of stupidity and greed. The tongues above our prayers utter the pain of entire races to the darkness of a Manichean God: *Dominus illuminatio mea*, for what was brought to this New World under the guise of divine light, the light of the sword blade and the light of *Dominus illuminatio mea*, was the same irridescent serpent brought by a containing Adam, the same tortured Christ exhibited with Christian exhaustion, but what was also brought in the seeded entrails of the slave was a new nothing, a darkness which intensified the old faith.

In time the slave surrendered to amnesia. That amnesia is the true history of the New World. That is our inheritance, but to try and understand why this happened, to condemn or justify is also the method of history, and these explanations are always the same: This happened because of that, this was understandable because, and in those days men were such. These recriminations exchanged, the contrition of the master replaces the vengeance of the slave, and here colonial literature is most pietistic, for it can accuse great art of feudalism and excuse poor art as suffering. To radical poets poetry seems the homage of resignation, an essential fatalism. But it is not the pressure of the past which torments great poets but the weight of the present:

> there are so many dead,
> and so many dikes the red sun breached,
> and so many heads battering hulls
> and so many hands that have closed over kisses
> and so many things that I want to forget.
>
> *Neruda*

The sense of history in poets lives rawly along their nerves:

> My land without name, without America,
> equinoctial stamen, lance-like purple,
> your aroma rose through my roots
> into the cut I drained, into the most tenuous
> word not yet born in my mouth.
>
> *Neruda*

It is this awe of the numinous, this elemental privilege of naming the New World which annihilates history in our great poets, an elation common to all of them, whether they are aligned by heritage to Crusoe and Prospero or to Friday and Caliban. They reject ethnic ancestry for faith in elemental man. The vision, the 'democratic vista' is not metaphorical, it is a social necessity. A political philosophy rooted in elation would have to accept belief in a second Adam, the re-creation of the entire order, from religion to the simplest domestic rituals. The myth of the noble savage would not be revived, for that myth never emanated from the savage but has always been the nostalgia of the Old World, its longing for innocence. The great

[356]

poetry of the New World does not pretend to such innocence, its vision is not naive. Rather, like its fruits, its savour is a mixture of the acid and the sweet, the apples of its second Eden have the tartness of experience. In such poetry there is a bitter memory and it is the bitterness that dries last on the tongue. It is the acidulous that supplies its energy ... For us in the archipelago the tribal memory is salted with the bitter memory of migration.

To such survivors, to all the decimated tribes of the New World who did not suffer extinction, their degraded arrival must be seen as the beginning, not the end of our history. The shipwrecks of Crusoe and of the crew in *The Tempest* are the end of an Old World. It should matter nothing to the New World if the Old is again determined to blow itself up, for an obsession with progress is not within the psyche of the recently enslaved. That is the bitter secret of the apple. The vision of progress is the rational madness of history seen as sequential time, of a dominated future. Its imagery is absurd. In the history books the discoverer sets a shod foot on virgin sand, kneels, and the savage also kneels from his bushes in awe. Such images are stamped on the colonial memory, such heresy as the world's becoming holy from Crusoe's footprint or the imprint of Columbus' knee. These blasphemous images fade, because these hieroglyphs of progress are basically comic. And if the idea of the New and the Old becomes increasingly absurd, what must happen to our sense of time, what else can happen to history itself, but that it too is becoming absurd? This is not existentialism. Adamic, elemental man cannot be existential. His first impulse is not self-indulgence but awe ... To most writers of the archipelago who contemplate only the shipwreck, the New World offers not elation but cynicism, a despair at the vices of the Old which they feel must be repeated. Their malaise is an oceanic nostalgia for the older culture and a melancholy at the new, and this can go as deep as a rejection of the untamed landscape, a yearning for ruins. To such writers the death of civilisations is architectural, not spiritual, seeded in their memories is an imagery of vines ascending broken columns, of dead terraces, of Europe as a nourishing museum. They believe in the responsibility of tradition, but what they are in awe of is not tradition, which is alert, alive, simultaneous, but of history, and the same is true of the new magnifiers of Africa. For these their deepest loss is of the old gods, the fear that it is worship which has enslaved progress. Thus the humanism of politics replaces religion. They see such gods as part of the process of history, subjected like the tribe to cycles of achievement and despair. Because the Old World concept of God is anthropomorphic, the New World slave was forced to remake himself in His image, despite such phrases as 'God is light, and in Him is no darkness', and at this point of intersecting faiths the enslaved poet and enslaved priest surrendered their power. But the tribe in bondage learned to fortify itself by cunning assimilation of the religion of the Old World. What seemed to be surrender was redemption. What seemed the loss of tradition was its renewal. What seemed the death of faith was its rebirth.

(1974)

James Berry

Introduction to Bluefoot Traveller

These poems illustrate the combined influences of an African, West-indian and British background: and more particularly they present something of the Westindians' response to life in British society. They show their incorporation into the society and their isolation within it. They reflect their settled and unsettled condition, their insecurity and, also, an underlying explosiveness.

The important human experiences between black and white in Britain take place quietly on a personal level. Publicly, British society is often different: on the one side it subtly excludes blacks and on the other tries indulgently to 'integrate' them, but quietly, as if wishing their non-existence. There is no nourishing atmosphere for the development of black distinctiveness. Neither does Britain show any desire for cultural fusion. Westindians here are a long way away from the dynamic cultural activities of American blacks or their fellow Westindians at home. They are grossly underexplored, underex-pressed, underproduced and undercontributing. They have not yet managed to create any steadily developing cultural activity with both a deepening and widening upward trend. Racial minority fears still lead to a protest orientation. And that orientation consumes too much creative energy; it undermines sensitive development and fulfilment.

The Westindian in Britain finds himself in a situation that amounts to a continuation of the old ways of life. Around him white people are still dominant, still in control. He hardly participates in the evolu-tion of his society. Demands are not made on his talents. Society generates no clamour to see him in new dimensions. He cannot unlid himself as his fellow Westindian at home does. He has missed out on the exciting process of rediscovery. He has missed out on the real experience of Independence, of being his own master, and can be part of the new life there only by proxy. At the same time, in reality, life in Britain is no longer a reserve of a big white tribe. And some-thing of the new relationship stimulates a new awareness and confidence which seeps through into the poetry here.

A new situation of freedom to think and act is always interesting to observe. Pursuits to develop Westindian art forms are a recent activity. A few years of political independence have turned each

Caribbean country into an exhibitor of its own arts. Each country continues to assemble and develop the various forms of its cultural heritage. Demands for Caribbean literature push writers to new achievements. A discarding of aspects of British culture that were restrictive, and limiting to natural development, came spontaneously. This means that Westindians at home are going through the incredible excitement of satisfying starved aspects of their personality. And it is what began in Africa and the Caribbean and Asia that excites and engages their artistic interest.

Westindies Talk, Westindian dialect or Westindian English, which had been the shame of village people suddenly became the pride of university students and city intellectuals. And it is now largely accepted that Westindian English did not develop out of a failure to learn correct English but was a successful response to the need to communicate naturally and well in a new tongue, without formal instruction . . . Westindian English has a directness, rhythm and swift imagery that readily leads to poetry.

(1976)

1980–89

Introduction

Nation Language: New Soundings in Caribbean Poetry

The 1980s saw the consolidation of more established voices in Caribbean poetry such as Walcott's, with the publication of *Selected Poems* in 1981 and *Collected Poems* in 1986, and with poets such as **Carter** (1980), **Brathwaite** (1982a, 1982b, 1987a) and **Walcott** (1984, 1987) all publishing important new collections in this decade. However, the 1980s were most strikingly characterized by the arrival of a new generation of poets, many more of whom were confidently handling creole (**Berry**, Bloom, D'Aguiar, M. Collins, David Dabydeen, Amryl Johnson, **Nichols**, F. Williams, Matthews) and experimenting with poetry as 'sounded voice' (Agard, **Breeze**, **Smith**, **Linton Kwesi Johnson**, Brother Resistance), a practice which Brathwaite surveyed mid-decade in his seminal *History of the Voice* (1984).

Of these writings in creole, we include a selection of poems by James Berry and an interesting example of a nation language prose monologue by Guyanese **Harry Narain**. Berry's **'Lucy's Letter'** is a good example of the continued use of the letter home format much used by **Louise Bennett** and also adapted by Valerie Bloom and **David Dabydeen** in the 1980s. Berry migrated from Jamaica to Britain in 1948 and the poems in this collection deal with migratory experience and the crossing of different worlds, which is a common theme in much early diasporic writing (e.g. Rhys 1934, Selvon 1956) and more recent texts such as Dabydeen (1987, 1988, 1991), Kincaid (1991), Phillips (1987), Riley (1985, 1987). Although 'Lucy's Letter' hovers on the verge of nostalgia, it is strengthened by its vigorous creole idiom. **'From Lucy: Holiday Reflections'** is part of another recurrent theme in Caribbean literature, 'going home' or revisiting the Caribbean, and can be usefully read alongside **Linton Kwesi Johnson (1984)**, Phillips (1986), and Amryl Johnson (1987).

Berry's **'Caribbean Proverb Poems'** attest to the effective use of folklore and communal wisdom as an imaginative and formal resource. Indeed, from the beginning of the century collections of Anancy Stories and other traditional resources form a veritable sub-genre of Caribbean literature (Sherlock (1936, 1956, 1959, 1966), Salkey (1973), Berry (1988). However, in contrast to the *Labrish* (or gossip) tradition (of which Bennett's **'Proverbs'** might still be regarded as part), Berry's poems exemplify the tempering of what Nettleford has called the Caribbean 'high propensity for words' (1966) to the taut, epigrammatic measure and necessary mnemonic economies of the oral proverb. This is an interesting recuperation of an oral traditional resource to a textual form but, as in Bennett's case, it is still a poetry which demands a speaking voice and the perpetual present tense of the creole idiom in these poems, as in Bennett's **'Beeny Bud'**, testifies to the oral origins of such texts.

Both Berry and Bennett's work provide a useful context against which to read Harry Narain's **'A Letter to the Prime Minister'**. We include this satirical 'open letter', in the tradition of mamaguy (a culturally specific narrative mode which makes use of structural irony), as an interesting and comparatively rare example of a creole prose monologue. It can be profitably read against other texts which deal with an Indo-Caribbean peasant experience (Monar 1985, **Dabydeen** 1984, 1988, **1995**), and alongside other satirical texts (see calypsos in this volume). It can also be located in a protest tradition in Caribbean literature alongside poets such as **Campbell**, Carter and the dub poets (see Asein 1972). Indeed, this is a pertinent reading, given Narain's close attention to the political and economic climate of early 1980s Guyana. British Guiana had gained its independence in 1966 and Prime Minister Forbes Burnham announced that the co-operative would be the instrument to 'revolutionize the colonial economy Guyana had inherited' (Daly 1974: 307) and make 'the small man the real man'. Guyana was declared a 'Co-operative Republic' in 1970, but by 1980 cracks in the system were already evident. In that year, general elections were boycotted by a new multi-racial independent Marxist party, established in 1979, The Working Peoples' Alliance; and its leader Dr Walter Rodney was assassinated. In the punitive years which followed, Guyana suffered extensive food shortages, industrial strikes, a reduction in production and exports and the breakdown of social and public services. In this context, **Narain**'s creole monologue reads as an immediate and courageous, politically committed literary text.

This increase in creole or nation language writing in the 1980s can be linked partly to literary developments in the late 1970s. The emergence of the first dub and other young poets during this period marked not only a newly confident poetic use of creole but also the start of a new receptiveness to literature in a creole idiom. This was largely, but by no means exclusively, facilitated by the new wave of performance poetry being popularized by poets such as **Linton Kwesi Johnson**, **Michael Smith** and Oku Onuora who attracted worldwide audiences, and by the work of touring troupes such as The Bluefoot Travellers in Britain and the 'All O' We' group in Guyana (Ken Corsbie, Marc Matthews, John Agard, Henry Muttoo) (Markham 1989: 14).

In the scholarly tradition, David Dabydeen's **'On Not Being Milton: Nigger Talk in England Today'** focuses on creole and the performative form in Black British writing and this piece may be read as a useful introduction to the field. Dabydeen argues that creole is a 'private reordering of "standard English"' and looks at dub's 'deliberate exploitation of high-tech to serve black "jungle-talk" [as] a reversal of colonial history . . . Caliban is tearing up the pages of Prospero's magic books and repasting it in his own order, by his own method and for his own purpose' (**Dabydeen 1989**: 129–30). This piece also makes an interesting and provocative intervention in debates concerning the politics of identity and of naming (in) Caribbean writing (see also **Singh 1973**). Against the over-refined sensibilities and aesthetic excesses of much early Caribbean poetry, Dabydeen probes the new 'deliberate wearing of the "primitive" label' and discusses the depressing longevity of 'the pressure . . . towards mimicry', re-inflected in the politics of the 1980s publishing marketplace as a new pressure to drop 'the epithet "black"' for that of 'writer', cease '*folking* up the literature', and become 'universal' or 'be sentenced to perish in the backwater of small presses' (Dabydeen 1989: 134).

Lawson Welsh (1991) also examines the background to the creative use of creole, seen as 'broken english' in earlier periods (**McFarlane 1957**: 58). Using the 1984 collection *Slave Song* by David

Dabydeen as her textual locale, she suggests how this concept of brokenness may be viewed as an aesthetic of deliberate unevenness, disturbance or interruption operating in the work. Brokenness is read as experimental linguistic medium, literary trope, historical and experiential paradigm in Caribbean literature. This piece also examines the problematic relationship between orality (voice) and textuality (script), creole and standard idioms and literary and critical texts. These same concerns are also explored, in different ways, by **Cooper (1990)** and remain both productive and vexed areas of inquiry for critics in the field today.

Anthologizing for the 1980s

Although the 1950s were boom years for the publication of Caribbean fiction, they were less so for poetry. Anthologies of Caribbean writing had steadily appeared throughout the 1960s and 1970s with particular clusters of anthologizing activity in 1966–67 and 1970–71 (see General Introduction). However, Caribbean and Black British poets were rarely included in anthologies of new writing in Britain (see Markham 1989: 22) and rarely adopted by the mainstream metropolitan presses in these decades. In the 1980s this was to change, as an unprecedented range of new writing appeared in print and as Caribbean poets were taken on by metropolitan presses and recording studios in increasing numbers. Significant anthologies include the general or territory-specific anthologies, such as Seymour ed. (1980), Ramchand ed. (1982), *Pacific Quarterly Moana* (1983), Burnett ed. (1986), Figueroa ed. (1986), Mordecai ed. (1987), Markham ed. (1989), Elliot ed. (1985), Cyril Dabydeen ed. (1987), Jones ed. (1987), Hamblestone ed. (1987), Turner ed. (1987a, 1987b). The Indo-Caribbean-based anthologies include Birbalsingh ed. (1988) and collections of women's writing include Morris ed. (1980), Cobham and Collins ed. (1987), Mordecai and Wilson eds (1989). The oral or performance-based anthologies include Stewart Brown ed. (1984), Habekost (1986) and Brown, Morris and Rohlehr *et al.* eds (1983). and (1984) Berry ed. represents 'Black British' compilations.

There were also notable Caribbean and Black British contributions to 1980s anthologies such as Paskin, Ramsay and Silver (1986), Linthwaite (1987) and Allnut, D'Aguiar, Edwards and Mottram eds (1988). Seemingly, the dynamic atmosphere and 'steadily developing cultural activity with both a deepening and widening upward trend' which James Berry felt to be present in the Caribbean in 1976 but lacking in Britain, had now arrived.

The 1980s saw the re-issuing of Caribbean prose 'classics' by Harris, **Lamming, Mais, Selvon**, Patterson, Roy, Allfrey, **Hodge** and others. Yet there were also important new voices to be heard, with the appearance of a number of highly significant first novels and short story collections from writers such as Brodber, **Kincaid**, Collins, Edgell, Senior and Monar in the Caribbean, Cliff and Bissoondath in the United States and Canada, and Scott, Shinebourne, Phillips and Riley in Britain.

Critical concerns

The foundations for a more receptive critical terrain in the 1980s had been laid partly by 'cultural commentators' such as **Rohlehr** (**1972–3**) and **Brathwaite** (**1979**) who had argued for a Caribbean literary aesthetic which would be based on a broad spectrum of cultural practices. The polemical tradition of Caribbean writing, to which Brathwaite and Rohlehr are important contributors, found lively continuation in the 1980s in the hands of writers such as **David Dabydeen** (**1989**), D'Aguiar (1989) and **Kincaid** (1988). Earlier influential critical works such as Ramchand (1970) appeared in updated editions (1983) and others such as Brathwaite (1974) were reissued.

Certainly the 1980s saw the launch of some new Caribbean journals such as *Carib*, *The Journal of Caribbean Studies*, *Antilia* and *The Journal of West Indian Literature*, as well as the publication of a number of critical works with an exclusively Caribbean focus (Gilkes 1981, Lloyd Brown 1984, Smilowitz and Knowles ed.s 1984, McWatt ed. 1985, Dance ed. 1986, Dabydeen and Samaroo ed.s 1987, Saakana 1987, Butcher ed. 1989) with a significant clustering of works on women's writing appearing at the end of the decade and in 1990 (Boyce Davies and Savory Fido eds 1990, Cudjoe ed. 1990). However, it is worth noting that these were both predominantly metropolitan publications and far outnumbered by the publication of critical works with a broader post-colonial remit during this period.

Indeed, the critical praxis of the 1980s was also characterized by an increasingly sophisticated articulation and interrogation of key post-colonial issues (e.g. Ashcroft, Griffiths and Tiffin 1989, Slemon and Tiffin eds 1989) which were catered for in journals such as *Ariel*, *World Literature Written in English*, *New Literature Review* and a number of newly emergent critical presses and specialist journals, including Dangaroo and the journal *Kunapipi*. The relationship between Caribbean literature and other post-colonial literatures, as well as that between Caribbean literature and predominantly European theory, continues to be a thorny one, as does the future of theory itself, with a series of debates and positions 'finding their feet' in the 1990s.

Beyond the 'riddum prison': new directions in dub

We include poems by **Linton Kwesi Johnson** and by the late **Michael Smith** which demonstrate the power but equally the versatility of the dub form at its best. Dub and performance poetry still often suffer low critical regard, not least because of the poor image created by some poems which rely on overworked themes or which privilege performance to the detriment of the poem. As Brathwaite has observed with characteristic wordplay, there is a tendency for some dub poets to become:

> captured by ye claps into a riddum prison out / of which he beats & beats & beats in vain / ut utter utterly like butterfly un / beat un / beat & utt / early be / atified.

The dub poet is presented with the problem that:

> sound poetry is one thing pun stage / another on the page Both must perform / yes Both will have form / yes but how trans / late trans / fer trans / form

especially when the 'oral / aura . . . can be corrupted by the too-fresh laurels of applause, the audience too thirsty / greedy for the same / too same effects' (Brathwaite 1987b). Poems such as Johnson's **'Reggae fi Dada'** or the frequently anthologized Smith's 'Me Cyaan Believe It' (1986), constitute some of the most striking and skilful examples of the 'oraliterary' in Caribbean literature. These poems suggest careful formulation in terms of both language and structure, but also an awareness of the power and potentialities of the oral/aural form with its characteristically additive and repetitive structures and

[366]

its allusive or resonant use of language. This sense of working within an 'oraliterary' framework rather than an exclusively oral or scribal one is also supported by the varying composition methods of the poets themselves (Morris 1982a, 1982b, 1986, 1992).

Jamaican-born Johnson, who came to Britain in 1963 as an eleven-year-old, has been the most enduring and maturing presence not only in dub, but also in Black British poetry more generally and has progressively widened the scope and formal experimentation of his poetry. We include **'Street 66'** as an early Johnson poem, grounded in the particular Blues Party culture of 1970s Black Britain, and indicative of a wider 'reggae culture' in its use of a reggae rhythm, Rasta lexical items and allusions to Reggae DJs (see Sutcliffe and Wong 1986: 52–68). 'Street 66' describes the ganja-induced atmosphere of a London Blues party and the onset of an unexpected visit from the police. In his poem, the overt violence of the better-known 'Five Nights of Bleeding' has become more subtle and subliminal, adding an undercurrent of threatened or imminent violence which makes the poem powerfully evocative and atmospheric. As with all Johnson's poetry, 'Street 66' is more effective when heard rather than read and rhythmic control and careful pacing are crucial – especially when, as at the end of this poem, dramatic effect is called for.

The publication of the 1987 anthology *Voiceprint* (Brown *et al.*) brought the range and interrelatedness of songs, calypsos, oral and performance poetry to a non-specialist audience. The editors devote a whole section of their anthology to elegy and lament, pointing out that 'the elegy has become a predominant mode in West Indian poetry' (1987: 17). However, until fairly recently there were still relatively few elegies in creole. Johnson's 'Reggae fi Dada' is perhaps the finest creole elegy to date, combining as it does a deep sense of personal loss in its elegiac address to his father, a lament for the decay of a society and a razor-sharp indictment of the violence, corruption, and economic privations which the poet sees as afflicting contemporary Jamaica. The biblical imagery and cadences in this poem are striking, as is the use of repetition, an incrementally shifting refrain and extended runs of rhyming clauses which are simultaneously characteristic of the strong oral culture of the Caribbean and of the Bible as an orally residual text. Indeed, Johnson has spoken, as have fellow Jamaican poets **Bennett** and **Breeze**, of the central influence of the Bible on his work – especially the action of reading it aloud (Morris 1982a).

Similar features are found in St Lucian Jane King's **'Intercity Dub'**, dedicated to dub poet Jean Binta Breeze. Like Berry's 'Lucy' poems included in this section, it explores a British diasporic experience, but King's London is much harsher: a Dantean 'hell / in many parts'. Breeze's creativity and her 'singing' of the body are celebrated as healing and reconciliatory acts, in stark contrast to the actions of the 'Brixton-battered sisters', hissing their 'bitterness and hate', because they 'don't want to build / No bridge, no gate'; in this moving exploration of human barriers and the problems of racial and cultural separatism, King explores the power of words to build or destroy, connect or isolate individuals and communities. Particularly note-worthy is the mimetic use of the rhythm of the train, a technique reminiscent in many ways of **Lamming's** similar experimentation in *The Emigrants* (see Brathwaite 1967: 48–9). Less openly intertextual than the extract from Kincaid's *Annie John* included in this section, the poem nonetheless makes use of a reiterated refrain of 'it will come', which is also the uplifting celebratory ending to the first novel of Erna Brodber, *Jane and Louisa Will Soon Come Home* (1980).

We include Michael Smith's **'Black and White'** with its pared-down syntax, its carefully controlled tempo and its characteristic wordplay from Smith's only collection, *It a Come* (available in textual and recorded form) as another poem which challenges the common belief that dub poetry is necessarily restrictive and monotonous. Instead it offers dub which is expressive, compact and highly controlled. Smith was stoned to death at a political rally in Kingston in 1983, thus foreclosing the career of one of the most promising poets of a generation.

Women's writing in the 1980s

One of the most significant developments of the 1970s was the increased publication of Caribbean women's writing and in the 1980s some highly significant new voices came into print. We include a prose extract from Antiguan-born, United States-based, Jamaica Kincaid's *Annie John*; poems by Jamaican **Lorna Goodison** and British-based poets Jamaican **Jean Binta Breeze** and Guyanese **Grace Nichols**, as examples of this generation of writers who were mostly

[368]

born in the late 1940s and 1950s and who produced their first major works in the 1980s.

Ramabai Espinet's critical piece **'The Invisible Woman in West Indian Literature'** complements earlier Caribbean women's writing by **Das** and **Singh** as well as male-authored texts dealing with an Indo-Caribbean experience, such as Monar (1985) and **Dabydeen (1995)**. Espinet explores the 'invisibility' of East Indian woman in Caribbean literature, a figure who is marginalized by virtue of her ethnicity and her gendered representation in limited or fixed ways. Her piece refers primarily to V.S. and Shiva Naipaul's fiction, Indo-Caribbean male writers whose paternal great-grandmother, like Per Ajie, made the journey across the *Kala pani* or 'black water' and yet remain unable to represent her descendants in complex or interesting ways. Although a rather crude developmental framework characterizes parts of this piece, it does constitute an important examination of a critically neglected area in Caribbean literature and criticism.

Grace Nichols's *i is a long memoried woman* is a seminal long poem which takes as its project the reconstructing and re/membering of (black) Caribbean women's histories. In its poem-cycle structure and its merging of the particular and the universal, the concrete and the mythical, it can be seen as parallel in some ways to **Brathwaite**'s long trilogies (1982a, 1982b, 1987a). This is especially true of parts of *The Arrivants* and *Mother Poem* which explore similar subject-matter: African cultural legacies in the Caribbean, the role of Caribbean women in relation to male histories, the geography or 'geo-psyche' of the Caribbean and how the landscape might be gendered in certain ways (**Nichols 1983**: 32–5). *i is a long memoried woman* also connects with the concerns of other Caribbean women writers such as Brodber (1980) in its affirmation of the multiple inheritances of the Caribbean woman – 'all [her] lives' – and in its emphasis on taking control of future(s) and new trajectories, and with African-American texts such as Toni Morrison's *Beloved* (1988), which explores a similar terrain of complex female subjectivities and of the experiences of motherhood within a context of slavery.

The centrality of the mother figure is most evident in Nichols's **'Your Blessing'**; however the possible defamiliarization of the mother figure, as representing neither nurture or security, is glimpsed in the fleeting ambiguity of the phrase 'motherland'; here Africa seems to be implied but the traces of a less welcoming 'mother', the Britain to which Nichols emigrated as a young woman, are also registered. 'Your Blessing' is a poem in which the daughter-figure craves benediction from her mother/land, and is appropriately antiphonal in structure. However, the prayer-like cadences shift to an increasingly imperative syntax and insistent tone, with a similar kind of increase in pace and experimentation with rhythm as is found in a poem such as 'Wings of a Dove' (Brathwaite 1973: 42–5).

Mothers and mothering are also prominent in our selection from Lorna Goodison's second collection *I Am Becoming My Mother* (1986). The title poem is concerned with immediate ancestry and mythologies of the self. This and the following poem, **'For My Mother (May I Inherit Half Her Strength)'** may be productively read against (or alongside) the male-authored 'grand/father poems' (**Johnson 1984** and **Scott 1987**) and clearly connect with the elegiac tradition and strong autobiographical strand running through Caribbean literature. **DeCaires Narain (1994)** notes the 'sensual merging of two lives' in the title poem and this celebration of the body and of sensual life as well as the strongly articulated need to 'connect' are salient features of the poem. Arguably, **Johnson (1984)** and **Scott (1987)** also act to 'recuperat[e] and validat[e]' the immediate ancestor, as Narain observes, but in different ways to those utilized by Goodison. The centrality of female creativity as the sustaining element is reminiscent of Alice Walker's *In Search of Our Mother's Gardens*, Narain reminds us, but such creativity is not exclusively matrilineal, and is also found in Scott's poem and to an extent in the framing of Johnson's father as a skilled and ingenious provider for his children. In its concern to ground the self and stabilize the interior landscapes of the self, **'For My Mother'** plots a kind of revisionist history of its own which is more directly woman-centred: 'Even at this death there was this "Friend" who stood by her side, but my mother is adamant that that has no place in the memory of my father.'

'On Houses' extends the familiar trope of building identified in the mainly androcentric canon of Caribbean literature of the 1950s into new territory of spiritual and psychological habitation. As in so much Caribbean poetry, this poem has biblical echoes: 'My father's mansion has many rooms', is domesticated to 'I have built many houses ...', with an intertextual nod to Naipaul (1961). However, as Biswas in Naipaul's key fictional work *A House for Mr Biswas* discovers, inhabiting one's own house is not an unequivocally liberating experience, as images of imprisonment take over from those of dispossession. However, in **Goodison** belonging is gendered. Just as in **Napier (1951)** the men at the pension are all transitory guests, sailors whose journeyings to distant places the protagonist can only imagine, so in Goodison's poem man journeys ('you went to sea') and woman remains. That this domesticated containment is an echo of slavery within a patriarchal post-colonial culture is strongly suggested by the phrase: 'the fingering of chains'.

Goodison's **'My Late Friend'** can be read as an update (in which depressingly little has changed) to **Marson's 'Kinky Hair Blues'**. However, the compulsion to blunt racial difference ironically accepted in Marson's poem is here mediated through the poem's persona who (perhaps spuriously) is differentiated from the subject of the poem. **DeCaires Narain** argues that this poem is a good example of Goodison's option 'not to speak of the body and to articulate a poetic identity which transcends this particular pain in the projection of a disembodied poetic voice'. As in **'On Houses'** there are ironic echoes of enslavement, in the gendered tyranny of the friend 'disciplin[ing] her hair till it lies in exhausted submission' and, in a novel variation on the paradigm of exile, flees 'the tropics / because the sun darkens her / my friend wants to be one with the snow'. **'Guyana Lovesong'** makes interesting use of images of textuality, a recurrent strategy in Caribbean literature (see Walcott 1981: 18–20, and many other of his poems; **Rhys 1960** and **Kincaid 1985**) and its blurring of space and time is reminiscent of Harris's more complex fictional experimentation with the same and, more recently, of Pauline Melville's short story 'Eat Labba and Drink Creek Water' (1990).

Resistant subjects: Jamaica Kincaid's 'Columbus in Chains'

If a new emphasis on resistance (both in reading and writing practices) within post-colonial theory emerges in the 1980s there are also other forms of resistance which were brought to critical attention during this period: most notably to dominant male forms and to acts of cultural (African–Caribbean) cultural homogenization. Jamaica Kincaid's **'Columbus in Chains'**, from *Annie John*, a novel about a young girl growing up in a Caribbean island, stages these multiple resistances. The standard critical response to this text and others which cover childhood narratives in the Caribbean is to equate the growth of the individual with that of the island and to draw out examples of colonial oppression in the processes of schooling and socialization, often with the exceptionally bright child feeling isolated from the community and society and migrating to the metropolis abroad (e.g. 'G', in Lamming 1953). However, we wish to foreground instead the ways in which Kincaid resists narratives which can be reduced to 'national allegories' (after Jameson) or tales of victims, and to encourage exploration of the effects and intellectual consequences of her resistance.

Arguably, Kincaid's contribution to this sub-genre in the 1980s demonstrates how far such writing has 'moved on'; the mentality in this text might be termed a post- 'post-colonial' one – an independent/ence mind. However, fields of enquiry and models of interpretation have been slower and more reluctant to move on: when we read Caribbean literature we often bring critical expectations that colonialism will act as an almost universal referent and decoder in the text and it is this assumption and this construction of the post-colonial which Kincaid so skilfully plays with and disrupts.

The chapter begins and ends with Annie thinking about her mother and, indeed, it is clear that it is the problems of maternal bonding which are the primary determinants of Annie's consciousness. The issues of colonialism surface very interestingly within the passage and are in no way denied or suppressed, but they do not take pre-eminence in terms of her psychological agenda. This dis-placing of colonial subjectivity, in which the ideas of colonization and its resultant cultural horror are seen as prime determinants, is both imposed and, to a certain degree, outdated.

The ironic narrative voice of this chapter questions the boundaries which construct the psychology of the colonized. It is a confident and centred voice, indicative on one level of the ways in which post-colonial peoples themselves have found ways to approach and deal with colonialism that the intellect of the colonizing power cannot. Here, Kincaid problematizes expectations of a narrative which sees colonialism as a model of conquest and resistance. It is the colonizers who are in crisis now and Annie who derives cultural confidence from her position as a post-colonial West Indian who is in control of and morally content with her history. Accordingly, Annie's act of textual defilement is much more complex than it initially appears. In a deft ironic reversal Annie 'discovers' Columbus rather than the other way round; however, she frees herself from the tyranny of this founding meta-narrative and recasts it as fictional construct. Moreover, she resists the colonial construction of her subjectivity within an outmoded framework of patriarchal and imperial domination in which the female subject is considered to be necessarily doubly oppressed.

Indeed, in an important fictional episode Kincaid is able to make a valuable and positive intervention within Caribbean literary critical and feminist debates, helping, like Annie, to rewrite the texts for her own time. Like many writers and critics in the 1980s, Kincaid is involved in the project of revisiting and reinvigorating a literature which, having found a certain solidity, had also acquired its own orthodoxies.

Linton Kwesi Johnson

Street 66

de room woz dark-dusk howlin softly
six-a-clack,
charcoal lite defyin site woz
movin black;
de soun woz muzik mellow steady flow,
an man-son mind jus mystic red,
green, red, green . . . pure scene.

no man would dance but leap an shake
dat shock thru feelin ripe;
shape dat soun tumblin doun
makin movement ruff enough;
cause when de muzik met I taps,
I felt de sting, knew de shock,
yea had to do an ride de rock.

outta dis rock
shall come
a greena riddim
even more dread
dan what
de breeze of glory bread.
vibratin violence
is how wi move
rockin wid green riddim
de drout
an dry root out.

de mitey poet I-Roy woz on de wire,
Western did a scank an each one laaf:
him feelin I-ry, dread I.
'Street 66,' de said man siad,
'any policeman come yah
will get some righteous rass klaat licks,
yea man, whole heap a kicks.'

hours beat de scene movin rite
when all of a sudden
bam bam bam a knockin pan de door.
'Who's dat?' asked Western feelin rite.
'Open up! It's the police! Open up!'
'What address do you want?'
'Number sixty–six! Come on, open up!'
Western feelin high reply:
'Yes, dis is Street 66;
step rite in an tek some licks.'

(1975)

Reggae fi Dada

galang dada
galang gwaan yaw sah
yu nevah ad noh life fi live
jus di wan life fi give
yu did yu time pan ert
yu nevah get yu jus dizert
galang goh smile inna di sun
galang goh satta inna di palace af peace

o di waatah
it soh deep
di waatah
it soh daak
an it full a hawbah shaak

di lan is like a rack
slowly shattahrin to san
sinkin in a sea af calimity
where fear breeds shadows
dat lurks in di daak
where people fraid fi waak
fraid fi tink fraid fi taak
where di present is haunted by di paas

a deh soh mi bawn
get fi know bout staam
learn fi cling to di dawn

an wen mi hear mi daddy sick
mi quickly pack mi grip an tek a trip

mi nevvah have noh time
wen mi reach
fi si noh sunny beach
wen mi reach
jus people a live in shack
people livin back-to-back
mongst cackroach an rat
mongst dirt an dizeez
subjek to terrorist attack
political intrigue
kanstant grief
an noh sign af relief

o di grass
turn brown
soh many trees
cut doun
an di lan is ovahgrown

fram country to toun
is jus thistle an tawn
inna di woun a di poor
is a miracle ow dem endure

di pain nite an day
di stench af decay
di glarin sights
di guarded affluence
di arrogant vices
cole eyes af kantemp
di mackin symbals af independence

a deh soh mi bawn
get fi know bout staam
learn fi cling to di dawn
an wen di news reach me
seh mi wan daddy ded
mi ketch a plane quick

[376]

an wen mi reach mi sunny isle
it woz di same ole style
di money well dry
di bullits dem a fly
plenty innocent a die
many rivahs run dry
ganja plane flyin high
di poor man im a try
yu tink a lickle try im try
holdin awn bye an bye
wen a dallah cant buy
a lickle dinnah fi a fly

galang dada
galang gwaan yaw sah
yu nevah ad noh life fi give
just di wan life fi give
yu did yu time pan ert
yu nevah get yu jus dizert
galang goh smile inna di sun
galang goh satta inna di palace af peace

mi know yu couldn tek it dada
di anguish an di pain
di suffahrin di problems di strain
di strugglin in vain
fi mek two ens meet
soh dat dem pickney coulda get
a lickle someting fi eat
fi put cloaz pan dem back
fi put shoes pan dem feet
wen a dallah cant buy
a lickle dinnah fi a fly

mi know yu try dada
yu fite a good fite
but di dice dem did loaded
an di card pack fix
yet still yu reach fifty-six
before yu lose yu leg wicket

[377]

'a noh yu bawn grung here'
soh wi bury yu a Stranger's Burying Groun
near to mhum an cousin Daris
not far fram di quarry
doun a August Town.

(1984)

Mikey Smith

Black and White

went to an all black school
with an all black name
all black principal
black teacher

graduated
with an all black concept

with our blackety blackety frustration
we did an all black march
with high black hopes
and an all black song

got a few solutions
not all black

went to a show
and saw our struggles
in black and white

Lawwwwwd have mercy.

(1986)

James Berry

Lucy's Letter

Things harness me here. I long
for we labrish' bad. Doors
not fixed open here.
No Leela either. No Cousin
Lil, Miss Lottie or Bro'-Uncle.
Dayclean doesn' have cockcrowin'.
Midmornin' doesn' bring
Cousin-Maa with her naseberry tray.
Afternoon doesn' give a ragged
Manwell, strung with fish
like bright leaves. Seven days
play same note in London, chile.
But Leela, money rustle regular.

Me dear, I don' laugh now,
no't'like we thunder claps
in darkness on verandah.
I turned battery hen
in 'lectric light, day an' night.
No mood can touch one
mango season back at Yard.
At least though I did start
evening school once.
An' doctors free, chile.

London isn' like we
village dirt road, you know
Leela: it a parish
of a pasture-lan' what
grown crisscross streets,
an' they lie down to my door.
But I lock myself in.
I carry keys everywhere.
Life here's no open summer,
girl. But Sat'day mornin' don'
find me han' dry, don' find me face

a heavy cloud over the man.
An though he still have
a weekend mind for bat'n'ball
he wash a dirty dish now, me dear.
It sweet him I on the Pill.
We get money for holidays
but there's no sun-hot
to enjoy the cool breeze.

Leela, I really a sponge
you know, for traffic noise,
for work noise, for halfway
intentions, for halfway smiles,
for clockwatchin' an' col' weather.
I hope you don' think I gone
too fat when we meet.
I booked up to come an' soak
the children in daylight.

(1982)

NOTE

1 Labrish: to gossip without restraint

From Lucy: Holiday Reflections

I'm here an' not here. Me head's
too full of mornin' sun
an' sea soun' an' voices
echoin' words this long long
time I never have.

Seeing home again, Leela chile,
I bring back a mind to Englan'
tha's not enough to share. For how
I eat a mango under a tree,
a soursop ripened for me,
a pawpaw kept, brings back
the whole taste of sunshine
an' how our own love ripen.

[381]

O I glad to see hard times
ease off some faces a little.
I glad to see the stream still
goin' in the gully, though
where it gives up to sea
is a different face now.

Big fig tree gone as ghost.
whole breed of nana midwives
gone. Givin'-for-not'n' gone
mixed with cash. I had to ask
a-where walled bank of fire an'
wood ashes gone from kitchen
for paraffin smell? Then I see
me head lost the account
of everything and everybody.

I meet a young face I get
the pain we don't know each other.
An' I see cousin John fine-shin boy
stretch up to sixfoot man. I see
Puppa is bones in the groun',
Mumma can't see to climb mount'n
lan'. An smellin' of pee, Aunty
Meg's in bed all through sunhot.
Then old Granny Lyn an' kids have
no regular man voice about.

Leela, sweetheart, I glad glad
I came home. I glad you still
have wasp waist an', funny,
that you' hair still short.
You see how food fill me out:
I promise to slim.

I glad you don't grow bitter.
I glad how the sun still ripen
evenin', so strong in colour.
An' there, where I did go
to school with one piece of book,
I came, I walked in darkness,

an' it was a soothin' blot.

Too many sea waves passed between
us, chile. Let us remind the other,
'Length of time gets length of rope buried'.

(1982)

Caribbean Proverb Poem 1

Dog mornin prayer is, Laard
wha teday, a bone or a blow?

Tiger wahn fi nyam[1] pickney[2], tiger sey
he could-a swear e woz puss.

If yu cahn mek plenty yeyewater[3]
fi funeral, start a-bawl early mornin.

(1984)

Caribbean Proverb Poem 2

1

Hungry belly an Fullbelly
dohn walk same pass.

Fullbelly always a-tell Emptybelly
'Keep heart'.

2

Yu fraid fi yeye
yu cahn nyam cowhead.

Yeye meet yeye
an man fraid!

3

Yu si yu neighbour beard
ketch fire, yu tek water
an wet fi yu.

When lonely man dead
grass come grow a him door.

[383]

4

Satan may be ol
but Satan not bedridden.

Man who is all honey,
fly dem goin nyam him up.

(1984)

NOTES

1 nyam: eat
2 pickney: child or children
3 yeye: eye

Jane King

Intercity Dub, for Jean

(for Jean Binta Breeze)

Brixton groans –
From the horror of the hard weight
Of history
Where the whites flagellate
In their ancestry
And the blacks hold the stone
And they press it to their hearts
And London is a hell
In many many parts.
But your voice rings true
From the edge of hell
Cause the music is the love
And you sing it so well.

And I travel through the country
On the inter-city train
And the weather may be bad
But the sperm of the rain
Wriggles hope, scribbles hope
Cross the windows of the train
And the autumn countryside
Has a green life still
And the rain-sperm says
It will come again, it will
It will come, it will come,
It will come again
New rich life from the bitter
And dark and driving rain –
And you run like water
Over Brixton soil
Writing hope on the windows
Bringing light through the walls
Like the water you connect

[385]

With the light above
Like the water writing making
The green life swell
Cause the music is the love
And you sing it so well.

Now I cannot give to you
What you gave to me
But one small part
Of your bravery
Makes me stand up to say
That I want to make them see
That you showed me the way
That the way is me
Like the way is you
And the way is we.
And the love is in the water
In the wells pooled below
And the love is in the light
And the cold cold snow
And the rain lances down
From the light to the well
And it points to heaven
And it points to hell
And the love is real
Make the music swell
Cause the music is the love
And you sing it so well.

There's a factory blowing smoke-rings
Cross the railway line
You know it took me time to learn
That this country wasn't mine
And I want to go back home
To swim in the sunset bay
Feel the water and the light
Soft-linking night and day
Like the music makes a bridge –
But there's joy here too
And I might not have seen it

If I hadn't heard you.
And I hope now I'll be writing
This poem all my life
For the black city world
Where the word is a knife
That cuts through the love
And divides up the life.
For you saved me from a trap
Just before I fell
Cause the music is the love
And you sing it so well.

The Brixton-battered sisters
Hissed their bitterness and hate
With their black man the oppressor
And death the white race fate
And they don't want to build
No bridge no gate –
And I nearly turned away
In pain and rage and fear
Till I heard your voice
Ringing clarion-clear
And you burst like a flower
From the sad sad soil
And you blew like a breeze
Round the shut-tight hall
And you danced like a leaf
And you sang like a bell –
You said Music reaches heaven
And music changes hell
Cause the music is the love
And you sing it so well.

(1988)

Grace Nichols

One Continent/To Another

Child of the middle passage womb
push
daughter of a vengeful Chi
she came
    into the new world
birth aching her pain
from one continent/to another

moaning

her belly cry sounding the wind

and after fifty years
she hasn't forgotten
hasn't forgotten
how she had lain there
in her own blood
lain there in her own shit

bleeding memories in the darkness

how she stumbled onto the shore
how the metals dragged her down
how she thirsted . . .

But being born a woman
she moved again
knew it was the Black Beginning
though everything said it was
the end

And she went forth with others of her kind
to scythe the earth knowing that bondage
would not fall like poultice from the
children's forehead

But O she grieved for them
walking beadless
in another land

From the darkness within her
from the dimness of previous
incarnations
    the Congo surfaced
so did Sierra Leone and the
Gold Coast which she used to tread
searching the horizons for lost
moons
her jigida guarding the crevice
the soft wet forest
    between her thighs

Like the yesterday of creation morning
she had imagined this new world to be –
bereft of fecundity

No she wasn't prepared
for the sea that lashed
fire that seared
solid earth that delivered
her up
birds that flew
not wanting to see the utter
rawness of life everywhere

and the men who seed the children
she wasn't prepared for that look
in their eye

that loss of deep man pride

Now she stoops
in green canefields
piecing the life she would lead

                (1983)

Your Blessing

Aie
the very first
time she knew
she was carrying
she wanted to
cry out

her throat
was a fist
of fear

she wanted
to crush
the weaving
blood mystery

to retch
herself
empty

days passed
she resigned
herself to
silence

eye water
trickling
down
her
face

Cover me with the leaves of your
blackness Mother

shed tears

for I'm tainted with guilt and
exile

I'm burden with child and maim

Heal me with the power of your
blackness Mother

shed tears

for I'm severed by ocean and
longing

I'm mocked I'm torn I fear

Cover me
Heal me
Shield me

With the power of your blessings

Uplift me
Instruct me
Reclothe me

With the power of your blessings

Mother I need I crave your blessing
Mother I need I crave your blessing

Mother I hear your voice
I hear it far away
breaking the wildness of my
thoughts
calming me to childhood presence
once again

As we have known Victory
As we have known Death
As we have known –
neither to rely on happiness
nor sorrow for our existence

So rise you up my daughter

Mother I need I crave your blessing
Mother I need I crave your blessing

Like the bamboo cane that groans
and creeks in the wind . . .
but doesn't break

Like the drumskin that is beaten
on the outside . . .

but keeps its bottom whole

So be you my daughter

Cast your guilt to the wind
Cast your trials to the lake
Clasp your child to your bosom
Give your exile to the snake

Mother I need I crave your blessing
Mother I need I crave your blessing

By the drumming of rain
and the running of stream
by the beating of sun
and the flash of steel
by the ripple of flesh
and despairing of dream

Heal, my daughter, heal

By the hot sun's eye
and the green cane stalk
by the root of blade
and the sweat of mind

Heal

Cast your guilt to the wind
Cast your trials to the lake
Clasp your child to your bosom
Give your exile to the snake

Mother I need I have your blessing
Mother I need I have your blessing

(1983)

Lorna Goodison

On Houses

I have built many houses
made warm smells in as many kitchens
created content within
according to the colour of the season.

The first were by definition rooms,
with corners I squared into other rooms
encouraged by this success
the time for the season approached me.

You later led me to believe
I led you to the house
of seasonal white
down the garden deep with dreams.

But, the kitchen grew electric
spun me away from it.
When you were not looking
flung me against the dowry chest,
I went upstairs to rest.

To lie in the bedroom adrift
with white curtains blowing you
goodbye as you went to sea
in a boat lined with careful money.
yet that house was not the last,
you commissioned one of newest glass
I tinkled,
and tried to creat[e] calm smells
in that transparent kitchen.
You fenced it in when I was not looking
I finger chains and make clinking noises
in key.
And watch the garden grow reproaches.

I'm inclined to think I'll build no more houses.

(1980)

My Late Friend

My friend is on the surface, black.
Africa's eyes and lips.
My friend is softest midnight black
and no Rap-Brown-Rhetoric, beautiful.

She's fled the tropics
because the sun darkens her
my friend wants to be one with the snow.

She's disciplined her hair till it lies
in exhausted submission

And each night from her sheets of white,
she thanks a WASP God for bleaching cream.
She has a white lover
'they treat you better'

each day my friend grows whiter.

When I admire lean evil princes
with crowns of Afro

she smiles at me in pity
and tells me how good it is to go skiing
and of the pearls her lover gave her.

She never wears colours like ghettogreen

or Colouredpeoplepurple.

I lost my friend somewhere between
strange Continents
my love for the sun
and the eternal peace
I can find only on islands.

(1980)

Guyana Lovesong

I, torn from the centre of
some ladies novel
drift a page across strange
landscape

resting on openfaced lily pads
melting in slow rain canals
Sliding by sentinel grass in
a savanna
I crossed the mighty Rupununi
River,
returned limp on the bow of
a ferry.
Timheri
The way to calm in your eyes.
the river without guile in your
eyes.

Wash over the edges of your woman's
sorrow

Time is one continent till tomorrow.

(1980)

For My Mother
(May I Inherit Half Her Strength)

My mother loved my father
I write this as an absolute
in this my thirtieth year
the year to discard absolutes

he appeared, her fate disguised,
as a Sunday player in a cricket match,
he had ridden from a country
one hundred miles south of hers.

She tells me he dressed the part,
visiting dandy, maroon blazer
cream serge pants, seam like razor,
and the beret and the two-tone shoes.

[395]

My father stopped to speak to her sister,
till he looked and saw her by the oleander,
sure in the kingdom of my blue-eyed grandmother.
He never played the cricket match that day.

He wooed her with words and he won her.
He had nothing but words to woo her,
On a visit to distant Kingston he wrote,

'I stood on the corner of King Street and looked,
and not one woman in that town was lovely as you'.

My mother was a child of the petite bourgeoisie
studying to be a teacher, she oiled her hands to hold pens.
My father barely knew his father, his mother died young,
he was a boy who grew with his granny.

My mother's trousseau came by steamer through the snows of
     Montreal
where her sisters Albertha of the cheekbones and the
perennial Rose, combed Jewlit backstreets with French-
turned names for Doris' wedding things.

Such a wedding Harvey River, Hanover, had never seen
Who anywhere had seen a veil fifteen chantilly yards long?
and a crepe de chine dress with inlets of silk godettes
and a neck-line clasped with jewelled pins!

And on her wedding day she wept. For it was a brazen bride
     in those days
who smiled.
and her bouquet looked for the world like a sheaf of wheat
against the unknown of her belly,
a sheaf of wheat backed by maidenhair fern, representing
     Harvey River
her face washed by something other than river water.

My father made one assertive move, he took the imported
     cherub down
from the heights of the cake and dropped it in the soft
     territory
between her breasts . . . and she cried.

When I came to know my mother many years later, I knew
   her as the figure
who sat at the first thing I learned to read : 'SINGER', and
   she breast-fed
my brother while she sewed; and she taught us to read while
   she sewed and
she sat in judgement over all our disputes as she sewed.

She could work miracles, she would make a garment from a
   square of cloth
in a span that defied time. Or feed twenty people on a stew
   made from
fallen-from-the-head cabbage leaves and a carrot and a
   cho-cho and a palmful of meat.

And she rose early and sent us clean into the world and she
   went to bed in
the dark, for my father came in always last.

There is a place somewhere where my mother never took the
   younger ones
a country where my father with the always smile
my father whom all women loved, who had the perpetual
   quality of wonder
given only to a child ... hurt his bride.

Even at his death there was this 'Friend' who stood by her
   side,
but my mother is adamant that that has no place in the
   memory of my father.

When he died, she sewed dark dresses for the women
   amongst us
and she summoned that walk, straight-backed, that she gave
   to us
and buried him dry-eyed.

Just that morning, weeks after
she stood delivering bananas from their skin
singing in that flat hill country voice

she fell down a note to the realization that she did

not have to be brave, just this once
and she cried.

For her hands grown coarse with raising nine children
for her body for twenty years permanently fat
for the time she pawned her machine for my sister's
Senior Cambridge fees
and for the pain she bore with the eyes of a queen

and she cried also because she loved him.

(1986)

I Am Becoming My Mother

Yellow/brown woman
fingers smelling always of onions

My mother raises rare blooms
and waters them with tea
her birth waters sang like rivers
my mother is now me

My mother had a linen dress
the colour of the sky
and stored lace and damask
tablecloths
to pull shame out of her eye.

I am becoming my mother
brown/yellow woman
fingers smelling always of onions.

(1986)

Jamaica Kincaid

'Columbus in Chains' from Annie John

Outside, as usual, the sun shone, the trade winds blew; on her way to put some starched clothes on the line, my mother shooed some hens out of her garden; Miss Dewberry baked the buns, some of which my mother would buy for my father and me to eat with our afternoon tea; Miss Henry brought the milk, a glass of which I would drink with my lunch, and another glass of which I would drink with the bun from Miss Dewberry; my mother prepared our lunch; my father noted some perfectly idiotic thing his partner in housebuilding, Mr Oatie, had done, so that over lunch he and my mother could have a good laugh.

The Anglican church bell struck eleven o'clock – one hour to go before lunch. I was then sitting at my desk in my classroom. We were having a history lesson – the last lesson of the morning. For taking first place over all the other girls, I had been given a prize, a copy of a book called *Roman Britain*, and I was made prefect of my class. What a mistake the prefect part had been, for I was among the worst-behaved in my class and did not at all believe in setting myself up as a good example, the way a prefect was supposed to do. Now I had to sit in the prefect's seat – the first seat in the front row, the seat from which I could stand up and survey quite easily my classmates. From where I sat I could see out the window. Sometimes when I looked out, I could see the sexton going over to the minister's house. The sexton's daughter, Hilarene, a disgusting model of good behavior and keen attention to scholarship, sat next to me, since she took second place. The minister's daughter, Ruth, sat in the last row, the row reserved for all the dunce girls. Hilarene, of course, I could not stand. A girl that good would never do for me. I would probably not have cared so much for first place if I could be sure it would not go to her. Ruth I liked, because she was such a dunce and came from England and had yellow hair. When I first met her, I used to walk her home and sing bad songs to her just to see her turn pink, as if I spilled hot water all over her.

Our books, *A History of the West Indies*, were open in front of us. Our day had begun with morning prayers, then a geometry lesson, then it was over to the science building for a lesson in 'Introductory

Physics' (not a subject we cared much for), taught by the most dingy-toothed Mr Slacks, a teacher from Canada, then precious recess, and now this, our history lesson. Recess had the usual drama: this time, I coaxed Gwen out of her disappointment at not being allowed to join the junior choir. Her father – how many times had I wished he would become a leper and so be banished to a leper colony for the rest of my long and happy life with Gwen – had forbidden it, giving as his reason that she lived too far away from church, where choir rehearsals were conducted, and that it would be dangerous for her, a young girl, to walk home alone at night in the dark. Of course, all the streets had lamplight, but it was useless to point that out to him. Oh, it would have pleased us to press and rub our knees together as we sat in our pew while pretending to pay close attention to Mr Simmons, our choirmaster, as he waved his baton up and down and across, and how it would have pleased us even more to walk home together, alone in the 'early dusk' (the way Gwen had phrased it, a ready phrase always on her tongue), stopping, if there was a full moon, to lie down in a pasture and expose our bosoms in the moon-light. We had heard that full moonlight would make our breasts grow to a size we would like. Poor Gwen! When I first heard from her that she was one of ten children, right on the spot I told her that I would love only her, since her mother already had so many other people to love.

Our teacher, Miss Edward, paced up and down in front of the class in her usual way. In front of her desk stood a small table, and on it stood the dunce cap. The dunce cap was in the shape of a coronet, with an adjustable opening in the back, so that it could fit any head. It was made of cardboard with a shiny gold paper covering and the word 'DUNCE' in shiny red paper on the front. When the sun shone on it, the dunce cap was all aglitter, almost as if you were being tricked into thinking it was a desirable thing to wear. As Miss Edward paced up and down, she would pass between us and the dunce cap like an eclipse. Each Friday morning, we were given a small test to see how well we had learned the things taught to us all week. The girl who scored lowest was made to wear the dunce cap all day the following Monday. On many Mondays, Ruth wore it – only, with her short yellow hair, when the dunce cap was sitting on her head she looked like a girl attending a birthday party in *The Schoolgirl's Own Annual*.

It was Miss Edward's way to ask one of us a question the answer to which she was sure the girl would not know and then put the same question to another girl who she was sure would know the answer. The girl who did not answer correctly would then have to repeat the correct answer in the exact words of the other girl. Many times, I had heard my exact words repeated over and over again, and I liked it especially when the girl doing the repeating was one I didn't care about very much. Pointing a finger at Ruth, Miss Edward asked a question the answer to which was 'On the third of November 1493, a Sunday morning, Christopher Columbus discovered Dominica.' Ruth, of course, did not know the answer, as she did not know the answer to many questions about the West Indies. I could hardly blame her. Ruth had come all the way from England. Perhaps she did not want to be in the West Indies at all. Perhaps she wanted to be in England, where no one would remind her constantly of the terrible things her ancestors had done; perhaps she had felt even worse when her father was a missionary in Africa. I could see how Ruth felt from looking at her face. Her ancestors had been the masters, while ours had been the slaves. She had such a lot to be ashamed of, and by being with us every day she was always being reminded. We could look everybody in the eye, for our ancestors had done nothing wrong except just sit somewhere, defenceless. Of course, sometimes, what with our teachers and our books, it was hard for us to tell on which side we really now belonged – with the masters or the slaves – for it was all history, it was all in the past, and everybody behaved differently now; all of us celebrated Queen Victoria's birthday, even though she had been dead a long time. But we, the descendants of the slaves, knew quite well what had really happened, and I was sure that if the tables had been turned we would have acted differently; I was sure that if our ancestors had gone from Africa to Europe and come upon the people living there, they would have taken a proper interest in the Europeans on first seeing them, and said, 'How nice,' and then gone home to tell their friends about it.

I was sitting at my desk, having these thoughts to myself. I don't know how long it had been since I lost track of what was going on around me. I had not noticed that the girl who was asked the question after Ruth failed – a girl named Hyacinth – had only got a part of the answer correct. I had not noticed that after these two attempts Miss Edward had launched into a harangue about what a worthless bunch we were compared to girls of the past. In fact, I was no longer on the same chapter we were studying. I was way ahead, at the end of the chapter about Columbus's third voyage. In this chapter, there was a picture of Columbus that took up a whole page, and it was in color – one of only five color pictures in the book. In this picture, Columbus was seated in the bottom of a ship. He was wearing the usual three-quarter trousers and a shirt with enormous sleeves, both the trousers and shirt made of maroon-colored velvet. His hat, which was cocked up on one side of his head, had a gold feather in it, and his black shoes had huge gold buckles. His hands and feet were bound up in chains, and he was sitting there staring off into space, looking quite dejected and miserable. The picture had as a title 'Columbus in Chains,' printed at the bottom of the page. What had happened was that the usually quarrelsome Columbus had got into a disagreement with people who were even more quarrelsome, and a man named Bobadilla, representing King Ferdinand and Queen Isabella, had sent him back to Spain fettered in chains attached to the bottom of a ship. What just deserts, I thought, for I did not like Columbus. How I loved this picture – to see the usually triumphant Columbus, brought so low, seated at the bottom of a boat just watching things go by. Shortly after I first discovered it in my history book, I heard my mother read out loud to my father a letter she had received from her sister, who still lived with her mother and father in the very same Dominica, which is where my mother came from. Ma Chess was fine, wrote my aunt, but Pa Chess was not well. Pa Chess was having a bit of trouble with his limbs; he was not able to go about as he pleased; often he had to depend on someone else to do one thing or another for him. My mother read the letter in quite a state, her voice rising to a higher pitch with each sentence. After she read the part about Pa Chess's stiff limbs, she turned to my father and laughed as she said, 'So the great man can no longer just get up and go. How I would love to see his face now!' When I next saw the picture of Columbus sitting there all locked up in his chains, I wrote under it the words 'The Great Man Can No Longer Just Get Up and Go.' I had written this out with my fountain pen, and in Old English lettering – a script I had recently mastered. As I sat there looking at the picture, I traced the words with my pen over and over, so that the letters grew big and you could read what I had written from not very far away. I don't know how long it was before I heard that my name, Annie John, was being said by this bellowing dragon in the form of Miss Edward bearing down on me.

I had never been a favorite of hers. Her favorite was Hilarene. It must have pained Miss Edward that I so often beat out Hilarene. Not that I liked Miss Edward and wanted her to like me back, but all my other teachers regarded me with much affection, would always tell my mother that I was the most charming student that they ever had, beamed at me when they saw me coming, and were very sorry when they had to write some version of this on my report card: 'Annie is an unusually bright girl. She is well behaved in class, at least in the presence of her masters and mistresses, but behind their backs and outside the classroom quite the opposite is true.' When my mother read this or something like it, she would burst into tears. She had hoped to display with a great flourish, my report card to her friends, along with whatever prize I had won. Instead, the report card would have to take a place at the bottom of the old trunk in which she kept any important thing that had to do with me. I became not a favorite of Miss Edward's in the following way: Each Friday afternoon, the girls in the lower forms were given, instead of a last period, an extra-long recess. We were to use this in ladylike recreation – walks, chats about the novels and poems we were reading, showing each other the new embroidery stitches we had learned to master in home class, or something just as seemly. Instead, some of the girls would play a game of cricket or rounders or stones, but most of us would go to the far end of the school grounds and play band. In this game, of which teachers and parents disapproved and which was sometimes absolutely forbidden, we would place our arms around each other's waists or shoulders, forming lines of ten or so girls, and then we would dance from one end of the school grounds to the other. As we danced, we would sometimes chant these words: 'Tee la la la, come go. Tee la la la, come go'. At other times we would sing a popular calypso song which usually had lots of unlady-like words to it. Up and down the schoolyard, away from our teachers, we would dance and sing. At the end of the recess – forty-five minutes – we were missing ribbons and other ornaments from our hair, the pleats of our linen tunics became unset, the collars of our blouses were pulled out, and we were soaking wet all the way down to our bloomers. When the school bell rang, we would make a whooping sound, as if in a great panic, and then we would throw ourselves on top of each other as we laughed and shrieked. We would then run back to our classes, where we prepared to file into the auditorium for evening prayers. After that, it was home for the weekend. But how could we go straight home after all that excitement? No sooner were we on the street than we would form little groups, depending on the direction we were headed in. I was never keen on joining them on the way home, because I was sure I would run into my mother. Instead, my friends and I would go to our usual place near the back of the churchyard and sit on the tombstones of people who had been buried there way before slavery was abolished, in 1833. We would sit and sing bad songs, use forbidden words, and, of course, show each other various parts of our bodies. While some of us watched, the others would walk up and down on the large tomb-stones showing off their legs. It was immediately a popular idea; everybody soon wanted to do it. It wasn't long before many girls – the ones whose mothers didn't pay strict attention to what they were doing – started to come to school on Fridays wearing not bloomers under their uniforms but underpants trimmed with lace and satin frills. It wasn't long before an end came to all that. One Friday after-noon, Miss Edward, on her way home from school, took a shortcut through the churchyard. She must have heard the commotion we were making because there she suddenly was, saying, 'What is the meaning of this?' – just the very thing someone like her would say if she came unexpectedly on something like us. It was obvious that I was the ringleader. Oh, how I wished the ground would open up and take her in, but it did not. We all, shamefacedly, slunk home, I with Miss Edward at my side. Tears came to my mother's eyes when she heard what I had done. It was apparently such a bad thing that my mother couldn't bring herself to repeat my misdeed to my father in my presence. I got the usual punishment of dinner alone, outside under the breadfruit tree, but added on to that, I was not allowed to go to the library on Saturday, and on Sunday, after Sunday school and dinner, I was not allowed to take a stroll in the botanical gardens, where Gwen was waiting for me in the bamboo grove.

That happened when I was in the first form. Now here Miss Edward stood. Her whole face was on fire. Her eyes were bulging out of her head. I was sure that at any minute they would land at my feet and roll away. The small pimples on her face, already looking as if they were constantly irritated, now ballooned into huge, on-the-verge-of-exploding boils. Her head shook from side to side. Her strange bottom, which she carried high in the air, seemed to rise up so high that it almost touched the ceiling. Why did I not pay attention, she said. My impertinence was beyond endurance. She then found a hundred words for the different forms my impertinence took. On she went. I was just getting used to this amazing bellowing when suddenly she was speechless. In fact, everything stopped. Her eyes stopped, her bottom stopped, her pimples stopped. Yes, she had got close enough so that her eyes caught a glimpse of what I had done to my textbook. The glimpse soon led to closer inspection. It was bad enough that I had defaced my schoolbook by writing in it. That I should write under the picture of Columbus 'The Great Man ...' etc. was just too much. I had gone too far this time, defaming one of the great men in history, Christopher Columbus, discoverer of the island that was my home. And now look at me. I was not even hanging my head in remorse. Had my peers ever seen anyone so arrogant, so blasphemous?

I was sent to the headmistress, Miss Moore. As punishment, I was removed from my position as prefect, and my place was taken by the odious Hilarene. As an added punishment, I was ordered to copy Books I and II of *Paradise Lost*, by John Milton, and to have it done a week from that day. I then couldn't wait to get home to lunch and the comfort of my mother's kisses and arms. I had nothing to worry about there yet; it would be a while before my mother and father heard of my bad deeds. What a terrible morning! Seeing my mother would be such a tonic – something to pick me up.

When I got home, my mother kissed me absent-mindedly. My father had got home ahead of me, and they were already deep in conversation, my father regaling her with some unusually outlandish thing the oaf Mr Oatie had done. I washed my hands and took my place at table. My mother brought me my lunch. I took one smell of it, and I could tell that it was the much hated breadfruit. My mother said not at all, it was a new kind of rice imported from Belgium, not breadfruit, mashed and forced through a ricer, as I thought. She went back to talking to my father. My father could hardly get a few words out of his mouth before she was a jellyfish of laughter. I sat there, putting my food in my mouth. I could not believe that she couldn't see how miserable I was and so reach out

[405]

a hand to comfort me and caress my cheek, the way she usually did when she sensed that something was amiss with me. I could not believe how she laughed at everything he said, and how bitter it made me feel to see how much she liked him. I ate my meal. The more I ate of it, the more I was sure it was breadfruit. When I finished, my mother got up to remove my plate. As she started out the door, I said, 'Tell me, really, the name of thing I just ate.'

My mother said, 'You just ate some breadfruit. I made it look like rice so that you would eat it. It's very good for you, filled with lots of vitamins.' As she said this, she laughed. She was standing half inside the door, half outside. Her body was in the shade of the house, but her head was in the sun. When she laughed, her mouth opened to show off big shiny, sharp white teeth. It was as if my mother had suddenly turned into a crocodile.

(1985)

Harry Narain

A Letter to the Prime Minister

Essequibo Coast,
Guyana.
October, 1978.

Dear Comrade Prime Minister,

This letter I writ[t]ing you is not really to ask fo' anything. Is just to tell you what's going on, and I left it to the kindness of you heart to mek we small man something lil mo'better than dey-bad. I don't want it sound like a complaint either, but I got few things on me mind because I see the situation going bad to wo'ss in the rice industry.

You always say when we see things go bad complain. Mek report. Down here who I gon complain to, the police? They gon sey they not concern with the rice industry; go talk to Mr Burnett, the big boss man at the local rice board. Mr Burnett office lock up whole day, you don't know whether he in or he out. And with the crowd that brace that office you might give Mr Burnett all right to protect heself. Any time he pull the bolt it might be like if hydro dam you tell we' bout break. Complain to the radio? Cde. P.M., how you go about that? My radio does only talk, it don't listen. The Chronicle? The only person I know connected with the newspaper down here is the lil boy who does bring it round. And the way he behaving he already got one foot in Berbice, if you know what I mean.

Cde. P.M., you don't know me, but I know you. I see you picture on all me chil'ren exercise books. And like the saying sey, is not who I know that's important, but who know me. So I dey bad a'ready. Anyway, me parents and me, all awe navel string bury here in this Guyanese soil. And since I know meself we all been wo'king the land. We the true offspring of the soil. I's a rice farmer and I live pon the Essequibo Coast. I do some wrong things in recent times, and the fust one is cultivate fifteen acres of rice. Really, fo' poor man like I plant too much. But Comrade, a man must wo'k, and a man must wo'k hard if he don't want he wife to go pon the street or he chil'ren to beg. And that's the big problem fo' me in the rice industry. I wo'k too hard. I support the gov'ment policy. I wo'k hard to keep me and me family belly full. I plant the 'N'. That's the next mistake I mek.

Cde. P.M., you might'n know the 'N', because whenever you chance visit me down here you does always come by aeroplane, and from up there I guess all the rice does look alike. And then you drive in them fast fast ministry vehicle that does only bruk up the road. You say two word fo' let we feel we in utopia, and you talk to them big wheels who can't feel how we the cogs straining to keep them, turning. They spread red loam over the trenches in the road. You land-rover bounce pon it and you don't even suspect that is just dey all them lorry does bust down and cut they axle and spill they paddy, we living in the hole. They say everything a'right, and you gone. But ask Mr Burnett. If he don't want fabricate he gon tell you. is the 'N' creating all the distress in the rice industry, the 'N' block up the place. The mill can't tek it off.

Cde. P.M., you might'n know the 'N'. It is as hybrid variety the rice board encouraging farmers to grown. It a'right, but it got several faults. One of them is that it bear too mucho. It bear so well that of things don't improve it on mek all we dey-bad farmers beggars . . .

Poor men you gon dead bad. You gon got to watch you wife go slave fo' rich man and you chil'ren go beg naked. And you gon got to put rope pon you neck or drink momoncrotophos because it gon be too much to bear. You and you mattie ain't got unity to come together to hire a tractor to fetch in al'you paddy. All ayou in the same rat race. Every one o' you want you paddy go in fust. So the rich man get the trailer because he got he own tractor. Though he paddy only cut last night. Last night paddy is fo' he holiday over-seas. You one is still you living and it done two weeks in the bag. Another week or two if it don't spread out and get some sun it gon tu'n powder.

So now I go to the private miel. I can't do better, I done gone low a'ready. The proprietor relaxing in he office watching them young girls sweeping paddy pon the drying floor. Now and then the breeze blow up they skirt and the view is good. He ain't seeing me come, but he expecting me. Since last week me son turn out to wo'k on the concrete he been looking out fo' me. He knows things really bad at home and this the opportunity he waiting fo'. I pass me lil boy raking paddy and he shout, 'Daddy!' I hear, but I shame to watch he, because I wilfully keep he back from school; and the sun like fire over he old hat, and the concrete like a tawa under he foot. And I mo' shame because he only thirteen and he wo'king like thirty and must accept a small boy pay.

The proprietor grin and touch me a little with, 'How long this paddy cut?' And then he touch me a little mo', 'You wind out the paddy?' I stagger under them touches. Then he start to talk fat; how he barn full, and he don't really want 'N', how the gov'ment ain't giving he a fair price with the 'N' rice, how he can't afford to buy bad paddy. Now he jam me with the bag weight and nearly throw me down. And again he come. This time with the price, and he knock me cold. I feel me legs move out from under me. I want to cry but me lil boy can see me through the door. So I turn and beg this proprietor to tek the paddy off me hand.

He walk round the compound. He drive round the estate. He spend one hour eating he lunch. He rest from the sun, and then later in the afternoon he notice me again. He say a'right, he gon send he lorry. But before I left the office he touch me up little with the lorry freight.

Proprietor, you still one saviour of me. So now I go home an bust the news. Everybody glad because Christmas coming. They smile tek over they whole face. But me daughter, I go can't buy them ear-rings till after next crop, hear Bettie? And son, the track boots I promise yu . . . I understand you run better in the athletic sports barefoot. Wife, you gon got to find wo'k if you really want new blinds fo' Christmas. You all don't ask me, 'Why Daddy?' I tell you a' ready things dear in the shop and then the gov'ment ban them fancy things. You think I don't know you all wo'k hard in the rice fields. true, I did say when we cut rice. Alright, definite next crop when we cut rice.

Cde. P.M., I sorry I give the picture so raw, and I hope you understand. Do, try help out.

Yours Respectfully,
Rice Farmer.

(1981)

David Dabydeen

On Not Being Milton: Nigger Talk in England Today

One of the many ways in which young British blacks have resisted white domination is in the creation of a patois evolved from the West Indian creole of their parents. The poetry that has emerged from the black communities is expressed in the language of this patois, and one of its greatest exponents is Linton Kwesi Johnson:

> Shock-black bubble-doun-beat bouncing
> rock-wise tumble-doun soun music:
> foot – drop find drum blood story;
>
> bass history is a moving
> is a hurting black story.
> ('Reggae Sounds')

Johnson's poetry is recited to music from a reggae band. The paraphernalia of sound-systems, amplifiers, speakers, microphones, electric guitars and the rest which dominate the stage and accompanies what one critic has dismissed as 'jungle-talk', is a deliberate 'misuse' of white technology. 'Sound-systems', essential to 'dub-poetry', are often home-made contraptions, cannibalized parts of diverse machines reordered for black expression. This de/reconstruction is in itself an assertive statement, a denial of the charge of black incapacity to understand technology. The mass-produced technology is re-made for self-use in the way that patois is a 'private' reordering of 'standard' English. The deliberate exploitation of high-tech to serve black 'jungle-talk' is a reversal of colonial history. Caliban is tearing up the pages of Prospero's magic books and repasting it in his own order, by his own method and for his own purpose.

A feature of Black British poetry is a sheer delight in the rhythm and sound of language that survives technology, and this joyousness is revealed in poems like Mikey Smith's 'R-ooTs' (the line 'lawwwwwwd', as Edward Brathwaite says, sounding like the exhaust roar of a motorcycle), or in the writings of Jimi Rand. There is a deliberate celebration of the 'primitive' consciousness of sound in:

> Me was fas asleep in me bed
> wen a nok come pun me door,

[410]

bright and early, fore day morning
before dawn bruk.
Nock nock – nock nock,
badoombadoom nock nock
badoombadoom nock nock
badoombadoom nock badoom nock.
Who dat; a who dat nock?

('Nock – Nock')

This deliberate wearing of the 'primitive' label is even more explicit in his 'Nigger Talk' poem:

Funky talk
Nitty gritty grass – root talk
Dat's wha I da talk
Cause de talk is togedder talk,
Like right on, out-a-sight, kind-a-too-much.
Ya hip to it yet?
Ya dig de funky way to talk
Talk talk?
Dis na white talk;
Na white talk dis.
it is coon, nignog samba wog talk.

The use of language is inextricably bound up with a sense of being black. Hence John Agard's poem 'Listen Mr Oxford Don' is conscious of the way creole suffers from the charge of being surly and indecent ('Muggin de Queen's English') and Agard links this literary indictment to attitudes in the wider society where blacks are accused of a host of criminal activities:

Dem accuse me of assault
on de Oxford dictionary /
imagine a concise peaceful man like me /
dem want me serve time for inciting rhyme to riot
so mek dem send one big word after me
i ent serving no jail sentence
I slashing suffix in self-defence
i bashing future wit present tense
and if necessary

I making de Queen's English accessory/to my offence

Johnson, Agard and others are reacting against the 'rational structure and comprehensible language' which Robert Conquest saw as a distinguishing feature of the Movement poets and which still afflicts contemporary English verse. The charge that Alvarez levelled against the Movement – the disease of gentility – is still relevant today. Andrew Motion for instance can visit Anne Frank's room and on emerging can conclude that all Anne Frank wanted was to

> leave as simply
> as I do, and walk at ease
> up dusty tree-lined avenues, or watch
> a silent barge come clear of bridge
> settling their reflections in the blue canal

There is glibness and gentility disguised as understatement but really amounting to a kind of obscenity. As Michael Hulse has commented, 'to go as a tourist to a house which, like many similar houses in Amsterdam, focused human hope and suffering, and then to parade the delicacy of one's response, savours somewhat of an opportunism that is slightly obscene'. The quiet understatement of Motion's response to human tragedy is as obscene as Conrad's heated, insistent rhetoric ('It was the stillness of an implacable force brooding over an inscrutable intention', etc.): both belong to a tradition of colonizing the experience of others for the gratification of their own literary sensibilities.

The pressure of the same racism that destroyed Anne Frank, and encounter with the thuggery that lurks beneath the polite surface of English life and letters, force black writers into poetry that is disturbing and passionate. The play of the light of memory upon pine furniture, touching vignettes of domestic life, elegiac recollections of dead relatives, wonderment at the zig-zag fall of an autumnal leaf, none of these typical English poetic concerns are of special relevance to them. They participate in a West Indian literary tradition which seeks to subvert English canons by the use of lived nigger themes in lived nigger language. Their strategies of 'rants, rudeness and rhymes' look back half a century to the West Indian struggle to establish 'black' expression. In March 1931, a new Trinidadian journal, *The Beacon*, attempted to instigate a movement for 'local' literature, encouraging writing that was authentic to the West Indian landscape and to the daily speech of its inhabitants. 'We fail utterly to understand', an editorial of January/February 1932 commented on the quality of short stories received for publication, 'why anyone should want to see Trinidad as a miniature Paradiso, where grave-diggers speak like English M.P.s'. Emphasis was placed on the use of creole, and on a realistic description of West Indian life, for political and aesthetic reasons. To write in creole was to validate the experience of black people against the contempt and dehumanizing dismissal of white people. Celebration of blackness necessitated celebration of black language, for how could a black writer be true to his blackness using the language of his/her colonial master? The aesthetic argument was bound up with this political argument, and involved an appreciation of the energy, vitality and expressiveness of creole, an argument that Edward Brathwaite has rehearsed in his recent book, *The History of the Voice*. For Brathwaite the challenge to West Indian poets was how to shatter the frame of the iambic pentameter which had prevailed in English poetry from the time of Chaucer onwards. The form of the pentameter is not appropriate to a West Indian environment: 'The hurricane does not roar in pentameters. And that's the problem: how do you get a rhythm which approximates the natural experience, the environmental experience?' The use of creole, or Nation language, as he terms it, involves recognition of the vitality of the oral tradition surviving from Africa, the earthiness of proverbial folk speech, the energy and power of gestures which accompany oral delivery, and the insistence of the drumbeat to which the living voice responds.

England today is the third largest West Indian island – there are over half-a-million of us here, fewer only than Jamaica and Trinidad – and our generation is confronted by the same issues that Brathwaite and other writers faced in their time. The pressure then was to slavishly imitate the expressions of the Mother Country if a writer was to be recognised. Hence the vague Miltonic cadence of Walter MacA. Lawrence, one of our early Guyanese writers, in describing, quite inappropriately, the native thunder of the Kaiteur Falls:

And falling in splendour sheer down from the heights
that should gladden the heart of our eagle to scan,
That lend to the towering forest beside thee the semblance
of shrubs trimmed and tended by man –
That viewed from the brink where the vast, amber volume
that once was a stream cataracts into thee,
Impart to the foothills surrounding the maelstrom beneath
thee that rage as this troublous sea.

[413]

Brathwaite and others eventually rescued us from this cascade of nonsense sounds. The pressure now is also towards mimicry. Either you drop the epithet 'black' and think of yourself as a 'writer' (a few of us foolishly embrace this position, desirous of the status of 'writing' and knowing that 'black' is blighted with negative connotations), meaning cease dwelling on the nigger/tribal/nationalistic theme, cease *folking* up the literature, and become 'universal' – or else you perish in the backwater of small presses, you don't get published by the 'quality' presses and don't receive the corresponding patronage of media-hype. Put bluntly, this is how the threat against us is presented. Alfred Ford, summarizing these issues, puts them in a historical context: the pressure is to become a mulatto and house-nigger (Ariel) rather than stay a field-nigger (Caliban).

I cannot however feel or write poetry like a white man, much less serve him. And to become mulattos, black people literally have to be fucked (and fucked up) first. Which brings us back to the pornography of Empire. I feel that I am different, not wholly, but sufficient for me to want to contemplate that which is other in me, that which owes its life to particular rituals of ancestry. I know that the concept of 'otherness' is the fuel of white racism and dominates current political discourse, from Enoch Powell's 'In these great numbers blacks are, and remain, alien here. With the growth of concentrated numbers, their alienness grows not by choice but by necessity', to Margaret Thatcher's 'swamped by people of a different culture'. I also know that the concept of 'otherness' pervades English literature, from Desdemona's fatal attraction to the body of alien culture, to Marlow's obsession with the thought that Africans are in one sense alien but in a more terrible sense they are the very capacities within Europeans for the gratification of indecent pleasures. But these are not my problem. I'm glad to be peculiar, to modify the phrase. I'd prefer to be simply peculiar, and to get on with it, to live and write accordingly, but gladness is a forced response against the weight of insults, a throwing off of white men's burdens.

As to 'universality', let Achebe have the last word, even if in the most stylish of English:

> In the nature of things the work of a Western writer is automatically informed by universality. It is only others who must strain to achieve it. So-and-so's work is universal; he has truly arrived! As though universality were some distant bend in the road which you must take if you

travel out far enough in the direction of Europe or America, if you put adequate distance between yourself and your home. I should like to see the word 'universal' banned altogether from discussion of African literature until such time as people cease to use it as a synonym for the narrow, self–serving parochialism of Europe, until their horizon extends to include all the world.

(1989)

Sarah Lawson Welsh

Experiments in Brokenness:
The Creative Use of Creole in David Dabydeens's
Slave Song

In many European travellers' accounts of visits or residence in the West Indies from the eighteenth century onwards, creole languages are figured as 'broken English', 'degenerate' linguistic forms which were thought to reflect the alleged 'depravity' and 'uncivilized' or 'childlike' status of their speakers. This article explores some of the permutations of brokenness as experimental linguistic medium, literary trope, historical and experiential paradigm, and considers the creative potentialities of these permutations as they are realized in *Slave Song*. The collection, as a whole, inscribes but also resists different readings of brokenness. For example, Dabydeen writes in his introduction of the brokenness of creole as a 'naturally tragic language ... no doubt reflecting the brokenness and suffering of its original users – African slaves and East Indian indentured labourers' (Dabydeen 1986: 13). However, this concept of a doubled broken-ness is resisted, in practice, by a number of dominant and defiant voices in the poems, voices which refuse to be broken (e.g. 'Slave Song'), which are not beaten or reduced to despair and which are markedly fluent rather than faltering. *Slave Song* is also characterized by a certain formal and generic brokenness or unevenness and the problematic relationship between the poems and the self-generated critical apparatus which is included within the collection, is analyzed in this context ...

Until relatively recently, there has been little confluence between the linguistic study of creoles and the study of the potentialities of creoles as an expressive medium (Rickford 1986 and Brathwaite 1984 are important exceptions) ... However, as Dabydeen points out, 'the potentiality for [creole] literature is very great indeed', for creole is 'capable of expressing the full experience of its users which is a very deep one' (Dabydeen 1984: 15).[1] The number of contemporary Caribbean or Black British poets utilizing creole in a creative capacity, has increased dramatically in the last fifteen years. Significantly their work has also enabled a number of stereotypes surrounding the use of creole to be broken down: first that it is employed primarily for comic effect; second that it is an attempt merely to effect verisimilitude and third, that it is the medium only of politicized protest poetry – often of the most mediocre kind. On the contrary, creole has proven a medium resourceful enough to encompass a range of poetic effects: elegiac, lyrical, robust, dramatic and satiric.

The poems in Dabydeen's *Slave Song* are more than Browningesque voice-portraits transferred to a Caribbean context – they are, as the title suggests, first and foremost songs: songs of resistance. Songs were the Caribbean's first poems (Burnett 1986: xxix), an important locus of linguistic and communal resistance in slave populations on plantations throughout the Caribbean and North America. Dabydeen has spoken of the overall concept behind *Slave Song* as 'in the title, slave and song, the contradiction between the two. What I wanted to show was the way of life that survived brilliantly and wickedly, mischievously and tragically, in spite of certain experiences of violence and brutality' (Dabydeen 1989: 75). The continued close relationship between music and word is a salient feature of Caribbean poetry and in *Slave Song* Dabydeen explores the creative potentialities of song in many forms and dimensions: slave work-song, call and response and choric forms, adapted folk song and bawdy, celebratory songs of domestic ritual, voice portraits of frustration and defiance, love-song and elegy . . .

Slave Song is also an imaginative attempt to assert the music and linguistic traces of a very different ancestry and cultural inheritance . . . including talismanic words with a specifically Hindu notation (Dabydeen, 1990). Whereas a range of Indo-Caribbean experiences have been well documented in West Indian fiction . . . Dabydeen is one of a much smaller number of Caribbean *poets* whose writing seeks to redress the Afro-centric, ethno-cultural imbalance of West Indian literature. *Slave Song* re-invokes both the Afro-centrist narratives which have traditionally dominated Anglophone Caribbean writing and its frequently limited or essentialist representations of an Indo-Caribbean experience; however, the collection also recognizes the need to mediate between these narratives and to speak with a thoroughly creolized as well as creole voice.

The directness and robust defiance of many of Dabydeen's poems in this collection stand in sharp relief to the elegiac tone, the images of fragile cultural transfer and quietly atrophying Indian culture which are central to Derek Walcott's depiction of an Indo-Caribbean community in 'The Saddhu of Couva' (Walcott 1979: 33–5). Indeed the dominant tone of *Slave Song* ... is rather 'overwhelmingly that of public protestation' (Parry 1988: 3) often combined, as in the title poem, with a celebratory and defiant sexuality. Yet amongst the more problematic poems of 'corrosive sexuality' (Dabydeen 1989a: 121) and 'starkly pornographic experiences' (Dabydeen 1989b: 75), there are intervals of lyrical tenderness and poignant introspection (e.g. 'Men and Women' and 'Elegy') ...

The brutality and violence of the slave's everyday life, and the harsh realities of hunger, exhaustion and pain are reflected in many of the poems, by the use of abrupt, contracted creole forms and images of violation, degradation and brokenness. This use of creole ... renders the physicality or immediacy of a moment with particular intensity (an effect created by predominantly present tense and imperative formulations in the collection) but it also 'speaks the dislocations and oppressions of its history' (Parry 1988: 1) as a linguistic form. However, the lyrical use of creole is not restricted to the expression of loss, regret or pain; it is also central to those poems in which the slave is seen to yearn for transfiguration, imagining his or her release from bound existence through death ('Song of the Creole Gang Women'), or through individual or collective sexual fantasy ('Love Song' and 'The Canecutter's Song'). In such cases the long vowel sounds of creole ('straang', 'laang', 'haan') and soft endings of words such as 'deh', 'wheh' and 'leh' are emphasized or a gently flowing alliterative effect ('Leh we go sit dung riverside, dip, dodo, die – / Shade deep in cool deh' (Dabydeen 1984: 17–18) is deliberately juxtaposed with the harsh, staccato effect creole can also produce ...

It is important not to assume Dabydeen's adaptation of Guyanese, creole is a naturalistic – or even a necessarily representative – one. The literary reconstruction of this medium of vocalization is necessarily an artifice, a self-conscious process. Even writers such as Selvon, whose fictional use of creole was considered naturalistic by many of his earliest (British) critics, has openly acknowledged the need to 'modify the dialect' (Selvon 1982: 60); the creative use of the raw material of Caribbean speech involves, for him at least, a carefully constructed adaptation, even simulation of the language as heard.

Dabydeen's use of creole in *Slave Song* may be a political choice but it is also highly artful. The poet accords his creole-speaking poetic personae an autonomy of voice, a subject position within a discourse which was historically denied their real-life counterparts. Intense individual experience thus becomes the platform from which Dabydeen launches his powerful examination of what (fellow Guyanese writer) Wilson Harris has termed the 'pornography of Empire', his exploration of the various means of self-expressive resistance open to the slave – linguistic, gestural and sexual. In his introduction to the collection, Dabydeen speaks of a 'criss-cross of illusions' (Dabydeen, 1984: 9) between England and Guyana, mythically figured as 'El Dorado'; this notion of illusion as public mythology is neatly mirrored by Dabydeen's admission that the poems are, in part 'an imaginative rendition . . . a private fantasy' (Dabydeen 1984: 10). Indeed, illusion and fantasy run through the collection as organizing motifs but the ultimate irony is that the 'autonomy' of Dabydeen's creole-speaking personae and of his poetic use of creole itself are also illusory, fantastical. They are contained, challenged, even silenced, by the translations and notes in Standard English provided by Dabydeen at the end of the collection.

Such Standard English translations might be seen as the ironic legacy of a whole colonial history of indigenous voices being represented, mediated through the colonizer and attenuated or obfuscated in the process. Dabydeen has spoken of the Standard English speaker's use of creole as necessitating a painful 'unsheathing of the tongue' in preparation for a 'language uncomfortably raw' (Dabydeen 1984: 14), yet paradoxically the energy and radicalism of the poems themselves, powerfully disruptive of linguistic hegemonies and canonical modes, are smothered by the Standard English translations and the eurocentric critical apparatus which encases them. It is as if 'the reader's need to consult the scholarly appendages to the poems was essentially in order to distance and detoxify the emotional effects of their message' (McWatt 1989: 87). The notes and translations are, in their own way, as insistent as the creole voices of *Slave Song*; as competing voices they act as a kind of metacommentary on the continuing problematic relationship between First and Third World literatures, the 'criss-cross of illusions' and the relationship of inequality which shadows all interpretative acts in this arena. Mark McWatt makes a similar point when he observes how *Slave Song*'s incorporation of its own critical apparatus effectively anticipates the hermeneutic requirements of a metropolitan audience (as the images

[419]

of the conspicuous consumption of 'peasant' literature by Oxbridge diners at the end of 'Coolie Odyssey' will make even more overt): '*Slave Song* [draws] attention to interesting problems of poetic form and voice, of the ways in which the projected audience of the poem modified the craft itself, so that the poet of ex-colonial societies bears the multiple burden of messenger, translator, apologist, explicator' (McWatt 1989: 87). However, it could be argued that the notes and translations are a deliberate and integral part of the text rather than a subtext incorporated under any such 'burden' or obligation; Dabydeen assumes different roles and modes of discourse – historian, polemicist, poet and critic among them – quite deliberately, in order to subvert conventional generic boundaries and to problematize definitions of historical documentation and imaginative reconstruction, primary text and secondary text, testimony and artifact in relation to *Slave Song*.

McWatt argues that Dabydeen 'emphasizes his separation from the lives of the singers by adopting the pose of scholar and translator' (McWatt 1989: 86), but this appropriation of the 'authoritative' voice of the metropolitan critic can be read more subversively; not only does it allow Dabydeen to speak tellingly of the double worlds he inhabits as Indo-Caribbean writer and (Black) British critic/academic but it also effectively breaks down the dualities between centre and periphery, critic and writer, literate and illiterate, literary and non-literary, standard and creole by showing that the authority of the critic is illusory, provisional and, moreover, one which is readily mimicked – mimicry as 'spectacular resistance' being one of the characteristics of post-colonial discourse, as defined by Homi Bhabha (Bhabha 1984: 162). Dabydeen inhabits all these modes in *Slave Song* and the Dabydeen of the notes and translations to *Slave Song* is merely assuming the last in a series of masks in the collection – there are no originary voices in *Slave Song*, only re-constructed, re-presented, mediating ones . . .

It is in the notes and translations, more than anywhere else in the collection, that the real artfulness of *Slave Song* is evidenced: a postmodernist concern with parody and playfulness which both flirts with and critiques the experiments of modernism, mediating constantly between the particularities of a creole/creolized Guyanese experience and the universalizing orthodoxies of much Western literary criticism. In this respect, Dabydeen's experiments in brokenness are not only linguistic but formal and generic also: *Slave Song* as a whole raises the question of boundary demarcation between writer and critic, poetry and its interpretation, elucidation and obfuscation.

Slave Song is a text – like T.S. Eliot's *The Waste Land* before it and Brathwaite's *X-Self* after it – which moves toward self-reflexive interpretation and which inscribes its own, wider, problematic positioning within conflicting discourses, different linguistic, literary and cultural legacies. Brathwaite's inclusion of extensive notes to *X-Self* opens up similar 'problems' to those generated by T.S. Eliot's notes to *The Waste Land* ... The initial effect of Eliot's Notes, as in *Slave Song*, is to detract from the possibility of an internal teleological logic: the poem's own syncretic movement toward greater understanding and to foreground instead the reductive, extra-textual 'scrabbling for significance' of a Western critical *modus operandi*. The tantalizing suggestion that the notes provide the keys or interpretative codes to unlock the text is little short of a tease; rather than providing closure, they displace our search for authoritative source materials and mythic ur-narratives into an inward and increasingly futile spiral of self-referentiality; if the notes reveal nothing else, they reveal the strength of our hermeneutic desires and the ease with which they can be mocked ...

The ambiguous and ultimately subversive function of Eliot's Notes to *The Waste Land* has not been without its imitators (e.g. Basil Bunting's *Briggflatts* (1966)) ... and the relationship between Eliot's and Brathwaite's poetry has been well documented (Rohlehr, 1981) ... However, Brathwaite's genius in his long poem *X-Self* is to reduce the modernist experimentation in brokenness as fragmentation to the level of aesthetic dalliance, by inscribing on this palimpsest the much more powerful trope of fragmentation as historical experience, paradigmatic of the African diasporic experience – and of the Caribbean condition more generally[2] ...

Brathwaite openly admits that he provides the notes:

> With great reluctance, since the irony is that they may suggest the poetry is so obscure in itself that it has to be lighted up; [that] it is so lame, that it has to have a crutch; and (most hurtful of all) that it is bookish, academic, 'history'.

The same kind of tension between the desire to make use of those essentially oral features of his linguistic and cultural heritage and the contrary appearance given by the notes, of them 'coming from a learned [and significantly written] treatise', is explored in *Slave Song* but to a different end ...

One senses something of the same experimental quality (without the same degree of artistic anxiety) in the notes to *Slave Song*, published some three years earlier, but they are altogether less transparent, more artful. That a playful relationship between poems and the notes/translations was evidently intended, is made clear by Dabydeen's comment: 'People like Brathwaite have been arguing for years that creole is a different language, sufficiently different from English to be considered its own language. So therefore the logic would be to provide a translation, which is what I did' (Dabydeen 1989b: 75) ...

If we take Dabydeen's comments to their logical conclusion it is possible to arrive at a very different reading of *Slave Song*, one which sees the introduction, notes and translations as self-aggrandizing texts which claim their own 'autonomy', asserting their dominance by adopting a separate – and privileged – language. The distinction between subverting the linguistic hegemonies and canonical modes of the centre and reproducing them, is often a very fine one, and in *Slave Song* it is possible to see the standard English voices, asserting a re-constituted cultural supremacy, slipping into the easy grooves of long established literary and linguistic hegemonies, falling back on the Western privileging of standardized forms over dialectal ones, the privileging of interpretative over primary materials ...

The prose notes to *Slave Song* may enrich the poems' meanings, but the translations of the poems into standard English tend to have the opposite effect. Dabydeen himself acknowledges that such translation attenuates the creole language which is not merely the vehicle, but indeed the substance, of thought. Alongside this is lost the 'Creole choreography' (Dabydeen 1984: 65) of the rhythms of song, work and life; a whole world of gesture and kinetic energy contained in the language is at once made 'lame'. A similar pull between enrichment and impoverishment of understanding, between explication and obfuscation which characterized Eliot's notes, can thus be seen to be enacted in *Slave Song*, albeit in a milder form.

An alternative is to read the notes/translations as a deliberate and organic part of the collection. The mediating voices of white amanuenses, who introduced (socially and textually) the published narratives and oral testimonies of slaves and ex-slaves in the last two centuries, especially in North America, are replaced in *Slave Song* by a self-generated critical introduction which parodically 'authorizes' the text for white or non-creole-speaking consumption. Superficially the notes/translations gesture towards the interpretative possibilities of the poems whilst in fact circumscribing the range of meanings; on a deeper level, they engage with more fundamental critical issues such as the problematic 'consumption' and reception of the post-colonial text in Europe, the need to decentre outmoded binaries and to re-appropriate the role of critic, self-reflexively. The critical apparatus of *Slave Song* also enacts the radical subversion of generic categories by skilfully inhabiting and impersonating multiple modes of discourse (literary and sociological analysis, polemic, translation). Arguably, the fluency and continuities of the notes, the 'access' to the poems which they apparently facilitate, is only superficial; their hybridized 'authority', the radical disjunction of their linguistic power base and milieu from the creole experience which the poems inscribe, encourages an awareness of brokenness operating as an aesthetic of deliberate unevenness, disturbance or interruption in the collection as a whole. *Slave Song*, viewed in this light, is a text playfully self-conscious of the illusory or provisional nature of its own autonomies and of textual 'authority' generally (as is enacted in the reconstitution of dominant voices in the notes); its different voices (creole, standard, slave, poet, critic) reveal the paradoxical nature of power and subjectivity to be never truly autonomous, always determined. Moreover, *Slave Song* inscribes its own subversiveness only to reinscribe the old hegemonies; for example, the collection is characterized by a vigorous orality but also a deeply interiorized – and ultimately stronger – textuality; like the published text of Sistren's *Lionheart Gal* (1986), it is a radical experimental text of mediated voices which 'somewhat ironically affirms the authority of the written word' (Cooper 1989: 51). The 'new indenture' (McWatt 1989: 88) for the post-colonial writer, as Mark McWatt suggests, may well be no less than literature itself.

(1994)

NOTES

1 David Dabydeen has spoken (Dabydeen, 1989b: 76) of this 'resourcefulness [of creole] in conveying certain experiences ... In the brokenness of the language resides not just a certain barbaric energy, but also the capacity to be

experimental with a language; it is almost like Shakespearean English. You can make up words, play with words, and you can rhyme in much more adventurous ways than you can in Standard English. The brokenness has a capacity to convey a greater sense of tragedy and pain, of energy, but you can also reconstruct it in your own way, you can play with the language with a greater degree of freedom'.

2 Walcott has recently used the analogy of reassembling a broken vase in a similar way (Walcott 1992: 9).

Ramabai Espinet

The Invisible Woman in West Indian Fiction

Over the last twenty-five years the presence of the Indian community in the Caribbean has made itself felt as a fit subject for fiction. The most famous writer of fiction which utilizes the Indian experience as its raw material is undoubtedly V. S. Naipaul. Other novelists such as Sam Selvon, Shiva Naipaul, Ismith Khan, Wilson Harris, and Edgar Mittelholzer have treated the subject in a variety of ways. But a searching look at the novels and stories ... will reveal that the characters ... who have provided us with explorations of the lives lived as Indians in the West Indian context are almost all male. Tiger, Hat, Bogart, Mr Biswas, Kripalsingh and Pundit Ganesh Ramsumair are fully made artistic representations of this experience, recognizable, identifiable to the reader as participants in a common human drama and furnished with physical descriptions which allow pictures of themselves as individuals to achieve form. But their female counterparts are less successful. Characters such as Urmilla, Shama and Leela play only pallid supporting roles ...

The Indian woman is invisible because no novelist has yet been able to regard her existence in the West Indies and give voice to the peculiarities and perceptions of that particular existence ... We live in a cultural situation where Anglophile and Americanized attitudes and values are thought to be desirable and the movement towards 'creolization' is inevitable. Gradually, repressive Indian attitudes towards women are being jettisoned along with other items of cultural baggage, and are being replaced, predictably enough, by other equally repressive though different attitudes which prevail in the dominant culture of the West. The change in dress and behaviour has made room for a freer assertion of individual personality which is visible in the society at large. But evidence is accumulating from historical and sociological studies that the prevalent notion of Indian female personality as submissive, shy and timid is a fallacy and that from the earliest waves of immigration, the majority of women who made the journey across the *Kala pani* did so independently, some even with small children – legitimate and illegitimate. V.S. Naipaul reveals in *Finding the Centre* that his paternal great-grandmother was one of these. These women came, for the most part, because they were less than passive recipients of an unendurable fate. Some of them had been forced by circumstances such as widowhood or inadequate dowries into prostitution; many were young widows. They came voluntarily or were sent, as a kind of banishment, to find new lives in an unknown land. So the picture of Indian womanhood which emerges from contemporary novels, that composite of compliance, obedience and domestic virtue, is far from complete. A more vigorous and psychologically exciting tale is needed to deal with the truth of this experience. The Indian who exists in the Caribbean today is very different from the figure which appears in the region's art. She is more varied and complex ...

The presence of the Indian community in the literature of the region continues to grow. It is a large and dispersed community, attended by the myriad discomforts of recently liberated colonials, uneven in its abilities to accommodate to the demands of a plural society and, surprisingly, mostly male, if one is to judge by its literary output. All of the published writers of Indian origin are male, with the exception of Rajkumarie [sic] Singh of Guyana, and they are pre-occupied with the pressing concerns of the Indian male in the West Indian social context. The Indian woman is located in a largely peasant, village culture, firmly attached to the traditional values of the home and seeking no active combat with the external, non-Hindu world. Safe in the ascriptions of the female Hindu role, she lives as an extension of the dominant male figure in her environment, and she transmutes all her needs into those which he can fill. Selvon's Urmilla is a good example of this. And although she and Tiger are equally inexperienced at the beginning of their relationship, he develops into a figure of paternal authority, capable of punishing her or of extending pardon and generosity, while she remains childlike and at the mercy of his whim ...

John Stuart Mill's cautionary reminder that 'whatever is usual appears natural' is more necessary than ever as we survey critically the real experience of Indian women in the Caribbean away from the idealized stereotypes of the good Hindu wife and the mainstream ideal of the petted and pampered 'Stepford' wife. The other stereotypes worth mentioning are those of the whore, the scold, the managing elderly aunt and the older woman whose lewdness is tolerated because of her age ...

Accommodation to the dominant culture of the West, now asserting a West Indian manifestation, has caused numerous changes in the external appearance of Indians in the diaspora. Interesting changes are also evident, indeed, inevitable, in the aesthetic sensibilities and moral codes of the individuals concerned. The novelists of the region have grappled with these ideas and memorable characterizations, possessed of varying degrees of subtlety, have emerged as a result. These characters reveal something of the anxieties of Indian males in a society in which they are still largely unplaced. But perceptions about the existence of Indian men project themselves, together with an absence of real seeing in considering the feminine side of the equation. And this is the major flaw in the characterization of the Indian female in the West Indian novel as a whole. She is a fleeting, unseen creature, functioning unambiguously within the constraints of the tight familial structure. The world outside is not her domain: still protected by the veil, she exists in that area of the Indian sensibility which is private, unrevealed even to one's self, and about which exploration is tentative.

This is a sad and critical state of affairs. It is damaging to the health of the society as a whole and to this sub-group in particular. The distance between the real existence of hundreds of women and the images thrown up by the fiction of the region needs to be bridged. We need to eliminate the falsehoods. Indian women have paid the price of psychic uncertainty, loneliness and guilt for the imperative of adjustment to the demands of their lives in the West Indies. And too often, their attempt at accommodation is satirized because of its gauche external manifestations, while sensitive probing is absent . . .

Almost every fictional instance of Indian womanhood yields these blinding stereotypes. It is a cause for wonder that so many writers in a society can be insensitive to the true nature of at least half of the people they are writing about . . .

It seems clear that the relations between the sexes among people of Indian background, as reflected in the region's fiction, suffer from an ohrni-blinkered sensibility which dictates that it is against custom to actually *see* Indian women. That this deeply conditioned psychological reticence has transferred itself into fictional character- izations is a predictable result. An examination of the fiction of the three Naipauls, V.S., Shiva and Seepersad, confirms this hypothesis. Seepersad Naipaul's stories in *The Adventure of Gurudeva* are an attempt at constructing a gentle, idyllic village pastoral . . . Men such

[427]

as Gurudeva, Dilraj and My Uncle Dalloo launch themselves into the world of the village in Trinidad with varying levels of success. Women like Ratni, Bipti and Moonia are the passive receptors of beatings and abuses, the result of conflicts encountered by their husbands in the course of their more demanding confrontations with the larger world . . . A brief glimpse of the village idyll occurs, though, in the story of Dookhani and Mungal. Seepersad Naipaul approaches the angle of the love story surreptitiously . . . for the idea of a blossoming romance coming out of an arranged marriage, a tentative but still defiant note in the settled process of Hindu family life.

Possibly something of the shyness and brevity of Hindu romance is re-echoed by V.S. Naipaul in *The Mystic Masseur* and in *A House for Mr Biswas* . . .

The episode which involves Shama in *A House for Mr Biswas* is described in comic terms, but the undercurrent of teasing and tenderness in its narration is unmistakable. Mr Biswas is hired to paint a sign for the Tulsi's shop and it is while he works there that he catches a glimpse of Shama. He is attracted to her because she is slim and pretty and is somewhat more retiring than the other noisy youngsters swarming around Mrs. Tulsi's counter. The telling detail emerges even then, though. He finds her voice harsh and hateful. The incident reveals a side of Shama's personality which is never enlarged upon and which concerns a black female customer who has entered the shop. It seems that there was a current vogue for flesh-coloured stockings and Shama produced a pair of unambiguously black cotton stockings in response to the customer's demand for the flesh-coloured articles. Naipaul digs here at many of the neuroses afflicting the aesthetic sensibilities and indeed, the self-perception of the colonized West Indian. The woman, a victim of the pre-'Black is beautiful' era, is deeply insulted. Shama reveals herself as a prankster who is nevertheless secure in her own superior sense of being Indian, Brahmin, and sufficiently pale-coloured to make fun of a darker pigment.

When Shama erupts into this aspect of her personality later in the novel, however, we find that her spirited responses have become those of a shrewish and discontented wife . . . The character Shama moves uncertainly between the various roles assigned to the Indian woman. Of her internal life, her desires, fears, agonies, we know nothing. Her motivations are not probed. Between loyal wife, dutiful daughter and resourceful custodian of household economy we know almost nothing of her personality. The mischievous girl in the shop resurrects herself in Mr. Biswas's memory, occasionally. He marvels at how ordered life is for his wife and reasons that for Shama and women like her, life resolved itself easily into a series of negatives which were to be avoided at all costs. Not to be married, not to bear children, not to be a dutiful daughter etc.

The role of the Hindu woman is defined here with clarity and simplicity. Mr Biswas's curiosity and his author's go no further. The idea that women like these might be driven by a sense of anguish or hopelessness, or that they might possess dreams beyond their capacity for achievement, is an unconsidered one . . .

A quick survey of V.S. Naipaul's female Indian characters reveals more unflattering versions of the stereotype – cardboard cutouts, for the most part, serving a functional novelistic purpose, but unexamined in themselves. An illuminating comparison can be made between Naipaul's Indian women and his other main women characters who are European. And chronology may provide another clue in assessing this writer's treatment of female character. It is significant that both Seeta and Nalini are products of his first two novels and both possess attractive qualities in personality and physical charm . . .

Seeta, Nalini and Naipaul's European women Sandra, Jane and Yvette, are the more fully developed female characters in his novels, and they are all unencumbered by the demands of children. Mrs Baksh in *The Suffrage of Elvira* . . . provides a dramatic contrast. Her outlines are definite, square and unattractive with a meanness of spirit which is endlessly visited upon the little Bakshes and her patient husband. Our artist here insists upon wide-angled lenses for his unsympathetic camera and Mrs Baksh becomes simply a literary device for illustrating the powerlessness of the oppressed Indian male. So the ritualised world of Hindu wifehood is invoked, and the writer's own reticence at exploring and revealing the internal world of the Indian woman triumphs . . .

In *The Mimic Men* . . . although the male protagonists are individualized, differentiated versions of colonized men seeking a sense of self in a confused and often destructive global environment which offers no guideposts, the important female functions [only] as a composite of a fairly static entity, labelled European woman.

Sandra, Jane and Yvette are really very slightly differing forms of the same woman. But there are major differences between the realization of these characters and that of the earlier Indian ones. There is adequate physical description, even a noticeable delight in the physical attributes of these women. And there is erotic detail ... there are feet – white, slender, beautifully shaped, and deserving of extravagant caresses, even in public, as in Kripalsingh's relationship with Sandra. These feet are symbolic of a passage to another, more civilized world, far from the mud of the canefields and the squabbling of dozens of meaningless progeny, piled like litter, in Hanuman House ... And although the analysis is concentrated upon one type of European woman only, it is for an understanding of a personality which disturbs and fascinates that this writer seeks. Sandra, Jane and Yvette are people who are caught in a vacancy, and they are voracious for some sense of selfhood which would, if realized, give point to their existence. They are also people who have freed themselves from certain conventional restraints ... so they can assume the recklessness of those who have nothing much to lose. And in the end, they can always reclaim their safe place in an ordered society. Jane's story in *Guerillas* is that of an excess of confidence in these assumptions, really the unbending arrogance of the white woman towards the black or brown colonial man ... in spite of their destructive natures, these women are infused with a real life, removed from the shortcut of caricature ...

The Indian female, seen at an earlier period through ritualized and indirect perception, remains frozen in that frame. [However, Naipaul's] maturer analyses of women, no doubt the result of daily contacts and experiences, are occurring in a setting in which the developing Indian woman is not present. This may be one of the reasons for the absence of this character in Naipaul's later fiction.

What remains abundantly clear is that there is much more scope to the personalities of Indian women than has been manifested in the fiction of the Caribbean region. And the resurgence of interest in the early history of Indian immigrants provide actual evidence of this. The simplified fictional accounts of Indian fleeting girlhood, acquiescent and resigned wifehood, and shrewish matronhood are not equal to the demands of the complex plural society which we inhabit ...

(1989)

Denise deCaires Narain

Delivering the Word:
the Poetry of Lorna Goodison

Lorna Goodison has published three volumes of poetry: *Tamarind Season* (1980); *I Am Becoming My Mother* (1986) and *Heartease* (1988).[1] In an interview with *The Guardian* newspaper, cited in *I Am Becoming My Mother*, Goodison says:

> I'm a poet, but I didn't choose poetry – it chose me ... it's a domi-nating, intrusive tyrant. It's something I have to do – a wicked force.

In many of her poems, poetry is represented as a physically abusive force with the poet as an embattled figure. Sometimes parallels are drawn between the pain involved in delivering a child and the pain of 'delivering' a poem. So, for example, in 'My Last Poem (Again)' in *Heartease* (p. 14), the anxiety and effort experienced in life and in *recording* that life are evoked in the vivid physicality of the following image:

> Goodbye poems, you bled me shiny bottles of red feelings.
> Poems you were blood leeches attaching yourself to me

and later in the same poem:

> When the King of Swords gutted me
> and left me for dead, in my insides were found
> clots of poems, proving that poets are made of poems

The reference to the 'King of Swords' points to another arena – that of sexual relationships – in which the woman's body is configured as a site of painful invasion; in the poem 'Ceremony For the Banishment of the King of Swords' (*Heartease* pp. 51–5), the attentions of the itinerant lover are described graphically, 'He unsheathes the sword aligned with his backbone and sinks it into your chest'. While in 'On Becoming a Mermaid' (*I Am Becoming My Mother* p. 30), the speaker seeks the solace of an asexual, mermaid's existence:

> Your sex locked under
> mother-of-pearl scales
> you're a pixie now, a mermaid
> a green tinged fish/fleshed woman/thing

[431]

If, as I've argued, both poetry and sex are configured as painful invasions of the (woman's) body, then one of the ways in which Goodison attempts to override this is to opt increasingly *not* to speak of the body and to articulate a poetic identity which transcends this particular pain in the projection of a disembodied poetic voice. This shift away from the body can be traced in the changing focus of her three collections of poetry – a change in focus which I am characterising as a shift from a more reproductive/woman-centred *delivery* of the word to a more asexual/spiritual notion of *deliverance* via the word. I shall now offer a discussion of this, using the title poems of each of these collections, as emblematic of this shift in poetic identity.

In 'Tamarind Season' the fruits on the tamarind tree encased in their hard brown shells are used as a metaphor for the spinster woman (though, in Jamaican culture, 'tamarind season' is also a more generalised reference to hard times). The regularly indented shape of the long, brown tamarind pod is exploited for its similarities to the shapely contours of the non-pregnant woman and the indented layout on the page reiterates this visually:

> The skin atrophies
> to a case of spinster brown.
>
> the soft welcome within
> needs protecting
> so she grows wasp-waisted
> again
> wasp-waisted

Goodison draws a parallel between the fruit and female sexuality, using the hard case of the tamarind to represent the spinster's protective abstinence. In the third stanza, the poet uses the image of the wizened fruit rattling in its now too-big case to evoke the barrenness of the spinster in linguistic – as well as sexual – terms:

> The welcome turns sour
> she finds a woman's tongue
> and clacks curses at the wind
> for taking advantage
> box her about this way
> and that is the reason
>
> wait is the reason
>
> Tamarind Season

Unfulfilled sexually, the spinster becomes that other female stereo-type, the shrew, whose tongue is her only weapon. The ambiguity of this stanza – is the wind being cursed by the frustrated spinster who wants to be taken or because it *is* taking advantage of her im-mobility by buffeting her as it likes? – leaves the reader with a sense that the moment of 'delivery of the word', paralleling the spinster's sexual impotence, is also deferred and we are left with the image/sound of the impotently clacking spinster – to 'wait'.

This sourly self-contained image of woman is in sharp contrast to the fecund plenitude of the mother in the title poem of the collec-tion *I Am Becoming My Mother* ... The poem celebrates creative processes in a series of deft, painterly strokes, in which the identi-ties of mother and daughter overlap sensuously. All of the senses are written into the poem: we feel the texture of the lace and linen; we smell and taste the onions; we hear the birth waters singing. The focus on hands 'smelling always of onions' draws attention to the idea of woman as creator/maker – of babies, homes, gardens, meals and, because the poem itself is a creation, of *poems*.

The cyclical movement of the poem, beginning and ending as it does with the same two lines (except for the subtle shift in order of the yel-low/brown combination) emphasizes the sensual merging of the two lives. This fluidity in movement is echoed, thematically, in the refer-ences to the birth waters singing and, more generally, to the focus on *process* and *becoming* which the poem celebrates. The woman-centred-ness and the powerful presence of the mother in this poem, as well as the fluidity of its movement and imagery, invites a reading in the light of the kind of textual strategies associated with *écriture féminine*. While such a reading *is* productive, I would place this poem more firmly in the context of the stress in many black women's texts on affirming maternal connections and continuity. The title essay of Alice Walker's collection, 'In Search of Our Mother's Gardens,'[2] is perhaps the most explicit outline of recuperating and validating the black mother. In this essay, Walker argues that black women writers who seek to place them-selves in a tradition of black female creativity have to broaden their definitions of 'artistry' to include such practices as quilt-making, cook-ing, gardening and so on. She argues:

> How was the creativity of the black woman kept alive, year after year
> and century after century, when for most of the years black people

have been in America, it was a punishable crime for a black person to read or write? And the freedom to paint, to sculpt, to expand the mind with action did not exist.

In the context of black women's writing that Walker describes, then, there is no clear boundary between the creation of 'Art' and other, more everyday, forms of artistry; this is precisely the kind of context Goodison's poem evokes. This contrasts interestingly with the much more ambivalent mother/daughter relationship described by feminists such as Adrienne Rich as a fraught, antagonistic battle: 'Matrophobia . . . the fear not of one's mother or of motherhood but of *becoming one's mother*'.[3]

Where the very short title poems of Goodison's first two volumes focus quite specifically on questions of identity in relation to womanhood, in *Heartease* the title poems are a suite of three which increase in length as the poet catalogues the hardships faced by the poor of her own society and of powerless people everywhere; the poems take on an increasingly apocalyptic tone and spread out to speak of and for Biblical crowds:

> In this year of cataclysm pre-predicted
> being plagued with dreams
> of barefoot men marching
> and tall civilisations crumbling
> forward to where the gathering, gathering.
> Crowdapeople, Crowdapeople weep and mourn,
> crowdapeople I have seen
>
> (*Heartease*, p. 36)

Goodison then clearly articulates her own role as poet within this materially deprived situation providing healing images, evoking possibilities to keep the spirit and imagination alive:

> I speak no judgement
> this voice is to heal
> to speak of possibility

And later in the same poem

> No judgement I speak
> that function is not mine
> I come only to apply words
> to a sore and confused time.

Goodison's voice is powerful and confident, demanding to be read
aloud. She draws on a range of discourses in these poems, collapsing
boundaries between them but privileging none consistently, thus
creating a fluid polyphonic voice. Goodison *speaks in tongues*, as it
were, and it is in this sense of *delivering* the word that she might
easily be categorised as a 'performance poet'. Goodison exploits a
style of delivery when she performs her poems which powerfully
consolidates her role as poet-priestess, for she carefully establishes a
calm context by first reading the poem, 'I Shall Light A Candle to
Understanding In Thine Heart Which Shall Not Be Put Out'
(*Heartease*, p.7) and by reading many of her poems in a subdued,
rhythmic – an almost trance-inducing, incantatory manner.

   In the 'Heartease' poems, the poet draws on the discourses of the
Bible, of Jamaican Creole, and of the Rasta as well as using more
obviously lyric/poetic language. She uses 'I' when making her obser-
vations or 'testifying', but uses 'we' when mapping the healing
possibilities, including herself in this process. Goodison's voice in
these poems is very much a public, speaking voice and the sense of
a live audience is inscribed within the poems at several points. The
result is that at the level of content and, more fundamentally of form,
Goodison's poetic identity is one in which she so strongly allies herself
with 'the people' that her poetic voice is a collective one; she *is* the
body politic. The poet's carefully constructed poetic role of healer
draws both on the kind of divining traditionally associated with
women but also on the linguistic power of the Biblical Word and
other patriarchal discourses. Interestingly, in another poem in
Heartease, 'My Father Always Promised Me', the poet explicitly links
her artistry as healer/poet to her father, describing him as the axis
of her world:

> Almost too late I learnt the flying steps
> father, look see me rising, lighter
> in the name of my father, dreamer
> who said I should be
> Of all worlds and a healer

Here the father's association with the power of the symbolic order
is made explicit; it is an order within which Goodison as woman poet
must negotiate a space and empower her own voice. As argued above,
Goodison does this by attempting to speak with the authority of her

fathers – Biblical and biological – but she also derives power by attempting to speak with the authority of the voices of the people too.

This speaking of the body politic within the body of her own texts is achieved at some cost: in 'Heartease New England 1987' the poet explores her doubts and vulnerabilities in relation to her own role as poet before affirming the importance of drawing strength from her community: 'I too can never quite get the measure of this world's structure / somewhere I belong to community'. But perhaps the greatest area of tension lies in the suppression of her sexuality as woman which her role as Poet/Priestess/healer seems to imply. The poem, 'Wild Woman (I)' begins:

> I seemed to have put distance
> between me and the wild woman
> she being certified bad company.
> Always inviting me to drink
> bloody wine from clay cups
> and succumb to false promise
> in the yes of slim dark men.

And 'Wild Woman (II)' begins:

> Sometime in this first half
> the wild woman left.
> Rumour spreads a story
> that bad love killed her
> kinder ones swear
> that just like that,
> she dreamed herself
> off precipices
> sheer as her dresses.

The two 'Wild Woman' poems point to a contradictory pull in Goodison's work between the private and the public; between the 'private' world of female sexuality and her 'public' role as Healer/Poet. Where many of the poems in Goodison's two earlier volumes might be described as womanist/feminist, focusing on explorations of woman's identity and the anxiety involved in writing as woman, there are fewer of these poems in *Heartease*. Instead, what seems to happen is that Goodison increasingly jettisons the focus on 'women's issues', including those associated with the body, and opts instead for a poetic identity and voice in which she attempts to transcend the limitations and difficulties of her woman's body to represent the body politic, rather than the individual, or even the representative woman. The association with spiritual delivery of the word is one which frees her from the kind of wounding associated with the more sexual/repro-ductive use of the word delivery and she empowers herself as poet/priestess to speak with and for the community from which that power derives.

(1995)

NOTES

1 Lorna Goodison, *Tamarind Season* (Kingston: Institute of Jamaica, 1980); *I Am Becoming My Mother* (London: New Beacon Books, 1986); *Heartease* (London: New Beacon Books, 1988).
2 Alice Walker, *In Search Of Our Mother's Gardens* (London: The Women's Press, 1984).
3 Adrienne Rich, *Of Woman Born; Motherhood as Experience and Institution* (London: Virago, 1977), p. 235.

The 1990s

Introduction

It is certainly true that in the 1990s Caribbean literature appears to be achieving more prominence in the academic domain of literary studies. However, it is also clear that the academy has exerted its own pressures on Caribbean literature. This is perhaps most evident in the shaping of Caribbean literature to the contours of a canon, often a post-colonial one, as this manageable entity appears to be crucial in gaining institutional recognition. Indeed, one of the most important consequences in terms of the reception of Caribbean literature in the 1990s is the consolidation of post-colonial literature as a cogent field of academic scholarship. Under the auspices of metropolitan universities, post-colonial criticism and theory has become the dominant paradigm through which Caribbean literature is constructed and read outside the Caribbean. Many Caribbean journals 'face very uncertain futures' (Breiner 1986: 141), and many Caribbean critics and writers find themselves publishing in the increasing number of Western academic journals specializing in post-colonial issues.

There appears to be a serious question mark over the survival of Caribbean literature given the generalizing and homogenizing tendencies of 'Post-Colonial Studies'. The Caribbean, like all other post-colonial cultures, has several unique features which can be erased in this larger conceptual framework; these include the absence of alter/native languages, and of a common pre-colonial culture, as well as the extraordinary cultural admixture. There is also an immense diversity within the Caribbean region which necessitates detailed analysis that is often difficult to achieve within an over-arching theoretical model. Indeed, although the post-colonial umbrella has enabled the academic recognition and widespread teaching of many formerly marginal literatures and writers, it can function according to a rather reductive agenda of resistance, rewriting and revisionism which irons out the cultural specificity of the different regional writings. As a term which is applied to Canada and Africa, to New Zealand and India, it is a term with complex and varied references and its multiple meanings need to be carefully discussed if it is to remain an intellectually enabling paradigm.

This re-centring of Caribbean literature within Western academic institutions is further complicated by the fact that the majority of Caribbean writers themselves are now based, or partly based, in these diasporic centres. Does this situation bear testimony to a postmodern world with no frontiers, to a new cosmopolitanism in which the boundaries of the nation state do not define their subjects? If this is the case then perhaps Caribbean literature as a distinct body of writings is no longer viable and we need to rethink the whole issue of regional literatures? Or perhaps, rather than being symptomatic of a contemporary global trend, this re-centring of Caribbean literature is a troubling move towards cultural neo-imperialism, and one made more acute by the migration of many writers? Indeed, it could be argued that Caribbean literature is now, more than ever, being written and published for outside consumption, and that there is an urgent need to counter the Western metropolitan re-absorption and reconstruction of Caribbean literature (see **Lamming 1960, Cooper 1989, Hodge 1990,** Griffiths 1991).

The way in which Western academic structures and media have sought to construct Caribbean writers according to particular, although varied, cultural iconographies certainly merits attention. The appropriation of **Derek Walcott** into 'the mainstream of world literature' (Busby 1992) clearly has implications for the reception of Caribbean literature in the 1990s, as a 'world literary canon' offers a new means of championing the few and neglecting the many. In contrast to the minimizing of Walcott's Caribbean identity, the blackness, indeed 'otherness', of certain Caribbean writers has become the main focus of their constructed image for a white audience. **John Vidal's** article on **Benjamin Zephaniah (1988),** offers a brief biography of Zephaniah, almost as an explanatory narrative for his poetry, in which he highlights the socially disruptive elements of this streetwise, post-criminalized artist. It is ironic that Vidal quotes Zephaniah's stated refusal to play up to the establishment's desired image of blackness ('a Rastafarian Lenny Henry'), as the image which he constructs of the radical and the political is also in danger of becoming an institutionalized icon of blackness which promises difference and excitement in a marketable form. It is not incidental that Vidal concentrates on the political status of Zephaniah's work, with no mention of the aesthetic qualities, a critical bias which is a marked problem in the reception of dub and performance poetry more generally.

These iconographies point to a wider issue concerning the aesthetic and cultural status of Caribbean literature. The critical policing of the post-colonial perimeter fence for writers and texts which stray from assigned identities remains a serious issue which readers of the literature need to address. The practice of regulating the post-colonial proper has led not only to narrow constructions of Caribbean writers and texts, but also to the exclusion of certain works (see **Breeze 1990**). The attachment which post-colonial theory has to resistant and rebellious subjects may have begun to exercise similar constraints to those imposed by colonial cultural authorities, with strict expectations and boundaries of literary acceptability which merely substitute the insurgent for the imitative.

It would be naïve to underestimate the influence which Western academic centres can exert on Caribbean literature through the processes of canonization and theorization, as well as by editing texts and buying archives. Nevertheless, it could be argued that Caribbean culture has responded creatively to many fierce situations of encounter and there appears to be good reason to suggest that the encounters with the academy and theory will not end any differently.

Theoretical debates

As our emphasis upon the writer–critic tradition demonstrates, Caribbean writers have always theorized, and their critical discourse has been as varied and creative as the literature itself. However, this theorizing may not take the same forms as 'high' Western theoretical discourses, indeed, it may even seek to define itself against these models in a statement of cultural and political difference. The problems and possibilities of theory with reference to post-colonial writings have been carefully explored by Stephen Slemon and Helen Tiffin in their Introduction to *After Europe* (1989). They point out how, at worst, theory functions as a: '"eurovision" set loose upon a field of difference, and one which fixes its exoticizing, objectifying knowledge-producing gaze wherever and whenever it pleases' (Slemon and Tiffin 1989: xii). They also indicate that, at best, theory can operate self-consciously as knowledge which: 'has to be negotiated' and which is 'always grounded to a cultural specificity' (Slemon and Tiffin 1989: xviii–xix).

The critical work of Wilson Harris, which blends the metaphysical, the philosophical and the creative, needs to be considered in any discussion of Caribbean theory. Harris's complex and engaging theoretical meditations on flux, process, self-reflexivity, and the 'erosion of bias' through 'infinite rehearsal' towards a new 'universalism' have been instrumental in establishing a vocabulary for discussing Caribbean culture (Harris 1981, 1983). However, as with an emergent Caribbean literary canon, certain writers and writings have been more readily admitted into a Caribbean critical tradition. Gareth Griffiths argues that until recently Wilson Harris's work suffered from marginalization as it was regarded as 'apolitical' and 'obscure' when politically committed, realist texts were critically endorsed. Moreover 'the eccentric bias of his criticism and its oddly ambivalent relationship at different times in its history with the dominant forms of the critical discourses on the Caribbean has seen his work frequently consigned to the fringe' (Griffiths 1991: 62).

Sometimes, as in Harris's case, a writer's marginalized status within a Caribbean critical tradition is at odds with her/his international reputation and participation in a wider nexus of intellectual exchange. The importance of the 'international' contributions of key Caribbean theorists such as Edouard Glissant, Aimé Césaire, **C.L.R. James** and Wilson Harris are indisputable. However, the powerfully appropriative tendencies of the dominant Western theoretical discourses to which their writings are frequently co-opted need to be recognized. These new hegemonies display, as noted, a tendency to flatten out cultural specificities; more insidiously, they may also act to 'Europeanize' individual theorists by foregrounding their European 'intellectual indentureship' (Wynter 1990: 365), as well as a more specific web of affiliations to Europe. In fact, the interactions between these Caribbean theorists and Western theoretical discourses are always more complex and often less one-way than is usually suggested (Henry and Buhle eds 1992: 62, Griffiths 1991: 67).

One of the most unambiguous and vituperative statements concerning the dynamics between (Caribbean) literature and the critical facility of what Gayatri Chakravorty Spivak terms 'the teaching machine' (Spivak 1993) is Derek Walcott's 'Caligula's Horse' (1989). In mock-theoretical mode, Walcott speaks directly about French (post-structuralist) theories in a coded language:

> the fish are French fish, and off their pages there is the reek of the fishmonger's hands. I have a horror not of that stink, but of the intellectual veneration of rot, because from the far-off reek which I get from the stall of the Academy, there is now a school of fishermen as well as schools of fish, and these fishmongers are interested in examining the disembowelled entrails of poetry, of marketing its guts and surrounding conversation with flies.
>
> (Walcott 1989: 141)

In his explicit refusal of post-structuralism and deconstruction as valuable critical avenues, Walcott actually forces a consideration of how theory can be used in an enabling way in reading post-colonial texts. It is a crucial question and one which is being answered in interesting ways.

Carolyn Cooper's creole critique of the work of Sistren, the Jamaican women's theatre collective, represents one alternative model of Caribbean literary theory. Her conscious code-switching from standard English to creole in order to offer a reading of the text is instrumental in breaking down residual prejudices concerning the suitable role and status of creole. In this way it takes up the same debates which **Mervyn Morris (1967)** situated thirty years earlier in relation to **Louise Bennett's** poetry. However, given the reminder which Hodge (1990) issues concerning the vital function of creole in the lives of Caribbean people (see p. 495), Cooper goes further in order to point out the serious consequences of the virtual exclusion of creole from the realm of academic discourse. Her evaluation *in creole* dramatically foregrounds and participates in the project of replacing a standard eurocentric critical discourse with a creole indigenous one. Her critique seeks to reconfigure the hierarchies of value informing the relationships between the oral and the written, the personal and the political, the creative and the academic, and the serious and the popular: 'plenty a dem who never go a none a Sistren play, dem same one a go read Sistren book, because book high'

(**Cooper 1989**: 56). We would argue that Cooper's important affirmative piece paves the way towards a new stage in Caribbean literature: a critical praxis in creole, even a creole (not just a creolized) theory. It is also interesting that Cooper's piece is animated by questions of gender politics as well as language politics, as this area of enquiry has been particularly lively in the 1990s.

Forging a Caribbean women's poetics

Perhaps the most highly charged debates concerning theoretical models for Caribbean literature have emerged in relation to feminist theory and women's writing. At the close of the 1980s and into the 1990s, there has been a flurry of articles and books addressing the issue of reading and evaluating women's writing from the region.

W.D. Ashcroft's 1989 article, 'Intersecting Marginalities: Post-colonialism and Feminism', traces the parallel and overlapping interests between these two. He offers a breakdown of the analogous features of post-colonialism and feminism under headings such as 'An "Authentic" Language' and 'Writing the Body/Writing Place'. By intimating how these two bodies of knowledge might work alongside each other, Ashcroft seeks to open up spaces for a post-colonial feminism to write itself. Possibly aware of his own position as a Western male critic, he does not suggest how this might proceed but merely that he considers there to be fertile ground as yet uncultivated. Although the tandem model which he offers is useful for establishing common ground, it inevitably reduces the tension between feminist and post-colonial discourses and in doing this overlooks some of the most productive ground which has since been claimed. Ashcroft's mediation between French feminists (Luce Irigaray, Hélène Cixous and Julia Kristeva) and male Caribbean writers and theorists (particularly Wilson Harris) is also problematic, as it effaces the post-colonial woman's voice entirely.

Ketu Katrak's 'Decolonizing Culture: Toward a Theory for Post-colonial Women's Texts' (1989) casts a wide net over India, Africa and pauses in the Caribbean to examine the work of Olive Senior and Sistren. Katrak usefully takes issue with the various temptations to validate, to obfuscate and to circumnavigate post-colonial texts which post-colonial theory can beguile one into. She does not, however, discuss the role which feminist or womanist theory might

[443]

play in an evaluative model. Like Carolyn Cooper, Katrak looks to Sistren in order to locate a culturally specific and resilient creative work. The reading of Sistren's *Lionheart Gal* (1986) may venture a new critical emphasis on the voice and bodies of post-colonial women, but it does not offer a helpful or transferable theoretical model for reading post-colonial women's texts, many of which are neither radically oral nor personal. Perhaps more importantly, the recourse to 'heavy-weight' male thinkers such as Frantz Fanon and Ngugi wa Thiong'o both speaks of and joins in the muffling of women theorists in the process of formulating theories relating to post-colonial women's texts.

The 1990 anthology of pan-Caribbean women's writing, *Her True True Name* edited by Pamela Mordecai and Betty Wilson, takes its title from **Merle Hodge**'s novel *Crick Crack Monkey* (1970). In this text, the young Tee never discovers the 'true, true name' of her great-great-grandmother because of her 'defection' to the europeanized cultural world of her Aunt Beatrice. As this allusion would suggest, the 1990 anthology is designed to recuperate a self-determined cultural identity which is denied to Tee, an identity outside middle-class and European values which the editors describe as 'providing her with roots, a source of goodness, wholeness and reality' (Mordecai and Wilson 1990: xv). To the editors 'The focus of most of the women's writing – especially recent writing – has been on grass roots concerns and ordinary people' (xiii). Yet these proposals for a common agenda for Caribbean women's writing and a single 'true' identity are constraining frameworks which cannot accommodate the diversity of interests and styles represented in the writings collected.

It is interesting to note the relative contentment with which Mordecai and Wilson, and Ashcroft, employ the term 'feminism' alongside the confident exclusion of this term from Katrak's theory for post-colonial women's texts. These critical agendas belie the significant friction which has been generated by the application of Western-oriented feminist theories in readings of Caribbean women's writing. The problems associated with the application of Anglo-American, French and even African-American feminist theory, all of which have been developed in relation to their own specific cultural contexts, clearly need to be negotiated with respect to Caribbean literature. However, there is equally a need to move beyond simply raising questions and problems concerning post-colonial feminism,

an‚ defining this against other models. In the 1980s there remained
little sense of what a theoretical framework for evaluating Caribbean women's writing might look like. In the 1990s there have
been several publications which have addressed this vexed question.
Out of the Kumbla: Caribbean Women and Literature (1990) edited by
Carole Boyce Davies and Elaine Savory Fido, is a comprehensive
volume which surveys different modes of gender-based scholarship,
offering a range of critical approaches and an historical perspective.
Caribbean Women Writers: Essays From the First International Conference
(1990) edited by Selwyn R. Cudjoe is also eclectic, with a section
devoted to discussions by women writers about their own work and
concerns. In this way, it continues an important tradition of representing the Caribbean writer–critic, a tradition dominated by male
writers in earlier decades. **Evelyn O'Callaghan**'s *Woman Version*
(1993) is much more focused on the project of establishing a theoretical framework for a reading of Caribbean women's writing.
However, as O'Callaghan wishes to emphasize:

> I do not attempt to construct a single theoretical model for West
> Indian women's writing but, rather, to suggest the need for plural and
> syncretic theoretical approaches which can take account of the multi-
> plicity, complexity, the intersection of apparently conflicting orienta-
> tions which we find in the writing: approaches which can combine
> heterogeneity and commonality while refusing to be ultimately formal-
> ized under any one 'ism'.
>
> (O'Callaghan 1993: 15)

O'Callaghan terms this foregrounding of plural, syncretic, heteroge-
neous theoretical configuration 'versioning': 'a kind of remix or dub
version, which utilizes elements from the "master tape" of Caribbean
literary discourse' (O'Callaghan, 1993: 11). She encourages readers
not to employ theoretical positions as totalizing grand narratives but
rather to accept the provisional and culturally determined nature of
each and therefore the particular possibilities and limitations which
they present in relation to Caribbean women's writing.

This need for a flexible and fluid model is echoed in Pamela
Mordecai's 'prismatic form' which is capable of envisaging plurality
released from a linear framework (Mordecai 1986). Elaine Savory
Fido's 'image of the crossroads' at which writer and critic stand similarly seeks to endorse the multiple possibilities for making meaning

(Boyce Davies and Savory Fido 1990: 30). All of these models share a preoccupation with exploding the myth of a monolithic master discourse and exploring the intersections and negotiations between various different textual and theoretical strategies. All stress the concepts of plurality, syncretism and creolization which might be perceived as the 'key words' to a Caribbean culture, and all are clearly rooted in this cultural context.

Possibly the most provocative and challenging piece of writing by a Caribbean scholar to seriously contest the appropriation of Caribbean women as 'ideal others' is Sylvia Wynter's essay **'Be-yond Miranda's Meanings: Un/silencing the "Demonic Ground" of Caliban's "Woman" '** (1990). In its refusal to be content with received assumptions and established European ideas, Wynter's piece confirms the strength and insightfulness of her contribution to critical debates concerning Caribbean literature present in her **1968** and **1969** articles on this subject.

Wynter traces how Western Europe's post-sixteenth-century colonization of the New World offered not only a new form and rationale for oppression, but also instigated a crucial shift from anatomy (sex) to physiognomy (race) in the construction of essential otherness. Using the post-colonial Shakespearean text, *The Tempest*, as a textual locale in which to play out the implications of this shift, Wynter points out that 'the most significant absence of all, [is] that of Caliban's Woman, of Caliban's physiognomically complementary mate'. However, her particular line of analysis does not lead her to concur that 'native' women are doubly colonized in relation to the single colonization of European women (a fairly wide-spread formu-lation) but rather that the silencing of this new category of the inferior other 'enables the partial liberation of Miranda's hitherto stifled speech' (Wynter 1990: 363). For Wynter, it is this model of white women's enfranchisement of voice being acquired at the expense of black women's silencing and obliteration which makes the position of feminist thinking so difficult to negotiate within the Caribbean context.

However, as the 'Afterword' to a volume of essays on Caribbean women and literature, Wynter's essay is also attempting to find strate-gies and spaces through which the seemingly textually absent 'native' woman can be spoken of without being spoken for. Locating a posi-tion from which this project can proceed is evidently difficult. Wynter proposes a 'demonic ground' beyond the now consolidated epistemologies (ways of knowing) of both patriarchal and feminist thought. Her argument here is well executed and persuasive, as well as being a defiant demonstration of her ability to 'theory-speak' and of her refusal to be a theory-taker.

Earlier in the century **C.L.R. James** faced, but did not engage with in any sustained way, the problem of taking on a Marxist framework in which class oppression was privileged over that of race. Suitably enough, Sylvia Wynter, whom James described in 1984 as 'second to nobody' (Cumber Dance, 1992: 118) does carefully unravel the politics of eurocentric feminism in such a way as to fully explore the significance of racial difference without denying that gender too makes a 'difference', even within groups which have been primarily defined according to 'race'. Wynter's essay is instructive in illustrating that 'racial' difference cannot be, and should not be, overlooked by a desire for gender 'sameness'. It is an extreme corrective perspective to that offered by Ashcroft (1989), who implies that post-colonial feminism will emerge from the shared concerns of women and post-colonial subjects. The problem with Ashcroft's approach is that it can conflate cultural difference with sexual difference under the banner of alterity, almost implying that one difference is equivalent to the other. Read in the context of this theoretical proposition, Wynter's essay is a genuine attempt to address the bewildering complexity of the intersection between cultural and gender oppression and identities. In this sense, Wynter's critical piece works alongside Caribbean women's creative writing in its assertion of a subjectivity which is 'too complex to be articulated simply by feminist or colonial discourse theories ... which are too often predicated on a belief that the other can easily be understood by the methodologies constructed by the self in order to "discover" difference' (**Donnell 1992**: 51). However, the density of argument which Wynter adopts is a gesture against Western theory, the discourse of which she deliberately takes to extremes in order to force questions about reader accessibility, who can speak and what manner of voice is granted authority (see also **Kincaid**'s very different intervention in the latter debate, Kincaid 1988).

Wynter's model is less accessible and more difficult to apply than the models put forward by **O'Callaghan**, Savory–Fido and Mordecai, although **Cooper**'s work could be read as a response to Wynter's call for a 'theoretical interpretative model' which can '"voice" the hitherto silenced ground of the experience of the "native" Caribbean woman' (1990: 363). Wynter's model might be termed 'meta-theory' (a theoretical discourse which is conscious of the relationship between power and discourse and seeks to make an intervention which disrupts this relationship as Western-owned). Despite its 'difficulty' we believe that Wynter's piece offers an important intellectual framework for reading Caribbean women's writing. Moreover, Wynter's radical dissent from simple formulae and received patterns of interpretation issues a timely and significant reminder to readers of Caribbean literature searching for a theoretical model.

These models of fluid-theory and of meta-theory are important gestures towards a specifically Caribbean women's poetics from within the region. They mark the beginning of a new phase of indigenous theorizing which promises to be both intellectually challenging and enabling. There is a third model of theorizing Caribbean women's writing which also seeks to privilege the nuances and specificities of Caribbean (women's) writing above those of Western theoretical discourse. Moreover, this model of creative theorizing suggests that literary texts are not merely passive recipients of theoretical discourse, but active participants in the acts of negotiating meaning and capable of 'theorizing back' (Slemon and Tiffin 1989: xvii). It is this proposition which **Donnell** explores in her reading of Jamaica Kincaid's *Lucy* (1992). Realigning the hierarchy of meaning which exists between text and theory, Donnell explores how **Kincaid**'s text: 'might help us to understand the limitations of certain theories' (**Donnell 1992**: 45). This new model of a 'literary theory' which gives agency back to the literary has also been explored by Helen Tiffin in her work on Caribbean women's writing (Tiffin 1989, 1992).

This creative response to intellectual orthodoxies is demonstrated in the way in which **Jean Binta Breeze** discusses her own work in answering the question **'Can a Dub Poet be a Woman?'** (1990). Breeze confidently stakes her claim on a traditionally 'male' form, here dub. It is important that she acknowledges her indebtedness to **Louise Bennett** and therefore to a tradition of women's poetry in the Caribbean which is seldom critically attended to. As a female antecedent who 'had broken so totally out of the literary and academic circles of recognition, had forced them to accept her' (**Breeze 1990**: 47), Bennett prefigures Breeze who has similarly worked both outside and against academic expectations in order to erode these. If dub poetry already has a marginal status in the canon of Caribbean literature, then women's dub poetry, with its reclamation of a female body and voice, is particularly difficult to accommodate within canonical boundaries. However, despite its radical initiation as a form, Breeze recognizes that dub is now in danger of becoming a new poetic uniformity 'as constraining in its rhythms as the iambic pentameter' (Breeze 1990: 48). However, she herself in *Spring Cleaning* (1992), and other dub poets such as **Linton Kwesi Johnson** in *Tings and Times* (1991), and **Benjamin Zephaniah** in *City Psalms* (1992) are now experimenting with the form.

In her consideration of critical standards, Breeze hits a particularly sore point of Caribbean literary reception when she discusses the rejection of her first album on the basis that it was 'far too personal and there were too many pieces dealing with love' (Breeze 1990: 48). Not only does this point to the framing of dub as a public, politically committed form, but it also speaks to a wider issue concerning the construction of Caribbean (and other post-colonial) literature as a literature of social and political engagement. As Breeze and other Caribbean writers are aware, the post-colonial subject is constructed to resist rather than to reconcile, to loathe rather than to love. It is a fixed criterion which has led to the neglect of **Una Marson** and many other writers. However it is not a criterion which Breeze has accepted. Her work still retains a strong sense of the personal and she has, like Bennett before her, succeeded in surpassing the narrow biases of academic expectations to realign and broaden the definitions of both personal and political writing. Her poem **'Testament'** demonstrates this redefinition in its affirmation of the domestic and maternal dimensions of women's lives (see **Lorna Goodison**'s **'On Houses'**), and in its celebration of matrilineal continuities in a diasporic context. The poem weaves speech with song, a strategy integral to much performance poetry, but it is a vital and expressive element of Breeze's work to sing (with) the body in a gendered act of reclaiming a body denigrated and erased within the dominant discourse.

New cultural authorities

We have already made the case that Western theory is arguably the most powerful and threatening cultural authority to impact on

Caribbean literature in the late twentieth century. Perhaps one of the most subtle and interesting problems which theory poses for readers of Caribbean literature is the seduction towards the intellectual 'post-colonial' ideal. By this we mean that the Caribbean, with its lived reality of co-presence and comingling, of hybrid and syncretic social and cultural formations, is almost the post-colonial intellectual utopia – an ethical model in which difference is seen as multiple, positive, and creative. This ideal is problematic because it is purely intellectual and not lived. It is certainly true that Caribbean cultural identities and cultural forms are excitingly full of promise in their syncretic and fluid configurations. However, it is also true that this ideal has been limited by certain post-colonial, neo-colonial cultural influences which continue to militate against cultural self-definition in a post-Independence Caribbean.

This is a point which Derek Walcott makes wonderfully in his Nobel prize acceptance speech, **'The Antilles: Fragments of Epic Memory'**:

> The Caribbean is not an idyll, not to its natives. They draw their working strength from it organically, like trees, like the sea almond or the spice laurel of the heights. Its peasantry and its fishermen are not there to be loved or even photographed; they are trees who sweat, and whose bark is filmed with salt, but everyday on some island, root-less trees in suits are signing favourable tax breaks with entrepreneurs, poisoning the sea almond and the spice laurel of the mountains to their roots.
>
> (Walcott 1992: 28–9)

As Walcott intimates, one of the most ubiquitous neo-colonial powers in the contemporary Caribbean is tourism, a profitable industry which many post-colonial governments 'support'. The tourist industry not only perpetuates an economic reliance upon the West, it also perpetuates the manufacture of cultural identities for the Western eye. Under this new cultural authority, Caribbean identities are either the 'smiles and serviettes' model of cruise-ship tourism, or the 'ganga and reggae' model of those on the 'encounter-the-other' trip. Consequently tourism promotes the commodification of cultural identity and of cultural products for outside consumption (see **Mighty Chalkdust 1968**, Kincaid 1988, Rohlehr 1989, and **Zephaniah 1992**).

In other ways, too, the global economy of late capitalism (which drives tourism and the drugs industry) and the global culture of fast food chains and satellite television work against the development of an 'independent' post-colonial Caribbean culture, as they represent: 'a new and more vicious era of cultural penetration' (**Merle Hodge 1990**: 205). However, there is also a sense in which these cultural 'outsiders', whether beamed in or shipped in, are now part of Caribbean culture and it may be the challenge of our time to trace the culture which emerges from the intersection of powerful global influences alongside local movements. The fact that Bermuda elected to remain under British sovereign rule in 1995 usefully disrupted the notion of a post-colonial subject as necessarily resistant. However, it also importantly indicated the need to rethink notions of Caribbean culture by unsettling the idea that decolonization is a central process of post-colonial cultural and political definition.

However, if in the 'post-colonial' 1990s battles over possession of the land have shifted, those over possession of the mind remain vital. With the peddlers of 'dead fish' theory in mind, Walcott's point that 'the imagination is a territory as subject to invasion and seizure as any far province of Empire' (1990: 141) is a reminder of the powerful occupational force of Western epistemologies, which **Wynter** refers to as 'intellectual indentureship' (1990: 365). This problem of intellectual and cultural occupation within the 'post-colonial' era is most fiercely articulated by Merle Hodge in her suggestion of continued 'mental desertion' within the Caribbean. As a writer and academic situ-ated in the Caribbean, **Hodge**'s essay, '**Challenges of the Struggle of Sovereignty**', is a strident and committed argument in support of activist writing, a position which has achieved academic prominence with post-colonial critics such as Edward Said and Gayatri Chakravorty Spivak, who have also sought to reconnect cultural products to the possibilities for political change. Indeed, Hodge draws on images of warfare in order to clearly articulate the power struggles at stake in this battle for cultural ownership: 'in this situation writing becomes for me, a guerrilla activity' (**1990**: 206). She advocates that 'the power of the creative word to change the world is not to be underestimated' (1990: 202) and she discusses the need to develop 'a modern tradition of popular literature' which can bridge the gulf between the educated writer and the audience, a key preoccupation of Caribbean writers throughout the century. This is clearly a prescriptive and polemical piece which offers a limited agenda to Caribbean writers, but which nevertheless addresses with conviction and urgency the problems of audience and of responsibility in the writing of Caribbean literature in the 1990s.

The work of **Benjamin Zephaniah**, a Caribbean-British dub poet, has both the popular base and the political dimension which Hodge calls for. In his **'A Modern Slave Song'**, which admonishes the white audience and reader to 'remember me', Zephaniah sings out against the erasure of a culture and its people. However, the 'yu' and 'I' divide, around which the poem is structured, is not directed from one individual to another. This refrain rehearses the binarism of colonial power structures and calls for an act of cultural re-memorying which allows the human subjects exploited and negated by slavery and indentureship to be 'I's – to claim a presence and identity. The poem makes explicit that the driving ideologies of colonialism (capitalism and self-aggrandizement) remain powerful political realities in the modern world. Zephaniah points to the tourist and music industries as two neo-colonial structures which continue to efface and dispossess black people from their own culture:

> When yu lying on me beach
> Remember I exist
> . . .
> When yu selling me me music
> Remember I exist
> (Zephaniah 1992: 52)

Past, present and future

A consideration of the neo-colonial powers which operate in the Caribbean may appear to point to the inescapable legacies of the colonial experience, both materially and culturally. However, this is not the only lens through which to view the present and future of Caribbean culture and literature. Indeed, many critics would argue that to foreground oppression is to perpetuate the classification of Caribbean literature as simply a literature of opposition. Moving beyond the reactive role, Caribbean writers are now writing for and to each other, outside the context of 'white man's meaning'.

Both **Lawrence Scott (1995)** and **David Dabydeen (1995)** imaginatively excavate a history. Their works could be read as re-staging primal scenes of a cultural imagination, going back and re-inscribing history in order to go forward. Scott's short story revisits the recurrent concern with narratives of childhood in Caribbean literature and explores the complex cultural and familial interrelationships. Dabydeen's piece can be linked to his poetic works which similarly recuperate Indo-Caribbean experience for a written archive and reclaim his ancestry (Dabydeen 1984, 1988, 1994). In Dabydeen's fictional account, the promise of the journey from India to the Caribbean (of economic empowerment and of release from the caste system) achieves neither spiritual nor material fulfilment. This reality is underlined by the barrenness of Rohini whose body is now reduced to commodity status.

A rather different sense of the Indo-Caribbean experience is given by Derek Walcott in his account of the contemporary situation in **'The Antilles: Fragments of Epic Memory' (1992)**. Walcott draws on the experience of witnessing the Hindu *Ramleela* (a dramatization of the *Ramayana*) performed in a small Trinidadian village in order to discuss the cultural complexity of the Caribbean and the relationship with its past. This episode is significant in Walcott's choice of an Indo-Caribbean village and festival as the base from which to theorize his ideas on cultural identities and the relation to history, as few writers have seen this experience as central to these debates. Walcott's position in relation to history is interesting here. He privileges the present and the unconscious (rather than the deliberate) recovery of the ancient, the ancestor and the traditions which are grounded in pre-Caribbean experience. He confesses that as witness he is almost deceived by the conditioned expectations of the Caribbean writer concerning historical loss, but that

I misread the event through a visual echo of history – the cane fields, indenture, the evocation of vanished armies, temples, and trumpeting elephants – when all around me there was quite the opposite ... a delight of conviction, not loss ... I, out of the writer's habit searched for some sense of elegy, of loss, even of degenerative mimicry, in the happy faces.

(Walcott 1992: 6)

This confession is an admission of the constraining expectations which still govern notions of Caribbean experience and culture. It prompts Walcott to reiterate his argument from **'the Muse of**

History' (1974) that: 'we make too much of that long groan which underlines the past' (Walcott 1992: 7–8). The simultaneity of present and past in the performance is grasped by Walcott as indicative of the liberating potential of the Caribbean more generally to free itself of a history characterized only as oppression and loss. Walcott sees 'one of the greatest epics in the world performed not with that desperate resignation of preserving a culture, but with an openness of belief that was as steady as the wind bending the cane lances of the Caroni plain' (Walcott 1992: 7). Indeed, Walcott's emphasis upon openness, process and creolization here perhaps suggests the new status of Caribbean literature as a proactive rather than a reactive tradition of writing. It anticipates a culture of change and of newness which is distinct and yet mongrel, a culture which generates a literature as instructive and inspirational to the rest of the globe as Walcott's poetry itself has been. Walcott's commitment to and affirmation of the Caribbean as a place of emotional possibility and of enormous creative resources is evident in his image of Caribbean culture as a broken vase in which: 'the love that reassembles the fragments is stronger than that love which took its symmetry for granted when it was whole' (Walcott 1992: 9).

The growing impact of the Amerindian population upon the political and cultural life of Guyana is a particularly important fragment which needs to be restored in the reconstruction of Caribbean culture for the 1990s. Readers of Caribbean literature need to revise the blanket historical narrative which suggests that the native peoples of the Caribbean and the Amerindian cultures (Macusi, Arawak, Carib) were totally eradicated in the process of European conquest. Indeed, Amerindians do not simply figure in the literature's mythologies but exist as producers of Caribbean literature (both oral and scribal). The writers Wilson Harris, Pauline Melville, Mark McWatt and the late artist Aubrey Williams are all part Amerindian. The material difficulties of locating and obtaining permission for Amerindian works such as proverbs and prayers are undeniable. However, we are conscious that we have not included any Amerindian works in this Reader, particularly as the repeated omission of such texts is symptomatic of the fact that few Caribbeanists have met Amerindians, or engaged in a serious and scholarly fashion with their languages and literatures. Indeed, the inclusion and understanding of Amerindian texts demands more than the literal journeys into the hinterland of

Guyana. It demands intellectual journeys beyond the conceptions of Caribbean culture and literature founded on readings of non-'native' texts. The fact that Amerindian works are entirely effaced by the Western academic and publishing worlds (the University of the West Indies in Guyana has an Amerindian Research Unit) is clearly an indication of their perpetual reliance on a narrow canon. However, this local literature which is unknown, and perhaps in an intellectual sense unknowable, to metropolitan academics has an interesting status and value in itself. **David Dabydeen** suggests that 'The Amerindians, the most invisible of West Indian peoples, are paradoxically signposts of the future'. For Dabydeen, this future is one which brings a 'recognition that West Indian peoples are not merely creatures of Britain, forged by British cultural values ... [and] an emphasis on the cultural values and practices that survived British colonization' (Dabydeen 1995: 12).

At the time of writing, we are only mid-way through the 1990s and already there have been crucial and invigorating interventions into long-standing debates concerning the literary value, the cultural status, the theoretical apparatus and the future of Caribbean literature. Caribbean literature is a literary tradition shaped by discensus and diversity (geographic, formal, cultural) and it is for us, as readers, to accept and enjoy the fact that it will always exceed its definitions.

Jean Binta Breeze

Testament

sing girl
sing
dere's more to you
dan skin

my fingers witlow
from years of cleaning corners
where brush an dustpan
couldn' reach
same han
use to plait yuh hair
wid pride
oil it thickness
wid hope an dreams
tie it up wid ribbons
of some rainbow future

mi apron was a canvas
all de greases
from rubbin down all yuh bodies
an cooking plenty greens
ah use to smell it
before ah roll it up
tek it to de laundry
smell de action a mi days
de sweat a mi action
mekking likkle time
fi yuh all
an yuh fadda
mekking time
fi a likkle formal prayer
to de heavens
fah dese days ah fine

every thought is a prayer
dat de pot won't bwoil over
while ah pull myself upstairs

[456]

to scrub de bath
dat de cooker
won't start play up
an de smell a gas
come leaking troo
dat someting teacha sey
would register
an yuh all could see a way
to stretch yuh brain
an move yuh han
pas idleness
to de honour a yuh work

ah can feel it
now yuh gettin older
steppin pas my likkle learning
dat yuh tink ah stupid
ah see how yuh fadda
embarrass yuh frens
wid im smell a oil
from de London trains
so yuh now stop bringing dem home

ah don't talk to yuh much no more
outside de house
ah never did have time
to soun de soun
a de madda tongue
or mek mi way wid ease
troo dem drawing room
but in yuh goings girl
don't mind we smell

we memories of back home
we regular Sunday church
in de back a de local hall
we is jus wat we is
watching you grow
into dis place
an ah want yuh to know

dis is yuh own
we done bleed fi it
yuh born here
in de shadow a Big Ben
im strike one
as de waters break
an you come rushing troo

ah don't move far as yuh
is nat mi duty to
an de cole does bad tings
to mi knee
I is ole tree girl
rough outside
wid years of breaking bark
feeling de damp
yuh is seed
burstin new groun

so sing girl
sing
dere's more to you
dan skin

ah see yuh eye turn weh
anytime yuh see mi han
an at my age
ah really kean worry
who ah belch in front a
an if ah see someting good
in a skip
ah know it embarrass yuh
wen ah tek it out
but in dis place
dem trow weh nuff good tings
an waste is someting
drill out a me
from young
we had to save weself
from a shoestring

[458]

to a likkle lef over
an yuh know
how ah keep all yuh tongue sweet
wen ah tun mi han
to mek something special
out a nutten

ah nat trying to mek yuh feel sorry
believe me
ah just want yuh to understan
dat we come as far as we can
an we try to arm yuh
wid all de tings
dat in fi we small way
we could see dat yuh might need
an nat telling yuh look roun
jus

sing girl sing
dere's more to you
dan skin

yuh granmadda
was Nana
mountain strong
fighting pon er piece a lan
she plant er corn
one one
two two
in likkle pool a dirt
between hard cockpit stone
reap big ears
er grata was sharp
use to talk dry corn
to flour
needed for de trail
de long hard journey
carving out somewhere
jus like we come here

we done pay de dues
but don't tink nobody
owe yuh nutten
jus stan yuh groun
is yuh born lan
yuh navel string cut yah

so sing girl sing
dere's more to you
dan skin

(1992)

Benjamin Zephaniah

A Modern Slave Song

When yu cosy in yu house
Remember I exist,
When yu drink expensive drink
Remember I exist,
When yu lying on me beach
Remember I exist,
When yu trying to sell me beans to me
Remember I exist.

When yu loving each other to death
Remember I exist,
When yu selling me me music
Remember I exist,
When yu sell dat cotton shirt
Remember I exist,
When yu interviewing me
Remember I exist.

I was de first inventor – remember
I am black an dread an luv – remember
I am poor but rich, don't mess – remember
I made history – remember.
Yu tried to shut me mouth – remember
Yu studied me an filmed me – remember
Yu spending me money – remember
Yu trying to feget me but remember,
Remember I am trained to not give in,
So don't feget.
Remember I hav studied studying
So don't feget.
Remember where I come from, cause I do.
I won't feget.
Remember yu got me, cause I'll get yu.
I'll mek yu sweat.

(1992)

Mutabaruka

dis poem

dis poem
shall speak of the wretched sea
that washed ships to these shores
of mothers cryin for their
young swallowed up by the sea
dis poem shall say nothin new
dis poem shall speak of time
time unlimited time undefined
dis poem shall call names names
like lumumba kenyatta nkrumah
hannibal akenaton malcolm garvey
haile selassie
dis poem is vex about apartheid racism fascism
the ku klux klan riots in brixton atlanta
jim jones
dis poem is revoltin against 1st world 2nd world
3rd world   division man made decision
dis poem is like all the rest
dis poem will not be amongst great literary works
will not be recited by poetry enthusiasts
will not be quoted by politicians nor men of religion
dis poem is knives bombs guns blood fire
blazin for freedom
yes dis poem is a drum
ashanti mau mau ibo yoruba nyahbingi warriors
uhuru uhuru
uhuru namibia
uhuru soweto
uhuru afrika
dis poem will not change things
dis poem need to be changed
dis poem is a rebirth of a people
arizin awakin understandin
dis poem speak is speakin have spoken
dis poem shall continue even when poets have stopped writin

dis poem shall survive u me it shall linger in history
in your mind
in time   forever
dis poem is time only time will tell
dis poem is still not written
dis poem has no poet
dis poem is just part of the story his-story her-story our-story
      the story still untold
is now ringin talkin irritatin
makin u want to stop it
but dis poem will not stop
dis poem is long cannot be short
dis poem cannot be tamed cannot be blamed
the story is still not told about dis poem
dis poem is old new
dis poem was copied from the bible your prayer book
playboy magazine the n.y. times readers digest
the c.i.a. files the k.g.b. files
dis poem is no secret
dis poem shall be called borin stupid senseless
dis poem is watchin u tryin to make sense from dis poem
dis poem is messin up your brains
makin u want to stop listenin to dis poem
but u shall not stop listenin to dis poem
   u need to know what will be said next in dis poem
      dis poem shall disappoint u
         because
            dis poem is to be continued in your mind
                  in your mind in your mind your mind

                                             (1992)

David Dabydeen

The Counting House

'Plantation Albion not enough,' Rohini fretted as she scrubbed pots and prepared to cook. Waterfrogs croaked like anxious old men cracking and re-cracking their knuckles. Fireflies massed at the pond behind the row of huts, illuminating the surface for no apparent reason. All evening they scratched themselves alight, but the dampness of the air overcame them and they fell into the water to die.

In the early months, at harvest time, she would join the gathering of children at the dam to watch the foreman pour kerosene into a trough running through a patch of cane. He struck a match, the cane-trash kindled and the fields soon blazed. The heat reached a flock of doves nesting in the cane and they scattered upward in a cloud of cinder, leaving their young behind. That was the best time to hunt: the children let loose their slingshots and several birds fell. The fire would roast them thoroughly, and when it was out, the feasting would begin. The cruelty of such scenes once distressed her but she soon grew accustomed to the rituals of cane: fire consuming the trash to make the cane easier to harvest; killing off scorpions and snakes to make it safer to work; cooking birdmeat to fill their bellies. The soil was manured, the cane was planted, the fields were weeded, the cane was harvested, and then the cycle of nurturing and killing began again. The factory's machinery was never idle, crushing, boiling, fermenting, distilling, making sugar and rum, molasses and bagasse. Boatloads of new coolies arrived to clear new fields or to replace those who succumbed to diseases. Many of them died rapidly of the same epidemics, but there was no shortage of ships from India to replenish the workgangs.

She spent the first year in Guiana in a state of exhilaration. She gave herself completely to her domestic tasks, finding time too to work in the manager's kitchen, bringing in her own small sum of money to add to Vidia's wages. At the end of each week she sat with him as he counted and recounted their earnings, organising the coins into separate piles: one to be sent back to India for Finee, the second for his parents, the third for the week's food, the last to be buried under the calabash tree as savings. At the end of five years, when Gladstone would reward him for his service with a free plot of land, he would have accumulated enough to buy wood to build their first home.

'You can wait that long? Five years is long you know?' he asked anxiously, wishing he could make speedier progress by finding extra work to do on the estate, if only the day was twice as long, and the night twice as short. Already he had measured his period of sleep, cutting it down from seven to six to five hours. Five hours affected him though: he barely had strength to chew the food she brought to him in the evening, so swallowed it in lumps – this gave him belly-ache the next day but he grinded his teeth and bore it, for there was a wealth of cane to be cut and if he didn't the rest of the gang would earn his share and overtake him in possessions. Moreover he couldn't please her in that state for he collapsed and slept as soon as he lay on the blanket beside her. No, he would give himself two extra hours on Sunday, to count his money correctly and to make her a baby. She could have the baby on a Sunday – work was slack then because Gladstone, being a Christian, limited it. Even if he wanted to work the two extra hours he would have to do it illegally, in the nearby village where the niggers were so downright lazy they would pay him in corn, or strips of sheep-skin, to help clear pond and canal. But what would happen if Gladstone found out, the niggers being so lazy and yet so envious they could easily tell on him? Licks! One month in jail for breaking the contract of his indenture. He didn't mind the licks, even the shame of it, because no-one ever beat him but his Pa; and licks healed soon-soon. But not jail! One month without wages! Rohini would have to survive on his savings! The jar would be half empty, worms might as well eat the rest. He might as well die and be buried in the ground and spare the money by giving over his body to the worms.

'Five years will go quick-quick,' she said, wanting to relieve his sudden gloom, 'I can wait ten years if you ask me.'

'Ten years? True? You can live ten years in here?' It was a single room in a sequence of rooms, and she could barely rest: the walls were so thin she could hear every grunt and scratch. When rain fell it dripped through holes in the troolie roof, so they had to huddle for days in one small corner, sharing it with ant and cockroach and centipede. The rain swelled the trough outside the logie which served an open toilet and refuse dump for everyone; it overflowed, flooding the yards with worms fat and pink as prawns.

[465]

'Ten years. Twenty even,' she lied, listening supportively as he outlined plans for their future. Afterwards, in bed, she succumbed to him, letting him vent his ambitions, each novel sensation or man-oeuvre marking a further distancing from India and from the past. She was nineteen now, a wife with no-one to shackle her. Without Droopatie, Vidia was even more unprotected, even more obedient to her moods. She knew there was a shortage of women on the plan-tation, that many of his fellow canecutters would scheme with money to bribe her, or with poison to kill him, if only she consented to it. But what could she gain by them, these uncouth coolies who would throw a few coppers her way and expect to devour her in return, then when she had grown shabby and exhausted, put her out to work for other men? She had avoided them from the time they were shep-herded on to the ship in Calcutta, each man squeezing against the next at the narrow hatchways, trying to get below quickly to find the best berth. They had with them all their belongings – lengths of cloth, knives, glass mirrors, brass pots, crude bracelets and coins secreted in the hem of their dhotis, in the lining of their blankets, in their stomachs. She fancied she could tell who had swallowed their wealth for safety – in calm weather they sat on deck with a pleasing look, as if listening to the jewellery jingling in their bellies; when the sea was distressed they clenched their mouths, swallowing and re-swallowing whilst all around the other coolies abandoned their stomachs, colouring the deck with massala, tumeric and dhall. The recruiter had promised romance, comparing it to the story of Lord Bharrat's journey to Dandaka forest to meet his bride, but in the three long months to Guiana and the two long years following she met only with the sickness of greed. That was all there was though, and she might as well find a way of profiting from it. What else could she do, except return to India, to Droopatie's clutch? Here at least she could flatter men or stir them into rage by a mere glance. She could make them forget their sun-baked blistered faces or the jigga eating away their feet. All they wanted was to grow frantic inside her. Although she would not dream of rejecting Vidia for such men, she still tormented him with the prospect of betrayal. She rubbed oils into her skin to keep it fresh and scented. She massaged her breasts and nipples, as Finee had taught her, to encourage growth. Miriam, the nigger maid in Mr Gladstone's house, showed her how to make curls in her hair, like the white ladies in the photographs decorating Mr Gladstone's chamber. Miriam gave her pieces of bright African cloth with which to make headbands. By these means she would goad Vidia into achievement. Why should she walk barefooted all her life with nothing but plain cotton to decorate her body? In exchange for his labour she would maintain her body and make children for him, not many . . . one boy, perhaps another, then she would stop before growing misshapen and outworn.

So why, Rohini brooded as she dabbed oil on the tawa, why was their room still empty after two years? Month succeeded month, gladness hardened and bruised within, her belly soaked up his milk, her breasts stretched in expectancy . . . but these were only false announcements of child. Month succeeded month, one jar filled up, then another, and was corked tight, and was buried under compact ground but all the time her body was slackening and emptying. They called in pandit to pray but there was still no baby, and Miriam gave her bush potions but they might as well be Kumar's doing for they all failed.

It was Kumar who kept awakening her to the guilt of her barrenness. When Vidia had done his counting and settled into bed she made excuses to delay joining him, remembering suddenly some task in the kitchen which she had neglected to complete. She was afraid to sleep for one dream in particular recurred to humiliate her. Lord Rama was leading her through a throng of worshippers, making her pause to allow women to garland her. The air was thick with incense pluming from their mouths. They pressed against her as if to deny her breath and deafen her with their chanting. She felt on the point of collapse when a thousand hands reached to raise her, carrying her like a bier towards a platform which held two thrones, one for Lord Rama, one for his bride. She struggled to escape, summoning Finee to help her but Finee chided her instead for her ingratitude. They deposited her on a platform before a throne embellished with more stones than all of Kumar's stars and a thousand voices urged her to sit, but she would not, ashamed of her simplicity and peasant's clothing. The moles on her face and neck, which she used to pride as ornaments of beauty, became magnified in her own sight. The more they gazed upon her, the more coarse she became, her blemishes evident to all. Lord Rama stood before her, His hands raised over her head in an attitude of benediction. Her eyes fixed on the bangles of light around His wrist, which blinded her to her own

[467]

appearance, but when she was about to yield to His forgiveness, He suddenly slapped her across the mouth, churlishly, like an ordinary bully. The chanting and adulation stopped. She reeled back and fell to the ground. When she recovered and looked out the worshippers had vanished. Only Lord Rama remained, radiant and ordinary. He reached down gently, as if to comfort her, but when she raised her face He slapped her again, drawing blood. The light cracked on his face so that she saw herself in so many fragments bound only by a cord of pain. The edges of broken light sought to cut the cord and shatter her irretrievably. She called out to Finee but no-one answered. She scrambled away from His feet as she had done when the recruiter tried to gather her up from the ground, and she fell from the platform into a garden of stones, where Kumar waited, dying, a slick of venom at the side of his mouth. 'Chamar crab-louse,' he cursed, 'nasty-pokey nimakarran bitch!' accusing her of taking Vidia from him. She ran blindly from him, following the sound of her feet, and she fell into a trough, into a temple of bone, into a white space bound by arches and spirals and columns. It was Kumar's boar, she knew instantly, the stomach of which had been cut open and ransacked; the British seeking nothing but the thrill of degradation, scattering its monumental bones like so many ransacked mosques they had seen in Calcutta, on the way to the emigrants' depot.

(1996)

Lawrence Scott

Mercy

The girl had the week-end off.

Sybil had left the house after putting the pot of split peas soup to boil slowly on the kerosene stove. She left the rice simmering.

Jonathan could not find his mother behind the pall of dark filling the recesses of the porch, the drawing room, dining room and the four bedrooms where he now wandered frantically in from play. Where was she? 'Mummy,' he cried, fleeing the dark corridor from the bedrooms, nothing familiar in his fear. He feared the kitchen's night before the Delco lights brought their weak orange glow, the colour of rum, to the lamps of the cavernous bungalow.

The fear of night. 'Mummy!'

That ultimate fear had not quite descended, it still being that brief twilight when the east side of the house was all in shadow, so that he could not even see his mother's tuberoses which were like the ones in St Joseph's arms in the chapel of The Holy Innocents down the hill. Nor could he see the clumps of palms which were sinister and looked like jumbies, no longer the hiding places for a child's games in the bright sunshine of day time. All was still in shadow, before the transient miracle of fireflies on the gravel avenue of casuarinas which ended in what his mother called, eternity.

Neither was she under the house, that labyrinth of wire clothes' lines with still damp washing; sheets and clammy, long khaki pants his father wore for work.

Then he heard the crunch on the gravel. Sybil had already gone. The watchman had not as yet come. He turned, saw nothing, but continued to hear the rhythmic pace, its ongoing meditation into what he was sure was eternity. Foot steps like in *O'Grady says* . . .

The west side of the house was battered with the last of the shattering sunset which illuminated the sky over the gulf and undulating sugarcane fields of Endeavour Estate like a canvas depicting creation, or God Almighty coming down from heaven on Judgement Day.

His mother was not there, not part of that illumination.

Where was she? 'Mummy!'

The crunch on the gravel was on the other side in the shadows and the increasing darkness. He didn't know who it was.

Down the gravel gap he saw the last of the servants making their way home to the overseers' bungalows, pushing their prams and pulling along the toddlers. He heard their cries, and the little ones breaking away from one last game of *Brown girl in the ring, tralalala, brown girl in the ring tralalala ... she looks like a sugar and a plum plum plum* ... the little ring of children in best frocks and sun suits.

'Mummy, mummy, where are you?' He hoped that his cry from where he was hidden, and even he thought, lost for a moment amidst the clammy washing, which, except for the damp, his mother liked to call the hole of hell, or the black hole of Calcutta, preferring the servants to go down there, would reach her wherever she was. Hell smelt of oil where his father's landrover dripped oil at the entrance on the concrete.

But it smelt mostly of washing and scrubbing boards and tubs and blue soap and Mercy's body, bent like a crooked stick over the ironing board. Mercy could not bend her legs. She stood stock still on them. She had to raise them one by one to walk as if they were perpetually in splints. Had she tried to heed the words of the gospel? *Take up your bed and walk, and come follow me.* She walked like this every week day from Hope village along the pitch road in the heat, and then up the gravel gap from the Chiney shop to do the washing and the ironing at the manager's house of Endeavour Estate. She could not get up the back stairs and so was sentenced to the thraldom of hell, or the black hole of Calcutta, both for work and her breakfast of bread and butter and hot cocoa-tea. Here she left her smell, her work clothes hanging on a rusty nail. '*Nigger sweat*', the child had heard others call it. Sweat and blue soap. There was the smell of ironing on damp clothes and starch still sticky in an old chipped, blue rimmed, enamel basin. Light into hell came through the west lattice which filtered in streams of God's creation setting.

Still, he could not find his mother. 'Mummy, mummy, where are you?'

'Darling, I'm here.' And, for a moment, it sounded like she was playing hide-and-seek with him, come and get me I'm here, hiding in the clumps of palms, which he was sure had now completely disappeared, or turned into those whispering presences he saw out of his bedroom window when he looked out before getting into bed to check that no one from the barrack rooms was shinnying up the bathroom pipes to steal or murder.

His father refused to believe the house could be broken into by the *coolies*. Though they, the grown ups, said, '*Can't trust a coolie*', when they clinked ice on glasses of rum and soda on evenings when the sun went down and uncles and aunts came to visit from town, or, now and then, English people from the company came for drinks, '*Trust a nigger any day, lazy breed, never trust a coolie.*'

There were no visitors this evening.

Jonathan followed the direction of his mother's voice away from the crunch on the gravel, wondering about those *O'Grady* steps which went on and on into eternity, coming back on themselves. Could you do that? Go into eternity and come back? Jesus was only coming back to take us all to him, the penny catechism said. By now he wished that his mother would be there where he could find her.

Her voice came from the kitchen and he ventured through the pantry into the darkness. 'Where are you? Where are you?'

'My pet.'

Then he saw her standing over the stove.

'The girl's off for the weekend.' She was standing over a pot of split peas soup, stirring. Rice was boiling away in another pot. He went and stood beside her, feeling safe after the run back from the Eccles where he used to play after school. Where was his father? 'Where is dad?'

She continued to stir, and then she looked at him, and then at the dirty wall of the kitchen. 'He's outside, poor dear, he's wrestling with the devil.' She stirred and he continued to stand next to her. 'You mustn't annoy your father, poor darling, he's in such a torment. I'm sure it's the devil. It can't be anything else but evil and the devil trying to dissuade him from the faith.'

Suddenly, they saw each other vividly. But with their shadows grotesquely enlarged and looming over them on the wall. They felt their presences beyond them. The Delco had been turned on at the Eccles. They could hear the drone of the generator across the sugar-cane fields. It brought a sudden illumination, revealing them and their dark selves, enlarged like on a film screen. 'Run along and have a shower. Get dressed before supper, shoes and socks and a shirt, don't annoy your father. Poor darling.'

Jonathan turned on the light of his bedroom and looked out of the window where he could hear his father pacing up and down outside along the gravel avenue of casuarina trees ending in darkness and eternity. Looking out from his lit room, the darkness was more tangible. He saw his father in the darkness when he turned the bedroom light off, but he could not see the devil.

He whipped his clothes off for a shower, hurriedly tying a towel around his waist and ran into the kitchen. 'Mummy I can't see the devil and dad is walking all alone in the darkness outside.'

'Don't come near this stove in your nakedness. Watch that towel. Now take care and leave the kitchen, go and wash and bathe yourself before supper. Leave your father alone. You should know better, knowing your catechism the way you do, that you can't see the devil, but that does not mean he doesn't exist.' She turned to the sink by the window. Then, the scream of her child wrenched her round once more to face him, where he stood next to the stove yelling. His face contorted with absolute terror.

'Mummy, mummy, mummy,' Jonathan stood and bawled and stamped up and down, the pot of boiling rice had tipped over his right shoulder and down the side of his body and right leg, the sticky rice clinging to his skin. His face was burnt.

'Darling, my pet,' she brushed off, and picked the pearly grains off his skin, pulling the naked child close to her, his sobs and screams smothered in her lap. 'What have you done? That stupid girl, Sybil, leaving the handle sticking out.'

She could see the immediate inflammation and the blisters puckering the child's soft skin.

Then he fainted. The last words he heard his mother saying, were, 'Offer it up, dear,' And then, 'That stupid girl, Sybil.'

Jonathan lay in bed. A white cotton sheet was pulled up over his naked body, tented by a small table which straddled his legs, so the sheet would not touch the blisters. He was burnt down the right side: thigh, leg and face livid, distended with water blisters. He lay under the cotton sheet naked from the waist down.

It seemed that he had to lie like this for an eternity.

The doctor came in the morning. He heard his steps crunching on the gravel. He came to break the water blisters. 'Offer it up, now, dear,' his mother said.

Mercy came into the gravel yard lifting up her legs. Her steps had another rhythm and she never came up the back stairs. She could not lift the legs like splints. She stayed below, in hell, that black hole of Calcutta. One day, she called from under the window. 'You up there, Mister Jonathan? God bless you child. I bring you some sugar-cake. Sybil go bring it up for you.'

'Yes Mercy,' He did not know whether she heard him from where he lay on his back. 'Thanks, Mercy.'

In the evening there were no more beams of light filtered through the jalousies, and he could not see the tip tops of the flowering palmiste because their green was now part of the darkness. A cool evening breeze came through the window at the same time that his mother came in smelling of eau de cologne. She patted his forehead with her hanky. He inhaled her.

Then he heard the watchman coming up the gap. He knew the steps.

But still he heard the pacing steps of his father wrestling with the devil, he presumed. He hardly saw him. He would stick his head around the bedroom door. 'You okay old man?' Why did he call him, old man? He was the old man.

His mother sat in the evening by his bed to read stories and fed him egg custard. She left when Sybil rang the brass bell for supper. 'Sleep well, dear.' She made the sign of the cross on his forehead with her thumb.

Weeks went by. Would he get better? He would have a scar for life.

Then, one afternoon, the steps on the pitchpine floor were unfamiliar. They were like someone humping furniture across the drawing room. He had dozed off. The house creaked. The wind whistled outside. Still the hump, thump across the drawing room, like someone carrying a bed. His mother was having her siesta. His father was out. He listened as the steps came closer. He thought of the devil who fought with his father, the devil was coming up from his mother's hell.

The steps stopped. He knew someone was at the door. He heard heavy breathing. But lying, looking up at the ceiling where the mosquito net was tied up, he smelt her, the smell of blue soap. He turned his head on the pillow. She was standing holding on to the door.

'Mister Jonathan.'

'Mercy!'

'Yes, is me, boy.'

'You've climbed the stairs, Mercy?'

'So long I not see you, child. I call. You hear me call under the window?'

'Yes Mercy, I hear you calling me. I call back. You didn't hear me?'

'You voice small, child. And I getting deaf.' She scratched the inside of her left ear with her index finger. She was bending over the child lying in the bed. On his forehead he saw beads of fresh sweat, beads like his mother's crystal rosary.

'Thanks for the sugarcake, Mercy.' She smiled and leant over him smelling of coconut milk.

'Let me see your scar.' She folded back the white cotton sheet, and he was shy because she could see his *totee*. She smiled, recognising his shyness. 'I have boy children too, Mister Jonathan, I see my little boy's *totee*. You lucky the boiling rice didn't burn it off.' She joked and laughed. Jonathan stared up at the ceiling, the thought of what might have happened, dawning, and the realisation as big as the afternoon sky outside. 'Don't be fraid, don't be shy,' and she traced her bony finger round the edges of the largest burn on his thigh. It tickled and itched. With her other hand she dabbed her neck with a cotton kerchief which smelt of her fresh sweat and bay rum. She patted his brow with it. It made him feel better.

'Take care, child.' Mercy turned, lifting her legs like sticks and humped them like heavy furniture across the room, disappearing around the door.

'You going to come back up the stairs again, Mercy?'

'No need child, no need,' her voice echoed and faded as she humped and thumped across the pitchpine floor. There was a thunder in the tread of her retreat down the back stairs.

The geography of Jonathan's scars shifted and set. They faded on his arms and legs. The small one on his face disappeared. Only where Mercy had traced her finger, only that jagged map of puckered pink on his thigh, remained.

When he went out to play again, his scar was hidden under his khaki pants. But, when in secrecy, he looked down at it, noticing what a close shave he had had, he always smelt Mercy's fresh sweat and the bay rum from her hanky. It tickled and itched where Mercy had etched out his scar with her finger.

His father too, had stopped wrestling with the devil.

And now the house smells of coconut milk all the time.

(1995)

Sylvia Wynter

Beyond Miranda's Meanings: Un/silencing the 'Demonic Ground' of Caliban's 'Woman'

The point of departure of this *After/Word* is to explore a central distinction that emerges as the dynamic linking sub-text of this, the first collection of critical essays written by Caribbean women. This distinction is that between Luce Irigaray's purely Western assumption of a universal category, 'woman', whose 'silenced' ground is the condition of what she defines as an equally universally applicable, 'patriarchal discourse', and the dually Western and post-Western editorial position of a projected 'womanist/feminist' critical approach as the unifying definition of the essays that constitute the anthology. The term 'womanist/feminist', with the qualifying attribute 'womanist' borrowed from the Afro–American feminist Alice Walker, reveals the presence of a contradiction, which, whilst central to the situational frame of reference of both Afro-American and Caribbean women writers/critics, is necessarily absent from the situational frame of reference of both Western-European and Euro-american women writers. Thus whilst at the level of the major text these essays are projected within the system of inference-making of the discourse of Feminism, at the level of the sub-text which both haunts and calls in question the presuppositions of the major text, the very attempt to redefine the term *feminist* with the qualifier 'womanist', expresses the paradoxical relation of Sameness and Difference which the writers of these essays, as members of the Caribbean women intelligentsia, bear to their Western European and Euro-american peers . . .

The central point I want to make in this After/Word is that the contradiction inserted into the consolidated field of meanings of the ostensibly 'universal' theory of feminism by the variable '*race*', and explicitly expressed by the qualifiers of 'womanist' and 'cross-roads situation', of these essays points toward the emergent 'downfall' of our present 'school like mode of thought' and its system of 'positive knowledge' inherited from the nineteenth century and from the Industrial epoch of which it was the enabling mode of rationality and participatory epistemology[1]; and that it does this in the same way as feminist theory itself had earlier inserted the contradiction of the variable *gender* into the ostensibly 'universal' theories of Liberal Humanism and Marxism–Leninism² . . .

For with Western Europe's post-medieval expansion into the New World (and earlier into Africa), and with its epochal shift out of primarily *religious* systems of legitimation, and behaviour – regulation, her peoples' expropriation of the land/living space of the New World peoples was to be based on the secular concept of the 'non-rational' inferior, *'nature'* of the peoples to be expropriated and governed; that is, of an ostensible difference in 'natural' substance which, for the first time in history was no longer *primarily* encoded in the male/female gender division as it has been hitherto in the symbolic template of all traditional and religiously based human orders, but now in the cultural-physiognomic variations between the dominant expanding European civilization and the non-Western peoples that, encountering, it would now stigmatize as 'natives'. In other words, with the shift to the secular, the primary code of difference now became that between 'men' and 'natives', with the traditional 'male' and 'female' distinctions now coming to play a secondary – if none the less powerful – reinforcing role within the system of symbolic representations, Lévi-Strauss's totemic schemas,³ by means of which, as governing charters of meaning, all human orders are 'altruistically' integrated.⁴

Nowhere is this mutational shift from the primacy of the *anatomical* model of sexual difference as the referential model of *mimetic* ordering, to that of the *physiognomic* model of racial/*cultural* difference, more powerfully enacted than in Shakespeare's play *The Tempest*, one of the foundational endowing⁵ texts both of Western Europe's dazzling rise to global hegemony, and at the level of human 'life' in general, of the mutation from primarily religiously defined modes of human being to the first, partly secularizing ones. Whilst on the other hand, both mutations, each as the condition of the other, are nowhere more clearly put into play than in the relations between Miranda the daughter of Prospero, and Caliban, the once original owner of the island now enslaved by Prospero as a function of the latter's expropriation of the island. That is, in the relations of enforced dominance and subordination between Miranda, though 'female', and Caliban, though 'male'; relations in which *sex-gender attributes* are no longer the primary index of 'deferent' difference,⁶ 'and in which the discourse that erects itself is no longer primarily 'patriarchal', but rather 'monarchical' in its Western-European, essentially post-Christian, post-religious definition. Therefore, in whose context of behaviour-regulatory inferential system of meanings, as the essential condition of the mutation to the secular, Caliban, as an incarnation of a new category of the human, that of the subordinated 'irrational' and 'savage'[7] *native* is now constituted as the lack of the 'rational' Prospero, and the now capable-of-rationality Miranda, by the Otherness of his/its *physiognomic* 'monster' difference, a difference which now takes the *coding* role of sexual-anatomical difference, with the latter now made into a mimetic parallel effect of the former, and as such a member of the *set* of differences of which the former has now become the primary 'totemic-operator'[8] . . .

And here, we begin to pose in this context a new question . . . This question is that of the most significant absence of all, that of Caliban's Woman, of Caliban's physiognomically complementary mate. For nowhere in Shakespeare's play, and in its system of image-making, one which would be foundational to the emergence of the first form of a secular world system, our present Western world system, does Caliban's mate appear as an alternative sexual-erotic model of desire; as an alternative source of an alternative system of meanings. Rather there, on the New World island, as the only woman, Miranda and her mode of physiognomic being, defined by the philogenically 'idealized' features of straight hair and thin lips is canonized as the 'rational' object of desire; as the potential genitrix of a superior mode of human 'life', that of 'good natures' as contrasted with the ontologically absent potential genitrix – Caliban's mate . . .

To put it in more directly political terms, the absence of Caliban's woman, is an absence which is functional to the new secularizing schema by which the peoples of Western Europe legitimated their global expansion as well as their expropriation and their marginalization of all the other population-groups of the globe, including, partially, some of their own national groupings such as, for example, the Irish[9] . . .

In consequence if, before the sixteenth century, what Irigaray terms as *'patriarchal discourse'* had erected itself on the 'silenced ground' of women, from then on, the new primarily silenced ground (which at the same time now enables the partial liberation of Miranda's hitherto stifled speech), would be that of the majority population-groups of the globe – all signified now as the 'natives'

(Caliban's) to the 'men' of Prospero and Fernando, with Miranda becoming both a co-participant, if to a lesser *derived* extent, in the power and privileges generated by the empirical supremacy of her own population; and as well, the beneficiary of a mode of privilege unique to her, that of being the metaphysically invested and 'idealized' object of desire for all classes (Stephano and Trinculo) and all population-groups (Caliban).[10]

This therefore is the dimension of the contradictory relation of Sameness and Difference, of orthodoxy and heresy which these Caribbean critical essays must necessarily, if still only partially, inscribe, and inscribe with respect to the theory/discourse of feminism, (as the latest and last variant of the Prospero/Miranda ostensibly 'universally' applicable meaning and discourse-complex); the relation of *sameness* and *difference* which is expressed in the diacritical term '*womanist*'. And if we are to understand the necessity for such an *other* term (projected both from the perspective of Black American women (U.S.) and from that of the 'native' women intelligentsia of the newly independent Caribbean ex-slave polities) as a term which, whilst developing a fully articulated theoretical/interpretative reading model of its own, nevertheless, serves, diacritically to draw attention to the insufficiency of all existing theoretical interpretative models, both to 'voice' the hitherto silenced ground of the experience of 'native' Caribbean women and Black American women as the ground of Caliban's woman, and to de-code the system of meanings of that other discourse, beyond Irigaray's patriarchal one, which has imposed this mode of silence for some five centuries, as well as to make thinkable the possibility of a new 'model' projected from a new 'native' standpoint, we shall need to translate the variable 'race', which now functions as the intra-feminist marker of difference, impelling the dually 'gender/beyond gender' readings of these essays, out of the epistemic 'vrai'[11] of our present order of 'positive knowledge',[12] its consolidated field of meanings and order-replicating hermeneutics. Correspondingly, this order/field is transformative, generated from our present purely secular definition of the human on the model of a natural organism, with, in consequence this organism's 'ends' therefore being ostensibly set extra-humanly, by 'nature' . . . we shall need to move beyond this founding definition, not merely to *another* alternative one, non-consciously put in place as our present definition, but rather to a frame of reference which parallels the 'demonic models' posited by physicists who seek to conceive of a vantage point outside the space-time orientation of the humuncular observer ... The possibility of such a vantage point, we argue, towards which the diacritical term 'womanist' (i.e. these readings as both gender, and not-gender readings, as both Caribbean/Black nationalist and not-Caribbean/Black nationalist, Marxian and not-Marxian readings)[13] point can only be projected from a 'demonic model' generated, parallely to the vantage point/demonic model with which the laity intelligentsia of Western Europe effected the first rupture of humans with their/our supernaturally guaranteed narrative schemas of origin,[14] from the situational 'ground' or slot of Caliban's woman, and therefore of her systemic behaviour regulatory role or function as the ontological 'native/nigger', within the motivational apparatus by means of which our present model of being/definition-of-the-human is given dynamic 'material' existence, rather than from merely the vantage point of her/our gender, racial, class or cultural being.[15] In other words, if the laity intelligentsia of Western Europe effected a mutation by calling in question its own role as the ontological Other of 'natural fallen flesh' to the theologically idealized, post-baptismal Spirit (and as such incapable of attaining to any knowledge of, and mastery over, either the physical processes of nature or its own social reality, except such knowledge was mediated by the then hegemonic Scholastic *theological* interpretative model), and by calling this role in question so as to clear the ground for its own self-assertion which would express itself both in the political reasons-of-state humanism (enacted in *The Tempest*), as well as in the putting in place of the *Studia Humanitatis* (i.e. as the self-study of 'natural man'), and in the laying of the basis for the rise of the natural sciences,[16] it is by a parallel calling in question of our 'native', and most ultimately, nigger women's role as the embodiment to varying degrees of an ostensible 'primal' human nature. As well, challenging our role as a new 'lay' intelligentsia ostensibly unable to know and therefore to master our present sociosystemic reality, (including the reality of our 'existential weightlessness' as an always 'intellectually indentured'[17] intelligentsia), except as mediated by the theoretical models generated from the vantage point of the 'normal' intelligentsia, clears the ground for a new self-assertion ... In effect, rather than only voicing the 'native' woman's hitherto silenced voice[18] we shall ask: What is the systemic function of her own silencing, both as women and, more totally, as 'native'

[480]

women? Of what mode of speech is that absence of speech both as women (masculinist discourse) and as 'native' women (feminist discourse) as imperative function? . . .

(1990)

NOTES

1 For the concept of 'participatory epistemology' see Francisco Varela, *Principles of Biological Autonomy* (New York, North Holland Series in General Systems Research, 1979).

2 At the theoretical level 'feminist' theory developed on the basis of its rupture with the purely economic and class-based theory of Marxism, thereby calling into question both the 'universalisms' of Marxian Proletarian identity and of the Liberal humanist 'figure of man'.

3 See C. Lévi-Strauss, *Totemism* (Harmondsworth: Penguin, 1969).

4 See J.F. Danielli, 'Altruism: The Opium of the People', *Journal of Social and Biological Structures* 3, no. 2 (April 1980): 87–94.

5 See D. Halliburton, 'Endowment, Enablement, Entitlement: Toward A Theory of Constitution' in *Literature and the Question of Philosophy*, ed. A.J. Cascari (Baltimore: John Hopkins University Press, 1986) where he develops this concept of 'endowment'.

6 A play on the Derridean concept of 'difference' where the temporal dimension is replaced by the stratifying/status dimension, making use of the concept of 'deferent' behaviour which functions to inscribe difference, and to constitute 'higher' and 'lower' ranking.

7 See in this respect, the book by Jacob Pandian, *Anthropology and the Western Tradition: Towards an Authentic Anthropology* (Prospect Heights, Illinois: Waveland Press, Inc., 1985).

8 See for an excellent analysis of this concept, the book by Claude Jenkins, *The Social Theory of Claude Lévi-Strauss*, (London: The Macmillan Press Ltd, 1979).

9 Recent work by political scientists have begun to focus on the parallels between the discourses by means of which the New World Indians were expropriated and those by which the Cromwellian conquest and partial occupation of Ireland were also legitimated i.e. by the projection of a 'by nature difference' between the dominant and the subordinated population groups.

10 The sailors' dream too, is to be king on the island and to marry Miranda.

11 The term is used by Foucault in his talk, 'The Order of Discourse' given in December 1970 and published as an Appendix of the *Archaeology of Knowledge* (New York: Harper and Row, tr. A.M. Sheridan-Smith, 1972). Here Foucault notes that Mendel's findings about genetic heredity were not hearable at first because they were not within the 'vrai' of the discipline at the time.

12 In *The Order of Things*, Foucault points out that because 'Man' is an object of 'positive knowledge' in Western Culture, he cannot be an 'object of science'.

13 The force of the term *womanist* lies in its revelation of a perspective which can only be *partially* defined by any of the definitions of our present hegemonic theoretical models.

[481]

14 With respect to the functioning of the narrative of origins in human orders, including the 'evolutionary' narrative of origin of our own which also functions as 'replacement material for genesis', see Glyn Isaacs, 'Aspects of Human Evolution' in D.S. Bendall, ed., *Evolution from Molecules to Men* (Cambridge University Press, New York, 1983), pp. 509–43.

15 The contradiction here is between 'cultural nationalism' i.e. the imperative to revalue one's gender, class, culture and to constitute one's literary counter-canon, and the scientific question. What is the function of the 'obliteration' of these multiple perspectives? What role does this play in the stable bringing into being of our present human order?

16 See Walter Ullman, op. cit. and Hans Blumenberg, op. cit. as well as Kurt Hubner, *The Critique of Scientific Reason* (Chicago: University of Chicago Press, 1983), for the linkage of the rise of the natural sciences to the overall secularizing movement of humanism.

17 The term is Henry Louis Gates's, and is central to the range of his work. See for example, his use of a variant of this term ('interpretative indenture') in his essay, 'Authority (White) Power and the (Black) Critic' in *Cultural Critique*, Fall 1987, no. 7. pp. 19–46.

18 In a paper given as a panel presentation at the 1988 March West Coast Political Science Conference, Kathy Ferguson of the University of Hawaii pointed to the contradiction, for feminist deconstructionists, between the imperative of a fixed gender identity able to facilitate a unifying identity from which to 'voice' their presence, and the deconstructionist program to deconstruct gender's oppositional categories.

Carolyn Cooper

Writing Oral History:
Sistren Theatre Collective's Lionheart Gal

Lionheart Gal: Life Stories of Jamaican Women is an experiment in narrative form that exemplifies the dialogic nature of oral/scribal and Creole/English discourse in Jamaican literature. For *Lionheart Gal* is dialogic in the old-fashioned, literal sense of that word: the text, with three notable exceptions, is the product of a dialogue in Creole and English between each woman of Sistren and Honor Ford Smith, the sister confessor, who herself confesses all in solitary script, immaculate in English.

In the fashionably modern, Bakhtinian sense of the word dialogic, *Lionheart Gal* is impeccably subversive. For it engenders an oral, Creole subversion of the authority of the English literary canon. Further, its autobiographical form – the lucid verbal flash – articulates a feminist subversion of the authority of the literary text as fiction – as transformative rewriting of the self in the *persona* of distanced, divine omniscience. *Lionheart Gal*, like much contemporary feminist discourse, does not pretend to be authoritative. Indeed, the preferred narrative mode of many feminist writers is the guise of intimate, understated domestic writing by women: letters, diaries or what Sistren, in an oral, Creole context, simply calls testimony. The simultaneously secular and religious resonances of 'testimony' intimate the potential for ideological development from the purely personal to the political that is the usual consequence of this process of communal disclosure.

It is important to distinguish between actual letters and diaries written by women, and the literary use of this sub-genre as fictional frame. For the artifice of these feminist narrative forms is that they are artless, the author having receded in Joycean detachment to pare, and perhaps paint her fingernails, leaving the tape-recorder or word-processor on automatic . . .

With *Lionheart Gal* this feminist illusion of narrative artlessness is complicated by the mediating consciousness of Honor Ford Smith, the editorial persona who performs a dual function in the making of the text. As testifier, Honor records her own story in 'Grandma's Estate'. As amanuensis, she transcribes the testimonies of the other

[483]

Sistren (except for 'Ava's Diary' and 'Red Ibo'), shaping the women's responses to her three leading questions: 'How did you first become aware of the fact that you were oppressed as a woman? How did that experience affect your life? How have you tried to change it?' . . .

Editorial intervention in the making of the text is clearly an important issue in *Lionheart Gal*. Evelyn O'Callaghan argues that 'the life stories related in *Lionheart Gal* stand somewhere *between* fiction and research data. These stories have been so shaped by selection, editing, rewriting and publication that they have become to a large extent . . . "fictionalized"'. As editor, Honor seems to doctor the text – less in the pejorative sense of that word and more in the sense of obstetrician. This metaphor signifies both the active creativity of the labouring woman telling her story, and the somewhat more passive efficiency of the enabling mid-wife dilating the passage of the text. This distinction between text and story, between ideological necessity and narrative autonomy, is central to the problem of authorship and authority in *Lionheart Gal* . . . .

As story, *Lionheart Gal* is for the most part clearly oral. The language of narration is Creole, employing proverb, earthy metaphors and folk tale structures, particularly repetition and apparent digression. In addition, the rural setting of many of the stories reinforces the sense of a 'folk' perspective. The life stories illustrate what Derek Walcott calls the 'symmetry' of the folk tale: 'The true folk tale concealed a structure as universal as the skeleton, the one armature from Br'er Anancy to King Lear. It kept the same digital rhythm of three movements, three acts, three moral revelations.' In the case of *Lionheart Gal*, narrative structure is shaped by Honor's three informing questions which compress female experience into riddle. Decoding the riddle is the key to identity and the moral of the fable.

As text, *Lionheart Gal* somewhat ironically affirms the authority of the written word. Documenting the ideological development of the women of the Sistren Theatre Collective cannot, apparently, be fully accomplished in the medium of theatre. The plays do not adequately speak for themselves: thus the scribal intention of the original project. Further, the search for what Honor calls a 'throughline for each story' (p. xxviii) superimposes on these misbehaving oral accounts a decidedly scribal narrative necessity. The circular line of oral narration becomes diametrically opposed to the ideological, scribal throughline . . .

This oral/scribal contradiction is quintessentially Creole/English . . .

Recognising the dialogic nature of oral/scribal and Creole/English discourse in the story/text *Lionheart Gal* and seeking to narrow the social distance between the language of the stories and the language of textual analysis, I wish to engage in an experimental Creole subversion of the authority of English as our exclusive voice of scholarship. My analysis of the testimonies of the women of Sistren – their verbal acts of introspective self-disclosure – will now proceed in Creole.

'We come together and talk our life story and put it in a lickle scene' (p. 72). A so Ava seh Sistren start off: a tell one anodder story. So yu tell, me tell, so tell di whole a we find out seh a di one story we a tell. Oman story. Di same ting over an over. But it no easy fi get up tell people yu business ma! It tek plenty heart. So Foxy seh eena fi her story. She seh:

> Plenty women used to talk bout di children dat we have and di baby-faada problem. At first me was shy to talk about myself. Di impression women always give me is dat dem is a set of people who always lap dem tail, tek yuh name spread table cloth. Mer did feel sort a funny at di time, having children fi two different man, especially since me never like Archie. Me never discuss it wid nobody. When me come meet Didi and hear she talk bout her baby faada and how she hate him after she get pregnant, me say, 'Well if yuh can say your own me can say mine, for we actually deh pon di same ting.' Me and she start talk bout it.
>
> (p. 253)

An a di same Foxy she come find out seh dat di tings dem dat happen to we jus because we a oman, dem deh tings supposin fi call 'politics', jus like any a di odder big tings deh, weh a gwan enna 'politricks' as di one Tosh him seh. Den wat a way dem kill him off ee! Me no know if a big Politics dat, or a lickle politics, but someting mus eena someting. But dat is anodder story. An di ile dat fry sprat cyaan fry jack, so small fry all like me no suppose fi business eena dem deh tings.

So hear how Foxy seh she start fi find out bout dis oman politics:

> Tings develop so-till we start meet more people and talk bout woman and work and woman and politics. We discuss what is politics and how it affect woman. After we done talk ah get to feel dat di little day-to-day tings dat happen to we as women, is politics too. For instance, if

yuh tek yuh pickney to hospital and it die in yuh hand – dat is politics. If yuh do someting to yuh own child dat damage him or her fi di future, dat is politics. If yuh man box yuh down, dat is politics. But plenty politicians don't tink dose tings have anything to do wid politics.

(p. 253)

A true. For yu cyaan understan 'di little day-to-day tings dat happen to we as women' if yu no understan seh dat di whole ting set up gainst plenty oman from di day dem born. Tek for instance how so much a di oman dem weh a tell dem story eena *Lionheart Gal* jus find out seh dem pregnant. Yes! It come een like a big surprise. Grab bag. A no nuttin dem plan for. A no like how yu hear dem people pon radio and t.v. a tell yu seh 'Two is better than too many' – like seh pickney is sums: add an multiply an divide an subtract! Wear yu down to nuttin. Nought. Dat a weh pregnant do plenty oman. Not even oman good. Young gal. Force ripe an blighted ...

A so it go. *Lionheart Gal* is a serious book. An oonu better read it. It might a lickle hard fi ketch di spellin fi di first, but after yu gwan gwan, it not so bad. Den one ting sweet me: Yu know how some a fi we people simple; from dem see sinting set down eena book dem tink it important. So now plenty a dem who never go a none a Sistren play, dem same one a go read Sistren book, because book high. Dem a go get ketch. For a six a one, half a dozen a di odder: oman problem, man problem, pickney problem. Plenty politics. An whole heap a joke! For yu know how we know how fi tek bad tings mek joke. Stop yu from mad go off yu head. Doreen know how it go. Hear her nuh:

> All my life, me did haffi act in order to survive. Di fantasies and ginnal-ship were ways of coping wid di frustration. Now me can put dat pain on stage and mek fun a di people who cause it.

Go deh, Sistren! Last lick sweet.

(1989)

Alison Donnell

Dreaming of Daffodils:
Cultural Resistance to the Narratives of Theory

Many critics have pointed to Jamaica Kincaid as one of the most innovative and interesting of contemporary Caribbean writers, and there have been several articles engaging with her fiction through contemporary literary theory ... I wish to shift the critical axis away from the application of theory to Kincaid's writing, in order to explore the way in which her writing itself could be seen as an alternative theory, a 'literary' theory which questions the assumptions within orthodox modes of interpretation, including feminist and psychoanalytical models. In other words, my interest lies with the ways in which post-colonial literature might help us to understand the limitations of certain theories, rather than with the ways in which theory can help us to understand post-colonial literature ...

As a focus for my reading of Kincaid's creative theoretical strategies, I wish to look at the way in which she problematises and theorizes popular cultural and intellectual narratives of the late twentieth century by rehearsing them through the eyes of Lucy, her latest Caribbean female protagonist in the novel of that name ...

For Lucy, her arrival in the United States is not to be the entry into Eden, or opportunity for personal genesis, which she had anticipated. Instead, she enters a land which is situated, both seasonally and morally, after the fall. America, in its wintering phase, presents profound disappointment to Lucy who had dreamt of a land where 'all these places were points of happiness to me; all these places were lifeboats to my small drowning soul'. Lucy has been betrayed by colonial indoctrination into believing the imperial narrative which couples 'discovery' of a land with self-discovery ...

In a text which constantly denies us the happy endings which feed our cultural imaginations, it is made explicit that the closure or fulfilment of that old colonial tale which depicts the 'other' land as the site on which to achieve aspirations and desires inaccessible at home is still dependent upon economic and social power. The dinner party guests of Lucy's employers had been, seen and consummated their fantasies of fun and frolics in 'the islands', but, journeying in the opposite direction, she is not so comfortably accommodated in her new environs. Although warmly embraced by the family for whom she works, Lucy remains acutely aware of her positioning within all structures of American society, including the home.

> The room in which I lay was a small room just off the kitchen – the maid's room. I was used to a small room, but this was a different sort of small room. The ceiling was very high and the walls went all the way up to the ceiling, enclosing the room like a box – a box in which cargo travelling a long way should be shipped. But I was not a cargo. I was only an unhappy young woman living in a maid's room, and I was not even a maid.
>
> (p. 7)

While the spatial configuration of Lucy's room evidently denotes containment, it more specifically evokes the iconography of the slave ship in which the captured Africans were transported as chattels across the ocean to America. This representation is suggestive of the fact that Lucy's respectable position of service as a nanny is a not so distant echo of her ancestor's enforced servitude in this land.

Yet as the reality of American society intrudes upon Lucy's dream, so other dreams begin to intrude upon her reality. The subsumed slave narrative emerges most dramatically within Lucy's dreams, one of which she relates to her employers, Lewis and Mariah, one evening at the dinner table.

> Lewis was chasing me around the house. I wasn't wearing any clothes. The ground on which I was running was yellow, as if it had been paved with cornmeal. Lewis was chasing me around the house, and though he came close he could never catch up with me. Mariah stood at the open windows saying, Catch her Lewis, catch her. Eventually I fell down a hole, at the bottom of which were some silver and blue snakes.
>
> (p. 14)

Images of plantation life and slave capture emerge alongside that of the yellow brick road to present a montage of the colliding and conflicting messages within this ambivalently informed cultural imagination. The conflation of seemingly opposing cultural signifiers, of desired future and denied past, of hope and fear, signals the complex matrix of competing claims within a migrant consciousness informed by both metropolitan expectations and ancestral histories.

[488]

As well as revealing the America of oppression buried beneath the dream of the land of the free, Lucy's dream and the response of her American employers to it, 'Lewis made a clucking noise, then said, Poor, poor Visitor. And Mariah said, Dr Freud for Visitor, and I wondered why she said that, for I did not know who Dr Freud was', point to the way in which Kincaid's fiction foregrounds the limitations of Western theoretical models. I would suggest that the description of Lucy's dream actually serves to question the value of dominant Western psychoanalytical theories, which see dreams only as ciphers for issues of sexual difference and conflict. While the heavily inscribed Freudian imagery of holes and snakes might seem to invite or endorse this reading, the images of running naked and of cornmeal clearly suggest that cultural difference and conflict are also primary determinants within this consciousness. The denial of issues of cultural difference in the development of psychoanalytical theory means that the proposed Dr Freud would be, at best, an inadequate model through which to interpret the dreams of an adolescent Caribbean female. Evidently the cultural context of the Caribbean makes the baffling nature of the already 'dark continent' of female sexuality even more inaccessible to Freudian interpretation.

In terms of the theorizing narrative, the depiction of Lucy's dream collapses or de-constructs the space which Western theory often seeks to construct between ideas of cultural difference and sexual difference, in order to present the way in which these two models of differentiation are intimately bound within the construction of a female post-colonial subjectivity.

It is this same denial of cultural difference which also necessitates Lucy's resistance to the discourse of Anglo-American feminism within the novel. Mariah, Lucy's supposedly liberal and liberated white employer, who constructs her as the 'poor visitor' and in need of rescue attempts to offer her this through the supposedly more authentic voice of a feminist language.

> Mariah left the room and came back with a large book and opened it to the first chapter. She gave it to me. I read the first sentence. 'Woman? Very simple, say the fanciers of simple formulas: she is a womb, an ovary; she is female – this word is sufficient to define her.' I had to stop. Mariah had completely misinterpreted my situation. My life could not really be explained by this thick book that made my

hand hurt as I tried to keep it open. My life was at once something more simple and more complicated than that . . .

(p. 132)

To Lucy, the text is meaningless and burdensome as it refuses context. Lucy must reject the language of the surrogate mother because it rejects her specific cultural and historical positioning. The language of the text, like that of Mariah herself, speaks to middle class white women, with little awareness of its exclusivity. The generalised statements concerning gender, which Mariah's feminism advocates, do not correlate to the cultural differences between women which Lucy has already observed.

Although I would not wish to deny the very real marginalisation, which the novel clearly reveals, that Lucy does experience as a woman within her home society, her Caribbean cultural heritage is clearly womanist/feminist both in ethos and in practice. Baffled by American women's obsessions with ageing and beauty, Lucy asserts her own code which confidently articulates a positive female subjectivity: 'Among the beliefs I held about the world was that being beautiful should not matter to a woman, because it was one of those things that would go away, and there wouldn't be anything you could do to bring it back' (p. 57). From her childhood in the Caribbean, Lucy has also learnt of the herbal abortifacients from her mother and thus is in possession of one of the primary objectives of the early American women's movement – control over fertility. Moreover, her Caribbean upbringing has instilled into Lucy the significance of solidarity among women: 'It was my mother who told me that I should never take a man's side over a woman's . . . It was from her own experience that she spoke' (p. 48). As well as exposing the alienating ethnocentric bias of a certain type of Anglo-American feminism, Lucy's simple statements seem to suggest that within Caribbean womens' lives theory and practice are not discrete, as Kincaid juxtaposes gender politics which are to be lived with those which are to be argued.

Here and throughout the novel, Lucy's thoughts and dreams testify to the ways in which certain intellectual spaces remain colonised within Western thought. It is Mariah who is trapped within the mono-logic narrative unable to negotiate the differences between language and living and self and other, not Lucy. It becomes clear that the narratives of opportunity and belonging (of having arrived) and of

[490]

liberation (here through feminism) have been transculturally marketed in versions which are deeply ethnocentric and exclusive, and which, moreover, with a certain cultural complacency, deny the coexistence of alternative models, such as those which Lucy brings with her from the Caribbean.

However, as well as revealing the cultural biases and blind spots within existing theoretical models, Kincaid's novel also explores the basis upon which we evaluate, by rehearsing the way in which we judge our notions of the aesthetic and the ideological. This process is staged most crucially within the narrative when Mariah initiates Lucy into the joys of Spring by telling her of a field of daffodils.

> She [Mariah] said, 'Have you ever seen daffodils pushing their way up out of the ground? And when they're in bloom and all massed together, a breeze comes along and makes them do a curtsy to the lawn stretching out in front of them. Have you ever seen that? When I see that, I feel so glad to be alive' ... I remembered an old poem I had been made to memorize when I was ten years old and a pupil at Queen Victoria's Girls' School. I had been made to memorize it, verse after verse, and then had recited the whole poem to an auditorium full of parents, teachers, and my fellow pupils. After I was done, everybody stood up and applauded with an enthusiasm that surprised me, and later they told me how nicely I had pronounced every word, how I had placed just the right amount of special emphasis in places where that was needed, and how proud the poet, now long dead, would have been to have heard his words ringing out of my mouth. I was then at the height of my two-facedness: that is, outside false, inside true. And so I made pleasant little noises that showed both modesty and appreciation, but inside I was making a vow to erase from my mind, line by line, every word of that poem.
>
> (pp. 17–18)

Mariah's admiration for the seemingly simple field of flowers acts as a powerful catalyst for Lucy's memories of cultural imperialism. What is essentially an aesthetic experience for Mariah constitutes a powerful ideological situation for Lucy. Her retrospective vision of reciting Wordsworth's poem works as both a literal example of colonial education and as a metonym for the colonial apparatus, promotion of an aesthetic which is ideologically motivated in its very essence of seeming to be devoid of ideology. 'Daffodils' was promoted pedagogically as an apolitical text and yet becomes highly politicised when analysed within the colonial context in which Kincaid places it. The poetic subject (daffodils) signifies the forced adoption of the motherland and the attendant suppression of difference. In addition, the process of learning by heart further supports the hegemony's underlying need for mimicry which Lucy publicly performs but privately attempts to negate.

Her double consciousness, or two-facedness as she calls it, is testimony to her ambivalent position as black and female in relation to colonial cultural authority, which is represented by the poem, the poet, and the institutions of the school. By appearing to subscribe to the version of aesthetics pedagogically promoted, but internally reacting against it, Lucy has clearly politicised and resisted the stifling appropriation of a culturally inauthentic voice. Indeed, when Mariah at last takes her to see the daffodils, which she had so carefully and painfully eulogised as a young girl, Lucy's reaction is a spontaneous and most vehement desire to cut them all down. 'It wasn't her fault. It wasn't my fault. But nothing could change the fact that where she saw beautiful flowers, I saw sorrow and bitterness, the same thing could cause us to shed tears, but those tears would not taste the same. We walked home in silence' (p. 30). Although Mariah's and Lucy's bewilderment at the situation may be mutual, from her analysis of their conflicting responses, it is evident that Lucy experiences and comprehends the politics of cultural difference in a way her American employer cannot ...

However, Kincaid does not appear to be bidding for a reading which emphasises the aesthetic as simply a frivolous position, an Anglo-centric luxury denied to, and irrelevant to, those outside the dominant economic group, as later in the book she neatly inverts the line of judgement. As Lucy watches Mariah and her adulterous husband posture romantically, she notices how 'She leaned her head backwards and rested it on his shoulder (she was a little shorter than he, and that looked wrong; it looks better when a woman is a little taller than her husband), and she sighed and shuddered in pleasure' (p. 47). Lucy's observation that it is aesthetically pleasing for a wife to be taller that her husband is a particularly playful and incisive context for the inversion of the divide, as this is a statement which Mariah, with her criteria of Western feminism, would clearly interpret as ideologically motivated ...

ALISON DONNELL

By re-presenting and unravelling the politics of certain national and intellectual narratives, Kincaid reveals that a Caribbean or a post-colonial female subjectivity is too complex to be articulated simply by feminist or colonial discourse theories or by national allegories, all of which are too often predicated on a belief that the other can easily be understood by the methodologies constructed by the self in order to 'discover' difference, and which further have a tendency to theorize that other into the self.

By arguing for a more complex subjectivity, both syncretic and shifting, Kincaid's novel *Lucy* not only offers a compelling and engaging presentation of the Caribbean migrant consciousness, but it also makes us question our confidence in making judgements which fail to encompass a consideration of cultural and gender orientation, although it very clearly does not deny the significance of working through the process of cross-cultural communication.

(1992)

Merle Hodge

Challenges of the Struggle for Sovereignty: Changing the World versus Writing Stories

My very dear friend Michael Anthony, one of the writers of the Caribbean for whom I feel a great deal of respect and affection, once said to me, expressing alarm at the activist role I seemed to have opted for: 'But you have to devote your time to writing stories – you can't change the world!'

I am very confident that it is people who change the world and that people must continually engage in actions aimed at changing the world for the better. For me, there is no fundamental contradiction between art and activism. In particular, the power of the creative word to change the world is not to be underestimated.

Fiction has immense political power. Its power can be revolutionary or, of course, the opposite: it is a prime weapon of political conservatism. That is why it was important for us to study the literature of the British Isles during the colonial era; that is why today, in the era of independence, it is important to saturate the Caribbean people with American soap-opera and situation comedy and Rambo-style adventure.

I began writing, in my adult life, in protest against my education and the arrogant assumptions upon which it rested: that I and my world were nothing and that to rescue ourselves from nothingness, we had best seek admission to the world of *their* storybook. (I first began writing in childhood, and those pieces which survive are a testimony to the power of the fiction to which I was exposed: namely, the power of the storybook.) The genesis of modern Caribbean writing lies, I think, in such a reaction, conscious or unconscious, against the enterprise of negating our world and offering us somebody else's world as salvation.

The protest against this imposition has developed, in my case, into an abiding concern with the issue of cultural sovereignty and beyond that, into an unapologetic interest in the political development of our region. Cultural sovereignty is an abstraction to a vagrant digging in dustbins for food on the streets of Port of Spain or a family that cannot send its children to school because there is no money for books . . .

And what, in all of this, is the use of writing stories? The potential of Caribbean literature for positively affecting the development of the Caribbean is an untapped resource. Caribbean fiction can help to strengthen our self-image, our resistance to foreign domination, our sense of the oneness of the Caribbean and our willingness to put our energies into the building of the Caribbean nation.

The cultural penetration of the Caribbean which we are witnessing today is a serious business. It is as serious as the invasion and continuing occupation of Grenada. It is perhaps even more serious, for you can recognize a military invasion when you see one. Invasion and occupation in the guise of entertainment are another kettle of fish.

And there are direct links between the continuing underdevelopment of the Caribbean and the continued – the renewed – suppression of Caribbean culture . . .

Governments of the region recognize and pay attention to one aspect of the culture – the performing arts – not because they have any interest in the people who created the steelband and calypso and reggae and Carnival but because in the development of tourism and the quest for foreign exchange, these things can be turned into commodities, packaged, and sold. (Right now the government of Trinidad and Tobago is talking about 'selling steelband to the world') . . .

Creole is the main medium of communication in the Caribbean. Almost everybody uses Creole. But the attitude of the Caribbean people to the language they speak is incredible. Parents who speak nothing but Creole severely reprimand their children for speaking Creole. Educators at the highest level become too hysterical to argue rationally when they are presented with the very simple proposition that Caribbean people can be armed with *both* standard English and their mother tongue, Creole; that the teaching of English must never be accompanied by efforts to discredit Creole – just as the education system of, say, Denmark or Nigeria seeks to equip its people with an international language in addition and with no detriment to its mother tongue. Think of the implications for our mental health – we speak Creole, we need Creole, we cannot function without Creole, for our deepest thought processes are bound up in the structure of Creole, but we hold Creole in utter contempt . . .

From the colonial era to the present time, one of the weapons used to subjugate us has been fiction. The proper role of fiction in

human societies includes allowing a people to 'read' itself – to deci-
pher its own reality. The storyteller offers a vision of the world which
is more coherent, more 'readable', than the mass of unconnected
detail of everyday experience. Fiction also brings to our attention and
puts in place parts of our reality that are not visible to us or are
normally overlooked, allowing us to form a more complete picture
of our environment than our own observation allows . . .

Caribbean people have only very limited exposure to their own
literature. Caribbean literature courses are available at the University
of the West Indies, and some texts have been introduced into
the curriculum of secondary schools through the CXC (Caribbean
Examinations Council) Exam. But access to secondary education
remains limited, and the great majority of students study literature
only in the first three years of secondary school, during which time
they are likely to read all of three Caribbean texts, if indeed so many.

If we recognize the process by which fiction validates reality, it
becomes clear that people steeped in imported fiction are not likely
to develop a healthy relationship with themselves or their environment. They are more likely to reject the real, palpable world in which
they live in favour of the world presented to them in fiction. Indeed
Caribbean people are capable of a kind of 'mental desertion' of their
own environment, which is not matched, I think, by any other people
on earth.

Such was our situation during the colonial era, and such is our
situation today. In this situation creative writing becomes, for me, a
guerrilla activity. We are occupied by foreign fiction. Fiction which
affirms and validates our world is therefore an important weapon of
resistance . . .

If we agree that Caribbean literature can contribute to the political process of empowering Caribbean people, then we must set about
solving another problem: how do we deliver Caribbean literature to
the Caribbean people? How do we compete with the great volume
of foreign fiction that our people consumes?

One of the problems is that in speaking of Caribbean literature
we are referring to a body of writing which is, in general, highly
accomplished and very sophisticated, by any literary criteria. The
Caribbean can boast of a relatively literate population, but our people
are no more *literary* than any other . . .

We might have to consider developing a modern tradition of

popular literature ... The idea of developing such a literature in the Caribbean may be fairly controversial. But I do not think that it necessarily involves a complete compromise of literary standards. A great deal of what is today revered as classical literature started out as fiction aimed at a mass audience rather than a highly educated elite ...

One of my specific concerns or ambitions is to one day be able to participate in the development of a strong popular theatre ... in much of the Caribbean – the theatre is perceived as an urban, middle-class activity. We have a duty, I think, to restore theatre to its popular roots.

(1990)

Jean Binta Breeze

Can a Dub Poet be a Woman?

In 1978, when I first moved from rural Jamaica into Kingston to study at the Jamaica School of Drama, I made closer contact with the dub poets, Mikey, Oku and Mutabaruka. I was already writing, but refused to read with them publicly at that time as I didn't feel my work was ready. It wasn't until 1981 that I first took to the stage with Muta in Montego Bay and he decided to record my work. This led to the acclaim of being, as one magazine termed it, 'the first female dub poet in the male-dominated field'.

I hadn't really taken on what the title meant as I had grown up as a young child performing the works of Louise Bennett on stages all over Jamaica in the annual festival. I had read and performed works from other women writers in Jamaica, but Miss Lou had not only drawn on the characters, experiences and languages of the people, she had also managed to give the people's poetry back to them in a way that made the nation celebrate itself. No other woman poet had taken on the popular stage, no other had broken so totally out of the literary and academic circles of recognition, indeed, had forced them to accept her and so opened the way for all of us who now work in our own language with ease.

I was therefore quite at home in the arena of dub poetry. It satisfied my personal political concerns about whom I was talking with and the voice became my instrument, not the page, although I do recognise the need for documentation. I enjoy the works of many writers but I am always aware of what in the text is available to me because of my own educational background which is not yet, for economic and political reasons, the background of the majority of my people. And I hasten to say here that this does not mean producing a kind of work that patronises, but a work so simple in its truth and in its details that it becomes as big as the universe. This is something quite natural to the peasantry I grew up within, as can quite easily be seen in our proverbs.

For this, I salute the coming of dub poetry. My criticism at this point in time is that there is not enough experimentation with the form and it is becoming as constraining in its rhythms as the iambic pentameter. My first voice in poetry, therefore, was largely political and I was not aware at the time of what difference it actually made being a woman in the field. However, there are three comments I remember as moments when I really had to stop and think.

The first of these was when Mutabaruka offered to re-record some of my work in his voice and many people thought they were lyrics much more suited to a male voice and someone even suggested that they had been written by a man. This was with particular reference to 'Aid travels with a bomb', my anti-IMF poem, and seemed to suggest that it was much more masculine to achieve such distance from the subjective or personal.

The second comment came after playing my first Reggae Sunsplash with a full band and dancing across the stage while performing. I was told by many people that a radical dub poet should not be 'wining up her waist' on the stage as it presented a sexual image rather than a radical one. This led me into an era of wearing military khaki uniforms for performing, but I soon realised that even if I wore sackcloth it would not reduce the sexual energy I carry normally as an individual and which becomes a source of creative energy on the stage. I still do not wear a G-string, but I dress in a way in which the woman in me is totally at ease in motion so the body can also sing and I dare anyone to say that for a woman to be accepted as a radical voice she cannot celebrate her own sensuality.

Thirdly, when I had my first album turned down by the American company that had put out my previous work, on the grounds that my new work was becoming far too personal and there were too many pieces dealing with love. For me, the coming of 'Riddym Ravings', the madwoman's poem, broke form so completely that it was impossible to return to the shape of my earlier work. It was a time of self-searching, and I allowed my pen its freedom when I realised that my politics had never been learned through the study or acceptance of any ideology. I have never read Marx totally and came to C.L.R. James through my love of cricket. My politics were shaped by my personal experiences and those of the people round me in their day-to-day concerns. The closest concerns I shared were obviously those of women. I lost the need to teach or preach, especially to audiences already converted, and found the courage to tell, and I will not manipulate the voices that work through me or the truth they bring.

Now, I am told, my work has advanced beyond the confines of dub poetry, but that is not to say I am achieving as much as other women writers in conventional poetry, and to tell you the truth, I don't much care. I like this space, there are no rules here.

(1990)

*'By Word of Mouth' – John Vidal Gets in Tune with
Dub Poet, Benjamin Zephaniah*

Benjamin Zephaniah couldn't read or write when his first book was
published. 'That's the kind of poet I am,' he says. The kind of poet
who prefers to walk the streets, to sleep four in a room, to live in
what he calls London's racist East End rather than in a 'safe' black
area like Ladbroke Grove, the kind of poet who created all hell at
Trinity College, Cambridge, last year [1987] when his candidacy for
a visiting fellowship was only narrowly defeated. The kind of poet
who can make people dance.

And think. His poetry is politically sharp; streetwise portraits of the
sort of poverty and urban depression that Thatcher and the whole pack
at Westminster turn away from. 'I'd like to play at the Tory Party
conference,' he says. He's serious. 'Preaching to the converted is the
easiest thing in the world to do but I'd like to speak to the people my
poetry is really addressing, the people I call the "downpressor".'

The downpressor has had a lot of time for Zephaniah. Approved
school, Borstal and then a spell in Winson Green in Birmingham,
all before he was 20. Mostly it was petty thefts, like stealing car
radios, but then he was accused of affray in the Bull Ring in
Birmingham with a gang of others. 'I stood there in the dock,' he
says, 'trying to tell the judge it really wasn't me who'd affrayed. But
he gave us all two years and honestly I wasn't there.'

So he went to jail and he still didn't write anything. He just watched
and 'learned who the enemy was' and when he came out he found
that his 'wordability' could be a powerful tool for change, even more
than mainstream politics which appals him and which he believes in
no way addresses the blacks in Britain who are having to break new
ground all the while.

'For the younger people,' he says, and he laughs again because he's
30 now, 'music and poetry can sway you more than politics.'

The dub poets, of which he is one, have been doing so for years.
His pitch is slightly different. 'If people are living in the shit you
can't keep telling them about the shit. People ask me how I can do
a poem about people dying in New Cross [London] followed by a
poem about condoms. And how can they work together, but they do.

'But there are two sides of my work and myself,' he says. 'The one is very serious. Political . . . If it was a perfect world and there was no poverty I'd be a comedian.'

The BBC, he says, want him to be just that. 'They'd just love to have a Rastafarian Lenny Henry¹, someone like me who can tell a joke and mimic Jagger, Marley and Jimi Hendrix. But I turn the offers down because I don't just want to be seen as a comedian. There's more to it than that.'

For a start, poverty inspires him. All his best work – as an artist, an organiser and a citizen – has come out of the hard times. In Stratford in the East End of London he couldn't believe the poverty and the racism he found after Birmingham . . .

His real work, the most satisfying, he says, is in the performances he still plays to schools and psychiatric wards, to kids on work schemes and miners' groups in Wales and Scotland, for little or no money.

Next month his first radio play, Hurricane Dub, will be played. It's a reappraisal – at times hilarious and at times deadly serious – in music and poetry of last year's storm [1987], and is part of the BBC's young playwright's festival. He's proud that it will be the first full play on Radio One. 'When I was younger I set myself a lot of goals – one was to make poetry news another was to make people dance to it. This is another.' . . .

Now he wants to write a serious book on the black experience in Britain. 'I'm going to night classes to learn English,' he says. He's serious.

(1988)

NOTE

1 A popular Black British comedian.

Derek Walcott

The Antilles: Fragments of Epic Memory

Felicity is a village in Trinidad on the edge of the Caroni plain, the
wide central plain that still grows sugar and to which indentured cane
cutters were brought after emancipation, so the small population of
Felicity is East Indian, and on the afternoon that I visited it with
friends from America, all the faces along its road were Indian, which,
as I hope to show, was a moving, beautiful thing, because this Saturday
afternoon *Ramleela*, the dramatization of the Hindu epic the
Ramayana, was going to be performed, and the costumed actors from
the village were assembling on a field strung with different-coloured
flags, like a new gas station, and beautiful Indian boys in red and
black were aiming arrows haphazardly into the afternoon light. Low
blue mountains on the horizon, bright grass, clouds that would gather
colour before the light went. Felicity! What a gentle Anglo-Saxon
name for an epical memory.

Under an open shed on the edge of the field, there were two huge
armatures of bamboo that looked like immense cages. They were
parts of the body of a god, his calves or thighs, which, fitted and
reared, would made a gigantic effigy. This effigy would be burnt as
a conclusion to the epic. The cane structures flashed a predictable
parallel: Shelley's sonnet on the fallen statue of Ozymandias and his
empire, that 'colossal wreck' in its empty desert . . .

Deities were entering the field. What we generally call 'Indian
music' was blaring from the open platformed shed from which the
epic would be narrated. Costumed actors were arriving. Princes and
gods, I supposed. What an unfortunate confession! 'Gods, I suppose'
is the shrug that embodies our African and Asian diasporas. I had
often thought of but never seen *Ramleela*, and had never seen this
theatre, an open field, with village children as warriors, princes and
gods. I had no idea what the epic story was, who its hero was, what
enemies he fought, yet I had recently adapted the *Odyssey* for a theatre
in England, presuming that the audience knew the trials of Odysseus,
hero of another Asia Minor epic, while nobody in Trinidad knew any
more than I did about Rama, Kali, Shiva, Vishnu, apart from the
Indians, a phrase I use pervertedly because that is the kind of remark
you can still hear in Trinidad: 'apart from the Indians'.

It was as if, on the edge of the Central Plain, there was another plateau, a raft on which the *Ramayana* would be poorly performed in this ocean of cane, but that was my writer's view of things, and it is wrong. I was seeing the *Ramleela* at Felicity as theatre when it was faith.

Multiply that moment of self-conviction when an actor, made-up and costumed, nods to his mirror before stepping onstage in the belief that he is a reality entering an illusion and you would have what I presumed to be happening to the actors of this epic. But they were not actors. They had been chosen; or they themselves had chosen their roles in this sacred story that would go on for nine afternoons over a two-hour period till the sun set. They were not amateurs but believers. There was no theatrical term to define them. They did not have to psych themselves to play their roles. Their acting would probably be as buoyant and as natural as those bamboo arrows crisscrossing the afternoon pasture. They believed in what they were playing, in the sacredness of the text, the validity of India, while I, out of the writer's habit, searched for some sense of elegy, of loss, even of degenerative mimicry in the happy faces of the boy-warriors or the heraldic profiles of the village princes. I was polluting the afternoon with doubt and with the patronage of admiration. I misread the event through a visual echo of history – the cane fields, indenture, the evocation of vanished armies, temples, and trumpeting elephants – when all around me there was quite the opposite: elation, delight in the boys' screams; a delight of conviction, not loss. The name Felicity made sense.

Consider the scale of Asia reduced to these fragments: the small white exclamations of minarets or the stone balls of temples in the cane fields, and one can understand the self-mockery and embarrassment of those who see these rites as parodic, even degenerate. These purists look on such ceremonies as grammarians look at a dialect, as cities look on provinces and empires on their colonies. Memory that yearns to join the centre, a limb remembering the body from which it has been severed. Like those bamboo thighs of the god. In other words, the way that the Caribbean is still looked at, illegitimate, rootless, mongrelized. 'No people there', to quote Froude, 'in the true sense of the word'. No people. Fragments and echoes of real people, unoriginal and broken.

The performance was like a dialect, a branch of its original language, an abridgment of it, but not a distortion or even a reduction of its epic scale. Here in Trinidad I had discovered that one of the greatest epics of the world was seasonally performed, not with that desperate resignation of preserving a culture, but with an openness of belief that was as steady as the wind bending the cane lances of the Caroni plain. We had to leave before the play began to go through the creeks of the Caroni Swamp, to catch the scarlet ibises coming home at dusk. In a performance as natural as those of the actors of the *Ramleela*, we watched the flocks come in as bright as the scarlet of the boy archers, as the red flags, and cover an islet until it turned into a flowering tree, an anchored immortelle. The sigh of History meant nothing here. These two visions, the *Ramleela* and the arrowing flocks of scarlet ibises, blended into a single gasp of gratitude. Visual surprise is natural in the Caribbean; it comes with the landscape, and faced with its beauty, the sigh of History dissolves.

We make too much of that long groan which underlines the past. I felt privileged to discover the ibises as well as the scarlet archers of Felicity.

The sigh of History rises over ruins, not over landscapes, and in the Antilles there are few ruins to sigh over, apart from the ruins of sugar estates and abandoned forts. Looking around slowly, as a camera would, taking in the low blue hills over Port of Spain, the village road and houses, the warrior-archers, the god-actors and their handlers, and music already on the soundtrack, I wanted to make a film that would be a long-drawn sigh over Felicity. I was filtering the afternoon with evocations of a lost India, but why 'evocations'? Why not 'celebrations of a real presence'? Why should India be 'lost' when none of these villagers ever really knew it, and why not 'continuing', why not the perpetuation of joy in Felicity and in all the other nouns of the Central Plain: Couva, Chaguanas, Charley Village? Why was I not letting my pleasure open its windows wide? I was entitled like any Trinidadian to the ecstasies of their claim, because ecstasy was the pitch of the sinuous drumming in the loudspeakers. I was entitled to the feast of Husein, to the crêpe-paper temples of the Muslim epic, to the Chinese Dragon Dance, to the rites of that Sephardic Jewish synagogue that was once on Something Street. I am only one-eighth the writer that I might have been had I contained all the fragmented languages of Trinidad.

Break a vase, and the love that reassembles the fragments is stronger than that love which took its symmetry for granted when it was whole. The glue that fits the pieces is the sealing of its original shape. It is such a love that reassembles our African and Asiatic fragments, the cracked heirlooms whose restoration shows its white scars. This gathering of broken pieces is the care and pain of the Antilles, and if the pieces are disparate, ill-fitting, they contain more pain than their original sculpture, those icons and sacred vessels taken for granted in their ancestral places. Antillean art is this restoration of our shattered histories, our shards of vocabulary, our archipelago becoming a synonym for pieces broken off from the original continent.

And this is the exact process of the making of poetry, or what should be called not its 'making' but its remaking, the fragmented memory, the armature that frames the god, the rite that surrenders it to a final pyre; the god assembled cane by cane, reed by weaving reed, line by plaited line, as the artisans of Felicity would erect his holy echo.

Poetry, which is perfection's sweat but which must seem as fresh as the raindrops on a statue's brow, combines the natural and the marmoreal; it conjugates both tenses simultaneously; the past and the present, if the past is the sculpture and the present the beads of dew or rain on the forehead of the past. There is the buried language and there is the individual vocabulary, and the process of poetry is one of excavation and of self-discovery. Tonally the individual voice is a dialect; it shapes its own vocabulary and melody in defiance of an imperial concept of language, the language of Ozymandias, libraries and dictionaries, law courts and critics, and churches, universities, political dogma, the diction of institutions. Poetry is an island and breaks away from the main. The dialects of my archipelago seem as fresh to me as those raindrops on the statue's forehead, not the sweat made from the classic exertion of frowning marble, but the condensations of a refreshing element, rain and salt.

Deprived of their original language, the captured and indentured tribes create their own, accreting and secreting fragments of an old, an epic vocabulary, from Asia and from Africa, but to an ancestral, an ecstatic rhythm in the blood that cannot be subdued by slavery or indenture, while nouns are renamed and the given names of places accepted like Felicity village or Choiseul. The original language dissolves from the exhaustion of distance like fog trying to cross an ocean, but this process of renaming, of finding new metaphors, is the same process that the poet faces every morning of his working day, making his own tools like Crusoe, assembling nouns from necessity, from Felicity, even renaming himself. The stripped man is driven back to that self-astonishing, elemental force, his mind. That is the basis of the Antillean experience, this shipwreck of fragments, these echoes, these shards of a huge tribal vocabulary, these partially remembered customs, and they are not decayed but strong. They survived the Middle Passage and the *Fatel Rozack*, the ship that carried the first indentured Indians from the Port of Madras to the cane fields of Felicity, that carried the chained Cromwellian convict and the Sephardic Jew, the Chinese grocer and the Lebanese merchant selling cloth samples on his bicycle.

And here they are, all in a single Caribbean city, Port of Spain, the sum of history, Froude's 'non-people', a downtown babel of shop signs and streets, mongrelized, polyglot, a ferment without a history, like heaven. Because that is what such a city is, in the New World, a writer's heaven.

(1992)

Bibliography

Anon (1952) 'Review of Sam Selvon's *A Brighter Sun*', *Times Literary Supplement*, 15 Feb.: 121.

Anon (1955) 'Caribbean Voices', *Times Literary Supplement*, 5 Aug.: xvi–xvii.

Anon (1957) 'New Fiction', *The Times*, 23 May: 15.

Anon (1958a) 'Review of Sam Selvon's *Ways of Sunlight*', *Times Literary Supplement*, 31 Jan.: 57.

Anon (1958b) 'Review of Sam Selvon's *Turn Again Tiger* and Jan Carew's *The Wild Coast*', *The Times*, 27 Nov.: 13.

Anon (1960a) 'Review of Andrew Salkey's *Escape to an Autumn Pavement*', *The Times*, 7 July: 15.

Anon (1960b) 'Review of George Lamming's *The Pleasures of Exile*', *Times Literary Supplement*, 29 July: 47.

Abrahams, R.D. (1983) *The Man of Words in the West Indies – Performance and the Emergence of Creole Culture*, Baltimore & London: Johns Hopkins University Press.

Adisa, O. Palmer (1989a) *Bake-Face and other Guava Stories*, London: Fontana.

—— (1989b) *Travelling Woman*, Oakland, CA: Jukebox Press.

Agard, J. (1985) *Mangoes and Bullets – Selected and New Poems*, London & Sydney: Pluto Press.

—— (1986) *Say it Again Granny: 20 Poems from Caribbean Proverbs*, London: Bodley Head.

Allfrey, P. Shand (1940) *In Circles: Poems*, London: Raven Press.

—— (1950) *Palm and Oak: Poems*.

—— (1953) *The Orchid House*, London: Constable, republished in London by Virago, 1982.

—— (1955) *Contrasts I*, Barbados.

—— (1973) *Palm and Oak II*, Roseau, Dominica: The Star Printery.

Allis, J. (1982) 'A Case for Regional Criticism of West Indian Literature', *Caribbean Quarterly*, 28,1 & 2: 1–11.

Allnutt, G., D'Aguiar, F., Edwards, K., and Mottram, E. (eds) (1988) *The New British Poetry – 1968–88*, London: Paladin.

Angier, C. (1990) *Jean Rhys*, London: André Deutsch.

Anthony, M. (1963) *The Games Were Coming*, London: André Deutsch.

—— (1965) *The Year in San Fernando*, London: André Deutsch.

—— (1967) *Green Days by the River*, London: André Deutsch.

Asein, S.O. (1972) 'The Protest Tradition in West Indian Poetry from George Campbell to Martin Carter', *Jamaica Journal*, 6,2: 40–5.

Ashcroft, B., Griffiths, G. and Tiffin, H. (eds) (1989) *The Empire Writes Back: Theory and Practice in Post-Colonial Literatures*, London: Routledge.
—— (eds) (1994) *The Post-Colonial Studies Reader*, London: Routledge.
Ashcroft, W.D. (1989) 'Intersecting Marginalities: Post-Colonialism and Feminism', *Kunapipi*, XI,2: 23–35.
Austin, R.L. (1976) 'Understanding Calypso Content: A Critique and an Alternative Explanation', *Caribbean Quarterly*, 22: 74–83.
Ayres, P. (1978) Introduction to Reinhard Sander (ed.) *From Trinidad: An Anthology of Early West Indian Writing*, London: Hodder & Stoughton.
Bailey, B. (1966) *Jamaican Creole Syntax*, Cambridge: Cambridge University Press.
Banham, M., Hill, E. and Woodyard, G. (eds) (1994) *The Cambridge Guide to African and Caribbean Theatre*, Cambridge: Cambridge University Press.
Baugh, E. (1971) *West Indian Poetry, 1900–1970; a Study in Cultural Decolonization*, Kingston, Jamaica: Savacou.
—— (ed.) (1978) *Critics on Caribbean Literature: Readings in Literary Criticism*, London: Allen & Unwin.
Beasley, P. (1994) *Hearsay – Performance Poems Plus*, London: Bodley Head.
Beckwith, M. (1924) *Jamaica Anansi Stories*, New York: American Folk-lore Society.
—— (1924) 'The English Ballad in Jamaica: a Note upon the Origin of the Ballad Form', New York: Modern Language Association of America.
—— (1925) *Jamaica Proverbs*, New York: Negro Universities Press.
—— (1929) *Black Roadways*, Poughkeepsie, NY: Vassar College.
Bell, V. (1948) 'Ancestor on the Auction Block', *Focus*: 187.
Bennett, L. (1940) *Dialect Verses*, compiled by G. Bowen, Kingston, Jamaica: Herald Publishers.
—— (1943) *Jamaican Humour in Dialect*, Kingston, Jamaica: Jamaica Press Association.
—— (1948) *Jamaica Dialect Poems*, Kingston, Jamaica: Gleaner.
—— (1957) *Anancy Stories and Dialect Verse*, Kingston, Jamaica: Pioneer Press.
—— (1961) *Laugh With Louise*, Kingston, Jamaica: Gleaner Co.
—— (1966) *Jamaica Labrish*, Kingston, Jamaica: Sangsters.
—— (1968) 'Bennett on Bennett – Louise Bennett interviewed by Dennis Scott', *Caribbean Quarterly*, 14,1 & 2: 97–101, reprinted in E.A. Markham (ed.) *Hinterland – an Anthology of Poetry from the West Indies and Britain*, Newcastle-upon-Tyne, UK: Bloodaxe Books, 1989.
—— (1982) *Selected Poems*, edited by Mervyn Morris, Kingston, Jamaica: Sangsters.
—— (1983) 'Jamaica Philosophy,' in Mervyn Morris (ed.) *Focus*, Kingston, Jamaica.
Bennett, W. (1974) 'The Jamaican Theatre: A Preliminary Overview', *Jamaica Journal* 8,2 & 3: 3–9.
Berry, J. (ed.) (1976) *Bluefoot Traveller – An Anthology of West Indian Poets in Britain*, London: Limestone Publications.
—— (1979) *Fractured Circles*, London: New Beacon Books.
—— (1982) *Lucy's Letters and Loving*, London: New Beacon Books.
—— (ed.) (1984) *News for Babylon: The Chatto Book of Westindian–British Poetry*, London: Chatto & Windus.
—— (1985) *Chain of Days*, Oxford: Oxford University Press.

—— (1986) 'The Literature of the Black Experience', in David Sutcliffe and Ansel Wong (eds) *The Language of the Black Experience*, Oxford: Basil Blackwell.

—— (1995) *Hot Earth, Cold Earth*, Newcastle-upon-Tyne, UK: Bloodaxe Books.

Bhabha, H. (1984) 'Representation and the Colonial Text: A Critical Exploration of Some Forms of Mimeticism', in Frank Gloversmith (ed.) *The Theory of Reading*, Brighton: Harvester Wheatsheaf.

Bickerton, D. (1973) 'On the Nature of a Creole Continuum', *Language*, 49: 641–69.

Birbalsingh, F. (1988a) *Passion and Exile: Essays in Caribbean Literature*, London: Hansib.

—— (1988b) (ed.) *Jahaji Bhai: An Anthology of Indo-Caribbean Literature*.

—— (ed.) (1996) *Frontiers of Caribbean Literature in English*, London & Basingstoke: Macmillan Caribbean.

Bisoondath, N. (1985) *Digging Up the Mountain*, Toronto: Macmillan.

Bissundyal, C. (1986) *Cleavage: A Poem on East Indian Immigration to British Guyana* [sic], Demerara, Guyana: the author.

—— (1994) *Whom the Kiskadees Call*, Leeds, UK: Peepal Tree Press.

Blackman, P. (1948) 'Is There a West Indian Literature?', *Life and Letters* 59.135: 96–102.

—— (1949) 'Is There a West Indian Literature?', *Sunday Gleaner* (Jamaica), 28 Jan.: 7.

Bliss, E. (1931) *Saraband*, republished in London by Virago, 1986.

—— (1934) *Luminous Isle*, republished in London by Virago, 1984.

Bloom, V. (1983) *Touch mi: Tell mi!*, London: Bogle d'Ouverture.

Blundell, M. (1966) 'Caribbean Readers and Writers', *Bim*, 11,43: 163–7.

Boissiere, R. de (1952) *Crown Jewel*, Melbourne: Australasian Book Society.

Boxhill, A. (1979) 'The Beginnings to 1929' in B. King (ed.) *West Indian Literature*, Basingstoke and London: Macmillan.

Boyce Davies, C. (1990) '"Woman is a Nation . . ." Women in Caribbean Oral Literature', in C. Boyce Davies and E. Savory Fido (eds) *Out of the Kumbla: Caribbean Women and Literature*, Trenton, NJ: Africa World Press: 165–93.

Boyce Davies, C. and Savory Fido, E. (eds) (1990) *Out of the Kumbla: Caribbean Women and Literature*, Trenton, NJ: Africa World Press.

Brathwaite, K. (1957) 'Sir Galahad and the Islands', *Bim*, 25: 8–16.

—— (1960) 'The New West Indian Novelists – I', *Bim*, 8,31: 199–210.

—— (1961) 'The New West Indian Novelists – II', *Bim*, 8,32: 271–80.

—— (1967a) 'Jazz and the West Indian Novel – I', *Bim* 12,44: 275–84.

—— (1967b) 'Jazz and the West Indian Novel – II', *Bim* 12,45: 39–51.

—— (1968a) 'West Indian Prose Fiction in the Sixties: a Survey', *Bim* 12,47: 157–65.

—— (1968b) 'Themes from the Caribbean', *Times Educational Supplement*, 6 Sept.: 396.

—— (1968–9) 'Jazz and the West Indian Novel – III', *Bim* 12,46: 115–26.

—— (1970) 'Timehri', *Savacou* 2: 35–44.

—— (1970/1971) Foreword to *Savacou*, 3 & 4: 5–9.

—— (1971) *Folk Culture of the Slaves in Jamaica*, London: New Beacon Books.

—— (1973) *The Arrivants, A New World Trilogy: Rights of Passage, Islands & Masks*, Oxford: Oxford University Press.

—— (1977a) 'The Love Axe: Developing a Caribbean Aesthetic 1962–1974 – I', *Bim*, 16,61: 53–65.

—— (1977b) 'The Love Axe: Developing a Caribbean Aesthetic 1962–1974 – II', *Bim* 16,62: 100–6.

—— (1978a) 'The Love Axe: Developing a Caribbean Aesthetic 1962–1974 – III', *Bim* 16,63: 181–92.

—— (1978b) *The Development of Creole Society in Jamaica 1770–1820*, Oxford: Oxford University Press.

—— (1979a) 'The African Presence in Caribbean Literature', *Bim* 17,65: 33–44.

—— (1979b) Introduction to *Savacou New Poets from Jamaica Anthology*, *Savacou* 14 & 15.

—— (1981) 'English in the Caribbean: Notes on Nation Language and Poetry', in Leslie A. Fiedler and Houston A. Baker Jr. (eds) *English Literature – Opening up the Canon, Selected Papers from the English Institute 1979*, New Series 4, Baltimore and London: John Hopkins University Press.

—— (1982a) *Sun Poem*, Oxford: Oxford University Press.

—— (1982b) *Mother Poem*, Oxford: Oxford University Press.

—— (1984) *History of the Voice*, London: New Beacon Books.

—— (1986) *Jah Music*, Mona, Jamaica: Savacou Cooperative.

—— (1987a) *X-Self*, Oxford: Oxford University Press.

—— (1987b) 'What Marcus Tellin Us', Introduction to Marc Matthews' *Guyana, My Altar*, London: Karnak House.

—— (1993) *Middle Passages*, Newcastle-upon-Tyne, UK: Bloodaxe Books.

—— (1994) *Dreamstories*, Harlow, U.K.: Longman.

—— (1995) 'A Post-Cautionary Tale of Helen of Our Wars', *Wasafiri*, Autumn: 69–78.

Breeze, J. Binta (1986) 'An Interview with Jean Breeze', *Commonwealth*, 8: 51–8.

—— (1988) Mervyn Morris (ed.) *Riddym Ravings and Other Poems*, London: Race Today Publications.

—— (1990a) 'Can a Dub Poet be a Woman?', *Women: a Cultural Review*, 1,1: 47–9.

—— (1990b) Interview with Jean Binta Breeze in Carol Dix, 'Rhythm Method – the Lot of Today's Female Bards', *Options*: 60–4.

—— (1992) *Spring Cleaning*, London: Virago.

Breiner, L.A. (1986) 'Is There Still a West Indian Literature?', *World Literature Written in English* 26.1: 140–50.

Brereton, B. (1981) *A History of Modern Trinidad 1783–1962*, London: Heinemann Educational Books.

Brodber, E. (1980) *Jane and Louisa Will Soon Come Home*, London: New Beacon Books.

—— (1982) 'Perceptions of Caribbean Women: Towards a Documentation of Stereotypes', Cave Hill, Barbados.

—— (1988) *Myal*, London: New Beacon Books.

—— (1994) *Louisiana*, London: New Beacon Books.

Brother Resistance (1986) *Rapso Explosion*, London: Karia Press.

Brown, L. (1978) *West Indian Poetry*, New York: Twayne.

Brown, S. (ed.) (1984) *Caribbean Poetry Now*, London: Hodder & Stoughton.

—— (1990) *Caribbean New Wave – Contemporary Short Stories*, Oxford: Heinemann.

—— (1992) *The Heinemann Book of Caribbean Poetry*, Oxford: Heinemann.

—— (ed.) (1995) *The Pressures of the Text: Orality, Texts and the Telling of Tales*, Birmingham, UK: Centre of West African Studies.

Brown, S., Morris, M. and Rohlehr, G. (eds) (1989) *Voice Print – An Anthology of Oral and Related Poetry from the Caribbean*, Harlow, UK: Longman.

Brown, W. (1970) 'West Indian Poetry of the 1940s', *Sunday Guardian* (Trinidad), 13 Sept.: 9.

Brydon, D. (1989) 'New Approaches to the New Literatures in English: Are We in Danger of Incorporating Disparity?', in H. Maes-Jelinek, K. Holst Peterson and A. Rutherford (eds) *A Shaping of Connections*, Coventry, UK: Dangaroo Press.

Brydon, D. and Tiffin, H. (1993) *Decolonising Fictions*, Coventry, UK: Dangaroo Press.

Burford, B. (ed.) (1984) *A Dangerous Knowing: Four Black Women Poets*, London: Sheba.

Burnett, P. (ed.) (1986) *The Penguin Book of Caribbean Verse*, Harmondsworth, UK: Penguin.

Busby, M. (1992) 'High Tide of a Caribbean Odyssey', *The Guardian*, 9 Oct.

—— (ed.) (1993) *Daughters of Africa: An International Anthology of Words and Writings by Women of African Descent from the Ancient Egyptian to the Present*, London: Jonathan Cape.

Cambridge, J. (1987) *Clarise Cumberbatch Want to Go Home*, London: The Women's Press.

Cameron, N. (ed.) (1931) *Guianese Poetry, 1831–1931*, Georgetown, British Guiana: The Argosy Co. Ltd.

Campbell, G. (1945) *First Poems*, Kingston, Jamaica.

Carew, J. (1958) *The Wild Coast*, London: Secker & Warburg.

Caribbean Voices (1950) 'A West Indian Symposium', *Caribbean Voices* Broadcast, 9 July.

Carr, E.A. (1933) 'Art and Tradition', *The Beacon*, III.4.

Carrington, L. (ed.) (1983) *Studies in Caribbean Language*, The University of the West Indies, St Augustine, Trinidad: The Society of Caribbean Linguistics.

Carter, M. (1954) *Poems of Resistance from British Guiana*, London: Lawrence & Wishart.

—— (1977) *Poems of Succession*, London and Port of Spain: New Beacon Books.

—— (1980) *Poems of Affinity: 1978–1980*, Georgetown, Guyana: Release Publishers.

Cassidy, F.G. (1961) *Jamaica Talk: Three Hundred Years of the English Language in Jamaica*, London: Macmillan.

—— and Le Page, R.B. (eds) (1967) *Dictionary of Jamaican English*, Cambridge: Cambridge University Press.

Chamberlain, J.E. (1993) *Come Back to Me My Language – Poetry and the West Indies*, Urbana: University of Illinois Press.

Chapman, E. (1927) *Punch and Judy*, London: Constable & Co.

—— (1928) *A Study in Bronze: A Novel of Jamaica*, London: Constable & Co., republished in London by Chantry, 1952.

—— (1938) 'The Truth about Jamaica', Kingston, Jamaica: *West Indian Review*.

—— (1939) *Pied Piper*, London: Constable & Co.

—— (1953) *Too Much Summer*, London: Chantry.

—— (1954) *Development in Jamaica* (third edition). Kingston, Jamaica: Arawak Press.

Chen, W. (1988) *King of Carnival and Other Stories*, London: Hansib.

Childs, P. and Williams, P. (1996) *Post-colonial Theory: A Critical Introduction*, Hemel Hempstead: Harvester Wheatsheaf, Prentice-Hall.

Christian, B. (1989) 'The Race for Theory' in L. Kauffman (ed.) *Gender and Theory: Dialogues on Feminist Criticism*, Oxford: Basil Blackwell, 113–32.

Clarke, H. (1929) 'Miss Jamaica', *Planters' Punch*, 2: 5.

Clarke, S. (ed.) (1978) *New Planet: Anthology of Modern Caribbean Writing*, London: Caribbean Culture International.

—— (1980) *Jah Music – The Evolution of the Popular Jamaican Song*, London: Heinemann.

Cliff, M. (1984) *Abeng*, Trumansburg, NY: Crossing Press.

—— (1985) *The Land of Look Behind*, Ithaca, NY: Firebrand Books.

—— (1987) *No Telephone to Heaven*, New York: Dutton.

Cobham, R. (1984) Introduction to Alfred Mendes' *Black Fauns*, London: New Beacon Books.

—— (1990) 'Women in Jamaican Literature 1900–1950' in C. Boyce Davies and E. Savory Fido (eds) *Out of the Kumbla: Caribbean Women and Literature*, Trenton, NJ: 195–222.

Cobham, R. and Collins, M. (eds) (1987) *Watchers and Seekers – Creative Writing by Black Women in Britain*, London: The Women's Press.

Cobham, S.N. (1907) *Rupert Gray, A Tale of Black and White Trinidad*.

Cobham-Sander, R. (1981) 'The Creative Writer and West Indian Society Jamaica 1900–1950', unpublished PhD dissertation, University of St Andrews.

Collier, G. (1985) 'Artistic Autonomy and Cultural Allegiance: Aspects of the Walcott–Brathwaite Debate Re-examined', *The Literary Half Yearly*, 26,1: 23–41.

Collins, M. (1985) *Because the Dawn Breaks!*, London: Karin Press.

—— (1987) *Angel*, London: The Women's Press.

—— (1990) *Rain Darling*, London: The Women's Press.

—— (1992) *Rotten Pomerack*, London, Virago.

—— (1995) *The Colour of Forgetting*, London: Virago.

Collymore, F.K. (1960) 'Writing in the West Indies: A Survey', *The Tamarack Review*, 14: 111–23.

Coombes, O. (ed.) (1974) *Is Massa Day Dead?*, New York: Anchor Press/ Doubleday.

Cooper, C. (1978) 'Noh Lickle Twang: An Introduction to the Poetry of Louise Bennett', *World Literature Written in English* 17: 317–27.

—— (1984) 'Proverb as Metaphor in the Poetry of Louise Bennett', *Jamaica Journal* 17,2: 21–4.

—— (1987) Review of Michael Smith's *It a Come* (London: Race Today Publications 1986), in *Journal of West Indian Literature* 1 & 2: 94–7.

—— (1988) ' "That Cunny Jamma Oman." The Female Sensibility in the poetry of Louise Bennett', in K. Owusu (ed.) *Storms of the Heart – An Anthology of Black Arts and Culture*, London: Camden Press.

—— (1989) 'Writing Oral History', in S. Slemon and H. Tiffin (eds) *After Europe*, Coventry, UK: Dangaroo Press.

—— (1992) 'Words Unbroken by the Beat: The Performance Poetry of Jean Binta Breeze and Mikey Smith', in A. Rutherford (ed.) *From Commonwealth to Post-Colonial*, Coventry, UK: Dangaroo Press.

—— (1993) *Noises in the Blood – Orality, Gender and the 'Vulgar' Body of Jamaican Popular Culture*, London & Basingstoke: Macmillan Caribbean.

—— (1995) *Noises in the Wrist: The Writer and the Oral Tradition in Jamaica*, London and Basingstoke: Macmillan Caribbean.

Corsbie, K. (1984) *Theatre in the Caribbean*, London: Hodder & Stoughton.

Coulthard, G.R. (ed) (1966) *Caribbean Literature – An Anthology*, London: University of London.

Craig, C. (1984) *Quadrille for Tigers*.

—— *Mint Tea and Other Stories*, Oxford: Heinemann.

Crozier, J. (1969) 'The Beginnings of Bim', *Bim* 48: 245–8.

Cruickshank, J.G. (1916) *Black Talk – Being Notes on Negro Dialect in British Guiana with (Inevitably) a Chapter on the Vernacular of Barbados*, Demerara, British Guiana: The Argosy Company Ltd.

Cudjoe, S.R. (ed.) (1990) *Caribbean Women Writers: Essays from the First International Conference*, Wellesley, MA: Calaloux.

Cumber Dance, D. (ed.) (1986) *Fifty Caribbean Writers: A Bio-bibliographical Critical Sourcebook*, New York: Greenwood Press.

—— (1992) *New World Adams – Conversations with Contemporary West Indian Writers*, Leeds, UK: Peepal Tree Press.

Cunningham, J. (1989) 'Rock of Sages – the Poetry of E.K. Brathwaite', *The Guardian* 14 Apr: 35.

D'Aguiar, F. (1985) *Mama Dot*, London: Chatto and Windus, The Hogarth Press.

—— (1989) *Airy Hall*, London: Chatto and Windus Ltd.

—— (1992) 'Sweet Thames' printed in booklet for TV Series, *Words on Film* (first broadcast Autumn 1991), London: BBC Education.

—— (1993a) *British Subjects*, Newcastle-upon-Tyne, UK: Bloodaxe Books.

Dabydeen, C. (1986) *Islands Lovelier Than a Vision*, Leeds, UK: Peepal Tree Press.

—— (ed.) (1987) *A Shapely Fire – Changing a Literary Landscape*, Oakville, Canada: Mosaic Press.

—— (1989) *Coastland – New and Selected Poems 1973–1977*.

—— (1994a) *Berbice Crossing*, Leeds, UK: Peepal Tree Press.

—— (1994b) *Crossing Columbus*, Leeds, UK: Peepal Tree Press.

Dabydeen, D. (1986a) *Slave Song*, Coventry, UK: Dangaroo Press.

—— (1986b) 'On Writing Slave Song', *Commonwealth* 8,2: 46–50.

—— (1988) *Coolie Odyssey*, Coventry, UK: Dangaroo Press.

—— (1989) David Dabydeen Interviewed by Wolfgang Binder, *Journal of West Indian Literature* 3,2: 67–80.

—— (1991) *The Intended*, London: Minerva.

—— (1993) *Disappearance*, London: Martin Secker & Warburg Ltd.

—— (1994) *Turner*, London: Jonathan Cape.

—— (1995) 'Teaching West Indian Literature in Britain', (unpublished) paper, published in *Teaching British Culture*, London: Routledge, 1996.

—— (1996) *The Counting House*, London: Jonathan Cape.

—— and Samaroo, B. (eds) (1987) *India in the Caribbean*, London: Hansib.

—— and Wilson-Tagoe, N. (1987) *A Reader's Guide to West Indian and Black British Literature*, Coventry, UK: Rutherford Press/Dangaroo Press.

Dalphinis, M. (1985) *Caribbean and African Languages – Social History, Language, Literature and Education*, London: Karia Press.

Daly, V.T. (1974) *The Making of Guyana*, London & Basingstoke: Macmillan Caribbean.

Das, M. (1976) *I Want to be a Poetess of My People*, Georgetown: Guyana National History and Arts Council.

—— (1982) *My Finer Steel Will Grow*, US: Samsidat, 31,2.

—— (1988) *Bones*, Leeds, UK: Peepal Tree Press.

Dathorne, O.R. (1967) *Caribbean Verse: an Anthology*, London: Heinemann.

Davies, B. (1972) 'The Sense of Abroad: Aspects of the West Indian Novel in England', *World Literature Written in English* 11,2: 67–80.

Dawes, N. (1960) *The Last Enchantment*, London: MacGibbon & Kee.

deCaires Narain, D. (1995) 'Delivering the Word: The Poetry of Lorna Goodison'.

De Lisser, H.G. (1913) *Twentieth Century Jamaica*, Kingston, Jamaica: Jamaica Times Ltd.

—— (1914) *Jane's Career*, London: Methuen.

—— (1915) *Susan Proudleigh*, London: Methuen.

—— (1917) *Triumphant Squalitone: a Tropical Extravaganza*, Kingston, Jamaica: The Gleaner Co.

—— (1919) *Revenge. A Tale of Old Jamaica*, Kingston, Jamaica: the author & The Gleaner Co.

—— (1929) *The White Witch of Rosehall*, London: E. Benn.

—— (1937) *Under the Sun: a Jamaica Comedy*, London: E. Benn.

—— (1953a) *Morgan's Daughter*, London: E. Benn.

—— (1953b) *Psyche*, London: E. Benn.

—— (1956) *The Cup and the Lip*, London: E Benn.

—— (1958) *The Arawak Girl*, Kingston, Jamaica: Pioneer Press.

Devonish, H. (1986) *Language and Liberation – Creole Language Politics in the Caribbean*, London: Karia Press.

Dodd, E.A. [E. Snod] (1905) *Maroon Medicine*.

Donnell, A. (1992) 'Dreaming of Daffodils: Cultural Resistance in the Narratives of Theory', *Kunapipi*, 4: 18–26.

—— (1995) 'Contradictory (W)omens? Gender Consciousness in the Poetry of Una Marson', *Kunapipi*, XVII, 3: 43–58.

Drayton, A. (1970) 'West Indian Consciousness in West Indian Verse', *Journal of Commonwealth Literature*, 9: 66–8.

Durie, A. (1939) *One Jamaica Gal*, Kingston: *Jamaica Times*.

Edgell, Z. (1982) *Beka Lamb*, London: Heinemann.

—— (1991) *In Times Like These*, Oxford: Heinemann.

Edwards, P. and Dabydeen, D. (eds) (1991) *Black Writers in Britain 1760–1890*, Edinburgh: Edinburgh University Press.

Egbert, M. (Leo) (1883) *Poetical Works*, London: privately printed.

Elder, J.D. (1966) 'Evolution of the Traditional Calypso of Trinidad and Tobago: A Socio-Historical Analysis of Song Change', unpublished PhD dissertation, University of Pennsylvania.

—— (1968) 'The Male–Female Conflict in Calypso', *Caribbean Quarterly*, 14: 23–41.

Espinet, R. (1989a) 'The Invisible Woman in West Indian Literature', *World Literature Written in English* 29,2: 116–26.

—— (1989b) (ed.) *Creation Fire – A CAFRA Anthology of Caribbean Women's Poetry*, Toronto: Sister Vision – Black Women and Women of Colour Press.

Estevez, C.C. and Paravisini, L. (eds) (1991) *Green Cane, Juicy Flotsam*, New Brunswick: Rutgers University Press.

Ferguson, M. (1993) *Colonialism and Gender from Mary Wollstonecraft to Jamaica Kincaid – East Caribbean Connections*, New York: Columbia University Press.

Fido, E. (1984) 'Radical Woman: Woman and Theatre in the Anglophone Caribbean' in Smilowitz and Quarles (eds) *Critical Issues in West Indian Literature*, Parkesburg, USA: Caribbean Books.

Figueroa, J. (1966) *Caribbean Voices 1: An Anthology of West Indian Poetry*, London: Evans.

—— (1970) *Caribbean Voices II*, London: Evans.

—— (ed.) (1982) *An Anthology of African and Caribbean Writing in English*, Oxford: Heinemann Education.

Foucault, M. (1977) *Language, Counter-Memory, Practise: Selected Essays and Interviews*, trans. D.F. Bouchard and S. Simon, Ithaca, NY: Cornell University Press.

Fowler Wright, S. (ed.) (1924) *From Overseas: An Anthology of Dominion and Colonial Verse*, London: The Merton Press Ltd.

French, J. (1988) 'Colonial Policy Towards Women After the 1938 Uprising: The Case of Jamaica', *Caribbean Quarterly*, 34: 38–61.

Froude, A. (1888) *The English in the West Indies or the Bow of Ulysses*, London: Longmans, Green & Co.

Garvey, A. (1925) 'Women as Leaders', editorial in *Negro World*, reprinted in Busby (ed.) (1993) *Daughters of Africa*, London: Jonathan Cape: 209–11.

Gates Jr., H.L. (1984) *Black Literature and Literary Theory*, New York & London: Methuen.

Gikandi, S. (1991) *Writing in Limb(o)?: Modernism and Caribbean Literature*, Ithaca & New York: Cornell University Press.

Gilroy, B. (1986) *Frangipani House*, London: Heinemann.

—— (1989) *Boy-Sandwich*, London: Heinemann.

—— (1994) *Sunlight on Sweet Water*, Leeds, UK: Peepal Tree Press.

Gilkes, M. (1981) *The West Indian Novel*, Boston: Twayne.

—— (1975) *Wilson Harris and the Caribbean Novel*, London & Basingstoke: Longman.

—— (ed.) (1989) *The Literate Imagination: Essays on the Novels of Wilson Harris*, London & Basingstoke: Macmillan Caribbean.

Glaser, M. and Pausch, M. (1994) *Caribbean Writers – Between Orality and Writing* (special edition of *Matatu*), Amsterdam & Atlanta, GA.

Glissant, E. (1989) *Caribbean Discourse: Selected Essays*, trans. J. Michael Dash, Charlottesville: University Press of Virginia.

Gomes, A. (1933a) 'A West Indian Literature', *The Beacon*, II, 12 June.

—— (1933b) 'Literary Clubs', Editorial, *The Beacon*, II, 12 June.

—— (1934) *From Trinidad: A Selection from the Fiction and Verse of the Island of Trinidad*.

—— (1974) *Through a Maze of Colour*, Port of Spain, Trinidad: Key Caribbean Publications Ltd.

Gonzalez, A. (1973) *Trinidad and Tobago Literature On Air*, Port of Spain, Trinidad: The National Cultural Council.

Goodison, L. (1980) *Tamarind Season*, Kingston, Jamaica: Institute of Jamaica Publications.

—— (1986) *I Am Becoming My Mother*, London: New Beacon Books.

—— (1989) *Heartease*, London: New Beacon Books.

—— (1990) *Baby Mother and the King of Swords*, Harlow, UK: Longman.

Griffiths, G. (1978) *A Double Exile: African and West Indian Writing Between Two Cultures*, London: Boyars.

—— (1991) 'Post-Colonial Space and Time – Wilson Harris and Caribbean Criticism', in Hene Maes Jelinek (ed.) *Wilson Harris – The Uncompromising Imagination*, Coventry, UK: Dangaroo Press, 61–9.

Guptara, P. (1986) *Black British Literature – An Annotated Bibliography*, Coventry, UK: Centre for Caribbean Studies, The University of Warwick.

Habekost, C. (ed.) (1986) *Dub Poetry: 19 Poets from England and Jamaica*, Neustadt, West Germany: Michel Schwinn.

Hamner, R.D. (ed.) (1993) *Critical Perspectives on Derek Walcott*, Washington DC: Three Continents Press.

Haniff, N.Z. (1988) 'Louise Bennett' in *Blaze a Fire*, Toronto: Sistervision.

Harris, W. (1960) *Palace of the Peacock*, London: Faber & Faber.

—— (1961) *The Far Journey of Oudin*, London: Faber & Faber.

—— (1962) *The Whole Armour*, London: Faber & Faber.

—— (1963) *The Secret Ladder*, London: Faber & Faber.

—— (1964) *Heartland*, London: Faber & Faber.

—— (1965) *The Eye of the Scarecrow*, London: Faber & Faber.

—— (1967a) *Tradition, The Writer & Society: Critical Essays*, London and Port of Spain: New Beacon Books.

—— (1967b) *The Waiting Room*, London: Faber & Faber.

—— (1968) *Tumatumari*, London: Faber & Faber.

—— (1970a) *Ascent to Omai*, London: Faber & Faber.

—— (1970b) *The Sleepers of Roraima, A Carib Trilogy*, London: Faber & Faber.

—— (1971) *The Age of the Rainmakers*, London: Faber & Faber.

—— (1972) *Black Marsden*, London: Faber & Faber.

—— (1975) *Companions of the Day and Night*, London: Faber & Faber.

—— (1977) *Da Silva da Silva's Cultivated Wilderness* and *Genesis of the Clowns*, London: Faber & Faber.

—— (1978) *The Tree of the Sun*, London: Faber & Faber.

—— (1981) *Explorations: A Selection of Talks and Articles 1966–1981*, edited by H. Maes-Jelinek, Mundelstrup, Denmark: Dangaroo Press.

—— (1982) *The Angel at the Gate*, London: Faber & Faber.

—— (1983) *The Womb of Space: The Cross-Cultural Imagination*, Westport, CT: Greenwood Press.

—— Review of David Dabydeen's *Slave Song*, *CRNLE Reviews Journal*.

—— (1985) *Carnival*, London: Faber & Faber.

—— (1987) *The Infinite Rehearsal*, London: Faber & Faber.

—— (1990) *The Four Banks of the River of Space*, London: Faber & Faber.

Hearne, J. (1950) 'Ideas on West Indian Culture', *Public Opinion* (Jamaica), 14 Oct.: 6.

Hendriks, A.L. and Lindo, Cedric (ed.) (1962) *Independence Anthology of Jamaican Literature*, Kingston, Jamaica: Jamaica Arts Celebration Committee of the Ministry of Development and Welfare.

[517]

Henriques, F. (1967) 'The West Indies', bibliographic entry, *Journal of Commonwealth Literature*, 4: 91–8.

Henry, P. and Buhle, P. (eds) (1992) *C.L.R. James's Caribbean*, Durham, NC: Duke University Press.

Herdeck, D.E. (1979) *Caribbean Writers: A Bio-bibliographical Critical Encyclopedia*, Washington, DC: Three Continents Press.

Hill, E. (ed.) (1964) 'The Artist in West Indian Society: a Symposium', Port of Spain, Trinidad: Department of Extra-Mural Studies, University of the West Indies, Trinidad.

—— (1971) 'Calypso', *Jamaica Journal* 5,1: 23–27.

—— (1992) *The Jamaican Stage 1655–1900 – Profile of a Colonial Theatre*, Amherst: University of Massachusetts Press.

Hodge, M. (1970) *Crick Crack Monkey*, London: André Deutsch.

—— (1990) 'Challenges of the Struggle of Sovereignty' in Selwyn Cudjoe (ed.) *Caribbean Women Writers*, Wellesley, MA: Calaloux/University of Massachusetts Press.

Hollar, C. (ed.) (1932) *Songs of Empire*, Kingston, Jamaica: Gleaner.

—— (1941) *Flaming June*, Kingston, Jamaica: New Dawn Press.

Holst Peterson, K. and Rutherford, A. (eds) (1988) *Displaced Persons*, Coventry, UK: Dangaroo Press.

hooks, b. (1982) *Ain't I A Woman – Black Women and Feminism*, London: Pluto Press.

Hosein, C. (1980) *The Killing of Nelson George and Other Stories*, London: London Magazine Editions.

Howes, B. (ed.) (1967) *From The Green Antilles*, London: Souvenir Press.

Huggan, G. (1989) 'Opting out of the (Critical) Common Market: Creolization and the Post-Colonial Text' in Stephen Slemon and Helen Tiffin (eds) *After Europe*, Coventry, UK: Dangaroo Press, pp. 27–40,

Hutton, A.C. (1930) *A Life in Jamaica*, London: Arthur Stockwell.

—— (1932) *Hill Songs and Wayside Verses*, Kingston, Jamaica: The Gleaner Co. Ltd.

Hymes, D. (ed.) (1971) *Pidginization and Creolization of Languages*, Cambridge: Cambridge University Press.

Iremonger, L. (1951) *Creole*, London: Hutchinson.

—— (1955) *The Young Traveller in the West Indies*, London: Phoenix House.

Ismond, P. (1971) 'Walcott vs. Brathwaite', *Caribbean Quarterly*, 17.3 & 4: 54–70.

Jackson, L.A. (1986) 'Proverbs of Jamaica' in D. Sutcliffe and A. Wong (eds) *The Language of the Black Experience*, Oxford: Basil Blackwell.

James, A.M. (1920) *The Cacique's Treasure, and Other Tales*, Kingston, Jamaica: The Gleaner Co. Ltd.

James, C.L.R. (1938) *The Black Jacobins: Toussaint L'Ouverture and the San Domingo Revolution*, republished in New York by Vintage Books, 1963.

—— (1962) 'The Artist in the Caribbean', Open Lecture Series, University College of the West Indies, Mona, Jamaica.

—— (1963) *Beyond a Boundary*, London: Hutchinson.

—— (1969) 'Discovering Literature in Trinidad', *Journal of Commonwealth Literature*, 7: 73–80.

—— (1971) *Minty Alley*, London: New Beacon Books.

—— (1980) *Spheres of Existence*, London: Allison & Busby.

Jekyll, W. (1907) *Jamaican Song and Story – Anancy Stories, Digging Songs, Ring Tunes and Dancing Tunes*, London: D. Nutt for the Folklore Society; reprinted in 1966.

—— (1912) Preface to C. McKay's *Songs of Jamaica*, Kingston, Jamaica: A.W. Gardner & Co.

Jin, M. (1985) *Gifts from my Grandmother*, London: Sheba Feminist Publishers.

—— (1995) *The Song of the Boatwoman*, Leeds, UK: Peepal Tree Press.

Johnson, A. (1982) *Long Road to Nowhere*, London: Sable Publications.

—— (1987) *Sequins for a Ragged Hem*, London: Virago.

Johnson, L.K. (1975) *Dread Beat and Blood*, London: Bogle d'Ouverture.

—— (1980) *Inglan is a Bitch*, London: Race Today Publications.

—— (1991) *Tings an Times – Selected Poems*, Newcastle-upon-Tyne: Bloodaxe Books.

—— (1987) Interviewed by Mervyn Morris in *Jamaica Journal* 20,1: 17–27 and E.A. Markham (ed.) (1989) *Hinterland*, Newcastle-upon-Tyne: Bloodaxe Books.

Jones, E. (ed.) (1987) *Tales of the Caribbean*.

Jones, M. Patrick (1973) *Pan Beat*, Port of Spain, Trinidad: Columbus Publishers.

—— (1976) *J'Ouvert Morning*, Port of Spain, Trinidad: Columbus Publishers.

Katrak, K. (1989) 'Decolonizing Culture: Toward a Theory for Postcolonial Women's Texts', *Modern Fiction Studies*, 35: 157–179.

Kay, J. (1991) *The Adoption Papers*, Newcastle-upon-Tyne: Bloodaxe Books.

—— (1993) *Other Lovers*, Newcastle-upon-Tyne: Bloodaxe Books.

Khan, I. (1961) *The Jumbie Bird*, London: Hutchinson.

—— (1964) *The Obeah Man*, London: Hutchinson.

—— (1985) *The Crucifixion*, Leeds, UK: Peepal Tree Press.

—— (1994) *A Day in the Country*, Leeds, UK: Peepal Tree Press.

Khemraj, H. (1994) *Cosmic Dance*, Leeds, UK: Peepal Tree Press.

Kincaid, J. (1983) *At the Bottom of the River*, London: Picador.

—— (1985) *Annie John*, London: Picador.

—— (1988) *A Small Place*, London: Virago.

—— (1991) *Lucy*, London: Virago.

Kindermann, W. (1984) 'From Babylon to Eden: Afro-Caribbean Responses to Metropolitan Culture', *World Literature Written in English* 24,1: 100–7.

—— (ed.) (1995) (revised edition), London & Basingstoke: Macmillan Educational.

King, B. (ed.) (1979) *West Indian Literature*, London & Basingstoke: Macmillan.

—— (1980) *The New English Literatures – Cultural Nationalism in a Changing World*, London & Basingstoke: Macmillan.

—— (ed.) (1995) *West Indian Literature* (revised edition), London & Basingstoke: Macmillan Educational.

King, J. (1988) 'Intercity Dub, For Jean' in *Confluence: Nine St Lucian Poets*, Castries, St Lucia: The Source.

Ladoo, H.S. (1972) *No Pain Like This Body*, Toronto: House of Anansi.

—— (1974) *Yesterdays*.

Lamming, G. (1953) *In the Castle of My Skin*, London: Michael Joseph.

—— (1954) *The Emigrants*, London: Michael Joseph.

—— (1958) *Of Age and Innocence*, London: Michael Joseph.

— (1960a) *The Pleasures of Exile*, London: Michael Joseph.
— (1960b) *Season of Adventure*, London: Michael Joseph.
— (1972a) *Natives of My Person*, London: Longman.
— (1972b) *Water With Berries*, London: Longman.
Latin America Bureau (1984) *Guyana: Fraudulent Revolution*, London: Latin America Bureau Research & Action Ltd.
Lawrence, W. MacA. (1929) *Meditations*, Georgetown, Guiana: privately published.
— (1948) *The Poet of Guyana*, edited by P.H. Daly.
— (n.d.) *Futility and Others*
Lawson Welsh, S. (1991) 'New Wine in New Bottles: the Reception of West Indian Writing in Britain in the 1950s and Early 1960s', extract from unpublished PhD dissertation, 'Language and Literature in the Caribbean: Orality, Literacy and the "Creole – Standard Debate"', University of Warwick, 1992.
— (1991) 'Experiments in Brokenness: the Creative Use of Creole in David Dabydeen's *Slave Song*', unpublished paper.
— (1996) '(Un)Belonging Citizens – Unmapped Territory: Immigration and Black British Identity in the post 1945 period', in Stuart Murray (ed.) *Not On Any Map – Essays on Postcolonial Cultural Nationalism*, Exeter, UK: Exeter University Press.
Leo (Martin Egbert) (1883) *Poetical Works*, London: privately printed.
Lehmann, J. (1957) Foreword to *The London Magazine*, 4,1: 9.
Lindo, A. (ed.) (1940) *Year Book of the Poetry League of Jamaica*, Kingston: New Dawn Press.
— (1941) *Year Book of the Poetry League of Jamaica*, Kingston: New Dawn Press.
Linthwaite, I. (1987) *Ain't I A Woman! – Poems by Black and White Women*, London: Virago.
Loncke, J. (1978) 'The Image of Woman in Caribbean Literature', *Bim*, 64: 272–81.
— (1986) 'The Female Presence in Caribbean Literature', *Bulletin of Eastern Caribbean Affairs*, 11.
Long, E. (1970) *History of Jamaica*, London: Frank Cass.
Look–Lai, W. (1968) 'The Road to Thornfield Hall', *New World Quarterly* 4.2: 17–27.
Lovelace, E. (1959) *While Gods are Falling*, London: Collins.
— (1979a) *The Dragon Can't Dance*, London: André Deutsch.
— (1979b) *The Schoolmaster*, London: Heinemann.
— (1979c) *The Wine of Astonishment*, London: André Deutsch.
— (1989) *A Brief Conversation and Other Stories*, Oxford: Heinemann.
MacDermot, T. (1904) *Becka's Buckra Baby* with Foreword 'The All Jamaica Library', Kingston, Jamaica: The All Jamaica Library.
— (1909) *One Brown Girl And–*, Kingston, Jamaica: The All Jamaica Library.
McFarlane, J.E.C. (1918) *Beatrice*, Kingston, Jamaica: Times Printery.
— (1924) *Poems*, Jamaica: privately printed.
— (ed.) (1929) *Voices from Summerland*, London: Fowler Wright.
— (1931) *Daphne; a Tale of the Hills of St Andrew*, London: F. Wright.
— (1935) 'The Challenge of Our Time', in *The Challenge of Our Time*, Kingston, Jamaica: New Dawn Press.

—— (1937) *Jamaica's Crisis*, Jamaica: privately printed.
—— (1945) 'The Poetry of Jamaica II', an address delivered in April 1940, in *The Challenge of Our Time*, Kingston, Jamaica: New Dawn Press.
—— (1945) *The Challenge of Our Time*, Kingston, Jamaica: New Dawn Press.
—— (ed.) (1949) *A Treasury of Jamaican Poetry*, London: University of London Press.
—— (1953) 'The Prospect of West Indian Poetry', *Kyk-over-al* 5,16: 125–7.
—— (1956) *A Literature in the Making*, Kingston, Jamaica: Pioneer Press.
—— (1957) *The Magdalen – the Story of a Supreme Love*, Kingston, Jamaica: Pioneer Press.
MacKay, A.C. (1912) *Poems*, Kingston, Jamaica: the author.
McKay, C. (1912) *Songs of Jamaica*, Kingston, Jamaica: A.W. Gardner & Co.
—— (1912) *Constab Ballads*, London: Watt & Co.
—— (1920) *Spring in New Hampshire & Other Poems*, London: Grant Richards.
—— (1922) *Harlem Shadows; the Poems of Claude McKay*, with an introduction by Max Eastman, New York: Harcourt, Brace.
—— (1928) *Home to Harlem*, New York & London: Harper.
—— (1929) *Banjo, a Story without a Plot*, New York: Harper.
—— (1932) *Gingertown*, New York: Harper.
—— (1933) *Banana Bottom*, New York and London: Harper & Brothers.
—— (1953) *Selected Poems*, with a biographical note by Max Eastman, New York: Harcourt, Brace & World Inc.
—— (1970) *A Long Way from Home*, New York: Brace & Jovanovitch Inc.
—— (1979) *My Green Hills of Jamaica*, Kingston, Jamaica & Port of Spain, Trinidad: Heinemann Caribbean.
McLeod, A.L. (1979) 'Memory and Edenic Myth: Claude McKay's *Green Hills of Jamaica*' in Daniel Massa (ed.) *Individual and Community in Commonwealth Literature*, Malta: Malta University Press.
—— (1980) 'Claude McKay's Adaptation to Audience', *Kunapipi* 2,1: 123–39.
McNeill, A. (1971) *Hello Ungod – Poems*, Baltimore: Peaceweed Press edited by M. McWatt, 1985.
—— (1972) *Reel from 'The Life Movie'*, Kingston, Jamaica: Savacou Publications.
—— (1979) *Credence at the Altar of Cloud*, Kingston, Jamaica: Institute of Jamaica Publications.
—— (1989) Review of D. Dabydeen's *Coolie Odyssey*, *Journal of West Indian Literature*, Sept.: 89–90.
McTurk, M. ('Quow') *Essays and Fables in the Vernacular*, edited by Vincent Roth, Georgetown, British Guiana: The Daily Chronicle Ltd.
McWatt, M. (ed.) (1985) *West Indian Literature and its Social Context* (Proceedings of Fourth Annual Conference on West Indian Literature, U.W.I.), St Michael, Barbados: Dept. of English, U.W.I., Cave Hill.
Maes-Jelinek, H. (1976) *The Naked Design*, Aarhus, Denmark: Dangaroo.
—— (ed.) (1991) *Wilson Harris: The Uncompromising Imagination*, Coventry, UK: Dangaroo Press.
Mais, R. (1940) 'Where the Roots Lie', *Public Opinion*, March 9: 12.
—— (1946) *Face and Other Stories*, Kingston, Jamaica: Universal Printery.
—— (1953) *The Hills Were Joyful Together*, London: Jonathan Cape.
—— (1954) *Brother Man*, London: Jonathan Cape.
—— (1955) *Black Lightning*, London: Jonathan Cape.

—— (1971) 'Listen, the Wind' in Barbara Howes (ed.) *The Green Antilles*, London: Souvenir Press.

—— (1986) *Listen, the Wind*, selected stories edited by K. Ramchand, London: Longman Caribbean.

Malik, A. (Delano De Coteau) (1988) *The Whirlwind*, London: Panrun Collective.

Markham, E.A. (ed.) (1989) *Hinterland – Caribbean Poetry from the West Indies and Britain*, Newcastle upon Tyne: Bloodaxe Books.

Marshall, P. (1959) *Brown Girl, Brownstones*, New York, republished in New York by Avon Books, 1970 and by Feminist Press, 1983.

—— (1968) *The Chosen Place, the Timeless People*, New York: Harcourt, Brace and World, republished by Vintage, New York, 1984.

Marson, U. (1930) *Tropic Reveries*, Kingston, Jamaica: Gleaner.

—— (1931) *Heights and Depths: Poems*, Kingston, Jamaica: Gleaner.

—— (1937a) *The Moth and the Star*, Kingston, Jamaica: the author.

—— (1937b) 'Wanted Writers and Publishers', *Public Opinion*, June 12: 6.

—— (1945) *Towards the Stars*, London: University of London Press.

—— (1949) 'We Want Books – But Do We Encourage our Writers?', *Daily Gleaner*.

Martin, E. ('Leo') (1883) *Poetical Works*, London: privately printed.

Matthews, M. (1987) *Guyana, My Altar*, London: Karnak Press.

Melville, P. (1990) *Shape-Shifter*, London: The Women's Press.

Mendes, A.H. (1973) In Interview, *World Literature Written in English* 12,1.

—— (1935) *Black Fauns*, London: Duckworth.

—— (1934) *Pitch Lake*, London: Duckworth.

—— (1978) 'Her Chinaman's Ways' (1929) in R. Sander (ed.) *From Trinidad, An Anthology of Early West Indian Writing*, London: Hodder & Stoughton.

Mighty Chalkdust (1968) 'Brain Drain', reprinted in P. Burnett (ed.) (1986) *The Penguin Book of Caribbean Verse*, Harmondsworth: Penguin, 46–7.

Mighty Sparrow (Slinger Francisco) (1963) 'Dan is the Man', reprinted in S. Brown, M. Morris and R. Rohlehr (eds.) (1989) *Voiceprint*, Burnt Mill, UK: Longman, 120–30.

Mittelholzer, E. (1950) *A Morning at the Office*, London: The Hogarth Press.

—— (1955) *My Bones and My Flute*, London: Secker & Warburg.

Monar, R. (1985) *Backdam People*, Leeds, UK: Peepal Tree Press.

Moore, G. (1969) *The Chosen Tongue*, London and Harlow: Longmans, Green & Co.

—— (1974) 'Review: Use Men Language', *Bim* 15,57: 69–76.

Mordecai, P. (1986) ' "A Crystal of Ambiguities": Metaphors for Creativity and the Art of Writing in Derek Walcott's *Another Life*', in *West Indian Poetry: Proceedings of the Fifth Annual Conference on West Indian Literature*, St Thomas: 106–21.

Mordecai, P. (ed.) (1987a) *From Our Yard. Jamaican Poetry Since Independence*, Kingston, Jamaica: Institute of Jamaica Publications Ltd.

Mordecai, P. and Morris, M. (eds) (1980) *Jamaica Woman – An Anthology of Poems*, Jamaica: Heinemann Caribbean.

Mordecai, P. and Wilson, B. (eds) (1989) *Her True-True Name – An Anthology of Women's Writing from the Caribbean*, London: Heinemann.

Morgan, A. (1990) 'Beat and Dub and Us and Dem', preview article on appearance of Allen Ginsberg and Benjamin Zephaniah at the Royal Festival Hall, 15 June 1990, *The Guardian* 15 June: 37.

Morris, M. (1967) 'On Reading Louise Bennett, Seriously', *Jamaica Journal* 1,1: 69–74.
—— (ed.) (1971) *Seven Jamaican Poets*, Kingston, Jamaica: Bolivar Press.
—— (1972) 'The All Jamaica Library', *Jamaica Journal*, 6: 47–9.
—— (1975) 'The Arts in Jamaica: When "a Freedom was Released and the Desert Flowered"', *Commonwealth*: 9–11.
—— (1984) 'Little Magazines in the Caribbean', *Bim* 17,68: 3–9.
—— (1986) Editor's Notes to Michael Smith's *It A Come*, London: Race Today publications: 9–11.
—— (1987) Interview with L.K. Johnson, *Jamaica Journal*, 20.1: 17–27, reprinted in E.A. Markham (ed.) (1989): 250–61.
—— (1988) Interview with Michael Smith, *Jamaica Journal*, 18.2: 38–45, reprinted in Markham (ed.) 1989: 275–83.
—— (ed.) (1990) *The Faber Book of Contemporary Caribbean Short Stories*, London: Faber and Faber.
—— (1992) 'Gender in some performance poems', *Critical Quarterly*, 35.1: 78–84.
Munro, I. and Sander, R. (eds) (1972) 'Interviews with Three Caribbean Writers in Texas: George Lamming, C.L.R. James and Wilson Harris', *Kas-Kas*, Occasional Publication of the African & Afro-American Research Institute, The University of Texas at Austin.
Mutabaruka, A. (1973) *Outcry*, Kingston, Jamaica: Swing.
—— (1980) *The First Poems*, Kingston, Jamaica: Paul Issa Publications.
—— (1992) 'dis poem', *Jamaica Journal*, 24.2: 52.
—— and Faybienne (1976) *Sun and Moon*, Kingston, Jamaica: privately published.
Naipaul, Seepersad (1943) *Gurudeva and other Indian Tales*, Trinidad: privately published.
Naipaul, V.S. (1957) *The Mystic Masseur*, London: André Deutsch.
—— (1958) *The Suffrage of Elvira*, London: André Deutsch.
—— (1959) *Miguel Street*, London: André Deutsch.
—— (1961) *A House for Mr Biswas*, London: André Deutsch.
—— (1962) *The Middle Passage: Impressions of Five Societies*, London: André Deutsch.
—— (1963) *Mr Stone and the Knights Companion*, London: André Deutsch.
—— (1967) *The Mimic Men*, London: André Deutsch.
—— (1968) *A Flag on the Island*, London: André Deutsch.
—— (1971) *In a Free State*, London: André Deutsch.
—— (1972) *The Overcrowded Barracoon*, London: André Deutsch.
—— (1974) 'Without a Place, Naipaul Interviewed by Ian Hamilton', *Savacou* 9,10: 120–26.
—— (1975) *Guerillas*, London: André Deutsch.
—— (1979) *A Bend in the River*, London: André Deutsch.
—— (1984) *Finding the Centre: Two Narratives*, London: André Deutsch.
—— (1987) *The Enigma of Arrival*, Harmondsworth: Penguin.
—— (1989) *A Turn in the South*, Harmondsworth: Penguin.
—— (1995) *A Way in the World*, London: Minerva.
Napier, E. (1951) 'Carnival in Martinique', *Bim* 4.15: 155–7.
Narain, H. (1981) *Grass-Root People: Thirteen Stories on One Theme*, Cuba: Casa de las Americas.

Nasta, S. (ed.) (1988) *Critical Perspectives on Sam Selvon*, Washington DC: Three Continents Press.

—— (ed.) (1991) *Motherlands – Black Women's Writing from Africa, the Caribbean and South Asia*, London: Women's Press.

—— (1995) 'Setting Up Home in a City of Words: Sam Selvon's London Novels', *Kunapipi* XVIII.I (special edition on Selvon): 78–95.

Nazareth, P. (1979) Interview with Sam Selvon, *World Literature Written in English* 18,2: 420–37.

Nettleford, R. (1966) Introduction to Louise Bennett's *Jamaica Labrish*, Kingston, Jamaica: Sangsters.

—— (1978) *Caribbean Cultural Identity: The Case of Jamaica*, Kingston: Institute of Jamaica.

—— (1994) *Inward Stretch, Outward Reach, A Voice from the Caribbean*, Basingstoke: Macmillan.

Ngcobo, L. (1987) *Let It Be Told: Black Women Writers in Britain*, London: Virago.

Nichols, G. (1983) *i is a long memoried woman*, London: Karnak House.

—— (1984) *The Fat Black Woman's Poems*, London: Virago.

—— (1986) *Whole of a Morning Sky*, London: Virago.

—— (1989) *Lazy Thoughts of a Lazy Woman*, London: Virago.

Nugent, M. (1907) *Lady Nugent's Journal of Her Residence in Jamaica, from 1801–1805*, Kingston, Jamaica: Institute of Jamaica Publications Ltd, reissued in a revised edition with a foreword by Phillip Wright, 1966.

O'Callaghan, E. (1984a) 'Selected Creole Sociolinguistic Patterns in the West Indian Novel' in Smilowitz and Knowles (eds) *Critical Issues in West Indian Literature* Parkesburg, US: Caribbean Books.

—— (1984b) 'Literature and Transitional Politics', *World Literature Written in English*, 24.2: 349–59.

—— (1986) 'The Outsider's Voice: White Creole Women Novelists in the Caribbean Literary Tradition', *Journal of West Indian Literature*, 1,1: 74–88.

—— (1987) '"Vive la Difference!": Political Directions in Short Stories by West Indian Women Writers', paper presented at 7th Annual Conference on West Indian Literature, University of Puerto Rico.

—— (1993) *Woman Version – Theoretical Approaches to West Indian Fiction by Women*, London and Basingstoke: Macmillan Caribbean.

Oakley, L. (1970) 'Ideas of Patriotism and National Dignity in Some Jamaican Writings', *Jamaica Journal* 4: 16–21.

Olsen, T. (1980) *Silences*, London: Virago.

Omotusu, K. (1982) *The Theatrical into Theatre: a Study of Drama in the English-speaking Caribbean*, London: New Beacon Books.

Onuora, O. (Orlando Wong) (1977) *Echo*, Kingston, Jamaica: Sangsters.

Orderson, J.W. (1842) *Creolana*.

Ormsby Marshal, H.V. (ed.) (1956) *Seed and Flower: An Anthology of Prose and Poetry by the Ormsby Family of Jamaica*, Kingston, Jamaica: The Gleaner Co. Ltd.

Owens, R.J. (1961) 'West Indian Poetry', *Caribbean Quarterly* 7: 120–7.

Owusu, K. (ed.) (1988) *Storms of the Heart – An Anthology of Black Arts and Culture*, London: Camden Press.

Pacific Quarterly Moana (1983) One People's Grief: Recent Writing from the Caribbean.

Parry, B. (1987) 'Problems in Current Theories of Colonial Discourse', *Oxford Literary Review* 9: 27–58.

—— (1988) 'Between Creole and Cambridge English: The Poetry of David Dabydeen', *Kunapipi* 10,3: 1–17.

Paskin, S., Ramsay, J. and Silver, J. (1986) *Angels of Fire – An Anthology of Radical Poetry in the 80s*, London: Chatto & Windus.

Patterson, O. (1964) *Children of Sisyphus*, London: Hutchinson.

Persaud, L. (1991) *Butterfly in the Wind*, Leeds, UK: Peepal Tree Press.

—— (1993) *Sastra*, Leeds, UK: Peepal Tree Press.

Pioneer Press (1950) *Fourteen Jamaican Short Stories*, Jamaica: Pioneer Press.

—— (1953) *Caribbean Anthology of Short Stories*, Jamaica: Pioneer Press.

Philip, M.N. (1988) *Harriet's Daughter*, London: Heinemann.

—— (1989) *She Tries Her Tongue Her Silence Softly Breaks*, Charlottestown, Canada: Ragweed Press.

—— (1991) *Looking for Livingstone: An Odyssey of Silence*, Toronto: The Mercury Press.

Phillips, C. (1985) *The Final Passage*, London: Faber & Faber.

—— (1986) *A State of Independence*, London: Faber & Faber.

—— (1989) 'Living and Writing in the Caribbean: An Experiment', *Kunapipi*, XI.2: 44–52.

—— (1991) *Cambridge*, London: Bloomsbury Publishing Ltd.

—— (1993) *Crossing the River*, London: Bloomsbury Publishing Ltd.

Pollard, V. (1982) 'Social History of Dread Talk', *Caribbean Quarterly* 28,4: 17–40.

—— (1983) 'Figurative Language in Jamaican Creole', *Carib* 3.

—— (1984) 'Word Sounds – The Language of Rastafari in Barbados and St Lucia', *Jamaica Journal* 17,1: 57–62.

—— (1986) 'Innovation in Jamaican Creole. The Speech of Rastafari', in M. Gorlach and J.A. Holm (eds) *Focus on the Caribbean*, Amsterdam & Philadelphia: Benjamins.

Poynting, J. (1985) 'Literature and Cultural Pluralism: East Indians in the Caribbean', unpublished PhD dissertation, University of Leeds.

—— (1990) '"You Want to Be a Coolie Woman?": Gender and Ethnic Identity in Indo-Caribbean Women's Writing' in Selwyn Cudjoe (ed.) *Caribbean Women Writers*, Wellesley, MA: Calaloux Publications.

Quayle, A. (1957) *The Mistress*, London: MacGibbon & Kee.

Quevedo, R. (Atilla the Hun) (1983) *Atilla's Kaiso – a Short History of Trinidad Calypso*, St Augustine, Trinidad: Department of Extra-Mural Studies, The University of the West Indies.

Raiskin, J. (1996) *Snow on the Cane Fields – Women's Writing and Creole Subjectivity*, Minneapolis: University of Minnesota Press.

Ramchand, K. (1968) 'Dialect in West Indian Fiction', *Caribbean Quarterly*, 14: 1–2: 27–43.

—— (1969) 'The West Indies', bibliographic entry, *Journal of Commonwealth Literature*, 8 (Dec.): 79–88.

—— (1970a) 'The West Indies', bibliographic entry, *Journal of Commonwealth Literature*, 10 (Dec.): 115–22.

—— (1970b) *The West Indian Novel and its Background*, London: Heinemann, second edition, Heinemann, 1983.

—— (1971) (ed. with Cecil Gray) *West Indian Poetry*, London: Longman.

—— (1978) 'The West Indies', bibliographic entry, *Journal of Commonwealth Literature*, 13.2 (Dec.): 168–75.

—— (ed.) (1982) *Best West Indian Stories*, Walton-on-Thames: Nelson Caribbean.

—— (ed.) (1985) *Tales of the Wide Caribbean*, London: Heinemann, 1985.

Reddock, R. (1990) 'Feminism, Nationalism and the Early Women's Movement in the English-Speaking Caribbean' in Selwyn Cudjoe (ed.) *Caribbean Women Writers*, Wellesley, MA: Calaloux Publications, 61–81.

Reid, V.S. (1949) *New Day*, New York: Alfred A. Knopf.

—— (1978) 'The Cultural Revolution in Jamaica after 1938', address delivered at the Institute of Jamaica.

Resistance, Brother (1986) *Rapso Explosion*, London: Karia Press.

Rickford, J. (1987) *Dimensions of a Creole Continuum. History, Texts and Linguistic Analysis of Guyanese Creole*, Stanford, CA: Stanford University Press.

Rhys, J. (1927) *Left Bank and Other Stories*, New York: Freeport.

—— (1928) *Postures*, London: Chatto & Windus, republished as *Quartet* in London by André Deutsch, 1969.

—— (1930) *After Leaving Mr MacKenzie*, London: Cape.

—— (1934) *Voyage in the Dark*, London: André Deutsch.

—— (1939) *Good Morning Midnight*, London: Constable.

—— (1960) 'The Day They Burnt the Books', *London Magazine*, 7 July: 42–46, reprinted in K. Ramchand (ed.) *Tales of the Wide Caribbean*, London: Heinemann, 1985.

—— (1966) *Wide Sargasso Sea*, London: André Deutsch.

—— (1968) *Tigers are Better Looking*, London: André Deutsch.

—— (1969) *Quartet*, London: André Deutsch.

—— (1975) *My Day*, Berkeley, CA: Frank Hallman.

—— (1976) *Sleep it Off Lady*, London: Deutsch.

—— (1979) *Smile Please: An Unfinished Autobiography*, London: André Deutsch.

Rodriguez, E. (1983) 'An Overview of Caribbean Literary Magazine: its Liberating Function', *Bim* 17,66–7: 121–8.

Rohlehr, G. (1970) 'Sparrow and the Language of Calypso', *Savacou* 2: 87–99.

—— (1971) 'Some Problems of Assessment: A Look at New Expressions in the Arts of the Contemporary Caribbean', *Caribbean Quarterly* 17,3 & 4: 92–113.

—— (1972a) 'West Indian Poetry: Some Problems of Assessment: I', *Bim* 14,54: 80–8.

—— (1972b) 'West Indian Poetry: Some Problems of Assessment: II', *Bim* 14,55: 134–44.

—— (1973) 'Afterthoughts', *Bim* 14,56: 227–32.

—— (1975) 'A Carrion Time', *Bim* 15,58: 92–109.

—— (1976) 'My Strangled City: Poetry in Trinidad 1964-75', *Caliban* 2,1: 50–122.

—— (1978) 'Samuel Selvon and the Language of the People', in Edward Baugh (ed.) *Critics in Caribbean Literature*, London: George Allen & Unwin.

—— (1981) *Pathfinder: Black Awakening in the Arrivants of Edward Kamau Brathwaite*, Trinidad: the author.

—— (1986) 'The Problem of the Problem of Form: The Idea of an Aesthetic Continuum and Aesthetic Code-switching in West Indian Literature', *Anales del Caribe* 6.

—— (1988) 'Images of Men and Women in 1930s Calypsoes' in P. Mohammed and C. Shepard (eds) *Gender in Caribbean Development*, U.W.I. Women and Development Project 3 pp. 232–306, reprinted in G. Rohlehr, *Calypso and Society in pre-Independence Trinidad*, 1990.

—— (1989) Introduction to *Voiceprint – An Anthology of Oral and Related Poetry from the Caribbean*, Harlow, UK: Longman, 1–23.

—— (1990) *Calypso and Society in pre-Independence Trinidad*, Port of Spain, Trinidad: the author.

Rutherford, D. (1985) *Speak to Me of Love*, London: Akira Press.

Saakana, A.S. (1987) *The Colonial Legacy in Caribbean Literature*, London: Karnak House.

Said, E. (1989) 'Representing the Colonized: Anthropology's Interlocutors', *Critical Inquiry*, 15: 205–25.

Salkey, A. (1959) *A Quality of Violence*, London: New Authors.

—— (1960a) *Escape to An Autumn Pavement*, London: Hutchinson.

—— (1960b) (ed.) *West Indian Stories – An Anthology*, London: Faber.

—— (1965) (ed.) *Stories from the Caribbean – An Anthology*, London: Elek Bros.

—— (1967) (ed) *Caribbean Prose – An Anthology*, London: Evans Bros.

—— (1973) *Anancy's Score*, London: Bogle l'Ouverture.

Sander, R. (1973) 'The Turbulent Thirties in Trinidad: An Interview with Alfred Mendes', *World Literature Written in English*, 12.1: 66–79.

—— (1975) 'The Impact of Literary Periodicals on the Development of West Indian Literature and the Modern World', in Hena Maes-Jelinek (ed.) *Commonwealth Literature and the Modern World*, Duxelles: Didier, 25–32.

—— (1978) *From Trinidad – An Anthology of Early West Indian Writing*, London: Hodder & Stoughton.

—— (1988) *The Trinidad Awakening – West Indian Literatures of the Nineteen-Thirties*, Westport, CN: Three Continents Press.

Sander, R. and Munro, I. (1971) 'The Making of a Writer – a Conversation with George Lamming at the University of Texas, Nov. 1970', *Caribbean Quarterly*, 17.3 & 4: 72–82.

Savacou (1977) *Savacou Special Issue: Caribbean Woman*, 13.

—— (1979) *Savacou New Poets from Jamaica*, 14/15.

Scott, D. (1973) *Uncle Time*, Pittsburg: Pittsburg University Press.

Scott, L. (1992) *Witchbroom*, London: Allison & Busby.

—— (1995) *Ballad for the New World*, London: Heinemann.

Sealy, C. (1958) 'My Fathers Before Me', *Bim* 7.27: 135–138, reprinted in A. Salkey (ed.) *West Indian Stories*, London: Faber, 1960.

Searle, C. (1984) *Words Unchained – Language and Revolution in Grenada*, London: Pluto Press.

Selvon, S. (1952) *A Brighter Sun*, London: Allan Wingate.

—— (1955) *An Island is a World*, London: Allan Wingate.

—— (1956) *The Lonely Londoners*, London: Allan Wingate.

—— (1957) 'Waiting for Aunty to Cough' in *Ways of Sunlight*, London: MacGibbon and Kee.

—— (1958) *Turn Again Tiger*, London: MacGibbon & Kee.

—— (1975) *Moses Ascending*, London: Davis–Poynter.

—— (1982) 'Sam Selvon Talking – A Conversation with Kenneth Ramchand' *Canadian Literature*, 95: 56–64.

—— (1987) 'Finding West Indian Identity in London', *Kunapipi*, IX/3: 34–8.

—— (1987) 'Three into One Can't Go – East Indian, Trinidadian, Westindian', in David Dabydeen & B. Samaroo (eds) *India in the Caribbean*, London and Coventry: Hansib & University of Warwick.

—— (1988) 'Talking of *Moses Ascending* with Samuel Selvon' – An Interview with Jean–Pierre Durix, *Commonwealth*, 10,2: 11–13.

Senior, O. (1985) *Talking of Trees*, Kingston, Jamaica: Calabash.

—— (1986) *Summer Lightning and Other Stories*, Harlow, UK: Longman.

—— (1989) *Arrival of the Snake-Woman and Other Stories*, Harlow, UK: Longman.

—— (1995) *Discerner of Hearts*, Toronto: McClelland & Stewart.

Seymour, A.J. (1937) *Verse*, Georgetown, Guyana: Guyana Chronicle.

—— (1940) *More Poems*, Georgetown, Guyana: Guyana Chronicle.

—— (1944a) *Over Guiana Clouds*, Georgetown, Guyana: Guyana Chronicle.

—— (1944b) *Suns in My Blood*, Georgetown, Guyana: Guyana Standard.

—— (1945) *Poetry in These Sunny Lands*, Georgetown, Guyana: Caribia.

—— (1946) *Six Songs*, Georgetown, Guyana: Caribia.

—— (1948) *The Guiana Book*, Georgetown, Guyana: The Argosy Co.

—— (1950) 'Poetry in the West Indies', *Kyk-over-al* (Special Issue: 'The Literary Adventure of the West Indies'), 2.10: 1–44 and whole issue.

—— (1951) *Leaves from the Tree*, Georgetown, Guyana: Miniature Poets, Series A.

—— (1952a) 'The West Indies of the Future and the Writer', Editorial, *Kyk-over-al*, 5.15: unpaginated.

—— (ed.) (1952b) *Kyk-over-al Anthology of West Indian Poetry*.

—— (1953/4?), 'The Creation of Quality in the West Indies', *Kyk-over-al*, 5.17: 43.

—— (ed.) (1954) *Kyk-over-al Anthology of Guianese Indian Poetry*.

—— (1965) *Selected Poems*, Georgetown, Guyana: the author.

—— (1966) 'The Novel in the British Caribbean', Part 1, *Bim*, 11.42: 83–5.

—— (1967–7) 'The Novel in the British Caribbean', Part 2, *Bim*, 12.46: 75–7.

—— (1968) *Monologue – Poems*, Georgetown, Guyana: the author.

—— (1971) *My Lovely Native Land*, London: Longman.

—— (ed.) (1972) *New Writing in the Caribbean*.

—— (ed.) (1980) *A Treasury of Guyanese Poetry*, Guyana.

Seymour, E. (ed.) (1973) *Sun is a Shapely Fire*, Georgetown, Guyana: the author.

Sherlock, P. (1932) *The New Age Poetry Books*, with A.J. Newman, London: Longmans Green & Co.

—— (1936) *Anancy Stories*, London: Ginn & Co.

—— (1937) 'Introduction' to U. Marson's "The Moth And The Star", Kingston, Jamaica.

—— (1953) *Ten Poems*, British Guiana: Master Printery.

—— (1956) *Anansi – The Spider Man*, London: Macmillan.

—— (1959) *The Man in the Web*, New York: T.Y. Crowell.

—— (1966) *West Indian Folk Tales*, London: Oxford University Press.

Shinebourne, J. (1986) *Timepiece*, Leeds, UK: Peepal Tree Press.

—— (1988) *The Last English Plantation*, Leeds, UK: Peepal Tree Press.

Showalter, E. (1977) *A Literature of Their Own.*

Sibley, I. (1968) *Quashie's Reflections in Jamaican Creole*, Jamaica: Bolivar Press; first published 1939 as *Quashie's Reflections* (in native dialect), under the pseud. 'Pennibb', Kingston, Jamaica: The Herald Ltd. Printers.

Singers Quarterly, II, III, IV, bound manuscripts held at West India Reference Library, Institute of Jamaica, Kingston, Jamaica.

Singh, R. (1960) *A Garland of Stories*, Ilfracombe, UK: Arthur J. Stockwell & Co.

—— (1971) *Days of the Sahib Are Over*, Georgetown, Guyana: the author & Whirl of Papers.

—— (1973) 'I am a Coolie', *Heritage* 2: 25–7, Georgetown, Guyana.

—— (1976) *Collection of Poems*, Georgetown, Guyana: privately published.

Sistren Theatre Collective (1986) *Lionheart Gal: Life Stories of Jamaican Women*, London: The Women's Press.

Slemon, S. & Tiffin, H. (eds) (1989) *After Europe – Critical Theory and Post-Colonial Writing*, Coventry, UK: Dangaroo Press.

Smilowitz, E. and Knowles, R.Q. (1984) *Critical Issues in West Indian Literature*, Parkesburg, Iowa: Caribbean Books.

Smith, M. (1986) *It a Come*, London: Race Today Publications.

—— (1985) 'Mikey Smith – Dub Poet, Interviewed by Mervyn Morris', *Jamaica Journal*, 18.2 38–45.

Smith, P. (1899) *Anancy Stories*, New York: R.H. Russell.

—— (1905) *Chim-Chim: Folk Stories from Jamaica*, London: 'The Green Shelf'.

Spivak, G. (1993) *Outside the Teaching Machine*, London: Routledge.

Stone, J.S.J. (1994) *West Indian Theatre*, London: Macmillan Caribbean.

Stuart, A. (1988) 'Riddym Ravings', *Marxism Today*, Nov. Issue: 44–5.

Sulter, M. (1985) *As a Blackwoman – Poems 1982-1985*, London: Akira Press.

Sutcliffe, D. and Wong, A. (eds) (1986) *The Language of the Black Experience*, Oxford: Basil Blackwell.

Swanzy, H. (1949) 'Caribbean Voices – Prolegomena to a West Indian Culture', *Caribbean Quarterly*, 1.1: 21–8.

—— (1956) 'The Literary Situation in the Caribbean', *Books Abroad*, 30: 266–74.

Thieme, J. (1987) *The Web of Tradition – Uses of Allusion in V.S. Naipaul's Fiction*, Aarhus, Denmark and Coventry, UK: Dangaroo Press/Hansib Publications.

—— (1994) 'Pre-Text and Con-Text: Rewriting the Caribbean', paper given at University of York Day School on Post-Colonial Literatures, May 1994.

Thomas, E. (1986) *Word Rhythms from the Life of a Woman*, London: Karia Press.

—— (1988) *Before They Can Speak of Flowers*, London: Karia Press.

Thomas, J.J. (1889) *Froudacity*, London: T. Fisher Unwin, reprinted London: New Beacon Books, 1969.

Thorpe, M. (1975) 'Beyond the Sargasso: the Significance of the Presentation of the Woman in the West Indian Novel', unpublished PhD thesis, Queen's University.

Tiffin, H. (1978) 'Mirror and Mask: Colonial Motifs in the Novels of Jean Rhys', *World Literature Written in English* 17.

—— (1983) 'Post-Colonial Literatures and Counter-Discourses', *Kunapipi*, IX.3: 17–34.

—— (1989) 'Rites of Resistance: Counter-Discourse and West-Indian Biography', *Journal of West Indian Literature*, 3: 23–46.

—— (1992) 'Travelling Texts: Intertextuality and Resistance', paper delivered at Ninth Triennial ACLALS Conference, UWI, Mona, Kingston, Aug. 1992.

Tropica (Mary Adella Wolcott) (1904) *Island of Sunshine*, New York: Knickerbocker Press.

Turner, T. (ed.) (1987a) *Climbing Clouds: Stories and Poems from The Bahamas*, Basingstoke: Macmillan Caribbean.

—— (1987b) *Once Below a Time: Bahamian Stories*, Basingstoke: Macmillan Caribbean.

Vidal, J. (1988) 'By Word of Mouth. John Vidal Gets in Tune with the Dub Poet Benjamin Zephaniah', *The Guardian* 15 Sept.

Virtue, V.L. (1938) *Wings of the Morning*, Kingston, Jamaica: New Dawn Press.

Walcott, D. (1948) *25 Poems*, the author, Bridgetown.

—— (1949) *Epitaph for the Young*, the author, Bridgetown.

—— (1962) *In a Green Night*, London: Jonathan Cape.

—— (1964) *Selected Poems*, New York: Farrar, Straus & Co.

—— (1965) *The Castaway and Other Poems*, London: Jonathan Cape.

—— (1965) 'The Figure of Crusoe', Paper presented at The University of the West Indies, St Augustine, Trinidad, 27 Oct. 1965, in R.D. Hamner (ed.) *Critical Perspectives on Derek Walcott*, Washington, DC: Three Continents Press, 1993.

—— (1966) 'Is Bad Verse Forgivable at a Certain Stage of Our Evolution?', *Sunday Guardian* (Trinidad), 11 Sept.: 5.

—— (1969) *The Gulf and Other Poems*, London: Jonathan Cape.

—— (1970a) 'Meanings', *Savacou* 2.

—— (1970b) *The Gulf*, New York: Farrar, Straus & Giroux.

—— (1970c) 'What the Twilight Says: An Overture' in *Dream on Monkey Mountain and Other Plays*, New York: Farrar, Straus & Giroux: 3–40.

—— (1973) *Another Life*, London: Jonathan Cape.

—— (1973) 'Rights of Passage: Drama in Itself', *Trinidad Guardian* 25 Apr.

—— (1974) 'The Muse of History' in O. Coombs (ed.) *Is Massa Day Dead*, New York: Doubleday/Anchor Press.

—— (1976) *Sea Grapes*, London: Jonathan Cape.

—— (1979) *The Star-Apple Kingdom*, New York: Farrar, Straus & Giroux.

—— (1981a) *Selected Poems*, edited by W. Brown, London: Heinemann.

—— (1981b) *The Fortunate Traveller*, New York: Farrar, Straus & Giroux.

—— (1984) *Midsummer*, London: Faber & Faber/New York: Farrar, Straus & Giroux.

—— (1986) *Collected Poems, 1948–1984*, New York: Farrar, Straus & Giroux.

—— (1987) *The Arkansas Testament*, New York: Farrar, Straus & Giroux.

—— (1990) *Omeros*, London: Faber and Faber.

—— (1992) *The Antilles: Fragments of Epic Memory* (The Nobel Lecture), London: The Nobel Foundation and Faber and Faber.

Walker, A. (1983) *In Search of Our Mother's Gardens: Womanist Prose*, New York: Harcourt Brace Jovanovich.

Walmsley, A. (1992) *The Caribbean Artist's Movement, 1966–72*, London: New Beacon Books.

Warner, K. (1982) *Kaiso: A Study of the Trinidad Calypso as Oral Tradition*, Washington, DC: Three Continents Press,

—— (1983) *The Trinidad Calypso – A Study of the Calypso as Oral Literature*, London: Heinemann.

Warner-Lewis, M. (1982) 'Sam Selvon's Linguistic Extravaganza: Moses Ascending', *Caribbean Quarterly* 28,4: 60–9.

Waters, E.J. (1994) *New Writing from the Caribbean*, Basingstoke: Macmillan.

Watts, M. (ed.) (1990) *Washer Woman Hangs her Poems in the Sun*, Trinidad: Gloria V. Ferguson Ltd.

Waugh, A. (1972) Review of Wilson Harris' *Black Marsden*, *The Spectator*.

Weaver, R. and Bruchas, J. (eds) (1977) *Aftermath: An Anthology of Poems in English from Africa, Asia and the Caribbean*.

Webb, B. (1992) *Myth and History in Caribbean Fiction – Alejo Carpentier, Wilson Harris & Edouard Glissant*, Amherst, MA: University of Massachusetts Press.

Webber, A.R.F. (1917) *Those That Be in Bondage – A Tale of Indian Indentures and Sunlit Western Waters*, Georgetown, Guyana: The Daily Chronicle Printing Press, reprinted, Wellesley, MA: Calaloux Publications, 1988.

—— (1931) *A Centenary History and Yearbook of British Guiana*, Georgetown, Guyana: The Argosy Company.

Wickham, J. (1970) 'West Indian Writing', *Bim* 13,50: 68–86.

Williams, P. (1989) 'Difficult Subjects: Black British Women's Poetry', in D. Murray (ed.) (1989) *Literary Theory and Poetry*, London: Basil Blackwell.

Williams, P. and Chrisman, L. (eds) (1993) *Colonial Discourse and Post-Colonial Theory*, Hemel Hempstead, UK: Harvester Wheatsheaf.

White, H. (1973) *Metahistory: The Historical Imagination of Nineteenth-Century Europe*, Baltimore: John Hopkins Press.

Wickham, John (1993) *Discoveries*, Harlow, UK: Longman.

Wolcott, M.A. (Tropica) (1904) *The Island of Sunshine*, New York: Knickerbocker Press.

Wong, A. (1986) 'Creole as a Language of Power and Solidarity', in David Sutcliffe and Ansel Wong (eds) *The Language of the Black Experience*, Oxford: Basil Blackwell.

Wyke, C.H. (1991) *Sam Selvon's Dialectal Style*, Vancouver: University of British Columbia Press.

Wynter, S. (1966) *The Hills of Hebron*, London: Jonathan Cape.

—— (1968) 'We Must Learn to Sit Down and Discuss a Little Culture: Reflections on West Indian Writing and Criticism I', *Jamaica Journal* 2,4: 23–32.

—— (1969) 'Reflections on West Indian Writing and Criticism II', *Jamaica Journal* 3,1: 27–42.

—— (1972) 'Creole Criticism: A Critique', *New World Quarterly* 5,4: 12–36.

—— (1978) 'The Necessary Background', in Edward Baugh (ed.) *Critics on Caribbean Literature*, London: George Allen & Unwin.

—— (1990) 'Beyond Miranda's Meanings: Un/silencing the "Demonic Ground" of Caliban's "Woman"', in C. Boyce Davis and E. Savory Fido (eds) *Out of the Kumbla: Caribbean Women and Literature*, Trenton, NJ: Africa World Press.

Yardan, S. (1976) *This Listening of Eyes*, Georgetown, Guyana.

Zephaniah, B. (1985) *The Dread Affair*, London: Arena.

—— (1992) *City Psalms*, Newcastle upon Tyne, UK: Bloodaxe Books.

Index

Page numbers in bold for an author indicate where an extract by that author is featured in the book.

Printed in the United States
98431LV00001B/28-39/A